The American
Public Library
Handbook

On October 11, 1897, the new Chicago Public Library opened its doors to the public. In the center of the building there was a room devoted to circulation. It contained a dome and hanging lamps designed by the Tiffany Glass and Decorating Company of New York. Today, the dome, recently refurbished, crowns Preston Bradley Hall, a venue for concerts and events in what has been since 1977 the Chicago Cultural Center.

* * *

"Don't permit your library ever to be a dismal, bibliographical cave, in charge of a dragon.... Let it be one of the most attractive places in town; let it outshine in attractiveness the vulgar and harmful attractions of the bar-room and the gambling den; let it [be] a place resorted to by all, loved by all, a blessing to all."

—Moses Coit Tyler, speaking at the dedication of the West Bay City (Michigan)
Public Library, January 16, 1884.

The American Public Library Handbook

Guy A. Marco

 LIBRARIES UNLIMITED

AN IMPRINT OF ABC-CLIO, LLC
Santa Barbara, California • Denver, Colorado • Oxford, England

Library of Congress Cataloging-in-Publication Data

Marco, Guy A.
  The American public library handbook / Guy A. Marco.
    p. cm.
  Includes bibliographical references and index.
  ISBN 978-1-59158-910-5 (acid-free paper) — ISBN 978-1-59158-911-2 (ebook)
1. Public libraries—United States—Handbooks, manuals, etc. 2. Public libraries—United States—Directories. 3. Librarians—United States—Biography. 4. Library science—United States—Encyclopedias. I. Title.
Z731.M29 2012
027.473—dc23   2011033377

ISBN: 978-1-59158-910-5
EISBN: 978-1-59158-911-2

16 15 14 13 12   1 2 3 4 5

This book is also available on the World Wide Web as an eBook.
Visit www.abc-clio.com for details.

Libraries Unlimited
An Imprint of ABC-CLIO, LLC

ABC-CLIO, LLC
130 Cremona Drive, P.O. Box 1911
Santa Barbara, California 93116-1911

This book is printed on acid-free paper ∞

Manufactured in the United States of America

To Karen

Contents

Acknowledgments

I am indebted to a great many people for assistance and information. My thanks go first of all to my advisory board members for their guidance. Let me offer special gratitude to those board members who read draft entries and provided me with valuable critiques: Loriene Roy, Connie Van Fleet, Virginia Walter, and Wayne A. Wiegand. Stephen Bero wrote two entries: "Buildings and Facilities" and "Fixtures, Furnishings, and Equipment." Connie Van Fleet (with Danny P. Wallace) wrote "Research" and "Evaluation."

Apart from advisory board members, several experts read draft entries and improved them greatly:

Everett Henderson, Statistical Analyst, U.S. Institute of Museum and Library Services

Eric J. Hunter, Professor Emeritus of Information Management, Liverpool John Moores University

Peter Jacso, Professor and Chairman, Library and Information Science Program, University of Hawaii

Christopher Millson-Martula, Director of the Library, Lynchburg College, Virginia

James P. Scanlan, Professor Emeritus of Philosophy, The Ohio State University

These individuals kindly responded to my inquiries with facts about their libraries or other information:

Andra Addison (Seattle Public Library), Marti Anderson (Boulder Public Library, CO), Shirley Apley (Fort Worth Public Library, TX), Angela Arnold (Charlotte Mecklenburg Library, NC), Cheryl Baker (Tulsa City-County Library System, OK),

Douglas Baldwin (Cranbury Public Library, NJ), Brenda Baxter (Washoe County Library, NV), Gretchen Beatty (Nederland Community Library, CO), Julie Beno (Lincoln City Libraries, NE), Nancy Berkowitz (Town of Indian Lake Public Library, NY), Alan Bern (Berkeley Public Library, CA), Louise P. Berry (Darien Library, CT), Kelly Bird (Lettie W. Jensen Library, Amherst, NY), Elaine L. Birkinshaw (St. Petersburg Public Library System, FL), David Blake (Birmingham Public Library, AL), Maria Blake (Indianapolis-Marion County Public Library), Helen Blumberg (Enoch Pratt Free Library, Baltimore, MD), Stephen Boggs (New Carlisle-Olive Township Public Library, IN), Rich Boulet (Blue Hill Public Library, ME), Laura Bramble (Indianapolis-Marion County Public Library, IN), Patricia Brown (Atglen Public Library, PA), Sherie Brown (Massillon Public Library, OH), Gretchen Browne (Plainview-Old Bethpage Public Library, NY), Alice Calabrese (Metropolitan Library System, IL), Michelle Callahan (Pickaway County District Public Library, Circleville, OH), Jean Campbell (Forsyth Library, IL), Amy K. Caviness (Mid-Continent Public Library, Independence, MO), Claudia Cayne (Scoville Memorial Library, Salisbury, CT), Judy Center (Cambridge Public Library, NY), Katharine Chilcoat (Town Historian, Salisbury, CT), Beverly Choltco-Devlin (Mid-York Library System, Poland, NY), Laurel N. Coccio (Sarah Hull Hallock Free Library, Milton, NY), Stephanie Conarton (Delta Township District Library, Lansing, MI), Beth Curran (Providence Public Library), Eva Davis (Canton Public Library, OH), Elberta De Jager (Runals Memorial Library, MN), Tom Dillie (Minerva Public Library, OH), Terri Dood (Bozeman Public Library, MT), Julie Drengson (Jackson County Library, OR), Jeremy Drouin (Kansas City Public Library, MO), Lawrence Dugan (Free Library of Philadelphia), Lois Dulavitch (Clarion State University, PA), Michelle Enke (Wichita Public Library, KS), Frank S. Faulkner Jr. (San Antonio Public Library, TX), Missi Felio (Calcasieu Parish Library, LA), Jean Fisher (Tacoma Public Library, WA), Willow Fitzgibbon (Fayetteville Public Library, AR), Erica Freudenberger (Red Hook Public Library, NY), Janette Friesen (Meade Public Library, KS), Debra Futa (St. Joseph County Public Library, MN), Olivia Morales Geaghan (Brooklyn Public Library, NY), Sue Glad (St. Charles Public Library District, IL), Norman Gluckman (Avalon Free Public Library, NJ), Donna Golden (Chula Vista Public Library, CA), Jean M. Gosebrink (St. Louis Public Library), Grace Gouveia (Frankfort Community Public Library, IN), Julie Greene (Hampton Library, Bridgehamton, NY), Deborah Grodinsky (Skokie Public Library, IL), Ellen Gruber (Wagnalls Memorial Library, Lithopolis, OH), Janel Haas

(Way Public Library, Perrysburg, OH), Kelly Haley (Fayetteville Public Library, AR), Barbara Hansen (Lincoln City Libraries, NE), Sarah Hartman (Middleton Public Library, WI), Carey Hartmann (Laramie County Library System, WY), Gina Hebert (Houma Public Library, LA), Maria Hernandez (Phoenix Public Library), Thomas Hutchens (Huntsville-Madison County Public Library, AL), David Jennings (Akron-Summit County Public Library, OH), Teresa Jensen (San Antonio Public Library, TX), Cole Johnson (San Antonio Public Library, TX), Wayne Johnson (Lexington Public Library, KY), Ebony Jones-Crowder (Chicago Public Library), Jane Jorgenson (Madison Public Library, WI), Marilyn Kahn (Montclair Public Library, NJ), Jeff Kaplan (Santa Monica Public Library, CA), Bo Kinney (Seattle Public Library), Cindy Kolaczynski (Maricopa County Library, Phoenix, AZ), Pat Kosuth (Marinette County Consolidated Public Library Service, Marinette, WI), Leah Krotz (Belleville Public Library, KS), Sandra K. Lang (North Canton Public Library, OH), Kathleen Lanigan (Evanston Public Library, IL), Sandra Licks (New London Public Library, NH), Robert Lipscomb (Harrison County Library System, Gulfport, MS), Georgia Lomax (Pierce County Library System, Tacoma, WA), Michael Madden (Flint Public Library, MI), Naomi Hurtienne Magola (New Orleans Public Library), Daniel Masoni (Unalaska Public Library, AK), Lee Maternowski (Elk Grove Village Library, IL), Grace Mattioli (San Francisco Public Library, CA), Gwendolyn Mayer (Hudson Library and Historical Society, OH), Darren McDonough (Oberlin Public Library, OH), Susie McIntyre (Great Falls Public Library, MT), Dwight McInvall (Georgetown County Library, SC), Michael McLaughlin (Los Angeles Public Library), Heather McLeland-Wieser (Seattle Public Library), Mary W. McMahon (Mary Riley Styles Public Library, Falls Church, VA), Peggy McPhillips (Norfolk Public Library, VA), Nancy Milford (Cuyahoga Falls Public Library, OH), Ben Miller (Slater Public Library, IA), Jeanne Christie Mithen (Topeka and Shawnee County Public Library, KS), Bobbie Morgan (Cameron Parish Library, LA), Melanie Motchenbacher (Womelsdorf Community Library, PA), Karen Muller (American Library Association Library, Chicago), Roz Napier (Jordan Bramley Library, NY), Victoria L. Norman (Public Library of Cincinnati and Hamilton County), Sandy Nozick (Kern County Library, Bakersfield, CA), Deborah O'Connor (Geauga County Public Library, Chardon, OH), Nancy Park (Glendale Public Library, CA), Margaret Peebles (Gail Borden Public Library District, Elgin, IL), Jennifer Petersen (American Library Association, Chicago), Bernice Piechowski (Browns Valley Public Library, MN), May Plazo (Akron-Summit County Public Library, OH), Laura Preston (Hennepin

County Library, MN), Anne Ramos (Texas State Library and Archives Commission, Austin), Mary Reuland (Snow Library, Orleans, MA), Melissa Rice (Frankfort Public Library District, IL), Lisa Richland (Floyd Memorial Library, Greenport, NY), Carol Riley (Lincoln Public Library, NH), Carol Roark (Dallas Public Library), Jeanelle Romo-Lucero (Taos Public Library, NM), Kevin Rosswurm (Cuyahoga Falls Public Library, OH), Sylvia Rowan (San Francisco Public Library), Robert J. Rua (Cuyahoga County Public Library, OH), Mary Jo Ruppert (Cherokee Public Library, IA), A. Ryan (Vineyard Haven Public Library, MA), Dee Santoso (Manchester Public Library, NH), Sharon Saye (Bridgeport Public Library, WV), Mary Jane Schmaltz (Bismarck Veterans Memorial Library, ND), Robert Seal (County of Los Angeles Public Library), John Shipley (Miami-Dade Public Library System), Trent Sindelar (St. Louis Public Library), Ann Snively (Wright Memorial Public Library, Dayton, OH), Eric Soriano (Jacksonville Public Library, FL), Tim Spindle (Tulsa City-County Library, OK), Tom Stack (Milwaukee Public Library, WI), Lynn Stainbrook (Brown County Library, WI), Juliette Swett (Evanston Public Library, IL), Cheryl Swihart (Crestline Public Library, OH), Theresa Tyner (North Manchester Public Library, IN), Lorna Van Maanen (Rock Valley Public Library, IA), Meredith Stanton Vaselaar (Adrian Branch Library, Nobles County Library, MN), Dee Vasquez (Pike's Peak Library District, CO), Gerry Vogel (Avon Lake Public Library, IL), Marsha Wagner (Canal Fulton Public Library, OH), Marge Walker (Amesbury Public Library, MA), Ann Webster (American Indian Library Association), MaryBeth Wheeler (Boston Public Library), Luann Whirl (Tappan-Spaulding Memorial Library, Newark Valley, NY), Dennis Williams (Rochester Public Library, NY), Lesley A. Williams (Evanston Public Library, IL), Cindy Wilson (Butler Public Library, IN), Leslie Perrin Wilson (Concord Free Library, MA), Dwight Woodward (Williamsburg Regional Library, VA), Jennifer Worrells (Greensboro Public Library, NC), Annie M. Wrigg (Pelican Rapids Public Library, MN), Laura Zupko (Chicago Public Library)

I am especially grateful to MaryFrances Watson for her technical assistance and general guidance. And I am indebted to my editor at Libraries Unlimited, Barbara Ittner, for her encouragement, patience, and flexibility.

Introduction

Purpose of This Book

Patrick Wilson has said that "the point of making reference works is to replace a large body of literature by a very much smaller body, containing only what is worth repeating" (*Public Knowledge, Private Ignorance*, 1977, 27). I thought of this handbook in those terms; however, I did not think of "replacing" the extensive literature on American public libraries. I intended, rather, to assemble and organize key facts and thoughts from that literature in order to form a précis of the subject. I have looked at the subject, the American public library, from four perspectives: topical, biographical, institutional, and bibliographical. The topical perspective offers essays on 65 subjects that, taken together, enclose the history, philosophy, and problems of public libraries as well as their daily operations. The biographical perspective summarizes the contributions to public librarianship of 75 individuals. In the institutional perspective, there are current factual snapshots, and in some cases historical outlines, of 1,200 libraries; these vignettes may serve to illustrate the present situation. The bibliographical perspective gives citations and references in the topical essays. The references include important writings on the topic of the entry, even if they are not specifically cited in the entry. In a sense the whole book is a bibliographic essay, a guide to the public library literature.

In pursuing these aims, I soon observed that librarians have been inconsistent in their professional terminology, often with results that impeded their work. I thought it would be useful to bring up definitional problems as appropriate and endeavor to clarify them. The "Prologue on Terminology" explicates this approach.

The public library as I define it is "a library that is open without charge for reference and circulation to all members of the community that is taxed to support it." It is America's preeminent gift to world society. I hope that this volume, compressing into a "smaller body" the great corpus of literature about public libraries, will contribute to a wide appreciation of that gift.

Structure and Methodology of This Book

There are three types of entries (topical, biographical, and institutional), interfiled in one alphabetical sequence. I wrote all but a few of them (see "Contributors"). In many cases, I profited from expert guidance by members of the advisory board and other specialists. In all cases, I searched the print and online literature and read what seemed to be the most useful contributions.

In most of the 65 topical essays, there are three subdivisions: Terminology, Historical Summary, and Current Issues. Discussion of terminology begins with definitions given in *Merriam-Webster's Collegiate Dictionary*, 11th edition, 2003 (cited as *Merriam*); *American Heritage College Dictionary*, 4th edition, 2007 (cited as *American Heritage*); *Online Dictionary for Library and Information Science*, by Joan M. Reitz (cited as *ODLIS*); and a few subject dictionaries. The historical summary section presents the facts and issues of the past in a chronological framework. Current issues are those that have appeared in the recent professional literature. I have opinions on many of these topics, but I have endeavored, in true librarian fashion, to construct neutral, balanced presentations. Nevertheless, I have included references to some of my published articles when I thought they fit into that balanced concept.

The presentations on individuals are limited to 76 persons who died before January 1, 2000. They include only persons who made direct contributions of major significance to public libraries. Entries are brief: they review the main career points and touch on the person's ideas. Citations identify sources of more extensive treatments, such as *Dictionary of American Biography*, *American National Biography*, and *Dictionary of American Library Biography* with its two supplements. There is notice of a person's inclusion in "A Library Hall of Fame," *Library Journal*, March 15, 1951.

Entries are made for individual libraries that belong to one or more of these clusters:

1. Libraries serving the 100 largest (by population) U.S. cities; the list of those cities appears in *World Almanac 2010*.
2. Libraries that have been awarded recognition in the *Library Journal*'s "LJ Index of Public Library Service" ("star libraries") in 2009 and/or 2010 or in *Hennen's American Public Library Ratings (HAPLR)* published in 2009 and/or 2010. Both *LJ* and *HAPLR* are described in the entry EVALUATION.
3. Libraries of major national or regional historical significance or with current programs of special interest.

Each entry for a library gives, as a minimum, this information: correct name of the library, street address, founding date, population served, circulation in a recent year, holdings in total volumes or items, number of branches, and number of bookmobiles. For certain libraries, there is also a historical survey, identification of notable services, and attention to recent issues of national interest.

Correct names of libraries were taken from the library websites. Libraries with distinctive names are entered under those names (e.g., Ferguson Library) with see references from the city names (e.g., Stamford, CT).

Facts and data in the library entries have variable reliability. Much of the information comes from *American Library Directory* (ALD), 62nd ed., 2009–2010 (Medford, NJ: Information Today, 2009) and the online *lib-web-cats*, a component of *Library Technology Guides* (www.library technology.org), accessed at various times in 2009 and 2010. ALD gets its information from the libraries listed (questionnaires) and public sources. lib-web-cats uses information from the U.S. Institute of Museum and Library Services and the libraries themselves. One would expect considerable uniformity between the reports of ALD and lib-web-cats, but this is not the case: the two sources differ, sometimes widely, in what they tell about a given library. Some discrepancies are explicable on the basis of different years covered (neither source gives a year for its data). Other discrepancies no doubt arise from different interpretations given to certain data elements. For example, population served may be read as the city population of a municipal library or as everyone eligible to use the library. Circulation may be read to include books only or all items, and holdings may likewise reflect the traditional measure of bound volumes or a larger scope that includes CDs and DVDs. I looked at websites for all the libraries entered in this volume (except for a few smaller libraries that had none), checking for circulation and holdings information. If websites did not give such data, I queried the libraries by email. Websites and personal communications often yielded more discrepant figures for the elements involved. I tried to sort all this out in the entries, giving preference to numbers that came from the library websites or the librarians and indicating in parentheses the source of the data. In the end, the most dependable source was lib-web-cats; that is the source in a given case unless noted otherwise.

One fact that is hard to pin down is the year in which a library was established as a free, tax-supported institution. Founding dates in ALD and in secondary literature often refer to the year of a precursor subscription or social library. Library websites are sometimes clear about this matter, sometimes less so. Direct queries to the libraries always brought courteous answers when they got through, but too often the website's email address was inhospitable, rejecting my query. I have tried to set down as founding date the correct year of free, tax-supported status, but my notes at that point will indicate how well I succeeded. In doubtful cases I have given no date at all in preference to a questionable one.

The number of branches and bookmobiles are taken from ALD and library websites.

Notable services and recent issues of national interest were identified through the library press. Library websites usually fail to mention these matters, so I verified the situations as I thought necessary by queries to the libraries. Again, responses to the queries that got through to the libraries were cordial and informative.

Prologue on Terminology

Librarianship, like any other field of activity, has developed a vocabulary of its own. Some words and phrases in that vocabulary identify specialized concepts and practices that are distinctive to the work of a librarian. They are scarcely to be found elsewhere, such as "subject heading," "reference desk," and "interlibrary loan." Other components of the vocabulary are words or phrases that have wide application beyond librarianship, such as "value," "privacy," "censorship," "children," and "information."

As persons engaged in the practice of librarianship and in thinking or writing about it, we have considerable latitude in saying what we mean by our specialized concepts. We have decided that interlibrary loan "is the process by which a library requests material from, or supplies material to, another library" (Interlibrary Loan Code 2001, 318), and we know what we are talking about when we use that statement, even though it is not found in *Merriam-Webster's Collegiate Dictionary*. If there are disagreements of some kind that touch upon interlibrary loan, they are not terminological.

However, when we take up the more general words and phrases, those that are used in other fields and appear in the dictionary, we are not so free in deciding what they mean. If we talk about our "professional values," for example, we cannot just make up a definition of "values": that term is already established in a wider usage with a significance that sticks to it as it moves in various contexts. Michael Gorman's value—applying the term in librarianship—is "something that is of deep interest (often and quite reasonably self-interest) to an individual or group" (Gorman 2000, 5). This is a definition that relies on subjectivity: on how someone feels about something. It leaves the door ajar for such "deep interests" as having a good job, winning a competition, or concealing a misdeed. In contrast, we have this view from a philosophical dictionary: "a theory of value is a theory about what things in the world are good, desirable, and important. The theory implies action, since to conclude that a state of affairs is good is to have a reason for acting so as to bring it about, or if it exists already, to maintain it" (Flew 1979, 338). The second description of value is more dense and difficult than the first, but it would serve us better as a platform for assembling our professional values. (For more on values, see the entry PHILOSOPHY OF PUBLIC LIBRARIANSHIP.)

We want to be clear about what we mean when we talk about values because the discussion may carry import in the practice of librarianship. Values underlie issues like "privacy" or "censorship." The meaning we ascribe to such ideas affects our policies and determines how we behave in given situations. Do library patrons have a "right to privacy" that librarians must defend at all costs, even in defiance of legal authority? Is the U.S. Patriot Act invalidated by the position of the American Library Association (a private organization, after all) as expressed in "Privacy: An Interpretation of the *Library Bill of Rights*"? What, then, is "privacy" and "the right" to it? If we are vague about the terminology—as we have certainly been vague in library practice—our values and possibly our place in society will be damaged. (Further on this matter is in the entry PRIVACY AND CONFIDENTIALITY.)

For example, "children" should be an easy word to define. Everyone knows what a child is. But our *Merriam* dictionary gives us twists and tangles, saying that a child is "an unborn or recently born person" or "a young person, esp. between infancy and youth." Putting aside that first segment, we can deal with "child" as someone between infancy and youth if we know what "infancy" and "youth" are. *Merriam* says infancy is early childhood, which would mean a part of childhood rather than a stage before childhood as stated earlier. And youth is the period "between childhood and maturity." So there is not much we can gain from studying these dictionary efforts.

In librarianship, Virginia Walter (1992) has promoted the definite age span of 14 years or younger as descriptive of a child. She concurs with the definition given in a report by the National Center for Education Statistics. Accepting that, it would follow that a "youth" is someone over 14, but when does a youth become an adult? In fact, library parlance does not often employ "youth," preferring "young adult." In the *World Encyclopedia of Library and Information Services*, Jill L. Locke (1993) observes that "young adults are generally defined as persons between the ages of 12 and 18." She says further that the term "young adults" is "used interchangeably" with "adolescents," "kids," "teenagers," and "teens" in the professional literature. But age 12 is not a teen, and age 19 is. In any case, we have an overlap suggested, in the age 12–14 range, between child and young adult. This kind of inconsistent attribution brings about chaos in use studies. Catherine Sheldrick Ross (2006, 104) has noted that "young people" (= young adult, it seems) is "variously defined, usually signifying those under the age of 24 years." But she has seen actual use studies of "teens" that vary in age range covered: 14–17, 12–18, 12–16, 15–24, and 15–19 years. To make comparisons among studies that are looking at different groups of young persons is a task that requires statistical juggling and is probably best not undertaken.

So we are in the rough terrain of the definition world. Philosophers stroll happily here, and some of them warn us not to leave it for greener pastures. David Hume (1748) put it thus:

> [If] a controversy has been long kept on foot, and remains still undecided, we may presume that there is some ambiguity in the expression, and that the disputants affix different ideas to the terms employed in the controversy . . . it were impossible, if men affix the same ideas to their terms, that they could so long form different opinions of the same subject. . . . A few intelligible definitions would immediately have put an end to the whole controversy.

A great deal of the time and energy that librarians expend in disputes about the correct approach to challenged materials, to the place of information science in library education, in the making of "plans," or on "library ethics" (or to the issues already cited above) would be saved by a "few intelligible definitions."

I will not go further at this point; definitions are best taken up as a topic in the entry PHILOSOPHY OF PUBLIC LIBRARIANSHIP. But I will endeavor, in all the entries of this handbook, to present clear and unambiguous statements that define the concepts of the topic.

References

Flew, Antony [sic]. 1979. *A Dictionary of Philosophy*. New York: St. Martin's.

Gorman, Michael. 2000. *Our Enduring Values: Librarianship in the 21st Century*. Chicago: American Library Association.

Hume, David. 1748. *An Enquiry concerning Human Understanding*. Edinburgh.

Interlibrary Loan Code. 2001. Interlibrary loan code for the United States. Reference and User Services Association, for the American Library Association. *Reference & User Services Quarterly* 40, no. 4 (Summer): 318–19.

Locke, Jill L. 1993. Children's services. In *World Encyclopedia of Library and Information Services*. 3rd ed., 190–95. Chicago: American Library Association.

Ross, Catherine Sheldrick, et al. 2006. *Reading Matters: What the Research Reveals about Reading, Libraries, and Community*. Westport, CT: Libraries Unlimited.

Walter, Virginia A. 1992. *Output Measures for Public Library Service to Children: A Manual of Standardized Procedures*. Chicago: American Library Association.

Abbreviations

ALD—*American Library Directory, 2009–2010.* Medford, NJ: Information Today.

American Heritage—*The American Heritage College Dictionary.* 4th ed. Boston: Houghton Mifflin, 2007.

ANB—*American National Biography Online.* www.anb.org/articles.

Appleton's Cyclopaedia. Appleton's Cyclopaedia of American Biography. New York: Appleton, 1894–1900. 7 vols.

DAB—*Dictionary of American Biography.* New York: Scribner, 1928–1937. 20 vols. Supplements 1–7, 1944–1981. Index, 1937.

DALB—*Dictionary of American Library Biography*, ed. Bohdan S. Wynar. Littleton, CO: Libraries Unlimited, 1978. Supplement 1, ed. Wayne A. Wiegand, 1990. Supplement 2, ed. Donald G. Davis Jr., 2003.

FY—fiscal year.

HAPLR—Hennen's American public library ratings, by Thomas J. Hennen, Jr., 1999– (annual). Publisher varies.

IMLS—U.S. Institute of Museum and Library Services.

lib-web-cats—*lib-web-cats: A Directory of Libraries throughout the World.* www.librarytechnology.org/libwebcats.

LJ—America's star libraries: the LJ index of public library service, 2009– (frequency varies). *Library Journal*, February 15, 2009–. www.library journal.com.

LJ Library of the year—citations by the *Library Journal*, years 1992–. Full list at entry LIBRARY JOURNAL/GALE LIBRARY OF THE YEAR.

Merriam—Merriam-Webster Collegiate Dictionary. 11th ed. Springfield, MA: Merriam-Webster, 2003.

ODLIS—Online Dictionary for Library and Information Science, by Joan M. Reitz. Santa Barbara, CA: Libraries Unlimited. www.lu.com/odlis/index/cfm.

A

A. K. SMILEY PUBLIC LIBRARY, REDLANDS, CA 125 W. Vine St., Redlands, CA 92373. Founded 1894. Population served: 70,324. Circulation: 305,000. Holdings: 112,000 volumes. The main library, a Moorish/Mission-style structure designed by Myron Hunt (1926, 1930), was included in the National Register of Historic Places in 1976. A 1990 addition includes a conservatory.

ABBOT, ABIEL, 1765–1859 Teacher, minister, public library promoter. Born Wilton, NH, December 14, 1765. Educated at Phillips Academy, Andover, NH, and Harvard (graduated 1787). Taught at Phillips Academy, and then did missionary work in Maine. Greek tutor at Harvard, 1794. Minister of a church in Coventry, CT, 1795–1811; dismissed over theological views. Taught at Dummer Academy (CT) to 1819, farmed to 1827. Pastor at Peterborough, NY, 1827 to retirement in 1848. Died at West Cambridge, MA, January 31, 1859. In January 1833 he led a group of farmers and small manufacturers in establishing a social library in Peterborough, selling shares at two dollars with a membership fee of 50 cents a year. On April 9, 1833, "the town, apparently under the inspiration of the same Rev. Abbot, voted to set aside for the purchase of books a portion of the state bank tax which was distributed among New Hampshire towns for literary purposes. This was the way the first American town library to be continuously supported over a period of years was begun" (Ditzion 1947, 5). *Appleton's Cyclopaedia.*

Reference

Ditzion, Sidney. 1947. *Arsenals of a Democratic Culture.* Chicago: American Library Association.

ACQUISITIONS

Terminology

"The term acquisitions refers to the function of obtaining all materials to be added to a library's collection" (McSweeney 1993, 31). This function commences after the selection of items to be obtained; the selection process is treated in the entry COLLECTION DEVELOPMENT. "Acquisitions" has rightly replaced "order work" as the descriptor of this activity (note Francis Drury's text of 1930 titled *Order Work for Libraries*) since some materials are acquired without being ordered (e.g., through gifts, exchanges, and various approval plans). Nevertheless, the older term "order" has survived in a number of components of the acquisitions process. Libraries still have" on-order" or "orders-out" files, "standing orders," and so on.

Organization and Routines

An acquisitions department is found in most libraries, generally as a unit within technical processes, collection management, or collection development. The fundamental routines of the department have not changed over the years: they were described in the early professional literature (e.g., Bostwick 1929) and remain in place, albeit with technological applications. These are the steps in acquisition as outlined in recent writings:

1. Notice of a selected title comes to the department. In a public library this notice is in the form of a request from a staff member. The request may have originated as a patron's suggestion. Some requests are categorical (e.g., all new books by Anne Tyler or all new editions of the *World Almanac*).

2. Verification of the requested title in terms of correct spelling and bibliographic data.

3. Searching present holdings. Acquisitions personnel consult appropriate catalogs to determine that a requested item is not already in the library.

4. Searching order files. Staff examine card and computer files to be sure the requested item has not already been ordered.

5. Placing the order. This involves a decision about vendors. An order may go to a publisher or to a middleman (variously identified as an agent, jobber, or dealer). A formal "purchase order" completes the process, which may have been preceded by an inquiry about price, availability, and so forth.

6. Recording the order. A file of "on-order" (or "orders-out") titles is maintained in card or computer format. This is one of the files searched before new orders are placed.

7. Receipt of the item. Careful checking is necessary at this point to be sure the delivered item is the one ordered. (Note: Acquisitions

may seem like a dry process, but opening a package of new books is a bright spot in any librarian's day.)

8. Receipt of the invoice. This statement needs checking against the original purchase request. If there is no discrepancy, the invoice is marked as approved for payment and sent on to the office that handles the checks.

9. Forwarding the item. Usually the path is to the cataloging department.

10. Clearing the order. The "orders-out" record is transferred to another file, named "orders in" or the like.

11. Notification. The original requestor is notified that the title has gone to cataloging. Other staff may be notified as well (e.g., reference librarians when new information sources come in).

12. Statistics. Records are kept, according to practice in the individual library, of expenditures and numbers of items acquired.

If requested materials are not available or cannot be funded for the moment, they are listed in the "desiderata file" or "want list." Items in this file can be ordered later or can be sent to dealers of out-of-print or hard-to-find materials. In large libraries or systems, it may be routine for acquisitions staff to maintain all requests in a want list, arrange them in priority sequence, and forward the list to purchasing. There, depending on available funds and higher-level priorities, decisions are made about what to order. The above steps are modified in the case of gifts or materials received through exchange.

The acquisitions procedure is labor intensive. Probably one person-hour, at least, is required to deal with a single item. Librarians have given attention since the first days of the profession to means of expediting the acquisitions routine. One approach, suggested in the first issue of *American Library Journal* (1876) was for cooperation among libraries in ordering (Welch 1968, 69) (for the story of that continuing enterprise, *see* COOPERATION). Another important timesaving method, ever more popular since the 1960s, has been sharing the work with vendors. This idea has various implementations.

Vendors now accept orders for multiple materials. Such arrangements may be "blanket orders," which cover all publications by a certain publisher or in certain categories. Materials that fall within the scope of the blanket, as agreed in advance between library and vendor, are shipped automatically with the understanding that all items will be retained and paid for. A modification of the blanket order is the "approval plan," through which the vendor ships items that the library may consider for purchase; since those items fall under a scope determination, as with blanket orders, it is likely that the library will accept all or most of them. But those materials that are not wanted can be returned to the vendor. Approval shipments may arrive monthly or weekly or by agreement at any interval.

The staff time saved by blanket orders and approval plans is clearly considerable. Indeed, the inclination of many librarians has been to turn over more and more responsibility for selecting materials in those arrangements to the vendors. What has emerged is the procedure called outsourcing, which is discussed below in "Recent Issues."

As noted above, the routines of acquisition have been fairly well fixed over the years. Technology has offered new approaches to those routines, with favorable impact on staff time and precision of record keeping. One of the first applications of technology to acquisitions arrived with the databases of OCLC and RLIN in the 1970s. OCLC (originally the Ohio College Library Center, later the Online Computer Library Center) was available to the public in 1971. It offered a union catalog of holdings of cooperating Ohio libraries in machine-readable format, giving acquisitions librarians a ready tool for verification of bibliographic information. This service has expanded to international coverage, as *WorldCat*, and it includes procedures to facilitate actual ordering as well as verification. RLIN (Research Libraries Information Network), which provides comparable services, is used primarily by academic and research libraries.

Automation of vendor activities has been extensive since the 1980s. Major dealers have compiled computer databases of materials in many categories, ready for librarians to examine in the selection and acquisition processes. Files are interactive, allowing direct click-on ordering of desired materials. The items ordered may be sent (as per library specifications) with cataloging data and even shelf labels. Automatic invoicing and payment procedures may be included as well. Some details on the programs offered by several vendors are given here; the information is drawn from the respective websites accessed in December 2009.

The largest of the services is Baker & Taylor (B&T), based in Charlotte, NC. The firm offers access to over 4.5 million book, movie, and music titles; 500,000 full-text reviews; and downloaded MARC records. On-screen search pages are customized for relevance to the individual library. When a title is selected for examination, all available reviews appear with it. Notifications and proposed selection lists may be prepared by B&T staff to meet the specifications of the client library. In addition to MARC records for cataloging, the firm offers theft protection devices, Mylar jackets, book pockets, spine labels, label protectors, bar-code labels, and automated records. All services are customized. Music, DVD, and video games are covered. In December 2009, B&T acquired Blackwell North America, another provider of acquisition services.

Midwest Library Service, Bridgeton, MO, offers many of the same programs as B&T. Users may select titles for ordering from a database of 100,000 newly published titles. Customized searching is possible through advance filtering. Abbreviated MARC records may be downloaded for input into the local system. Users may prepare library profiles that Midwest will apply in providing a selection of newly published materials.

OCLC (Online Computer Library Center), based in Dublin, OH, offers integrated, automated materials selection through its *WorldCat selection* program. The system allows selection of titles from multiple materials vendors in one central system, with downloadable MARC records.

The richness of such offerings by vendors has drawn most libraries into arrangements with one or more of them. As the range of services has increased, with attendant prospects for saving staff time, questions have arisen about what is going on. Some of these questions are taken up in the next section.

Recent Issues

The only concern about acquisitions expressed by librarians in the professional press has to do with the vendor role. This matter is embedded in the larger issue of outsourcing (*see* MANAGEMENT AND ORGANIZATION). The main point in dispute over outsourcing centers on competence; while this arrow is aimed at the vendor, library staff must take some responsibility as well. It would seem reasonable for outsourcing to be implemented for those activities that require relatively little library professional expertise and experience. For example, contracting with a security firm to look after checkpoints and other safety matters would draw on outside expertise and would relieve library staff of tasks for which they have no special competence. Similar situations apply in regard to library publications, marketing, user surveys, building and facilities, and computer installations. In the areas of collection development and acquisitions, however, there are spheres of activity in which staff have specialized education and experience, and outside contractors are normally less qualified. So the assignment of selection/acquisition responsibilities to an outside firm seems to involve a reduction in the level of knowledge and experience relevant to the work. This sacrifice has to be justified on the basis of cost savings.

An interesting case of vendor incompetence was reported some years ago. A study found that when the same acquisition profile, covering science and technology materials, was sent to four vendors, results were disturbing. After five months, "only 4 percent of the titles would have been supplied by all four vendors" (Grant 1999, 154). This curious outcome may have been grounded in a poorly designed profile, in vendor inability to interpret the profile, or in vendor interest in promoting certain titles or categories of titles (e.g., by particular publishers). It may be that similar results in other cases would stem from similar considerations.

Baker & Taylor was involved in a notable case of problematic outsourcing. In June 1996, the Hawaii State Public library System outsourced its entire book budget, for its 49 branches, to B&T. A five-year contract obliged the vendor to supply 60,000 units of library materials during the first year, for $1.2 million, charging $20.94 per title regardless of the list price. No returns were permitted. (Alvin 1997, 276–80, is the source for this account.) Librarians in the system, who had not been consulted about the deal, objected on the grounds that collection development was a staff responsibility. They criticized many of the B&T choices as they arrived in terms of quality and appropriateness. There was also a civil suit by two unions, alleging that the government could not privatize civil service jobs. The furor caused the state librarian to terminate the contract in July 1997. What was learned? The arrangement had been made without staff input, the contract was put together hastily, and poor planning had penetrated the whole process. The lesson seems to be: move slowly, consult widely, get legal counsel, and include a short-term trial period in the contract. But the underlying question remains: who should do this work?

Among recent texts with useful details on acquisition are Chapman (2008), Holden (2010), and Wilkinson (2003).

References

Alvin, Glenda. 1997. Outsourcing acquisitions: Methods and models. In *Understanding the Business of Library Acquisitions*, 2nd ed., ed. Karen Schmidt, 262–84. Chicago: American Library Association.

Bostwick, Arthur E. 1929. *The American Public Library*. 4th ed. New York: Appleton. 1st ed. 1910.

Chapman, Liz. 2008. *Managing Acquisitions in Library and Information Services*. Rev. ed. New York: Neal-Schuman.

Drury, Francis K. 1930. *Order Work in Libraries*. Chicago: American Library Association.

Grant, Joan. 1999. Approval plans: Library-vendor partnerships for acquisitions and collection development. In *Understanding the Business of Library Acquisitions*, 2nd ed., ed. Karen Schmidt, 143–56. Chicago: American Library Association.

Holden, Jesse. 2010. *Acquisitions in the New Information Universe*. New York: Neal-Schuman.

McSweeney, Marilyn G. 1993. Acquisitions. In *World Encyclopedia of Library and Information Services*, 3rd ed., 32–34. Chicago: American Library Association.

Schmidt, Karen, ed. 1999. *Understanding the Business of Library Acquisitions*. 2nd ed. Chicago: American Library Association.

Welch, Helen M. 1968. Acquisitions. In *Encyclopedia of Library and Information Science* 1: 64–73. New York: Marcel Dekker.

Wilkinson, Frances C., and Linda K. Lewis. 2003. *The Complete Guide to Acquisitions Management*. Westport, CT: Libraries Unlimited.

ACTON PUBLIC LIBRARY, OLD SAYBROOK, CT   60 Old Boston Post Rd., Old Saybrook, CT 06475. Founded 1873. Population served: 10,520. Circulation: 251,591. Holdings: 251,591. LJ February 15, 2009: 3-star library.

ADMINISTRATION. *See* MANAGEMENT AND ORGANIZATION.

ADVOCACY. *See* PUBLIC RELATIONS.

AHERN, MARY EILEEN, 1860–1938   Librarian and editor. Born near Indianapolis, IN, October 1, 1860. Assistant state librarian, Indiana, then state librarian, 1889–1895. Studied at Armour Institute of Technology, Chicago, 1895–1896. Founding editor of *Public Libraries* 1896; she was the only editor of the journal, which was published to 1931 (name changed to *Libraries* in 1926). In 1889 promoted establishment of the Indiana Library Association. Relocated to Illinois and was president of the Illinois Library Association in 1908, 1909, and 1915. Died on a train in Georgia, May 22, 1938. Ahern, like many public librarians of her generation, supported some censorship of fiction, singling out "novels of neurotic exploration" and those that made no contribution to the "happiness of mankind." She felt that excluding such items should not trouble librarians (Boyer 2002, 115). LJ Hall of Fame; *DALB*.

Reference

Boyer, Paul S. 2002. *Purity in Print: Book Censorship in America from the Gilded Age to the Computer Age*. 2nd ed. Madison: University of Wisconsin Press.

AIMS AND OBJECTIVES. *See* PLANNING.

AKRON-SUMMIT COUNTY PUBLIC LIBRARY   60 S. High St., Akron, OH 44326. Founded 1874. Population served: 386,433. Circulation: 4,744,124. Holdings: 1,553,106. 17 branches. LJ February 15, 2009; November 15, 2009; and October 1, 2010: 5-star library. Directors: Theron A. Noble, 1874–1875; Horton Wright, 1875–1882; Joseph A. Beebe, 1882–1889; Mary Pauline Edgerton, 1889–1920; Maude Herndon, 1920–1927; Herbert S. Hirshberg, 1927–1929; Will H. Collins, 1929–1944; R. Russell Munn, 1944–1967; John H. Rebenack, 1967–1980; Steven Hawk, 1980–2004; David Jennings, 2004–.

ALAMEDA COUNTY LIBRARY   2450 Stevenson Blvd., Fremont, CA 94538. Founded 1910. Population served: 527,926. Circulation: 5,637,420. Holdings: 1,082,638. 11 branches.

ALBERT CITY PUBLIC LIBRARY   215 Main St., Albert City, IA 50510. Founded 1939. Population served: 709. Circulation: 12,214. Holdings: 14,800. LJ February 15, 2009, and November 15, 2009: 3-star library; October 1, 2010: 4-star library.

ALBUQUERQUE BERNALILLO COUNTY LIBRARY SYSTEM   501 Copper Ave., Albuquerque, NM 87102. Population served: 626,054. Circulation: 4,834,137. Holdings: 1,315,791. 16 branches.

ALEXANDRIA BAY, NY. *See* MACSHERRY LIBRARY, ALEXANDRIA BAY, NY.

ALGONQUIN AREA PUBLIC LIBRARY DISTRICT, ALGONQUIN, IL   2600 Harnish Dr., Algonquin, IL 60102. Population served: 39,456. Circulation: 800,556. Holdings: 159,130. 1 branch. HAPLR 2010.

ALLAIN, ALEX P., 1920–1994   Library trustee; promoter of intellectual freedom. Born near Jeanerette, LA, June 27, 1920. Law degree, Loyola University, New Orleans. Public library trustee in 1950s. In 1963 led the establishment of the Library Freedom Committee in the American Library Trustee Association of ALA. Chaired Louisiana Library Association Intellectual Freedom Committee in 1964. At ALA he helped create the Office for Intellectual Freedom (1967) and the Freedom to Read Foundation (1969). Allain died on January 5, 1994. Among his numerous awards were ALA Honorary Membership and the Roll of Honor Award of the Freedom to Read Foundation. He was named one of the 100 library leaders in *American Libraries*, December 1999. *Louisiana Libraries*, Winter 2006; *DALB*, 2nd supplement.

ALLEN COUNTY PUBLIC LIBRARY, FORT WAYNE, IN   Public Library Plaza, Fort Wayne, IN 46802. Founded 1895. Population served: 337,512. Circulation: 5,267,742 (library annual report 2009). Holdings: 2,780,289. 13 branches. LJ February 15, 2009, and November 15, 2009: 4-star library; October 1, 2010: 5-star library. HAPLR 2009, 2010.

AMAGANSETT FREE LIBRARY, NY   215 Main St., Amagansett, NY 11930. Founded 1916. Population served: 1,328. Circulation: 38,221. Holdings: 39,383. LJ November 15, 2009, and October 1, 2010: 5-star library.

AMERICAN LIBRARY ASSOCIATION   The American Library Association (ALA) is the world's oldest and largest organization in the field of librarianship. This entry emphasizes those activities of the association with the most significant relation to public libraries.

Historical Summary

In 1853 a group of 82 librarians, meeting in New York, laid the plans for a professional association. Charles Jewett, one of the men present (there were no women), stated the reason for the meeting: "We meet to provide for the diffusion of a knowledge of good books and for enlarging the means of public access to them. Our wishes are for the public, not for ourselves" (Utley 1926, 9). Eventually the proposed conference took place, during the 1876 Centennial in Philadelphia, resulting in the formation of the ALA. Melvil

Dewey was the force behind this conference; he brought together 103 individuals, 13 of them women, 30 of them from public libraries. On October 6 the assembly adopted a resolution:

> For the purpose of promoting the library interests of the country, and increasing reciprocity of intelligence and good will among librarians and all interested in library economy and bibliographical studies, the undersigned formed themselves into a body to be known as the "American Library Association." (Stevenson 1968, 267)

The first version of Dewey's decimal classification system was made available at the conference, along with Charles Cutter's cataloging rules. Samuel Swett Green's paper (Green 1876) on "personal relations" initiated discussion of what came to be reference work. Dewey observed later that "Through all coming time 1876 will be looked upon as the most eventful year in the history of libraries" (Thomison 1978, 10).

Justin Winsor was elected president (serving nine years) and Melvil Dewey secretary (also serving 1879–1890 and 1897–1898). The association grew slowly: a year after its foundation, 66 persons registered for the second annual meeting in New York. (Attendance figures and membership numbers are from www.ala.org, accessed December 2009.) At the Boston meeting in 1879, attendance was 162. Only 70 were at the Washington, D.C., meeting of 1881, but for the tenth anniversary of ALA, 133 librarians attended the Milwaukee conference. At the Columbian Exposition in Chicago, 1893, ALA set up a model public library, exhibiting 5,000 books. In 1900, the earliest year for which a count is available, there were 874 ALA members. At the 1904 international conference in St. Louis, delegates joined the ALA from 16 countries; there were 1,228 ALA members by then. As a facilitator for Europeans coming to American conferences and Americans going to Europe, a Committee on International Relations was set up in 1900. Activities of the young association focused on "cooperative activities, standardization of library procedures and forms, and debating the merits and demerits of stocking fiction" (Wiegand 1993, 848). A publication program was initiated in 1886, intending to promote the preparation of catalogs, indexes, and bibliographies. With a grant of $100,000 by Andrew Carnegie in 1902, the publication of in-house materials was energized. Melvil Dewey edited the first edition of the *ALA Catalog: 8,000 Volumes for a Popular Library* in 1904; it had six subsequent editions to 1943, evolving into the H. W. Wilson Company's "standard catalog" series. A number of serials were issued: the official journal of ALA was *American Library Journal* (1876–1877), name changed to *Library Journal* (1877–1907); it was edited or coedited by Dewey up to 1880. As this serial passed to a commercial publisher, the association commenced a new one: *Bulletin of the American Library Association* (1907–1938; name changed to *ALA Bulletin in 1939*, then *American Libraries* in 1970, later supplemented by a weekly e-publication, *ALDirect*). *ALA Booklist* (1905), a selection guide for general materials, became *Booklist* in 1917. It merged with *Subscription Books Bulletin* (1930–1956), a partner guide for larger reference publications, as *Booklist and Subscription Books Bulletin* in 1956, appearing under that name to 1969. Since then it has been simply *Booklist* again, with a section on reference books included from 1983. *Guide to the Study and Use of Reference Books*, by Alice Bertha Kroeger, appeared in 1902, with annual supplements through 1907. New editions have been compiled since by various authors and title changes. After the eleventh edition (1996), the *Guide to Reference Books* became an online work titled *Guide to Reference*. The publishing program has expanded to included handbooks and monographs across the spectrum of library interests. A major work of 1980, *The ALA World Encyclopedia*, reached a third edition under the name *World Encyclopedia of Library and Information Services* (1993).

The association scored a success in 1899 by influencing the choice of a new Librarian of Congress. On February 3, William C. Lane, president of ALA, and publisher R. R. Bowker had a personal meeting with President McKinley at the White House, promoting the appointment of Herbert Putnam. Although other persons were interested in the post, including ex-Congressman Samuel G. Barrows, ALA made the point that a professional librarian should be selected. McKinley agreed, and after some intervening complications, he nominated Putnam on March 13. Unfortunately, no enduring tradition for selecting professional librarians to head the Library of Congress was created.

Meanwhile, membership moved up. There were 2,005 persons in the association as it met on Mackinac Island in 1910, 533 of them at the conference. Membership reached 3,024 in 1915 and 4,464 in 1920. Theresa West Elmendorf was the first woman to be elected president of ALA, serving 1911–1912. Specialized units within ALA were emerging, precursors to the present structure of divisions, round tables, and committees. Those units represented particular interests of state librarians (1889), college and reference librarians (1889), trustees (1890), children's librarians (1900), and catalogers (1900).

It is remarkable that the association functioned in its first 30 years with no permanent office and no salaried personnel; headquarters was simply the home base of the ALA secretary, whose "compensation was a good conscience for having served well a worthy cause" (Utley 1926, 15). The first salaried executive secretary was engaged in 1909. At that time the association had settled in its second headquarters office in the new (1897) building of the Chicago Public Library. An earlier office had been located in Boston (1906–1909). ALA remained in the Chicago Public Library until 1924, then moved across the street to the John Crerar Library and in 1929 to an office building at 520 N. Michigan Ave. By then there was a substantial paid staff of 50 persons. In 1946 a final move took place to 50 E. Huron St. The offices were in a remodeled mansion at first, but in 1963 ALA replaced it with a new building at the same address. There were 164 staff at that time.

ALA was commendably active in serving the military during World War I. By June 1918, it was reported that ALA, through its War Service Committee, could claim the following among its achievements: it had purchased 300,000 books, sent 1,349,000 gift books to camps and stations, and distributed 5,000,000 magazines. A total of 36 camp library buildings had been erected. Library service was available in 464 camps, stations, and vessels (Thomison 1978, 66).

After World War I, the association developed priority activities in adult education, library education, position classification, extension of library service to unserved areas, professional standards, library legislation, and intellectual freedom. Carl H. Milam was the dynamic executive secretary from 1920 to 1948; he "dominated the association as no one had since Melvil Dewey's time" (Holley 1993, 47). Membership reached 6,055 in 1924, with a record conference attendance, at Saratoga Springs, of 1,888.

The topic of library education was first brought before the ALA at the annual conference of 1883 in Buffalo. Dewey reported that Columbia College, where he was librarian, was considering the establishment of a library school. Those at the conference (attendance was 72) expressed their interest via a formal resolution. In due time the proposed school did open (1887), the first of its kind, under Dewey's direction, albeit without ALA involvement. What did come from ALA at the time was a committee that was to consider all aspects of education of librarians; it was the ancestor of the current Committee on Accreditation (COA, 1955). Interim units were a Committee on Library Training (1900) and the Board of Education for Librarianship (1924) (*see* EDUCATION OF PUBLIC LIBRARIANS).

In 1923 the ALA undertook serious consideration of library personnel issues. Reports on position classification and pay plans were made; the 1927 submission by the Committee on Schemes for Library Service proposed a personnel classification in seven grades. Further work in the area of personnel by ALA and others is described in STAFFING.

Another resolution passed at the 1923 conference expressed interest by ALA in the growth of county library systems, based on the belief that the county is the logical unit of library service for most parts of the nation. This early attention to the skewed public library map of the time seems to have shaped no particular path of action, although the association did publish a significant book by Louis Round Wilson: *The Geography of Reading* (1938). The story of county libraries in summarized in the entry COUNTY AND REGIONAL LIBRARIES (*see also* OUTREACH).

Beginning in the 1930s, ALA devoted much effort to creation of standards for service in various types of libraries. *Standards for Public Libraries* was adopted in 1933. Other public library standards were issued later, as *Post-War Standards for Public Libraries* (1943), *Public Library Service, a Guide to Evaluation with Minimum Standards* (1956), *Interim Standards for Small Public Libraries* (1962), *Standards for Library Functions at the State Level* (1963), and *Minimum Standards for Public Library Systems* (1966). Documents that offered standards were often blended with statements about the purposes of public libraries. The 1933 *Standards* emphasized education and recreation; the 1943 *Post-War Standards* identified the purposes of education, recreation, information, and democracy. A *National Plan* (1946) announced two objectives for public libraries: "to promote enlightened citizenship and to enrich personal life" (Williams 1988, 55; Williams is the source for many of these appraisals of purpose). A novel purpose was ascribed to public libraries by ALA in the 1953 *Freedom to Read* statement: librarians were identified as "guardians of the people's freedom to read" who must "contest encroachments upon that freedom." This role remains at the forefront of ALA philosophy and action today (see "Recent Issues" below and INTELLECTUAL FREEDOM). Nevertheless, in 1956 the ALA's *Public Library Service* restated earlier goals of libraries: education, recreation, and information, adding "appreciation."

Association membership had passed 10,000 in 1927; it was 10,526 in 1928. A record conference attendance was 2,743 in 1929, in Washington, DC. By 1929, ALA membership reached 11,833; however, during the Depression, ALA programs were curtailed. Membership dropped and conference attendance slipped for several years. However, public library use increased—a phenomenon displayed since then in times of economic downturn. An upturn occurred in the later 1930s, as 5,312 persons went to the New York City meeting of 1937. Successful lobbying, mostly by Forrest Spaulding, resulted in the creation of a Library Division in the U.S. Office of Education in fiscal year 1936–1937. In order to facilitate communication with legislators and officials, ALA opened an office in Washington in 1945. Three of the World War II years passed with no conferences, and it took time for attendance to build up when meetings resumed in 1946.

During World War II, ALA demonstrated a fresh interest in library development overseas, especially in the Third World. The International Relations Office opened in August 1943 with a grant from the Rockefeller Foundation. There had been earlier international activities by the association, and—as noted above—a Committee on International Relations (CIR) had been formed in 1900. A significant international episode was the advisory assignment to China in 1925 by Arthur Bostwick. He "made a seven-week visit, traveling widely and promoting the concept of the public library as a means to further popular education. As a result of his official visit, the China Foundation for Education and Culture ... made a grant of $5 million for the establishment of a national library in Peking and proposed to create six demonstration public libraries throughout China" (Brewster 1976, 220). Such advising became common in the late 1930s and 1940s, at which time American public libraries were held up to universal esteem. There was considerable attention to Latin America and Hispanic Europe, with a committee having that sphere of interest created in 1921 (it had numerous titles), concentrating on smoothing acquisitions and exchanges of publications. In 1939, J. Periam Danton, chair of the CIR, and Carl Milam, ALA executive secretary, secured a $60,000 grant from the Rockefeller Foundation to plan and activate a "Books for Europe" project that—despite war conditions—supplied books to nine countries.

International Relations Office administered projects in the 1940s that promoted library education in Ecuador, Peru, Brazil, Mexico, and Chile and that established American-style public libraries in Mexico, Nicaragua, and Uruguay (Brewster 1976, 231). Advisers were sent to the state library in Guadalajara and the national library in Rio de Janeiro to assist in reorganizing and recataloging projects. After World War II, IRO was involved with numerous programs, sponsored by USAID and several foundations that provided technical assistance for libraries in underdeveloped areas. ALA began in the 1970s to take a prominent role in the International Federation of Library Associations and Institutions.

Membership climbed to 20,177 in 1954 and 24,690 in 1960. The major achievement of ALA in the 1950s was successful promotion of the first federal legislation, with funding, on behalf of public libraries. The Library Services Act (LSA) of 1956 was supported by ALA and 16 national organizations. It called for funds to strengthen inadequate public library services and to extend service to unserved (primarily rural) areas. Reluctance to advance this legislation in Congress was based on the long understanding that education is a function reserved for individual states in the U.S. Constitution; a public library, as an educational institution, was therefore a state responsibility. Congress finally decided to take on that responsibility, in a limited way, and the act was signed into law on June 19, 1956. A maximum of $7.5 million per year was to be appropriated, and state matching funds were required. The act has been renewed periodically, with increased funding. After four years, accomplishments under the act were considerable: 34 million persons in rural areas had improved service, 1.5 million of them served by libraries for the first time; 6 million books had been added to rural resources, along with 250 bookmobiles; and the number of personnel in state library agencies had doubled (Lorenz and Carl 1961, 536–40) (for details on the LSA and successor legislations, see GOVERNMENT ROLE).

Success in lobbying, or "public relations" as it was termed then, made that activity a favored one. National Library Week was created in 1958. In that year the National Defense Education Act (NDEA) was signed into law, secured at least in part by the lobbying of ALA. Funding for school library materials was a significant component of NDEA. Later legislation with library benefits included the Higher Education Act and Elementary and Secondary Education Act, both passed in 1965. A further federal contribution to librarianship was the establishment in 1970 of the National Commission on Libraries and Information Science.

The ALA president, Emerson Greenaway, emphasized in a 1959 speech that the public library idea "must still be 'sold' to a great majority of the population" (quoted in Williams 1988, 91). Looking for the widest possible readership has been an enduring theme in ALA. The concept encountered in the 1950s a serious impediment: the *Public Library Inquiry*, a set of studies published by Columbia University. Those studies concluded that the rightful audience for public libraries was just a small minority of the population, a self-selected group of educated persons. Only 10 percent of the population accounted for 70 percent of circulation. It would be impossible to make library service universal, and libraries should concentrate on serious users (see PHILOSOPHY OF PUBLIC LIBRARIANSHIP). This elitist concept ran head on into the ALA's populist stance.

Another effort to reach more people was the adult education movement. Mostly supported by the Ford Foundation's Fund for Adult Education, ALA opened an Adult Education Office in 1953. The office administered grants and gave support to workshops and events in public libraries. Results were dubious, and Ford ceased funding; ALA closed the office in 1964.

Beginning in the 1960s, ALA's leadership was much affected by social movements and political actions. At the 1964 conference, E. J. Josey called for a change in policy regarding the scheduling of meetings in sites that supported racial segregation (see SERVICES TO AFRICAN AMERICANS). Disruption and disturbance over the Vietnam War and over civil rights were the eye of the storm, but there were issues over education, sexual conduct, and migrant workers. This populist revolt produced massive demonstrations and riots. ALA—and the library community in general—was divided about what to do in the midst of this turmoil. Go on with business as usual, providing a neutral base of information on the topics of concern or choose sides and join the battle? The decision was made at the 1968 Kansas City conference, where "a new urgency about social concerns, and the relevance of libraries and ALA to them; a swelling impatience with 'the establishment' and a demand for the involvement of youth; a veritable barrage of criticism ... an insistent, rumbling awakening: that's what was happening in Kansas City" (*Library Journal* editorial, quoted in Williams 1988, 103). There were 6,849 persons at that conference out of a membership that had reached 35,666.

In the 1969 Atlantic City conference, young activists were noisy and disruptive. They wanted ALA to condemn the Vietnam War, and they wanted ALA to reform itself. Those present were uncertain about the nature of that reform, and it seems the activists were too; nothing much came of it except the creation of some committees and the Social Responsibilities Round Table. But on the point of ALA official statements regarding political matters outside the immediate sphere of librarianship—on that point the rebellion was triumphant. ALA political positions have become the norm, as illustrated in the *Recent Issues* section below. Nevertheless,

> the rise of special socially oriented groups within ALA was clearly viewed with hostility by a large segment of the membership and leadership ... This lack of support seemed to indicate a feeling that the problems were outside the sphere of a professional association and that society alone could solve them. (Thomison 1978, 247)

One campaign of the activist librarians was to promote public library service to the disadvantaged persons of society: essentially, these were the urban poor. A worthy effort was carried on for several years, under the name of "outreach," to attract the poor citizens to the library. The movement (see OUTREACH) ran its course and folded up by 1972, although the term "outreach" is still used in a more general sense to identify programs and services for unserved or underserved users, such as the visually impaired, home-bound, institutionalized, illiterate, or non-English speaking (*ODLIS*). The end of outreach overlapped the onset of a new project entitled "information and referral." This was a supplement to traditional reference service that assisted patrons in contacting agencies appropriate to their particular needs. The concept drifted on a cloud of poor definitions, and a 1978 survey indicated that it had never been securely operating (Williams 1988, 106; *see* REFERENCE AND INFORMATION SERVICES).

In addition to these political-social complications, library life in the 1970s was distressed and confused by the spread of computer use, for automated services at first and then for access to databases like DIALOG and the birth of something new with an old name: "information" (see the section "Recent Issues" below). After some declines in membership during the early 1970s, the number rose again to 35,524 in 1979. In 1980, ALA issued *A Planning Process for Public Libraries*. It urged library planners to ascertain "community information needs and resources" but did not explain how that was to be done, especially since "information" was defined to include "all knowledge, ideas, facts, and imaginative works of the mind." Nevertheless the document's conclusions were essentially to assert the benefits of traditional library services, with an emphasis on meeting popular demands (Williams 1988, 120–24).

ALA in recent decades has published numerous guidelines for different aspects of service, a code of ethics (1995; *see* ETHICS FOR LIBRARIANS), an interlibrary loan code (*see* INTERLIBRARY LOAN), policy statements, standards, output measures (*see* EVALUATION), an *Intellectual Freedom Manual* (2010; *see* INTELLECTUAL FREEDOM), and a valuable data series, "State of America's Libraries." All these are available on the ALA website at www.ala.org.

Structure

ALA is organized in accordance with its Constitution and Bylaws. Article II of the Constitution states that "the object of the American Library Association shall be to promote library service and librarianship." The mission of ALA is "to provide leadership for the development, promotion, and improvement of library and information services and the profession of librarianship in order to enhance learning and ensure access to information for all" (www.ala.org is the source for the statements in this paragraph, accessed November 2009). Article VI states that the governing body of the association, with authority to set all policies, is the council, although actions of the council may be overruled by a three-fourths vote of the membership at large. Article VII provides for an executive board to administer policies and programs, with day-to-day operations delegated to an executive director. Article VIII calls for a president and a treasurer, both elected by the membership. The Bylaws set out rules and procedures for classifying members; holding meetings; elections; establishing divisions, round tables, and committees; and handling of finances.

ALA Policy Manual gives the full texts of position statements and policies of the association. An account of this collection of statements is in "Recent Issues" below.

As of September 2009, there were 11 divisions and 17 round tables. The divisions are named here. Each of the divisions has one or more serial publications. Since these publications are of value to public librarians, they are identified here by division:

American Association of School Librarians (AASL). Principal serial publication: *Knowledge Quest*, 1997—(5 per year). This title succeeds *School Libraries*, 1952–1972, which continued as *School Media Quarterly*, 1972–1981, and *School Library Media Quarterly*, 1981–1997.

Association for Library Collections & Technical Services (ALCTS). Principal serial publication: *Library Resources & Technical Services*, 1957—(quarterly).

Association for Library Service to Children (ALSC). Public library children's work was first discussed at an ALA conference in 1897. ALSC makes the annual Caldecott and Newbery Awards and publishes numerous lists of recommended books and other media. Principal serial publication: *Children and Libraries: The Journal of the ALSC*, 2003—(3 per year). Continues in part *Journal of Youth Services in Libraries*, 1987–2002.

Association of College and Research Libraries (ACRL). Principal serial publications: *College Research Libraries*, 1939—(quarterly); *Choice*, 1964—(monthly).

Association of Library Trustees, Advocates, Friends and Foundations (ALTAFF). Formed on February 1, 2009, through the union of the Friends of Libraries U.S.A. and the Association of Library Trustees and Advocates (ALTA, founded 1890). Principal serial publication: *The Voice*, 2000—(quarterly).

Association of Specialized and Cooperative Library Agencies (ASCLA). Represents several types of library and activities. Most relevant to public libraries are sections for Interlibrary Cooperation and Networking, Libraries Serving Special Populations, and the State Library Agency Section. Serial publication: *Interface*, 1978—(quarterly).

Library Leadership & Management Association (LLAMA). Founded in 1957 as Library Administration and Management Association (LAMA). Aims to nurture leaders and promote good management practices. Various sections reflect interest areas relevant to public libraries: Buildings and Equipment; Fund Raising and Financial Development; Human Resources; Organization and Management; Measurement, Assessment, and

Evaluation; and Public Relations and Marketing. Principal serial publication: *Library Administration & Management*, 1987— (quarterly).

Library and Information Technology Association (LITA). Founded in 1966 as Information Science and Automation Division; changed to present name in 1978. Active in promotion of MARC; proposed ISBN in 1967. Principal serial publication: *Information Technology & Libraries*, 1982—(quarterly). Continues *Journal of Library Automation*, 1968–1981.

Public Library Association (PLA). Founded in 1944 as Division of Public Libraries. Concerns include the range of public library issues, many dealt with by virtual groups called "communities of practice." Holds biennial conferences separate from ALA conferences. Principal serial publications: *Public Library Data Service*, 1988—(annual); *Public Libraries*, 1947—(bimonthly).

Reference and User Services Association (RUSA). Founded in 1972 as merger of Adult Services Division (ASD) and Reference Services Division (RSD), both of which date from 1957. Change to present name in 1996. Concerns include reference practice, readers' advisory, interlibrary loan, literacy, and service for seniors. RSD prepared the ALA *National Interlibrary Loan Code* of 1968 and had major responsibility for the *Interlibrary Loan Procedure Manual* of 1970. Principal serial publication: *Reference & User Services Quarterly*, 1997—(quarterly). Continues *RQ*, 1960–1997.

Young Adult Library Services Association (YALSA). Founded in 1957. Aims to advocate and strengthen library service to persons ages 12 to 18, to nurture teen literacy, and to promote young adult literature. Issues book lists and descriptions of excellent services. Principal serial publication: *Young Adult Library Services*, 2002—(quarterly). Continues *Top of the News*, 1942–1987; continues in part *Journal of Youth Services in Libraries*, 1987–2002.

Divisions may have sections, which are groups devoted to special concerns under the umbrella topic of the division. Examples are the State Library Agency Section of ASCLA and the Measurement Analysis and Evaluation Section of LAMA. Another type of subdivision, forum, is found in ASCLA (e.g., the Library Service to Prisoners Forum). PLA has some clusters, such as the Library Development Cluster.

Round tables are membership units that promote a specific field of librarianship; they may recommend policy and action to other units. ALA has the following round tables: Ethnic and Multicultural Information Exchange; Exhibits; Federal and Armed Forces Librarians; Gay, Lesbian, Bisexual, and Transgendered; Government Documents; Intellectual Freedom;

International Relations; Learning Round Table; Library History; Library Instruction; Library Research; Library Support Staff Interests; Map and Geography; New Members; Social Responsibilities; Staff Organizations; and Video. While any of these units may deal with topics of concern to public librarians, some—as suggested by their names—have a closer relationship than others. The Social Responsibilities Round Table (SRRT) has had a considerable impact; it is discussed in the "Recent Issues" section below.

A number of membership committees operate outside the divisional structure: Budget Analysis and Review Committee, Council Committee on Minority Concerns and Cultural Diversity, Legislation Committee, Council Committee on Diversity, Committee on Accreditation, Committee on Organization, Committee on Status of Women in Librarianship, Chapter Relations Committee, Intellectual Freedom Committee, and International Relations Committee.

All these membership groups benefit from coordination and support by designated offices (and officers) maintained by ALA. In December 2009 the ALA offices were Office for Accreditation; Office of Government Relations; Office for Intellectual Freedom; Office for Information Technology Policy; Office for Library Advocacy; Office for Literacy and Outreach Services; Office for Human Resources, Development, and Recruitment; and Office for Research and Statistics. ALA operates various administrative offices as well; they carry on the business of the association. Freedom to Read Foundation is a quasi-independent unit. This considerable organization is staffed by 301 persons under the leadership of the executive director (formerly titled secretary). Executives with long tenure in office have included George B. Utley (1911–1920), Carl H. Milam (1920–1948), David H. Clift (1951–1958), and Robert Wedgeworth (1972–1985). The present (2011) officeholder is Keith Michael Fiels.

Recent Issues

Growth of the association has been most impressive. In five-year snapshots after the 1979 figure of 35,524, we see 40,761 in 1985, 50,509 in 1990, 56,444 in 1995, 61, 103 in 2000, 66,075 in 2005, and 66,624 in 2008. The year 2010 showed a decline to 61,198, probably caused by library economic conditions. Conference attendance has climbed apace, reaching a high mark of 22,762 at the Chicago meeting of 2009.

One who follows the history of ALA in the 1960s and 1970s and reads the "Structure" section above may find the two rather disconnected. ALA's stated mission expresses two venerable tenets of librarianship, aimed at education and information. (Recreation is missing.) However, a list of ALA "priorities" (voted by council in 1998) steps outside this mission to include "diversity" and "intellectual freedom." The association's "key action areas" also include "advocacy." A mission is what an organization is sent to do by its community. In the public library context, it is what the taxpayers who support the library expect from it. It is necessary to understand the mission and to match plans and actions to it. (This problem is discussed in the entry

PLANNING.) There is no evidence in user surveys that diversity is such an expectation, nor is intellectual freedom. The library profession has simply supplied these wishes, presumably on the basis that they are good for the people. In practice, the profession also supplies "recreation," another absent element in the mission but on strong grounds: recreational reading is one thing library patrons do want.

Another ALA policy that needs examination is found in the "strategic plan": *ALA Ahead to 2010*. The plan consists of "goal areas" and "strategic objectives." (The objectives are simply vague goals, with no specific outcomes attached.) In Goal Area III, it is written that "ALA plays a key role in the formulation of national and international policies and standards that affect library and information services." All the strategic objectives under this head relate to library policy issues. But the association has for many years entered into debates about nonlibrary issues as well, offering resolutions and statements. A few examples may suffice. *American Libraries* reported in June/July 2007 that ALA had joined a group of 43 organizations campaigning against the proposed national identification called Real ID. ALA's concern was about "potential privacy implications for library users, as well as the increased potential for identity theft for all individuals." In November 2008, *American Libraries* reported that ALA was strongly opposing the legislative proposal for the U.S. Treasury to purchase mortgage-related assets, the so-called Financial Bailout Bill. "ALA calls for public option in health care reform" is the heading of a report in *American Libraries* (November 2009). The text of the ALA position, presented in a letter to Congress from the ALA Washington Office, shows some sensitivity to the problem of mission by attaching the association's views to the health care problems of librarians: "Libraries must be able to offer affordable and comprehensive health care insurance to assure healthy employees, to manage library budgets, and to promote healthy communities that our libraries serve." No concerted opposition to such policies has emanated from the membership at large. Council has been less than assertive: in endorsing the SRRT in 1968, it anticipated a forum in which social change would be the main subject and that ALA would help make libraries "more responsive to current social needs" (Joyce 2008, 38). But in reviewing recommendations of the new Activities Committee on New Directions for ALA (ACONDA) in 1970, council did not approve one that said that ALA "should take a position on current critical issues," and council did not take up that matter again. Neutrality on social issues (except those directly affecting library activity) was a position declared by David Berninghausen in a series of articles: taking a stand on such nonlibrary matters was, he said, to act in opposition to intellectual freedom (Joyce 2008, 42). These two principles, neutrality and intervention, formed an uneasy duality in the 1970s and 1980s. Neutrality remained the "largely unspoken standard" (Joyce 2008, 50), but it was open to criticism as a policy that maintained "an inequitable status quo created by and in the interests of the dominant forces within society" (Joyce 2008, 54).

The word "information" acquired an expanded meaning for librarians in the late 1960s. The dictionaries still say that it means "knowledge obtained from investigation, study, or instruction" (*Merriam*), but the new library sense seems to cover everything contained in printed, recorded, or digital documents. Shakespeare gives us information, and so do Mozart and Picasso. Since the care and provision of such documents has been the role of libraries since antiquity, there seems to be no need for a new descriptor. Information entered the library field as a part of "information retrieval" around 1950, which referred to the storage and dissemination of data by computer. The term "information science" came into the language around 1960, signifying "the collection, classification, storage, retrieval, and dissemination of recorded knowledge treated both as a pure and as an applied science" (*Merriam*)—a definition obviously overlapping the work of librarianship. The topic of information is examined in the entry INFORMATION SCIENCE and will not be followed here except to note how the terminological shift has affected ALA and by extension the public library domain.

A trend in American library schools has been to incorporate "information" or "information science" into their academic names. Since uncertainty prevailed about the actual meaning of those expressions, the practice has been accepted, and ALA has had nothing to say about it (*see* EDUCATION OF PUBLIC LIBRARIANS). It is the marginalization and in some cases of elimination of library education from the names of library school programs. Among the U.S. programs accredited by ALA are such academic units as Department of Information Studies (State University of New York, Albany, and University of California, Los Angeles), College of Information (Florida State University), College of Information Studies (University of Maryland), and School of Information (University of Michigan and University of Texas at Austin). No program is titled simply "School of Library Science." Generally, these names of programs have been accepted quietly by ALA and by librarians, but in 2009 the New Jersey Library Association asked Rutgers University not to change the name of its program as planned from School of Communication, Information and Library Studies, to School of Communication and Information (omitting the library component); nevertheless, the change was made (reported in *Library Journal*, May 1, 2009, 12). ALA took no position on the matter.

It should be noted that despite this array of nonlibrary titles for academic units, the degrees awarded retain, for the most part, a library element: master of library and information science is common. Some programs offer multiple master's degrees, including one that is more librarian focused. And the courses offered often enough include the traditional subjects of librarianship (cataloging, reference, administration, and collection development) albeit under new names and usually as electives. What, if anything, ALA should do about the apparent demise of librarianship in the accredited schools remains an open question. COA has been criticized by some for doing nothing; Michael Gorman, ALA president in 2005–2006, wrote that ALA accreditation had become "a farce" (Gorman 2000, 68). Bill Crowley has said that ALA has failed to monitor, via accreditation practice, the current system of library education (Crowley 2008, 25). Indeed such critiques go back 30 years at least: the decline of the traditional core curriculum was noted in 1978 (Marco 1978), and an "erosion of library education" was identified in 1983 (Eshelman 1983). Recently, an attempt to regain control of the situation has developed through "Core Competencies of Librarianship," an ALA policy approved by council in 2009 and passed on to COA with recommendations. These competencies, if they are required in some form to be in the curriculum of a program seeking ALA accreditation, may be useful in reviving the "library" in library education. However, the competencies may also be met by resistance from the schools, which generally oppose rigid, prescriptive curricular requirements. And another perspective on the reduction of traditional library science in the programs is that they are preparing graduates for a broader range of employment scenarios.

A convenient way to discover what ALA members are most concerned about is to look over the programs and papers at an annual conference. The Chicago conference of 2009 displayed an emphasis on presentations about advocacy and marketing of libraries, cultural diversity, information literacy, readers' advisory service and reading studies, new digital technologies, staff development, services to seniors and disadvantaged, and the new idea of library as a place. Many of these subjects are also prominent in current library periodicals. *See also* EDUCATION OF PUBLIC LIBRARIANS; INTELLECTUAL FREEDOM; PHILOSOPHY OF PUBLIC LIBRARIANSHIP.

References

Much of the information about ALA structure and policy was drawn from the association's website, www.ala.org, accessed on various dates in 2009 and 2010.

Asheim, Lester. 1966. *Librarianship in the Developing Countries*. Urbana: University of Illinois Press.

Brewster, Beverly J. 1976. *American Overseas Technical Assistance, 1940–1976*. Metuchen, NJ: Scarecrow Press.

Crowley, Bill [William A.]. 2008. *Renewing Professional Librarianship: A Fundamental Rethinking*. Westport, CT: Libraries Unlimited.

Eshelman, William R. 1983. The erosion of library education. *Library Journal* 108, no. 13 (July): 1309–12.

Gorman, Michael. 2000. *Our Enduring Values: Librarianship in the 21st Century*. Chicago: American Library Association.

Green, Samuel Swett. 1876. Personal relations between librarians and readers. *American Library Journal* 1, no. 2 (October): 74–81.

Holley, Edward G. 1993. American Library Association. In *World Encyclopedia of Library and Information Services*, 3rd ed., 46–52. Chicago: American Library Association.

Joyce, Steven. 2008. A few gates redux: An examination of the social responsibilities debate in the early 1970s and 1990s. In *Questioning Library Neutrality: Essays from Progressive Librarian*, 33–66. Duluth, MN: Library Juice Press.

Lorenz, John G., and Herbert A. Carl. 1961. The Library Services Act after four years. *ALA Bulletin* 55, no. 6 (June): 34–40.

Marco, Guy A. 1978. Recent adventures of the American core curriculum. *Unesco Bulletin for Libraries* 32, no. 4 (July/August): 279–83.
Stevenson, Grace T. 1968. American Library Association. In *Encyclopedia of Library and Information Science* 2: 267–303. New York: Marcel Dekker.
Thomison, Dennis. 1978. *The American Library Association, 1876–1972.* Chicago: American Library Association.
Utley, George. 1926. *Fifty Years of the American Library Association.* Chicago: American Library Association.
Wiegand, Wayne A. 1993. United States. In *World Encyclopedia of Library and Information Services*, 3rd ed., 840–49. Chicago: American Library Association.
Williams, Patrick. 1988. *The American Public Library and the Problem of Purpose.* New York: Greenwood Press.

AMES TOWNSHIP, OH. *See* NELSONVILLE PUBLIC LIBRARY, OH.

AMESBURY PUBLIC LIBRARY, MA   149 Main St., MA 01913. Founded 1889 (communication from the library). Population served: 15,737. Circulation: 127,724. Holdings: 68,235. The library of the Amesbury Flannel Co. was given to the town in 1856 as a subscription library, charging one dollar per borrower. John Greenleaf Whittier was a strong supporter of the library, but subscriptions declined steadily. In March 1889 the town voted to take over the library, resulting in an immediate rise in circulation (Ditzion 1947, 42–43).

Reference

Ditzion, Sidney. 1947. *Arsenals of a Democratic Culture.* Chicago: American Library Association.

AMHERST, WI. *See* LETTIE W. JENSEN PUBLIC LIBRARY, AMHERST, WI.

ANAHEIM PUBLIC LIBRARY, CA   500 W. Broadway, Anaheim, CA 92805. Population served: 345,317. Circulation: 689,744. Holdings: 492,320. 4 branches.

ANCHORAGE PUBLIC LIBRARY, AK   3600 Denali St., Anchorage, AK 99503. Founded 1945. Population served: 278,241. Circulation: 1,438,887. Holdings: 600,000. 5 branches.

ANDERSON, EDWIN HATFIELD, 1861–1947   Librarian. Born Zionsville, IN, September 27, 1861. He attended New York State Library School, Albany, 1890–1891. Worked as a cataloger, Newberry Library, Chicago, 1891, then librarian, Braddock (PA) Public Library, 1892. He was the first librarian of the Carnegie Library of Pittsburgh, 1895. Anderson was state librarian of

NY, 1906–1907; assistant director, then director, New York Public Library, 1908–1934. At Carnegie Library of Pittsburgh, Anderson established children's departments in the main library and branches. He created a library training program there in 1900 that later became the Carnegie Library School, forerunner of the University of Pittsburgh library school. In 1911 he established the library school of the New York Public Library, which later transferred to Columbia University. LJ Hall of Fame. *DAB*, supplement 4; *DALB*.

ANDOVER PUBLIC LIBRARY, OH   142 W. Main St., Andover, OH 44003. Population served: 7,837. Circulation: 132,103. Holdings: 19,741. LJ November 15, 2009: 5-star library; October 1, 2010: 4-star library.

ANGEL FIRE, NM. *See* SHUTER LIBRARY OF ANGEL FIRE, ANGEL FIRE, NM.

ANN ARBOR DISTRICT LIBRARY, MI   343 S. Fifth Ave., Ann Arbor, MI 48104. Founded 1916. Population served: 155,611. Circulation, fiscal year 2008–2009: 9,200,000 (library website). Holdings: 335,192. 4 branches. LJ February 15, 2009; November 15, 2009; and October 1, 2010: 5-star library. HAPLR 2009, 2010.

APPROVAL PLANS. *See* ACQUISITIONS.

ARCHITECTURE AND BUILDINGS. *See* BUILDINGS AND FACILITIES.

ARDMORE FREE LIBRARY, PA   108 Ardmore Ave., Ardmore, PA 19003. Population served: 58,740. Circulation: 1,368,824. Holdings: 38,694. LJ October 1, 2010: 4-star library.

ARLINGTON HEIGHTS MEMORIAL LIBRARY, IL   500 Dunton, Arlington Heights, IL 60004. Founded 1926. Population served: 70,031. Circulation: 2,472,790. Holdings: 480,000. 1 bookmobile. LJ February 15, 2009, November 15, 2009, and October 1, 2010: 5-star library.

ARLINGTON PUBLIC LIBRARY, VA   2100 Clarendon Blvd., Arlington, VA 22201. Population served: 198,267. Circulation: 2,408,395. Holdings: 624,769. 10 branches.

ARLINGTON PUBLIC LIBRARY SYSTEM, TX   101 E. Abram St., Arlington, TX 76010. Population served: 359,467. Circulation: 1,500,000. Holdings: 500,000. 5 branches.

ASHLEY, OH. *See* WORNSTAFF MEMORIAL PUBLIC LIBRARY, ASHLEY, OH.

ASHTABULA HARBOR, OH. *See* HARBOR-TOPKY MEMORIAL LIBRARY, ASHTABULA HARBOR, OH.

ASKEW, SARAH BYRD, 1863–1942   Librarian. Born Dayton, OH, February 15, 1863. She attended Pratt Institute Library School in 1903 and worked as an assistant in Cleveland Public Library. In January 1905 she moved to New Jersey and organized the state public library commission, promoting library development; there were 66 public libraries in the state in 1905 and 316 at her death in 1942. Askew drove her own horse and buggy around the state to encourage library growth. In 1920 she secured legislation to create county libraries, reaching remote areas with book trucks. She was president of the New Jersey Library Association in 1913–1914 and 1939–1940. Askew died on October 20, 1942. LJ Hall of Fame; *DALB*.

ASPEN, CO. *See* PITKIN COUNTY LIBRARY, ASPEN, CO.

ASSOCIATIONS

Terminology

Merriam states that an association is "an organization of persons having a common interest." A common interest in libraries is reflected in the creation and maintenance of numerous associations. The *Encyclopedia of Associations* (48th ed., Gale-Cengage, 2009) includes 123 organizations with "library," "librarian," or "information" (or their derivatives) in their names. The 2010 supplement added 23 more.

The value of such associations is extensive. They promote connections among colleagues, provide a discussion forum, facilitate and often publish research, establish policies and guidelines for practitioners, present programs and in many cases conferences, lead in advocacy for libraries, and act as links to nonlibrary agencies (Fisher 1997).

In the United States there are national associations, state and municipal associations, and associations with special focus on types of collections, services, or clientele. The principal national organization is the American Library Association (ALA), with more than 60,000 members. ALA has 11 divisions that function as semi-independent associations; the most relevant to public libraries is the Public Library Association (*see* AMERICAN LIBRARY ASSOCIATION). Special focus organizations have been founded as affiliates of ALA. They include the following:

> American Indian Library Association (1979). Serves the interests of American Indians and Alaska natives. Issues a newsletter and holds annual meetings at ALA conferences. There were 193 members in June 2010.

> Asian/Pacific American Librarians Association (1980). Speaks to concerns of librarians who serve communities of Asian and

Pacific patrons. Issues a newsletter and holds annual meetings at ALA conferences.

Black Caucus (BCALA, 1970). Advocates "development, promotion and improvement of library services and resources to the nation's African American community; and provides leadership for the recruitment and professional development of African American librarians" (BCALA website). Issues a newsletter and holds annual meetings at ALA conferences.

Chinese American Librarians Association (1973). Has had various names: took present name in 1983. Has members in the United States, Canada, China, Hong Kong, Singapore, and Taiwan. Promotes interests of patrons and librarians of Chinese background and maintenance of appropriate collections. Issues a newsletter and holds annual meetings at ALA conferences.

REFORMA (1971). Promotes Spanish and Latino oriented collections, recruitment (scholarship program), and development of appropriate programs. Has 26 chapters and 896 members (from its website, June 2010).

Echavarria and Wertheimer (1997) discuss ethnic library associations.

Other national associations that contribute to public librarianship include the following:

American Society for Information Science and Technology (ASIS&T; 1937). Founded as American Documentation Institute; became American Society for Information Science in 1968 and took current name in 2000. Provides "focus, opportunity, and support to information professionals and organizations" (from its website, June 2010). Structured with elected officers, executive office, and 56 chapters in the United States and abroad. Holds annual conference; issues *Journal of the American Society for Information Science and Technology* (1950–; original title *Journal of the American Society for Information Science* changed to current title in 2000). There were about 4,000 members in June 2010.

Association for Library and Information Science Education (ALISE, 1945). Founded as Association of American Library Schools, changed name in 1960. Aims to "promote excellence in research, teaching, and service, and to provide an understanding of the values and ethos of library and information science" (from its website, June 2010). Has about 500 individual members and more than 60 institutional members. The institutions are U.S. and Canadian graduate programs that offer degrees in library and information science or "cognate fields." Programs do not need to be accredited by ALA. ALISE issue *Journal of Education*

for Library and Information Science (1960–; original title
Journal of Education for Librarianship changed to current title
in 1960). Other publications include a faculty directory and
annual statistics of library and information science programs. A
conference is held annually.

Two substantial regional associations are the following:

Pacific Northwest Library Association (PNLA, 1909). Represents
Alaska, Alberta, British Columbia, Idaho, Montana, Oregon, and
Washington. Provides "opportunities for communication, education, and leadership that transcend political boundaries" and aims
to "develop stronger library networks and networking in the
region" (from its website, June 2010). PNLA holds an annual
conference and publishes *PNLA Quarterly* (1989; issued in
electronic form only from 2008). There were 165 personal
members and 35 institutional members in June 2010.

Southeastern Library Association (1930). Represents Alabama,
Arkansas, Florida, Georgia, Kentucky, Louisiana, Mississippi,
North Carolina, South Carolina, Tennessee, Virginia, and West
Virginia. Most of the members are in academic libraries. Holds
biennial conferences and issues the quarterly journal *South-
eastern Librarian* (1951–).

Public library development is a key concern in state library associations.
They usually have elected officers, an executive office, divisions, committees,
publications, and conferences. They typically work closely with their respective state libraries or state library agencies. The New York Library Association, founded in 1890 by Melvil Dewey, was the first of these state
organizations; it served as a "model for librarians from other states"
(Wiegand 1996, 197). Other early state associations were the Iowa Library
Society (1890), Massachusetts Library Club (1890), New Jersey Library Association (1890), Wisconsin State Library Association (1891), Connecticut
State Library Association (1891), Maine Library Association (1891),
Michigan Library Association (1891), Library Association of Indiana
(1891), Colorado Library Association (1892), Library Association of Wash-
ington City (1894), Vermont Library Association (1894), California Library
Association (1898), Nebraska Library Association (1895), Illinois State
Library Association (1896), and Georgia Library Association (1897).

References

Echavarria, Tami, and Andrew B. Wertheimer. 1997. Surveying the role of ethnic-
American library associations. *Library Trends* 46, no. 2 (Fall): 373–92.
Fisher, William. 1997. The value of professional associations. *Library Trends* 46,
no. 2 (Fall): 320–31.
Wiegand, Wayne A. 1996. *Irrepressible Reformer: A Biography of Melvil Dewey*.
Chicago: American Library Association.

ATGLEN PUBLIC LIBRARY, PA   413 Valley Ave., Atglen, PA 19310. Founded 1945. Population served: 1,217. Circulation in 2008: 35,334 (communication from the library). Holdings: 9,707. LJ February 15, 2009, and November 15, 2009: 4-star library; October 1, 2010: 3-star library.

ATHENS, GA. *See* PINEWOODS LIBRARY, ATHENS, GA.

ATHENS COUNTY PUBLIC LIBRARIES, OH. *See* NELSONVILLE PUBLIC LIBRARY, OH.

ATKINSON PUBLIC LIBRARY, NE   113 W. State St., Atkinson, NE 68713. Population served: 1,244. Circulation: 27,597. Holdings: 18,075. LJ February 15, 2009, November 15, 2009, and October 1, 2010: 5-star library.

ATLANTA-FULTON COUNTY LIBRARY SYSTEM, GA   Margaret Mitchell Square, Atlanta, GA 30303. Population served: 832,000. Circulation: 2,700,000. Holdings: 3,700,000. 33 branches. LJ February 15, 2009: 3-star library. *See also* SERVICES TO AFRICAN AMERICANS.

AUDIOVISUAL COLLECTIONS

Terminology

"Audiovisual" or "audio-visual" has been in use since 1937 (*Merriam*), originally as a term describing classroom teaching aids. That sense of the word remains in the *Merriam* definition: "designed to aid in learning or teaching by making use of both hearing and sight." *American Heritage* has a broader view: "of or relating to materials, such as films, that present information in audible and pictorial form ... an aid, other than printed matter, that uses sight or sound to present information." Whether a given item needs to have both audio and visual elements to be "audiovisual" is unclear; both dictionary definitions seem to say both, but there are media commonly grouped in the audiovisual category that are audio only (sound recordings) or visual only (silent films, filmstrips, and slides).

ODLIS offers this definition: "a work in a medium that combines sounds and visual images, for example a motion picture or video recording with a sound track or a slide presentation synchronized with audiotape," supporting the dual aspect. In this handbook, visual media (with or without sound) are discussed in the present entry, and all totally audio media are discussed in the entry MUSIC COLLECTIONS.

The early visual media were 8-mm films, filmstrips, and slides. Today's public library has replaced them with videotapes and, more recently, digital videodiscs. Videotapes, once sold in two competing formats, became standardized in the VHS format. This medium, "a magnetic tape used to record visual images and associated sound for playback or broadcasting" (*American Heritage*), was dominant in public libraries (and video rental stores) from the 1980s to around 2003. With up to six hours of playing time, VHS tapes are suitable for feature films as well as documentaries and teaching functions. They present difficulties to the user in locating specific places on the tape and to the librarian in allowing the patron to erase parts of the material at home. The digital videodisc (DVD) was developed by several companies in 1995. It was introduced in Japan in November 1996 and in the United States in March 1997. A DVD is the same size as a compact disc (CD) but with greater storage capacity. A dual-layer DVD holds 240 minutes of playing time; a double-sided DVD holds 266 minutes. Compared to the six-hour playing time of a videotape, these capacities are not enough to drive the industry, but the newer format has advantages in definition and in capability of indexing to specific locations. The capacity weakness has been addressed by the Blu-ray format, introduced by SONY in 2006. This is a high-definition optical disc that stores up to 50 gigabytes (five times the standard DVD). By 2009, Blu-rays were circulated by 10 percent of public and academic libraries despite playback problems. In 2010 the basic DVD remained the medium of choice in public libraries.

Current Situation

Many librarians were skeptical at first about collecting videocassettes because of what appeared to be their exclusively entertainment nature and because of competition concerns of video rental shops in the community. Informal agreements were achieved in some cases whereby recent movies would be left to the rental shops, and materials of more enduring interest (like classic films and documentaries) would be acquired by the library. Eventually, librarians came to accept the value of comprehensive collecting as circulation figures for videos soared. The impact of the DVD format on circulation has been impressive. In surveys of Normative Data Project libraries covering the years 2003–2006, the percent of book circulation achieved by DVDs rose from 6.27 to 20.04 percent. In 2005 circulation of DVDs exceeded for the first time circulation of videocassettes (*Bowker Annual* 2007, 405).

Public library holdings of video formats doubled in the 10-year period from 1999 to 2008 in terms of items per capita. Figures released in June 2010 by the Institute of Museum and Library Services show that public libraries held 73.5 video items per 1,000 population in 1999 and 166.7 video items per 1,000 population in 2008 (Institute of Museum and Library Services 2010).

Expenditures for video materials by public libraries were reported as 9.47 percent of total acquisition expenditures in 2005. This figure approximates the proposed standard 10 to 15 percent for audiovisual expenditures by public libraries announced in 1975 by the Public Library Association (*Guidelines* 1975), but one needs to keep in mind the difference between audio and audiovisual categories.

All the data exhibit a growing importance of visual formats. Several problem areas have developed along with this surge. One concern is longevity and how to extend it through appropriate storage. No one knows the life span of a DVD, which is essentially a CD, on the market only some 25 years. Studies of CD longevity are noted in the entry MUSIC COLLECTIONS. At present public libraries do not take special pains to store CDs or DVDs in the best environmental conditions; they are simply treated as parts of the general materials collection. Time will tell whether this is a wise policy. Access to the videotape and DVD collection is another troublesome matter. Videotapes come in cartons that are more or less book size and can stand spine out on regular shelves. DVDs and CDs are better displayed frontally in browser bins, but these consume more space than shelves. And what does the patron find in the browser bin? Either an empty container—with the actual disc kept at the circulation desk—or a container sealed in a plastic jacket that obscures the written material on the item. The plastic jacket is used to deter theft, which is otherwise simple enough if the thief is content to take the disc without its container.

If a patron wants to see a videotape or DVD in the library, equivalent to reading a book there, a listening-viewing station needs to be provided. Large libraries will want several: a costly investment.

Selection of video materials remains awkward. Sections of reviews in the library magazines give useful guidance over a limited range of new materials. But the video field is outside bibliographic control so that librarians cannot make choices from the whole output in all formats as they can with printed books. A new addition to the H. W. Wilson core collections series offers a recommended list of about 2,300 electronic resources, including videos, with useful critical annotations (*Nonbook Materials* 2008). Equipment needed is found in *Audio Visual Market Place*.

Cataloging of video items follows AACR2 (1978) with various later changes. Like book cataloging, it is mostly a venture of locating catalog copy in national databases (all aspects of audiovisual cataloging are taken up by Olson 2008).

Interlibrary loan of videos and other nonprint media brings up issues of possible damage plus increased costs of special shipping. Recent efforts by the American Library Association press libraries to lend all formats: "Supplying libraries are encouraged to lend audiovisual material, newspapers, and other categories of material that have traditionally been noncirculating," and "audiovisual materials should be lent to other libraries and agencies as freely as possible" (Hicks 2005).

References

Audio Visual Market Place. 2009. 37th ed. Medford, NJ: Information Today.

Bowker Annual of Library and Book Trade Information. 2007. New York: R. R. Bowker.

Guidelines for Audiovisual Materials and Services for Large Public Libraries; Recommendations for Audio Visual Materials and Services for Small and Medium Sized Public Libraries. 1975. Chicago: Public Library Association.

Hicks, Avery. 2005. Interlibrary loans of audiovisual materials: breaking the taboo. *Virginia Libraries* 51, no. 2 (April/May/June): 25–28.

Nonbook Materials Core Collection: A Selection Guide. 2008. New York: H. W. Wilson.

Olson, Nancy B., et al. 2008. *Cataloging of Audiovisual Materials and Other Special Materials.* 5th ed. Westport, CT: Libraries Unlimited.

U.S. Institute of Museum and Library Services. 2010. Public library visits, circulation spike while staff numbers stay the same. Press release, June 30, 2010. Washington: Institute of Museum and Library Services. www/imls.gov/news/2010/0063010/shtm. Accessed August 2010.

AURORA PUBLIC LIBRARY, CO   14949 Alameda Parkway, Aurora, CO 80012. Population served: 295,775. Circulation: 843,000. Holdings: 440,000. 7 branches (4 of them closed in 2009).

AUSTIN PUBLIC LIBRARY, TX   800 Guadalupe St., Austin, TX 78701. Population served: 692,102. Circulation: 3,373,408. Holdings: 1,705,805. 21 branches. LJ library of the year, 1993.

AUTOMATION. *See* INFORMATION TECHNOLOGY.

AVALON FREE PUBLIC LIBRARY, NJ   235 32nd St., Avalon, NJ 08202. Founded 2005. Population served: 6,274 (communication from the library). Circulation in 2007: 105,984 (communication from the library). Holdings: 32,539. LJ February 15, 2009, November 15, 2009, and October 1, 2010: 5-star library.

AVON LAKE PUBLIC LIBRARY, OH   32649 Electric Blvd., Avon Lake, OH 44012. Founded 1937. Population served: 18,761. Circulation: 648,707. Holdings: 94,577. HAPLR 2009, 2010.

B

B. B. COMER MEMORIAL LIBRARY, SYLACAUGA, AL   314 N. Broadway, Sylacauga, AL 35150. Founded 1936. Population served: 12,616. Circulation: 150,000. Holdings: 65,000. IMLS award, 2000.

BAINBRIDGE, GA. *See* SOUTHERN GEORGIA REGIONAL PUBLIC LIBRARY SYSTEM, BAINBRIDGE, GA.

BAKER, AUGUSTA BRAXTON, 1911–1998   Librarian. Born Baltimore, MD, April 1, 1911, the granddaughter of a slave. After study at the University of Pittsburgh and Albany State Teachers College (NY), she began working in 1937 at New York Public Library (NYPL), remaining 36 years. Baker was a noted storyteller and collector of books for children on the black experience and folklore. She was the first black in upper administration at NYPL, serving as assistant coordinator of children's services, then supervisor of storytelling in 1953. She was named coordinator of children's services in 1961. Baker made radio and television broadcasts and was a consultant for *Sesame Street*. She taught at library schools of Rutgers, Columbia, and South Carolina. NYPL published her bibliography of *The Black Experience in Children's Books* (1971). She died February 22, 1998. *DALB*, 2nd supplement.

BAKERSFIELD, CA. *See* KERN COUNTY LIBRARY, BAKERSFIELD, CA.

BALTIMORE, MD. *See* ENOCH PRATT FREE LIBRARY, BALTIMORE, MD.

BALTIMORE COUNTY PUBLIC LIBRARY, TOWSON, MD   320 York Rd., Towson, MD 21204. Founded 1948. Population served: 754,291. Circulation: 10,017,547. Holdings: 1,633,710. 17 branches, 3 bookmobiles. LJ February 15, 2009: 4-star library; LJ November 15, 2009: 3-star library. HAPLR 2008, 2009, 2010. The library played an important role in promotion of popular reading during the 1960s and 1970s. Directors: Richard D. Minnich, 1949–1963; Charles W. Robinson, 1963–1996; James H. Fish, 1996–.

BANCROFT PUBLIC LIBRARY, BANCROFT, IA   208 E. Ramsey St., Bancroft, IA 50517. Population served: 1,416. Circulation: 26,894. Holdings: 15,400. LJ October 1, 2010: 4-star library.

BARRINGTON PUBLIC LIBRARY DISTRICT, IL   505 N. Northwest Highway, Barrington, IL 60010. Founded 1913. Population served: 42,127. Circulation: 705,222. Holdings: 259,592. LJ February 15, 2009, November 15, 2009, and October 1, 2010: 3-star library.

BARTLESVILLE PUBLIC LIBRARY, OK   600 S. Johnstone, Bartlesville, OK 74003. Founded 1913. Population served: 50,000. Circulation: 450,000. Holdings: 120,000. In 1950 the library attracted national attention when librarian Ruth Brown, who had been in office since 1919, was dismissed by the board for subscribing to "subversive periodicals." Her involvement with racial integration was another factor (Boyer 2002, 286). Efforts by the American Library Association on her behalf were not successful. Brown was the subject of a Columbia film, *Storm Center*, in 1956.

Reference

Boyer, Paul S. 2002. *Purity in Print: Book Censorship in America from the Gilded Age to the Computer Age.* 2nd ed. Madison: University of Wisconsin Press.

BARTRAM TRAIL REGIONAL LIBRARY, WASHINGTON, GA   204 E. Liberty St., Washington, GA 30675. Also known as the Mary Willis Free Library. Founded 1889 (the first free public library in the state). Population served: 33,165. Circulation: 89,505. Holdings: 98,889. 2 branches, 1 bookmobile.

BATON ROUGE, LA. *See* EAST BATON ROUGE PARISH LIBRARY, BATON ROUGE, LA.

BATTLE CREEK PUBLIC LIBRARY, NE   103 E. Main St., Battle Creek, NE 68715. Population served: 1,158. Circulation: 35,386. Holdings: 19,089.

LJ October 1, 2010: 3-star library. In December 2009 the new building, financed by a donation from the Lied Foundation and Trust, was named Lied Battle Creek Public Library.

BAY ST. LOUIS, MS. *See* HANCOCK COUNTY LIBRARY SYSTEM, BAY ST. LOUIS, MS.

BAYPORT PUBLIC LIBRARY, MN   582 N. Fourth St., Bayport, MN 55003. Founded 1960. Population served: 3,162. Circulation: 82,583. Holdings: 28,555. LJ February 15, 2009: 3-star library.

BEAUFORT COUNTY LIBRARY SYSTEM, BEAUFORT, SC   311 Scott St., Beaufort, SC 29902. Founded 1918. Population served: 135,725. Circulation: 516,992. Holdings: 216,295. Dorothy Canfield Fisher Award, "outstanding small library," 1963.

BEE CAVE PUBLIC LIBRARY, TX   4000 Galleria Parkway, Bee Cave, TX 78738. Population served: 2,300. Circulation: 162,000. Holdings: 23,000. LJ October 1, 2010: 5-star library.

BEER, WILLIAM, 1849–1927   Librarian, mining engineer. Born Plymouth, United Kingdom. He studied in Paris (medicine, languages, and art), 1871–1877. Returning to England, he studied mining engineering and antiquities and worked in Newcastle Public Library. Beer was a mining engineer in the United States and in 1889 a librarian, Topeka (KS) Public Library. He was librarian, Howard Memorial Library, New Orleans, 1891, then of the New Orleans Free Public Library, a consolidation of the Fisk Free Library and Lyceum Library. Beer resigned 1906, returning to Howard Memorial; he developed it as a reference library. At his death, the library had 80,000 volumes. *DAB, DALB.*

BELCAMP, MD. *See* HARFORD COUNTY PUBLIC LIBRARY, BELCAMP, MD.

BELDEN, CHARLES FRANCIS DORR, 1870–1931   Librarian. Born October 5, 1870, in Syracuse, NY. He earned bachelor's and law degrees from Harvard and was assistant law librarian there, 1902–1908. He was chairman of the Massachusetts Free Public Library Commission, 1909–1931. He served as librarian of the Boston Public Library, 1917–1931, a period of greatly increased circulation; an annex to the main building (1917); and a business library (1930) and a developed system of 32 branches. Belden was president of the American Library Association in 1926. His beliefs were that the library is everyman's university, that library research is necessary, and that cooperation among libraries is essential and in the freedom to read. In a 1926 article he wrote that "the true public library must stand for intellectual freedom of access to the printed word." *DALB*.

BELL MEMORIAL LIBRARY, MENTONE, IN   306 N. Broadway, Mentone, IN 46539. Founded 1916. Population served: 3,678. Circulation: 158,394. Holdings: 25,711. LJ February 15, 2009; November 15, 2009; and October 1, 2010: 5-star library. HAPLR 2009, 2010.

BELLEVILLE PUBLIC LIBRARY, KS   1327 19th St., Belleville, KS 66935. Founded 1930. Population served: 1,983. Circulation: 44,987. Holdings: 21,045. LJ February 15, 2009; November 15, 2009; and October 1, 2010: 3-star library.

BELLEVILLE PUBLIC LIBRARY, WI   130 S. Vine St., Belleville, WI 53508. Founded 1878. Population served: 2,909. Circulation: 62,365. Holdings: 22,777. HAPLR 2009, 2010.

BERESFORD PUBLIC LIBRARY, SD   115 S. Third St., Beresford, SD 57004. Population served: 4,500. Circulation: 56,000. Holdings: 33,000. HAPLR 2010.

BERKELEY PUBLIC LIBRARY, CA   2090 Kittredge Way, Berkeley, CA 94704. Founded 1893. Population served: 104,534. Circulation: 1,486,307. Holdings: 454,147. 4 branches. LJ February 15, 2009; November 15, 2009; and October 1, 2010: 4-star library. The art deco–style central library building, by architect James Plachek, opened January 31, 1931. Extensive renovations were completed in 2002. In 1982 the building was listed on the National Register of Historic Places.

BERNARDSVILLE PUBLIC LIBRARY, NJ   One Anderson Hill Rd., Bernardsville, NJ 07924. Population served: 7,345. Circulation: 219, 613. Holdings: 84,128. LJ February 15, 2009; November 15, 2009; and October 1, 2010: 5-star library.

BEVERLY HILLS PUBLIC LIBRARY, CA   444 N. Rexford Dr., Beverly Hills, CA 90210. Founded 1929. Population served: 35,969. Circulation: 620,909. Holdings: 293,813. LJ February 15, 2009: 4-star library; November 15, 2009: 5-star library; October 1, 2010: 4-star library.

BIBLIOGRAPHIC INSTRUCTION. *See* INFORMATION LITERACY INSTRUCTION.

BILLINGS, JOHN SHAW, 1838–1913   Librarian, surgeon, army officer. Born April 12, 1839, in Cotton Township, IN. He graduated in 1857 from Miami

(Ohio) University, then earned an MD 1860 from Medical College of Ohio, Cincinnati. An army surgeon in the Civil War, he remained in uniform to 1895, ranked deputy surgeon general. In 1880–1895, Billings prepared the important *Index Catalogue of the Surgeon General's Office*. He went to the New York Public Library (NYPL) as director, January 15, 1896, organizing the Astor and Lenox Libraries. He was largely responsible for the interior layout of the new building, 1911. NYPL staff grew from 42 to nearly 1,000 by 1913. Billings retired on March 3, 1913, and died a week later. He was buried with military honors at Arlington Cemetery. *DALB*.

BIRMINGHAM PUBLIC LIBRARY, AL   2100 Park Pl., Birmingham, AL 35203. Founded 1902. Population served: 403,327. Circulation: 1,436,303. Holdings: 880,682. 20 branches. LJ October 1, 2010: 3-star library.

BLACK BRIDGE LIBRARY, DIME BOX, TX   1079 Austin Blvd., Dime Box, TX 77853. Founded 2003. Population served: 1,333. Circulation: 30,036. Holdings: 9,600. LJ February 15, 2009, and November 15, 2009: 5-star library.

BLOOMFIELD PUBLIC LIBRARY, NE   121 S. Broadway, Bloomfield, NE 68718. Founded 1915. Population served: 1,126. Circulation: 16,175. Holdings: 8,376. LJ November 15, 2009: 4-star library; October 1, 2010: 3-star library.

BLOOMINGTON, IN. *See* MONROE COUNTY PUBLIC LIBRARY, BLOOMINGTON, IN.

BLUE, THOMAS FOUNTAIN, 1866–1935   Librarian. Born March 6, 1866, in Farmville, VA, the son of former slaves. He graduated from Hampton Normal and Agricultural Institute in 1888 and taught school. He earned a bachelor of divinity degree, Richmond Theological Seminary, in 1898. Blue worked with the YMCA as the organization's secretary in Louisville, KY, 1899–1905. Although untrained as a librarian, he joined the Louisville Free Public Library (KY) in 1905 as branch librarian, Western Colored Branch. The branch was the first in the United States to serve black patrons with a black staff, and Blue was the first black to hold an administrative position in an American public library. He established a training program for black librarians which drew students from the libraries of Houston, Birmingham, Atlanta, Evansville (IN), Memphis, Knoxville, Nashville, and Chattanooga. A second branch for African Americans opened in Louisville in 1915. Blue was named head of the library's "Colored Department" in 1919, directing a staff of eight persons. The department had two branches, 80 classroom collections, two junior high school locations, and 15 other stations. Blue remained with Louisville until his death. In 1929 he was the first African

American to make a program appearance at an American Library Association conference. *DALB.*

BLUE HILL PUBLIC LIBRARY, ME   5 Parker Point Rd., Blue Hill, ME 04614. Founded 1938, with antecedent subscription libraries dating back to 1796. Population served: 3,781. Circulation: 110,418. Holdings: 35,526. LJ February 15, 2009, and November 15, 2009: 4-star library.

BOISE PUBLIC LIBRARY, ID   715 S. Capitol Blvd., Boise, ID 83702. Founded 1905. Population served: 193,161. Circulation: 1,510,530. Holdings: 330,131. 1 branch.

BOLINGBROOK, IL. *See* FOUNTAINDALE PUBLIC LIBRARY DISTRICT, BOLINGBROOK, IL.

BOLTON FREE LIBRARY, BOLTON LANDING, NY   4922 Lakeshore Dr., Bolton Landing, NY 12814. Population served: 2,117. Circulation: 48,558. Holdings: 19,132. LJ October 1, 2010: 4-star library.

BOLTON LANDING, NY. *See* BOLTON FREE LIBRARY, BOLTON LANDING, NY.

BONNERS FERRY, ID. *See* BOUNDARY COUNTY DISTRICT LIBRARY, BONNERS FERRY, ID.

BOOK SELECTION. *See* COLLECTION DEVELOPMENT.

BOOKMOBILES

Terminology

American Heritage defines bookmobile as "a truck, trailer, or van serving as a mobile lending library." The National Center for Educational Statistics (NCES) elaborates: "A bookmobile is a traveling branch library. It consists of at least all of the following: (1) a truck or van that carries an organized collection of library materials; (2) a paid staff, and (3) regularly scheduled hours (bookmobile stops) for being open to the public" (U.S. National Center for Education Statistics 2007, notes to table 2). NCES is redefining bookmobile operation; the truck or van is still a bookmobile whether or not it has a paid staff and so on. *ODLIS* offers "a branch on wheels" or "a mobile library." A "traveling library" of the late nineteenth century was simply a conveyance for shipping rotating collections of books to schools or other libraries; originally there was no public service element, but this was added later. "Field libraries" in "book wagons" were promoted by Melvil Dewey, who operated them in New York State in the 1890s; they did offer public access. "Book wagon" remained the term of choice for the horse-drawn vehicles that undertook those tasks. "Bookmobile," drawn from "automobile," replaced it with the emergence of motorcars.

Historical Summary

Melvil Dewey, as state librarian of New York, initiated book wagons in the state in 1892. He wrote, "No one who fully appreciates the great influence of books and reading can doubt that the money required to equip such a book wagon and to pay the salary of such a traveling librarian would yield very great educational dividends" (quoted in Pennell 1970, 4; for details on the project, see Wiegand 1996, 148, 203). Around 1905 two notable efforts by two notable women took place. In Wisconsin, Lutie Eugenia Stearns established a system of "traveling libraries" with around 100 books in a "strong book case which had a shelf, double doors with a lock and key, a record book for loans, printed copies of the few simple rules, borrowers' blanks, and so complete a line of equipments that it could be set up anywhere on a table, a box or a counter" (Pawley 2007, 267). Stearns (*see* STEARNS, LUTIE EUGENIA) herself was the mobile librarian, utilizing "stage coach, buggy, wagon, passenger coach and caboose" to transport her stock, dedicated book wagons being as yet unavailable. In winter she used a sleigh, wearing a "black bear-skin to wear over my fur-lined muskrat coat" (Pawley 2007, 268).

The other distinguished pioneer was Mary L. Titcomb, librarian of the Washington County Free Library, Hagerstown, MD (*see* TITCOMB, MARY L.). She began with traveling collections sent out on hired wagons but in 1905 arranged for a wagon to be converted specifically for books, capacity around 200 volumes. At first the driver handled public service tasks, then a library assistant began to accompany him. In 1915 the library bought a large bookmobile with a capacity of 500 books on its shelves. The library is still operating bookmobile service.

Bookmobile activity became national, and vehicles became larger. In Hibbing, MN, in 1919, there was a walk-in van with room for a librarian's desk and space for 12 patrons to look at the shelves. Evanston (IL) Public Library set up a service in 1920, with a standard Chevrolet truck converted to book use with donated funds and local workers. It made stops "in sections of town farthest from the streetcar line" (Pennell 1970, 9). Areas covered expanded. Countywide service began in New York's Monroe County in 1923, guided by Ruth B. Drake. She and an assistant drove the truck, making several weekly trips in all weather, visiting country stores, schoolhouses, and farm homes. Beulah K. Eyerly, with experience in Washington County, MD, headed a mobile effort in Susquehanna County, PA, in 1924. She reported 32 trips in her first year, circulating nearly 4,000 books.

Ohio made extensive use of bookmobiles from the 1930s. By 1962, a fourth of the state's libraries were operating them, accounting for 14.2 percent of total public library circulation. In 1935 there were five vehicles running, while in 1966 there were 99. Other states showed similar patterns of use and growth. The Library Services Act of 1956 and its later renewals provided funds and impetus for bookmobile activity. By 1965, funds from that legislation had been used to acquire 487 vehicles.

The number of bookmobiles in service peaked in the 1960s and then began to decline, as these figures show:

1943	300
1950	603
1956	919
1962	1,334
1989	921
1991	1,125
1993	1,035
1996	966
2000	884
2005	825
2008	797

(Data from Pennell 1970 and NCES reports.)

One reason for the diminishing number of vehicles is the increase in number of public library branch outlets. Branches tend to replace bookmobiles when patron demand is sufficient at certain locations. There were 7,017 branches in the United States in 1993, 7,503 in 2005, and 7,629 in 2008 (*see* BRANCH LIBRARIES).

Current Situation

NCES reported that in 2008, 670 American libraries were sending out bookmobiles. The most active states have been California, Florida, Illinois, Indiana, Kentucky, Louisiana, North Carolina, Ohio, Pennsylvania, South Carolina, Utah, and Virginia. Maine is the only state without bookmobile service. According to figures in the *American Library Directory* for (American Library Association 2010), these public libraries are operating more than one bookmobile: Stark County District Library (OH), 4; Seattle Public Library, 4; Baltimore County Library (MD), 3; Carroll County Library (MD), 3; Louisville Free Library (KY), 3; Pierce County Library (WA), 3; Topeka and Shawnee County Public Library (KS), 3; Charleston County Library (SC), 2; Chicago Public Library, 2; Columbus Metropolitan Library, 2; Detroit Public Library, 2; Harford County Public Library (MD), 2; Miami-Dade Public Library, 2; San Antonio Public Library, 2; San Diego County Library, 2; Toledo-Lucas County Library (OH), 2; Wadsworth Public Library (OH), 2; and Williamsburg Regional Library (VA), 2. One of the pioneer cities noted above, Evanston (IL), dropped its bookmobile service in 1997.

Leading manufacturers of the vans are Gerstenslager Company, Wooster, OH, and Farber Specialty Vehicles, Columbus, OH. Gerstenslager entered the library field after long experience in making trucks for many uses, including postal and military. Their 1948 "Pioneer" was acquired by Mansfield Public Library (OH) and displayed there. Lois Pennell was the supervising librarian. The van could carry up to 2,000 books. It was exhibited nationally in 1949 and became the industry standard. In 1957 the company provided Hagerstown, MD, with the eleventh vehicle used there in the 52-year history of bookmobile service (see above). The new one was 33 feet long, with desks for two librarians and 143 feet of shelves. Some later vehicles carry up to 6,000 volumes and have air-conditioning plus computer access. Both Gerstenslager and Farber offer custom-built vans in a variety of sizes and optional features.

Clarion University of Pennsylvania had a Center for the Study of Rural Librarianship from 1998 to 2008. A journal, *Bookmobile and Outreach Services*, issued 1998–2008, had brief articles on the practical side of bookmobile operation.

Most of the book stock in bookmobiles has always been adult fiction, with children's books as a second category. The bulk of material would be classed as recreational. While this factor might be a source of concern, it has not been an area of complaint in the literature.

References

Alloway, Catherine S., ed. 1990. *The Book Stops Here: New Directions in Bookmobile Service*. Metuchen, NJ: Scarecrow Press.

American Library Association. 2010. Bookmobiles in the U.S. Chicago: American Library Association. www.ala.org/ala/ors/statsaboutlib/bookmobiles. Accessed September 2010.

Bookmobile and Outreach Services. Clarion University of Pennsylvania, Department of Library Science, 1998–2008. Semiannual.

Brown, Eleanor Frances. 1990. *Bookmobiles and Bookmobile Service*. Metuchen, NJ: Scarecrow Press.

Dilger-Hill, Jeannie, and Erica MacCreaigh, eds. 2010. *On the Road with Outreach: Mobile Library Services*. Santa Barbara, CA: Libraries Unlimited.

Pawley, Christine. 2007. Blood and thunder on the bookmobile: American public libraries and the construction of "the reader," 1950–1995. In *Institutions of Reading*, ed. Thomas Augst and Kenneth Carpenter, 264–82. Amherst: University of Massachusetts Press.

Pennell, Lois G. 1970. Bookmobiles. In *Encyclopedia of Library and Information Science* 3: 11–57. New York: Marcel Dekker.

U.S. National Center for Education Statistics. 2007. *Public Libraries in the United States: Fiscal Year 2005*. Washington, DC: National Center for Education Statistics.

Wiegand, Wayne A. 1996. *Irrepressible Reformer: A Biography of Melvil Dewey*. Chicago: American Library Association.

BOSTON PUBLIC LIBRARY, MA   Copley Square, Boston, MA 02116. Opened March 20, 1854. Population served: 569,165. Circulation: 2,848,813 (library website, fiscal year 2007). Holdings: 15,686,902. 26 branches. LJ February 15, 2009: 3-star library. The first American large-city public library, Boston Public Library (BPL) resulted from the vision and efforts of several men. Alexandre Vattemare, a Frenchman, visited Boston in 1841 as part of his promotion of international understanding through sharing of books and creation of libraries. His influence and numerous gifts of books to Boston led to the creation of a City Council committee charged with exploring the idea of library. Mayor Josiah Quincy strongly supported the initiative and secured state authority with enabling legislation. The statute that passed on March 18, 1848, was the first of its kind in the country. No further official action followed until May 1852, when the council appointed Edward Capen as librarian and selected a board of trustees. The board was notable for its distinguished and dedicated membership, including Edward Everett (former governor of Massachusetts and president of Harvard—later to be secretary of state) and George Ticknor, former Harvard professor. Ticknor, "the true founder of the Boston Public Library" (Curley 1994, 85), was principal author of the "Report of the Trustees of the Public Library of the City of Boston" (July 6, 1852), which announced the intention to provide a library free to all, with home circulation of materials, serving both scholars and the general public. This report has been acclaimed as the "charter of the American public library movement" (Lord 1970, 101). It presented what came to be called the "ladder theory" of book selection and public reading, holding that taste for the best books would develop step-by-step with a beginning in popular fiction (see COLLECTION DEVELOPMENT; PHILOSOPHY OF PUBLIC LIBRARIANSHIP).

Gifts and endowments came in, and the library opened in its first location, two rooms in the Adams School on Mason Street, on March 20, 1854. Public acceptance was pronounced: by May 1854, 6,590 persons had registered, and 35,389 items had circulated to them. An accession book was available, with a shelf list, official card catalog, and a printed alphabetical catalog (Stone 1977, 158). After four years on Mason Street, a new building was dedicated on Boylston Street on January 1, 1858. By this time BPL had 70,000 volumes, ranking as the second-largest public collection after the Library of Congress. Charles Coffin Jewett became "superintendent" in 1858, remaining to 1868; Edward Capen remained as librarian under Jewett. Innovations in the Jewett era included publication of classified lists from 1866 (covering fiction, history and politics, theology, medicine, law, biography, and travel) and acquisition of the DeKondelka music collection in 1858 (see MUSIC COLLECTIONS). Justin Winsor directed the library from 1868 to 1877. A card catalog, the first U.S. Braille collection, and a branch library program were highlights of his tenure. The branches constructed were East Boston (1870), South Boston (1872), Roxbury (1873), Charleston (1874), Brighton (1874), Dorchester (1875), and Jamaica Plain (1877). By 1877, BPL was "the largest library in the country, the most used, and probably the best" (Williams 1988, 7). The collection had reached 300,000 volumes, and circulation was above 1 million per year.

A dispute with the trustees prompted Winsor's resignation in 1877, and the post was vacant for 18 years, with the library administered by committees of the trustees. In March 1887, a contract was negotiated with the architectural firm of McKim, Mead and White for a new building; they started work in the following year and completed the structure for opening on February 1, 1895. The building, still in use, is remarkable for its design, artwork, and sculptures. It was named to the National Register of Historic Places in 1973 and designated a National Historic Landmark in 1986 (photos and floor plans are in Wick 1977). With the new building there was a new librarian in charge, Herbert Putnam, later to be Librarian of Congress. Under Putnam, BPL displayed an orderly administration, a new children's room, and interlibrary loan service. Putnam's successor was Horace G. Wadlin, who remained to 1917.

Charles F. D. Belden was librarian, 1917–1931. It was a prosperous period just before the Depression: an annex to the main building opened in 1917; a special branch for business opened in 1930. Thirty-two branches were in operation by 1930. The *Boston Public Library Quarterly* was published (1926–1948, 1949–1960).

Administrative reorganizations under Milton E. Lord, librarian 1932–1965, included new offices for a "keeper of rare books" and "keeper of prints." Lord's organizational plan was a simple one, with main units for circulation, reference, and administration. Philip J. McNiff was librarian, 1965–1983. An important addition to the main building was designed by Philip Johnson in 1972; it housed circulation functions, leaving the research activity in the 1895 building. The original structure was renovated in the tenure of Arthur Curley (1983–1996), who also took a successful initiative in adjusting staff salaries. Bernard A. Margolis assumed the directorship in 1997 under the new title of president. Amy Ryan became president in 2008.

Elements of political interference in library matters have been a concern. It was said in 2001 that "the present municipal administration is attempting to curtail the library's formerly semi-independent status . . . the mayor wishes to have the library's business procedures more closely aligned to other city departments, whether or not this serves the ultimate goals and mission of the library" (Grealish 2001, 223). Budgetary difficulties have had their impact as well. In 2009, the Business Branch, founded in 1930, had to close, with an estimated saving of $4 million a year (its services moved into the central library). Service hours were reduced to 16 per week in the Music and Fine Arts Department (*Library Journal*, April 15, 2009, 12). In 2010, four of the 26 branches had to close, and at least 86 positions had to be eliminated (*Library Journal*, May 1, 2010, 12). On a happier note, there was a $10 million grant by Norman B. Leventhal in 2007 to enhance the map center that he had originally endowed in 2004 (*Library Journal*, October 1, 2007, 18).

References

Curley, Arthur P. 1994. Boston Public Library. In *Encyclopedia of Library History*, 85–86. New York: Garland.
Grealish, William. 2001. Boston Public Library. In *International Dictionary of Library Histories* 1: 218–23. Chicago: Fitzroy Dearborn.

Lord, Milton E. 1970. Boston Public Library. In *Encyclopedia of Library and Information Science* 3: 100–4. New York: Marcel Dekker.

Stone, Elizabeth. 1977. *American Library Development*. New York: H. W. Wilson.

Whitehill, Walter M. 1956. *Boston Public Library: A Centennial History*. Cambridge, MA: Harvard University Press.Wick, Peter Arms. 1977. *A Handbook to the Art and Architecture of the Boston Public Library*. Boston: Associates of the Boston Public Library.

Williams, Patrick. 1988. *The American Public Library and the Problem of Purpose*. New York: Greenwood Press.

BOSTWICK, ARTHUR ELMORE, 1860–1942   Librarian, editor. Born March 8, 1860, in Litchfield, CT. He took degrees from Yale University: BA, 1881; PhD in physics, 1883. He taught high school, 1884–1886. Then he took up editorial work with *Appleton's Cyclopaedia of American Biography* and the Funk and Wagnalls *Standard Dictionary of the English Language*. He was science editor, *Literary Digest*, 1891–1933. Bostwick entered the library field in 1895 as chief librarian of the New York Free Circulating Library. He was director, Brooklyn Public Library, 1899, then chief of the circulation department of the New York Public Library (NYPL). By 1909, NYPL was the world's premier lending institution, loaning 6.5 million items annually. Bostwick was president of the American Library Association (ALA), 1907–1908. In 1909 he moved to the St. Louis Public Library, remaining until his death. He expanded the branch system, tripled circulation, and occupied a new central building (1912), earning national recognition for the library. The library's training school (1917–1932) was also successful. Bostwick visited China as an ALA adviser in 1925. He published 19 books and pamphlets and hundreds of articles, the best-known monograph being *The American Public Library* (four editions, 1910–1929). He died in Oak Grove, MO, on February 13, 1942. Bostwick believed in the public library as a force for popular education. He was conservative in the areas of censorship, supporting the suppression of books with "immoral tendency" (Bostwick 1908, 264). However, he had no problem with the major circulation role of fiction: "so long as this is of good quality there is no reason for being ashamed of it" (Bostwick 1929, 152). He was satisfied with separate but equal library treatment of black citizens, finding that "the colored branch would seem the best solution" in the South, and it might be "desirable to adopt it in the North also" (Bostwick 1929, 63). *DALB*, LJ Hall of Fame.

References

Bostwick, Arthur E. 1908. The librarian as censor. *Library Journal* 33, no. 7 (July): 257–64.

Bostwick, Arthur E. 1929. *The American Public Library*. 4th ed. New York: Appleton. 1st ed. 1910.

BOULDER PUBLIC LIBRARY, CO   1000 Canyon Blvd., Boulder, CO 80306. Founded 1899. Population served: 97,469. Circulation: 1,088,504.

Holdings: 361,740. 3 branches. LJ February 15, 2009, and November 15, 2009: 4-star library.

BOUNDARY COUNTY DISTRICT LIBRARY, BONNERS FERRY, ID   6700 Koutenai, Bonners Ferry, ID 83805. Founded 1957. Population served: 10,619. Circulation: 118,204. Holdings: 35,127. IMLS award, 2002.

BOWERMAN, GEORGE FRANKLIN, 1868–1960   Librarian. Born Farmington, NY, September 8, 1868. BA, University of Rochester, 1892. Melvil Dewey engaged him as a reference librarian in the New York State Library in 1893; he attended the library school in Albany and earned a library degree in 1895. From 1901 to 1904 he was chief librarian of the Wilmington (DE) Public Library. In 1904 he became librarian of the District of Columbia Public Library, remaining to 1940. During his tenure, congressional support for the library was increased, and librarians gained professional status (as opposed to their former clerical ranking) and entry into the federal retirement system. Bowerman was a promoter of children's work and of the library as the "university of the people." He favored some censorship activity by librarians and relegating certain books to "the inferno": a location behind the desk holding risky materials that were available only to "aggressive" users (Geller 1984, 138). His approach to censorship emerged from the concept that the library board represents the opinion of the community and that board policy on restrictions reflect the wishes of the people served. His book *Censorship and the Public Library* (1931) was an important contribution to the debate of the time. *DALB*.

Reference

Geller, Evelyn. 1984. *Forbidden Books in American Libraries, 1876–1939*. Westport, CT: Greenwood Press.

BOYDEN PUBLIC LIBRARY, IA   609 Webb St., Boyden, IA 51234. Population served: 2,020. Circulation: 25,075. Holdings: 21,299. LJ February 15, 2009, and November 15, 2009: 4-star library.

BRANCH LIBRARIES

Terminology

This is the *ODLIS* definition of a branch library: "an auxiliary service outlet in a library system, housed in a facility separate from the central library, which has at least a basic collection of materials, a regular staff, and established hours, with a budget and policies determined by the central library." It should be added that the facility is in a fixed location to distinguish branch from bookmobile and that certain policies may be developed within the branch, supplementing or modifying policies of the central library.

Historical Summary

The first American public library to found a branch was Boston. East Boston opened in 1870, followed by South Boston, 1872; Roxbury, 1873; Charleston, 1874; Brighton, 1874; Dorchester, 1875; and Jamaica Plain, 1877. Branch service was an experimental idea in the 1890s. A survey conducted in 1898 found branch operation only in Boston, New York City (Free Circulating Branch, Aguilar Branch), Philadelphia, Baltimore, and Brooklyn. Detroit Public Library's Chauncy Hurlbut Branch opened after that survey was done, in 1898. Most libraries preferred local "delivery stations" (Bostwick 1929, 15). Chicago Public Library had 87 delivery stations in 1909 where patrons could pick up and return books, along with 15 small branch reading rooms; there was one full branch that circulated books. (There was also a branch reading room in Hull House in 1890.) But Henry Legler's term as librarian brought accelerated branch development so that by 1915 Chicago had 32 of them. Los Angeles Public Library began its branch program in 1900. At the Denver Public Library, eight branches opened during the tenure of Chalmers Hadley (1910–1924). San Jose (CA) had its first branch in 1911.

In San Francisco, the North Branch (1908) was the first library to collect books in the language of a minority population (Italian). San Francisco Public Library also developed a distinctive collection in the Chinatown Branch (1915) (*see* SERVICES TO IMMIGRANTS).

Branches devoted to business and industry were created in several cities. John Cotton Dana was the pioneer, with a facility of the Newark Public Library that was known as the Business Branch (1907).

Other cities followed this lead with business branches outside their main library buildings, notably Minneapolis (1916), Rochester (1917), Indianapolis (1918), Detroit (1920), and Boston (1930). Dr. Joseph Wheeler made history with the business community in Youngstown (OH) when he had build a small temporary building on its public square, housing a small collection but offering quick service with a few reference books there and daily supplementary service from the Main Library. The Cleveland Public Library initiated a similar service in the Terminal Tower building in 1968 (Vormelker 1970, 578). Brooklyn Public Library and the Carnegie Library of Pittsburgh have business branches (*see* SERVICES TO BUSINESS AND INDUSTRY).

"Separate but equal" branches were found in many city systems before the Civil Rights Act of 1965: they served black patrons, who were not welcomed in the main library (although their taxes helped to support it). The Western Branch of Louisville Public Library (1905) was managed by an African American, Thomas Fountain Blue. In some cases, those "colored branches" have been converted to research facilities on African American culture, such as the Auburn Avenue Research Library (1996) of the Atlanta-Fulton County Library System, which had opened in 1921 (*see also* SERVICES TO AFRICAN AMERICANS).

Other important branches include two of the New York Public Library—
the Schomburg Center for Research in Black Culture (1925) and the Library
and Museum of the Performing Arts at Lincoln Center (1965)—and the
Edwin Fleisher Collection of Orchestral Music, with the Art Branch of the
Free Library of Philadelphia (1929), and Denver Public Library's Blair-
Caldwell African American Research Library (2003).

Another example of specialty branches includes that of the Hoopa Branch
of the Humboldt County Library, Eureka, CA, which is located on an Indian
reservation. In addition, some libraries have their services for the blind and
people with disabilities located apart from their central buildings in
branches, such as in the Cleveland Public Library.

Current Situation

Of the 9,221 public libraries in the United States in 2008, 1,559 had at least
one branch. The total number of branches in 2008 was 7,629. The number
was 7,503 in 2005 and 7,017 in 1993—displaying a small but steady increase.
All the country's large public libraries have numerous branches. Those with
the greatest number of branches, as reported in the *American Library
Directory* (2009–2010), are Los Angeles County (88), Chicago (87), the city
of Los Angeles (71), Queens (70), Brooklyn (58), and Philadelphia (54). It
must be noted that some libraries give the name "branch" to what is actually
a division located in the central building; thus, the tally of branches for a given
library may exceed the number of locations. Branches typically offer the same
range of services as the central libraries. While branch policy is drawn from
central library policy, branch librarians often have a degree of autonomy in
such areas as staffing and collection development.

A study of circulation patterns made some years ago showed that branch
circulation varied with the population characteristics of the neighborhood
served, but circulation by subject area was about the same in all branches
of a system (Ottensmann 1995). Significant recent research on the branch
situation is lacking.

The financial difficulties of recent years have had a strong impact on public libraries. Fifty-five percent of urban libraries reported funding cuts
between fiscal years 2008 and 2009. Budgetary authorities have found it
more politically acceptable to cut back hours in branches or to close them
entirely than to take such steps against central libraries. Such budgetary
reductions have been nationwide. A few examples may be cited: All 54
branches of the Free Library of Philadelphia were scheduled to close in
2009, but they were saved in September when the state senate approved
funding for them. Charlotte Mecklenburg Library (NC) announced that all
12 branches (of 28) would close in April 2010. The six branches (of 15) of
the Phoenix Public Library that had been slated to close in 2010 were preserved at the last minute. In January 2010 all branches of the Chicago Public
Library went on reduced hours. Fort Worth announced the closing of three
(of 13) branches in summer 2010, and Newark closed two (of 10) branches
in August 2010. *See also* FUNDING OF PUBLIC LIBRARIES.

References

Bostwick, Arthur E. 1929. *The Public Library in the United States*. Chicago: American Library Association.

Ottensmann, John R., et al. 1995. Similarities in circulation patterns among public libraries serving diverse populations. *Library Quarterly* 65, no. 1 (January): 89–118.

Vormelker, Rose. 1970. Business and the public library. In *Encyclopedia of Library and Information Science* 3: 573–92. New York: Marcel Dekker.

BRETT, WILLIAM HOWARD, 1846–1918   Librarian. Born Braceville, OH, July 1, 1846. After high school he worked as a bookstore clerk in Warren, OH, then enlisted as a musician in the 196th Ohio Volunteer Infantry during the Civil War. Brett attended the University of Michigan and Western Reserve University (no degree), then returned to bookstore work in Cleveland, 1874–1884. Recognized in the city for his wide knowledge of books, he was invited to head the Cleveland Public Library in 1884. Brett developed a citywide library system of national repute. He advocated open shelves (effective 1890), a concept new in the profession and not widely accepted. He promoted neighborhood branches (15 constructed with funds from Andrew Carnegie); library stations in businesses, factories, and hospitals; and service to the blind (Braille collection, 1903). He urged attention to the library needs of children, eventually engaging the country's first children's librarian (Effie Power) in 1895 and creating a children's room in 1898. Brett was also busy recataloging and reclassifying the collection, leading to a printed catalog. In 1896 the library began to prepare a periodical index, soon covering 100 titles; this source merged with the *Readers' Guide to Periodical Literature* in 1898. In all aspects of his work, Brett displayed a devotion to serving the user. His attitude was shared by the library staff, who became known for their enthusiasm, a tradition carried forward by his successor, Linda Eastman. Yet he was conservative about what should be in the collection; he "excluded books of low moral tone unless they had distinct merits, literary or other, that warranted keeping a single copy as a restricted book ... available to mature readers" (Geller 1984, 89). Brett was founding dean of the library school at Western Reserve University, holding that responsibility from 1904 to 1918. He was president of the American Library Association in 1897 and first president of the Ohio Library Association. He was struck by a car and killed in Cleveland on August 24, 1918. *DALB*; LJ Hall of Fame.

Reference

Geller, Evelyn. *Forbidden Books in American Libraries, 1876–1939*. Westport, CT: Greenwood Press.

BRIDGEHAMPTON, NY. *See* HAMPTON LIBRARY, BRIDGEHAMTON, NY.

BRIDGEPORT PUBLIC LIBRARY, WV   1200 Johnson Ave., Bridgeport, WV 26330. Founded 1975 as an independent library, "mostly tax supported"; has been operating since 1956 "mainly supported by the Benedum Foundation" (communication from the library). Population served: 7,306. Circulation: 275,411. Holdings: 95,960. HAPLR 2009, 2010.

BRIDGEWATER, NJ. *See* SOMERSET COUNTY LIBRARY SYSTEM, BRIDGEWATER, NJ.

BRISTOL PUBLIC LIBRARY, BRISTOLVILLE, OH   1855 Greenville Rd., Bristolville, OH 44402. Founded 1912. Population served: 5,428. Circulation: 177,710. Holdings: 46,575. HAPLR 2009, 2010.

BRISTOLVILLE, OH. *See* BRISTOL PUBLIC LIBRARY, BRISTOLVILLE, OH.

BRONXVILLE PUBLIC LIBRARY, NY   201 Pondfield Rd., Bronxville, NY 10708. Founded 1906. Population served: 6,543. Circulation: 177,315. Holdings: 62,381. LJ November 15, 2009, and October 1, 2010: 4-star library.

BROOKLINE, MA. *See* PUBLIC LIBRARY OF BROOKLINE, MA.

BROOKLYN PUBLIC LIBRARY, NY   Grand Army Plaza, Brooklyn, NY 11238. Founded 1892. Population served: 2,465,326. Circulation: 15,370,209. Holdings: 6,809,959. 58 branches. 1 bookmobile. The library exists independently of the New York Public Library, which serves the Bronx, Manhattan, and Staten Island. It was the first U.S. public library with a music department (ca. 1885) and to circulate music scores. The central library building was constructed from 1912 to 1941. Between 1901 and 1923, Andrew Carnegie donated $1.6 million toward the development of 21 branch libraries. Directors: Mary E. Craigie, 1897–1898; Arthur E. Bostwick, 1899–1901; Frank P. Hill, 1901–1930; Milton J. Ferguson, 1930–1949; Francis R. St. John, 1949–1963; Margaret B. Freeman (acting), 1964; John A. Humphry, 1964–1967; John C. Frantz, 1967–1970; Kenneth F. Duchac, 1970–1986; Larry Brandwein, 1986–1994; Judith Faust (acting), 1994; Martin Gomez, 1995–2001; Siobhan Reardon (acting), 2001; Ginnie Cooper, 2002–2005; Dionne Mack-Harvin, 2005–2010; and Linda Johnson (acting), 2010–.

BROOKVILLE, FL. *See* HERNANDO COUNTY PUBLIC LIBRARY, BROOKVILLE, FL.

BROWARD COUNTY LIBRARIES, FORT LAUDERDALE, FL   100 S. Andrews Ave., Fort Lauderdale, FL 33301. Founded 1974. Population served:

1,750,000. Circulation: 11,000,000. Holdings: 3,408,774. 39 branches, 1 bookmobile. LJ Library of the Year 1996. LJ February 15, 2009, and November 15, 2009: 3-star library.

BROWN COUNTY LIBRARY, GREEN BAY, WI   515 Pine St., Green Bay, WI 54301. Founded 1889. Population served: 239,137. Circulation: 2,400,000. Holdings: 490,228. LJ Library of the Year 1994.

BROWNS VALLEY PUBLIC LIBRARY, MN   15 S. Third St., Browns Valley, MN 56219. Founded 1914. Population served: 901. Circulation: 18,116. Holdings: 30,972. HALPR 2009, 2010.

BRUMBACK LIBRARY, VAN WERT, OH   215 W. Main St., Van Wert, OH 45891. Population served: 29,141. Circulation 495,770. Holdings: 130,000. 5 branches. First county library in the United States.

BRUNSWICK PUBLIC LIBRARY, NE   303 Franklin, Brunswick, NE 68720. Population served: 179. Circulation 6,250. Holdings: 5,866. HALPR 2009, 2010.

BRYANT LIBRARY, ROSLYN, NY   2 Paper Mill Rd., Roslyn, NY 11576. Founded 1945 (state provisional charter; absolute charter in 1950). Population served: 18,221. Circulation: 285,140. Holdings: 155,253. LJ February 15, 2009, and November 15, 2009: 3-star library.

BUDGETING. *See* FUNDING OF PUBLIC LIBRARIES; MANAGEMENT AND ORGANIZATION.

BUFFALO AND ERIE COUNTY LIBRARY, NY   1 Lafayette Square, Buffalo, NY 14203. Population served: 920,625. Circulation: 7,619,902. Holdings: 3,624,615. 11 branches.

BUHLER PUBLIC LIBRARY, KS   121 S. Main St., Buhler, KS, 67522. Population served: 1,336. Circulation: 24,134. Holdings: 9,714. LJ February 15, 2009: 3-star library; November 15, 2009: 4-star library; October 1, 2010: 5-star library.

BUILDINGS AND FACILITIES

Historical Summary

As American public library architecture developed in the nineteenth century, it followed European library models. Those models favored buildings that looked like temples, palaces, or medieval churches. Both public and academic libraries in the United States accepted those styles, leading to ornate, monumental structures. Interiors were in "fixed-function" patterns, in which reading rooms were separate from closed areas that housed multi-tiered, iron-steel book stacks. Theatrical grand staircases were a common feature. Twenty-three large public library buildings appeared in 1876–1893 (Rogers 1976, 223). The typical library style of 1890 was "Romanesque, stone or brick and stone, with a separate ladies' reading room"; it had a circulation desk, a second-floor lecture hall and art gallery, and a stacks in a rear wing (Stone 1977, 320). Librarians did not have input into the design of their buildings until they demanded that opportunity. The battle was exemplified in the planning of the Newberry Library in Chicago (1892) and the insistence of librarian William Frederick Poole on certain interior plans over the resistance of architect Henry Cobb. Poole required a design that provided subject reading rooms and easy access to the books by the readers—and he won the points, although those features are not found in today's Newberry. The pace of public library construction "rose sharply in the 1890s and peaked in 1900, with a slightly declining plateau between 1900 and 1910 and a marked decline between 1910 and 1918" (Rogers 1976, 225). Fifty-nine large structures went up in 1894–1918. Architects had a special interest in libraries. The November 1897 issue of *Architectural Review* was devoted to library buildings, and the January 1902 issue had 50 pages of library building plans.

A turn toward simplicity of design was due largely to the benefactions of Andrew Carnegie, who donated funds for 1,679 American public library buildings in the early twentieth century; he favored functional, uncluttered designs, and issued guidelines to that effect (see entry for him). Architects and librarians got together for the first time at a conference of the American Library Association (ALA) in 1906. ALA began collecting library plans and formed a committee on the economics of library architecture.

As a cost reduction measure, the Depression fostered simplicity as well. Although the 1930s was a time of austerity, the period 1919–1945 was one of "substantial, sometimes even spectacular advance" (Rogers 1976, 228). Of 28 large public libraries constructed in that period, nine cost $1 million or more: John Crerar (1921), Detroit (1921), Cleveland (1925), Los Angeles (1926), Philadelphia (1927), Baltimore (1933), Rochester (1936), Brooklyn (1940), and Toledo (1940). The Baltimore library (Enoch Pratt Free Library) initiated a style that departed from the monumental: it had sidewalk-level entrances and display windows like those in department stores. It was an open-shelf library, with seven subject reading rooms, a general reference room, and three tiers of stacks below. A children's room was in the basement (for the place of children's rooms in public library buildings, *see* SERVICES TO CHILDREN AND YOUNG ADULTS). By this time librarians were typically involved in planning their buildings.

Since World War II there has been a trend toward "modular" design. It appeared in academic libraries first (Princeton, Iowa, and Massachusetts Institute of Technology), then in public libraries. Modular offers a plan for flexibility in which all spaces of a building can be adapted for any use. While modular meant simple at first, it became more embellished and complex in the 1960s. Recent structures have illustrated postmodern styles. They are colorful, carpeted, air-conditioned, and suitable for disabled persons. Librarians with experience in planning are called on to advise others, creating a career title of building consultant.

From 1969 to 2003 the number of library building projects averaged 214 per year (U.S. National Center for Education Statistics 2007, 16). The American economic recession that began in 2008 was not reflected in library building projects since they had been planned and financed earlier. Between July 1, 2007, and June 30, 2008, 183 public library buildings were completed (Fox 2008). In fiscal year 2009, 80 new public libraries were built in the United States, and there were 90 additions, renovations, or remodeling—with a total cost of $1,138,235.728 (*State of America's Libraries* 2010, 1).

This chronology notes important events in the emergence of American public library architecture:

> 1745—James Logan built a library for his private collection on Sixth Street between Walnut and Chestnut in Philadelphia, granting access to any Philadelphian "with proper introduction." It was the first building in the United States devoted to the use of a public library.
>
> 1750—Redwood Library, Newport, RI, completed; the oldest structure in the United States continuously used as a library; architect Peter Harrison.
>
> 1788—In a competition for design of the Library Company of Philadelphia, Thomas Jefferson was one of the entrants. The winner was William Thornton, architect of the U.S. Capitol. The Philadelphia structure was completed in 1790 and used to 1880, then demolished.
>
> 1878—North Easton Public Library (MA), by H. H. Richardson.
>
> 1879—San Francisco Public Library by George K. Kelham; Woburn Public Library (MA), by H. H. Richardson.
>
> 1883—Crane Memorial Public Library, Quincy, MA, by H. H. Richardson.
>
> 1890—Carnegie Library, Allegheny City (Pittsburgh), by Smithmeyer and Pelz.
>
> 1892—Newberry Library, Chicago, by Henry Cobb; Library of Congress main building, by Smithmeyer and Pelz.
>
> 1895—Boston Public Library, by McKim, Mead and White.
>
> 1897—Chicago Public Library, by Shepley, Rutan & Coolidge.
>
> 1911—New York Public Library, by Carrère and Hastings; Andrew Carnegie's guidelines on economical use of space.
>
> 1912—St. Louis Public Library, by Cass Gilbert.

1917—Indianapolis-Marion County Public Library, by Paul Cret; San Francisco Public Library, by George K. Kelham.

1921—Detroit Public Library, by Cass Gilbert.

1925—Cleveland Public Library, by Walker and Weeks.

1926—Los Angeles Public Library, by Bertram Goodhue.

1933—Enoch Pratt Free Library, Baltimore, by Edward Tilton.

1941—*The American Public Library Building* (Wheeler and Githens 1941).

1956—Denver Public Library, by Burnham Hoyt.

1965—*Planning Academic and Research Library Buildings* (Metcalf 1965), the first substantial work of its kind.

1991—Chicago Public Library, Harold Washington Center (main library), by Hammond, Beeby, and Babka.

1995—Denver Public Library, by Michael Graves.

1997—San Francisco Public Library, by Pei Cobb Freed & Partners, with Simon Martin-Vegue Winkelstein Moris.

2003—Salt Lake City Public Library, by Moshe Safdie.

2009—Minneapolis Public Library, by Pelli Clarke Pelli; Seattle Public Library, by Rem Koolhaas.

Since 1995 the ALA and the American Institute of Architects (AIA) have recognized outstanding library design with a library buildings award. All the winning architects are listed here, along with other architects of notable library structures. The names of the architects are given as they are in the award list on the ALA website (www.ala.org/ala/mgrps/divs/llama/awards/aiaalalibrarybuildings). Unless otherwise indicated, the buildings cited are the central library buildings.

Ackerman & Ross. District of Columbia Public Library, 1903.

Belluschi, Pietro. Corvallis (OR) Public Library, 1932.

Blackwell. Marion. Gentry Public Library (AZ). AIA/ALA award 2009.

Bohlin Cywinski Jackson. Seattle Public Library, Ballard Branch. AIA/ALA award 2007. King County Library System, Issaquah Public Library. AIA/ALA award 2005.

Breuer, Marcel. Atlanta-Fulton County Public Library, 1980.

Burnette, Wendell. Phoenix Public Library (AZ), Palo Verde Branch and Maryvale Community Center. AIA/ALA award 2009.

Carlson Architect. Belfair Public Library (WA). AIA/ALA award 2001.

Carrère and Hastings. New York Public Library, 1911.

Clint Pherson Architects. Amanda Park (WA), Timberland Library. AIA/ALA award 1995.

Cobb. Henry. Newberry Library (Chicago), 1892.

Cret, Paul. Indianapolis-Marion County Public Library, 1917.

Damon, Isaac. Lenox Library Association (MA), 1816 (on National Register of Historic Places).

Davis Brody Bond. New York Public Library, main reading room, AIA/ALA award 1999. New York Public Library, South Court, AIA/ALA award 2003.

Elliott & Elliott. Brooklin Public Library (ME). AIA/ALA award 2001.

Ferry & Clas. Milwaukee Public Library, 1898.

Fisher & Fisher/Burnham Hoyt. Denver Public Library, 1956.

Fletcher Farr Ayotte. Multnomah County Central Library, Portland (OR). AIA/ALA award 2001.

Fowler, Orson Squire. Red Hook Public Library (NY), 1935.

Gehry, Frank. Hollywood Public Library (CA), Frances Howard Goldwyn Branch, 1986.

Gilbert. Cass. St. Louis Public Library, 1912; Detroit Public Library, 1921.

Goodhue, Bertram. Los Angeles Public Library, 1926.

Graves, Michael. Denver Public Library 1995.

Gwathmey Siegel & Associates. New York Public Library, Science Industry and Business Library. AIA/ALA award 1997.

Hammond, Beeby and Babka. Chicago Public Library, Harold Washington Center (main library), 1991.

Hardy Holzman Pfeiffer Associates. Los Angeles Public Library, central library renovation. AIA/ALA award 1995.

Harrison, Peter. Redwood Library, Newport (RI), 1750.

Hoyt, Burnham. Denver Public Library, 1956.

Hunt. Myron. Pasadena Public Library, 1927; Redlands (CA), 1930.

Hunt, Richard Morris. Lenox Library, New York City, 1877.

Johnson/Burgee. Boston Public Library extension of main library, 1973.

Kelham. George K. San Francisco Public Library, 1917.

Klipp Colussy Jenks DuBois Architects. See Michael Graves & Associates.

Koolhaas, Rem. Seattle Public Library, 2009.

Lake/Flato. San Antonio Public Library, Great Northwest Branch. AIA/ALA 1997 award.

Litchfield. Electus. St. Paul Public Library (MN), 1917.

LMN Architects. Seattle Public Library, temporary central library facility. AIA/ALA award 2003.

Loysen + Kreuthmeier. Carnegie Library of Pittsburgh, Brookline Branch. AIA/ALA award 2005.

M. W. Steele Group. San Diego Public Library, Carmel Mountain Branch. AIA/ALA award 1999.

Mack Scogin Merrill Elam. Riverdale Public Library (GA), Lee B. Philmon Branch. AIA/ALA award 2003. The library is now the Riverdale Branch, Clayton County Library System.

Madison, Robert P. Cleveland Public Library, Langston Hughes Branch, 1998.

McKim, Mead and White. Boston Public Library, 1895.

Mies van der Rohe, Ludwig. District of Columbia Public Library, 1972.

Michael Graves & Associates, with Klipp Colussy Jenks DuBois Architects. Denver Public Library. AIA/ALA award 2001.

Office for Metropolitan Architecture and LMN Architects. Seattle Public Library. AIA/ALA award 2005.

Patton & Miller. More than 100 libraries, mostly Carnegie structures.

Pei, I. M. Columbus Public Library (IN), 1969.

Pei Cobb Freed & Partners, with Simon Martin-Vegue Winkelstein Moris. San Francisco Public Library, central library. AIA/ALA award 1997.

Pelli Clarke Pelli. Minneapolis Public Library. AIA/ALA award 2009.

Plachek. James. Berkeley Public Library, 1931.

Polshek Partnership. Queens Borough Public Library (NY), Flushing Branch. AIA/ALA award 1999.

Richard + bauer: Scottsdale Public Library (AZ), Arabian Branch. AIA/ALA award 2009. Phoenix Public Library, Desert Broom Branch. AIA/ALA award 2007.

Richard Fleishman Architects. Cleveland Public Library, Lake Shore Branch. AIA/ALA award 1995.

Richardson. H. H. Woburn Public Library (MA), 1876–1879; North Easton (MA), 1878; Crane Memorial Library, Quincy (MA), 1883.

Safdie. Moshe. Salt Lake City Public Library, 2003. AIA/ALA award 2005.

Scoggin, Elam and Bray. Atlanta-Fulton County Public Library, Buckhead Branch, 1989.

Shepley, Rutan & Coolidge: Chicago Public Library, 1897; Grand Rapids Public Library (MI), 1902.

Smithmeyer and Pelz: Carnegie Library, Allegheny City (Pittsburgh), 1886–1890; Library of Congress, main building, 1892..

Stephen D. Weinstein/John Ellis & Associates. New York Public Library, Tottenville Branch. AIA/ALA award 1997.

Steven Ehrlich Architects of Los Angeles. Los Angeles Public Library, Robertson Branch. AIA/ALA award 2001.

Stone. Edward Durrell. Palo Alto City Library (CA), 1958.

Thomas Hacker & Associates. Library Association of Portland (OR), Woodstock Branch. AIA/ALA award 2001.

Tigerman, Stanley. Pensacola Public Library (FL), 1978-1982.

Tilton. Edward. Enoch Pratt Free Library, Baltimore (MD), 1933.

Trumbauer, Horace, and Julian Abele. Free Library of Philadelphia, 1927.

Walker, Ralph. Montclair Public Library (NJ), 1955.

Walker and Weeks. Cleveland Public Library, 1925.

Wetherell, F. E. Cherokee (IA) Public Library, 1905.

William P. Bruder-Architect. Phoenix Public Library, central library. AIA/ALA award 1997.

Zimmer Gunsul Frasca Partnership. King County Library System (WA), Bellevue Regional Library. AIA/ALA award 1995.

Current Practice and Issues (by Stephen P. Bero)

Public library buildings and facilities are the instruments by which librarians deliver services. But more than just this utilitarian function, buildings and facilities embody the social institution of the shared library as a cultural good. For what is a library if not its building, even in this Internet age? In many communities the public library building presents itself as an iconic image that is a source of pride for community residents.

Program and Site.   The actual facilities are derived from the building program, which is a plan for constructing spaces to deliver library services, that is, the traditional core services of circulation, reference, readers' advisory, educational presentations, and support for reading and perhaps modern ancillary services, such as provision of meeting rooms, computers, photocopiers, and fax machines. The building program itself is derived from a space needs assessment and site plan. Once the governing body of the public library determines which services to provide, the body must assess the sizes and types of spaces needed to accommodate the facilities to deliver these services. Finally, the governing body must place the building on a suitable site. The governing body decides on a location for the library building by taking into account the broader needs of the community and the character of the populace, weighing community preferences for a library situated in a residential area as opposed to a business district or a municipal campus that includes other public service facilities.

The grounds must be able to bear the infrastructural and structural requirements of a massive building. A library, whatever its square footage, dints the ground deeply because of its need for extremely strong floors, high ceilings, large open spaces, and huge mechanical systems. Planners must take into account the needs for adequate parking spaces when delineating the total acreage of the site. Libraries in the twenty-first century are developing building programs that include plans to gain certification of environmental responsibility and sustainability by the United States Green Building Council through its "Leadership in Energy and Environmental Design" (LEED) program (*LEED Program* 2010). Although many libraries exist in facilities that were repurposed from their original functions (e.g., churches), it is highly desirable that a library be built anew from ground up.

Interior. The centerpiece of any public library has been and continues to be the traditional reading room. Present-day libraries rather than having one large central reading room allocate spaces throughout the public areas for tables and carrels for reading and writing. Because of the increased noise in high-traffic areas, many libraries also have a designated space or spaces for strict maintenance of silence.

Public libraries have seen a philosophical difference in approach to programming service areas. The first approach is based on the long-standing tradition of separating service areas by age, most commonly into areas for adult services and children's services. In recent years libraries have also provided additional separate areas for teens and for tweens. The second approach is differentiation of areas by type of service as opposed to age. Libraries have delineated spaces that concentrate on reference services or readers' advisory services regardless of age, that is, to serve all ages. The public service desks are also being designed to serve different purposes. There is a trend to break up the traditional, huge reference desk at which a number of librarians sat into smaller, individual desks designed for one-on-one reference interviews and modeled on the smaller service desks currently seen in some hotel and bank lobbies. In a similar fashion the customary long circulation desk with teller stations is being replaced by separate supermarket-style checkout counters. The decision of what style of service desk to employ affects the allocation of space.

Present space planning must accommodate equipment and machinery needed for radio-frequency identification (RFID), the technology that is the current standard for inventory control. Libraries utilizing RFID equip their facilities with express checkout terminals (self-checks) and mechanical sorters to handle returns. The self-checks can in many instances replace the traditional long circulation desk and can also be located in areas other than the circulation area. A mechanical sorter leaves more or less of a large footprint, depending on how many return bins it needs. The sorter's overall needs for space relate also to the length and figuration of the conveyor belts feeding into it.

The largest open areas for the public house the collection of materials, both circulating and reference. These areas require planning for shelving. As with most components of the modern public library, shelving units can be repositioned as the program needs of the space change. Even shelving units attached to the wall are designed to be removable. Other types of shelving may be less portable, but the principle of fairly easy relocation still applies. Some examples of these types of shelving are collapsible, compact shelving, and other automated shelving.

In summary, the primary directive that the archetypical modern library building program gives the architect is to design a flexible structure, that is, one in which library staff can easily relocate furnishings, shelving, and equipment. Detailed formulas for calculating the square footage required for every element of a building interior are available (*Building Blocks* 2001).

In recent years the public library has emerged as "third space," that is, the location where people choose to spend the bulk of their discretionary time after home and the workplace. A person seeks out the third space/library in order to be able to interact and collaborate with others. Thus, modern library buildings give spaces over to meeting rooms and group study rooms. To support the work done by visitors lingering in its third space, the library building provides areas for document processing, computer labs, and digital media labs. The virtual infrastructure of the third space is wireless network connectivity, the library as Wi-Fi hot spot. As the third space design of the library intentionally encourages people to linger in the building, the library must offer public amenities, such as refreshments in a café or food vending area and fireplaces surrounded by lounge-type furniture. Some public libraries have tried to follow the example of book superstores that incorporated cafés. Buildings must allocate spaces to supply these amenities.

Indirect natural light through northern exposures provides the best light for the public reading rooms. It is practically axiomatic in modern library design that artificial lighting be supplied by fluorescent bulbs reflected off the ceilings. With the exception of north windows, all windows need light control equipment such as shades, perforated vinyl blinds, and so on. Artificial light systems can be configured to harvest natural light, thereby making the building more energy efficient and meeting a requirement for LEED certification. Buildings save even more energy by installing motion-sensing light switches in areas like restrooms and staff workrooms. To control glare and increase the contrast needed for close reading and writing, task lighting can be used on tables, on workstations, and in study carrels in areas of a library where the general light may not be so bright (e.g., a very large room).

Although present-day libraries are generally noisier places than libraries of a generation ago, they still must favor silence throughout most of the interior and in many cases provide protected rooms where silence is strictly maintained as opposed to other spaces, such as the children's area and circulation desk, where greater and constant activity naturally produces more noise. In order to prevent the unwanted transmission of sound, acoustic ceilings are called for throughout the building. Best practice in multilevel library design avoids atriums, which easily transmit sound between floors.

As mandated by the Americans with Disabilities Act of 1990, amended in 2008 (ADA), library buildings and facilities must be accessible to the disabled as defined in the act. Designing a building to comply with the ADA translates to ensuring accessibility in particular to those in wheelchairs, the blind, and the deaf (see SERVICES TO PEOPLE WITH DISABILITIES).

To assist visitors in finding their way through the building, the building program must not neglect plans for signs. Libraries that can afford cutting-edge technology are installing computerized signs. Whatever the types of signs employed in the building, they must comply with the requirements of the ADA.

Most public libraries are fortunate to have a group of supportive volunteers called Friends of the Library. In planning a building one must keep in mind the needs of the Friends of the Library for storage space, a workroom, and possibly a bookstore to sell used books or a shop to sell library-related wares as ways to raise funds.

When attention turns from the public spaces to the spaces needed for library staff, spaces that are sometimes called the "back of house," the programming must solve the problems associated with not only sufficiently large office spaces but also the proximity of those offices to other. related offices; efficiencies of work flow between functional departments; and the inclusion of staff conference rooms and other collaborative spaces for interdepartmental work. In addition to proximity to other, related staff areas in the back of house, public service staff also need adjacencies to their points of service in the public areas along with a view of these public service areas in order to monitor activity and respond quickly to increases in business. An efficient library building also serves to keep staffing at a minimum. Any building program must fulfill the perennial desire of the staff for storage space sufficient not only for the present but also for the foreseeable future. The staff needs spaces to store not only supplies and records but also equipment, furniture, program props, and attic stock. Amenities for the staff should at minimum include a lounge and restrooms separate from the public. They could at maximum also include a quiet room with a couch or cot so that a staffer could repair there in case of illness and showers for those staffers who would, for example, walk or ride their bicycles to work. Showers used in these ways aid in securing LEED certification because they foster means of transit that reduce reliance on polluting cars, buses, and trains.

The back of house contains the rooms for the utilities, computer servers, custodial services, and mechanical control switches. A shipping-and-receiving dock is a necessity for the efficient handling of library business. The staff side of the building encompasses garages to shelter bookmobiles and other vehicles owned by the library. The bookmobile garage must be adjacent to the work areas of the staff who use and maintain the vehicle. A well-thought-out building design will show lines for electrical power, data, and telephone running throughout the building. A good design will place receptacles at convenient locations and intervals along these lines. Again the byword is ease of relocation of furniture.

Programming facilities also calls for planning for safety, security and disaster. The great combined value of a library building and its contents necessitates installing theft control systems, security video cameras, fire alarms, and intrusion alarms. A comprehensive disaster plan covers preparedness for a disaster, the actual response to the disaster, and the recovery after the disaster. Building programs must incorporate evacuation routes, with all doors on the exterior walls numbered according to the National Incident Management System.

Interior walls must be easily cleaned. The most washable materials for walls are vinyl wallpaper and oil-based paint. Carpets need to be laid as carpet tile, which affords easy replacement of small sections rather than whole roles.

The aesthetics of designing interiors of modern libraries varies over a wide range, from a Zen-like austerity to highly decorated and worked spaces on the order of those in modern museums. Along this line some public libraries have gone to the extent of programming the "experience" library, that is, a library designed for ambient learning and interactivity, fully adapting the museum model to the library. Perhaps the most prominent self-identified example of the experience library is the Cerritos Public Library (CA).

Exterior.   The programmed facilities must be wrapped in the skin of the building itself. While the look of the exterior of the building is an aesthetic choice, there are functional components to consider as well. Most if not all libraries provide outside materials return slots. More and more libraries complete the outside self-service cycle by offering materials lockers and materials vending machines. It is ideal to have a porte cochere over the main public entrance. Exterior signage and way finding for pedestrian and vehicle traffic are especially important for locations of the drive-up materials returns and the other points of service on the outside of the building. Lighting the building exterior meets both aesthetic and practical needs. As with the building interior, video cameras installed to monitor the areas around the building and any parking lot for the library serve to provide strong security.

If the grounds of the site permit, outdoor reading areas, such as gardens or patios, may fit adjacent to the building and may also be connected to service areas within. Building programmers must decide how to secure those outdoor areas to prevent theft of library materials and property.

As with the interior, the exterior of the building requires space dedicated to staff only. A secure waste disposal area will make life easier for both the staff and the public. As a finishing touch, it is a nice amenity to offer an outdoor picnic area for staff use, space on the grounds permitting.

More than fulfilling its utilitarian function, the exterior of the building is most important because it gives the library its iconic stature in the community. The experience of the library derives from the design of the interior and exterior of the building and the landscaping of the grounds and its relationship with surrounding landscapes and structures. Despite the time-honored truth that *de gustibus non est disputandum*, public library officials must meet the challenge to choose a qualified architect who can design to realize the building program and to please the community aesthetically without introducing undesirable "signature design" elements.

Resources. Current references to architects, construction companies, surveyors, engineers, furniture vendors, and other consultants appear in library journals. *American Libraries* publishes an annual "Library Design Showcase," typically in its April issue. *Library Journal* publishes a supplement titled "Library by Design." In addition to their directories of design and construction professionals, these journals review the most recent new and remodeled library buildings. The AIA and the ALA have presented biennial library buildings awards since 1999 (see the list of architects above); the awards identify many of the leading architects who work in the library field. *Library Journal* also sponsors an annual Design Institute, a one-day educational seminar in its eighth year as of this writing.

Libraries customarily draw up contracts and enter into agreements with architects, space planners, construction managers, and contractors using standard forms issued by the AIA. As comprehensive and time tested as the AIA forms are, libraries are nonetheless advised to seek legal counsel in the preparation of contract documents. Such counsel usually results in necessary changes to the AIA forms for the particular library's individual case.

References

Bryan, Cheryl. 2007. *Managing Facilities for Results: Optimizing Space for Services*. Chicago: American Library Association.

Building Blocks for Planning Functional Library Space. 2001. Prepared by the American Library Association, Library Administration and Management Association, Buildings and Equipment Section. Chicago: American Library Association.

Dewe, Michael. 2006. *Planning Public Library Buildings: Concepts and Issues*. Aldershot (England): Ashgate.

Fox, Bette-Lee. 2008. Library buildings 2008: Keeping the "ECO" in economy. *Library Journal* 133, no. 20 (December): 36–37.

Kahn, Miriam B. 2008. *The Library Security and Safety Guide to Prevention, Planning, and Response*. Chicago: American Library Association.

Khan, Ayub. 2009. *Better by Design: An Introduction to Planning and Designing a New Library Building*. New York: Neal-Schuman.

LEED Program. 2010. *Green Buildings and LEED: Core Concepts Guide*. Washington, DC: United States Green Building Council. E-book available through www.usgbc.org.

Metcalf, Keyes D. 1965. *Planning Academic and Research Library Buildings*. New York: McGraw-Hill.

Rogers, A. Robert. 1976. Library buildings. In *A Century of Service: Librarianship in the United States and Canada*, ed. Sidney L. Jackson et al., 221–42. Chicago: American Library Association.

Sager, Donald J. 2000. Interior design trends in libraries. *Public Libraries* 39, no. 3 (May/June): 137–142.

Sannwald, William W. 2009. *Checklist of Library Building Design Considerations.* 5th ed. Chicago: American Library Association.

State of America's Libraries. 2010. Chicago: American Library Association. www.ala.org/ala/newspresscenter. Accessed May 2010.

Stone, Elizabeth. 1977. *American Library Development.* New York: H. W. Wilson.

U.S. National Center for Education Statistics. 2007. *Public Libraries in the United States, FY 2005.* Washington, DC: U.S. Department of Education.

Wheeler, Joseph L., and Alfred Morton Githens. 1941. *The American Public Library Building.* New York: Scribner. Reprint, Chicago: American Library Association, 1951.

BURLINGAME COMMUNITY LIBRARY, KS   122 W. Santa Fe Ave., Burlingame, KS 66413. Founded 1970. Population served: 1,019. Circulation: 21,216. Holdings: 14,385. LJ November 15, 2009: 3-star library.

BURLINGTON, KS. *See* COFFEY COUNTY LIBRARY, BURLINGTON, KS.

BURTON PUBLIC LIBRARY, OH   14588 W. Park St., Burton, OH 44021. Founded 1937. Population served: 9,431. Circulation: 236,165. Holdings: 74,765. HALPR 2010.

BUTLER PUBLIC LIBRARY, IN   340 S. Broadway, Butler, IN 46721. Founded 1905, incorporated 1906 (communication from library). Population served: 2,725. Circulation: 50,941. Holdings: 29,381. LJ February 15, 2009, and October 1, 2010: 4-star library.

C

CALCASIEU PARISH LIBRARY, LAKE CHARLES, LA 301 W. Claude St., Lake Charles, LA 70605. Lake Charles Public Library opened 1904, Calcasieu Parish Library 1944; they merged into present form in 1973. Population served: 181,799. Circulation: 1,000,000. Holdings: 406,222. 14 branches. *See also* HURRICANES KATRINA AND RITA.

CAMBRIDGE PUBLIC LIBRARY, MA 359 Broadway, Cambridge, MA 02138. Founded 1874. Population served: 100,791. Circulation: 985,967. Holdings: 331,034. 6 branches. The library had one of the earliest children's rooms in 1894.

CAMBRIDGE PUBLIC LIBRARY, NY 21 W. Main St., Cambridge, NY 12816. Founded 1904. Population served: 1,925. Circulation: 46,484. Holdings: 11,729. LJ November 15, 2009: 3-star library; October 1, 2010: 4-star library.

CAMDEN PUBLIC LIBRARY, ME 55 Main St., Camden, ME 04843. Founded 1928. Population served: 5,452. Circulation: 155,841. Holdings: 51,854. LJ February 15, 2009, and November 15, 2009: 4-star library; October 1, 2010: 5-star library.

CAMERON PARISH PUBLIC LIBRARY, LA 469 Marshall, Cameron, LA 70631. Founded 1958. Population served: 9,558. Circulation: 74,185.

Holdings: 78,626. 6 branches, 1 bookmobile. *See also* HURRICANES KATRINA AND RITA.

CAMPBELL, JANE MAUD, 1869–1947   Librarian. Born in England of Scottish parents; she was brought to New Jersey as a child. In 1901, with no library training, she was employed as a library assistant in Newark Public Library, then as librarian at Passaic. The majority of population served there was immigrant. Campbell promoted services to them, working with community groups and developing a collection in 11 foreign languages. Her 1904–1905 annual report noted that the 550 foreign books held had circulated 11,114 times. In 1906 she was appointed to the New Jersey Immigration Commission, where she promoted evening schools. She left library work in 1910, joining the North American Civic League for Immigrants, pressing for educational and recreational activities in construction camps, leading to legislation. In 1913, Campbell directed work with foreigners of the Massachusetts Free Public Library Commission, establishing traveling libraries of foreign books. She took up directorship of the public library in Lynchburg, VA, and remained 25 years.

Reference

Jones, Plummer Alston, Jr. 1999. *Libraries, Immigrants, and the American Experience*. Westport, CT: Greenwood Press.

CANAAN, CT. *See* DAVID M. HUNT LIBRARY, CANAAN, CT.

CANAL FULTON PUBLIC LIBRARY, OH   154 E. Market St., Canal Fulton, OH 44614. Founded 1937. Population served: 9,502. Circulation: 344,730. Holdings: 55,131. HAPLR 2010.

CANTON, OH. *See* STARK COUNTY DISTRICT LIBRARY, CANTON, OH.

CANTON PUBLIC LIBRARY, MI   1200 S. Canton Center Rd., Canton, MI 48188. Founded 1980. Population served: 76,000. Circulation: 2,015,317 in 2009 (library website). Holdings: 223,750. LJ February 15, 2009, and November 15, 2009: 3-star library.

CAREY, OH. *See* DORCAS CAREY PUBLIC LIBRARY, CAREY, OH.

CARMEL, CA. *See* HARRISON MEMORIAL LIBRARY, CARMEL, CA.

CARMEL, IN. *See* CARMEL CLAY PUBLIC LIBRARY, CARMEL, IN.

CARMEL CLAY PUBLIC LIBRARY, CARMEL, IN   55 Fourth Ave. SE, Carmel, IN 46032. Population served: 64,709. Circulation: 1,681,974. Holdings: 282,931. HAPLR 2009, 2010.

CARNEGIE, ANDREW, 1835–1919   Industrialist, philanthropist. Born Dunfermline, Scotland, November 25, 1835. His family came to the United States in 1846, settling in Allegheny, PA, a suburb of Pittsburgh. He had minor positions in factories and then worked for the Pennsylvania Railroad, rising to an official position. In 1865 he entered the iron and steel business. Carnegie achieved ownership of Homestead Steel Works, which he consolidated with other holdings in 1899 to create Carnegie Steel Corporation. He sold his company to J. P. Morgan in 1901 and retired. His life thereafter was devoted to philanthropy, acting out his philosophy that the wealthy have a responsibility to support the public good. He focused his attention on public education, libraries, and international peace. He died in New York City on August 11, 1919. An estimate placed his total benefactions, including those of the Carnegie Corporation after his death, at $350 million.

Carnegie funding (ca. $41 million) resulted in the construction of 1,679 American public library buildings. His decisions on which projects to fund were at first subjective but came to rely on quantitative procedures. Buildings were not required to follow any architectural design, although the dome and temple–front style was a favorite of local officials. Carnegie's name did not need to be inscribed anywhere on the structure. He did promote open stacks and public service and sharing of reading rooms by men and women. Controversy was always present with respect to "tainted money" that Carnegie had amassed by alleged exploitation of his workers, and some library boards refused his assistance. Carnegie also contributed more than $4 million to the construction of 108 American academic library buildings. He has been credited with full or substantial financing of 2,509 library buildings in the English-speaking world. The Carnegie Corporation also gave major assistance to the American Library Association, funded the establishment of the Graduate Library School at the University of Chicago, and funded important research in public libraries and library education. *DAB; DALB.*

References

Bobinski, George. 1969. *Carnegie Libraries: Their History and Impact on American Public Library Development.* Chicago: American Library Association.
Van Slyck, Abby. 1995. *Free to All: Carnegie Libraries and American Culture, 1890–1920.* Chicago: University of Chicago Press.

CARNEGIE LIBRARIES. *See* BUILDINGS AND FACILITIES; CARNEGIE, ANDREW, 1835–1919.

CARNEGIE LIBRARY OF PITTSBURGH, PA   4400 Forbes Ave., Pittsburgh, PA 15213. Founded 1895, but a predecessor library in Allegheny City (which became part of Pittsburgh in 1909) had been built with funds by Andrew Carnegie in 1890. President Benjamin Harrison attended the opening ceremony for the structure, which was named the Carnegie Library and Music Hall. Smithmeyer and Pelz were the architects, presenting a Romanesque design and clock tower. The Allegheny Library merged with the Carnegie Library of Pittsburgh in 1956. The Pittsburgh main building opened November 5, 1895, and was greatly enlarged in 1907. Population served today: 1,300,000. Circulation: 2,975,000. Holdings: 3,000,000. 16 branches. Historical highlights: 1897—first U.S. library to have a director of children's work (Frances Olcott); 1899—first library story time, West End Branch, and first organized children's department, main library; 1900—first training class for children's librarians, main library, became Carnegie Library School in 1916, part of Carnegie Tech, 1930–1962, then part of University of Pittsburgh; 1902—first U.S. science and technology department, main library (published *Technical Book Review Index*, 1917–1928, then turned it over to the Special Libraries Association). It was announced in November 2009 that all branches would close in January 2010 because of financial crisis, but the closings were later postponed for one year. Directors: Edwin H. Anderson, 1895–1904; Anderson H. Hopkins, 1905–1908; Harrison W. Craver, 1908–1917; John Hopkins Leete, 1917–1928; Ralph Munn, 1928–1964; Keith Doms, 1964–1969; Anthony A. Martin, 1969–1985; Robert B. Croneberger, 1986–1998; Herb Elish, 1999–2005; and Barbara K. Mistick, 2005–.

CARNOVSKY, LEON, 1903–1975   Library educator and consultant. Born St. Louis, MO, November 28, 1903. He earned a BA, University of Missouri, 1927. After completing the training class at St. Louis Public Library, he was employed as assistant librarian at Washington University of St. Louis. At the Graduate Library School, University of Chicago, he earned a PhD in 1932 and joined the faculty as an instructor; he was a professor in the school, 1944–1971, when he retired. Carnovsky was managing editor of the *Library Quarterly*, 1943–1961. His direct contributions to public libraries came from surveys and advising. He worked with dozens of libraries, writing important studies of West Chester County (1936), Cleveland Public Library (1939), and Chicago Public Library (1940), among others. He died in Oakland, CA, December 6, 1975. *DALB*.

CARPENTER MEMORIAL LIBRARY, CLE ELUM, WA   302 Pennsylvania Ave., Cle Elum, WA 98922. Population served: 1,785. Circulation: 19,089. Holdings: 14,001. LJ February 15, 2009: 3-star library.

CARR, JOHN FOSTER, 1869–1939   Advocate of library service to immigrants, born in New York City. He studied at Yale and Oxford. As a journalist in New York he often wrote about immigration issues, advocating Americanization rather than preservation of native cultures. Carr taught school in La Porte, IN, 1909–1911. He published an Italian-language guide to the United States for Italians in 1910; although it was described as "patronizing" and having "potentially offensive language" (Jones 1999, 73), the book was well received in public libraries. Polish and Yiddish versions followed. In 1913, Carr joined the American Library Association (ALA) and spoke regularly at conferences. He founded the Immigrant Publication Society in 1914 and published (with ALA) a guide for librarians working with Italians. He chaired the ALA Committee on Work with the Foreign Born, 1919–1920. Carr helped to create a positive attitude toward immigrants among public librarians.

Reference

Jones, Plummer Alston, Jr. 1999. *Libraries, Immigrants, and the American Experience*. Westport, CT: Greenwood Press, 1999.

CARROLL COUNTY PUBLIC LIBRARY, NEW WINDSOR, MD   115 Airport Dr., New Windsor, MD 21157. Founded 1958. Population served: 160,000. Circulation: 3,100,000. Holdings: 805,000. 5 branches, 3 bookmobiles. LJ February 15, 2009; November 15, 2009; and October 1, 2010: 4-star library.

CASCADE PUBLIC LIBRARY, ID   105 Front St., Cascade, ID 83611. Population served: 1,025. Circulation: 10,257. Holdings: 14,713. LJ February 15, 2009: 4-star library; November 15, 2009: 3-star library.

CASTAGNA, EDWIN, 1909–1983   Librarian. Born Petaluma, CA, May 1, 1909. He earned a BA, University of California, Berkeley, 1935, and a library certificate, 1936. He was an assistant in Alameda County Library, then city librarian Ukiah Public Library (CA). In 1940, Castagna was director of Washoe County Library, Reno, NV. He volunteered for army service in World War II, earning a Purple Heart and a Bronze Star. He was city librarian, Glendale, CA, in 1949, then librarian at Long Beach in 1950, where he was a successful fund-raiser and extended the branch system. Castagna was president of the California Library Association in 1954 and a lecturer in the library school of the University of Southern California. He became director of the Enoch Pratt Free Library in Baltimore in 1960, remaining to 1975. He led library outreach efforts into poor communities and promoted the creation of a library school at the University of Maryland. Active in the American Library Association, he was elected president in 1964. Castagna was a strong advocate of intellectual freedom. He published many articles, mostly on practical administrative matters. After retirement in 1975 he took an assignment for six months as city librarian in San Francisco. He died in Baltimore, MD, on November 26, 1983, an apparent suicide. *DALB*, 1st supplement.

CASTINE, ME. *See* WITHERLE MEMORIAL LIBRARY, CASTINE, ME.

CASTLE ROCK, CO. *See* DOUGLAS COUNTY LIBRARIES, CASTLE ROCK, CO.

CASTLETON PUBLIC LIBRARY, CASTLETON-ON-HUDSON, NY   85 S. Main St., Castleton-on-Hudson, NY 12033. Founded 1909. Population served: 1,619. Circulation: 31,098. Holdings: 16,405. LJ February 15, 2009, November 15, 2009, and October 1, 2010: 5-star library.

CASTLETON-ON-HUDSON, NY. *See* CASTLETON PUBLIC LIBRARY, CASTLETON-ON-HUDSON, NY.

CATALOGING   This entry focuses on cataloging issues of most importance in American public libraries. Developments outside the United States, such as the classified form of the catalog (which was the predominant form in the United Kingdom), are excluded.

Terminology

"Catalog" is now the preferred spelling, having replaced "catalogue," but the latter is still used in the United Kingdom. As a noun, a "catalog" is "a complete enumeration of items, arranged systematically, with descriptive details" (*Merriam*). In the library context, that definition would be more accurate without the "complete" since all a library's items may not be in the catalog. *ODLIS* has this definition of cataloging: "the process of creating entries for a catalog." A standard textbook, *Introduction to Cataloging and Classification*, by Arlene G. Taylor (2006), gives a more elaborate perspective: "the process of creating surrogate records for information packages by describing the information package, choosing name and title access points, conducting subject analysis, assigning subject headings and classification numbers, and maintaining the system through which the records are made available." A "surrogate record" is "a presentation of the characteristics (e.g., title, creator, physical description if appropriate, date of creation, subject(s), etc.) of an information package," and an "information package" is "an instance of recorded information (e.g., book, article, video, Internet document or set of 'pages,' sound recording, electronic journal, etc.); also called information resource" (Taylor 2006, 528, 545, 536). The term "entity" is used in this entry as more comprehensive than information package since it includes objects of all kinds. "Classification" in Taylor's longer definition is a part of cataloging, but traditionally it has held a separate court of its own; indeed, the title of Taylor's text seems to maintain that distinction (in this handbook there is a separate entry for CLASSIFICATION).

In any case, the work of the cataloger—the person who does the cataloging—deals with the subject matter of the entity as well as its overt characteristics. These are the fundamental cataloging tasks:

- Descriptive cataloging—the presentation, based on established rules, of overt characteristics of an entity, such as may be discerned by examination of it (e.g., author, title, medium, date and place of publication, publisher, edition, place in a series [if any], pagination, dimensions, and other physical features).

The cataloger may do research to amplify the information given in the entity itself (e.g., to discover the date of publication of a sound recording).

- Subject analysis—the selection and presentation of terms from a standard list (of "subject headings") or the placement and presentation of an entity within an established taxonomy ("classification scheme" or "classification system") to best express the intellectual content or nature of an entity.

- Authority control—the creation and utilization of consistent terminology for the characteristics (e.g., personal names or titles of musical works) of entities.

- Catalog management—the creation and maintenance of organizational structures, policies, procedures, and cooperative agreements.

The process of cataloging may be original or derivative or may partake of both approaches. "Original cataloging" results when the cataloger examines the entity independently of the work of other catalogers. This is the traditional image: a cart of books (or other media) stands at the cataloger's desk, and she takes one at a time for careful study, finally writing her "entry." Derivative cataloging, usually termed "copy cataloging," presents a different image. In this perspective the cataloger treats each book as an item to be searched in some database where a catalog entry for it stands ready for use. Derivative cataloging is akin to cooperative cataloging, which, as the name implies, involves an agreement among a number of libraries to share the work. When a group of libraries is connected for the purpose of satisfying specified requirements, this is referred to as a "network." The derivation or exchange of cataloging information constitute possible network objectives.

There remains an original component in copy cataloging since the cataloger may wish to alter the entry located in a database to suit local library practice in some way. Copy cataloging works best in libraries with general collections since there are likely to be database entries for items in them. Libraries that acquire highly specialized materials will probably be doing original cataloging for them.

The "rules" referred to above represent a current cataloging paradigm, reached by wide agreement among practitioners; a set of such rules is a "code." American librarians at this time rely on a code named *Anglo-American Cataloguing Rules, Second Edition* (AACR2) with its various revisions. AACR2 is the culmination of work on cataloging rules that extends back to 1841 (Taylor 2006, 25-27 summarizes the history of those rules).

Three formats for catalog entries are in use among American public libraries:

- Card catalogs
- Book catalogs
- Online catalogs

A card catalog consists of stiff paper cards, approximately three by five inches in dimension, each carrying one catalog entry; the cards are arranged alphabetically. In a "dictionary catalog," cards for author, title, and subject entries are interfiled. In a "divided catalog," there are separate sections for authors/titles and subjects. A book catalog consists of bound or loose-leaf volumes with each page displaying one or more catalog entries, the entries being in either "dictionary" or "divided" arrangement. An online catalog (online public access catalog [OPAC]) allows the user to sit at a computer terminal and access catalog records directly from the digitized base. It is also possible to access the catalogs of other libraries via remote access. In American practice, book catalogs came first and were more or less replaced by card catalogs by the end of the nineteenth century; since the 1980s, OPACs have eclipsed card catalogs.

The terminology of cataloging has been greatly expanded in the computer age as librarians have sought to accommodate earlier goals and procedures to digital formats. Machine-readable cataloging (MARC) was the earliest of those endeavors. It is "the international standard digital format for creation and dissemination of computerized cataloging among libraries" (*ODLIS*). The latest, current version is MARC 21, a consolidation of the previous USMARC and CAN/MARC formats, intended to adopt them to the needs of the twenty-first century. UNIMARC is an "international format for the exchange of machine readable cataloging records between national bibliographic agencies" (Taylor 2006, 547). Despite its widespread use, the MARC record, based as it is on AACR, remains an automated version of a manual catalog entry. Therefore, whether it is the most suitable format for machine-based systems is questionable. Resource Description and Access (RDA) is the new standard for resource description and access designed for the digital world. "RDA provides a comprehensive set of guidelines and instructions, based on the foundations of AACR2, for resource description and access covering all types of content and media" (www.rdatoolkit). Functional Requirements for Bibliographic Records (FRBR) is "a conceptual model of the bibliographic universe . . . that provides a way of describing entities and relationships between them" (Taylor 2006, 283).

"Metadata" is a system of describing "information resources—such as websites, electronic texts, digital artifacts, and so on—through the compilation of descriptions that are structured according to a specific framework (called a scheme) and are placed together to serve an indexing function in information retrieval" (Smiraglia 2005, 2). Metadata provides "a level of data at which choices can be made as to which information resources one wishes to view or search, without having to search massive amounts of irrelevant full text" (Taylor 2006, 538).

The cataloging vocabulary includes hundreds of terms. A useful list of them appears in the glossary section of Taylor (2006, 525–48).

Historical Summary

This is a chronology of significant events in the development of cataloging in the United States.

1833 (or 1848)—Harvard College created the first American card catalog as a supplement to its printed book catalog (Pope 1975).

1850s—Boston Public Library and the Library Company (Philadelphia) made "slip catalogs" available to the public; these were interfiled like cards. The main purpose of slips was to make supplements—originally for staff use—for printed book catalogs.

1853—First publication of catalog rules in the United States by Charles Coffin Jewett for the Smithsonian Institution Library (Jewett 1853). Jewett based his rules on those written by Anthony Panizzi at the British Museum. He gave instruction on entering titles, imprint data, headings, and cross-references (Stone 1977, 249).

1854—First dictionary catalog in the United States created by William Frederick Poole for the Boston Mercantile Library (Poole 1854). It was the earliest card catalog with entries interfiled for subject, author, and title.

1858—Jewett's rules applied in Boston Public Library cataloging, as he became superintendent there. Boston was the first public library to catalog according to standard rules.

1871—Boston Public Library card catalog made available to users.

1874—Charles Ammi Cutter, librarian of the Boston Athenaeum, issued the *Catalogue of the Library of the Boston Athenaeum* in five volumes, 1874–1882 (*Catalogue* 1874). It was acclaimed as the "best catalogue extant" by Justin Winsor. The work followed Cutter's cataloging rules (see next item). Printed book catalogs were the typical form of presentation of library holdings in the mid-nineteenth century, but the card catalog gained acceptance by 1876.

1876—*Rules for a Printed Dictionary Catalogue* by Charles Ammi Cutter was published in the United States Bureau of Education *Public Libraries in the United States*. Under various names and editors, this compilation became the standard American text (Cutter 1876).

1876—Melvil Dewey published the first edition of his *Decimal Classification*.

1877—The American Library Association (ALA) settled on a standard size for catalog cards, 2.95 by 4.92 inches, or 75 by

125 millimeters. This became known as the 3-by-5-inch card. It replaced a welter of different sizes used by libraries up to that time (Pope 1975).

1883—The ALA issued its first catalog rules.

1895—The ALA published *List of Subject Headings for Use in a Dictionary Catalogue.*

1895—John Shaw Billings completed his *Index Catalogue of the Library of the Surgeon General's Office.*

1896—A survey found that the card catalog had become the dominant format in U.S. libraries; typed cards were coming into favor, replacing those in "library hand"; printed cards were sold by the Library Bureau and used by a few libraries.

1901—The Library of Congress (LC) began selling printed catalog cards. Cutter's rules were followed. Distribution of cards ceased in 1997.

1901—LC established the National Union Catalog.

1908—*Cataloging Rules: Author and Title Entries.* The Anglo-American "joint code" was created. It was the first attempt to bring uniformity to the cataloging process in English-speaking countries.

1909–1914—LC published its list of subject headings used in the library's catalogs.

1938—H. W. Wilson Company began selling printed catalog cards, offering a simpler format than the LC cards. Wilson cards became popular in public libraries, especially smaller libraries. Distribution ceased in 1975.

1942–1946—LC published a printed catalog of its holdings, consisting of photocopies of the catalog cards, in 167 volumes.

1949—LC published *Rules for Descriptive Cataloging* (1949).

1949—ALA published cataloging rules, following the 1949 LC rules.

1950s—Printed book catalogs issued by various libraries, including King County Public Library (WA), Los Angeles County Public Library, and Baltimore County Public Library.

1953—*Cataloging Rules and Principles* by Seymour Lubetzky. Argued for rules based on principles: "conditions" rather than "cases." Paved the way for the "Paris principles" of 1961 and the subsequent AACR of 1967.

1964—National Union Catalog at LC had 15 million cards for 8 million titles.

1967—MARC program initiated at LC (Avram 1975).

1967—Ohio College Library Center (OCLC) established; became the Online Computer Library Center. This was at first a computerized database of library holdings in Ohio, then an international compilation. See *WorldCat* at 2002 below.

1967—International Standard Book Number (ISBN) and International Standard Serial Number (ISSN) created by international agreement among publishers, providing unique identifiers for publications.

1967—*Anglo-American Catalog Rules* (AACR) published, promoting standard cataloging practice for the United States and the United Kingdom.

1967—LC reported sales of 74 million printed catalog cards to 20,000 libraries.

1968–1981—*National Union Catalog: Pre-1956 Imprints*, published by LC, provided photocopies of 11 million catalog cards in 1,500 research libraries; 754 volumes.

1971—OCLC went online in Ohio.

1971—Cataloging in Publication (CIP) program initiated, in cooperation between LC and publishers, printing LC catalog information on verso of title pages in new publications. This program culminated various earlier efforts to put catalog information into books (Pope 1970).

1974—International Standard Bibliographic Description (ISBD) finalized, following a draft of 1971.

1976—CONSER (Cooperative Online Serials Project) was created. A national database of serial records, it is now maintained by OCLC.

1977—UNIMARC program initiated at LC.

1978—*Anglo-American Catalog Rules* published in revised version by ALA, Canadian Library Association, and U.K. Chartered Institute of Library and Information Professionals (AACR2) (Maxwell 2004).

1978—OCLC, a national database, was created.

1980s—Online public access catalogs (OPACs) replace card catalogs in most American libraries.

1981—*The Concise AACR2*, by Michael Gorman, was published, providing a simplified version of the rules for smaller libraries.

1998—Functional Requirements for Bibliographic Records (FRBR) issued by the International Federation of Library Associations and Institutions (IFLA), creating a "new model of the bibliographic universe" (Maxwell 2008, 1), much resembling a new cataloging code (see also LeBoeuf 2005; Taylor 2006; Zhang and Salaba 2009).

1999—MARC 21 adopted by the United States, Canada, the United Kingdom, and others: a consolidation of previous MARC schemes.

2002—OCLC initiated *WorldCat*, an international database of library holdings. It is said to add a new entry every 10 seconds. Those entries, using the current version of AACR2, are provided by many libraries. Retrieval is possible by author, title, subject, classification number, ISBN, and so on.

2005—Metadata cataloging code issued by IFLA (Coleman 2005; Howarth 2005; Smiraglia 2005).

2005—RDA (Resource Description and Access) initiated by the U.S./Canadian/U.K. committee to revise AACR2 (Kraus 2007).

2010—RDA Toolkit launched (www.rdatoolkit).

Current Issues

Since the creation of FRBR in 1998 (see above), the concerns of catalogers have centered on new approaches to rules and codes. FRBR is not limited to library objects but includes everything that libraries, bookstores, museums, and other entities might collect (AACR2 had this wide coverage also; see next paragraph) and "all persons, bodies, or families that might interact with those collections in any way," plus "all concepts that might be needed to describe other entities in the bibliographic universe" (Maxwell 2008, 1). This far-ranging perspective was incorporated into RDA (see above) and influenced the IFLA "Statement of International Cataloging Principles." Library practice has not embraced FRBR: "There has been little apparent movement toward conversion of our cataloging databases" in accord with it (Maxwell 2008, 137). Online catalogs checked in public library websites, during the writing of this entry in August 2010, revealed adherence to traditional cataloging format. *WorldCat* entries are in AACR2 style. At this point, it appears that the new rules and codes remain in the theoretical realm.

There seem to be two key goals involved in the modernization endeavors. One is to extend the domain of cataloging beyond the library walls and beyond traditional objects like printed materials; the other is simplification. Regarding the extension idea, conservative opposition centers on the capability of traditional cataloging rules to handle digital media. "It is possible to catalogue *any* document in any format using AACR2, a major classification, the LC subject heading list, and MARC" (Gorman 2000, 115). Indeed, the scope of AACR2 was neatly illustrated in a book by one of its authors: it gave examples of catalog copy for such items as an alarm clock, a body exercise device, a flax display, a tractor, and a shoehorn (Hunter 1989, 197–99). Simplification may be applied to the work of the cataloger and to the task of the library user. The "Dublin Core" is a set of metadata elements and code conventions that relieves the cataloger of many research duties; in most cases, it takes all the facts needed to make an entry directly from the source. Thus, the old problems of verifying author information, creating conventional titles, and clarifying editions are put aside (Coleman 2005). "A blurring of lines" between traditional bibliographic description and the Dublin Core is likely (Howarth 2005, 45). And the whole Dublin Core/metadata process has been denounced as "a fancy name for an inferior form of cataloguing" and "unstandardized, uncontrolled, ersatz cataloguing" (Michael Gorman, quoted in Howarth 2005, 52). The controversy is summarized in Kraus (2007).

From the library user's point of view, it is desirable to make the lookup task as simple as possible. Library OPACs examined in the writing of this entry vary in their success at simplification. Search terms are not standardized, and some are ambiguous; a user may wonder what to do with a choice between "title browse" and "keyword browse." A certain computer literacy is prerequisite for using an OPAC, which eliminates a portion of the community from participating. But on the whole, surveys show user satisfaction with OPACs.

A radical effort toward simplification of cataloging is disposal of it to some degree or entirely. Public library experimentations in so-called bookstore or reader-interest approaches aim to relieve the patron of searching anything. Books are shelved in broad subject categories or just by title or author, which would seem to be practical in quite small collections but dubious in large ones. Such an arrangement does not necessarily replace the catalog; if an item is out on loan, for instance, the catalog is the only means of ascertaining whether it is in stock (for further explanation, *see* CLASSIFICATION).

Another simplification idea concerns subject headings. American libraries are accustomed to using either the subject heading lists of the Library of Congress (2008; first issued in 1897) or the less complex lists published under the name of Sears (2010). What is being discussed is dropping these formal lists, which require the user to adjust his topical searches to a controlled vocabulary, in favor of "natural language" and free-text searching. This notion came from the remarkable capability of search engines such as Google to find materials on a multitude of topics without a fixed list of headings. Although no tangible steps have been taken to eliminate subject headings in American libraries or to stop publishing revised lists of Sears and LC headings, resistance has been pronounced. Michael Gorman spoke for the conservative objectors: "if LCSH were to be replaced by uncontrolled free-text searching it would be a scholarly catastrophe" (Oder 2006, 14). But Karen Calhoun of Cornell University, speaking for the possibility of free text, noted that "it takes six months to a year to train someone in the complexities of how to use that controlled vocabulary. It's very, very costly" (Oder 2006, 15).

New theories in cataloging must lead to changes in the teaching of cataloging in library schools. However, it has been a long time since cataloging (or a course of whatever name that deals with cataloging) has been a required course (see Hill 2002; *see also* EDUCATION OF PUBLIC LIBRARIANS), so the impact of such changes does not strike all students. It is interesting that employers who seek catalogers tend to ask for skill in traditional cataloging standards, with much less concern for newer standards (Lussky 2008). The conclusion of one writer is that those programs that "teach traditional tools and sources as well as emerging technologies will produce professionals better able to contribute significantly throughout their careers" (Baca et al. 2008, 2). It is also significant for education that copy cataloging has become a task for library technicians rather than librarians.

Commercial vendors are available to relieve librarians of the entire cataloging activity. In arrangements similar to those found in purchasing (*see* ACQUISITIONS), they will provide catalog records ready for downloading into local OPACs, along with spine labels and other accessories. As the library order is placed with the vendor, catalog copy is ready to deliver. Outsourcing of cataloging is controversial on grounds of professional responsibility and of cost benefits. The former claim is cloudy in view of the change from original to copy cataloging. The latter element remains uncertain pending full research.

As a final note, cataloging must not be considered a self-contained unit; the catalog generally forms the basis of an integrated system with ordering, acquisition, and circulation control modules. The OPAC was in fact introduced as an offshoot of computerized circulation systems. Some form of inquiry module was provided for library staff, and as this facility was developed and became more powerful, it was a logical step to extend the provision to the user. *See also* AUDIOVISUAL COLLECTIONS; CLASSIFICATION; MUSIC COLLECTIONS.

References

Anglo-American Cataloguing Rules. 2005. Prepared under the direction of the Joint Steering Committee for Revision of AACR ... Chicago: American Library Association. Updates through 2005 of *AACR2*.

Avram, Henriette D. 1975. Machine-readable cataloging (MARC) program. In *Encyclopedia of Library and Information Science* 16: 380–413. New York: Marcel Dekker.

Baca, Murtha A. et al. 2006. *Cataloging Cultural Objects: A Guide to Describing Cultural Works and Their Images*. Chicago: American Library Association.

Baca, Murtha A. et al. 2008. Making the connection: Focusing on the disconnect between LIS education and employer expectations. *Journal of Education for Library and Information Science* 49, no. 2 (Spring): 91–92.

Broughton, Vanda. 2009. *Essential Library of Congress Subject Headings*. New York: Neal Schuman.

Catalogue. 1874–1882. *Catalogue of the Library of the Boston Athenaeum*. Prepared by Charles Ammi Cutter. Boston: Athenaeum.

Chan, Lois Mai. 2005. *Library of Congress Subject Headings: Principles and Application*. 4th ed. Westport, CT: Libraries Unlimited.

Chan, Lois Mai. 2007. *Cataloging and Classification: An Introduction*. 3rd ed. Lanham, MD: Scarecrow Press.

Coleman, Anita S. 2005. From cataloging to metadata: Dublin Core records for the library catalog. In *Metadata: A Cataloger's Primer*, ed. Richard P. Smiraglia, 153–81. Binghamton, NY: Haworth.

Cutter, Charles Ammi. 1876/1904. *Rules for a Dictionary Catalogue*. 4th ed. Edited by William Parker Cutter. Washington, DC: Government Printing Office. 1st ed. In United States Bureau of Education, *Public Libraries in the United States*, 1876.

Gorman, Michael. 2000. *Our Enduring Values: Librarianship in the 21st Century*. Chicago: American Library Association.

Gorman, Michael. 2004. *The Concise AACR2, 4th ed., through the 2004 Update*. Chicago: American Library Association.

Hill, Janet Swan. 2002. *Education for Cataloging and the Organization of Information: Pitfalls and the Pendulum*. Binghamton, NY: Haworth.

Hines, Theodore C. 1969. Book catalogs. In *Encyclopedia of Library and Information Science* 2: 659–657.

Howarth, Lynne C. 2005. Metadata and bibliographic control: Soul-mates or "two solitudes"? In *Metadata: A Cataloger's Primer*, ed. Richard P. Smiraglia, 37–56. Binghamton, NY: Haworth.

Hunter, Eric J. 1989. *An Introduction to AACR2: A Programmed Guide to the Second Edition of Anglo-American Cataloguing Rules 1988 Revision*. London: Bingley.

Hunter, Eric J. 1989. *Examples Illustrating AACR2 1988 Revision*. London: Library Association.

International Conference. 1963. *International Conference on Cataloguing Principles: Report, Paris, 9–18 Oct 1961*. London: Organizing Committee of the International Conference on Cataloguing Principles.

Jewett, Charles Coffin. 1853. *On the Construction of Catalogues of Libraries*. 2nd ed. Washington, DC: Smithsonian Institution.

Kraus, Daniel. 2007. Controversies in cataloging. *American Libraries* 38, no. 9 (October): 66–67.

Lane, W. C. 1892. Cataloging. In *Papers Prepared for the World's Library Congress Held at the Columbian Exposition*. Part 2, chapter 7, of the *Report of the Commissioner of Education, 1892–1893*. Washington, DC: Government Printing Office.

Library of Congress. 1949. *Rules for Descriptive Cataloging in the Library of Congress*. Washington, DC: Government Printing Office. Preliminary ed., 1947.

Library of Congress. 1998. *Library of Congress Subject Headings*. 31st ed. Washington, DC: Library of Congress, Cataloging Distribution Service. 5 vols. 1st ed., *Subject Headings Used in the Dictionary Catalogues of the Library of Congress*, 1897.

Lussky, Joan P. 2008. Employer demand for cataloger and cataloger-like librarians and implications for LIS. *Journal of Education for Library and Information Science* 49 (2, Spring): 116–28.

Maxwell, Robert L. 2004. *Maxwell's Handbook for AACR2: Explaining and Illustrating the Anglo-American Cataloging Rules through the 2003 Update*. Chicago: American Library Association.

Maxwell, Robert L. 2008. *FRBR: A Guide for the Perplexed*. Chicago: American Library Association.

Miksa, Francis. 2009. Chan, Taylor, and the future of cataloging texts (review article). *Library Quarterly* 79, no. 1 (January): 131–143.

Oder, Norman. 2006. The end of LC subject headings? *Library Journal* 131, no. 9 (May 15): 14–15.

Poole, William F. 1854. *Catalogue of the Mercantile Library of Boston*. Boston: John Wilson & Son.

Pope, Elspeth. 1970. Cataloguing in source. In *Encyclopedia of Library and Information Science* 4: 231–41. New York: Marcel Dekker.

Pope, Elspeth. 1975. Library catalog cards. In *Encyclopedia of Library and Information Science* 14: 448–64. New York: Marcel Dekker.

Ranz, James. 1964. *The Printed Book Catalogue in American Libraries, 1723-1900*. Chicago: American Library Association.

Sears, Minnie Earl. 2010. *Sears Subject Headings*. 20th ed. Edited by Joseph Miller. New York: H. W. Wilson. 1st ed., *List of Subject Headings for Small Libraries*, 1923.

Smiraglia, Richard P., ed. 2005. *Metadata: A Cataloger's Primer*. Binghamton, NY: Haworth.

Stone, Alva T. 2000. *The LCSHs: One Hundred Years with the Library of Congress Subject Headings System*. New York: Haworth.

Stone, Elizabeth. 1977. *American Library Development*. New York: H. W. Wilson.

Taylor, Arlene G. 2006. *Introduction to Cataloging and Classification*. 10th ed. Westport, CT: Libraries Unlimited.

Taylor, Arlene G., ed. 2007. *Understanding FRBR: What It Is and How It Will Affect Our Retrieval Tools*. Westport, CT: Libraries Unlimited.

Zeng, Marcia Lei, and Jian Quin. 2008. *Metadata*. New York: Neal Schuman.

Zhang, Yin, and Athena Salaba. 2009. *Implementing FRBR in Libraries: Key Issues and Future Directions*. New York: Neal-Schuman.

Significant portions of this entry were written by Eric J. Hunter.

CATALOGS. *See* CATALOGING.

CEDAR RAPIDS PUBLIC LIBRARY, IA   500 First St. SE, Cedar Rapids, IA 52401. Founded 1895. Population served: 120,758. Circulation: 525,755. Holdings: 78,480. 1 branch. There were severe losses in the flood of June 2008; 160,000 items were lost, and the central building was put out of use. The library operated from the West Side Branch and plans to do so until a new facility is ready, expected in 2011.

CENSORSHIP. *See* INTELLECTUAL FREEDOM.

CENTER MORICHES FREE PUBLIC LIBRARY, NE   235 Main St., Center Moriches, NY 11934. Founded 1950. Population served: 6,518. Circulation: 192,348. Holdings: 100,790. LJ February 15, 2009; November 15, 2009; and October 1, 2010: 4-star library.

CENTERBURG PUBLIC LIBRARY, OH   49 E. Main St., Centerburg, OH 43011. Founded 1924. It is an association library without taxing authority. Population served: 1,481. Circulation: 88,959. Holdings: 29,553. LJ February 15, 2009; November 15, 2009; and October 1, 2010: 5-star library. HAPLR 2009, 2010.

CENTEREACH, NY. *See* MIDDLE COUNTY PUBLIC LIBRARY, CENTEREACH, NY.

CENTERVILLE, OH. *See* WASHINGTON-CENTERVILLE PUBLIC LIBRARY, CENTERVILLE, OH.

CENTERVILLE COMMUNITY LIBRARY, SD   421 Florida, Centerville, SD 57014. Population served: 1,567. Circulation: 32,244. Holdings: 26,114. LJ February 15, 2009; November 15, 2009; and October 1, 2010: 5-star library.

CENTRAL CITY, IA. *See* J. C. CLEGG PUBLIC LIBRARY, CENTRAL CITY, IA.

CENTRAL CITY PUBLIC LIBRARY, NE   1604 15th Ave., Central City, NE 68826. Population served: 2,998. Circulation: 78,463. Holdings: 35,118. LJ February 15, 2009; November 15, 2009; and October 1, 2010: 5-star library.

CENTRAL RAPPAHANNOCK REGIONAL LIBRARY SYSTEM, FREDERICKS-BURG, VA   1201 Caroline St., Fredericksburg, VA 22401. Founded 1910 as Fredericksburg Public Library; became regional system 1971. Population served: 243,100. Circulation: 6,061,759. Holdings: 371,261. LJ November 15, 2009, and October 1, 2010: 3-star library. HAPLR 2009, 2010.

CENTRALIA PUBLIC LIBRARY, MO   210 S. Jefferson, Centralia, MO 65240. Founded 1941. Population served: 3,758. Circulation: 76,863. Holdings: 20,000. LJ February 15, 2009: 4-star library; November 15, 2009: 3-star library; October 1, 2010: 4-star library.

CERRITOS LIBRARY, CA   18925 Bloomfield Ave., Cerritos, CA 90703. Founded 1973. Population served: 55,000. Circulation: 970,000. Holdings: 238,000. LJ February 15, 2009; November 15, 2009; and October 1, 2010: 5-star library. The 1989 addition, by Fleischman Associates, is described in the library website as the first titanium clad building in the United States.

CHAMA, NM. *See* ELEANOR DAGGETT MEMORIAL LIBRARY, CHAMA, NM.

CHAMPAIGN PUBLIC LIBRARY, IL   200 N. Green, Champaign, IL 61820. Founded 1876. Population served: 75,254. Circulation: 2,392,033. Holdings: 372,841. LJ February 15, 2009; November 15, 2009; and October 1, 2010: 3-star library.

CHANDLER PUBLIC LIBRARY, AZ   22 S. Delaware, Chandler, AZ 85225. Founded 1954. Population served: 230,000. Circulation: 2,000,000. Holdings: 450,000. 3 branches.

CHANDLER WATTS MEMORIAL LIBRARY, STRATFORD, OK   340 N. Oak, Stratford, OK 74872. Population served: 1,478. Circulation: 38,265. Holdings: 21,551. LJ February 15, 2009, and October 1, 2010: 4-star library.

CHARDON, OH. See GEAUGA COUNTY PUBLIC LIBRARY, CHARDON, OH.

CHARLESTON COUNTRY PUBLIC LIBRARY SYSTEM, CHARLESTON, SC   68 Calhoun St., Charleston, SC 29401. Founded 1931. Population served: 326,762. Circulation: 3,256,863. Holdings: 1,084,483. 15 branches, 2 bookmobiles. Thomas Bray established a free public library in Charleston, 1698, the first in the United States (library website). LJ February 15, 2009: 3-star library.

CHARLOTTE MECKLENBURG LIBRARY, CHARLOTTE, NC   310 N. Tryon, Charlotte, NC 28202. Founded 1903. Population served: 768,789. Circulation: 6,000,000. Holdings: 1,950,500. 28 branches. The name of the library was changed from Public Library of Charlotte and Mecklenburg County in January 2010. IMLS award 2006. LJ Library of the Year 1995. LJ February 15, 2009, and November 15, 2009: 5-star library.

CHATHAM, MA. See ELDREDGE PUBLIC LIBRARY, CHATHAM, MA.

CHELSEA DISTRICT LIBRARY, MI   221 S. Main, Chelsea, MI 48118. Founded 1938. Population served: 14,098. Circulation: 313,295 in 2008 (library website). Holdings: 54,757 (library website). LJ February 2008: "best small library in America."

CHEROKEE PUBLIC LIBRARY, IA   215 S. Second St., Cherokee, IA 51012. Founded 1898. Population served: 5,369. Circulation: 62,634. Holdings: 42,869. LJ November 15, 2009: 4-star library. The 1905 building, by architect F. E. Wetherell, was placed on the National Register of Historic Places in 1986.

CHEYENNE, WY. See LARAMIE COUNTY LIBRARY SYSTEM, CHEYENNE, WY.

CHICAGO PUBLIC LIBRARY, IL   400 S. State St., Chicago, IL 60605. Founded 1872. Population served 2,896,016. Circulation 7,771,541. Holdings: 5,526,677. 87 branches, 2 bookmobiles. Chicago Public Library (CPL) was established by municipal ordinance on April 1, 1872; it opened to the public on January 1, 1873, but did not commence circulating books until May 1, 1874. CPL was originally housed on the third floor of City Hall and an adjacent abandoned water tank. There were various locations later until a new library was built; that structure was dedicated on October 9, 1897. Architects were Shepley, Rutan, and Coolidge (also designers of the Art Institute of Chicago). The building is distinguished for its ornate marble interiors and the remarkable glass dome by Tiffany (see the cover illustration of this book) that adorns what is now a concert hall. William F. Poole was the first librarian, serving from 1874 to 1887. When he went on to direct the Newberry Library, Frederick H. Hild was appointed, serving from 1887 to 1909. The library was slow to reach a large public. Annual circulation hovered around one per capita at the end of Hild's term. Growth was hampered by the absence of branches; there was only one in 1909 that circulated books, although there were also 15 small branch reading rooms and 87 "delivery stations" where patrons could pick up and return books. Services in general were poor until the appointment of Henry Legler as librarian on October 11, 1909. He concentrated on branch development, and by 1915 there were 32 of them, all circulating materials. Legler's death in 1917 led to the appointment of Carl Roden, who served to 1950. His tenure brought CPL success and many innovations. The number of branches increased to 58 by 1929. A Readers' Bureau, created in 1923, offered readers' advisory service that included personalized self-study courses. Classroom collections were set up in elementary schools, and 24 high school libraries were staffed and operated by CPL by 1928. Circulation soared during the early years of the Depression (as it tended to do in all public libraries), with 16 million reported for 1931 (4.57 per capita), the highest of any U.S. library. In the later 1930s, CPL lost ground in terms of circulation, in comparison with its own earlier records and with other large libraries. With 3.61 per capita in 1938, it was well behind Boston (4.85), Cleveland (10.29), Los Angeles (8.5), San Francisco (5.53), and Washington, D.C. (6.38). Staff had been growing rapidly—from 210 persons in 1908 to 521 in 1918, 1,053 in 1928, and 1,037 in 1938—but most employees had minimal qualifications. Only 4 percent of the staff in 1938 had a year or more of library school. There were also concerns about the limitations of space in the building. Roden arranged for a study of the library by two professors of the University of Chicago Graduate Library School. That survey, carried out by Carleton Joeckel and Leon Carnovsky (1940), is still regarded as a model of its kind. The surveyors recommended major changes in administrative structure, staffing, financing, and space allocations. Many of their ideas were implemented. One odd suggestion was for the replacement of the "old, unattractive building," a similar thought occurred to a later consultant, Lowell Martin, in 1968. Fortunately the building has been preserved; it was added to the National Register of Historic Places in 1972 and converted to new use as the Chicago Cultural Center. Instead of demolition, the building underwent a thorough renovation in 1974–1976 and was designated a Chicago landmark.

Before the end of Roden's term in 1950, CPL had reached another peak in circulation. The 1948 figure of 9 million was again the highest in the United States. There were 60 branches in that year. An art department was opened in 1945 and a music department in 1949. The high school libraries were transferred to the Board of Education in 1947. Circulation remained strong into the 1960s, then began a decline, both in absolute numbers and per capita. In 1995 circulation was 7,455,063 (2.67 per capita).

Gertrude Gscheidle was librarian, 1950–1967, followed by Alex Ladenson, 1967–1974; David L. Reich, 1975–1978; Donald Sager, 1978–1981 (title changed to commissioner); Amanda Rudd, 1982–1985; James Lowry (acting), 1985; John B. Duff, 1985–1992; Robert Remer (acting), 1992–May 1993; Karen Danczak-Lyons (acting), 1993 and 2005; and Mary Dempsey, 1993– (chief procurement officer, January 2005–September 2005). On July 29, 1987, the City Council approved a bond issue to finance a new library building and authorized a design competition. On June 20, 1988, the SEBUS group, a consortium of architects and engineers, was awarded the contract. Principal architect was Thomas Beeby of Hammond, Beeby and Babka. The new building, infelicitously isolated at the southern tip of the Loop, opened to the public on October 7, 1991. With more than 70 miles of shelves and 756,650 square feet of space, the "Harold Washington Library Center" was said to be the largest public library building in the world. The design brought much criticism: it is a forbidding stone castle in somewhat Romanesque style, a stark contrast to the airy, inviting public libraries being built in other cities. (Possibly the atmosphere created by the structure permeated within, resulting in remarkably restrictive policies of access and circulation.) In 1995 an online public access catalog was offered with research databases available; the catalog is accessible from home workstations. Extensive Internet access is provided at the main library and all branches.

References

Joeckel, Carleton B., and Leon Carnovsky. 1940. *A Metropolitan Library in Action: A Survey of the Chicago Public Library.* Chicago: University of Chicago Press.
Ladenson, Alex. 1970. Chicago Public Library. In *Encyclopedia of Library and Information Science*, 4: 530–539. New York: Marcel Dekker.
Spencer, Gwladys [sic]. 1943. "The Chicago Public Library: Origins and Background." PhD dissertation, University of Chicago.

CHILDREN'S LIBRARY SERVICES. *See* SERVICES TO CHILDREN AND YOUNG ADULTS.

CHILMARK FREE PUBLIC LIBRARY, MA   522 South Rd., Chilmark, MA 02535. Founded 1891. Population served: 934. Circulation: 50,995. Holdings: 29,172. HAPLR 2010.

CHULA VISTA PUBLIC LIBRARY, CA   Civic Center, Chula Vista, CA 91910. Founded 1912. Population served: 217,543. Circulation: 1,414,295. Holdings: 463,947. 2 branches.

CIMARRON CITY LIBRARY, KS   120 N. Main, Cimarron City, KS 67835. Population served: 2,035. Circulation: 40,648. Holdings: 35,858. 2 branches. LJ February 15, 2009: 4-star library; November 15, 2009: 5-star library.

CINCINNATI, OH. *See* PUBLIC LIBRARY OF CINCINNATI AND HAMILTON COUNTY, CINCINNATI, OH.

CIRCULATION SERVICES

Terminology

In *ODLIS* circulation is "the process of checking books and other materials in and out of a library." "Checking out" and "charging out" refer to the act of borrowing an item by a patron; "checking in" refers to the act of returning the item ("charging in" is not in use). The library's procedures and equipment devoted to circulation are its "circulation system." The term "circulation" also applies to the number of times an item—or all items in a category—is checked out over a given period of time—thus leading to "circulation statistics." A "circulating" item is one that may be checked out, while a "noncirculating" item may be used only in the library.

According to the definition of public library observed in this handbook, circulation of materials is a necessary service (*see* PUBLIC LIBRARY).

Historical Summary

From antiquity to modern times, libraries embraced a noncirculating policy, meaning that their stock was for use in the library only. This is still the practice in certain types of libraries in many countries. In the United States, materials in national and other federal government libraries and in state libraries may circulate—if at all—only to specified users. Privately supported libraries usually follow restrictive circulation policies. Home circulation of books began in the eighteenth century in Britain and the United States by rental agencies that were called circulating libraries. The earliest of these in the United States were active in Annapolis, MD (1762); New York City (1763); and Boston (1765). Their stock was essentially popular fiction. A second type of library permitted charging out materials: the social or subscription library. Benjamin Franklin's Junto, established in 1728 in Philadelphia, was the first. (It is still operating as the Library Company of Philadelphia.) Social libraries aimed at gathering collections of quality materials for their discriminating members, who were the only authorized users. Boston Public Library had home borrowing from its opening day in March 1854; two months later it had charged out 35,389 items.

The New York Free Circulating Library (1878) was a rental agency that gained wide acceptance. By 1886 it had a circulation of 200,000 items from a stock of 20,000 volumes. Another successful venture in New York was the Aguilar Free Library (1878), serving Jewish communities. The "free" in the names of these agencies meant only that they were open to all customers. The free libraries joined with two noncirculating research libraries, the Astor and the Lenox, to form the city's actual public library (*see* NEW YORK PUBLIC LIBRARY), which established a circulation department in 1901. Twenty years later the annual circulation was 9,658,977 items.

The American public library tradition has been unequivocally based on home circulation. A report in 1929 stated that "in most American public libraries" ... all books circulate except for "retention of a small group for use in the building for the users' convenience only" (Bostwick 1929, 9).

Libraries have kept track of their borrowed materials in various ways. The earliest method was with a ledger in which book titles and patron names were written. Next there were "dummy" approaches, in which some object with borrowing information was placed on the shelf in place of the book that was charged out. Then came the idea of a slip or card kept in each book, the slip being taken out and filed when the book circulated. Later elaborations of that concept included the two-card system (one put in a book file, the other in a patron file) and the three-card system. With three cards there were three files maintained, one by date due, one by book number, and one by borrower name; this invention of the Newark (NJ) Public Library (1896) dominated national practice for 30 years. In all the methods mentioned, the borrowed book carried a card or date stamp to remind the user of the return date. Devices to reduce charging time were sold by Dickman (in 1927) and Gaylord (in 1931). Punched cards appeared in a number of systems in the 1930s. Photo-chargers were popular for a while from the 1940s, although staff needed to examine reels of film to locate transaction data. (Details and illustrations of these systems are in Geer 1955 and Parker 1970.)

In the 1970s computer technology disposed of earlier manual methods. Integrated systems now offer staff and users a record that gives bibliographic information about a title along with circulation status (on shelf, charged out with due date, noncirculating). Bar codes in books and on readers' library cards make checkout or check-in an instantaneous event and generate complete patron records. Home access to online catalogs allows patrons to view their lists of items charged out and click for renewals. Some systems also permit users to queue for materials in circulation, with a "hold" or "reserve" request.

Current Situation

Technology has not solved all circulation problems. Each library still has to devise and publicize a circulation policy. Such policies usually cover requirements for borrowing (how to get a library card), loan periods, overdue fines, and library responses to theft, damaged, or lost materials. Library websites spell out these policies (for a detailed example, see the Tulsa City County Library System website *see also* POLICY STATEMENTS). There is no unanimity about loan periods. The tradition in the era of the printed book was a 14-day period with at least one renewal. As their collections grew, large libraries tended to increase the initial period to 21 days for books. But audio and visual items are almost always limited to shorter periods. Some libraries also have limits on the number of items to be charged out. A few examples may be useful:

- Cleveland Public Library: 21 days; but 7 days for entertainment videos and DVDs. Renewal if not reserved.
- Brooklyn Public Library: 21 days; but 7 days for videos, DVDs, and CDs. Renewal if not reserved. Charge-out limits: books 99, video and audio items 10.
- Naperville (IL) Public Library: 14 days; 3 to 14 days for DVDs and videos. Renewal if not reserved.
- San Diego Public Library: 21 days; 7 days for videos and DVDs. Only one renewal.
- Las Vegas-Clark County Library District: 21 days; 7 days for DVDs. 3 renewals unless reserved; no renewal for DVDs and bestsellers. Charge-out limit: 50 items.
- Dover Town Library (MA): 21 days; 14 for magazines; 7 days for videos and DVDs. One renewal.
- Harford County Public Library (MD): 21 days; 3 days for entertainment DVDs. 2 renewals. Charge-out limit: 10 DVDs.
- Tulsa City-County Library System (OK): 14 days. 2 renewals. Charge-out limit: 40 items.

None of the websites examined reveals a loan period above 21 days. Possibly this limitation is ripe for reexamination in view of the size of many library collections today.

Assessment of fines for overdue items is virtually a universal practice (Dover Town Library, MA, is one exception). Fines follow a complex pattern, with a base charge of 10 to 25 cents a day for most books, increasing to a dollar a day or more for audio and video materials and high-demand books.

An important issue regarding circulation is maintenance and availability of patron borrowing records. Such records could be of use to librarians in collection development and readers' advisory work, although there is no research to demonstrate the point. The risk of keeping records is the possibility of their misuse (*see* PRIVACY AND CONFIDENTIALITY). Most libraries have decided in favor of expunging individual circulation records when materials are returned, and computerized systems do it automatically.

It is possible with computerized circulation to keep elaborately categorized data. Those figures are of value in budgeting and publicity and for comparison purposes among libraries. The Institute of Museum and Library
Services issues periodic tabulations of circulation data. National per capita
circulation was 6.6 in 1997 and 7.7 in 2008 (*see* STATISTICS). In addition
to materials owned by an individual library, patrons have access to items in
other collections (*see* INTERLIBRARY LOAN).

References

Bostwick, Arthur E. 1929. *The American Public Library*. 4th ed. New York:
    Appleton. 1st ed. 1910.
Flexner, Jennie Maas. 1927. *Circulation Work in Public Libraries*. Chicago: Ameri-
    can Library Association.
Geer, Helen. 1955. *Charging Systems*. Chicago: American Library Association.
Parker, Ralph H. 1970. Charging systems. In *Encyclopedia of Library and Informa-
    tion Science* 4: 142–44. New York: Marcel Dekker.

CITY OF COMMERCE PUBLIC LIBRARY, CA   5655 Jilson St., Commerce, CA
90040. Population served: 13,504. Circulation: 259,861. Holdings:
131,182. 3 branches. LJ February 15, 2009, and October 1, 2010: 3-star
library.

CITY OF MESA LIBRARY, AZ   64 E. First St., Mesa, AZ 85201. Population
served: 450,000. Circulation: 3,500,000. Holdings: 816,314. 2 branches.

CLASSIFICATION   This entry deals only with classification matters of
concern to American public librarians.

Terminology

Merriam, tracing the word back to 1790, defines it as "a systematic
arrangement in groups or categories according to established criteria; = taxonomy." A library classification has three main parts:

- A schedule or table—a list of the classes (categories) and subclasses used, usually in hierarchical arrangement
- A notation—symbols that identify each class, the symbols
  typically being numerals, letters, or combinations thereof
  (the symbols are such that they can be arranged in a familiar
  order)
- An index—an alphabetical list of the classes and subclasses

Classification may be viewed as an aspect of cataloging or as a distinct
concept and operation. The work of classification is carried out by a classifier, who is usually the cataloger (*see* CATALOGING). The principles of
classification are elucidated in Hunter (2009, chaps. 1 and 2).

A "call number" is "a combination of characters assigned to a library book to indicate its place on a shelf" (*Merriam*). That combination consists first of the notation that identifies the subject of the book (or other entity); it is the class number. The rest of the call number is the "author number" or "book number," a letter plus decimal number that enables all books of the same class to be arranged systematically, usually according to author. There are infelicities connected to the term author number (which may well be a title or other main entry instead of an author) and the term book number (which fails to consider nonbook entities). The most common term in the United States for this part of the call number is "cutter number," after Charles Ammi Cutter, who invented it. A cutter number renders the author surname (or whatever word follows the class number in the call number) as an initial letter plus one or more numerals; the numerals represent those letters in the word after the initial and, by virtue of their numerical sequence, keep the words in alphabetical order. A second cutter number may follow. Various tables of cutter numbers were written by Cutter himself and others. The one most used today is the Cutter-Sanborn version (named for Kate E. Sanborn). Extra "work letters" may be added after the cutter number. All these complications boil down to a rather simple result. An example follows:

> Rattenbury, Ken. *Duke Ellington, Jazz Composer.* ML410 .E44 R3
>
> (ML 410 is the class for composers. E44 is the cutter number for Ellington, R3 the cutter for Rattenbury.)
>
> Copland, Aaron and Vivian Perlis. *Copland: Since 1943.* ML410 .C756 A3
>
> Copland, Aaron and Vivian Perlis. *Copland: 1900 through 1942.* ML410 .C756

The A3 is a "form number" for autobiography. These examples display the Library of Congress Classification (LCC; see below). Some call numbers incorporate dates that may refer to a book's edition or to some chronological aspect of the subject treated by the book.

Historical Summary

Of the many library classifications created in the nineteenth century, only two have had enduring interest to American public librarians. Both of them are "hierarchical." Another genre of classification, "faceted," is not used in American public libraries. (Descriptions of the two approaches are given in Hunter [2009], chaps. 3–6.) The Decimal Classification (DDC) devised by Melvil Dewey for use in the Amherst College Library was issued by the college in 1876 as Amherst College Classification and Subject Index. It consisted of 12 pages listing the classes and an 18-page index. It was soon adopted by libraries around the country, eclipsing the contemporary classification by Charles Ammi Cutter. DDC is said to be used in 200,000 libraries today, in 135 countries (Fister 2009, 6). The 22nd edition, in four volumes, was published in 2003 (Dewey 2003).

A rival to DDC, LCC, was developed by James C. Hanson and Charles Martel for use in the Library of Congress (LC). It was published in sections, by class, with an outline of all the classes appearing in 1903 (see *LC Classification* 2003). Revisions of the various sections have appeared from time to time. DDC was the early choice of public and academic libraries, many of which gave up local schemes to convert to it. But certain shortcomings of DDC for large collections became evident, and in the 1950s and 1960s there was a move to convert academic libraries from DDC to LCC. (It was a long process; for example, the University of Wisconsin, Madison, required 10 years for the task.) The problem that large libraries experienced with DDC had to do with the designation of only one main class to each of the sciences and technologies, a feature that led to overcrowding within subclasses and very long notations. LCC is more open ended, with indefinite potential for expansion in any class, but some notations are also lengthy.

As a clarification of this expansion issue, it is useful to have an overview of the schedules in both DDC and LCC.

> Dewey Decimal Classification: Main Classes
>
> 000—Computer science/information and general works
>
> 100—Philosophy/psychology
>
> 200—Religion
>
> 300—Social sciences
>
> 400—Language
>
> 500—Natural sciences/mathematics
>
> 600—Technology
>
> 700—Arts and recreation
>
> 800—Literature
>
> 900—History/geography

Each main class has 10 "divisions," known as the "second summary." For example, within the 300 class are the following:

> 310—General statistics
>
> 320—Political science
>
> 330—Economics
>
> 340—Law
>
> 350—Public administration
>
> 360—Social services
>
> 370—Education
>
> 380—Commerce, communications, transport
>
> 390—Customs, etiquette, folklore

Within each division there are "sections" (comprising the "third summary"). Under 370—Education, for example, the subdivisions (21st ed.) are the following:

371—Schools and their activities

372—Elementary education

373—Secondary education

374—Adult education

375—Curricula

376—Education of women

377—Schools and religion

378—Higher education

379—Public policy issues in education

These may have further subdivisions past the decimal point.

All materials about higher education would have the number 378, followed by a decimal extension to distinguish among subtopics in the area. For example, *Lecture Notes: A Professor's Inside Guide to College Success* by Philip Freeman (2010) is 378.170281. This is one of those long numbers that have caused trouble for DDC. The numbers are often split into groups of three for convenience and ease of use, such as 378.170.281. Catalogers may choose to restrict division to a set number of digits, thereby simplifying numbers and providing a broader classification. An abridged version of the DDC is available, recommended for libraries with fewer than 20,000 volumes (*Abridged Dewey* 2004).

At the same time, 379, about public policy issues, would be less crowded, while tendencies to crowd—more or less—are noticeable in the other main classes.

DDC specifies only a fraction of all possible class numbers but allows the classifier to build, or synthesize, numbers for a great many subjects (or aspects of subjects) not listed in the schedules. This is accomplished by the addition of extensions derived from various tables or by following specific instructions for number building in particular classes. The tables include forms of publication (dictionaries, periodicals, etc.) and "modes of treatment," such as the philosophy or history of a topic. Familiar extensions are .03 for dictionaries and encyclopedias and .09 or .9 for history (e.g., 780.03 for a dictionary of music and 780.09 for a history of music; a detailed account is given in Taylor 2006, 411). Number building always begins with a base number to which another number is added and instructions often begin "Add to base number ... " This enables one number to be divided in the same way as another and leads to economy of enumeration; thus, 636.082 is breeding animals, and 636.8082 is breeding cats, although the latter is not listed in the schedules.

The index of DDC is very detailed (more than 1,000 pages), and the fact that it is a "relative index" ensures that the various aspects of a given subject, found in many different places in the schedules, are collocated together here.

The entire content of DDC's 22nd edition, along with LC subject headings, authority records, and other aids, is offered as *WebDewey* by OCLC.

The Library of Congress Classification (LCC) was developed in the late nineteenth and early twentieth centuries to meet the specific needs of the library's collections. The system does not present taxonomy of knowledge; it is a practical scheme of 21 basic classes, each with its own structure and index. Nevertheless, LCC offers a comprehensive view of present knowledge as inscribed in documents of all kinds and is hospitable to new fields of knowledge as they appear. The system is used in most academic and research libraries in the United States and many public libraries as well. Published in 41 volumes, it is under continuing revision in the library's Cataloging Policy and Support Office, which posts weekly updates on its website (www.loc.gov/catdir/cpso/lcc; that website is the source for much of the account given in this entry).

LCC identifies each of its 21 classes with a single letter of the alphabet and further divides most of them into subclasses that are identified by two-letter or occasionally three-letter combinations. Thus, class N, Art, has subclasses NA, Architecture; NB, Sculpture; ND, Painting; and so on. Subclasses take the topic from general to more specific categories and to specific places, time periods, or forms (periodicals, biographies, etc.). The notation includes numerals that follow the letters from one to four digits in length. Thus, ND1700-2495 is Watercolor Painting, and ND2550-2888 is Mural Painting. Classes appear in separate volumes, revised at various intervals. Each volume has its own index, but there is no comprehensive index to the entire classification. LC subject headings refer, in many entries, to class numbers of the LCC, providing a partial index to the complete schedules. *Classification Web* is an online product issued by LC that facilitates use of LCC. It provides subject correlations between the LC subject headings and LCC and allows searching of the subject headings and up-to-date LCC schedules.

Library of Congress Classification: Main Classes

A—General works

B—Philosophy, psychology, religion

C—Auxiliary sciences of history

D—World history and history of Europe, Asia, Africa, Australia, New Zealand, and so on

E—History of the Americas

F—History of the Americas

G—Geography, anthropology, recreation

H—Social sciences

J—Law

L—Education

M—Music and books on music

N—Fine arts

Q—Science

R—Medicine

S—Agriculture

T—Technology

U—Military science

V—Naval science

Z—Bibliography, library science, information resources

Education is expanded to about 330 subclasses, including separate places for individual countries. This is the scheme for higher education:

LB2300-2430 Higher education

LB2326.4-2330 Institutions of higher education

LB2331.7-2335.8 Teaching personnel

LB2335.86-2335.885 Trade unions

LB 2335.95-2337 Endowments, trusts, and so on

LB2337.2-2340.8 Student financial aid

LB 2341-2341.95 Supervision and administration and business management

LB2351-2359 Admissions and entrance requirements

LB2361-2365 Curriculum

LB2366-2367.75 College examinations

LB2371-2372 Graduate education

LB2381-2391 Academic degrees

Further treatments of higher education appear later in the schedules, such as Higher education and the state (LC165-182).

The book by Freeman (2010), cited above under DDC, has this LCC classification: LB2343.3, which is just two spaces smaller than the DDC number. How much difference this makes in practice is debatable. Since the final resting place of the classification symbols is in the item's call number (see "Terminology" above), which is used to keep materials in sequence on the shelves, short numbers are easier to arrange and keep in order. In this case both DDC and LCC give lengthy numbers, conducive to misshelving and user challenges. (Libraries assign the duty of shelving to persons with little training and low pay. Yet shelving is a complicated business, considering that the call number has decimals and whole numbers in it and often includes dates or other extra elements. It is not surprising to find so many books out of order on public library shelves.)

The trend has been toward greater use of LCC in public libraries as well as academic and research libraries. For some time main libraries converted to LCC while branches remained in DDC, but the use of online public access catalogs (OPACs) that cover branch and main collections has required full conversion of branches as well. However, many smaller public libraries have kept DDC, as have at least two large ones: San Francisco and Philadelphia.

Current Issues

Efforts to simplify the task of the cataloger and of the library user have brought a reaction, in some public libraries, against DDC and LCC—against elaborate classification of any kind. The novel alternative is an arrangement according to broad categories such as appear in bookstores. (An approach of this kind was used from 1949 to 1967 in the Detroit Public Library as the "Reader Interest Classification.") Several public libraries have adopted the Book Industry Standards and Communications System (BISAC). BISAC is a subject heading list structured in 52 broad categories with some levels of specificity. Those categories may be subdivided into subgroups. A number of new books display BISAC categories on their back covers, but for the most part libraries that use the system choose the categories and label the books accordingly. The subjects are wide in scope, such as Current Affairs, Science, Psychology, Relationships, Self-Help, and True Crime. Books are arranged by title on the shelves within each category. There are no call numbers. A 2009 report mentioned that three libraries that have gone to BISAC: Perry Branch of the Maricopa County (AZ) Library; Frankfort Public Library District (IL), and Rangeview Library District (CO). They all spoke favorably of the results in terms of patron satisfaction (Fister 2009). Other participants include the Gail Borden Library in Elgin, IL, and the library in Lansing, MI.

A telephone conversation (August 25, 2010) with Melissa Rice, director of the Frankfort Public Library, clarified practical aspects of BISAC use. The library uses BISAC for its nonfiction collection of some 25,000 titles. Old books were converted by staff from DDC to BISAC, and all incoming materials are categorized by staff. Categories are extensively subdivided; "Health," for example, has 32 subcategories, including Aging, Care Giving, Diseases, and First Aid. The volumes have appropriate labels, and shelves are clearly signed. The OPAC gives BISAC subjects, with no DDC numbers. A customer survey found general satisfaction with the new system, and both trustee and staff opinions are also favorable. No problems were cited.

There is a BISAC/DDC partnership in the Delta Township District Library, Lansing, MI. An email communication from Stephanie Conarton, library services coordinator, explained,

> We categorize and print spine labels in-house. Books are shelved alphabetically by subject area name with prominent signage and within the subject by Dewey number. We are Dewey lite, not Dewey free like Frankfort—our spine labels show subject name on first line and Dewey number on second. We have not formally surveyed our patrons—our general sense is that those who understood Dewey in the first place were confused in the beginning but

caught on fast. Those who didn't understand Dewey anyway like it. It is easy to browse. (August 30, 2010)

In Maricopa County, AZ, there has been a comprehensive adoption of BISAC, covering all branches, all topics, and all media. Some highlights of the process were provided via email by Cindy Kolaczynski, deputy director, and Susan Varacsak, the transitions coordinator:

> All of our cataloging and processing for new materials is outsourced, thus the vendors follow our MCLD Neighborhood Scheme classification charts to classify any new materials we order for our "Deweyless" branches. For conversion of existing branch collections, our library transitions staff assigns the classifications.... At this time nine of our branch libraries are still on the Dewey classification system; the other eight branches have been either opened as a "Deweyless" building or have been converted to "Deweyless" by our library transitions staff.... This small staff of two people works on converting only one branch at a time.... Conversion of a collection consisting of approximately 12,000 items takes around six months.
>
> Items are shelved by the general classification, then by any subclasses, and finally by the book's title.... We hired a team to conduct a customer survey and staff survey. Results of the customer survey: 95 percent were satisfied with book organization.
>
> We continue to modify our classes and sub-classes.... Currently we have forty-six classifications. Music has the most second-tier or sub-classes with seventeen (the different styles of music contribute to this: classical, county, folk, inspirational, jazz, R&B, rock, etc.); history follows with twelve sub-classes. (September 10, 2010)

Results with BISAC have been favorable, but so far only medium-size libraries have taken it up. DDC can certainly sort large collections into specific groups more precisely than BISAC. Another concern is that BISAC is an English-word system, one that excludes persons unfamiliar with the vocabulary. DDC is numeral based and thus international. Some libraries have been trying to modify DDC along "bookstore" lines, enhancing shelf arrangements and using signage with user-friendly designations. The editors of DDC have shown interest in ways of incorporating BISAC principles: there is "a mapping underway between BISAC and Dewey to support the association of Dewey numbers with metadata early in the publication stream" (Fister 2009, 6).

Much of this discussion has centered on shelf arrangement. There are also "search" aspects of classification, particularly in online catalogs. Currently, libraries are developing "next-generation" catalogs that enable more refined searching by users. Among the features provided is an approach that resembles faceted classification. It allows the user to narrow results not only by subject but also by various other facets, such as author, language, and type of material. There are also facilities such as relevancy ranking and tagging. Commercial systems are available for such applications, such as Endeca and Primo. New York Public Library uses Encore (http://encoreforlibraries .com). There is emerging a distinction between the "classic catalog"—where users search online for library materials through formats developed for card catalogs, and "next-generation catalogs"—which have more sophisticated search possibilities equating more closely to Internet methodologies.

References

Abridged Dewey Decimal Classification and Relative Index. 2004. 14th ed. Dublin, OH: OCLC.
Broughton, Vanda. 2004. *Essential Classification.* New York: Neal-Schuman.
Chan, Lois Mai, et al. 1994. *Dewey Decimal Classification: A Practical Guide.* Albany, NY: Forest Press.
Chan, Lois Mai, et al. 1999. *A Guide to the Library of Congress Classification.* 5th ed. Englewood, CO: Libraries Unlimited.
Chan, Lois Mai, et al. 2007. *Cataloging and Classification: An Introduction.* 3rd ed., with the assistance of Theodora L. Hodges. Lanham, MD: Scarecrow Press.
Dewey. 2003. *Dewey Decimal Classification and Relative Index.* 22nd ed. Edited by Joan S. Mitchell et al. Dublin, OH: OCLC. 4 vols. Available with supplementary information as *WebDewey,* http://connexion.oclc.org.
Fister, Barbara. 2009. The Dewey dilemma. *Library Journal* 134, no. 16 (October 1): 22–29.
Hunter, Eric J. 2009. *Classification Made Simple: An Introduction to Knowledge Organization and Information Retrieval.* 3rd ed. Farnham (England): Ashgate.
LC Classification. 2003. *Library of Classification Outline.* 7th ed. Washington, DC: Library of Congress, Cataloging Policy and Support Office. 1st ed., *Outline Scheme of Classes,* 1903. Individual volumes issued separately, various dates. Weekly updates of the LCC are at www.loc.gov/catdir/cpso/lcc.
Taylor, Arlene G. 2006. *Introduction to Cataloging and Classification.* 10th ed. Westport, CT: Libraries Unlimited.
                    Significant portions of this entry were written by Eric J. Hunter.

CLAUD H. GILMER MEMORIAL LIBRARY, ROCKSPRINGS, TX   201 N. Highway 377, Rocksprings, TX 78880. Population served: 1,200. Circulation: 32,600. Holdings: 20,500. LJ February 15, 2009: 3-star library; November 15, 2009, and October 1, 2010: 4-star library.

CLE ELUM, WA. *See* CARPENTER MEMORIAL LIBRARY, CLE ELUM, WA.

CLEVELAND HEIGHTS-UNIVERSITY HEIGHTS PUBLIC LIBRARY, CLEVELAND HEIGHTS, OH   2345 Lee Rd., Cleveland Heights, OH 44118. Founded 1921. Population served: 61,194. Circulation: 1,547,414.

Holdings: 353, 733. 3 branches. LJ February 15, 2009, and November 15, 2009: 5-star library.

CLEVELAND PUBLIC LIBRARY, OH   325 Superior Ave., Cleveland, OH 44114. Founded 1869. Population served: 464,744. Circulation: 5,011,399. Holdings: 4,073,720. 29 branches, 1 bookmobile. A school district library, it is governed by a board of trustees appointed by the Cleveland Board of Education. Luther M. Oviatt was the first librarian, I. L Beardsley the second. The library flowered in the administration (1884–1918) of William Howard Brett. He developed the system of branches (15 constructed with funding by Andrew Carnegie); opened library stations in businesses, factories, and hospitals; developed services to the blind (Braille collection, 1903); and gave special attention to the needs of children, which his predecessors had considered irrelevant. The Cleveland Public Library (CPL) had the country's first children's librarian (Effie Power) in 1895 and a children's room in 1898. Brett advocated open shelves (effective 1890), a concept new in the profession and not widely accepted at the time. The collection was recataloged and reclassified. Alice Tyler was catalog librarian in 1895. The library prepared a periodical index covering 100 titles. Brett and his staff shared a sense of devotion to the needs of users. On his death in 1918, his assistant Linda Eastman succeeded him, remaining to 1938. The new central building opened on May 6, 1925, designed by Walker and Weeks in the style of other civic buildings, following Daniel Burnham's plans. A Business Information Bureau was established in 1926 under Rose Vormelker. The library set attendance records during the Depression. The collections continued to grow; as a result, the board acquired the adjacent building and used it to house the business and science departments.

John G. White was the library's greatest benefactor. His donations covered employee benefits as well as thousands of books. Two collections he developed, in folklore and chess, are among the principal research sources in their fields. When Linda Eastman retired in 1938, her successors were Charles E. Rush, 1938–1941; Clarence S. Metcalf, 1941–1950; L. Quincy Mumford, 1950–1954; Raymond C. Lindquist, 1955–1968; Edward D'Alessandro, 1969–1970; Fern Long (acting), 1970; and Walter W. Curley, 1970–1973.

CPL had been operating the city's school libraries since 1896, but that arrangement ended in 1968 as the board of education took them over. In the 1970s, library revenues were declining. Ervin J. Gaines, librarian 1974–1986, undertook a reorganization of the system and advocated increased funding; a successful city tax levy in 1975 supported a program to upgrade the branches. The card catalog was replaced by an online catalog in 1981. Marilyn Gell Mason became librarian in 1986, promoting further building improvements and construction, leading to a $90 million bond issue in 1991. The adjacent building that house business and technology was demolished and replaced (1997) by the Louis Stokes Wing, an 11-story structure.

When Mason resigned in 1999, Andrew A. Venable Jr., her deputy, became director. Innovative technology has marked his administration. CPL was the first U.S. public library to offer e-book downloads (2009). The library remains in the forefront of the public library endeavor; as recognized by LJ, February 15, 2009, and October 1, 2010: 5-star library.

COFFEY COUNTY LIBRARY, BURLINGTON, KS   401 Juniatta St., Burlington, KS 66839. Founded 1910. Population served: 8,759. Circulation: 262,000. Holdings: 173,227. 6 branches. LJ February 15, 2009: 4-star library; November 15, 2009, and October 1, 2010: 3-star library.

COGSWELL, JOSEPH GREEN, 1786–1871   Librarian, scholar. Born Ipswich, MA, September 27, 1786. He graduated from Harvard in 1806 and practiced law; also tutored in Latin at Harvard. In 1815–1820 he traveled and studied in Europe, visiting with Goethe. Back in the United States, Cogswell was appointed librarian at Harvard (1820) and professor of mineralogy and geology. He resigned in 1823. He was acquainted with John Jacob Astor and advised him regarding a proposed public library for New York City. In 1848 he became superintendent of the Astor Library, which opened in 1854, having made extensive buying trips in Europe. Cogswell resigned the post in December 1861 and retired to Cambridge, where he died on November 26, 1871. *DAB; DALB.*

COLD SPRING, NY. *See* JULIA L. BUTTERFIELD MEMORIAL LIBRARY, COLD SPRING, NY.

COLERAINE PUBLIC LIBRARY, MN   203 Cole Ave., Coleraine, MN 55722. Population served: 1,110. Circulation: 42,593. Holdings: 10,165. LJ February 15, 2009: 5-star library; November 15, 2009: 4-star library.

COLLECTION DEVELOPMENT

Terminology

The phrase "collection development" has more or less replaced "book selection" as a description of what librarians do in acquiring and disposing of books and nonbook materials. Recently the expression "collection management" has appeared, with a meaning that embraces collection development and adds attention to deployment of resources. Some writers have offered a new term, "content development," to account for the fact that online products are not part of the library collection.

Historical Summary

In the early days of libraries in Europe and the United States, the work of selection was highly subjective. The person in charge of a library simply tried to acquire the best books he knew about. His main task was to locate copies of those books and purchase them. Disposal of materials was not really considered. A classic manual that explicated this process was Gabriel Naudé's *Advis pour dresser une bibliothèque* of 1627 (Naudé 1960). In the American context the Naudé approach was dominant for more than two centuries. It was inherent in the thinking of those who attended the first national conference of librarians in 1853. Charles Coffin Jewett stated in the opening address that "we meet to provide for the diffusion of a knowledge of good books and for enlarging the means of public access to them" (quoted in Haines 1950, 15). Indeed, the great American library movement of the nineteenth century was focused on that idea: bringing people and good books together. It was Naudé's concept adapted to a democracy.

When the Boston Public Library opened to the public in 1854, the movement and its purposes were embodied for the first time in a vital institution. George Ticknor, one of the trustees, wrote in 1852 a preliminary report that announced what kinds of books would be in the library: reference books, "books that few persons will wish to read," and popular books (quoted in Williams 1988, 5). Jewett, the superintendent of the library, wrote in 1858 that while a substantial segment of the collection did consist of books "of a more popular character," the entire collection was "eminently suited to promote the ultimate design of the institution, the intellectual and moral advancement of the whole people" (Williams 1988, 6). Uneasiness about the popular category was already in the air; it has remained a factor in collection development to this day. Directors of the early public libraries—institutions that were a fresh phenomenon in the world—had trouble confronting popular reading and popular literature. They were learned men. Ticknor was a professor at Harvard, Jewett was at Brown; many other library leaders of the century were of similar background. They wanted to serve the ordinary citizen as well as the serious student, but their own tastes remained in the refined category. Their solution was to offer light fiction and popular nonfiction along with more "educational" books. They took up what came to be called "the ladder theory," which assumed that a person's reading habits would climb from books of lesser quality to those of presumed higher value (*see* READERS' ADVISORY SERVICES).

During the last quarter of the nineteenth century, the overarching principle of selecting public library materials was that book reading in itself was the primary goal. The readers should have what they wanted, although "improper" books were never provided (*see* INTELLECTUAL FREEDOM). And "quality" fiction was preferable to that of lesser substance. There was another angle to selection, namely, the provision of technical books to assist workers and students in the industrial fields. Librarians wanted to give a person reading matter that would enhance skills and improve earning power.

As the library movement spread steadily around the United States (*see* HISTORY OF PUBLIC LIBRARIES), the backgrounds of library directors began to vary greatly, and what may have been the elitist environment of the Boston library was not everywhere replicated. Urban growth, immigration, increase in wealth, and the development of public school systems influenced the general loosening of criteria for book selection. A beneficial aspect of the library movement was the separation of collection matters from political matters. By 1880 all the states had passed permissive legislation regarding public libraries, and in no case was there any restriction placed on library administrators on what they could put in their collections. Indeed, there was encouragement for the presentation of all viewpoints—a principle that remains operative today. The twentieth century brought forth an arena of dispute: the place, if any, of so-called immoral materials in the collection (*see* INTELLECTUAL FREEDOM).

With the establishment of the first academic program for educating librarians, at Columbia College in 1887, the practice of book selection began to be formalized. The Columbia program was wholly practical so that the teaching of book selection was focused on acquisition procedures ("order work"). A similar orientation applied in other library training programs (*see* EDUCATION OF PUBLIC LIBRARIANS). Textbooks on the subject emerged: a pioneer British work by Lionel McColvin appeared in 1925, with an American counterpart by Francis Drury (1930). The most distinguished early text was *Living with Books* by Helen Haines (1935; 2nd ed. 1950). Librarians became concerned about underlying principles of selection. The "demand theory" was the leading viewpoint in American texts and practice: it stated that what the public wanted should be provided. In fact this was an outgrowth of the original philosophy of the Boston Public Library and the early library movement. But other positions were announced as well. Pierce Butler's (1933) *An Introduction to Library Science* promoted the idea that selection should support primarily the benefits of society as a whole by providing for the needs of its leaders. An influential study published in 1949–1950 under the name of the *Public Library Inquiry* held that selection should function to serve "opinion leaders" of the community. These principles formed a sociological theory of selection (*see* PHILOSOPHY OF PUBLIC LIBRARIANSHIP). Helen Haines presented a compromise that brought together the demand advocates and the sociological advocates as well as the quality advocates. She said that the demand of patrons can be satisfied through quality materials if librarians know the books well enough to choose good things that readers will want. Good things here would include those of sociological merit, as per Butler's theory. In other words, there was a way to blend the wants of an individual with the needs of the individual and of society.

Dealing with wants and needs presents some difficulties. It was acknowledged by the pioneers of the profession that both concepts were relevant. The book selector must consider community "desires" and needs and should "select books that satisfy such desires and are at the same time good literature" (Bostwick 1929, 126, 149). A modern writer has drawn a distinction between wants and needs. "Needs are limited and practical. Their denial has definite, knowable consequences" (Williams 1990, 55). Failure to supply needs adversely affects the community. "No such consequences result when wants are not met." The public sector has to provide goods and services in response to needs—acting on the principle that public goods are a government responsibility. But the public sector has no responsibility to satisfy demands without needs and is guilty of diverting resources from where they are necessary if it does so. Satisfying wants is the business of the private sector.

It's all very well for public librarians to insist that they are populists, virtuously sympathetic to public demand. But until they clarify their position on wants and needs and which agencies should undertake to meet wants and needs and under what conditions, if any, no one can really tell what this dedication to public demand means (Williams 1990, 56).

This argument appears to identify public librarians as careless handlers of the funds entrusted to them if they buy materials according to demand. However, there is a counterargument that states that serving popular demand does serve a community need since recreational reading (the usual object of demand) has the function of unifying a society and articulating its values (see READERS' ADVISORY SERVICES).

In the last analysis, the selection of materials for a library is a responsibility assigned by society to the library profession. "It is here that we exert, however indirectly, our greatest influence on the public we serve and the total society of which that public is a part" (Asheim 1959, 14). Librarians are the only persons qualified to make the decisions involved in collection development. They make those decisions on the basis of informed judgments and with the courage to stand back of those decisions once they are made. "It is this that makes librarianship a true profession and not just a skilled trade ... of course it is difficult, and demanding, and challenging—would you really have it otherwise?" (Asheim 1959, 18).

Aids to Selection

Selection "tools" began to appear in the librarian's workshop in the late nineteenth century. Those tools are of two kinds: one kind simply lists new publications, the other kind evaluates them. Today they are named "current bibliographies" and "review media." A start was made in 1873 with the issue of *Publisher's Trade List Annual* (*PTLA*), a gathering of publisher catalogs, pasted together into a big binding. Without indexes, this collection was convenient but of limited value. The publisher of *PTLA*, R. R. Bowker, ultimately produced author and title indexes to it with a new annual, *Books in Print* (1948–) and then with a subject index, *Subject Guide to Books in Print* (1957–). With these volumes in hand and with the *Cumulative Book Index* issued by the H. W. Wilson Co. (1899 as *United States Catalogue*, then 1928–), a selector could see the totality of available titles. Since 1960, Bowker has also published a monthly (with annual and five-year cumulations) *American Book Publishing Record*, which lists new print materials as they appear, thus serving the function of something lacking in the United States: an official national bibliography.

The second type of selection tool gives the librarian guidance about the contents and worth of new books. The earliest of these were the *Book Review Digest* (H. W. Wilson, 1905–) and the American Library Association (ALA) *Booklist* (1905–). Critiques were also available in *Library Journal* (1876–) and the *New York Times Book Review* (1896–). A set of aids by H. W. Wilson is its standard catalog series, which gives selected, annotated lists of books, compiled by librarian specialists, for various types of library and materials: *Children's Catalog* (1909–), *Junior High School Catalog* (1965–), *Senior High School Catalog* (1926–), *Fiction Catalog* (1908–), and *Public Library Catalog* (nonfiction, 1934–). In 2008 the publisher added *Nonbook Materials Core Collection: A Selection Guide*. A "starter list" for new public library collections was issued by the ALA in 1971, with later updates. In 1921, Bowker published a *Reader's Adviser,* describing the core literature in many fields; this work has been revised and expanded since 1974 (specific tools for the selection of reference books are noted in the entry REFERENCE AND INFORMATION SERVICES). Specialized tools for various formats and purposes are cited in the appropriate entries.

Current Practice and Issues

Through the first half of the twentieth century, libraries created a structure for selection of books and other materials. Depending on the size of the library, staff members were connected to specific subjects and became proficient in evaluating publications in those areas. They examined new book lists and critical media and considered them in the context of what was already in the collection and what ought to be added. In many cases those staff specialists came together in periodic selection meetings to discuss new materials and made recommendations for purchase. As publication of new materials increased, another technique was added to the structure: standing orders with publishers (later with vendors who covered many publishers) for books in certain categories or requests for copies that would be considered for selection ("approval plans"). What came about gradually was selection by clusters of material rather than by individual titles alone. For example a library might enter an order with a vendor to supply all the books on the best-seller list of the *New York Times*. In time, librarians often entrusted to vendors much of the selection task by preparing a profile of needs in different areas and inviting the vendor to supply suitable items within cost parameters. Benefits and problems of this approach are taken up in ACQUISITIONS.

The last piece of the new structure is the collection development policy (CDP). This document expresses, in terms of varying specificity, the depth of coverage ("intensity level") that a library intends to have in given fields or categories. Actually this is an old idea. When Melvil Dewey was librarian of Columbia College (1883–1888), he formed a selection policy with five "grades" that correspond to intensities (Wiegand 1996, 87). ALA has prepared useful guidelines for librarians writing CDPs, using this terminology:

"comprehensive level" (a plan to acquire all significant works in all formats of a defined field), "research level" (a plan to acquire major published source materials in a field, such as those required for writing new research), "study level" (a plan to acquire what would be needed by college students or independent scholars), "basic level" (a plan to acquire enough material to introduce a reader to the field and guide further investigation), and "minimal level" (a plan to acquire only a few basic works in a field). In practice, this notion of intensity levels has been accepted by academic libraries, less so by public libraries. Indeed, many CDP's examined in connection with the writing of this article are merely general statements that cannot hold much value in the selection decision. One strong example that follows ALA guidelines is the policy of Topeka and Shawnee County Public Library, available on the library's website.

A thorough CDP includes a goal statement for the entire collection, narrower goal statements for subjects and formats (preferably with "intensities"), gift policy (see below), deaccession policy ("weeding"), duplication policy, policy on cooperative selection with other libraries, a statement on handling of controversial materials, and an evaluation and revision policy for the CDP itself. A CDP does not include individual titles of books, budget estimates, or acquisition procedures. Evaluation of the present collection may be a starting point in a CDP, or it may be a separate task.

Books and other items donated to a library are free and save staff time in acquisitions. Substantial gifts have formed the basis for important collections. However, gifts, whether large or small, produce extra tasks as well. Staff need to organize and tabulate large gifts. Any gift requires a check for duplication in present holdings. Donors should receive thank-you letters with estimates of the value of their gifts for tax purposes. Some librarians question the value of accepting routine gifts, supposing that most of what comes in would not have been acquired; that is, it was not wanted. Indeed, a large proportion of routine gift books go to the next book sale. These issues are best addressed in the CDP, where restrictions on accepting gifts should be spelled out. The key principle is that materials that fall into the collecting scope of the CDP are accepted and others are not, but of course a gift may involve a number of each (Carothers 1998; Carrico 1999).

Exchange agreements are useful if a library issues publications. Those products can be offered to other publishing libraries in exchange for theirs. Shipping costs are a deterrent, along with staff time for correspondence and processing (Carrico 1999).

Cooperation among libraries in collection development is more talked about than achieved. The idea is that by dividing up areas of responsibility, such as certain subjects, libraries would avoid duplicative purchases and could share their holdings through interlibrary loan. Major efforts have involved academic libraries, most famously the Farmington Plan (1954–1972). Such projects have encountered the desire of individual members in the plan to have important books on their own shelves. Another problem was the difficulty of evaluating the results (Hazen 1997; Wood 1997). Collaborative selection among public libraries is a venture for the future.

Internal cooperation should be easier to manage. A public library with branches should have clear understandings, documented in the CDP, about selection responsibilities. In general a central library ought to have a copy of any item in any branch, with the exception of branches with foreign language concentrations or subject specializations. One way to coordinate this situation is for branch selection to be done centrally. The idea that branch heads have a particular competence in selection for their own community has been described as an illusion; readers in all branches in fact exhibit the same reading interests (Gibson 1998).

Weeding, or deaccessioning, means removing items from the active collection. They may be moved to storage, used for exchange, offered for sale to the public, or simply discarded. The decision to weed an item is based on several criteria: frequency of use, intrinsic value of the item, relevance to the goals of the CDP, and physical condition. A book that has not circulated in 20 years is a good candidate for weeding, and one writer holds that noncirculation is sufficient cause for removal (Slote 1989). Physical condition may be viewed two ways: a badly deteriorated book should be taken from the active collection, but its condition is probably due to heavy use. Replacement is the answer if other copies are available, otherwise repair. Ideally, collection review and weeding should be systematic, periodic events (*see* EVALUATION).

In principle at least, it seems that book selection—now collection development—has reached a satisfactory stage of sophistication. With a solid CDP and the wide range of tools available, a librarian should be able to provide readers with an array of materials that will suit their wants and needs. Library education programs used to emphasize instruction in this activity. Selection was a part of the standard core curriculum in library schools until about 20 years ago when the core concept dissolved. Collection development is not a required subject for library school students now, but it is usually a recommended option.

Print materials have been the focus of this entry. Selection issues regarding other formats are covered in AUDIOVISUAL COLLECTIONS; DIGITAL MEDIA; INTERNET; MICROFORM; MUSIC COLLECTIONS; SERIALS. *See also* ACQUISITIONS; INTELLECTUAL FREEDOM; PHILOSOPHY OF PUBLIC LIBRARIANSHIP; READERS' ADVISORY SERVICES.

References

American Book Publishing Record. 1960– (monthly, cumulations). New York: Bowker.

American Library Association. 1996. *Guide for Written Collection Policy Statements*. 2nd ed. Chicago: American Library Association.

American Library Association. Collection Development Committee. 1979. *Guidelines for Collection Development*. Chicago: American Library Association.

American Library Association. Subcommittee on Guidelines for Collection Development. 1989. *Guide to the Evaluation of Library Collections*. Chicago: American Library Association.

Asheim Lester. 1959. The professional decision. In 2 *Library Lectures*, 14–24. Emporia: Kansas State Teachers College.

Berelson, Bernard. 1949. *The Library's Public: A Report of the Public Library Inquiry*. New York: Columbia University Press. *Book Review Digest*. 1905– (10 per year; cumulations). New York: H. W. Wilson.

Book Review Index. 1965– (bimonthly, cumulations). Detroit: Gale Cengage.

Booklist. 1905– (monthly). Chicago: American Library Association. Title varies.

Books in Print. 1948– (annual). New York: Bowker.

Boston Public Library. 1852. *Preliminary Report*. Boston: Trustees of the Boston Public Library.

Bostwick, Arthur E. 1929. *The American Public Library*. 4th ed. New York: Appleton.

Broadus, Robert N. 1980. Use studies of library collections. *Library Resources & Technical Services* 24, no. 4 (Fall): 317–24.

Butler, Pierce. 1933. *An Introduction to Library Science*. Chicago: University of Chicago Press.

Carothers, Frank. 1998. Gifts and exchanges. In *Technical Services Today and Tomorrow*, ed. Michael Gorman, 21–42. Englewood, CO: Libraries Unlimited.

Carrico, Steven. 1999. Gifts and exchanges. In *Understanding the Business of Library Acquisitions*, 2nd ed., 205–23. Chicago: American Library Association.

Children's Catalog. 1909– (quinquennial). New York: H. W. Wilson.

Cumulative Book Index: A World List of Books in the English Language, 1928/ 1932–. 1933– (11 per year; cumulations). New York: H. W. Wilson. Title varies.

Dilevko, Juris. 2008. An alternative vision of librarianship: James Danky and the sociocultural politics of collection development. *Library Trends* 56, no. 3 (Winter): 678–705.Disher, Wayne. 2007. *Crash Course in Collection Development*. Westport, CT: Libraries Unlimited.

Ditzion, Sidney. 1947. *Arsenals of a Democratic Culture*. Chicago: American Library Association.

Drury, Francis K. W. 1930. *Book Selection*. Chicago: American Library Association.

Evans, G. Edward, and Margaret Z. Saponaro. 2005. *Developing Library and Information Center Collections*. 5th ed. Westport, CT: Libraries Unlimited.

Fiction Catalog. 1908– (quinquennial). New York: H. W. Wilson.

Gibson, Catherine. 1998. "But we've always done it this way!"—Centralized selection five years later. In *Public Library Collection Development in the Information Age*, ed. Annabel K. Stephens, 33–40. Binghamton, NY: Haworth.

Goldhor, Herbert. 1942. A note on the theory of book selection. *Library Quarterly* 12, no. 2 (April): 151–74.

Gorman, G. E., and Ruth H. Miller, eds. 1997. *Collection Management for the 21st Century*. Westport, CT: Greenwood Press.

Haines, Helen H. 1950. *Living with Books: The Art of Book Selection*. 2nd ed. New York: Columbia University Press. 1st ed. 1935.

Hazen, Dan C. 1997. Cooperative collection development: Compelling theory, inconsequential results? In *Collection Development for the 21st Century: A Handbook for Librarians*, ed. G. E. Gorman and Ruth H. Miller, 263–86. Westport, CT: Greenwood Press.

Ingold, Cindy, and Susan E. Searing. 2007. Gender issues in information needs and services. *Library Trends* 56, no. 2 (Fall): 299–303.

Johnson, Peggy. 2004. *Fundamentals of Collection Development*. Chicago: American Library Association. *Junior High School Catalog*. 1965– (quinquennial). New York: H. W. Wilson.

Lambert, Dennis K. et al. 2002. *Guide to Review of Library Collections: Preservation, Storage, and Withdrawal*. 2nd ed. Collection and management guides, 12. American Library Association, Association for Collections and Technical Services. Metuchen, NJ: Scarecrow Press.

Lee, Lauren K. 1998. Five levels of vendor-assisted collection development. In *Public Library Collection Development in the Information Age*, ed. Annabel K. Stephens, 41–52. Binghamton, NY: Haworth.

Library Journal. 1876– (monthly). New York: Bowker.

Lunati, Rinaldo. 1975. *Book Selection: Principles and Procedures*. Trans. Luciana Marulli. Metuchen, NJ: Scarecrow Press.

Mack, Daniel C., ed. 2003. *Collection Development Policies: New Directions*. Binghamton, NY: Haworth, 2003.

McColvin, Lionel. 1925. *The Theory of Book Selection for Public Libraries*. London: Grafton.

Naudé, Gabriel. 1960. *Advice on Establishing a Library*. Translated Archer Taylor. Berkeley: University of California Press. Originally *Advis pour dresser une bibliothèque* (Paris: F. Targa, 1627).

New York Times Book Review. 1896– (weekly). New York: New York Times.

Nonbook Materials Core Collection: A Selection Guide. 2008–. New York: H. W. Wilson.

Public Library Catalog. 1934– (quinquennial). New York: H. W. Wilson.

Publisher's Trade List Annual. 1873– (annual). New York: Bowker.

Reader's Adviser: A Layman's Guide to Literature. 1921– (frequent revisions). New York: Bowker. Title varies.

Senior High School Catalog. 1926– (quinquennial). New York: H. W. Wilson.

Slote, Stanley J. 1989. *Weeding Library Collections*. 3rd ed. Littleton, CO: Libraries Unlimited.

Stephens, Annabel K., ed. 1998. *Public Library Collection Development in the Information Age*. Binghamton, NY: Haworth.

Subject Guide to Books in Print. 1957– (annual). New York: Bowker.

Sullivan, Michael. 2000. Giving them what they want in small public libraries. *Public Libraries* 39, no. 3 (May/June): 148–155.

Wellard, James Howard. 1937. *Book Selection: Its Principles and Practice*. London: Grafton.

White, Carl M. 1961. *The Origins of the American Library School*. New York: Scarecrow Press.

Wiegand, Wayne A. 1996. *Irrepressible Reformer: A Biography of Melvil Dewey*. Chicago: American Library Association.

Williams, Patrick. 1988. *The American Public Library and the Problem of Purpose*. New York: Greenwood Press.

Williams, Patrick. 1990. How should the public library respond to public demand? *Library Journal* 115, no. 17 (October 15): 54–56.

Wood, Richard J. 1997. The axioms, barriers, and components of cooperative collection development. In *Collection Development for the 21st Century: A Handbook for Librarians*, ed. G. E. Gorman and Ruth H. Miller, 221–48. Westport, CT: Greenwood Press.

Wortman, William A. 1989. *Collection Management: Background and Principles.* Chicago: American Library Association.

COLLECTION MANAGEMENT. *See* COLLECTION DEVELOPMENT.

COLONIAL LIBRARY, RICHBURG, NY   Main St., Richburg, NY 14774. Population served: 1,334. Circulation: 6,503. Holdings: 10,509. LJ October 1, 2010: 3-star library.

COLORADO SPRINGS, CO. *See* PIKES PEAK LIBRARY DISTRICT, COLORADO SPRINGS, CO.

COLUMBIA, MD. *See* HOWARD COUNTY LIBRARY, COLUMBIA, MD.

COLUMBIA, SC. *See* RICHLAND COUNTY PUBLIC LIBRARY, COLUMBIA, SC.

COLUMBIANA PUBLIC LIBRARY, OH   332 N. Middle St., Columbiana, OH 44408. Founded 1935. Population served: 6,952. Circulation: 340,709. Holdings: 67,767. LJ February 15, 2009; November 15, 2009; and October 1, 2010: 4-star library. HAPLR 2009, 2010.

COLUMBUS METROPOLITAN LIBRARY, OH   96 S. Grant Ave., Columbus, OH 43215. Founded 1872. Population served: 900,000. Circulation: 15,000,000. Holdings: 4,000,000. 21 branches, 2 bookmobiles. Established in 1873 as Public Library and Reading Room; 1903, became Columbus Public Library; 1975, became Public Library of Columbus and Franklin County; 1989, took present title. Directors: James L. Grover, 1872–1897; John J. Pugh, 1897–1946; Blanche C. Roberts, 1946–1947; Will H. Collins, 1947–1956; Margaret E. Carroll, 1956–1962; Edward B. Daniels, 1962–1974; James E. Ahlstrom, 1974–1975; Donald J. Sager, 1975–1978; Hoyt Rees Galvin, 1978–1979; Richard Sweeny, 1979–1984; Larry Black, 1984–2002; and Patrick Losinski, 2002–. LJ February 15, 2009; November 15, 2009; and October 1, 2010: 5-star library. LJ Library of the Year 2010. HAPLR 2009, 2010.

COLUMBUS VILLAGE LIBRARY, NM   112 W. Broadway Ave., Columbus Village, NM 88029. Population served: 1,846. Circulation: 8,853. Holdings: 13,166. LJ February 15, 2009; November 15, 2009; and October 1, 2010: 4-star library.

COMFREY COMMUNITY LIBRARY, MN   306 Brown St. W, Comfrey, MN 56019. Population served: 1,051. Circulation: 14,620. Holdings: 19,772. LJ October 1, 2010: 5-star library.

COMMERCE, CA. *See* CITY OF COMMERCE PUBLIC LIBRARY, CA.

COMPTON, CHARLES HERRICK, 1880–1966   Librarian. Born Palmyra, NE, October 24, 1880. He earned a BA, University of Nebraska, 1901, then went to the New York State Library School, 1905–1908. He was employed in Seattle Public Library as a reference librarian, 1910; also handled public relations. During World War I he worked with the American Library Association (ALA) in Washington, selecting and buying books for the army and navy. Compton was assistant to Carl Milam, ALA executive director, after the war, then went to St. Louis Public Library as assistant librarian under Arthur E. Bostwick, handling administrative tasks; he succeeded Bostwick in 1938, remaining to 1950. Compton promoted professional status and salaries for librarians. As president of the Missouri Library Association he influenced the place of public libraries in the revised state constitution and promoted bookmobile service. As ALA president in 1934–1935 he advocated the establishment of a federal library agency and federal aid to libraries. Compton wrote two books on the history of the St. Louis library. He retired October 24, 1950. In 1958 the annex to the main library building was named for him. *DALB.*

COMPUTERS. *See* INFORMATION TECHNOLOGY; INTERNET.

CONCORD FREE PUBLIC LIBRARY, MA   129 Main St., Concord, MA 01742. Founded 1873. Population served: 16,019. Circulation: 259,899. Holdings: 234,975. 1 branch. The first librarian, Ellen Frances Whitney (1873–1899), was one of four female U.S. public library directors at the time. Her successor had a somewhat similar name: Helen Whitney Kelley (1899–1919). The original building, with many renovations, remains in use.

CONFREY COMMUNITY LIBRARY, MN   305 Ochre St. W, Confrey, MN 56019. LJ November 15, 2009: 4-star library.

CONRAD PUBLIC LIBRARY, IA   102 E. Grundy, Conrad, IA 50621. Founded 1936. Population served: 1,055. Circulation: 49,515. Holdings: 18,346. LJ February 15, 2009: 3-star library.

CONSORTIA. *See* COOPERATION.

CONTRA COSTA COUNTY LIBRARY, PLEASANT HILL, CA   1750 Oak Park Blvd., Pleasant Hill, CA 94523. Founded 1913. Population served: 902,200. Circulation: 4,736,101. Holdings: 1,292,627. 23 branches. In 2009 the library installed book vending machines in BART train stations and shopping centers; each holds some 400 books. The library's refusal to make a meeting room available to a church group for a meeting that included worship service was upheld by the U.S. Supreme Court on October 1, 2007.

COONSKIN LIBRARY. *See* NELSONVILLE PUBLIC LIBRARY, OH.

COOPERATION

Terminology

To cooperate is "to associate with another or others for mutual benefit" and cooperation is "the action of cooperating" (*Merriam*). For librarians the concept is more specific: "Library cooperation—methods by which libraries and library systems work together for the mutual benefit of their users, including centralized processing, cooperative cataloging, international exchange of bibliographic information, union catalogs, resources sharing, etc." (*ODLIS*).

Cooperative activity among librarians may be ad hoc and informal, but it is more typically manifested through formal arrangements. Such arrangements are usually expressed in a consortium or network. A consortium is "an association of independent libraries and or library systems established by formal agreement, usually for the purpose of resource sharing," and a network is "a group of physically discrete computers interconnected to allow resources to be shared and data exchanged" (*ODLIS*). Of course a network is more than just connected computers; it is the organization that uses them. And the term may apply to a "group of people with similar interests or concerns who interact for mutual assistance or support" (*American Heritage*) whether or not computers are involved; for example, the Public Libraries International Network is a "think tank" for public librarians (*ODLIS*).

Another term in use is ambiguous: "library system." According to *ODLIS* it may be "a group of libraries administered in common, for example a central library and its branches," or "a group of independently administered libraries joined by formal or informal agreement to achieve a common purpose." The second definition is appropriate for this entry, but it does seem to occupy the same space as consortium or network.

Historical Summary

This is a chronology of developments in the United States that fall under library cooperation:

> 1876—Samuel Swett Green, in the first issue of *American Library Journal*, called on libraries to "lend books to each other for short periods of time."
>
> 1901—Library of Congress (LC) began cooperative cataloging and selling printed catalog cards; established the National Union Catalog.

1908—*Cataloging Rules: Author and Title Entries.* The Anglo-American "joint code."

1909—The earliest regional union catalog of public libraries, established in the California State Library.

1917—First interlibrary lending code issued by the American Library Association.

1927—First edition of the *Union List of Serials,* a cooperative compilation of 75,000 titles in 225 libraries.

1948—Farmington Plan, for cooperative acquisitions by research libraries; terminated 1972.

1949—Midwest Interlibrary Center, Chicago, organized to house infrequently used materials supplied by its members (originally 10 in number).

1965—Midwest Interlibrary Center, Chicago, became Center for Research Libraries.

1966—Title III, Interlibrary Cooperation, added to renewal of the Library Services and Construction Act.

1967—Ohio College Library Center (OCLC) established; became the Online Computer Library Center. It was originally a computerized database of library holdings in Ohio, then became an international compilation. See *WorldCat* at 2002 below.

1967—International Standard Book Number (ISBN) and International Standard Serial Number (ISSN) created by international agreement among publishers, providing unique identifiers for publications.

1967—*Anglo-American Catalog rules* (AACR) published, promoting standard cataloging practice for the United States and the United Kingdom.

1968–1981—*National Union Catalog: Pre-1956 Imprints* published by LC, providing photocopies of 11 million catalog cards in 1,500 research libraries; 754 volumes.

1971—Cataloging in Publication (CIP) program initiated, in cooperation between LC and publishers, printing LC catalog information on verso of title pages in new publications.

1974—International Standard Bibliographic Description (ISBD) finalized, following a draft of 1971.

1976—CONSER (Cooperative Online Serials Project). A national database of serial records, now maintained by OCLC.

1978—Revised version of *Anglo-American Catalog Rules* (AACR2).

1978—OCLC became a national database.

1979—Interlibrary loan system available in OCLC database.

2002—OCLC initiated *WorldCat*, an international database of library holdings.

Current Situation

The *American Library Directory 2009–2010* includes a list of about 300 "networks, consortia & other cooperative library organizations" that illustrates the wide scope of cooperative activity among libraries and its somewhat flexible vocabulary. Some examples are the following: Colorado Library Consortium (453 libraries; provides consulting, continuing education, support services); Central Florida Library Cooperative (84 libraries; promotes resource sharing, Internet access, continuing education); Cooperative Information Network (Idaho; 15 libraries; provides a shared automated database for cataloging, circulation OPAC); Center for Research Libraries (Chicago; 239 libraries; houses and circulates research materials for use by members); Suburban Library Cooperative (Michigan; 21 libraries; provides shared automated system, negotiates contracts and quantity discounts, continuing education, publicity and public relations).

Evidently, many services are offered by cooperative groups. The two cooperative services that are nearly universal are sharing of databases and interlibrary loan. Underlying those activities are the cooperative creation of cataloging codes and principles of bibliographic description.

For the most part cooperative ventures of public libraries involve other public libraries or in some cases academic and research libraries. Agreements between public libraries and school media centers are less common. A study of that combination in the state of Indiana revealed that only 17 (29 percent) public libraries and six (14 percent) elementary school media centers—of 91 libraries surveyed—reported "face-to-face interaction" (LaMaster 2005). This area of cooperation must be viewed as a work in progress. *See also* CATALOGING; INTERLIBRARY LOAN.

Reference

LaMaster, Jennifer. 2005, Collaboration of Indiana public and school media center youth services: a survey analysis of current practices. *Indiana Libraries* 24, no. 1: 38–41.

COPYRIGHT

Terminology

Copyright is "the legal right to exclusive publication, production, sale, or distribution of a literary, musical, or artistic work" (*American Heritage*). In the United States this right has been recognized by the courts, although it places a limitation on the free speech clause of the First Amendment. Copyright protection for the creator(s) of a covered work exists from the time it takes a fixed form. While registration is not a requirement for copyright protection, it offers many advantages to the copyright owner, primarily the right to file suit for infringement. Registration is made through the Copyright Office, Library of Congress, 101 Independence Ave. SE, Washington, DC 20559. The Copyright Act of 1976 (17 U.S.C., Public Law 94-533, 90 Stat.), the basic law governing copyright matters in the United States, explains which works are "protected" by copyright and the circumstances that permit some abridgement of that protection. (There is no international copyright protection, as each country has its own laws for this matter. However, certain treaties and conventions provide some protection in particular cases.)

Works that are copyrighted should contain a notice consisting of three elements: the symbol © or, for sound recordings, the symbol ℗; the year of first publication of the work; and the name of the owner of the copyright. Example: © 2010 by Libraries Unlimited.

Works in the "public domain" are not protected by copyright. In the United States all works published before 1923 are in the public domain. Works created before January 1, 1978, will be protected for 95 years, then pass into the public domain. Works created on or after January 1, 1978, are protected for the life of the author plus 70 years, then will pass into the public domain.

"Fair use" is an exemption from copyright protection, described in section 107 of the Copyright Act. It allows a nonowner of the copyright of a given work to utilize the work for "purposes such as criticism, comment, news reporting, teaching (including multiple copies for classroom use), scholarship, or research." However, there are numerous points that libraries need to consider.

Public Library Concerns

Two activities occur in most public libraries: patron copying of materials and interlibrary loan. The first is not a library responsibility (section 108f of the Copyright Act) as long as the library displays a notice—at all copiers and computer printers—that making copies may be subject to copyright law (Torrans 2004, 137). Interlibrary loan is a little more complicated. It is all right to borrow copyrighted materials but not for the "systematic reproduction or distribution of single or multiple copies." Generally, interlibrary loans are acceptable so long unless with the "purpose or effect of substituting for subscription or purchase" (section 108g). Guidelines stated by the National Commission on New Technological Uses of Copyrighted Works suggest that no more than five requests for a given periodical in its most recent five years of publication should be honored.

Another activity with copyright implications is replacement. A library wishing to replace all or part of a copyrighted work in its collections because of theft, damage, or deterioration should follow fair use principles. This may be awkward since "no real definition of the [fair use] concept has ever emerged ... and each case raising the question must be decided on its own facts" (U.S. Copyright Office, Circular 21). The main issue in the case of replacement copying is whether a substitute copy at a fair price is available; if so, the library should buy it, but if not, the library may copy what is needed from another library. A test question would be how the "amount and substantiality" of the portion used relates to the whole work and how the act of copying affects the potential marketing or value of the work (U.S. Copyright Office, Circular 21).

Most databases purchased by libraries are copyrighted and protected by license agreements.

References

Carson, Bryan M. 2007. *The Law of Libraries and Archives*. Lanham, MD: Scarecrow Press.

Heller, James S. 2004. *The Librarian's Copyright Companion*. Buffalo: William S. Hein.

Keogh, Patricia, compiler. 2008. *Copyright Policies*. Chicago: American Library Association. Concerned with academic libraries, but offers useful information for public libraries as well. Has policies of sixteen colleges.

Torrans, Lee Ann. 2004. *Law and Libraries: The Public Library*. Westport, CT: Libraries Unlimited.

U.S. Copyright Office. Circular 21. Reproduction of copyrighted works by educators and librarians. Washington, DC: U.S. Copyright Office.

CORDOVA DISTRICT LIBRARY, IL   402 Main Ave., Cordova, IL 61242. Founded 1878 as township library; 1991, became district library. Population served: 1,069. Circulation: 37,133. Holdings: 10,962. LJ February 15, 2009: 5-star library; November 15, 2009: 4-star library.

CORPUS CHRISTI PUBLIC LIBRARIES, TX   805 Comanche St., Corpus Christi, TX 78401. Founded 1909. Population served: 285,000. Circulation: 1,361,307. Holdings: 700,000. 5 branches.

CORVALLIS-BENTON COUNTY PUBLIC LIBRARY, CORVALLIS, OR   645 NW Monroe Ave., Corvallis, OR 97330. Founded 1899, city library from 1920. Population served: 83,000. Circulation: 1,500,000. Holdings: 300,000. 3 branches, 1 bookmobile. The original building (1932) was designed by Pietro Belluschi. A new building opened in 1992.

COUNTRYMAN, GRATIA ALTA, 1866–1953   Librarian. Born Hastings, MN, November 29, 1866. She attended the University of Minnesota and from 1889 worked in the Minneapolis Public Library under Herbert Putnam. She held the post of director, 1904–1936. Countryman was also secretary of the Minnesota Library Commission, 1899–1918. At the state level she was responsible for legislation in 1899 that enabled local communities to tax themselves for the support of public libraries. She was a firm advocate of the library as a social center, a welcoming place for clubs, unions, missionary societies, and immigrants—offering to all "the broadest spirit of hospitality; the atmosphere should be as gracious, kindly, and sympathetic as one's own home" (Countryman 1905). She was president of the American Library Association in 1933–1934. Death came in Duluth, MN, July 26, 1953. *DALB.*

Reference

Countryman, Gratia Alta. 1905. The library as a social centre. Address to the Minnesota Library Association, Red Wing, MN, October 12, 1905. Printed in *The American Public Library*, by Arthur E. Bostwick, 433–37. New York: Appleton, 1929.

COUNTY AND REGIONAL LIBRARIES

Terminology

The county is "the largest territorial division for local government within a state of the United States" (*Merriam*). A county library is a public library financed and operated by a county government. A region is "an administrative area, division, or district" (*Merriam*). A regional area may encompass two or more counties. A regional library is a public library financed and operated by a regional administrative area; most often that area is known as a district. Thus, a district library is a type of regional library. In Louisiana a county is known as a parish; in Alaska it is a borough. In New York City, the five boroughs are coterminous with counties: Manhattan = New York County, Brooklyn = Kings County, Bronx = Bronx County, Queens = Queens County, and Staten Island = Richmond County. There are 3,143 counties (or county equivalents) in the United States. There are 903 county libraries.

Historical Summary

Counties as subdivisions of state governments were found under various names in the U.S. colonies of the seventeenth century; for example, there were four "incorporations" in Virginia in 1617. County library development emerged only in the twentieth century, with one example at the end of the nineteenth. Many important county libraries were organized in the 1920s. Although most library planners came to regard the county as the proper "unit of service" by mid-century, the movement did not sweep the nation. One reason it did not was fragmentation of the concept. Gertrude Schenck (1954, 30–41) tabulated the great variety of approaches to library service below the state level:

- Library as part of county government (e.g., California)
- County service by contract with established municipal libraries
- Joint city-county libraries (e.g., Indiana, Ohio)

- Multicounty regional libraries (e.g., Georgia, North Carolina)
- Regional district libraries (e.g., Illinois, Washington)
- State regional supplementary service (e.g., Vermont, Massachusetts)
- Direct state service, provided in the form of funding to established libraries (Tennessee)
- State regional partial service (e.g., New York)
- State agency branch service, public service units operated by the state (Rhode Island, Delaware)
- State advisory service only (Michigan)

This chronology presents some of the important events in county library development:

1898—Library service from the city library of Brumback, OH, extended to the county of Van Wert, an area of 405 square miles.

1903—The Library Association of Portland, OR, began serving Multnomah County.

1909—Legislation In California, advocated by state librarian James Gillis, authorized county libraries.

1911—Kern County Library (CA) established, serving 8,152 square miles from Bakersfield.

1912—The County Library of Los Angeles established.

1913—San Diego County Library (CA) established.

1914—A survey reported the existence of 57 county libraries: California 22, Minnesota 11, Wyoming 9, Ohio 8, and Oregon 3 and one each in Illinois, Indiana, Maryland, and Missouri.

1917—Of California's 58 counties, 36 had complete library service.

1919—Orange County Library (CA) established.

1921—The Ohio legislature allowed areas of the state without free public library service to establish county district libraries with voter approval. Harris County Library (TX) established, centered in Houston.

1922—Cuyahoga County Library (OH) and Hennepin County Library (MN) established.

1929—Maricopa County Library (AZ) established, centered in Phoenix.

1939—Salt Lake County Library (UT) established, centered in Salt Lake City.

1954—*County and Regional Library Development,* by Gertrude Schenck, published by the American Library Association, the first substantial treatment of the subject.

1993—The U.S. National Center for Education Statistics (1995) reported that there were 1,071 county libraries in the United States.

2008—Hennepin County Library (MN) absorbed the Minneapolis Public Library, which became a branch of the county system.

Current Situation

There are 903 libraries that serve their entire counties with full or partial funding from county sources (U.S. Institute of Museum and Library Services 2010) Those with the greatest number of persons served are the County Library of Los Angeles (3,672,882), Kings County (NY, = Brooklyn, 2,465,326), Queens County (NY, = Queens County, 2,225,486), Miami-Dade Public Library System (FL, 2,1223,688), New York County (NY, = Manhattan Borough, 1,634,795), Orange County Library (CA, 1,503,961), Harris County Library (TX, 1,408,797), Las Vegas-Clark County Library District (1,400,000), and Tampa-Hillsborough County Public Library (FL, 1,131,546). Some of the largest U.S. counties do not have a county library. Service to their residents is the responsibility of individual communities. Examples are Cook County, IL, and Dallas County, TX.

A number of county libraries have received consistent recognition for excellent service. The 2010 list of "star libraries" in *Library Journal* gave five stars to Cuyahoga County Library, Columbus Metropolitan Library (serving Franklin County, OH), Spencer County Public Library (Rockport, IN), Middle Country Public Library (Center Reach, NY), Haines Borough Public Library (AK), Stark County District Library (Canton, OH), Elkhart/Morton County Library (KS), Mercer County Library (Lawrenceville, NJ), Akron-Summit County Public Library, and Allen County Public Library (Fort Wayne, IN). County libraries with four-star ratings in 2010 were Indianapolis-Marion County Public Library, Upton County Public Library (McCamey, TX), Tulsa City-County Library System, Public Library of Cincinnati and Hamilton County, Ocean County Library (Toms River, NJ), Douglas County Libraries (Castle Rock, CO), San Mateo County Library (CA), Harford County Public Library (Belcamp, MD), Real County Public Library (Leakey, TX), Toledo-Lucas County Public Library, and Santa Clara County Library (Los Gatos, CA). Other starred municipal libraries that give countywide service by contract are not cited here.

There has been a small decline in the number of county libraries since the National Center for Education Statistics report for fiscal year 1993. In that year there were 8,929 public libraries, 1,071 of them (12 percent) county libraries. The percent of county libraries has settled just below 10 percent; it is 9.8 percent for fiscal year 2008. Wide disparity appears among the individual states. Wyoming has reported that 100 percent of their libraries were county based, South Carolina 97.9 percent, and Maryland 95.8 percent. At the other extreme, none of the New England states have county libraries.

Library districts have increased in number. They accounted for just 6 percent of all public libraries in 1993, but they now represent 14.6 percent.

A cautionary note is needed with regard to all these official data. The terminology is complex, and it may be that reporting libraries tabulate county as city-county or even as regional. In many cases what is named a county library is legally a district library (e.g., King County Library System, WA). Ohio's city-county libraries and those of Indiana are legally district libraries and tabulated accordingly in the statistical tables.

References

Schenck, Gertrude. 1954. *County and Regional Libraries*. Chicago: American Library Association.
U.S. Institute of Museum and Library Services. 2010. *Public Libraries in the United States: FY 2008*. Washington, DC: U.S. Department of Education.
U.S. National Center for Education Statistics. 1995. *Public Libraries in the United States: 1993*. Washington, DC: U.S. Department of Education.

COUNTY OF LOS ANGELES PUBLIC LIBRARY, DOWNEY, CA   7400 E. Imperial Highway, Downey, CA 90242. Founded 1912. Population served: 3,672,882. Circulation: 15,368,606. Holdings: 6,091,825. 88 regional and community libraries, 4 bookmobiles. Service area is about 3,000 square miles (for a description of the American Indian Resource Center, *see* SERVICES TO NATIVE AMERICANS). The library approved the use of filters on Internet stations in 2006. Administration of three branches was outsourced to Library Systems and Services in 2010 (*New York Times*, September 26, 2010). Directors: Celia Gleason, 1912–1924; Helen E. Vogelson, 1924–1946; John D. Henderson, 1946–1963; William S. Geller, 1963–1973; Carol E. Moss, 1973–1980; Linda F. Crismond, 1980–1989; Sandra F. Reuben, 1989–2000, and Margaret Donnellan Todd, 2001–.

COWDEN, IL. *See* DRY POINT TOWNSHIP LIBRARY, COWDEN, IL.

CRAFTSBURY PUBLIC LIBRARY, VT   12 Church St., Craftsbury, VT 05827. Founded 1878. Population served: 1,155. Circulation: 15,857. Holdings: 11,531. LJ February 15, 2009: 3-star library; November 15, 2009, and October 1, 2010: 4-star library.

CRANBURY PUBLIC LIBRARY, NJ   23 N. Main St., Cranbury, NJ 08512. Founded 1906. Population served: 3,500. Circulation: 35,000. Holdings: 25,007. LJ February 15, 2009: 3-star library.

CRAWFORD PUBLIC LIBRARY, NE   601 Second St., Crawford, NE 69339. Population served: 1,270. Circulation: 11,458. Holdings: 14,705. LJ February 15, 2009: 4-star library.

CRESTLINE PUBLIC LIBRARY, OH   324 Thoman St., Crestline, OH 44827. Founded 1925. Population served: 12,000. Circulation: 178,991. Holdings: 69,000. LJ February 15, 2009: 3-star library; November 15, 2009: 4-star library; October 1, 2010: 3-star library. HAPLR 2009, 2010.

CRUNDEN, FREDERICK MORGAN, 1847–1911   Librarian. Born Gravesend, England, September 1, 1847. His parents moved to St. Louis, and he attended school there, going on to Washington University. He took a master's degree in 1872 and joined the faculty, remaining to 1876. In 1877, Crunden became librarian of the Public School Library, a subscription library established in 1865, and promoted its transformation to a free public library for the city. Operation of the library was transferred from the private library society to the board of education in 1869. It became independent of the board in 1893, when the citizens voted to support a free public library. Crunden was director of the St. Louis Public Library to 1909, establishing six branches and securing dependable support. He was president of the American Library Association in 1889 and first president of the Missouri Library Association. Crunden saw the role of the library as educational, meaning that it should be "lifting up of the great mass of humanity to an understanding of the significance of life, individual and social" (Williams 1988, 27). His words were inscribed over the main entrance to the library: "Recorded thought is our chief heritage from the past, the most lasting legacy we can leave to the future. Books are the most enduring monument of man's achievements. Only through books can civilization become cumulative." Crunden died in St. Louis on October 28, 1911. *DALB*.

Reference

Williams, Patrick. 1988. *The American Public Library and the Problem of Purpose.* New York: Greenwood Press.

CULVER, ESSAE MARTHA, 1882–1973   Librarian. Born Emporia, KS, November 15, 1882. She earned a bachelor's degree at Pomona College in 1904 and attended the New York State Library School in 1908. She directed the Salem (OR) Public Library, 1909–1912. From 1912 to 1925 she was librarian of three county libraries in California. When Louisiana received a Carnegie Corporation grant of $500,000 in 1925 to fund a rural library demonstration project, Culver was chosen to head the enterprise. She was Louisiana's first state librarian. Taking the county (parish) as the appropriate unit of service and building on her experience in California, she succeeded in gaining local funding after the demonstration project. She also convinced legislators to finance a state library agency. Eventually parish libraries were established throughout the state. Her model influenced library development across the United States. It was through her promotion that a library school was created at Louisiana State University in 1931. As American Library Association president in 1940–1941, she called for library extension to unserved areas. When she retired in 1962, the state library was housed in its own building near the Capitol. Culver died January 2, 1973. *DALB.*

CURLEY, ARTHUR, 1938–1998   Librarian. Born Boston, January 22, 1938. Attended Boston Latin, then Harvard (BA 1959). His MSLS was from Simmons College, 1962. He was director of these public libraries: Avon Lake, MA (1961–1964); Palatine, IL (1964–1968); Montclair, NJ (1968–1975); and Cuyahoga County, OH (1975–1976). Then he became deputy director Detroit Public Library (1977–1980) and New York Public Library (1980–1985). Curley's last position was librarian of the Boston Public Library (1985–1996). He was active in the American Library Association as a member of council and the executive board and president in 1994–1995. Curley's role in the profession was above all exhortative: he urged that librarians must "champion literature, ideas, learning, and the pursuit of wisdom" in order to balance "intellectual malaise." *DALB.*

CUTCHOGUE NEW SUFFOLK FREE LIBRARY, NY   27550 Main Rd., Cutchogue, NY 11935. Population served: 3,392. Circulation: 117,004. Holdings: 33,161. LJ February 15, 2009: 5-star library; November 15, 2009: 3-star library; October 1, 2010: 4-star library.

CUTTER, CHARLES AMMI, 1837–1903   Librarian. Born Boston, March 14, 1837. He entered Harvard College at age 14 and graduated in 1855; was engaged as library assistant there, 1860–1868. Appointed librarian of the Boston Athenaeum in December 1868, Cutter compiled a catalog of that library, published in five volumes, 1874–1882, described as "the best catalogue extant" by Justin Winsor. He then wrote *Rules for a Printed Library Catalogue* (1875), which became the world's leading text. His *Expansive Classification* (1891–1904) was highly regarded as well, considered the principal alternative to the classification of Melvil Dewey. Cutter's alphabetic-order tables based on authors' names are still widely used to organize books within class numbers. In October 1894 he began to develop the new Forbes Library, the public library of Northampton, MA. He wanted it to be "a new type of public library, which, speaking broadly, will lend anything to anybody in any desired quantity for any desired time." Forbes, where he remained until his death, had a department for art and music and a children's room. Cutter was one of the signers of the call to prominent librarians to meet in Philadelphia in 1876—the gathering that gave birth to the American Library Association. He advocated the "ladder theory": that once people came to the library and started to read, their tastes would be elevated over time. He wrote in 1878 that the public should prefer good reading, "but how is it to be done? ... What power is to compel them? Certainly nothing can be effected by a policy that will begin by driving them off. The true way is to get them in the habit of frequenting the library, and then to raise by personal influence the character of the reading" (Williams 1988, 17). He died in Walpole, NH, on a driving trip with his wife on September 6, 1903. *DAB; DALB.*

Reference

Williams, Patrick. 1988. *The American Public Library and the Problem of Purpose.* New York: Greenwood Press.

CUYAHOGA COUNTY PUBLIC LIBRARY, PARMA, OH   2111 Snow Rd., Parma, OH 44134. Founded 1922. Population served: 589,298. Circulation: 14,070,613. Holdings: 2,839,767. 28 branches. LJ November 15, 2009, and October 1, 2010: 5-star library. HAPLR 2009, 2010. In 1922 voters in Cuyahoga County passed a referendum authorizing the Cuyahoga County Public Library, the first county district library system organized under a state law of 1921. On March 4, 1924, the library began delivering service through the Cleveland Public Library. Today its 28 branches serve 47 communities. Directors: Margaret Wright Thayer, 1924–1941; Amy Winslow, 1941–1945; Raymond C. Lindquist, 1946–1955; Lewis C. Naylor, 1955–1969; Christopher Devan, 1970–1974; Arthur Curley, 1975–1976; James H. Pickering, 1976–1978; Patrick M. O'Brien, 1979–1984; Donald J. Napoli, 1985; Ronald S. Kozlowski, 1985–1989; Claudya [*sic*] Muller, 1990–1994; John A. Lonsak, 1995–2003; and Sari Feldman, 2003–.

CUYAHOGA FALLS LIBRARY, OH   2015 Third St., Cuyahoga Falls, OH 44221. Founded 1930. Population served: 50,515. Circulation: 772,236. Holdings: 149,443. The name was Taylor Memorial Library until January 2004.

D

DALLAS PUBLIC LIBRARY, TX   1515 Young St., Dallas, TX 75201.
Founded 1901. Population served: 1,210,393. Circulation: 7,333,191.
Holdings: 3,098,091. 23 branches, 1 bookmobile. The library opened a
library for teens ("Bookmarks") in a shopping center in 2008. Directors:
Rosa M. Leeper, 1901–1916; Betsy T. Wiley, 1916–1922; Cleora Clanton,
1922–1955; James D. Meeks, 1955–1961; Lillian Moore Bradshaw, 1961–
1984; Patrick O'Brien, 1984–1992; Ramiro Salazar, 1993–2004; Laurie
Evans, 2005–2010; and Connie Hill (interim): 2010–.

Reference

Hazel, Michael V. 2001. *The Dallas Public Library: Celebrating a Century of
Service, 1901–2001.* Denton: University of North Texas Press.

DALY CITY PUBLIC LIBRARY, CA   40 Wembley Dr., Daly City, CA 94015.
Founded 1925. Population served: 104,820. Circulation: 336,104. Holdings: 98,787. 3 branches.

DAMARISCOTTA, ME. *See* SKIDOMPHA PUBLIC LIBRARY, DAMARIS-
COTTA, ME.

DANA, JOHN COTTON, 1856–1929   Librarian, lawyer, civil engineer. Born
Woodstock, NY, August 19, 1856. He graduated from Dartmouth College,
1878, and studied law, 1878–1880. He was a surveyor in Colorado, 1881,
then practiced law in New York City and worked a year as civil engineer.

In 1889, Dana was appointed to head the new Denver Public Library. He remained eight years, promoting open access and service to children. He went to Springfield, MA, as city librarian in 1898, nearly doubling the circulation during his four years there. On January 15, 1902, Dana became librarian of the Newark (NJ) Public Library and soon made it the "most effective institution of its kind in the U.S." (*DAB*). The library grew to 392,000 volumes with 2 million circulation. Dana opened a business branch in the financial district in 1904. The library had open shelves. Dana promoted modern architecture for libraries, as opposed to temples and palaces, and urged librarians to practice public relations. He was elected president of the American Library Association in 1896. Among his writings were *Library Primer* (1896) and *Libraries: Addresses and Essays* (1910). He was in poor health for five years and died in New York City on July 21, 1929. Dana had doubts about the educational role of the library; he described it as a "hopeless task" and thought it impossible for librarians to do effective reader's advising (Williams 1988, 22, 45). But he was unequivocal about intellectual freedom and opposition to censorship, proclaiming that "liberty of thought . . . can only be maintained by those who have free access to opinion" (Geller 1984, 113). *DAB*; *DALB*; LJ Hall of Fame.

References

Geller, Evelyn. 1984. *Forbidden Books in American Libraries, 1876–1939*. Westport, CT: Greenwood Press.

Williams, Patrick. 1988. *The American Public Library and the Problem of Purpose*. New York: Greenwood Press.

DARIEN LIBRARY, CT   1441 Post Rd., Darien, CT 06820. Founded 1917. Population served: 20,547. Circulation: 757,221. Holdings: 171,082. LJ February 15, 2009, November 15, 2009, and October 1, 2010: 5-star library. HAPLR 2009, 2010.

DAVID M. HUNT LIBRARY, CANAAN, CT   108 Main, Canaan, CT 06018. Founded 1889. Population served: 1,106. Circulation: 15,092. Holdings: 27,281. LJ February 15, 2009, and November 15, 2009: 4-star library; October 1, 2010: 3-star library.

DAYTON METROPOLITAN LIBRARY, OH   215 E. Third, Dayton, OH 45402. Population served: 472,000. Circulation: 6,965,000. Holdings: 2,298,000. LJ November 15, 2009, and October 1, 2010: 3-star library. HAPLR 2009, 2010.

DE SMET, SD. *See* HAZEL L. MEYER MEMORIAL LIBRARY, DE SMET, SD.

DELTA COMMUNITY LIBRARY, DELTA JUNCTION, AK   2291 Deborah, Delta Junction, AK 99737. Founded 1960. Population served: 5,000. Circulation:

30,000. Holdings: 12,000. LJ February 15, 2009, and October 1, 2010: 5-star library.

DELTA JUNCTION, AK. *See* DELTA COMMUNITY LIBRARY, DELTA JUNCTION, AK.

DENNIS MEMORIAL LIBRARY ASSOCIATION, MA   1020 Old Bass River Rd., Dennis, MA 02638. Population served: 15,000. Circulation: 36,647. Holdings: 14,218. LJ November 15, 2009, and October 1, 2010: 4-star library.

DENVER CITY, TX. *See* YOAKUM COUNTY LIBRARY, DENVER CITY, TX.

DENVER PUBLIC LIBRARY, CO   10 W. 14th Ave., Denver, CO 80204. Founded 1889. Population served: 582,474. Circulation: 9,244,353. Holdings: 2,042,220. 22 branches, 1 bookmobile. LJ October 1, 2010: 5-star library. HAPLR 2009, 2010. Under its first director, John Cotton Dana (1889–1897), the library was recognized for its open access and services to children. The first circulating picture collection in the United States (1891) was primarily for children, and a separate children's room was established in 1894. A Carnegie building (1910) served as the central library until a new structure was built in 1956. Another new building was occupied in 1995. In 1913 the library opened its first bilingual branch, with materials in Dutch and English. Bilingual branches today feature materials in nine immigrant languages. There are important programs for the Hispanic communities in seven branches, with multimedia collections, Spanish-speaking staff, English classes, literacy programs, and life skills classes (Gross 2006). There are more than 5,000 items in the Vietnamese language at two locations (Eitner 2006). A major program to assist persons with disabilities has been operating since 1997 (Sarling 2002). Directors: John Cotton Dana, 1889–1897; John Parsons, 1898–1899; Charles R. Dudley, 1899–1910; Chalmers Hadley, 1911–1924; Malcolm Glenn Wyer, 1924–1951; John T. Eastlick, 1951–1969; Henry Shearouse, 1969–1984; Rick J. Ashton, 1985–2006; and Shirley C. Amore, 2006–.

References

Eastlick, John T. 1971. Denver Public Library. *Encyclopedia of Library and Information Science* 6: 588–592. New York: Marcel Dekker.

Eitner, Mike. 2006. The Vietnamese collection at the Denver Public Library: Evolving needs and preferences. *Colorado Libraries* 32, no. 4 (Fall): 19–20.

Gross, Barbara, et al. 2006. A library for all: Denver Public Library designs services to meet the needs of the Hispanic community. *Colorado Libraries* 32, no. 4 (Fall): 32–36.

Sarling, Jo, et al. 2002. Providing increased services and access to information for persons with disabilities at the Denver Public Library. *Colorado Libraries* 28, no. 4 (Winter): 16–19.

DES PLAINES PUBLIC LIBRARY, IL   1501 Ellinwood, Des Plaines, IL 60016. Founded 1907. Population served: 56,945. Circulation: 1,083,691. Holdings: 259,451. 1 bookmobile. LJ February 15, 2009: 3-star library.

DETROIT PUBLIC LIBRARY, MI   5201 Woodward Ave., Detroit, MI 48202. Founded 1865. Population served: 951,270. Circulation: 1,200,00. Holdings: 7,770,077. 23 branches, 2 bookmobiles. A business branch opened in 1920. The new main library, designed by Cass Gilbert, opened 1921 (plans and photos in Van Slyck 1995). Under the direction of Ralph Ulveling (see entry for him) in 1941–1967, the library gained national recognition. Clara S. Jones, appointed director in 1970, was the first black person to head a major American public library.

Reference

Van Slyck, Abby. 1995. *Free to All: Carnegie Libraries and American Culture, 1890–1920.* Chicago: University of Chicago Press.

DEWEY, MELVIL, 1851–1931   Librarian. Born December 10, 1851, Adams Center, NY. An advocate of simplified spelling, he adjusted the form of his name: dropping the final "le" from "Melville" in 1874, adopting the surname form "Dui" in 1879, and returning to "Dewey" in 1883. He attended Amherst College, 1870–1874; worked in college library as a student, then became acting librarian. He was disturbed by the time and effort wasted in the fixed location system of shelving books (typical in libraries of the time) and conceived the idea of a "relative location" based on a classification of the materials. Dewey's decimal classification was approved by the college for use in the library in 1873; it was published in the 1876 report on public libraries by the U.S. Bureau of Education. He also wrote a collection development policy for the library that included five grades of collecting intensity—a principle enacted in modern collection practice (Wiegand 1996, 87). Organizing and rationalizing the work of librarians became Dewey's life work. "Librarianship did not exist when Dewey set out on his self-assigned task. To be sure, there were libraries, and people worked in them, but no unified body of purpose and practice (which we call librarianship) existed to guide them" (Comaromi 1993, 250). He was one of the promoters of the meeting of librarians in Philadelphia, 1876, that resulted in the formation of the American Library Association (ALA); he was the unpaid secretary of the association, 1876–1890, and president, 1890 and 1892–1893. He was instrumental in establishing the *American Library Journal* and edited it from 1876 to 1881. He set up a library supply company that developed into the Library Bureau in 1881 and headed it for 25 years. He was the first to suggest that catalog copy be included in newly published books.

On May 7, 1883, Dewey was appointed librarian of Columbia College, New York City (later Columbia University). Among his innovations there were activities in public relations, open shelves, and subject specialists. He advocated a training school for librarians at Columbia, and it opened—the world's first formal library school—on January 1, 1887. Unfortunately Dewey's energy and creativity were counterbalanced by considerable egoism and impatience with the views of others; one might say that he failed in diplomacy. He alienated the Columbia faculty by charging them overdue fines and imposing apparently arbitrary rules. Budgets were also a problem. A resolution for his dismissal as librarian was passed by the board of trustees on November 5, 1888, but it was revoked on December 3. In a situation that was, to say the least, uncomfortable, Dewey had looked elsewhere. On December 12, 1888, the New York State Board of Regents appointed him director of the State Library and secretary of the board. With his resignation from Columbia on December 20, he arranged to transfer the library school to Albany; the move occurred on April 1, 1889.

Dewey held the post of secretary to December 22, 1899. He promoted a state law that supported higher education and public libraries. Library growth in the state was rapid: there were 238 public libraries in 1893 and 553 10 years later, and circulation increased in the period from 2,294,000 to 10,870,000 (Wiegand 1996, 203). As director of the State Library, Dewey initiated special collections for the blind and for children. He sent out traveling libraries (*see* BOOKMOBILES). The library in the mid-1890s was the fifth largest in the country, with half a million volumes. He advocated centralized cataloging at the Library of Congress. The first American state library association was the New York Library Association, for which Dewey was prime mover; he was the first president in 1890 of the organization, "a model for librarians from other states" (Wiegand 1996, 177). He was also instrumental in creating the Association of State Librarians (1891), serving as its first president. The journal *Public Libraries* appeared in 1896 with his support. The course of library education would have been changed if Dewey had accepted an 1892 offer from William Rainey Harper, president of the University of Chicago, to be dean of a proposed library school there.

Dewey could not escape conflicts with his superiors. His many achievements were blurred by disputes with the regents, the governor, and the legislature. At the end of 1905 he decided to leave library work, centering his later life on development of the Lake Placid (NY) Club (incorporated 1896). It became the base for his crusades for simple spelling, calendar reform, and the metric system. At the same time, the club grew from one rented house to 412 buildings on 10,600 acres in 1931. It was alive with cultural and educational activities and conferences, including an ALA conference. Melvil Dewey died at Lake Placid on December 26, 1931.

Philosophically, Dewey believed in the inclusion of women in the library profession as equals. He thought that reading tastes would be elevated as persons read simpler things: "These novels educate taste to better books" (Wiegand 1996, 21). Above all he served as a model and inspiration for librarians to organize, cooperate, standardize, publish, serve, and look always for a better way to do their work. *DAB; DALB;* LJ Hall of Fame.

References

Comaromi, John P. 1993. Dewey, Melvil. In *World Encyclopedia of Library and Information Services*, 3rd ed., 250–52. Chicago: American Library Association.
Linderman, Winifred B. 1972. Dewey, Melvil. *Encyclopedia of Library and Information Science* 7: 142–160. New York: Marcel Dekker.
Wiegand, Wayne A. 1996. *Irrepressible Reformer: A Biography of Melvil Dewey*. Chicago: American Library Association.

DIGITAL MEDIA

Terminology

"Digital: of or relating to a device that can read, write, or store information represented in numerical form" (*American Heritage*). The term "digital" is also applied to the items that the device (a computer) reads, writes, or stores; they are in digital format. And the adjective describes a kind of library as well, as defined in *ODLIS*: "A library in which a significant proportion of the resources are available in machine-readable format (as opposed to print or microform), accessible by means of computers." Terms derived from "digital" are "digitize," which is to translate an item into digital format, and "digitization," which is the process of digitizing.

"Electronic" is synonymous with "digital" in this context. Thus, a digital book = electronic book (or e-book), digital journal = electronic journal (or e-journal), digital magazine (or e-zine), and so on. Access to digital material may be online (by direct contact with a computer website or database) or offline through storage formats like CD-ROM.

Electronic publishing is "the publication of books, periodicals (e-journals, e-zines, etc.), bibliographic databases, and other information resources in digital format, usually on CD-ROM or online via the Internet, for in-house users, subscribers, and/or retail customers, with or without a print counterpart" (*ODLIS*). Public libraries are very interested in the electronic book, which may be an original publication in digital format or a digital version of a printed book. Such e-books are read with various kinds of software applications generally identified as e-book readers.

Current Situation

The early e-books, in the 1970s, were created for specialized audiences. The rise of the Internet made mass production and distribution possible, and U.S. public libraries began providing e-books in the late 1990s. Free, downloadable electronic publications were available from 2003. By 2010, 66 percent of public libraries were offering e-books to their patrons. Sophisticated e-book readers have been marketed by Sony, Barnes & Noble, Apple, and other companies.

Libraries have noted several advantages that electronic formats have over print and microform formats:

- Scope of selections. Some 2 million free downloads were available in 2009.

- Space saving. Thousands of titles can be accessed or stored by a single device.
- Immediate access. No time is spent by staff or patrons in finding items on shelves.
- Multiple access. Any number of users may access the same title simultaneously.
- Paper saved. No paper is consumed in printing or reading e-materials.

However, there are negative features of digital media:

- Changing technology. Hardware and software may require costly upgrades or may become unavailable.
- Shelf life. There is no conclusive research regarding the life span of digital media.
- Device problems. E-book readers may be damaged, or fall victim to malfunction.
- Toxic waste. E-book readers contain materials that are not biogradable.
- Privacy issues. Online reading can be tracked so that patron privacy may be jeopardized.

A lively issue today is preservation of digital materials. Apart from general considerations that apply to all formats (*see* PRESERVATION), digital media have particular challenges. Their intellectual content needs to be maintained rather than their physical expression. "Sometimes we must focus on maintain the ability to reproduce a record that is reliable and authentic over time. This is a different conceptual model from the artifactual model upon which conservation and preservation have been built" (Cloonan and Harvey 2007, 1). Of course it is difficult with digital media to be sure of what is "authentic." Authenticity had its methods of proof in the print world, but digital documents are easily altered, and the notion of an original is lost (Rosenzweig 2007, 318). Another difference between print and digital conservation is the rapidity of decay: print materials deteriorate gradually over time (except in disasters), lending themselves to systematic remedies, but digital records may fail completely in a moment. A further question comes from the vast corpus of digital material. A library concerned with preservation of printed items has a limited stock to deal with. But a library that wants to preserve its digital stock confronts billions of records—some of which are owned and others licensed from vendors or publishers. Do publishers have a responsibility of preserving their digital products, especially beyond the period of their copyright protection? Or do public domain materials fall into the guardianship of libraries?

Does digital preservation include attention to hardware and software needed to read electronic documents? A museum of old computers and floppy discs might be necessary for access to early products (Harvey 1997).

In 2004 the Library of Congress initiated a project, National Digital Information Infrastructure and Preservation Program to bring together organizations interested in sustaining access to digital information that is critical to scholarship and cultural heritage. The project addresses such issues as migration of digital content, interoperability, data transfer and storage, and the future of digital preservation systems (Cruse and Sandore 2009). UNESCO (2005) has moved in this area with *Preserving the Digital Heritage*. It is expected that digital preservation efforts in the future will be collaborative on national and international scales.

Another consideration, cost, cannot be readily classed as positive or negative. An e-book reader in 2010 costs as much as 5 to 10 times what a single book costs, but it can handle thousands of titles. However, printed books require no maintenance or upgrading, so they represent one-time costs. Digital materials sold by subscription, like most databases, are subject to price fluctuations according to market factors. No useful research has appeared to determine whether the use of electronic resources justifies their cost (Koehn and Hawamdeh 2010). A recent issue evolves around the number of times a library may check out an e-book. The standard agreement between a library and an e-book publisher has been that once the item is purchased, it may be loaned without limitations. However, HarperCollins began enforcing a new restriction in March 2011, requiring that its e-books be circulated only 26 times before they expire. The move aroused strong opposition among librarians, and the American Library Association assembled two task forces to study the problem. While other publishers are considering the question of restrictions, none have implemented them as of April 2011 (*New York Times*, March 15, 2011).

A recent study found that public libraries have not given adequate attention to publicizing their digital media (McKnight et al. 2008). Websites examined in the writing of this handbook are often uninformative about electronic materials and e-book readers that they may have ready for their patrons.

[Should we mention here a paragraph about the new issue arising between publishers (specifically HarperCollins) and libraries over the policy of licensing agreements running expiring after a specific number of checkouts and the additional cost to libraries this will cause.]

References

Cloonan, Michele V., and Ross Harvey. 2007. Preserving cultural heritage: introduction. *Library Trends* 56, no. 1 (Summer): 1–3.

Cruse, Patricia, and Beth Sandore. 2009. Introduction: The Library of Congress National Digital Information Infrastructure and Preservation Program. *Library Trends* 57, no. 3 (Winter): 301–15.

Harvey, Ross. 1997. The preservation of electronic records: what shall we do next? In *Collection Management for the 21st Century: A Handbook for Librarians*, ed. G. E. Gorman and Ruth H. Miller, 173–90. Westport, CT: Greenwood Press.

Koehn, Shona L., and Suliman Hawamdeh. 2010. The acquisition and management of electronic resources: Can use justify cost?*Library Quarterly* 80, no. 2 (April): 161–74.

McKnight, Cliff, et al. 2008. Making e-books available through public libraries: Some user reactions. *Journal of Librarianship and Information Science* 40, no. 1 (March): 31–43.

Rosenzweig, Roy. 2007. Scarcity or abundance? Preserving the past in a digital era. In *Institutions of Reading: The Social Life of Libraries in the United States*, ed. Thomas Augst and Kenneth Carpenter, 310–42. Amherst: University of Massachusetts Press.

UNESCO. 2005. *Preserving the Digital Heritage*. Geneva: UNESCO.

Woodyard-Robinson, Deborah, ed. 2005. *Digital Preservation*. An issue of *Library Trends*, 54, no.1.

DIME BOX, TX. *See* BLACK BRIDGE LIBRARY, DIME BOX, TX.

DISTRICT OF COLUMBIA PUBLIC LIBRARY, WASHINGTON, DC   901 G. St. NW, Washington, DC 20001. Founded 1896. Population served: 550,021. Circulation: 1,128,870. Holdings: 3,000,000. 25 branches, 3 bookmobiles. The library was created by act of Congress in 1896 and housed in temporary quarters at 1320 New York Ave. NW. A new central building at Mt. Vernon Square, 1903, designed by Ackerman and Ross, was built with a Carnegie grant. The first branch opened in 1912. A new central library, the Martin Luther King Jr. Memorial Library, Ninth and G Sts. NW, 1972, was designed by Ludwig Mies van der Rohe.

DIVERSITY. *See* STAFFING.

DORCAS CAREY PUBLIC LIBRARY, CAREY, OH   236 E. Findlay St., Carey, OH 43316. Population served: 5,610. Circulation: 155,626. Holdings: 47,823. LJ October 1, 2010: 3-star library.

DOUGLAS COUNTY LIBRARIES, CASTLE ROCK, CO   100 S. Wilcox, Castle Rock, CO 80104. Founded 1966, opened 1967. Population served: 250,000. Circulation: 7,911,290. Holdings: 708,797. 6 branches, 1 bookmobile (withdrawn 2009). LJ February 15, 2009; November 15, 2009; and October 1, 2010: 4-star library. HAPLR 2009, 2010.

DOVER TOWN LIBRARY, MA   56 Dedham St., Dover Town, MA 02030. Founded 1894. Population served: 5,657. Circulation: 150,944. Holdings: 55,999. LJ February 15, 2009: 4-star library.

DOWNEY, CA. *See* COUNTY OF LOS ANGELES PUBLIC LIBRARY, DOWNEY, CA.

DRUMMOND SCHOOL-COMMUNITY LIBRARY, MT   108 W. Edwards St., Drummond, MT 59832. Population served: 1,117. Circulation: 10,200. Holdings: 11,731. LJ February 15, 2009: 3-star library.

DRY POINT TOWNSHIP LIBRARY, COWDEN, IL   County Highway 651, Cowden, IL 62422. Population served: 1,085. Circulation: 5,919. Holdings: 7,114. LJ October 1, 2010: 4-star library.

DURHAM COUNTY LIBRARY, NC   300 N. Roxboro St., Durham, NC 27702. Population served: 236,789. Circulation: 1,359,711. Holdings: 553,517. 6 branches.

DVDS. *See* AUDIOVISUAL COLLECTIONS.

DYERSVILLE, IA. *See* JAMES KENNEDY PUBLIC LIBRARY, DYERSVILLE, IA.

E

EAGLE PUBLIC LIBRARY, AK   Second and Amundsen, Eagle, AK 99738. Population served: 137. Circulation: 4,809. Holdings: 8,823. HAPLR 2010.

EARLVILLE FREE LIBRARY, NY   5 W. Main St., Earlville, NY 13332. Population served: 883. Circulation: 31,120. Holdings: 33,362. HAPLR 2010.

EAST BATON ROUGE PARISH LIBRARY, BATON ROUGE, LA   7711 Goodwood Blvd., Baton Rouge, LA 70806. Population served: 412,447. Circulation: 2,486,503. Holdings: 1,543,337. 12 branches. *See also* HURRICANES KATRINA AND RITA.

EAST CLEVELAND PUBLIC LIBRARY, OH   14101 Euclid Ave., East Cleveland, OH 44112. Founded 1933. Population served: 29,939. Circulation: 528,351. Holdings: 195,202. LJ October 1, 2010: 3-star library.

EAST PALESTINE MEMORIAL PUBLIC LIBRARY, OH   Population served: 4,819. Circulation: 118,153. Holdings: 48,127. LJ November 15, 2009: 3-star library.

EASTMAN, LINDA ANNE, 1867–1963   Librarian. Born in Oberlin, OH, and spent most of her life in Cleveland. She had no college degree but attended a normal school and taught for six years. Then she became an apprentice in Cleveland Public Library, working in the first branch of the system, and took an extension course from the library school in Albany. When a second

Cleveland branch opened in 1894, Eastman was the librarian; two years later she became vice librarian of the Cleveland Public Library, serving under William Howard Brett. When Brett died in 1918, she was invited to succeed him. She carried on the innovative programs that brought the library national recognition, expanding all services and adding service to hospitals, the blind, and to the business community with the Business Information Bureau under the energetic direction of Rose Vormelker. A travel section was added in 1926. She maintained high staff morale in the Depression until her retirement in 1938. She died in Cleveland on April 3, 1963. Eastman was president of the Ohio Library Association, 1903–1904, and of the American Library Association, 1928–1929. She was a full professor at Western Reserve University despite a lack of academic qualifications. The reading garden between the main library and the annex of the Cleveland Public Library is named for her. *DALB.*

EASTMAN, WILLIAM REED, 1835–1925   Civil engineer, minister, librarian. Born October 19, 1835, in New York City. He earned a BA, 1854, and MA, 1857, from Yale University and was a graduate of Union Theological Seminary, 1862. He became a Presbyterian minister, an army chaplain in the Civil War, and a pastor in congregational churches. At age 55, Eastman entered librarianship, studying at the New York State Library School. After completing that program in 1892, he was appointed library inspector and supervisor of the public libraries in New York State, a position he held for 20 years. He developed specialized knowledge of library buildings and equipment, becoming "perhaps the first authority in his profession" in those areas (*DAB*). He gave library school lectures and served as president of the New York Library Association, 1904–1905. Eastman died on March 25, 1925. *DAB.*

EDGERTON PUBLIC LIBRARY, MN.   811 First Ave., Edgerton, MN 56128. Population served: 1,033. Circulation: 47,664. Holdings: 16,328. LJ October 1, 2010: 5-star library. HAPLR 2009, 2010.

EDUCATION OF PUBLIC LIBRARIANS

Terminology

A pair of terms were of consequence in the first generations of public librarianship: "education" and "training." At present the two concepts, as they are generally used, appear to have merged into a single meaning, as indicated by the reference dictionaries. For "to educate," *Merriam* has "to train by formal instruction or supervised practice," and for "to train," it has "to teach so as to make fit, qualified, or proficient." In *American Heritage*, "to educate" is "to provide with knowledge or training in a particular area or for a particular purpose," and "to train" is "to make proficient with specialized instruction and practice." But in the library context of the late nineteenth and early twentieth centuries, "training" carried the connotation of instruction in routines, while "education" pointed to instruction in principles. In a sense this division of concentration remains in the field of library education (no longer called training) today.

Historical Summary

The purpose of any educational program is always to change the knowledge base, skills, and attitudes of its students. "At the end of the course, the student will be able to . . . " is the typical language of a modern "educational objective." Something happens to the student as a result of the course (or program), marking a change that will enable him or her to express new knowledge, demonstrate new skills, or display new attitudes about what was taught. What makes education such a grand challenge is a dual problem. First, what *should* the student be able to do when the course is over? Second, what methods of instruction are most likely to achieve that result? Or what are the qualifications of a librarian, and what will produce them?

A profession that is unclear about the qualifications of its members will have a confused educational system. American librarianship was created by persons of high culture: scholars and book lovers. They learned on the job how to administer and operate libraries. Many of them were satisfied that this approach would serve young librarians as well. An informal apprentice system was in place, along with equally informal mentoring. William F. Poole was rather dismayed, while he was directing the Chicago Public Library in 1883, that "scarcely a day passes in which one or more of these tyros does not come to my library for information"(Poole 1883, 288). Nevertheless, Poole was among those who felt uncomfortable about formal instruction for new librarians ("there is no training school for educating librarians like a well-managed library"; 1883, 288), others being Justin Winsor and John Shaw Billings. It was Melvil Dewey who led the movement for actual schooling. But what he promoted was a program to teach basic library skills—"training" more than "education."

Inculcation of principles, as opposed to routines, was a much later priority. It is of interest that this focus on principles in professional education was expressed as early as 1901, applied to the field of business. When a school of business was being planned for the University of Chicago, J. Laurence Laughlin, professor of political economy, proposed that it should be one that would not tell a man "how to perform a task today without at the same time teaching him, by a training in fundamental principles, how to think out a new and better method if a new adjustment shall be needed tomorrow" (Storr 1966, 137). When Melvil Dewey opened the world's first library school at Columbia College, New York City, on January 5, 1887, his sights were set on "today" and its needs. His 20 students (taught by himself and six part-time instructors) had lectures and practice work dealing with the daily life of a library. As the program was revised and moved to the State Library in Albany, it became more formal, organized into a clear

curriculum and timetable. In 1901–1902 the subjects covered were cataloging, classification, bibliography, reference work, selection of books, accession, bookbinding, shelf work, loan department work, buildings,
"founding and government of libraries," supervision, history of libraries
and printing, and indexing (White 1961, 95). There was also instruction in
"library handwriting," but this gave way to typing in 1903.

The Albany school was a vivid success, drawing students from around the
country and overseas. Many registrants had college degrees; in 1902 the
school began to require a degree for admission. As other schools were established, they followed the "practical curriculum" pioneered in Albany.
Apprentice training was still viable, centered in public libraries. A survey in
1901 found that 61 percent of public libraries had such programs, meant
to develop staff for their own institutions.

Murmurs of discontent about the library schools were heard. As early as
1890, the librarian of Princeton University, Ernest Cushing Richardson,
noted that the Albany school was "teaching method without science, praxis
before principle" (White 1961, 109). Praxis flourished as more subjects were
added to the school curricula in order to reflect new specialties in library
work. "The additions included courses on library extension, county libraries, small libraries, large libraries, branch and department administration,
business methods, bibliographical cataloging, etc." (White 1961, 184). The
need was recognized, in the 1920s, for a grounding in professional principles
that would encompass such tight specialties. In the distinction noted above,
the schools were still training rather than educating.

The 10 schools of 1915 formed themselves into the Association of American Library Schools. In 1983 the name was changed to Association for
Library and Information Science Education (ALISE). Individual membership
is open to all interested persons, but institutional membership is limited to
ALA accredited programs. *Journal of Education for Library and Information Science* is published by ALISE.

On March 28, 1919, Charles C. Williamson was invited by the trustees of
the Carnegie Corporation to undertake a study of "training for library service." Williamson, who headed the Economics and Sociology Division at
the New York Public Library, visited and examined all the library schools
in the United States and issued a landmark report in 1923 (Williamson
1923). A listing of the schools, arranged by date of establishment, may be
useful toward an understanding of the American scene at the time:

- New York State Library School, Albany, NY. Founded 1887.
- Pratt Institute School of Library Science, Brooklyn, NY.
  Founded 1895.
- University of Illinois Library School, Urbana. Founded 1893 as
  the Armour Institute of Technology Library School.
- Carnegie Library School, Pittsburgh, PA. Founded 1900;
  organized as the Carnegie Library School in 1916.

- Simmons College School of Library Science, Boston, MA. Founded 1902.
- Library School of Western Reserve University, Cleveland, OH. Founded 1904.
- Library School, Carnegie Library of Atlanta, GA. Founded 1905 as the Southern Library School; renamed 1907.
- Library School of the University of Wisconsin, Madison. Founded 1906.
- Syracuse University Library School, Syracuse, NY. Founded 1908.
- Library School of the New York Public Library, New York, NY. Founded 1911.
- Library School, University of Washington, Seattle, WA. Founded 1917.
- Riverside Library Service School, Riverside, CA. Founded 1913.
- The Library School of the Los Angeles Public Library, Los Angeles, CA. Founded 1914.
- The St. Louis Library School, St. Louis, MO. Founded 1917.
- University of California, Courses in Library Science, Berkeley, CA. Founded in 1919.

Williamson found much disparity of purposes and methods among the programs. He recommended that they should teach only professional work, not clerical routines. He suggested that all library schools be located in universities, where they might be ranked with other professional schools. He asked for a course of study lasting two years. As guarantors of quality, he proposed national certification for librarians and a body that would accredit library schools.

The American Library Association (ALA), which had been a rather passive observer of the library training–education situation, was energized by Williamson to create a Board of Education for Librarianship (BEL) in 1924. In 1956, BEL was replaced by the Committee on Accreditation (COA) and the ALA Library Education Division. These units worked to develop standards by which library school quality could be measured and also did the measuring by direct inspection of the programs. Standards were at first quantitative, but they became more qualitative in later revisions. The 1951 standards called for schools to offer a fifth-year degree. In 1972 that credential was specified as a master's degree.

An important move toward establishment of library science as a learned profession took place in 1926 with the creation of the Graduate Library School (GLS) at the University of Chicago. A $1 million endowment by the Carnegie Corporation made it possible. With the opening of this school in 1928, the vision that had been voiced 27 years earlier for a business school (see above) came to life in a new field, for GLS did not resemble the practical training programs Williamson had found elsewhere. The emphasis was on discovery and teaching of principles and of research that would connect those principles to the real library world. A PhD was available, the first in librarianship. *The Library Quarterly*, the profession's first research journal, was issued by GLS from 1931. Douglas Waples, a GLS professor, listed the school's goals in the first issue:

- Meet the standards of other graduate departments in the university
- Build a research department
- Do not teach library routines but treat them as prerequisites
- Integrate librarianship with related fields
- Maintain a teacher-to-student ratio of one to five
- Publish monographs in the field

At first, students were expected to have a bachelor's degree and a year of library experience (Waples 1931, 23–26). Aspirations were lofty. F. W. Keppel, also writing in the first issue of *Library Quarterly*, wanted GLS to be esteemed on a level with the Harvard Law School and the Johns Hopkins Medical School (Keppel 1931, 23). Cross-disciplinary considerations aside, it may be said that GLS did achieve, within its own sphere, a position of eminence that lasted for a generation. Its graduates became the directors of great libraries and deans of library schools.

But all was not so well in the larger panorama of library education. In 1936 only five of the 26 library schools accredited by the BEL were "type one": set at postgraduate level (Chicago, Columbia, Illinois, Michigan, and California). Writing in 1946, J. Periam Danton of Columbia's library school noted that of the 32 accredited library schools, all but GLS were "still in the *basic* tradition with respect to curricula and approach that they were sixty years ago—this in spite of the facts that they are no longer apprenticeship affairs, their admission requirements are higher, their curricula 'more academic,' their faculties better and their standards improved in every way" (Danton 1946, 5). He noted the current criticisms of the schools: they were not preparing for leadership, their curricula were not "truly professional in content or approach," and faculties lacked adequate academic training. In general, Danton concluded, the schools continued to emphasize routines and paid little attention to principles and to the intellectual aspects of librarianship.

A report to the Carnegie Corporation by Joseph L. Wheeler, also in 1946, touched on many of Danton's concerns. It also brought up the issue of "core curriculum," which has been under discussion ever since. In general, said Wheeler (1946, 59), the essential subjects that ought to be required of all students are book selection, cataloging and classification, reference, administration, and the history of books and libraries (libraries and society).

Lacking such a core, the profession was without agreement on the fundamental point of education: what should the student know and be able to do
at the end of the program?

> The profession . . . needs a much clearer concept than it now has
> as to what librarianship is and what the heads and workers in
> public, college, school, and special libraries may fairly be
> expected to know and to do. Librarianship at the moment is like
> a harp of the winds, responding to every slight breeze. It lacks any
> certainty as to scope and purpose. (Wheeler 1946, 96)

In his closing words, Wheeler (1946, 97) called for a renewal of "books,
reading, study, and thinking" as the foundations of the field and that
"knowledge and love of books make the keystone to librarianship." Very little has been heard in later years about "love of books" as a professional
value. Helen Haines (1935/1950) brought it forward in *Living with Books*,
and Lawrence Clark Powell (1949, 133) proclaimed it ("passion for books
is the greatest single basic asset of the librarian") into the 1960s, then the
light went out.

"Book lover" suggests the humanities, and it was the humanities (primarily literature, classical languages, history, biography, and the arts) that
shaped the learning of most American public librarians into the 1930s. From
that point more librarians began to appear with backgrounds in the social
sciences. The field itself may be said to have begun shifting its center of grav-
ity, as the philosophy of library service to society (groups) took precedence
over the older intention of serving the individual. At GLS it was society first,
a viewpoint promoted by Pierce Butler and other faculty, and the position
was supported by authors of the *Public Library Inquiry* of the early 1950s
(*see* PHILOSOPHY OF PUBLIC LIBRARIANSHIP). Amidst the widespread
public unrest of the 1960s in the United States there flowered a student rights
movement that fostered the wish by university students to choose their own
courses: for a curriculum of electives rather than requirements. Many library
educators listened sympathetically to the student voices. They were also
aware of the changing role of public libraries in American society. It was a
time of outreach services, aimed at bringing nonusers into the library, and
a period of growth in group services.

"The Library in Society" (or a similarly named course) was found in the
library schools of the 1960s and 1970s, and many librarians thought of themselves as agents of social change. ALA began taking an activist role with
respect to political issues (*see* AMERICAN LIBRARY ASSOCIATION).
The impact of this movement on library education was the addition of
more courses, such as those dealing with research methods and outreach
services, and a loosening of the core curriculum concept. The core, up to the
1960s, had been more or less stabilized: library in society, book selection,
cataloging, administration, and bibliography or reference. At ALA, the COA
decided (in its 1972 standards for accreditation) to let the library schools
determine for themselves what their goals were and what programs to devise

in pursuit of those goals. There was only passing reference to the "foundation of general academic and professional education," without any elaboration of a model curriculum or a list of core subjects. Library schools, for all the reasons given above, were in the mood to experiment, and in doing so they eventually demolished the traditional core.

The 1960s were a boom era for library education. Enrollments grew, new PhD programs were offered, and the Higher Education Act of 1965 brought fellowships for students. Library technician programs were developed in community colleges. It was a period of harmony between educators and practitioners. However, the next decade was troubling. Library schools experienced falling enrollments, and many of them had to close. The ALA Office for Library Education closed in 1971, so the professional association took itself out of the philosophical arena. By 1978 it was clear that the curricula of the schools, in the process of giving up their core studies— cataloging was first to go—(Marco 1978) were like "harps in the wind, responding to every breeze." It may be noted that the 1976 "Standards for Library Schools" issued by the International Federation of Library Associations and Institutions (IFLA) called for a curriculum with "a division between fundamental 'core' subjects, and specialized subjects" and proposed that "fundamental subjects should be mastered first by all students in the school, and should serve as prerequisites for study of specialized subjects" (Standards 1976, 219). Indeed, American library educators also supported the core concept but with the sense that changes of emphasis are to be expected and that particular topics do not necessarily have to be shaped into specific courses. What was sought—and what has always been sought by educators—is a means of meeting objectives of student outcome that will connect to tasks to be performed (Marco 1978, 281). One approach that seemed promising in the 1970s was the "integrated core." This idea can be traced to the University of Pittsburgh in 1964, which required an orientation course for new students, covering library literature and history and the current situation; it was team taught (Horrocks 1968). In 1970, Drexel University offered a full term of "fundamentals," also dealing with several subjects (Oller 1974). Other schools provided similar integrations. However, the integration movement subsided within a few years.

A favorable development of the 1970s was the fresh attention to continuing education for librarians in the field. This focus was emphasized in a study by the National Commission on Libraries and Information Science (1973). ALA displayed growing interest in this area, culminating in the 1984 incorporation of the Continuing Library Education Network and Exchange (CLENE) as a Round Table. CLENE had been created in 1975 at the Catholic University of America. "Guidelines for Quality in Continuing Education for Information, Library, and Media Personnel" were adopted by ALA Council in 1988. National programs of continuing education, through one-day presentations and short courses, were offered in the early 1980s by private organizations (e.g., Library Development Consultants International) and library associations (e.g., Special Libraries Association). Library schools were active in providing such opportunities locally.

Another valuable enhancement of library education in this country was internationalization. Exchanges of students and faculty, and full-time engagement of Europeans as professors in American schools were notably frequent in the 1970s. And American educators participated in the international library school programs at the College of Librarianship Wales (1973) and the summer schools of the International Federation for Documentation. (The idea, often discussed in the 1970s, of a permanent, year-round international library school did not find fruition.) What comes from these mixtures of students and teachers from various nations is an arena representing a wide and varied library experience from which principles of practice may be extracted.

As the computer came into the library world, with "information" and "information science" tagging along, professional education was seriously distressed (*see* INFORMATION SCIENCE). The computer entered the curriculum quietly in the 1960s, with a course or two on "library automation" or "data processing." Then "information retrieval" appeared; soon computer-related courses were prominent, and traditional studies were pushed aside. In the 1970s many of the schools changed their names to include an "information" component; for example, the University of Maryland program became the College of Library and Information Services, the University of Pittsburgh program became the Graduate School of Library and Information Sciences, and the Syracuse University program became the School of Information Studies (from the 1977 COA list of accredited programs). It seemed that the profession itself had once again recast its pediment: from humanities to social science, now to computer science. (By 1985, 42 of the 61 accredited schools had "information" in their names.)

As enrollments continued to drop in the 1980s, COA came under criticism for failing to control the number of library schools. In a poor job market, many graduates found no employment. By liberal application of the liberal 1972 Standards for Accreditation, COA did not do what some thought it ought to do: disaccredit the weaker programs, thus reducing the number of graduates. It was found that COA membership was dominated by library school deans and faculty; in effect, the regulatory body had been captured by the schools it was to regulate (Eshelman 1983). There were 56 U.S. accredited schools in 1985 and seven in Canada; 21 U.S. schools and two Canadian schools offered the doctor's degree. A debate among educators turned on the idea of extending the master's program to two years, but that movement faded.

Recent Issues

In the 1990s library schools continued to emphasize information technology and did not revive the traditional core subjects. A 1994 article announced "the demise of the core curriculum" (Marco 1994). Students learned to search the cumbersome online databases (like DIALOG) that preceded Google. Graduates were finding employment. But the gap between what they were learning and what employers wanted them to know seemed to be widening. A study published in 1991 reported on the qualifications cited in job advertisements. Employers, it was found, were seeking librarians with the ability to carry out book selection, reference, and cataloging and with knowledge of computer applications. The study also showed that the required courses in 10 leading library schools did not cover those topics, except for "resources," which could include reference (Schlessinger et al. 1991, 19). An examination of programs in 47 library schools, done a few years later, supported those findings, and gave some egregious examples of core neglect. The University of North Carolina did not require cataloging, reference, selection, or management, and the University of California, Berkeley, did not require reference, selection, management, or research methods. Nineteen schools did not require management and so on (Marco 1994, 186). As the new century began, it could be said that "library educators are separated from practitioners by a gulf so wide that it seems each side is speaking a different language" and that "courses essential to the education of librarians who wish to work in libraries (reference work, cataloging, etc.) are now elective or shallowly introductory or both" (Gorman 2005, 125). A confusing array of degrees is offered for supposed careers like "information architect" and "information consultant." However, "much of the content of the new programs involves essentially a repackaging of the traditional curriculum of librarianship" (Leckie and Buschman 2009, 172).

The practitioner gulf has been further examined by recent studies of job ads. One review of ads for cataloging workers showed that employers were still looking for persons with the familiar skills: "The results provide an impetus for LIS programs to continue to teach the traditional cataloging tools as well as new emerging technology tools" (Lussky 2008, 128).

Yet the core concept has survived, in fresh garb. A proposal made by one writer in 2007 suggested a "new blended LIS core course stressing information, communication and technology infusion, delineating cross-disciplinary concepts that every LIS graduate should be required to study" (Miller 2007, abstract). Some schools have already moved in that direction. For example, the Information School at Drexel University requires six courses: Foundations of Information Systems, Information Resources and Services I and II, Action Research, Professional and Social Aspects of Information Services, and Managing Information Organizations. The University of Tennessee requires Information Environment, Information Representation and Organization, and Information Access and Retrieval. Many of these offerings appear to be old wine in new bottles, but others, like Information Environment, present novel approaches to the core. As for the names of the schools, 54 of 57 accredited programs now have "information" in their titles. A recent decision of Rutgers University changed the name of its library school from School of Communication, Information, and Library Studies to

School of Communication and Information. The deletion of "library" brought protests from the New Jersey Library Association and others (*Library Journal*, May 1, 2009, 12).

Attention returned to COA accreditation, described as "a farce" by one ALA president (Gorman 2000, 68). In March 2007, the ALA Executive Board established a Task Force on Library Education. The task force presented a list of "core competencies of librarianship" to the council "as an important component of the revision of the association's accreditation standards" in January 2009 (ALA 2009). The list defined "the basic knowledge to be possessed by all persons graduating from an ALA-accredited master's program in library and information studies." Its headings evoke the traditional core:

1. Foundations of the profession

2. Information resources

3. Organization of recorded knowledge and information

4. Technological knowledge and skills

5. Reference and user services

6. Research

7. Continuing education and lifelong learning

8. Administration and management

Each heading is elaborated by a number of specific topics; the whole document forms a clear platform for a library school program: course titles and content. Having gained council approval, the task force recommendations were passed on to COA. Although the library schools will need time to respond to these specific competence goals, they have been taking similar statements into account: "Content analysis of program presentation documents submitted to the ALA Committee on Accreditation and a survey of U.S. and Canadian LIS schools reveal that such statements are used in curriculum development, although specific use is not always documented in detail" (Lester and Van Vleet 2008, abstract).

A recent innovation is online study. The ability to take classes from home has made it possible for many persons to pursue degrees, persons who would otherwise be unable to do so because of employment or other anchoring responsibilities. Online programs are now widely available in the accredited schools (COA has found them acceptable).

An expansion of the LIS sphere of action has occurred with a renewed interest in undergraduate education. Bachelor's degrees in information topics are offered, as "preparation to work in all kinds of organizations"; they do not replace the master's degree in library and information science (LIS), which is "for professional librarians" (McInerney et al. 2002, 40). By joining other university departments that teach undergraduates as well as graduate students, the schools bring "LIS into the mainstream and thus advances library schools as full partners in the university's educational mission" (McInerney 2002, 4). And of course the increase in student full-time equivalency will mean better income for schools in universities where budgets are enrollment driven.

Despite the ongoing critiques of what they are doing and not doing, the above account of recent activities demonstrates that the library schools are ever thinking about their mission and of novel ways to accomplish it.

References

American Library Association. 2009. *Core Competencies of Librarianship*. Chicago: American Library Association. http://www.ala.org/ala/aboutala/governance/council/councildocuments/2009mw/councildoc/us/10.doc. Accessed February 2010.

Danton, J. Periam. 1946. *Education for Librarianship: Criticisms, Dilemmas, and Proposals*. New York: School of Library Service, Columbia University.

Eshelman, William R. 1983. The erosion of library education. *Library Journal* 108, no. 13 (July): 1309–12. Reprinted in *Library Lit. 14: The Best of 1983*, ed. Bill Katz. Metuchen, NJ: Scarecrow Press, 1984.

Gorman, Michael. 2000. *Our Enduring Values: Librarianship in the 21st Century*. Chicago: American Library Association.

Gorman, Michael. 2005. *Our Own Selves: More Meditations for Librarians*. Chicago: American Library Association.

Haines, Helen H. 1950. *Living with Books: The Art of Book Selection*. 2nd ed. New York: Columbia University Press. (1st ed. 1935).

Horrocks, Norman. 1968. Pitt's changed approach. *Journal of Education for Librarianship* 9, no. 1 (Summer): 13–17.

Keppel, F. W. 1931. The Carnegie Corporation and the Graduate Library School: An historical outline. *Library Quarterly* 1, no. 1 (January): 22–26.

Leckie, Gloria J., and John E. Buschman, eds. 2009. *Information Technology in Librarianship*. Westport, CT: Libraries Unlimited.

Lester, June, and Connie Van Fleet. 2008. Use of professional competencies and standards documents for curricular planning in schools of library and information studies education. *Journal of Education for Library and Information Science* 49, no. 1 (Winter): 43–70.

Lussky, Joan. 2008. Employer demand for cataloger and cataloger-like librarians and implications for library and information science. *Journal of Education for Library and Information Science* 49, no. 2 (Spring): 116–28.

Marco, Guy A. 1978. Recent adventures of the American core curriculum. *Unesco Bulletin for Libraries* 32, no. 4 (July/August): 279–83.

Marco, Guy A. 1994. The demise of the American core curriculum. *Libri* 44, no. 3 (September): 175–89.

McInerney, Claire, et al. 2002. Broadening our reach: LIS education for undergraduates. *American Libraries* 33, no. 2 (February): 40–43.

Miller, Michael J. 2007. Information communication technology infusion in 21st century librarianship: A proposal for a blended core course. *Journal of Education for Library and Information Science* 48, no. 3 (Summer): 202–17.

Oller, A. Kathryn. 1974. Education for librarianship: A new approach to the core. *Drexel Library Quarterly* 10, no. 3 (July). Entire issue.

Poole, William F. 1883. Remarks at American Library Association Conference, 1883. *Library Journal* 8 (September/October): 288–89.

Powell, Lawrence Clark. 1949. Education for academic librarianship. In *Education for Librarianship*, ed. Bernard Berelson, 133–46. Chicago: American Library Association.

Schlessinger, Bernard S., et al. 1991. Information science/library science education programs in the 1990s: A not-so-modest proposal. *Library Administration and Management 5*, no. 1 (Winter): 16–19.

Standards. 1976. Standards for library schools. *IFLA Journal 2*, no. 4: 209–24.

Storr, Richard J. 1966. *Harper's University: The Beginnings*. Chicago: University of Chicago Press.

U.S. National Commission on Libraries and Information Science. 1973. *Continuing Library and Information Science Education*. Washington, DC: National Commission on Libraries and Information Science.

Waples, Douglas. 1931. The Graduate Library School at Chicago. *Library Quarterly 1*, no. 1 (January): 26–36.

Wheeler, Joseph L. 1946. *Progress and Problems in Education for Librarianship*. New York: Carnegie Corporation of New York.

White, Carl M. 1961. *The Origins of the American Library School*. New York: Scarecrow Press.

Williamson, Charles C. 1923. *Training for Library Service: A Report Prepared for the Carnegie Corporation of New York*. New York: Carnegie Corporation of New York.

EDWARDS, MARGARET A., 1902–1988   Librarian. Born near Childress, TX, October 23, 1902. She attended Trinity University (BA 1937) and Columbia University (MA in Latin, 1928, and BSLS, 1937). As a librarian at Enoch Pratt Free Library (Baltimore), she organized the young adult department. Her view was the young readers should be encouraged to read adult books rather than books written for their age levels. She taught in several library schools and served on the American Library Association (ALA) Council. Her book *Fair Garden and the Swarm of Beasts*, 1969, is regarded as a classic of young adult services; ALA reissued it in 1994. She was editor of *Something about the Author* (1989). *DALB*, 2nd supplement.

EL PASO PUBLIC LIBRARY, TX   Civic Center Plaza, El Paso, TX 79901. Populating served: 613,190. Circulation: 1,426,115. Holdings: 974,235. 11 branches, 1 bookmobile. According to a 1930 survey, El Paso had the only racially integrated public library in the South (Marshall 1976, 68).

Reference

Marshall, A. P. 1976. Service to Afro-Americans. In *A Century of Service: Librarianship in the United States and Canada*, ed. Sidney L. Jackson et al., 62–78. Chicago: American Library Association.

ELA AREA PUBLIC LIBRARY DISTRICT, LAKE ZURICH, IL   275 Mohawk Trail, Lake Zurich, IL 60047. Population served: 32,419. Circulation: 747,376. Holdings: 175,986. LJ November 15, 2009: 4-star library.

ELBRIDGE FREE LIBRARY, NY　241 Main St., Elbridge, NY 13060. Population served: 1,103. Circulation: 32,836. Holdings: 24,191. LJ February 15, 2009; November 15, 2009; and October 1, 2010: 5-star library.

ELDREDGE PUBLIC LIBRARY, CHATHAM, MA　564 Main St., Chatham, MA 02633. Population served: 6,517. Circulation: 102,322. Holdings: 46,776. LJ February 15, 2009; November 15, 2009; and October 1, 2010: 4-star library.

ELEANOR DAGGETT MEMORIAL PUBLIC LIBRARY, CHAMA, NM　299 W. Fourth St., Chama, NM 87520. Population served: 1,167. Circulation: 36,435. Holdings: 9,206. LJ February 15, 2009, and November 15, 2009: 5-star library; October 1, 2010: 3-star library.

ELECTRONIC BOOKS. *See* DIGITAL MEDIA.

ELECTRONIC JOURNALS. *See* DIGITAL MEDIA.

ELECTRONIC NEWSPAPERS. *See* DIGITAL MEDIA.

ELGIN, IL. *See* GAIL BORDEN PUBLIC LIBRARY DISTRICT, ELGIN, IL.

ELK GROVE VILLAGE PUBLIC LIBRARY, IL　1001 Wellington Ave., Elk Grove Village, IL 60007. Founded 1959. Population served: 35,000. Circulation: 602,364. Holdings: 385,783 (communication from the library). HAPLR 2010.

ELKHART, KS. *See* MORTON COUNTY LIBRARY, ELKHART, KS.

ELLINWOOD SCHOOL-COMMUNITY LIBRARY, ELLINWOOD, KS　210 N. Schiller Ave., Ellinwood, KS 67526. Population served: 2,074. Circulation: 23,335. Holdings: 29,684. LJ February 15, 2009: 3-star library; November 15, 2009: 4-star library; October 1, 2010: 3-star library.

ELMENDORF, THERESA WEST, 1855–1932　Librarian. Born in Pardeeville, WI, on November 1, 1855. Her family moved o Milwaukee, and she attended school there. In 1877 she worked as a library assistant in the Young Men's Association of Milwaukee, which became the Milwaukee Public Library a year later. In 1880 she was deputy librarian and head librarian in 1892. She married Henry L. Elmendorf in 1896 and went with him to Buffalo, NY, where he directed the new public library and she acted as an unofficial partner. They offered open shelves and a cooperative program with schools. In 1903 she was elected president of the New York Library Association. On the death of her husband in 1906, she was appointed vice librarian of the library, a title she retained for 20 years. In her view, public libraries existed "for the preservation and perfecting of democratic society" (Williams 1988, 31). Elmendorf was a prolific author of reading lists and articles in the library press and was an editor of the American Library Association (ALA) *Catalogue of Books for Small Libraries* (1904). Active in ALA, she was the first woman elected president (1911). She retired in 1926 and died in Buffalo on September 4, 1932. LJ Hall of Fame; *DALB*.

Reference

Williams, Patrick. 1988. *The American Public Library and the Problem of Purpose. New York: Greenwood Press.*

ELMHURST PUBLIC LIBRARY, IL   125 S. Prospect, Elmhurst, IL 60126. Founded 1916. Population served: 42,762. Circulation: 1,171,046. Holdings: 303,774. LJ October 1, 2010: 3-star library. HAPLR 2009, 2010.

ELY PUBLIC LIBRARY, MN   30 S. First Ave., Ely, MN 55731. Population served: 3,724. Circulation: 61,500. Holdings: 33,070. LJ February 15, 2009; November 15, 2009; and October 1, 2010: 3-star library.

ENNIS, MT. *See* MADISON VALLEY PUBLIC LIBRARY, ENNIS, MT.

ENOCH PRATT FREE LIBRARY, BALTIMORE, MD   400 Cathedral, Baltimore, MD 21201. Founded 1884. Population served 633,100. Circulation: 1,367,939. Holdings: 3,120,493. 20 branches. A young adult department was organized by Margaret Edwards, 1932. The new building was completed in 1933, designed by Edward Tilton; annex opened 2003. Directors: Lewis Henry Steiner, 1884–1892; Bernard C. Steiner, 1892–1926; Joseph L. Wheeler, 1926–1944; Emerson Greenaway, 1945–1951; Amy Winslow, 1951–1957; Arthur H. Parsons Jr., 1957–1959; Robert S. Ake (acting), 1959–1960; Edwin Castagna, 1960–1974; Ernest Siegel, 1974–1981; Anna Curry, 1981–1993; and Carla Hayden, 1993–.

EQUIPMENT. *See* FIXTURES, FURNISHINGS, AND EQUIPMENT.

ERIE CITY PUBLIC LIBRARY, KS   204 S. Butler, Erie City, KS 66733. Founded 1932. Population served: 1,173. Circulation: 12,852. Holdings: 14,676. LJ November 15, 2009, and October 1, 2010: 3-star library.

ESPAÑOLA, NM. *See* SANTA CLARA PUEBLO COMMUNITY LIBRARY, ESPAÑOLA, NM.

ESSEX, IA. *See* LIED PUBLIC LIBRARY, ESSEX, IA.

ETHICS FOR LIBRARIANS

> Was jeder Tag will, sollst du fragen; Was jeder Tag will, wird er sagen [Ask each day what it wants; It will tell you what it wants]—Goethe (1902)

Terminology

Ethics (sometimes "ethic") has several meanings; in *Merriam*: "(1) the discipline dealing with what is good and bad and with moral duty and obligation; (2) a set of moral principles: a theory or system of moral values; (3) the principles of conduct governing an individual or a group (professional ethics)." *American Heritage* offers, "(1) a set of principles of right conduct; a theory or system of moral values; (2) the study of the general nature of morals and of specific moral choices; moral philosophy; (3) the rules or standards governing the conduct of a person or the members of a profession." A more succinct statement appears in the *Cambridge Dictionary of Philosophy* (Cambridge 1999, 284): "The philosophical study of morality." In *Cambridge*, professional ethics is viewed as "applied ethics" (34). From this may be distilled the following: Ethics for librarians, as a specimen of professional ethics, is a statement of the moral principles that apply to the conduct of librarians. The first challenge faced by the framer of such a statement is rooted in the identification of those moral principles and in the connection of them to appropriate examples of conduct. Applied ethics requires a top-down approach, from ethical theory (principles) to practical issues.

Another challenge involved in writing a statement of ethics for librarians is the need to separate three related levels of attention: the individual librarian, the library or library system, and the total library enterprise. The assumption is that the three levels do not collapse into one another (Goodpaster 1992, 112).

While most statements of professional ethics are "normative" (expressing how matters ought to be), they may be "descriptive" (expressing how things are). A descriptive statement may be interpreted in normative terms or not. This point is taken up below with respect to the American Library Association's (ALA's) 1995 Code.

Conduct is defined by acts, or actions. *Merriam*: "act—the doing of a thing: deed; something done voluntarily." The voluntary aspect is significant in ethical appraisals since only voluntary actions by rational agents are subject to praise or blame (Aristotle 1941, section 1110b). Acts may be appraised on the basis of their intentions or their consequences or both.

What are desirable consequences of acts? The personal benefit of the agent may be one, as may be the benefit to select others of the agent (see agent-centered morality below). In contrast, there is the approach of utilitarianism: "a theory that the aim of action should be the largest possible balance of pleasure over pain or the greatest happiness of the greatest number" (*Merriam*).

Theoretical Considerations

If applied ethics is drawn from a higher body of principles of conduct, what are those principles? A difficult question: indeed, one that philosophers since Aristotle have answered in hundreds of ways. Goethe's response, given in the quote above, is that those principles are revealed to us as we live our lives. The circumstances of each day announce its demands on us and shape our conduct. This might be termed "commonsense morality." No statement of principles is needed, except those possessed by any rational person, whose feelings of right and wrong give adequate moral guidance. Morality is taken as similar to aesthetics, both being fields of interest without objective truths, dependent in their appraisals only on "the appropriateness of some object to one's own sensibility or intellectual powers" (Adams 1992, 71). In other words, the idea of codifying ethics is overdone. One librarian wrote, "I for one resent the implication that my behavior as a professional person of any kind must be codified for me. If I do not recognize my responsibilities to the structure of society by the time I am ready to face the world professionally, no formal code will ever provide this recognition" (Patricia Paylore 1961, quoted in Preer 2008, 15). This position does not deny the existence of objective truths in ethics; it is saying, rather, that ethical truths are obvious to the reasonable person and do not require spelling out.

Others have preferred a more formal framework for ethics. Two important frameworks are agent-centered morality and consequentialism. Agent-centered (or agent-relative) morality might express a person's duties and obligation with a set of rules like these:

- I can do whatever I like unless it restricts others from pursuing their universal needs (food, shelter, freedom of expression, etc.)

- I do not need to support others in pursuing those universal needs.

- I can do whatever I like even if it restricts others in pursuing preferences (nonuniversal needs).

- I do not need to support others in pursuing their preferences.

- I may exhibit special concern for the needs of certain persons or groups and support their pursuit of universal needs and some of their preferences.

- I treat others with respect for their needs even though I am not obliged to support them.

- I am satisfied if others follow these rules with regard to myself.

These rules are an expansion of the description of agent-centered morality by Thomas Nagel (1986, 165). Nagel observed further that "claims of others for me to further their projects (ends) are limited to impersonal projects (general good), not their personal projects" (173). Personal projects = preferences; general good = universal needs. A table of rules like these refers to the general conduct of life. Special situations may call for elaborations of the rules, and that is the root of professional ethics (see next section).

Consequentialism is the moral theory that evaluates acts solely on their consequences. It may be identified with utilitarianism, which advocates the greatest good for the greatest number (Mill [1863] 1952, chap. 2). Complexities surround this perspective: for example, how is the greatest good to be defined, and measured?

The significance of a specific theory as the foundation for a statement of applied ethics lies in the contrasting viewpoints of different theories, for to draw on theories with different outlooks would lead to a confused application. The conflict between agent-centered morality and consequentialism (especially utilitarianism) stems from the former's focus on the individual agent with her personal interests and the latter's focus on benefit to everyone. Agent-centered morality assigns limited duties or obligations to the agent (see the rules above); utilitarianism assigns the duty of promoting an overall good (vague as that may be).

It is only in statements of duty or obligation that ethical conflicts arise. The agent must choose, in determining any given act, whether to observe applicable obligation(s) (and, if so, to what degree) or to privilege his personal benefits. The issue may be simplified into a choice between duty and desire. In cases where the agent must choose between duties, since both cannot be met and neither exhibits a clear dominance, the result is a "moral dilemma." Such a situation (exemplified in "Sophie's choice") is perhaps insoluble, but it does not seem to be an ethical problem. Likewise, the need to choose, in a given situation, between acts that serve personal interest is a problem but not an ethical one; the approach to its solution lies more in the area of cost–benefit analysis. On the other hand, there may be a conflict when two duties are involved. For example, which takes precedence in a given situation: the duty to tell the truth (if there is such) or the duty to avoid harm to others (by telling a lie that prevents such harm)?

Another aspect of the act is its motivation. This is a layered issue that resists exploration in a brief survey. In the agent-centered orientation, all motivations may be considered "good" since the agent acts in her own interest (Bentham [1789] 1939, 816); in consequentialist orientations, motives are not ethically relevant since ethical judgments of actions are determined entirely by their consequences. A further complication appears when motives themselves are multiple in character. A classic library example of this difficulty emerged in the reactions to Andrew Carnegie's benevolence in the early twentieth century; Carnegie was criticized in some quarters for using his gifts as a means of self-aggrandizement or perhaps as atonements for the (assumed) fact that he had gained his wealth through mistreatment of workers. Carnegie's mental processes are not available for inspection, but the issue is troubling since a personal interest (desire) may obviously be satisfied by a "good" action; indeed, the performance of such good actions may constitute the desire itself.

Professional Ethics

The *Merriam* definition above lays the markers for this aspect of ethics: "the principles of conduct governing an individual or a group (professional ethics)." However, it is not universally accepted that professional ethics requires independent consideration apart from more general ethics. "While professions require knowledge and skills in high degree, there is not necessarily an ethical mode of reasoning in them that is different from ordinary morality" (Welch 1993, 10). It may be argued that all the situations encompassed in professional codes could as well be analyzed from the perspective of "ordinary ethics." If a code is written, it ought to be a specimen reflecting a higher order, one example of a general moral philosophy: it is an application of an ethical theory.

As an example, the rules for agent-centered morality listed above set up the conditions for a professional ethic. Taking the "I" in the rules to be "a librarian" and the "others" as the community served would give, in the second rule, a reading that relieves a librarian from supporting universal needs of people generally, including freedom of expression. However, the fifth rule takes precedence, for a librarian does exhibit special concern for certain groups (the community served) in pursuit of their universal needs and some of their preferences. It is this rule that energizes all professional ethics. Medical ethics gives special concern to a doctor's patients; it does not require a doctor to support, say, disease prevention in the Third World.

Given the propensity of professions to produce ethical codes, it may be useful to ponder what they tend to include. There seem to be four categories of guidance that appear in many professional codes: general morality, ideals, competence, and specific conflicts.

- An example of general morality would be an instruction to treat colleagues and patrons with respect and fairness. A statement of this nature (see ALA Code 1995, statement 5, below) may be regarded as redundant to ordinary ethics since it only tells librarians to behave the way everyone should behave. This issue of redundancy is one that is considered in the critique of the ALA codes below.

- Ideals of the profession are often voiced in ethics codes. Such pronouncements may serve a purpose in reminding members of the profession of the nature of their calling. They do not seem to have ethical application, unless as exhortations toward right conduct in vivifying those ideals. (ALA Code statement 1 is an example.)

- Statements dealing with competence—doing the job well—find a place in many professional codes. As in the case with ideals, they may serve to inspire members toward excellence in performing their tasks. It is not clear how they apply to ethical questions.

- Special conflicts may exist in any profession between personal interests and institutional aims. The issue revolves around a pair of assumptions. Fundamentally there is the acceptance that professionals, like any other persons, are entitled to act as they think best in service of their own interests (agent centered) or what they see to be the general good (utilitarianism). A profession does not have obedience rules like an army. The second assumption is that by joining an institution or an association, the individual tacitly accepts its essential way of doing things and that the institution trusts her to behave accordingly. These understandings stem from a larger category called "role obligations." Some role obligations grow out of societal needs (parents must take care of their children). Other role obligations are contractual, entered into voluntarily by rational agents as they join an enterprise (Hardimon 1994). A physician who must perform abortions contrary to his conscience is a familiar example of the kind of conflict arising from contractual obligations. Within the American medical profession and its service institutions (hospitals, clinics) the decision has been made that abortions will be performed. The doctor's choice is not whether to comply or not, but whether to remain in the profession or not—more precisely, whether to remain in that professional area where abortions are called for (the physician may electo specialize in dermatology or men's diseases). In other words the conscience issue should be settled at an earlier stage than the moment of decision about how to act in a given case.

• For a library example, no person who believes that a librarian should expunge all sexually oriented materials from a public library can rationally enter public library service, where the decision has been made to include such materials unless they are legally obscene. Such a person could still be a librarian, specializing in academic work, rare books, or other areas not likely to require actions on sexually oriented materials.

By including all the four categories described, the framer of a professional code of ethics would be taking a broad view of the task. By limiting attention in the code to special conflicts, the framer would be taking a narrow view. (Both are explicated in Marco 1996.) Broad views predominate, as exemplified in the ALA codes.

The ALA Codes of Ethics

As indicated above, professional ethics is a specimen of applied ethics, which is drawn from an ethical theory. It might be expected that persons formulating codes of professional ethics would have expert guidance by philosophers since ethical theory is not within the scope of a layperson. In the case of the ALA statements of ethics, it seems that such expert guidance was not involved; certainly none was acknowledged in the statements themselves and none in the documentation of the meetings that led to the code (Karen Muller, ALA librarian, personal communication, June 10, 2010). The statements do not describe any kind of moral theory as the foundation of the codes.

Limiting the present discussion to the ALA codes of 1981 and 1995, several problematic points stand out. A comparison of the codes shows first of all a change of perspective from normative to descriptive. In 1981 there were six statements beginning "librarians must . . . " and then identifying specific acts. In 1995 there were eight statements beginning "we . . . " followed by a verb that designated specific acts. While "librarians must" in 1981 included (presumably) all persons identifiable as librarians, the "we" in 1995 refers only to "members of the American Library Association." The newer statement is thus restrictive in application: it offers ethics of an organization rather than of a profession or professional enterprise. As stated in the beginning of this entry, this matter of "levels of attention" is one that calls for clarity in any statement.

By changing the tone of the code from normative to descriptive, the framers in 1995 created a statement of goals (or "values" as they say). The reader needs to recast the statement into normative form to instantiate a code of ethical behavior. It is not clear what was gained by this alteration of perspective in 1995.

Each of the eight statements in the 1995 code presents some issues:

1. We provide the highest level of service to all library users through appropriate and usefully organized resources; equitable service policies; equitable access; and accurate, unbiased, and courteous responses to all requests.

    Comment: As a descriptive account of present library service the statement is necessarily limited. For example, evidence is clear that accuracy in responses to information requests has been severely lacking in practice (*see* REFERENCE AND INFORMATION SERVICES). In any case, the goal of doing good work is not connected to ethical matters since there is no conflict in pursuing it (except the potential conflict that arises in any work situation: the wish to do something else instead of the task). The statement may serve a purpose in reminding librarians about the need for competence in their work.

2. We uphold the principles of intellectual freedom and resist all efforts to censor library resources.

    Comment: The situation in which a librarian decides to resist censorship may be an ethical case if such resistance runs counter to personal interests. Following an agent-centered principle, one could say that resistance to any outside pressures is contrary to autonomy: "I do not need to support others in pursuing those universal needs." Following consequentialist principles, however, one might question whether resistance will result in a better or worse overall situation. Another consideration would be whether the "effort to censor" is an official act of an authorized unit of government (*see* INTELLECTUAL FREEDOM) or an unofficial challenge from a community member. To resist the authorized unit may be illegal; to resist the community member brings up the question of public library mission: how far to go in telling the mission giver that the library will not observe its wishes? Is a recalcitrant library more beneficial to the community than a complaisant one?

3. We protect each library user's right to privacy and confidentiality with respect to information sought or received and resources consulted, borrowed, acquired or transmitted.

   Comment: There are many questions about right to privacy (*see* PRIVACY AND CONFIDENTIALITY). In general the code offers a useful intention, but when legal intrusions on privacy are involved, the library must comply with authority. Deciding whether to break the law is a moral consideration applicable to all rational persons; it is not necessary to include it in a professional code.

4. We respect intellectual property rights and advocate balance between the interests of information users and rights holders.

   Comment: These rights are established in copyright law, and librarians have the duty to observe them. The problem of understanding the law is formidable but not ethical (*see* COPYRIGHT).

5. We treat co-workers and other colleagues with respect, fairness, and good faith, and advocate condition of employment that safeguard the rights and welfare of all employees of our institutions.

   Comment: This statement would apply to interpersonal relations generally in the agent-centered approach but would not hold up in the consequentialist approach. In either case, it is a guide of wide application in all work situations, not a special library issue.

6. We do not advance private interests at the expense of library users, colleagues, or our employing institutions.

   Comment: This imprecation stems from utilitarianism, and seems sound enough in the library environment. The difficulty mentioned above, that of sorting out private interests with good general outcomes from private interests without such outcomes, remains in the choice situation and is not addressed.

7. We distinguish between our personal convictions and professional duties and do not allow our personal beliefs to interfere with fair representation of the aims of our institutions or the provision of access to their information resources.

   Comment: Here is a matter of separating levels of attention, as mentioned above. To distinguish between personal interests and professional duties is important, but the decision as to which should dominate a given choice situation is complex. It may be argued that by taking employment in a particular library, the librarian gives tacit agreement to support its aims and policies. But it may be that certain policies are not evident to a new staff member or that policies change in a way that troubles the moral view of the staff member. In extreme cases such gaps between institutional policy and personal belief lead to "whistle-blowing" or other public denunciations by the individual. Such actions would be in accord with agent-centered philosophy and perhaps utilitarian philosophy as well. Less vociferous opposition to library policy may of course occur in the normal course of events through participation in managerial decisions (*see* STAFFING). As for the conflict suggested in the statement between personal convictions and provision of access, it seems to lie in the area of professional competence, probably covered adequately by code statement 1.

8. We strive for excellence in the profession by maintaining and enhancing our own knowledge and skills, by encouraging the professional development of co-workers, and by fostering the aspirations of potential members of the profession.

   Comment: These are fine things to do. But it is hard to see that failing to do them would represent ethical lapses or just what situations would be involved in the decisions to do them or not. However, for the utilitarian any failure to maximize the common good is an ethical failure.

Information Ethics

With the rise of the computer, there have been concerns about novel problems that seem to fall into the area of morality. Information ethics is the name of the field that examines those problems. The range of attention is roughly congruent with that of librarian ethics, turning on such topics as information access and privacy, copyright, and intellectual freedom. The American Society for Information Science and Technology has not promulgated a code of ethics. The Association for Computing Machinery issued a code in 1992, including a number of "moral imperatives" like "avoid harm to others," "be honest and trustworthy," "acquire and maintain professional competence," and "know and respect existing laws pertaining to professional work" (Stanford 2001). There is an International Center for Information Ethics, which publishes *International Review of Information Ethics* (2004–).

References

Adams, E. M. 1992. Autonomy of ethics. *Encyclopedia of Ethics* 1: 69–71. New York: Garland.

American Library Association. 1995. *ALA Code of Ethics*. Chicago: American Library Association, 1995; modified 2008. www.ala.org.

Aristotle. 1941. *Nichomachean Ethics*. Translated by W. D. Ross. In *The Basic Works of Aristotle*, ed. Richard McKeon, 927–1112. New York: Random House.

Bentham, Jeremy. [1789] 1939. *The Principles of Morals and Legislation*. In *The English Philosophers from Bacon to Mill*, ed. Edwin A. Burtt, 791–852. New York: Modern Library.

Cambridge. 1999. *Cambridge Dictionary of Philosophy*. 2nd ed. Cambridge: Cambridge University Press.

Froelich, Thomas J. 1992. Ethical considerations of information professionals. *Annual Review of Information Science and Technology*, 291–324. Medford, NJ: Learned Information.

Goethe, Johann Wolfgang. 1902. Lebensregel. In *Goethes Sämtliche Werke. Jubiläums-Ausgabe*, 2: 168. Stuttgart: J. G. Cotta.

Goodpaster, Kenneth E. 1992. Business ethics. In *Encyclopedia of Ethics* 1: 111–15. New York: Garland.

Hardimon, Michael O. 1994. Role obligation. *Journal of Philosophy* 91, no. 7 (July): 333–63.

Marco, Guy A. 1996. Ethics for librarians: A narrow view. *Journal of Librarianship and Information Science* 28, no. 1 (March): 33–37.

Mill, John Stuart. [1863] 1952. *Utilitarianism*. In *Great Books of the Western World* 43, 445–76. Chicago: Encyclopaedia Britannica.

Nagel, Thomas. 1986. *The View from Nowhere*. New York: Oxford University Press.

Preer, Jean. 2008. *Library Ethics*. Westport, CT: Libraries Unlimited.

Stanford. 2001. *Stanford Encyclopedia of Philosophy*. Stanford, CA: Stanford University Press.

Tavani, Herman T. 2004. *Ethics and Technology: Ethical Issues in an Age of Information and Communication Technology*. New York: Wiley.

Welch, Don. 1993. Just another day at the office: the ordinariness of professional ethics. *Professional Ethics* 2, no. 3–4 (Spring/Summer): 3–14.

EUCLID PUBLIC LIBRARY, OH   631 E. 222nd St., Euclid, OH 44123. Population served: 51,106. Circulation: 1,345,215. Holdings: 279,392. LJ October 1, 2010: 4-star library. HAPLR 2009, 2010.

EUGENE PUBLIC LIBRARY, OR   100 W. 10th Ave., Eugene, OR 97401. Population served: 144,648. Circulation: 2,919,072. Holdings: 414,737. 2 branches. LJ November 15, 2009: 4-star library; October 1, 2010: 3-star library.

EUREKA, CA. *See* HUMBOLDT COUNTY LIBRARY, EUREKA, CA.

EVALUATION

Terminology

Evaluation has to do with determining the value, quality, or benefit of something. In a library context, this can range from evaluating a specific collection, service, or program to evaluation of the library as a whole. Lancaster (1993) emphasized the fundamentally pragmatic role of evaluation in librarianship: "An evaluation is performed not as an intellectual exercise but to gather data *useful* in problem-solving or decision-making activities" (1). Hernon and McClure (1990) provided a more detailed and action-centered definition: "Evaluation is the process of identifying and collecting data about specific services or activities, establish criteria by which their success can be assessed, and determining both the quality of the service or activity and the degree to which the service or activity accomplishes stated goals and objectives" (1).

Evaluation and Research

Evaluation is closely related to research. According to Wallace and Van Fleet (2001), "Systematic evaluation is the nexus between the need to conduct true research into library operations and the need to provide direct evidence of the value of libraries" (xix). The methods and tools of evaluation and research overlap extensively, but the purposes of evaluation and research are quite different. The intent of research is to add to understanding; although research may lead to action, research can be valid and useful if it simply yields information, knowledge, or interpretation that was previously absent. Research is at its best when it yields results that are broad, universal, and generalizable. Evaluation, on the other hand, is practical, purposeful, and focused on application. Evaluation is at its best when it yields results that contribute to confirming that an institution, service, activity, program, process, or set of materials is fulfilling its purpose or results that can lead to improvement. Evaluation results are usually specific, localized, and immediate (*see* RESEARCH).

The term *evaluation research* is sometimes used to describe the application of rigorous scientific research methods and tools to evaluation. Although this is for some purposes a useful concept, the nature of evaluation is not exclusively a function of the methods and tools used in the evaluation process. There are valid and useful approaches to evaluation that do not directly use scientific research methods. Another term that has come into use is *evidence-based librarianship*. "Evidence-based librarianship (EBL) provides a process for integrating the best available scientifically-generated evidence into making important decisions. EBL seeks to combine the use of the best available research evidence with a pragmatic perspective developed from working experiences in librarianship. EBL actively supports increasing the proportion of more rigorous applied research studies so the results can be available for making informed decisions" (Eldredge 2006, 342). This term is very closely parallel to *evaluation research* and is not sufficiently distinct from evaluation as it has been historically presented to constitute a unique endeavor. A third related term, *action research*, has found substantial favor among educators and has seen some use in the school library media context. The processes of action research are generally presented as being something of a fusion of evaluation research and evaluation broadly defined. Callison (2007) pointed out that the concept of action research is frequently described in a false light: "It is presented as a manageable short-cut to discovery of new insights that will dramatically change education, place library media programs at the forefront of curriculum design, and lead to such high degrees of respect that additional funding is certain to follow" (40). The term *action research* does not appear to have gained any traction in the public library literature.

Historical Summary

The history of public library evaluation is characterized by three prominent phases: (1) a development phase during which evaluation does not appear to have been an actively perceived needs, (2) a phase that emphasized development of national standards promulgated by the American Library Association (ALA), and (3) the current era, in which standards developed primarily at the state level are accompanied by localized planning and assessment based on principles and processes promulgated by the ALA.

Evaluation of products and services does not appear to have been a major interest of public librarians—or of librarians in general—until the profession had gained substantial maturity. The emphasis from the dawn of public libraries at the midpoint of the nineteenth century until after World War I was primarily on the funding and construction of library buildings, establishment of mechanisms for governance and sustenance, collection building, and defining various kinds of services. Andrew Carnegie's 36-year effort to provide community support to establish public library buildings did little to encourage evaluation except at the extremely broad level of requiring assurance that collections and services would be funded by local entities.

The ALA did not become a major force in library evaluation until the 1933 publication of the first standards for public libraries. Martin (1972) described the tone of the two-page 1933 standards as a statement that "hopefully called for few essential minima of service" (165). Subsequent revised standards were published by the ALA in 1943, 1956, and 1966. The 1943 standards were "a coming-of-age of public library standards" that "covered the whole range of objectives, government, organization and services, as well as collections, personnel and finance ... Many library administrators used it as a compact planning and administration guide in the postwar period when libraries were attempting to get back on their feet" (Martin, 1972, 165).

Where the 1933 and 1943 standards had attempted to set quantitative standards for community support and library performance, the 1956 standards deliberately veered away from quantitative measures in favor of more effective service based on systematic planning. Martin (1972) described the inclusion of standards in the title of the document, *Library Service: A Guide to Evaluation, with Minimal Standards* (1956), as "almost an afterthought" (166). The 1956 standards were revised in 1966 as "a replica of its predecessor ten years" (168), a move that Martin clearly viewed as a missed opportunity to create a new vision for a rapidly changing future. The 1966 standards both continued the deemphasis on quantification and the emphasis on the growth of library systems, as reflected in the title *Minimum Standards for Public Library Systems*.

Efforts to develop new standards or engage in a more significant revision of the existing standards carried out through the late 1960s and into the 1970s failed to come to fruition. The challenges of keeping standards up to date in a constantly evolving library universe, the need to address local accountability issues, and changes in philosophies and views of evaluation combined to impede the development of new national standards. Blasingame and Lynch (1974) presented an alternative model to national standards based directly on the principles of community-centered planning and assessment and a focus on processes rather than numeric formulas. Their argument was that public libraries and their administrations "cannot use standards but they do need instruments, more sophisticated and sensitive than any currently available, which will enable them to 1) understand the particular community they are serving; 2) choose objectives in the light of that understanding; and 3) measure the degree to which these objectives are being met" (Blasingame and Lynch, 1974, 6).

The principles set forth by Blasingame and Lynch became the drivers for a new era of public library evaluation based largely on local planning and decision making rather than national quantitative standards:

> The initial decision to replace quantitative national standards with a manual instructing librarians in a recommended step-by-step planning process and to develop a series of standardized "output" measures for local use in evaluating services was a significant one. It marked a major change in direction and thinking within the leadership of PLA [Public Library Association]. It led to a national dissemination effort by state associations and library development agencies that continues to the present time. In addition, it sparked considerable controversy in the field, even among those who recognized the inadequacy of national standards. (Pungitore 1989, 74–75)

This change in direction had its first concrete manifestation in the publication of *Performance Measures for Public Libraries* (DeProspo, Altman, and Beasley 1973), which presented the results of the PLA's Measurement and Effectiveness of Public Library Service Study. Although *Performance Measures* did not actively serve as a substitute for standards, it did provide thought and guidance on approaches to public library evaluation. The first direct substitute for earlier standards was *A Planning Process for Public Libraries* (Palmour, Bellassai, and DeWalt, 1980) and its companion work *Output Measures for Public Libraries: A Manual of Standardized Procedures* (Zweizig and Rodger 1982). Subsequent process-driven documents from the ALA have included *Planning and Role Setting for Public Libraries:*

A Manual of Options and Procedures (McClure et al. 1987), *Planning for Results: A Public Library Transformation Process* (Himmel and Wilson 1998), *Managing for Results: Effective Resource Evaluation for Public Libraries* (Nelson, Altman, and Mayo 2000), *The New Planning for Results: A Streamlined Approach* (Nelson 2001), *Creating Policies for Research: From Chaos to Clarity* (Nelson and Garcia 2003), *Strategic Planning for Results* (Nelson 2008), and *Implementing for Results: Your Strategic Plan in Action* (Nelson 2009).

Parallel to the development both of the four editions of ALA national standards and ALA's planning process documents, states were developing their own standards. Although some state standards were based directly on ALA standards, the development of state-level standards actually preceded the first ALA standards, and many states took directions that were noticeably different from the ALA's. State standards have taken on increasing importance since the shift to planning and process on the part of the ALA. Compliance with state standards is frequently tied to state fiscal support for public libraries, including state distribution of federal Library Services and Technology Act funding, which is normally managed by state library agencies. As of 2011, all but three states have state-level standards for public library services; funding is directly linked to standards compliance in 15 states (Public Library Standards by State 2011).

A more recent return to quantitative measures can be found in the annual indexes of public library performance provided by the Hennen American Public Library Ratings (HAPLR), summarized in *American Libraries* since 1998, and the *LJ* Index of Public Library Service, published in *Library Journal* since 2008. Both present aggregated data drawn from the Federal-State Cooperative System (FSCS), the oversight agency for state public library data.

The history of public library evaluation can be summarized in the context of Pungitore's (1989) comment:

> If the 1960s were a time of expansive growth, and the1970s were a time of retrenchment, the 1980s might be characterized as a period of questioning, of reassessment of the basic purpose and local objectives of public libraries. The recurring theme throughout the 1980s has been the importance of understanding the nature of the community in order to gear the library's services to local needs. The agenda for the 1990s and beyond appears to be a continued emphasis on community-based, long range planning and the development of local performance data as a means of measuring and evaluating public library services. (74)

The Characteristics of Evaluation

There are seven essential factors that characterize evaluation. Although the balance of these factors may vary from one evaluation need or activity to another, recognition of the totality of the seven factors is essential to understanding the nature of evaluation. The list of characteristics presented here is adapted from Wallace and Van Fleet (2001):

1. Evaluation is *intentional*. Assigning quality or value judgments is a natural part of the human experience. Every individual, as part of the experience of daily life, makes automatic assessments of the people, things, and events that affect that experience. This extends into professional life, as well. Any librarian who adheres to the principles that Schön (1983) referred to as those of the reflective practitioner is constantly assessing his or her own performance, the performance of other professionals, the needs of patrons, the availability of resources for assisting patrons, and myriad other factors. These reflexive assessments, however, do not constitute evaluation. Evaluation is a planned, formal activity that is more usually a group or institutional function rather than an individual one. Evaluation is a deliberate, formal process based on planning, design, thought, and attention to detail. Casual or careless approaches to evaluation lead to results lacking in the validity and reliability necessary for pragmatic application.

2. Evaluation is *purposeful*. Library evaluation has its origins in the mission, goals, and objectives of the library and is useful only to the extent that it advances the purposes of the library and is itself done with a defined purpose or goal in mind. Although the need for evaluation is sometimes imposed externally rather than arising from internal awareness of the need to evaluate, an evaluation done without a clearly understood and accepted purpose is at best cynical and at worst a waste of resources.

3. Evaluation is about *quality*. Understanding the extent to which a service or program is used, the perceptions of the public toward the library and its activities, or the comparative costs and advantages of different ways of doing things are all approaches to assessing quality. Any desire to maximize or improve quality requires establishment of a baseline and determination of the current level of quality. Any approach to evaluation that is not based on understanding levels of quality is empty and extraneous.

4. Evaluation is *interpretive*. Although measurement is frequently an essential component in evaluation, measurement in and of itself is not evaluation. The numbers that a public library annually reports to a state library agency do not constitute evaluation. Similarly, knowing that the library's reference transactions per week ranked tenth among public libraries in

the state for the most recent reporting year is a relative measure but still does not confer value. Evaluation is inherently relative and has meaning only in the context of the purpose of the evaluation. Knowing the reference transactions per week ranking is useful only to the extent that it can be interpreted as an indicator of quality and a target for action.

5. Evaluation is *varied in size and scope*. The complexity and extent of an evaluation activity is a function of the purpose of the evaluation and the nature of the data gathered for the evaluation. Expansiveness is not necessarily an indicator of the quality or usefulness of an evaluation. Having more data is not automatically better than having fewer data. Complicated or sophisticated data are not necessarily superior to straightforward, simple data. In many cases, the reverse is true. The key to determining the proper size and scope for any evaluation is estimation of what needs to be done to achieve the purposes of the evaluation.

6. Evaluation is *diverse in method*. There are many ways to conduct an evaluation and many methods and tools to support evaluation. There is no universal tool or tool kit for public library evaluation. Some measures, methods, and tools are imposed by reporting requirements from external agencies, but others are the result of internal planning, assessment of best practices, and immediate needs. The best approach to evaluation is the approach that meets the purposes and needs that motivate the evaluation.

7. Evaluation is *cyclical*. It is rarely—perhaps never—the case that a single evaluation of any product, process, or service will yield results that stand for all of time. Because evaluation has to do with assessing quality and improvement, there is a recurring impetus to evaluate. The best evaluation cycle is a carefully planned sequence in which the next round is predictable and scheduled. One of the benefits of a cyclical approach to evaluation is the ability to build comparative time series that show how quality has varied over time. In the absence of such time series, true improvement is nearly impossible to assess.

Targets for Evaluation

Data for use in evaluation fall into three categories of increasing power and complexity: inputs, outputs, and outcomes. The differential complexity and difficulty of assessing these three targets for evaluation creates a fundamental quandary: the most easily identified, defined, quantified, understood, and communicated data are the least expressive data, while the most expressive data and potentially most useful data are those that are the most difficult to identify, define, quantify, understand and communicate.

Inputs

Inputs are those resources that are available to achieve the library's mission, goals, and objectives. Physical facilities, collections, digital resources, equipment, and staff are all examples of inputs. To a considerable extent, the most important input for any enterprise is financial resources. Many of the other inputs to a library are direct or indirect functions of budgetary resources. Inputs are in general readily amenable to precise definition and categorization, easily quantified, subject to mathematical and statistical summarization, and presentable in tabular or graphical snapshots that are readily interpreted. Inputs clearly indicate something about the quality of the library, but their ability to directly convey quality is limited, and determining the meaning of inputs requires interpretation. There are public libraries that provide very high quality services from very limited resources. There are also public libraries with vast input availability that provide very poor services.

Outputs

Outputs are those products and services that constitute the library's deliverables. Circulation counts, attendance at programs, numbers of reference questions answered, and numbers of bookmobile visits are all outputs. Like inputs, most outputs are easily defined, categorized, quantified, and presented. Outputs, if carefully selected, may say something about the quality of the library, but careful interpretation is required. To a considerable extent, outputs are meaningful only in the context of the resources—the inputs—on which they are based.

Outcomes

A limitation of both inputs and outputs is that neither is likely to be directly reflective of a library's mission, goals, and objectives. A goal of supporting a collection of a particular size or answering a certain number of reference questions in a given period of time is in and of itself trivial. Such a goal becomes meaningful only when it is related to the impact of its achievement. Goals and objectives are typically expressed in terms of desired outcomes that, as Lancaster (1993) pointed out, "tend to relate to long-term, social, behavioral, or even economic objectives that are rather intangible and, therefore, not easily converted into concrete evaluation criteria" (3). Ultimately, most evaluation relies on carefully selected and designed measures of output to serve as indicators of outcomes (see PLANNING).

Approaches to Evaluation

There are many possible approaches to evaluation in the public library context. Five prominent approaches, in order of difficulty, are (1) list checking; (2) quantitative standards compliance; (3) surveys, interviews, and focus groups; (4) benchmarking; and (5) community-based planning and assessment.

List Checking.   List checking, also known as the checklist method, is one of the oldest approaches to evaluation of library collections. List checking is simply the process of matching a library's collection, usually as represented in the library's catalog, against some standardized or recommended list of resources. The goal is to determine the extent to which the library's collection is inclusive of the titles included in the list. "With this procedure the evaluator selects lists of titles or works appropriate to the subjects collected, to the programs or goals of the library, or to the programs and goals of consortia. These lists are then searched in the library files to determine the percentage the library has in its own collection" (Lockett 1989, 5). Lists can consist of standardized reference tools such as the *Public Library Catalog*, the *Children's Catalog*, the *Fiction Core Collection*, or *Magazines for Libraries* or more specialized bibliographies of subject-specific or genre-specific titles. The list checking approach has also been used to evaluate access to resources via full-text databases and other media (Nisonger 2008).

Quantitative Standards Compliance.   Although there are currently no national standards for public library performance in the United States, most states have standards or guidelines for public libraries that are in some cases linked to state funding for public libraries. The distinction between standards and guidelines is not always clear, although in general standards are enforceable and guidelines function as recommendations. State standards may be developed and revised under the aegis of governmental state library agencies or state library associations. The New York State Library, a division of the New York State Department of Education, is responsible for the state's "Standards for Registration of Public, Free Association and Indian Libraries," which are primarily minimum standards for the official recognition of public libraries. Florida's "Standards for Florida Public Libraries" were developed, revised, and published by the Florida Library Association. The "Standards for Louisiana Public Libraries" are a collaborative effort of the Louisiana Library Association and the State Library of Louisiana.

Library standards are generally thought of as "a tool to evaluate service, as a spur to improve service, and as a model description of what adequate service is" (Nelson Associates 1969, 21). Baker and Lancaster (1991, 321–22) identified two broad categories of standards. *Technical standards* are uniform practices that define ways in which tasks must be performed or functions must be accomplished. Standards for bibliographic description and electronic data transfer are obvious examples of technical standards. Compliance with technical standards is essentially a binary process: the standard is met, or it is not. *Performance standards* are general guidelines for assessing the quality or quantity of collections, services, programs, or other library activities. Compliance with performance standards is a more directly evaluative process in which compliance is a matter of the degree or extent to which the standard is met. By comparing itself to the standards, a library can determine areas of strength and weakness and develop targets for improvement, correction, or development. Baseline compliance with state standards can be an effective platform on which to build local library goals and objectives.

Pungitore (1989) identified four potential weaknesses of standards:

1. The validity and authority of standards are directly dependent on the manner in which they are developed and the association or agency responsible for their development. Standards are generally not based on research or true evaluation but instead represent a form of consensus within the professional community.

2. It is frequently unclear whether standards represent minimum performance, adequate performance, or excellence. Some state standards are tiered to reflect these differing interpretations, but not all are.

3. Differentiations in resources and sizes of public libraries tend to divide standards compliance into libraries that greatly exceed minimum standards, libraries with such limited resources that they are unlikely to ever meet minimum standards, and libraries that are challenged by meeting minimum standards but have a reasonable expectation of doing so.

4. The linkage of standards to local objectives and outcomes is questionable. Even when meeting standards is a fixed requirement, addressing standards frequently has no more than a superficial connection to planning and improvement (96–97).

Many state library standards are strongly influenced by the need to provide public library data for the Federal-State Cooperative System hosted by the national Institute of Museum and Library Services (IMLS). Among other things, the FSCS program provides a functional working definition of a public library:

A public library is established under state enabling laws or regulations to serve a community, district, or region and provides at least the following:

- An organized collection of printed or other library materials or a combination thereof
- Paid staff
- An established schedule in which services of the staff are available to the public
- The facilities necessary to support such a collection, staff, and schedule
- Is supported in whole or in part with public funds (Institute of Museum and Library Services 2011; *see also* PUBLIC LIBRARY)

The areas addressed in the "Standards for Louisiana Public Libraries" are typical and include reporting in the areas of planning, administration, and finance; access to library services; services; collection; technology; and facilities. The Louisiana standards function partially as a checklist for standards that are considered universal minimums for the state, such as completion of a systematic planning process at least every five years and tiered standards that represent differing levels of performance. The standard for the materials budget for a public library, for instance, defines three levels that describe the percentage of the total operating budget devoted to the library's collection, using the levels "Essential," "Enhanced," and "Comprehensive."

Surveys, Interviews, and Focus Groups.   Libraries employ many tools for gathering data, including recording volumes of activity such as circulation of materials, attendance at programs, sources and amounts of income, and categories and amounts of expenditures. These quantitative data may contribute to assessing compliance with state standards. Surveys, interviews, and focus groups are tools for gathering data regarding library performance, constituent perceptions, community needs, or other areas of interest that cannot be gained from routinely gathered data or assessment of compliance with standards.

The core commonality of surveys, interviews, and focus groups lies in the processes of identifying constituents who can reasonably be expected to contribute useful answers to questions, identifying and formulating questions to ask of those constituents, gaining access to the constituents from whom feedback and input are sought, asking questions, recording responses, and analyzing those responses. The processes for carrying out surveys, interviews, and focus groups are well established, and models for their application in library evaluation are readily available in the literature.

Benchmarking.   "Benchmarking refers to the practice of measuring a particular activity in one organization, such as a library, and comparing the result with comparable measurements from other organizations or libraries" (Smith 1996, 86). The availability of aggregated data about public libraries from state library agencies and IMLS facilitates such comparisons, which are an effective way of positioning a library within its actual or desired peer group. Benchmarking can be used at the level of a specific activity, program, or service but can also be done at a broader level to create a numeric picture of the library as a whole.

Smith (1996) outlines the steps involved in setting a benchmark, which include "identifying a problem area to study and improve, finding a library or libraries to benchmark against, working with the staff of the benchmark library to study and measure their process, setting targets, measuring your library's productivity against the benchmark measures, and analyzing the results" (87). Although this can seem an intimidating process, especially to staff unfamiliar with quantitative methods of analysis, once the routines of benchmarking are established, future iterations can be made nearly automatic.

Benchmarking can be used with both input and output measures and is frequently used with output/input ratios, such as registered borrowers per capita or circulation per item held. Many state library agencies provide annual reports that include selected rankings for both raw input and output measures and for predefined ratios. The PLA's annual Public Library Data Statistical Report provides comparative data for 800 public libraries in the United States and Canada. A companion PLDS Online database provides searchable data that can be used with a spreadsheet or local database software and allows for the generation of customized reports. Both the annual report and the database are available from the PLA at a fee. Hennen's HAPLR and the *LJ* Index of Public Library Service, also known as "America's Star Libraries," are also sources of data for benchmarking.

Benchmarking is especially effective as a means of visually presenting the results of evaluation. Comparisons of the local library to the peer group can be effectively presented in the form of bar or column graphs. Changes over time in benchmark data are readily amenable to presentation as time-series line graphs. Both raw counts and ratios can be effectively presented in visual formats. Visualization is especially useful in reporting library performance to external groups, such as library boards, government bodies, or constituents.

Community-Based Planning and Assessment.   The focus of public library evaluation since the move away from national standards that evolved in the late 1960s and early 1970s has been on community-based planning to identify local needs and assessment of achievement of localized goals and objectives. The series of planning guides produced by the PLA from 1980 to 2008 are based on three core assumptions:

1. Excellence must be defined locally. It results when library services match community needs, interests, and priorities.

2. Excellence is possible for both small and large libraries. It rests more on commitment than on unlimited resources.

3. Excellence is a moving target. Even when achieved, excellence must be continually maintained (Nelson 2008, xi).

As described in the current PLA planning guide, *Strategic Planning for Results*, the evolution of the PLA planning guides has been a sequential process in which each new guide added to the precedent established by its forebears. *A Planning Process for Public Libraries* (Palmour et al. 1980) was intended to introduce basic concepts of planning and guidelines for planning for public librarians who had previously not engaged in any kind of systematic or strategic planning. *Planning and Role Setting for Public Libraries: A Manual of Options and Procedures* (McClure et al. 1987) added the concept of defined library roles as a means of defining service priorities as targets for action. *Planning for Results: A Public Library Transformation Process* (Himmel and Wilson 1998) added the concept of service responses that define actions taken by a library to meet community needs and concentrated attention of implementation of the results of planning. *The New Planning for Results: A Streamlined Approach* (Nelson 2001) reduced the timeline of the planning cycle from 15 months to between four and five months in recognition of the rapid pace of technological change and its influence in library planning and service delivery (Nelson 2008, xi–xii). *Strategic Planning for Results* (Nelson 2008) replaced the previous expression "long-range planning" with *strategic planning* in recognition "that the future is too fluid to make firm 'long-range' plans'" (Nelson 2008, xii). The second major change in the 2008 planning guide is an enhanced emphasis on the need for change and change management (Nelson 2008, xiii).

The planning process outline in *Strategic Planning for Results* is divided into five fundamental phases: (1) planning to plan, (2) identifying service points, (3) setting the state, (4) describing the future, and (5) communicating the plan. This approach, grounded in a community-based planning philosophy, incorporates the key elements of evaluation discussed above and acknowledges the cyclical nature of the process. *See* PLANNING.

Summary

The current context of evaluation in public libraries is a mix of externally developed standards, nationally derived and reported measures, and internally created or adapted measures. These measures are generally selected in relation to local priorities discovered through a community-based planning approach. Public librarians use a rich amalgam of processes and measures to provide effective service to their local communities (*see also* RESEARCH).

—*Connie Van Fleet and Danny P. Wallace*

References

Baker, Sharon L., and F. Wilfrid Lancaster. 1991. *The Measurement and Evaluation of Library Services*. 2nd ed. Arlington, VA: Information Resources Press.

Blasingame, Ralph, and Mary Jo Lynch. 1974. Design for diversity: Alternatives to standards for public libraries. *Public Library Association Newsletter* 13 (June): 4–22.

Callison, Daniel. 2007. Action research. *School Library Media Activities Monthly* 23, no. 10 (June): 40–43.

DeProspo, Ernest R., Ellen Altman, and Kenneth E. Beasley. 1973. *Performance Measures for Public Libraries*. Chicago: American Library Association.

Eldredge, Jonathan. 2006. Evidence-based librarianship: The EBL process. *Library Hi Tech* 24, no. 3: 341–54.

Hennen's American Public Library Ratings. 2011. http://www.haplr-index.com/order.html. Accessed January 2011.

Hernon, Peter, and Charles R. McClure. 1990. *Evaluation and Library Decision Making*. Norwood, NJ: Ablex.

Himmel, Ethel, and William James Wilson. 1998. *Planning for Results: A Public Library Transformation Process*. Chicago: American Library Association.

Institute of Museum and Library Services. 2011. Library Statistics. Public Libraries. http://harvester.census.gov/imls/publib.asp. Accessed January 2011.

Lancaster, F. Wilfrid. 1993. *If You Want to Evaluate Your Library....* 2nd ed. Champaign: University of Illinois Graduate School of Library and Information Science.

Lockett, Barbara. 1989. *Guide to the Evaluation of Library Collections*. Chicago: American Library Association.

Martin, Lowell A. 1972. Standards for public libraries. *Library Trends* 21, no. 2 (October 1972): 164–77.

McClure, Charles R., et al. 1987. *Planning and Role Setting for Public Libraries: A Manual of Options and Procedures*. Chicago: American Library Association.

Minimum Standards for Public Library Systems. 1966. Chicago: American Library Association.

Nelson Associates. 1969. *Public Library Systems in the United States: A Survey of Multijurisdictional Systems*. Chicago: American Library Association

Nelson, Sandra S. 2001. *The New Planning for Results: A Streamlined Approach*. Chicago: American Library Association.

Nelson, Sandra S. 2008. *Strategic Planning for Results*. Chicago: American Library Association.

Nelson, Sandra S. 2009. *Implementing for Results: Your Strategic Plan in Action*. Chicago: American Library Association.

Nelson, Sandra S., Ellen Altman, and Diane Mayo. 2000. *Managing for Results: Effective Resource Evaluation for Public Libraries*. Chicago: American Library Association

Nelson, Sandra S., and June Garcia. 2003. *Creating Policies for Research: From Chaos to Clarity*. Chicago: American Library Association.

Nisonger, Thomas E. 2008. Use of the checklist method for content evaluation of full-text databases: An investigation of two databases based on citations from two journals. *Library Resources & Technical Services* 52, no. 1 (January): 4–17.

Palmour, Vernon E., Marcia C. Bellassai, and Nancy V. DeWath. 1980. *A Planning Process for Public Libraries*. Chicago: American Library Association.

Public Library Service: A Guide to Evaluation, with Minimum Standards. 1956. Chicago: American Library Association.

Public Library Standards by State. 2011. http://plsc.pbworks.com/w/page/7422647/Public-library-standards-by-state. Accessed January 2011.

Pungitore, Verna. 1989. *Public Librarianship: An Issues-Oriented Approach*. New York: Greenwood Press.

Rohlf, Robert H. Standards for public libraries. *Library Trends* 31, no. 1 (Summer 1982): 65–76.

Rubin, Rhea Joyce. 2006. *Demonstrating Results: Using Outcome Measurement in Your Library*. Chicago: American Library Association.

Schön, Donald A. 1983. *The Reflective Practitioner: How Professionals Think in Action*. New York: Basic Books.

Smith, Mark L. 1996. *Collecting and Using Public Library Statistics: A How-to-Do-It Manual*. New York: Neal-Schuman.

Standards for Public Libraries. 1933. *Bulletin of the American Library Association* 27, no. 10 (November): 513–514.

Wallace, Danny P., and Connie Van Fleet. 2001. *Library Evaluation: A Casebook and Can-Do Guide*. Englewood, CO: Libraries Unlimited.

Zweizig, Douglas, and Eleanor Jo Rodger. 1982. *Output Measures for Public Libraries: A Manual of Standardized Procedures*. Chicago: American Library Association.

EVANS, CHARLES, 1850–1935   Librarian. Born Boston November 13, 1850. At age 16 he took an apprentice position in the Boston Athenaeum, then directed by William F. Poole. In 1872, on Poole's recommendation, Evans was offered the directorship of the new Indianapolis (IN) Public Library. During his 23 years there, the library gained national recognition, having the sixth-largest circulation among American public libraries. Evans emphasized public relations and local history. He was the second person (after Melvil Dewey) to sign on to the new American Library Association in 1876 and one of 21 librarians to go to the first international library conference in London a year later. Evans had an undiplomatic temperament, leading to friction with superiors in most of his positions. He was terminated at Indianapolis in 1878 and had no substantial employment until 1884. Then Poole helped him to an appointment as assistant librarian in the Enoch Pratt Free Library, Baltimore, MD, effective January 1, 1885. Problems with the chief librarian ensued, and Evans was again out of work in December 1886. In a curious turn of events, the Indianapolis trustees invited him to return there in 1889. He developed a personnel plan and worked at reclassification of the collection, but again there was trouble with the trustees. Once more Poole stepped in, inviting Evans to the Newberry Library (which he was directing) to head reference and classification; he stayed from 1892 to 1895, then took the post of librarian at the Chicago Historical Society but was soon dismissed. Evans finally gave up library work and set about writing the landmark *American Bibliography*. He completed 12 of the ultimate 13 volumes while technically unemployed before his death on February 8, 1935. *DAB*; *DALB*; LJ Hall of Fame.

EVANSTON PUBLIC LIBRARY, IL   1703 Orrington, Evanston, IL 60201. Founded 1873. Population served: 74,239. Circulation: 180,561. Holdings: 492,448. 2 branches. The library had open shelves from 1898. In 1920 began bookmobile service (ended 1997). Main library building, 1908, replaced in same location by new building, 1961; new building, 1994. Evanston was the first American public library to circulate any kind of sound recording format (*see* MUSIC COLLECTIONS). The Sadie Knowland Coe music collection was established in 1907. It included books, printed music, periodicals, and piano rolls, all of which circulated. In the library's annual report for the year 1935, 609 "pianola rolls" were noted, but there were none cited in the following year. A communication from the library states that "at some point during 1936 the library seems to have divested itself of these pianola rolls. Unfortunately, we have no information about exactly when this occurred, or why."

EVANSVILLE-VANDERBURGH PUBLIC LIBRARY, IN   200 SE Martin Luther King Jr. Blvd., Evansville, IN 47713. Population served: 171,922. Circulation: 2,918,303. Holdings: 652,892. 9 branches, 1 bookmobile. LJ February 15, 2009: 3-star library; November 15, 2009: 5-star library; October 1, 2010: 4-star library. HAPLR 2009, 2010.

F

FACILITIES. *See* BUILDINGS AND FACILITIES.

FAIRFAX COMMUNITY LIBRARY, VT   75 Hunt St., Fairfax, VT 05454. Founded 1972. Population served: 3,929. Circulation: 57,016. Holdings: 35,651. LJ February 15, 2009: 4-star library. HAPLR 2009.

FAIRFAX COUNTY PUBLIC LIBRARY, VA   12000 Government Center Parkway, Fairfax, VA 22035. Population served: 1,200,000. Circulation: 13,931,027. Holdings: 2,460,395. 22 branches. The library has been recognized for a number of initiatives that bring library programs to segments of the community. There is an early literacy program for preschoolers in all the branches. There is a Center for the Book, which presents authors, discussions, seminars, and other book-related events. The most unusual effort is an alternative sentencing program for teen and adult offenders. It "consists of a demanding book discussion group that meets over a series of weeks and involves reading, reflecting, sharing, and contact with stable members of the community and their values. ... Participating probation officers and court personnel are impressed with the success of the program" (Clay and Bangs 2008).

Reference

Clay, Edwin S., III, and Patricia Bangs. 2008. Fairfax County Public Library—Reaching out to readers. *Virginia Libraries* 54, nos. 3/4 (July/December): 13–17.

FAIRPORT HARBOR PUBLIC LIBRARY, OH   335 Vine St., Fairport Harbor, OH 44077. Population served: 3,244. Circulation: 84,660. Holdings: 40,938. LJ October 1, 2010: 3-star library.

FALCONER PUBLIC LIBRARY, NY   101 W. Main St., Falconer, NY 14733. Founded 1922. Population served: 2,540. Circulation: 197,006. Holdings: 50,999. LJ February 15, 2009; November 15, 2009; and October 1, 2010: 5-star library.

FALLS CHURCH, VA. *See* MARY RILEY STYLES PUBLIC LIBRARY, FALLS CHURCH, VA.

FALLS CITY LIBRARY AND ARTS CENTER, NE   120 E. 18th St., Falls City, NE 68355. Population served: 4,071. Circulation: 72,021. Holdings: 39,015. LJ November 15, 2009: 4-star library; October 1, 2010: 5-star library.

FAYETTE, OH. *See* NORMAL MEMORIAL LIBRARY, FAYETTE, OH.

FAYETTEVILLE FREE LIBRARY, NY   300 Orchard, Fayetteville, NY 13066. Founded 1911. Population served: 10,192. Circulation: 277,066. Holdings: 34,315. LJ February 15, 2009; November 15, 2009; and October 1, 2010: 5-star library.

FAYETTEVILLE PUBLIC LIBRARY, AR   401 W. Mountain St., Fayetteville, AR 72701. Founded 1959 (year the city took it over; there had been a library in Fayetteville since 1916). LJ Library of the Year 2005.

FERGUSON, MILTON JAMES, 1879–1954   Librarian. Born April 11, 1879, in Hubbardstown, WV. He earned a BA, 1990, and MA, 1906, at the University of Oklahoma and a certificate, 1902, at the New York State Library School. He was appointed librarian, University of Oklahoma, 1902, and remained to 1907. From 1908 to 1917, Ferguson was assistant state librarian of California under James Gillis, then succeeded him as state librarian, serving 1917–1930. Ferguson went to the Brooklyn Public Library as librarian in 1930. He modernized the plans for the new building, reorganized the administration, rationalized procedures, created the regional branch system, opened a business branch, and enhanced professionalism of the staff with a pension system, sabbatical leaves, and released time for study. Ferguson was president of the American Library Association (ALA), 1938–1939, and also president of the California and New York library associations. He wrote the compilation *American Library Laws*, published by ALA in 1930, and edited the fifteenth edition of the *Dewey Decimal Classification*. He died on October 23, 1954. His philosophy of public librarianship must be cast as a minority position for its time. An article published in 1932 asserted that public libraries should serve financiers, manufacturers, and college students—not "those often so unfortunate as to be without a job, even in good times, whose coats, soaked in the rain, in mass formation give off an odor so unlike the perfumes of Araby" (Ferguson 1932, 418). *DALB*.

Reference

Ferguson, Milton James. 1932. Should the public library be for all the people? No! *American Library Association Bulletin* 26, no. 7 (July): 418–19.

FERGUSON LIBRARY, STAMFORD, CT   Public Library Plaza, Stamford, CT 06904. State charter 1880, free library 1911. Population served: 120,160. Circulation: 975,340. Holdings: 482,739. 3 branches, 1 bookmobile. The library has extensive collections and programs for minorities, including newspapers and resources in Spanish, Italian, French, Russian, Polish, Portuguese, Arabic, and Haitian Creole.

FILMS. *See* AUDIOVISUAL COLLECTIONS.

FINANCE. *See* FUNDING OF PUBLIC LIBRARIES; MANAGEMENT AND ORGANIZATION.

FIXTURES, FURNISHINGS, AND EQUIPMENT   If public library facilities are the instruments by which librarians deliver services, then the fixtures, furnishings and equipment within the facilities are the particular utilitarian features of these instruments. The selection of fixtures, furnishings, and equipment usually occurs at the end of the development of the building program (*see* BUILDINGS AND FACILITIES).

Fixtures

Fixtures, as the name implies, are functional parts of the library building and are designed simultaneously with the building. In traditional library building design, most of the functional components, such as shelving, furniture, and equipment, were designed as fixtures. In current building design, more and more of the furnishings and equipment have been freed from being affixed to the building and have become more portable and more easily relocated as areas of the library building have become more and more subject to recurring repurposing. Even telephone and electrical equipment are no longer considered fixtures. Thus, current library fixtures have been reduced to lighting fixtures, some electrical fixtures, and functional building extensions.

Best practice for lighting fixtures incorporates fluorescent light reflected off white ceilings throughout as much of the library as possible. These fixtures must be spaced to light ceilings as evenly as possible, with no streaks of light and dark and with full brightness at the perimeters. Track lighting fixtures will be used only where they are essential for exhibit areas. To control glare and increase the contrast needed for close reading and writing, task lighting can be used on tables, on workstations, and in study carrels in areas of a library where the general light may not be so bright, such as in a very large room.

Electrical and data conduits are still fixtures in current library building design, but even these fixtures are being phased out as wireless technology makes them obsolete.

Functional building extensions include desks and counters designed for specific, long-term use (e.g., a fixed point of public service, such as a circulation desk) or storage shelves attached to walls. Bulletin boards and display cases can also be considered functional extensions when they are built into the building structure.

Furnishings

Public Areas.   The most prominent furnishings for the public areas are the various service desks, such as the circulation and reference desks. Although in the past these desks were often fixtures of the building, current practice favors modular, portable desks of a flexible design and easily adaptable to plans, allowing for future relocation, new technology, or even elimination of the desk. Whereas traditional public service desks tended to be large pieces of furniture, the trend is to smaller individual desks on the order of what hotels and banks currently use for one-on-one interactions with customers. Despite this trend, though, there remains the legitimate concern of protecting staff from potential aggressive patrons, so larger service desks may still be preferred. Whatever the function, desks need to be sized for the staff manning the desk and for storage of supplies needed for the particular public service delivered at the desk. The locations of the desks in the public spaces must provide good sight lines both for the staff to monitor public activity and for members of the public to easily see the desks. Signs, then, provide an adjunct to lead people to the service desks. All desks should present a clean appearance with wires and equipment shielded.

Next in prominence after the public service desks are the furnishings that allow patrons to pursue their activities, whether that involves reading, writing, or computer work. Reader seating typically runs heavy to discourage casual rearrangement by patrons. However, there are some spaces in libraries, for example, spaces for young people, wherein it has become desirable for patrons to reposition the seating to allow for collaboration or greater comfort. The type of seating in these spaces is modular and lighter or with casters. This type of movable "seating" may even be balance balls or beanbags.

Seating throughout the library generally accommodates all ages. Senior citizens especially must be able to get in and out of chairs easily. Seating that is attractive, comfortable, and ergonomic encourages patrons to relax and read for an extended periods. Footstools or ottomans aid in inviting patrons to linger and read. Because of high usage, the fabrics covering the reader chairs must be sturdy, easy to clean, and easy to reupholster.

For patrons who need to write or work on computers, the library must offer attractive, heavy-duty tables and study carrels. Best current practice dictates that tables be of wood, with high-pressure laminate surfaces on both sides of their tops to prevent warping. Table legs will be anchored to tabletops with steel rods inside the legs welded to heavy-duty plates bolted to tabletops. Because of the requirements of the Americans with Disabilities Act, a library will select tables—such as Parsons design tables—with thin tops, without skirting, and without beams connecting the legs. A mixture of circular and rectangular tables as well as carrels for individual studying will provide patrons with sufficient variety of work spaces to meet their needs. Seating at tables and carrels will be more of the nature of task chairs.

By virtue of the sheer square footage covered in the public spaces, shelving for both the circulating and the reference collections may be the most important furnishing a public library has. This shelving must store books, audiovisual materials, and other regalia in the functional areas of the building whether those functions are designated by age or by type of service, such as reference, readers' advisory, or special collection. Shelving runs single faced and double faced in varying lengths. In keeping with the need for portability, the most useful shelving will be of cantilever design, fabricated of heavy-gauge steel, and manufactured by a company that specializes in library shelving. Such a company will also be best able to supply special features the may be needed, such as pullout shelves and periodical shelves.

The American Library Association contributed to the development of the standard for library shelving, ANSI/NISO Z39.73—Single-Tier Steel Bracket Library Shelving, in 1994 (revised 2001). To save space when necessary, libraries install movable-aisle compact shelving, operated either manually or electrically. Larger public libraries are emulating academic libraries in their use of automatic retrieval systems conjoined to shelving. When purchasing new factory-made furniture or shelving, libraries select standard sizes and finishes. Although custom designs and finishes are exciting and are often affordable at the time of a major order, the cost of adding an additional matching chair or table at a later time can be high. Because libraries frequently reposition furniture and shelving, colors that force items of furniture or equipment into particular groupings should generally not be selected. It is the rare "experience library" that can pull off such particular color/design groupings. For the typical public library, any chair or table of the right size should be suitable for any location in the library.

Staff Areas. Office furniture systems for library staff have moved from the relatively isolating cubicle farms to arrangements of desks with lower dividers in order to encourage more and closer collaboration in the workrooms. Again, "portability" and "flexibility of purpose" are the bywords in designing and choosing office furniture. Conference tables that have traditionally been large and bulky pieces are being supplanted by modular systems that can be put together and taken apart to accommodate the number of participants seated at the table. Task chairs need to be ergonomic and comfortable enough for long hours of sitting.

The bywords "portability" and "flexibility" apply as well to filing and storage systems. Modular, changeable, and resizable components that can handle documents and media of a wide variety of shapes and sizes are preferred over the comparative straitjackets of traditional letter-sized or legal-sized filing cabinets.

Equipment

The topic of technology dominates the discussion of how to equip 21st-century public libraries. Information technology has come to control all other equipment in the building. Indeed, anything powered by electricity is now considered a component of the computerized information system in a library. The domination of technology in the planning of library facilities means that a large portion of the building budget must be appropriated for hardware and other equipment for the information system and computer network. The list of such equipment shows servers, switches, routers, uninterruptible power supplies, personal computers, phone systems (Voice over Internet Protocol), cabling, public computers, printers, photocopiers, scanners, video monitors, kiosks, and telefax machines. The list can also be expanded to include the controls for heating, ventilating, and air-conditioning units and for fire and intrusion alarms, depending on the technological sophistication of the library.

The core technology for the public library is its integrated library system, tying together the various computerized modules necessary to maintain the patron and bibliographic databases, acquire and catalog materials, provide an online public access catalog, and deliver circulation services. State-of-the-art automated circulation services employ radio-frequency identification (RFID) technology, which consists of express checkout terminals and materials return sorters (i.e., conveyor belts and bins). Both the circulation and the technical services departments require antenna pads for processing the RFID-tagged items. Library cards themselves have been upgraded to incorporate RFID but may become obsolete soon as biometric identification technology improves. Plans to utilize RFID technology are incomplete without provisions for theft control systems tied into RFID.

The building program must incorporate an adequate equipment room for housing the central servers for the local area network (LAN). Public libraries are well known in current times as wireless local area network (Wi-Fi) hot spots. Wi-Fi antennae are necessary to be such a hot spot, the number and locations of the antennae determined by the square footage of the hot spot.

Cutting-edge technology has also started appearing in public libraries. Touch-screen monitors have made their way into libraries, at first used for self-contained (i.e., nonnetworked) information kiosks but now used for personal computers on the LAN. An exciting example of the evolved state of touch-controlled technology is Microsoft Surface, a flat tabletop the responds to fingers, hands, and "real-world objects." Wireless energy transfer or wireless power, which obviates the necessity of conduit and receptacles in a building, is poised to be the next big thing in technology. As of this writing, wireless-powered furniture has been around for a few years and has started appearing in libraries as a means for patrons to charge their electronic devices without plugging in to any outlets.

The public library has expanded its role as a traditional support for reading and writing to encompass support for technological work. Digital media labs for video production have rapidly become de rigueur in new public library buildings. These are modeled on similar labs that academic libraries have had for many years now and can be extensive multimedia (video, audio, photographic, artistic, graphic, and textual) production studios with equipment ranging from camcorders to musical instruments, all with the computers to support the recordings.

Perhaps the ultimate technologically equipped circulating library is a library that is itself a piece of equipment, that is, a fully automated self-service library machine. Successful examples of the total self-service library are Bokomaten from Distec and BranchAnywhere from Evanced Solutions.

Resources

Librarians can find the most current references to architects, interior designers, furniture vendors, and other consultants in regularly published library journals. In particular, *American Libraries* publishes an annual "Library Design Showcase," typically in its April issue. *Library Journal* publishes a supplement titled "Library by Design." In addition to their directories of design and construction professionals, these journals review the most recent new and remodeled library buildings and showcase the products of the major vendors, such as furniture vendors Brodart, Gale, KI, Agati, and LFI and technology vendors such as Innovative Interfaces, Inc.; SirsiDynix; the Library Corporation; Integrated Technology Group; 3M; Tagsys; and CDW. Catalogs of these and other vendors are available on the World Wide Web. Furniture vendors also have showrooms in many cities, for example, those in Chicago's Merchandise Mart. Contracts with furniture and equipment vendors specify not only purchase prices but also prices and terms of ongoing maintenance of the products.

—*Stephen Bero*

References

Dewe, Michael. 2006. *Planning Public Library Buildings: Concepts and Issues.* Aldershot (England): Ashgate.

Sannwald, William W. 2009. *Checklist of Library Building Design Considerations.* 5th ed. Chicago: American Library Association.

FLEMING COMMUNITY LIBRARY, CO   506 N. Fremont Ave., Fleming, CO 80728. Population served 1,024. Circulation: 10,335. Holdings: 11,245. LJ February 15, 2009; November 15, 2009; and October 1, 2010: 5-star library.

FLEXNER, JENNIE MAAS, 1882–1944   Librarian. Born Louisville, KY, November 6, 1882. She did not attend college; worked several years as a secretary. She was employed by Louisville Public Library from 1905, then enrolled in the library school at Western Reserve University in 1908. Returning to Louisville, she rose to head of circulation by 1912, promoting open shelves and readers' advisory services. As president of the Kentucky Library Association in 1923–1924 she was active in recruiting blacks to library work. She was author of the earliest textbook on circulation services, *Circulation Work in Public Libraries* (American Library Association, 1927), reporting on practices in outstanding libraries that she visited. In 1928, Flexner was invited to the New York Public Library (NYPL) to set up a readers' advisory service, and in 1929 she opened an office there for that purpose. She wrote reading lists and worked with groups as well as individual patrons. Flexner and Sigrid Edge wrote *A Readers' Advisory Service* (American Association for Adult Education, 1934). A special interest in immigrant needs developed as refugees from Nazism came to New York in the 1930s. Flexner conducted training classes for NYPL staff and wrote guides for other librarians engaged in readers' advisory. She died on November 17, 1944, in New York. LJ Hall of Fame; *ANB; DALB.*

FLINT PUBLIC LIBRARY, MI   1026 Kearsley, Flint, MI 48502. Founded 1885. Population served: 120,000. Circulation: 308,000. Holdings: 436,000. 3 branches, 1 bookmobile. IMLS award 2004.

FLOMATON PUBLIC LIBRARY, AL   608 McCurdy St., Flomaton, AL 36441. Population served: 1,588. Circulation: 111,609. Holdings: 22,534. LJ February 15, 2009; November 15, 2009; and October 1, 2010: 5-star library. HAPLR 2009, 2010.

FLOYD MEMORIAL LIBRARY, GREENPORT, NY   539 First St., Greenport, NY 11944. Founded 1907. Population served: 5,296. Circulation: 100,270. Holdings: 37,348. LJ November 15, 2009, and October 1, 2010: 3-star library.

FORBES LIBRARY, NORTHAMPTON, MA   20 West St., Northampton, MA 01060. Founded 1894. Population served: 26,037. Circulation: 307,464. Holdings: 234,689. Charles Ammi Cutter was the first librarian; he stayed nine years. His classification is still used at Forbes. In 1902, an art and music department was established, as was a children's room.

FORRESTON PUBLIC LIBRARY, IL   204 First Ave., Forreston, IL 61030. Population served: 1,469. Circulation: 16,786. Holdings: 12,181. LJ November 15, 2009: 3-star library.

FORSYTH COUNTY PUBLIC LIBRARY, WINSTON-SALEM, NC   600 W. Fifth St., Winston-Salem, NC 27101. Population served: 343,028. Circulation: 2,000,000. Holdings: 771,167. 11 branches.

FORSYTH PUBLIC LIBRARY, IL   268 S. Elwood, Forsyth, IL 62535. Founded 1983. Population served: 2,434. Circulation: 58,569. Holdings: 31,958. LJ November 15, 2009, and October 1, 2010: 3-star library.

FORT LAUDERDALE, FL. *See* BROWARD COUNTY DIVISION OF LIBRARIES, FORT LAUDERDALE, FL.

FORT WORTH PUBLIC LIBRARY, TX.   500 W. Third St., Fort Worth, TX 76102. Founded 1901. Population served: 603,337. Circulation: 4,471,122. Holdings: 1,153,854. 13 branches. Directors: Jennie Scheuber, 1901–1938; Helen P. Toombs (acting), 1938–1939; Harry Peterson, 1939–1948; Joseph S. Ibbotson, 1948–1954; Arless Nixon, 1954–1964; Wyman Jones, 1964–1971; Mabel Fischer, 1971–1981; Linda Allmand, 1981–1998; and Gleniece Robinson, 1999–.

FOSTER, WILLIAM EATON, 1851–1930   Librarian. Born June 2, 1851, in Brattleboro, VT. He graduated from Brown University in 1873 and took a master's degree in 1876. He headed Hyde Park Public Library (MA). He was one of the group who founded the American Library Association in 1876. Foster was invited to direct the new Providence Public Library (RI) in 1877 and set to work at once selecting and cataloging the initial collection for opening day, February 4, 1878 During his 53 years in Providence, he created one of the first public library children's sections, an art department, a music department, an industrial department, and a foreign department. He promoted use of the library by elementary school pupils, offering teacher loan collections for student use. Exhibiting a liberal view of selection, he asked for patron suggestions on what to buy. Foster was an early advocate of public relations, even to the point of listing ways that the city saved money by supporting the library (Foster 1891); for example, thousands of dollars would be saved in a contract negotiation if city officials consulted data in library reference works. He took up the theme, familiar in the twenty-first century, of tabulating how the library participated in the "life of the user": by supporting industries, societies, public lectures, college classes, schoolteachers, and parental reading for children (Foster 1880). When he retired, Providence Public Library was nationally respected. It had grown to a system of 12 branches, with 400,000 volumes and annual circulation of 1,300,000. He died September 10, 1930. LJ Hall of Fame; *DALB*.

References

Foster, William E. 1880. Methods of securing the interest of the community. *Library Journal* (September/October). Reprinted in *The American Public Library*, 4th ed., by Arthur E. Bostwick, 193–97. New York: Appleton, 1929.

Foster, William E. 1891. Arguments for public support of public libraries. Paper given at the American Library Association conference, San Francisco, 1891.

Printed in *The American Public Library*, 4th ed., by Arthur E. Bostwick, 215–30. New York: Appleton, 1929.

FOUNTAINDALE PUBLIC LIBRARY DISTRICT, BOLINGBROOK, IL   300 W. Briarcliff, Bolingbrook, IL 60440. Population served: 71,474. Circulation: 807,086. Holdings: 285,727. 1 branch, 1 bookmobile. LJ February 15, 2009; November 15, 2009; and October 1, 2010: 3-star library.

FRANKFORT COMMUNITY PUBLIC LIBRARY, IN   208 W. Clinton St., Frankfort, IN 46041. Founded 1884 as a free library operated by the city; earlier a subscription library from 1879. Population served: 31,030. Circulation: 275,616. Holdings: 194,492. 3 branches, 1 bookmobile. IMLS award 2006.

FRANKFORT PUBLIC LIBRARY DISTRICT, IL   21119 S. Pfeiffer Rd., Frankfort, IL 60423. Founded 1966. Population served: 25,254. Circulation: 292,037. Holdings: 92,559. 1 bookmobile. One of the libraries that converted to BISAC (*see* CLASSIFICATION).

FRANKLIN GROVE PUBLIC LIBRARY, IL   203 N. Elm St., Franklin Grove, IL 61031. Population served: 1,052. Circulation: 5,190. Holdings: 10,896. LJ October 1, 2010: 3-star library.

FRANKLINTON, LA. *See* WASHINGTON PARISH LIBRARY SYSTEM, FRANKLINTON, LA.

FREDERICKSBURG, VA. *See* CENTRAL RAPPAHANNOCK REGIONAL LIBRARY SYSTEM, FREDERICKSBURG, VA.

FREDONIA PUBLIC LIBRARY, KS   807 Jefferson, Fredonia, KS 66736. Founded "sometime between 1914 and 1925" (library website). Population served: 2,487. Circulation: 50,958. Holdings: 26,800. LJ February 15, 2009, and November 15, 2009: 4-star library.

FREE LIBRARY OF PHILADELPHIA   1901 Vine St., Philadelphia, PA 19103. Opened 1894. Population served: 1,517,550. Circulation: 6,294,313. Holdings: 8,144,478. 54 branches. The Free Library of Philadelphia (FLP) was incorporated in 1891 and opened in March 1894. Original quarters were three rooms in City Hall. On February 11, 1895, FLP moved to an old concert hall on Chestnut Street. The library moved again on February 1, 1910, to 13th and Locust streets. A Carnegie grant of $1.5 million was used to initiate establishment of branches in 1903. FLP occupied its present site on June 2, 1927, in a distinguished structure designed by Horace Trumbauer and Julian Abele.

Notable collections in FLP include rare books; maps; children's books printed in the United States, 1642–1850; prints and pictures; automotive history; and the Edwin A. Fleisher collection of orchestral scores and parts (1929). A library for the blind (now at 919 Walnut Street) dates from 1899.

On December 29, 2004, the mayor signed a bill approving a $30 million bond issue for renovation of the present building with a 160,000-square-foot expansion, the work to be designed by architect Moshe Safdie. Financial problems led to the closing of 11 branches in November 2008. However, the Pennsylvania Senate approved funding in 2009 that kept all 54 branches open.

FLP directors have been John Thomson, 1893–1916; John Ashhurst, 1916–1932; Franklin H. Price, 1934–1951; Emerson Greenway, 1951–1969; Keith Doms, 1969–1987; Elliot L. Shelkrot, 1987–2007; and Siobhan A. Reardon, 2008–.

Reference

Doms, Keith. 1973. Free Library of Philadelphia. In *Encyclopedia of Library and Information Science* 9: 105–111. New York: Marcel Dekker.

FREMONT, CA. *See* ALAMEDA COUNTY LIBRARY, FREMONT, CA.

FREMONT PUBLIC LIBRARY DISTRICT, MUNDELEIN, IL   1170 N. Midlothian Rd., Mundelein, IL 60060. Founded 1955. Population served: 29,620. Circulation: 508,286. Holdings: 122,858. LJ October 1, 2010: 4-star library.

FRESNO COUNTY PUBLIC LIBRARY, CA   2420 Mariposa St., Fresno, CA 93721. Founded 1893 as free library; subscription library from 1892. Population served: 856,667. Circulation: 2,991,108. Holdings: 2,223,842. 37 branches.

FUNDING OF PUBLIC LIBRARIES

Terminology

American Heritage says that "funding" is "to furnish a fund for" and that "fund" is "a sum of money or other resources set aside for a specific purpose."

Historical Summary

Two basic questions arise from this definition of funding: (1) who furnishes the fund for the specific purpose of supporting public libraries? and (2) how shall the appropriate amount of such a fund be determined? If libraries are "public" in the sense employed in this handbook, they are essentially supported by taxes (*see* PUBLIC LIBRARY). But the justification of such taxes rests on the assumption that libraries constitute a public good, or common good, and that assumption leads into problematic territory.

In *The Wealth of Nations*, Adam Smith stated that "the expense of the institutions for education and religious instruction is . . . no doubt, beneficial to the whole society, and may therefore, without injustice, be defrayed by the general contribution of the whole society" (357). Smith did not mention public libraries, which did not yet exist, so his concept must be expanded to include them as educational institutions. That expansion was made, with minimal resistance, by librarians and government in the pioneer period of public libraries. Smith also noted the appropriateness of individual contributions to the funding of common goods if "they most immediately benefited by them." So economics offers a rationale for schools funded by general taxation and schools funded at least in part privately—the latter being available to the limited clientele that pays for them. In the library domain, the same theory leads to free libraries open to all, funded generally, and to restricted-use libraries (subscription libraries and research libraries) funded privately.

Nobody in a modern state is excluded by policy from public goods. Every person, whether or not a contributor to the funding of a fire department or national defense, is entitled to the benefits of such services. Every child has access to schools, and every resident of a community has the use of its public library. So it would seem that the fundamental structure is evident: the government (federal, state, or local) will fund those libraries (as public goods) that are not privately supported. However, there are two obstacles to the execution of this principle. First, there is no solid information about the complete social benefits of library services. It seems fairly clear that schools render a social benefit in preparing young people to participate in society. But it is not obvious what libraries do in serving those same people when they have left school or serving children who are already being served in school. Some studies, such as those reported in the *Public Library Inquiry* of the 1950s, indicated that public libraries were usefully serving only a small minority of the people (*see* PHILOSOPHY OF PUBLIC LIBRARIANSHIP). Statistics of library use are impressive, but there is no research record to establish a social value for that use. That is one obstacle. The other is that there are competing services—other common goods that governments must consider in distributing funds.

As long as public libraries are regarded as educational institutions, accommodating adults with opportunities for lifelong learning, and supplementing the schools in assisting children to learn, the competing institutions are few. Museums may be mentioned, as may public television or radio. There are no commercial competitors. But if the public library is regarded as a recreational institution, competitors abound: movies, commercial television, theater, music, bookstores, and the Internet are examples. Government appraisal of public library interests in providing recreation in that context may well bring negative results. Public libraries as "information providers" encounter the same glut of competition, from radio and television media and the Internet.

The formative decades of the American public library movement displayed such issues in the hard light of actual legislation. Public libraries were broadly identified as common goods because they abetted democratic values. Among those values were human rights, political equality, individualism (supported by "self-culture"), moral duty, the informed voter, nationalism, and religious liberalism. The first question posed above, "Who furnishes the fund for the specific purpose of supporting a public library?," brought one clear response: the government. State and municipal governments met the challenge together as library laws were enacted by states permitting municipalities to tax themselves in order to establish and maintain libraries. The first state library law (in New Hampshire in 1849) placed no limit on the amount of tax that a town or city could levy for library purposes. In other states the scenario varied: some had maximum rates (Maine, 1854). Massachusetts (1851) had limitations at first, then, in 1866, none (Ditzion 1947, 30–31; this is the source for much of this section). Taxation was not the only means of support in mid-century. In New York State there was "a haphazard state of library affairs" with towns giving ad hoc funds to libraries, drawing on "liquor license fees, excise taxes on spirits, and from fines imposed for infractions of temperance laws" (Ditzion 1947, 34). And private gifts to libraries were an important if undependable fount of added revenue.

Overall, there existed a "rather cordial legislative acceptance of public libraries," but "in some cities it was only after a long period of uncertainty and fluctuating fortune that a city library partly or completely supported by subscribers' fees finally became a full-fledged tax-supported institution" (Ditzion 1947, 41). Salem, New Haven, Northampton, and Providence were among the slow-moving towns.

A refinement to the concept of the library as educator was the inclusion of children in its scope. Until the last years of the nineteenth century, most public libraries catered to adults only, refusing to deal with persons under 14 or in some cases under 16 years of age. While adult education (for school leavers) was a sturdy oak for public libraries, childhood education was a weaker sapling. Children's rooms and services were created only in the 1880s (*see* SERVICES TO CHILDREN AND YOUNG ADULTS).

That nineteenth-century perspective on funding remains the norm today. Public libraries are created through permissive, enabling state legislation and local funding. Taxes on property, income, or other assets (e.g., the former "intangibles tax" in Ohio) are the typical local devices for raising money. The taxing jurisdiction may be a municipality, a county, a region of several counties, or a specially constructed library district.

Modern adjuncts to the funding menu are bond issues, which are usually targeted to specific cause like a new building and which require voter approval. Additional revenue for libraries has flowed from federal programs since 1956, when the Library Services Act was passed (*see* GOVERNMENT ROLE).

The second question above, "How shall the appropriate amount of such a fund be determined?," was answered in helter-skelter fashion in the early days and still has not earned a clear response. Local authorities (municipal, county, region, and district) with taxing power determine appropriations for their public libraries, following no identifiable rules or principles. In placid economic times, libraries may anticipate receiving funds on the order of what they got the previous year; in rough times, they will face stagnation or reductions.

Current Situation

Total public library operating expenses in fiscal year (FY) 2008 were $10,724,925,000, or $36.36 per capita (U.S. Institute of Museum and Library Services 2010). Both total expenses and per capita figures have grown steadily in recent years. These numbers tell the story:

Data from Institute of Museum and Library Services and National Center for Education Statistics.

	Total Expenses	Per Capita Expenses
FY 1993	$4.7 billion	$19.16
FY 2004	$8.6 billion	$30.49
FY 2005	$9.1 billion	$31.65
FY 2008	$10.7 billion	$36.36

From FY 2008 to FY 2009, total operating expenses appear to have been fairly stable. A study issued in 2010 (American Library Association 2010) found that 25.9 percent of libraries had the same budget as the year before; 21.8 percent had an increase up to 2 percent, 20.1 percent had an increase of 2.1 to 4 percent, and 9.4 percent had an increase of more than 6 percent. These data represent the financial picture at the outset of the national recession.

Sources of library revenue have not changed much over the years. In FY 2005 local governments provided 81 percent, state governments 10 percent, and federal government 1 percent. In 1993 the comparable figures were 78 percent, 13 percent, and 1 percent.

City and library websites for several municipalities were examined in the preparation of this entry. The result was a picture of wide disparity across the range of values, with public library allocations averaging 2 to 3 percent of total city budgets. Per capita library allocations ranged from around $40 to around $90 in the libraries examined, while the per capita national average for FY 2008 was $36.36.

All that has been said so far about the current situation—taking "current" to mean the past few years—presents a favorable landscape of public library finance. But in the national recession climate of 2009 and 2010, the measures, in many libraries if not all of them, turned downward. Darkening budgets in state and local jurisdictions led to cuts in library shares. Indeed, such cuts were noted in earlier years as well but not generally. An account in the website of the Public Library of Cincinnati and Hamilton County is instructive about the recent situation:

The faltering state and national economy devastated library funding in 2009. As a result of both falling tax collections and a legislated reduction in the percentage designated to the Public Library Fund (from 2.22% to 1.97%), library income dropped significantly. Our library received $39 million in state funding in 2009—almost $8.5 million less than in 2008. The Public Library Fund remains our primary source of funding—91.6% of all funding received in 2009. But other income fell as well, most notably donations and investment income. Despite a $2.2 million reduction in expenditures, overall income was $11.8 million short of what we needed to operate the library system this year. ... The Ohio Department of Taxation estimates that funding will continue to drop in 2010. (Public Library of Cincinnati and Hamilton County 2010, 1)

Such income declines are reported nationally. Fifty-two percent of libraries report cuts in state funding from FY 2009 to FY 2010. At the same time, library usage continues to increase. Cincinnati had a 5 percent increase in circulation in 2009 over 2008, and library visits increased 8 percent.

Branch libraries are being targeted for closing or greatly reduced hours (*see* BRANCH LIBRARIES). But central libraries are also in difficulty, forced to reduce staff while trying to meet the rising demand for service. *Library Journal* initiated a series of reports in 2010 titled "Losing Libraries" to "map libraries' cuts/layoffs/closing and create a unified national picture" (Losing libraries 2010).

The answers to the two questions posed at the beginning of this entry have the same answers in 2010 as they had 100 years ago. No widespread doubts have been raised about the governmental responsibility for public library support. But as governments run out of money, they set up priorities that may exclude libraries, at least for the duration of the financial crisis. For example, in 2010, Hood River County, OR, closed all three locations of its public library (*Library Journal*, July 2010, 17). Nothing has been heard of the possibility of fee-based public libraries. Even the occasional attempt to raise funds by increasing overdue fines has not fared well (Oder 2006, 20). The second question, "How shall the appropriate amount of library funding be determined?," also has the same answer it always had. The amount is set by the funding authority in response to budget requests submitted by the libraries. The typical pattern—and the situation in the Chicago Public Library—is that "there are no set formulas, rather the budgets are based upon departmental requests and overall city needs." A burden of proof thus falls on the library to justify their requests. This is perhaps a healthy foundation for the public library. Many librarians have made calculations of the dollar value of their services and offer suggestions on their websites to patrons for estimating what they save by using the library. The most prominent response of public librarians to the threat of declining income has been advocacy (*see* PUBLIC RELATIONS).

Despite a dark economic climate and the possibility that they may be increasingly viewed as recreation centers, public libraries appear to be well established as public goods in the minds of funding agencies and the people at large. As long as that status is held, fluctuation in support can be absorbed, and higher levels of funding may be anticipated as conditions improve.

References

American Library Association. 2010. *Libraries Connect Communities: Public Library Funding & Technology Access Study, 2009–2010*. Chicago: American Library Association. http://www.ala.org/lplinternetfunding. Accessed October 2010.

Ditzion, Sidney. 1947. *Arsenals of a Democratic Culture*. Chicago: American Library Association.

Oder, Norman. 2006. Philadelphia backs off fine policy. *Library Journal* 131, no. 3 (February 15): 20.

Public Library of Cincinnati and Hamilton County. 2010. Library funding. http://www.cincinnatilibrary.org/info/funding. Accessed October 2010.

Smith, Adam. 1776/1952. *An Inquiry into the Nature and Causes of the Wealth of Nations* (1776). Chicago: Encyclopaedia Britannica, 1952. Pagination from the 1952 edition.

U.S. Institute of Museum and Library Services. 2010. *Public Libraries in the United States, Fiscal Year 2008*. Washington, DC: Government Printing Office.

FYAN, LOLETA DAWSON, 1894–1990   Librarian. Born May 14, 1894, Clinton, IA. She attended Wellesley College, 1911–1915, then taught school for one year. In 1916 she went to the public library in Davenport, IA, doing extension work. After a year at Western Reserve University library school in 1919, she was employed in the reference department at the Detroit Public Library. She headed the new Wayne County Library in 1921, staying to 1941. During her tenure, the staff grew to more than 100. Fyan was president of the Michigan Library Association, 1934–1935. She was active in promoting state legislation for libraries and from 1941 to 1961 served as state librarian. She chaired the coordinating committee for the Library Services Act in 1956–1959 and was a member of the library advisory committee to the U.S. commissioner of education in 1956–1961. As state librarian she helped initiate programs for the blind, and she herself became blind in the late 1960s. Fyan retired in 1961 and died in Lansing, MI, on March 15, 1990. *DALB*, 2nd supplement.

G

GAIL BORDEN PUBLIC LIBRARY DISTRICT, ELGIN, IL   270 N. Grove Ave., Elgin, IL 60120. Population served: 125,507. Circulation: 1,180,088. Holdings: 332,466. 1 branch. The Rakow Branch, which opened in 2009, is the library's first. It is "green," with a Zen garden, computer café, and family room with fireplace. LJ October 1, 2010: 3-star library. IMLS award 2009. One of the libraries that converted to BISAC (*see* CLASSIFICATION).

GARLAND, TX. *See* NICHOLSON MEMORIAL LIBRARY SYSTEM, GARLAND, TX.

GEAUGA COUNTY PUBLIC LIBRARY, CHARDON, OH   12701 Ravenwood, Chardon, OH 44024. Founded 1963. Population served: 85,787. Circulation: 2,100,000. Holdings: 600,000. 6 branches, 1 bookmobile. LJ February 15, 2009, and November 15, 2009: 3-star library.

GENESEO, NY. *See* WADSWORTH LIBRARY, GENESEO, NY.

GENEVA PUBLIC LIBRARY, NE   1043 G St., Geneva, NE 68361. Population served: 2,226. Circulation: 59,067. Holdings: 21,683. LJ February 15, 2009, and November 15, 2009: 3-star library.

GEORGETOWN COUNTY LIBRARY, SC   405 Cleland St., Georgetown, SC 29440. Subscription library 1799, tax supported "in the 1930s" (communication from the library). Population served: 59,790. Circulation: 210,649. Holdings: 134,250. IMLS award 2007.

GIFTS AND EXCHANGES. *See* COLLECTION DEVELOPMENT.

GILLIS, JAMES L., 1857–1917   Librarian. Born Richmond, IA, October 3, 1857. His family moved West by ox train, eventually settling in Sacramento, CA. He had no schooling after age 15. From 1872 to 1894, Gillis worked for the Sacramento Valley Railroad, rising to assistant superintendent. He was employed by the California state legislature, then appointed state librarian on April 1, 1899. He reorganized operations and upgraded state library law. In 1903 he was dispatching traveling libraries, in 1904 he was circulating books for the blind, and in 1905 he created an extension department. He began publishing *News Notes of California Libraries* in 1906. Gillis was president of the California Library Association for eight terms between 1906 and 1915, president of the National Association of State Libraries in 1906 and 1914, and a member of the American Library Association council in 1911. Most of his later career was devoted to promoting county libraries; he secured a state law authorizing them in 1909. By 1917, 36 of California's 58 counties had complete library service under direction of the state librarian. LJ Hall of Fame; *DALB*.

GLEN CARBON CENTENNIAL LIBRARY, IL   198 S. Main St., Glen Carbon, IL 62034. Founded 1992. Population served: 11,799. Circulation: 92,772. Holdings: 30,890. LJ best small library 2010.

GLEN ELLYN PUBLIC LIBRARY, IL   400 Duane St., Glen Ellyn, IL 60137. Founded 1912. Population served: 26,999. Circulation: 531,173. Holdings: 157,128. Glen Ellyn had the first Friends of the Library, 1922.

GLENDALE PUBLIC LIBRARY, AZ   5959 W. Brown St., Glendale, AZ 85302. Founded 1922. Population served: 251,522. Circulation: 2,631,465. Holdings: 600,000. 2 branches.

GOALS. *See* PLANNING.

GOVERNMENT ROLE   This entry deals with the role of the U.S. federal government in the realm of public libraries. For the role of state and local governments, *see* COUNTY AND REGIONAL LIBRARIES; PUBLIC LIBRARY; STATE LIBRARY AGENCIES.
    The federal government took no part in public library affairs until 1956. Its reticence was grounded in the Constitution and in the widely accepted view that public libraries are educational institutions. Since neither the Constitution nor its amendments authorizes federal involvement in education, the Tenth Amendment appears to reserve the educational sphere for

the individual states. This perspective remains alive, notably among Republican legislators; it underlies resistance to library and educational programs at the federal level.

Direct support by the federal government of its own agency libraries was never questioned. Public libraries have benefited from the work of those libraries, in particular the Library of Congress (1800), the National Library of Medicine (1956)—originally the library of the Surgeon General (1836)—and the National Agricultural Library (1962). Those libraries have created databases and catalog programs along with other services that libraries outside the government are utilizing.

The Department of Education was founded in 1867, primarily to collect and disseminate statistics on schools; it moved down a step in the hierarchy a year later to become the Office of Education (OE), then slipped again to the bureau level within the Department of the Interior. In 1939 it again took the name Office of Education, within the Federal Security Agency, then in 1953 within the new Department of Health, Education, and Welfare (HEW). Cabinet level was gained in 1980 as the Department of Education.

The first publication with library statistics was the *Report of the Commissioner of Education Made to the Secretary of the Interior for the Year 1870*. It included a list of 161 libraries, excluding academic libraries, with their founding dates, holdings, and annual acquisition figures. In 1876 the Bureau of Education published an important assemblage of data titled *Public Libraries in the United States*. This substantial inventory listed 3,647 libraries. According to general usage at that time, a public library was any collection open to a group larger than a family, whether or not there was a fee for access (for a detailed analysis of this report, see McMullen 2000, x.) Subsequently the bureau (and office) issued periodic collections of educational data with some account of public libraries. When a library services unit was established within the OE in 1939, the library statistical program was accelerated (*see* STATISTICS). In 1966 the OE combined all educational statistics units into the National Center for Educational Statistics (NCES), which set up a library statistics unit. NCES worked on standardization of statistics practices, organized demonstration surveys in the 1970s, and collected national data to 2007. In 2007 the Institute of Museum and Library Services (IMLS) absorbed the NCES role of public library statistics reporting, along with the administration of federal support programs for public libraries (*see* INSTITUTE OF MUSEUM AND LIBRARY SERVICES; STATISTICS).

Persistent lobbying for a decade by the American Library Association (ALA) resulted in the first federal funding for public libraries, as President Eisenhower signed the Library Services Act (LSA) on May 14, 1956. The act was a five-year demonstration project, providing for the "extension of public library service to rural areas without such service or with inadequate service," specifically excluding aid to towns of 10,000 population or more. There was a formula for state matching funds. Federal appropriations under LSA were gradually increased from $2,050,000 for January–June 1957 and $5,000,000 for July 1957–June 1958 to $25,000,000 for July 1963–June 1964. The act was renewed in 1960 to cover 1960–1966 and then amended as the Library Services and Construction Act (LSCA), signed by President Johnson on February 11, 1964. A separate title in LSCA allowed for funding of new buildings and renovations. A 1966 amendment added two new titles: one for interlibrary cooperation and one for state institutional library services (for patients and inmates of state institutions). Authorizations grew steadily; with the 1970 extension of LSCA, funding had surpassed $1 billion over a five-year period.

LSA produced remarkable results. As of June 1961 34,000,000 rural persons had improved public library service, 1,500,000 of them receiving service for the first time. Six million books were added to rural library collections, and 250 bookmobiles were put on the road. Some provisions of LSCA as amended, for fiscal years 1972–1976, were improvement of service to any areas (no longer exclusively rural) and groups (including patients and inmates, physically handicapped, and those in poverty), improvement of metro libraries that functioned as regional or national resource centers, and improvement of state library agencies (which doubled their personnel). Construction projects were funded on a matching basis. Cooperation projects were fully funded. All these programs had the healthy consequence of uplifting library practice in planning and data gathering. They all required state-level five-year plans and annual reports, which led in turn to local-level plans and systematic reports.

In addition to LSA and LSCA, legislation of the 1950s and 1960s with major library impact were the National Defense Education Act (NDEA) of 1958, the Elementary and Secondary Education Act (ESEA) of 1965, and the Higher Education Act (HEA) of 1965. NDEA provided funding for instructional materials, ESEA specifically for school library resources, and HEA for grants to library schools and fellowships for students. Support for these programs was strong in the 1960s. For fiscal year 1966, $55 million was authorized. However, in the 1970s, President Nixon vetoed appropriations for LSCA and ESEA II; his fiscal year 1974 budget request recommended ending all federal support for libraries. Congress funded the programs through HEW appropriations and opposed the executive branch efforts to eliminate library assistance. The fiscal year 1976 appropriations for education were vetoed by President Ford, but Congress overrode the veto. Funding for libraries under ESEA, LSCA, and HEA remained between $90 million and $100 million through fiscal year 1976.

Another name change occurred in 1996 as LSCA became the Library Services and Technology Act (LSTA). This legislation, advocated by the ALA, covered all types of libraries, emphasizing technology needs. It was reauthorized in 2003 and again in 2010 as part of the Museum and Library Services Act (see INSTITUTE OF MUSEUM AND LIBRARY SERVICES). Appropriations, administered by the IMLS, have been at high levels in the new century (but the impact of inflation must be considered): fiscal year 2001, $163,178,000; 2005, $199,292,000; and 2010, $213,523,000.

The depository program originated in 1895 with the Depository Library Act. That legislation authorized free distribution of Government Printing

Office (GPO) publications to libraries selected by senators and representatives in their states and districts. In 1962 the program was expanded to identify more libraries as depositories and to include federal agency publications that were not issued by the GPO. A depository library was permitted to choose series of publications for receipt and access to the public, with the understanding that the materials would be kept indefinitely (a weeding option was added later). Smaller libraries had difficulty with space demands of the program, private college libraries had problems with the public access requirement, and all libraries felt the impact of processing on staff time, but all things considered, the depository act was a useful gift to libraries. Now the digital age has introduced new considerations. "A small but increasing number of selective depositories are leaving the FDLP [Federal Depository Library Program], their directors citing the burden of processing publications that aren't used and the diminishing importance of maintaining tangible collections of government publications when most current federal publications are available online" (Ragains 2010, 37). "GPO is currently creating brief records from its retrospective shelflist, but will need assistance from libraries to create complete MARC records" (Ragains 2010, 38); the problem is with pre-1976 documents not available online.

President Nixon signed legislation on July 20, 1970, creating the National Commission on Libraries and Information Science (NCLIS), intended to advise the president and Congress on policy, to conduct surveys and research on library and information needs, to plan for meeting those needs, and to advise other agencies at state and local levels. NCLIS published numerous reports and held two White House conferences on library and information services. An account of NCLIS history, publications, and activities was issued as a farewell document by the commission in March 2008 (NCLIS 2008). On March 30, 2008, the NCLIS office closed, its duties transferred to the IMLS, which thus became the primary channel of federal concern, support, and data gathering for public libraries.

Two other pieces of federal legislation with major impact on public libraries may be mentioned. One is the Americans with Disabilities Act (1990; *see* SERVICES TO PEOPLE WITH DISABILITIES), which brings some work and planning but no hardship. The other is the USA Patriot Act (2001, reauthorized 2006 and 2010), which brings a serious challenge to library integrity. Efforts by the ALA and the Civil Liberties Union to remove provisions affecting libraries from the Patriot Act have been unsuccessful (*see* PRIVACY AND CONFIDENTIALITY).

References

Krettek, Germaine. 1975. Library legislation, federal. *Encyclopedia of Library and Information Science* 15: 337-354. New York: Marcel Dekker.

McMullen, Haynes. 2000. *American Libraries before 1876*. Westport, CT: Greenwood Press.

National Commission on Libraries and Information Science. 2008. *Meeting the Information Needs of the American People: Past Actions and Future*

Initiatives. Washington, DC: National Commission on Libraries and Information Science. http://www.nclis.gov.

Ragains, Patrick. 2010. Fixing the Federal Deposit Library Program. *American Libraries* 41, no. 5 (May): 36–38.

White House Conference on Library and Information Services. 1979. *Information for the 1980s: Final Report of the White House Conference on Libraries and Information Services, 1979.* Washington: National Commission on Libraries and Information Science, 1980.

White House Conference on Library and Information Services. 1991. *Information 2000: Library and Information Services for the 21st Century. Summary Report of the 1991 White House Conference on Library and Information Services.* Washington: Government Printing Office.

GRAND MARAIS PUBLIC LIBRARY, MN   104 Second Ave., Grand Marais, MN 55604. Population served: 1,409. Circulation: 59,464. Holdings: 19,302. LJ February 15, 2009; November 15, 2009; and October 1, 2010: 5-star library. HAPLR 2010.

GRAND RAPIDS PUBLIC LIBRARY, MI   111 Library St., Grand Rapids, MI 49503. Population served: 197,800. Circulation: 1,500,000. Holdings: 650,000. 7 branches. The central library, opened June 20, 1904, was designed by Shepley, Rutan, and Coolidge, who were architects of the Chicago Public Library. The structure was renovated in 2003.

GRAND VALLEY PUBLIC LIBRARY, ORWELL, OH   One N. School St., Orwell, OH 44076. Population served: 2,800. Circulation: 88,546. Holdings: 37,937. LJ February 15, 2009: 5-star library; November 15, 2009: 4-star library. HAPLR 2009, 2010.

GRANDVIEW HEIGHTS PUBLIC LIBRARY, OH   1685 W. First Ave., Grandview Heights, OH 43212. Founded 1924. Population served: 7,485. Circulation: 818,200. Holdings: 168,946. LJ February 15, 2009; November 15, 2009; and October 1, 2010: 5-star library. HAPLR 2009, 2010.

GRAVETTE PUBLIC LIBRARY, AR   407 Charlotte St. SE, Gravette, AR 72736. Founded 2006. Population served: 22,224. Circulation: 14,106. Holdings: 20,159. LJ October 1, 2010: 4-star library.

GREAT NECK LIBRARY, NY   159 Bayview Ave., Great Neck, NY 11023. Population served: 40,000. Circulation: 750,000. Holdings: 350,000. 3 branches. LJ February 15, 2009: 5-star library; November 15, 2009: 4-star library: October 1, 2010: 3-star library.

GREEN, SAMUEL SWETT, 1837–1918   Librarian, minister. Born Worcester, MA, on February 20, 1837. He was a graduate of Harvard, 1858, and the

Divinity School, 1864. He was a preacher, then a banker, and in 1871 librarian of the Worcester Free Library. He initiated Sunday openings at the library in 1872 as part of his strong motivation to satisfy patron needs. Green was active at the 1876 conference of librarians in Philadelphia that resulted in establishment of the American Library Association and served as its president in 1891. Appointed to the Massachusetts State Library Commission, he served there 19 years. In 1893 he presided over the World's Congress of Librarians at the Chicago Columbian Exposition. Although he retired from the Worcester library in January 1909, he continued to go to his office every day until shortly before his death. Green is often cited as the writer of the first article on reference work (Green 1876). He was a believer in the ladder theory of selection, expecting a person's reading tastes to rise over time, and promoted readers' advisory service in the form of lists of books designed to take patrons to higher levels. Another of his ideas was for public libraries to give service to business and industry. He also fostered cooperation between schools and public libraries. *DAB*; *DALB*; LJ Hall of Fame.

References

Green, Samuel Swett. 1876. Personal relations between librarians and readers. *American Library Journal* 1, no. 2 (October): 74–81.
Green, Samuel Swett. 1879. Sensational fiction in public libraries. *Library Journal* 4: 348–349.
Green, Samuel Swett. 1889. The library and its relation to persons engaged in industrial pursuits. *Library Journal* 14, no. 5/6 (May/June): 215–225.

GREEN BAY, WI. *See* BROWN COUNTY LIBRARY, GREEN BAY, WI.

GREEN TREE PUBLIC LIBRARY, PA   10 W. Manilla Ave., Green Tree, PA 15220. Founded 1964. Population served: 4,719. Circulation: 92,682. Holdings: 33,994. LJ February 15, 2009; November 15, 2009; and October 1, 2010: 3-star library.

GREENAWAY, EMERSON, 1906–1990   Librarian. Born May 25, 1906, in Springfield, MA. He graduated from Massachusetts Agricultural College in 1927 and found employment in the public library of Springfield as a reference assistant. He took the post of branch supervisor in Hartford and then went to the University of North Carolina for his library degree in 1934. Greenaway directed the library in Fitchburg, MA, for three years and then moved to the Worcester Public Library. In 1945 he became director of the Enoch Pratt Free Public Library in Baltimore, MD, remaining to 1951. He worked to upgrade the branches and the children's services. UNESCO invited him to survey the library situations in Czechoslovakia, Austria, and Poland; he was active thereafter in various international activities. From 1951 to his retirement in 1969, Greenaway directed the Free Library of

Philadelphia. He extended the branch system, doubled the size of the book collection, and saw the number of registrants rise from 227,000 to 575,000. His concurrent activities included library school lecturing and American Library Association (ALA) positions; he was president of the ALA in 1958–1959. In the area of materials selection, Greenaway was conservative. He wrote in 1950 that the public library should "encourage such use of leisure time as will promote personal development and social well-being, and tend increasingly to leave to commercial agencies the provision of trivial, purely ephemeral materials" (Williams 1988, 74). In Baltimore he refused to buy a best-seller named *Washington Confidential*, which he believed would not promote the development or social well-being of his patrons. He was a strong anticommunist, recommending at one time a periodical article supporting Senator Joseph McCarthy, but advocated collection of communist publications. Greenaway received numerous awards, including two citations for distinguished service from the ALA. He died in New London on April 8, 1990. *DALB*, 2nd supplement.

Reference

Williams, Patrick. 1988. *The American Public Library and the Problem of Purpose.* New York: Greenwood Press.

GREENE COUNTY PUBLIC LIBRARY, XENIA, OH   76 E. Market St., Xenia, OH 45385. Founded 1899. Population served: 151,996. Circulation: 2,900,000. Holdings: 650,000. HAPLR 2009.

GREENPORT, NY. *See* FLOYD MEMORIAL LIBRARY, GREENPORT, NY.

GREENSBORO PUBLIC LIBRARY, NC   219 N. Church St., Greensboro, NC 27402. Founded 1902. Population served: 345,694. Circulation: 1,680,000. Holdings: 729,147. 6 branches, 1 bookmobile. The library offers an unusual service for homeless persons. A local chapter of Food Not Bombs provides a meal at the central library each week. The library partners with them in winter with relevant programming and services. Events include health screening, computer classes, visits with public officials, art activities, and movies (information from the library).

GREENWICH LIBRARY, CT   101 W. Putnam Ave., Greenwich, CT 06830. Founded by an endowment, free to all, 1899; tax supported from 1917. There was a subscription library in the city in 1805. Population served: 62,317. Circulation: 1,407,570. Holdings: 374,502. 2 branches, 1 bookmobile. LJ February 15, 2009: 5-star library; November 15, 2009: 4-star library; October 1, 2010: 5-star library.

GUILFORD MEMORIAL LIBRARY, ME   4 Library St., Guilford, ME 04443. Population served: 1,494. Circulation: 31,942. Holdings: 15,831. LJ February 15, 2009, November 15, 2009, and October 1, 2010: 4-star library.

GULF SHORES, AL. *See* THOMAS B. NORTON PUBLIC LIBRARY, GULF SHORES, AL.

GULFPORT, MS. *See* HARRISON COUNTY LIBRARY, GULFPORT, MS.

GURNEE, IL. *See* WARREN-NEWPORT PUBLIC LIBRARY DISTRICT, GURNEE, IL.

H

HAGERSTOWN, MD. *See* WASHINGTON COUNTY FREE LIBRARY, HAGERSTOWN, MD.

HAINES BOROUGH PUBLIC LIBRARY, HAINES, AK   111 Third Ave. S, Haines, AK 99827. Founded 1928 as association library; borough support from 1970. Population served: 2,207. Circulation: 89,654. Holdings: 34,426. LJ February 15, 2009, November 15, 2009, and October 1, 2010: 5-star library.

HAMPTON LIBRARY, BRIDGEHAMPTON, NY   2478 Main St., Bridgehampton, NY 11932. Founded as subscription library 1877; part of the New York State Department of Education, 1905, no more fees (information from the library). Population served: 1,866. Circulation: 41,534. Holdings: 40,984. LJ February 15, 2009, and November 15, 2009: 5-star library.

HANCOCK COUNTY LIBRARY SYSTEM, BAY ST. LOUIS, MS   312 Highway 90, Bay St. Louis, MS 39520. Population served: 45,000. Circulation: 300,000. Holdings: 115,000. 3 branches. IMLS award 2001.

HARBOR-TOPKY MEMORIAL LIBRARY, ASHTABULA HARBOR, OH   1633 Walnut Blvd., Ashtabula Harbor, OH 44004. Founded 1924. Population served: 30,496. Circulation: 170,024. Holdings: 45,982. LJ October 1, 2010: 4-star library.

HARDTNER PUBLIC LIBRARY, KS   102 E. Central, Hardtner, KS 67057. Population served: 191. Circulation: 9,037. Holdings: 12,000. Outstanding small library award 1991. HAPLR 2009, 2010.

HARFORD COUNTY PUBLIC LIBRARY, BELCAMP, MD   1221-A Brass Mill Rd., Belcamp, MD 21017. Founded 1946. Population served: 230,600. Circulation: 4,466,496. Holdings: 1,050,759. 11 branches, 2 bookmobiles. LJ November 15, 2009 and October 1, 2010: 4-star library. The library board has decided to have a teenaged member at all times.

HARLOWTON PUBLIC LIBRARY, MT   13 S. Central Ave., Harlowton, MT 59036. Population served: 2,269 Circulation: 7,366. Holdings: 11,972. LJ October 1, 2010: 4-star library.

HARRIS COUNTY PUBLIC LIBRARY, HOUSTON, TX   8080 El Rio, Houston, TX 77054. Population served: 1,408,797. Circulation: 10,724,945. Holdings: 2,557,578. 26 branches.

HARRISON COUNTY LIBRARY SYSTEM, GULFPORT, MS   2600 24th Ave., Gulfport, MS 39501. Founded as association library, 1891; subscription library, 1893; free public library, 1912; became Harrison County Library, 1984. Population served: 193,810. Circulation: 632,433. Holdings: 175,851. 9 branches, including temporary libraries. The following report was received from the library director, Robert Lipscomb, on June 10, 2010:

> The Harrison County Library System currently consists of nine member libraries. On August 8, 1984, the Harrison County supervisors created ... the system with its five-member statutory board of trustees. On October 1, 1994, the cities of Biloxi, D'Iberville, Gulfport, and Pass Christian, and the County of Harrison signed a new contract that formalized the current library system. ... On August 29, 2005, we were hit with Hurricane Katrina. This very devastating event saw the destruction of four of our member libraries and the loss of more than 180,000 circulating items. Additionally, we lost approximately 103 computers. On November 5, 2005 the Pass Christian Library opened a temporary library in a trailer donated by the DuPont Corporation. In January of 2007 the D'Iberville Library reopened after repairing the extensive damage caused by the storm. Three other temporary trailer libraries (in Biloxi, Gulfport, and Woolmarket) were opened in June of 2007 as a result of a grant from the Bill and Melinda Gates Foundation.
>
> On February 20, 2009 construction began on the new 12,000 square foot Pass Christian Library. Three other new library buildings are planned for construction in the near future. They

are the Biloxi Library (21,000 square feet), the Downtown Gulf-port Library (10,000 square feet) and the new Headquarters Library (31,000 square feet). Obviously, we are going to need as much help as we can get to replace all that we have lost. Even with insurance, FEMA and local funding, we will still need a great deal of outside funding if we are to resume the level of public service we provided before the storm.

HARRISON MEMORIAL LIBRARY, CARMEL, CA   Ocean Ave. at Lincoln St., Carmel, CA 93921. Population served: 4,078. Circulation: 104,077. Holdings: 81,638. LJ February 15, 2009: 5-star library.

HARSH, VIVIAN GORDON, 1890–1960   Librarian. Born May 27, 1890, in Chicago. She entered library work as a clerk in Chicago Public Library (CPL) in 1919 and moved up the ranks, taking time off for a library degree (Simmons College) in 1921. Harsh was the first black person with a profes-sional position in CPL, 1924. From 1932 to 1958 she headed the George C. Hall Branch in a black neighborhood. There she developed a specialized collection and held literary events. She died on August 17, 1960, in Chicago. The collection she created was named the Vivian G. Harsh Collection and relocated to the Woodson Branch in 1975. It is the largest of its kind in the Midwest, with more than 75,000 items. *DALB*, 2nd supplement.

HARTFORD PUBLIC LIBRARY, CT   500 Main St., Hartford, CT 06103. There was a library as early as 1774; in 1892 the Hartford Library Associa-tion became free to all; in 1893 Hartford Public Library was established. Population served: 125,053. Circulation: 560,569. Holdings: 560,000. IMLS award 2002. Caroline Hewins was librarian from 1875 of the earlier libraries, then head of Hartford Public Library, one of only four female directors in 1878 (*see* HEWINS, CAROLINE).

HARTINGTON PUBLIC LIBRARY, NE   106 S. Broadway, Hartington, NE 68739. Population served: 1,640. Circulation: 43,591. Holdings: 17,612. LJ February 15, 2009; November 15, 2009; and October 1, 2010: 5-star library.

HAWAII STATE PUBLIC LIBRARY SYSTEM, HONOLULU, HI   478 S. King St., Honolulu, HI 96813. Population served: 1,288,198. Circulation: 7,228,276. Holdings: 3,657,735. 51 branches including the State Library. The state library evolved from an 1879 "library and reading room." Hawaii is the only state with a single statewide library system (borrow and return anywhere).

HAYS PUBLIC LIBRARY, KS   1205 S. Main, Hays, KS 67601. Founded in 1904 as a tax-supported library, evolving from a subscription library established in 1899. Population served: 19,827. Circulation: 1,112,167. Holdings: 145,842. LJ February 15, 2009; November 15, 2009; and October 1, 2010: 5-star library. HAPLR 2009, 2010.

HAZEL L. MEYER MEMORIAL LIBRARY, DE SMET, SD   111 First St., De Smet, SD 57231. Population served: 1,164. Circulation: 32,770. Holdings: 22,816. LJ February 15, 2009: 3-star library; November 15, 2009: 4-star library; October 1, 2010: 3-star library. HAPLR 2009.

HEALY, AK. See TRI-VALLEY COMMUNITY LIBRARY, HEALY, AK.

HENDERSON DISTRICT PUBLIC LIBRARIES, NV   280 S. Green Valley Parkway, Henderson, NV 89012. Founded 1956. Population served: 249,000. Circulation: 905,000. Holdings: 298,605.

HENDERSON MEMORIAL PUBLIC LIBRARY ASSOCIATION, JEFFERSON, OH   54 E. Jefferson St., Jefferson, OH 44047. Founded 1934. Population served: 5,500. Circulation: 135,000. Holdings: 44,984. LJ February 15, 2009: 4-star library.

HENNEPIN COUNTY LIBRARY, MINNETONKA, MN   12601 Ridgedale, Minnetonka, MN 55305. Founded 1922. Absorbed the Minneapolis Public Library (MPL), which became a branch, on January 2, 2008. Population served: 1,136,599. Circulation: 15,186,935. Holdings: 4,539,957. 41 branches. LJ February 15, 2009: 5-star library. HAPLR 2009, 2010. MPL was founded in 1887. It had a children's room in 1893 and a business branch in 1916. Its new central library building, designed by the firm Pelli Clarke Pelli, won an award from the American Institute of Architects and the American Library Association in 2009. It includes a children's library with materials in more than 30 languages and a "New Americans Center" for recent immigrants as well as a major business department. Directors of MPL: Herbert Putnam, 1888–1891; James K. Hosmer, 1892–1904; Gratia Countryman, 1904–1936; Carl Vitz, 1937–1946; Glenn M. Lewis, 1946–1957; Raymond E. Williams, 1957–1963; Margaret M. Mull (acting), 1963–1964; Ervin J. Gaines, 1964–1974; Mary L. Dyar (interim), 1974–1975; Joseph Kimbrough, 1975–1989; Susan Goldberg Kent, 1990–1995; Mary Larson, 1996–2002; Jan Feye-Stukas (interim), 2002–2003; Katherine G. Hadley, 2003–2007; and Jane Eastwood (interim), 2007–. Hennepin County Library directors: Gratia Countryman, 1922–1925; Ethel Barry, 1925–1947; Helen Young, 1947–1969; Robert H. Rohlf, 1969–1994; Charles M. Brown, 1994–2004; Ann Ryan, 2005–2008; and Lois Langer Thompson, 2009–.

HENRY CARTER HULL LIBRARY, CLINTON, CT   10 Killingworth Turnpike, Clinton, CT 06413. Founded as an association library 1910, supported by endowments to 1976, then tax supported. Population served: 13,638. Circulation: 436,236. Holdings: 62,690. HAPLR 2009, 2010.

HEWINS, CAROLINE MARIA, 1846–1926   Librarian. Born Roxbury, MA, October 10, 1846. After graduating from normal school, she worked in the Boston Athenaeum, 1866–1867, under William Frederick Poole. She taught in private schools, then became librarian of the Young Men's Institute in Hartford, CT. That organization was absorbed by the Hartford Library Association in 1878 and became the Hartford Public Library in 1892. Hewins remained as librarian, one of only four female public library directors at the time. She improved the children's collection and gave the first American story hours in 1882. Hartford had a separate children's room in 1904 and a full-time children's librarian in 1907. The American Library Association (ALA) published *Books for Boys and Girls: A Selected List* by Hewins in 1897 (revised 1904, 1915). In her work with children Hewins emphasized classics and opposed writings that condescended to young readers. Apart from her accomplishments in the children's field, she brought the Hartford library to prominence, with a collection of 150,000 volumes by 1925. She was vice president of ALA in 1891 and founder of the Connecticut Library Association (president 1912–1913). She gave papers at ALA conferences and in London and published numerous articles. Hewins died on November 4, 1926, in Hartford. *DALB*; LJ Hall of Fame.

HIALEAH, FL. *See* JOHN F. KENNEDY LIBRARY, HIALEAH, FL.

HIAWATHA, KS. *See* MORRILL PUBLIC LIBRARY, HIAWATHA, KS.

HISTORY OF PUBLIC LIBRARIES   In this volume the historical perspective on public libraries is for the most part dispersed among entries for relevant topics, institutions, organizations, and individuals. This entry refers to many of those presentations and places them in a chronological framework. Attention is limited to the public library as a library that is open without charge for reference and circulation to all members of the community that is taxed to support it. (Other definitions appear in PUBLIC LIBRARY.) A prehistory and, to some extent, a parallel history of the public library would include social or subscription libraries, private libraries with some public access, mercantile libraries, and circulation (rental) libraries. The story of those institutions is not told in this handbook.

    Libraries that accord with the definition offered above were primarily creations of the mid-nineteenth century. A few earlier examples are described in separate entries (*see* PETERBOROUGH TOWN LIBRARY, NH; SCOVILLE MEMORIAL LIBRARY, SALISBURY, CT; WITHERLE MEMORIAL LIBRARY, CASTINE, ME). It may be noted that a library's establishment date or founding date is often problematic. Many public libraries began as private libraries of some kind and only gradually developed into tax-based community resources—indeed, there are still public libraries that retain some private financing (*see* BRIDGEPORT PUBLIC LIBRARY, WV), and there are a great many that inhabit dwellings or offer special services born of private philanthropy.

The sustained public library movement originated with state legislation in New England that authorized municipalities to levy taxes for the operation of public libraries. New Hampshire (1849), Massachusetts (1851), and Maine (1854) took the initiative. Given this taxing authority, "the majority of town histories show a short direct course from the 'social' to the free library form" (Ditzion 1947, 37), although there were cases of inertia and even opposition to the library concept.

From its early years the public library movement has been a philosophical forum. If the fundamental American vision at the middle of the nineteenth century was one of progress, with general education as one of its strategies, there was also a conservative force that favored protection of elite values. Public libraries might be seen as bright torches leading the populace out of ignorance to an enlightened place in democracy or as dangerous rousers of unruly dullards best left to their simple ways. Fortunately the progressive attitude prevailed in time. Very likely the decisive concept was self-culture, which "embraced the idea of duty (the moral), the aspiration towards the true idea of God (the religious), the disinterestedness which follows the truth wherever it goes (the intellectual), the unfolding and purifying of the affections (the social), and lastly, the ability to make quick decisions when these were necessary for action (the practical)" (Ditzion 1947, 54). Libraries, as extensions of schools, presented the ideal fundament for self-culture.

With the emerging acceptance of the library idea there followed divisions over emphasis and methods. A key aspect of debate turned on the nature of library stock: whether "popular" materials (usually referring to current fiction) had a role to play in the educational enterprise (*see* PHILOSOPHY OF PUBLIC LIBRARIANSHIP). When the Boston Public Library (BPL) opened in a school house on March 20, 1854, these questions had already been debated for several years by its trustees; the outcome of their discussions was expressed in a seminal report of 1852 (*see* BOSTON PUBLIC LIBRARY). The gist of the report was an intent to provide a library free to all, with home circulation of materials, serving both scholars and the general public. Deeds followed words, and BPL prospered under the guidance of wise, liberal trustees, notably Edward Everett and George Ticknor, and outstanding library leaders beginning with Charles Coffin Jewett and Justin Winsor (see individual entries for Ticknor, Jewett, and Winsor). What came to be hallmarks of the American public library, open shelves, popular and serious books, children's services, and branch libraries were features of BPL within a few years. It was by far the most influential library in the national movement.

Libraries sprouted in small Massachusetts towns as well (see entries for Amesbury, Lawrence, Lowell, New Bedford, Northampton, Salem, and

Wayland). After the Civil War the library idea spread quickly westward. Economic and social conditions favored it:

> The country was on a long economic upswing, albeit with occasional short depressions. The population of the country was rapidly expanding, based on immigration and a rising birthrate. The Industrial Revolution, fueled by the seemingly endless mineral resources of the West, was transforming the nation from a rural agrarian nation to an urban, industrial state. Mechanization of the printing industry and the development of wood pulp paper meant that much more printed material was capable of being produced. The intellectual and industrial ferment of the nineteenth century radically overhauled the nature of education both primary and higher, producing a more literate populace which had more time available for reading at a time when no other media were competing for attention. The institution of the public library expanded with the times. (Seavey 1994, 520)

That expansion was energized by librarians themselves. They held a national meeting in 1853 and another in 1876 that resulted in the formation of the American Library Association (ALA). Melvil Dewey was a force in that organization, as well as a pioneer in classification and library education (*see* DEWEY, MELVIL). By 1876 two large cities had opened public libraries: Cleveland in 1869 and Chicago in 1873. An extensive survey report issued in 1876 by the U.S. Bureau of Education listed 3,647 libraries of various types. However, as noted by Haynes McMullen (2000, table 8.1), that count omitted libraries no longer extant and certain extant categories. He reckoned that there were—or had been—10,032 libraries in the country in 1876 or earlier, of which 1,995 were "free public libraries."

In the last quarter of the century, city libraries were established in Providence, RI (1878); Milwaukee (1878); San Francisco (1879); Philadelphia (1894); and New York (1895; see entries for those cities). The first great library building housed the BPL in 1895. This period was also important for the development of state libraries and agencies, many of them outgrowths of earlier law libraries. Melvil Dewey, state librarian of New York, 1888–1905, expanded the limited role of those libraries from serving legislative needs to giving assistance to public libraries in the state. "In 1893 Dewey sent out the first traveling libraries, boxes of 100 books each, to serve communities without public libraries. . . . The idea . . . quickly spread to other states" (Himmel 1994, 602). "Library development," as it came to be called, was soon assumed as a function of states, through their state libraries or separate state library commissions. California, under its state librarian James Gillis (in office 1899–1917), was a leader in offering a range of helpful services to local libraries, focusing on the county as the unit of service. By 1929 there were county libraries in 34 states (*see* COUNTY AND REGIONAL LIBRARIES).

Traveling libraries were joined and then supplanted by book wagons, later known as bookmobiles. The first of them were out on the muddy roads of Wisconsin (guided by Lutie Stearns) and Maryland (guided by Mary Titcomb) in 1905 (see entries for the two women; *see also* BOOKMOBILES). A half century later 919 of those vehicles were in service around the country, producing 11.1 percent of total public library circulation (Pennell 1970, 19), and in 2008 there were still 797 bookmobiles making their rounds.

The philanthropy of Andrew Carnegie, commencing in Pittsburgh in 1890, eventually led to the construction of 1,412 library buildings. By 1923 they served over 31 percent of the U.S. population (Bobinski 1969; Van Slyck 1995; *see* CARNEGIE, ANDREW).

Formal service to children can be traced to the 1890s, in Brookline, MA; Minneapolis; Denver; and Cambridge, MA (see entries for these cities). The BPL had the earliest service for the blind in 1882; followed by the New York Free Circulating Library for the Blind, opened in 1896, which joined the newly organized public library of the city in 1903; and Brooklyn Public Library in 1905.

All these achievements of the early decades of the twentieth century, the so-called progressive era, may be viewed as progeny of the public library driving force, which was a missionary zeal to bring good reading to everyone, everywhere. That great goal was implemented through book selection policies (*see* COLLECTION DEVELOPMENT) and staff guidance to patrons. The latter service, under the name "readers' advisory" (RA), took shape in the 1920s. Its purpose was to help readers fulfill their own purposes in reading, whether for recreation or for practical reasons. but RA has also been criticized as an effort to prod readers along preferred lines that supported approved values—to the use of "good books" (Pawley 2007; *see* READERS' ADVISORY SERVICES). A ground value of the period was moral conservatism, which underlay national attempts at censorship. Many librarians marched in that crusade against "pernicious and immoral books" (Electra Doren of Dayton Public Library, quoted in Geller 1984, 86; *see* INTELLECTUAL FREEDOM). World War I gave librarians the opportunity to set aside their "neutrality" and remove titles that were identified as "treasonous," or just insufficiently American (Wiegand 1989). However, much creditable work was performed by librarians in the war through book distribution. By the end of the war, "the public library had matured into a bon fide social service institution" (Wiegand 1993, 843). In the 1920s public library values were reconstituted around the concept of freedom to read (Geller 1984, 111–12, 127). A problem thus came to light, one not yet resolved, of how to "balance" the viewpoints in a collection.

During the Depression public libraries were heavily used, even as funding for them diminished. The desire to do as much as possible with fewer resources was an inspiration for studies of individual libraries by outside experts. Such investigations were a part of the fresh interest in scholarly research into library issues, much of it based in the new Graduate Library

School of the University of Chicago (1928) and its *Library Quarterly* (1931–) (*see* EDUCATION OF PUBLIC LIBRARIANS; RESEARCH).

World War II saw public libraries trying to strengthen the ideals of democracy. That theme was pervasive into the mid-1950s, promoted through extensive programming and exhibits. Such events were available in more than half the nation's public libraries (Bobinski 2007, 30). Equal opportunity to enjoy public library service was a democratic value, and in the 1940s it became clear that such equality was far from attainment. The ALA reported in 1943 that although there were some 6,000 public libraries in the United States, 3 million urban dwellers and 32 million rural dwellers had no access to one. Of 3,100 counties nationwide, more than 600 had no public library. The situation was more serious in some states than in others as a result of great disparity in library expenditures: California was spending 84 cents per capita on libraries and Arkansas five cents per capita. Other measures in the report substantiated the view that a grand uplift in national service was needed. The ALA proposed a one-dollar-per-capita annual expenditure as the minimum standard for city libraries (ALA 1943, 3, 4, 13).

The number of public libraries stood at 7,172 (plus branches) in 1948. Important research into the history of public libraries, including the movement itself (e.g., Ditzion 1947; Shera 1949) and individual libraries (e.g., Spencer 1943), was emerging. The ALA stimulated library development with statements of standards in 1943 and 1948, which pressed forward ideas of cooperation and larger units of service. In its 1956 standards the ALA pointed to cooperation as "the most important single recommendation of this document" (ALA 1956, 7). Interesting collaborative projects were soon under way, including the Midwest Interlibrary Center in Chicago (1950) and the ambitious Farmington Plan (1948). Both of these enterprises were carried out primarily by academic libraries, but a number of larger public libraries were included (*see* COOPERATION). The ALA had issued a number of interlibrary loan codes to help standardize the principles and practices involved. The first code was adopted in 1919; it was revised in 1940 and again in 1952. None of these statements—or any that have followed—solved the problems associated with interlending, but they did encourage cooperation. There were 7,569,000 interloans by public libraries in fiscal year (FY) 1993 and 36,048,000 in FY 2005 (*see* INTERLIBRARY LOAN).

During the 1950s public libraries began to face the shameful practice of segregation that was universal in the South and common in the North as well. "Colored branch" or "Negro branch" was a designation given to certain public library locations, and black people were either required or encouraged to use them. As late as 1956, the director of the public library in a large city of New York State said to the author of this entry while driving past its "colored branch," "They can go to any library, but this is the one they use." With the Supreme Court ruling in *Brown v. Board of Education* (1954), so-called separate but equal schools were cast out, affecting other public facilities as well, but it was not until the Civil Rights Act of 1964 that all public libraries were integrated (*see* SERVICES TO AFRICAN AMERICANS). An influx of immigrants, most of them Hispanic or Asian, came to the large American cities in the 1950s. As they occupied inner cities, many previous residents moved to the suburbs. The consequent disruption in service patterns was a major challenge to public librarians: the reading segment of the population served was greatly reduced, and a new nonreading segment became a core constituency. A fresh form of outreach developed, aimed at making readers and library users of the new (and older) inner-city dwellers; they were collectively identified as "disadvantaged." The effort to reach them had mixed results (*see* OUTREACH). Central libraries in the cities experienced collapsing circulation, while suburban libraries saw their metrics rising.

Pressure by the ALA resulted in the first federal aid programs to libraries in the 1956 Library Services Act. Although the original appropriation was only $7.5 million, intended for demonstration projects, the amount grew steadily over the years. In FY 2006, Congress appropriated $210,597,000 for library programs (*see* GOVERNMENT ROLE). A change of title to Library Services and Construction Act in 1964 allowed the use of funds for buildings. A trend away from the traditional style of large urban libraries, which was monumental and rather forbidding to some users, took place in the 1960s. Beginning with branches, then in central libraries, buildings became more open and inviting. At the same time library policies were relaxing, and patrons were allowed to speak and gather in groups—to treat the library as a social space (*see* BUILDINGS AND FACILITIES).

Federal funding was important, but local taxes and bond issues remained the essential sources of library finance. In the 1960s metropolitan areas had to deal with rising expenditures and lower income. Public librarians learned to emphasize public relations, and in time that project has become a key theme in the profession under the title "advocacy" (*see* PUBLIC RELATIONS).

The other great concern of the 1950s, extending into the 1960s, was about the kind of reader who should be the focus of public library attention. Historically the characterization of the library reader had been quite broad: it was Everyman, as long as he adhered to societal norms of behavior in the library. But a countervailing force entered the scene to disturb the old tradition: it was the idea, fostered by a set of studies published as *The Public Library Inquiry*, that public libraries were really serving a small minority of the people, and indeed that was a reasonable and proper function for them. By giving excellent service to the regular users, the "opinion leaders," libraries would—through a kind of trickle-down process—benefit everyone (*see* PHILOSOPHY OF PUBLIC LIBRARIANSHIP). The dispute dissolved rather quickly for two reasons: public library circulation was heavily weighted (as it still is today) toward popular novels and light nonfiction, so librarians could not accept a theory that would undermine the validity of such reading, and the federal government initiated financial assistance to libraries. Popular support for the Library Services Act of 1956 and subsequent legislation depended on the idea of equal service to all. The opinion leader faded into the background and has not returned.

One consequence of the new federal grant programs was the strengthening of state library agencies since they were the clearinghouses for grant applications and administrators of the funds (*see* STATE LIBRARY AGENCIES). Another was the stimulus to rational planning: library grant proposals were judged in part on the basis of their clearly stated goals, objectives, and strategies. Public libraries began to partake, up to a point, in scientific management (*see* GOVERNMENT ROLE; MANAGEMENT AND ORGANIZATION; PLANNING).

Library schools flourished in the 1950s and 1960s, aided by foundation scholarships and federal funding of assistantships. Under new ALA standards, library education was firmly settled at the postgraduate level (*see* EDUCATION OF PUBLIC LIBRARIANS). Publication of texts and other professional materials, centered before World War II on the ALA, H. W. Wilson, and R. R. Bowker, expanded substantially as new publishers entered the field, among them Scarecrow Press (1952), Shoe String Press (1952), and Libraries Unlimited (1964). Public libraries—and the profession generally—had become multifaceted fixtures of the American scene.

The library world was transformed by the computer. Machine-readable cataloging started in 1967. Lockheed's DIALOG (1972) was the first computerized database, followed by ORBIT, BRS, and Lexis-Nexis. These systems would produce bibliographies on many subjects from many sources but only if queried by trained searchers. Librarians went to classes and workshops to learn the intricacies. Patrons submitted to elaborate reference interviews before staff would undertake the searches, which were expensive. In the background, computers were used for accounting and other routines. There were no personal computers yet, no word processors, no monitors, no floppy discs, and no mice. The revolution took hold in the 1980s, with CD-ROM technology for offline database storage and the IBM microcomputer (personal computer) in 1981. But it was not until 1991, with OCLC First Search, that a large database was sufficiently user friendly for direct access by patrons (*see* INFORMATION TECHNOLOGY).

With the spread of the Internet in the late 1990s, public librarians acquired a new task: teaching patrons to use it. That teaching was more complex than the older kind of instruction, which had dealt with using the card catalog and basic reference books, and in its fully expansive form it aimed to create "information literacy" (*see* INFORMATION LITERACY INSTRUCTION). Accommodating the Internet into library practice is an ongoing project. There are issues of cost benefit (Koehn and Hawamdeh 2010) as well as concerns about the social role of the system (McClure and Jaeger 2009). Pervasive doubts are attached to the basic quality and reliability of information websites and databases (*see* INTERNET; REFERENCE AND INFORMATION SERVICES). There were 185,179 public Internet terminals in the nation's public libraries in FY 2005; electronic resources were used 376,549,000 times. The number of reference inquiries rose from 242 million in FY 1993 to 305 million in FY 2003.

In sheer numbers, public libraries have shown steady growth over the past two decades. In FY 1993, the U.S. National Center for Education Statistics (NCES 1995) reported 8,929 public libraries (administrative entities plus branches) in the country. The number was 9,221 in FY 2008. Central libraries numbered 9,042, branches 7,629. Circulation of materials was 1.6 billion (6.5 per capita) in FY 1993; it rose to 2.28 billion (7.7 per capita) in FY 2008. Staff size grew from 111,945 in FY 1993 to 137,855 in FT 2005 (a third of them being librarians; NCES 2007) and 145,243 in FY 2008. Public libraries reported collections of 656 million books and serial volumes (2.7 per capita) in FY 1993, and 816 million print materials in FY 2008. Despite perceptions of decline in finance in the early twenty-first century, operating revenues rose from $4.7 billion ($19.16 per capita) in FY 1993 to $9.1 billion ($31.65 per capita) in FY 2005 and $10.72 billion in FY 2008. Economic downturns in 2008–2010 will have eroded some of these gains. Nevertheless, the negative attitude toward public libraries, to the extreme of finding them on the way to extinction, is clearly out of phase with reality.

A 2009 report from the Institute of Museum and Library Services (IMLS) exhibited strong growth patterns in library visits (4.13 per capita in 1997 and 4.91 per capita in 2007), circulation (6.6 per capita in 1997 and 7.42 per capita in 2007), and number of Internet stations (1.9 per 5,000 residents in 2000 and 3.6 per 5,000 residents in 2007). That report also pointed out that the old disparity in service between urban and rural libraries is still a factor in the national scene.

> Even though about half of all public library administrative enti-
> ties are located in nonmetropolitan counties, metropolitan
> counties were still home to 84 percent of all individuals residing
> in library services areas in 2007. Libraries in metropolitan
> counties also accounted for 86 percent of all visits, 88 percent
> of all circulations, and 78 percent of all public Internet terminals
> in libraries in 2007 (Henderson 2009, 5).

This gap between metro and nonmetro service is being explored in current IMLS research. IMLS also noted in the report cited the importance of private initiatives in library support, notably that of the Bill and Melinda Gates Foundation.

A Harris telephone survey conducted in January 2010 substantiates the usage figures from NCES. Respondents were 18 years of age or older. Sixty-five percent had used their public library at least once in the past year. It was agreed by 96 percent that "because it provides free access to materials and resources, the public library plays an important role in giving everyone a chance to succeed, and ninety-four percent agreed that the library improves the quality of life in their community" (ALA 2010a, 2). Uses reported were the traditional set: school-related work, entertainment, and news or infor-mation along with a sign of the times: assistance in job searching.

As noted above, despite recent budget setbacks in many libraries, the aggregate financial picture has not been a disaster. Just 14.3 percent of reporting libraries in another study had budget decreases in FY 2009 compared to the prior year. Fifty-nine percent had increases, and 25.9 percent held even (ALA 2010b). Library construction went forward in 2009: there were 80 new public libraries, plus 90 additions, renovations, or remodeling (*see* BUILDINGS AND FACILITIES).

The most significant measure of success in the historical pageant of the public library is the way people feel about the institution. A 2006 survey found that nearly all respondents agreed that public libraries are essential for maintaining a productive community. Library users and non-users agreed that libraries are using their money well. A concluding statement of the report may serve as a capstone to this review of public library history:

> What we have heard loud and clear both from the leadership and the public was that the mission of libraries should remain much the same in terms of free and open access to all citizens and maintaining core library services—efficient and friendly librarians, current books and reference materials, programs for children, and well-maintained buildings. The research does not call for wholesale reinvention of libraries. (Public Agenda 2006, 35)

References

American Library Association. 1943. *The Equal Chance: Books Help to Make It.* Chicago: American Library Association. First published in 1936; revised in 1943; supplemented in 1947.

American Library Association. 1956. *Public Library Service: A Guide to Evaluation with Minimum Standards.* Chicago: American Library Association.

American Library Association. 2010a. *Libraries Connect Communities: Public Library Funding & Technology Access Study, 2009–2010.* Chicago: American Library Association. http://www.ala.org/plinternetfunding. Accessed May 2010.

American Library Association. 2010. *The State of America's Libraries.* Chicago: American Library Association. http://www.ala.org/ala/newspresscenter/mediapresscenter/americaslibraries. Accessed May 2010; summary in *American Libraries* 41, no. 5 (May 2010): 13–14.

Bobinski, George S. 1969. *Carnegie Libraries: Their History and Impact on American Public Library Development.* Chicago: American Library Association.

Bobinski, George S. 2007. *Libraries and Librarianship: Sixty Years of Challenge and Change, 1945–2005.* Lanham, MD: Scarecrow Press.

Ditzion, Sidney. 1947. *Arsenals of a Democratic Culture.* Chicago: American Library Association.

Geller, Evelyn. 1984. *Forbidden Books in American Libraries, 1876–1939.* Westport, CT: Greenwood Press.

Henderson, Everett. 2009. *Service Trends in U.S. Public Libraries, 1997–2007.* IMLS Research Brief 1. Washington, DC: Institute of Museum and Library Services.

Himmel, Ethel E. 1994. State library agencies in the United States. In *Encyclopedia of Library History*, 602–4. New York: Garland.

Koehn, Shona L., and Suliman Hawamdeh. 2010. The acquisition and management of electronic resources: Can use justify cost? *Library Quarterly* 80, no. 2 (April): 161–74.

McClure, Charles R., and Paul T. Jaeger. 2009. *Public Libraries and Internet Service Roles: Measuring and Maximizing Internet Services.* Chicago: American Library Association.

McMullen, Haynes. 2000. *American Libraries before 1876.* Westport, CT: Greenwood Press.

Pawley, Christine. 2007. Blood and thunder on the bookmobile: American public libraries and the construction of the reader, 1950–1995. In *Institutions of Reading*, ed. Thomas Augst and Kenneth Carpenter, 264–82. Amherst: University of Massachusetts Press.

Pennell, Lois G. 1970. Bookmobiles. In *Encyclopedia of Library and Information Science* 3: 1–57. New York: Marcel Dekker.

Public Agenda. 2006. *Long Overdue: A Fresh Look at Public Attitudes about Libraries in the 21st Century.* New York: Public Agenda.

Rebenack, John. 1978. Contemporary libraries in the United States. In *Encyclopedia of Library and Information Science* 24: 291–339. New York: Marcel Dekker.

Seavey, Charles A. 1994. Public libraries. In *Encyclopedia of Library History*, 518–28. New York: Garland.

Shera, Jesse H. 1949. *Foundations of the Public Library: The Origins of the Public Library Movement in New England, 1629–1855.* Chicago: University of Chicago Press.

Spencer, Gwladys [sic]. 1943. The Chicago Public Library, origins and background. PhD diss., University of Chicago.

U.S. National Center for Education Statistics. 1995. *E. D. TABS: Public Libraries in the United States: 1993.* Washington, DC: U.S. National Center for Education Statistics.

U.S. National Center for Education Statistics. 2007. *E. D. TABS: Public Libraries in the United States: Fiscal Year 2005.* Washington, DC: U.S. National Center for Education Statistics.

Van Slyck, Abby. 1995. *Free to All: Carnegie Libraries and American Culture, 1890–1920.* Chicago: University of Chicago Press.

Wiegand, Wayne A. 1989. *An Active Instrument for Propaganda: The American Public Library during World War I.* New York: Greenwood Press.

Wiegand, Wayne A. 1993. United States. In *World Encyclopedia of Library and Information Services*, 3rd ed., 840–49. Chicago: American Library Association.

HODGKINS PUBLIC LIBRARY DISTRICT, IL   6500 Wenz Ave., Hodgkins, IL 60525. Population served: 2,134. Circulation: 58,335. Holdings: 37,619. LJ February 15, 2009: 4-star library; November 15, 2009, and October 1, 2010: 3-star library.

HOMEWOOD PUBLIC LIBRARY, AL   1721 Oxmoor Rd., Homewood, AL 35209. Founded 1941. Population served: 25,043. Circulation: 532,095. Holdings: 92,084. LJ February 15, 2009: 3-star library; November 15, 2009: 4-star library.

HONOLULU, HI. *See* HAWAII STATE LIBRARY, HONOLULU, HI.

HOUSTON PUBLIC LIBRARY, TX   500 McKinney Ave., Houston, TX 77002. Founded 1904. Population served: 2,245,108. Circulation: 6,930,189. Holdings: 3,170,131. 42 branches. The library was racially segregated until 1953, when it changed its policy to "token integration" (Malone 2007). Directors: Julia Ideson, 1903–1945; Martha Schnitzer (acting) 1945; director 1948–1949; Harriet Dickson Reynolds, 1950–1967; Barbara Gubbin, 1994–2004; and Rhea Lawson, 2005–. *See also* HARRIS COUNTY PUBLIC LIBRARY, HOUSTON, TX.

Reference

Malone, Cheryl Knott. 2007. Unannounced and unexpected: The desegregation of Houston Public Library in the early 1950s. *Library Trends 55*, no. 3 (Winter): 665–74.

HOWARD COUNTY LIBRARY, COLUMBIA, MD   6600 Cradlerock Way, Columbia, MD 21045. Founded 1940. Population served: 282,169. Circulation: 6,591,841. Holdings: 949,573. 7 branches, 1 bookmobile. HAPLR 2009, 2010.

HUBBARD PUBLIC LIBRARY, IA   323 E. Maple St., Hubbard, IA 50122. Population served: 1,568. Circulation: 12,229. Holdings: 10,272. LJ November 15, 2009, and October 1, 2010: 3-star library.

HUDSON LIBRARY AND HISTORICAL SOCIETY, OH   96 Library St., Hudson, OH 44236. Founded 1941 (the year when it first received public money, $1,000). Population served: 23,054. Circulation: 594,566. Holdings: 105,122. LJ February 15, 2009; November 15, 2009; and October 1, 2010: 3-star library.

HUGOTON, KS. *See* STEVENS COUNTY LIBRARY, HUGOTON, KS.

HUMBOLDT COUNTY LIBRARY, EUREKA, CA   1313 Third St., Eureka, CA 95501. Founded 1878. Eureka was the first California city with a free public library, publicly funded. The county library was established in 1915. In 1972 the two libraries consolidated. Population served: 131,334. Circulation: 574,046. Holdings: 205,000. 11 branches. One branch, Kim Yerton Memorial Library, Hoopa, is on an Indian reservation. IMLS award 2007.

HUNTSVILLE-MADISON COUNTY PUBLIC LIBRARY, AL   915 Monroe St., Huntsville, AL 35801. Opened as free and tax supported in a new Carnegie building, February 29, 1916. Population served: 319,510. Circulation: 1,943,320. Holdings: 583,069. 12 branches.

HURRICANES KATRINA AND RITA   In 2005 the United States experienced the most active hurricane season ever recorded. Hurricane Katrina (August 25–30) and Hurricane Rita (September 20–25) caused extensive damage to libraries. This entry concerns the impact of Katrina and Rita on libraries of Louisiana. The status of repairs and reopenings gives the situation in July 2011 (for an account of damage in Mississippi, *see* HARRISON COUNTY LIBRARY SYSTEM, GULFPORT, MS). The following is a list of damage done to area libraries:

Cameron Parish Public Library, Rita destroyed four of the five branches. The main branch is currently housed in a temporary building while the new building is being designed and built. The Johnson Bayou Library reopened in February 2011. The Grand Chenier Library is currently in a temporary building. Construction on the new library is slated for early 2012. The Hackberry Library has been renovated and reopened in June 2009 (Morgan 2010).

Calcasieu Parish Public Library. Rita damaged all 13 branches. All of them except the Maplewood Branch reopened a week after residents were allowed back into the parish. Maplewood, which suffered extensive damage, had to be completely reconstructed; it was reopened within a year (Davidson 2010).

Jefferson Davis Parish Public Library. Rita destroyed one branch (Elton) and damaged three others. The three damaged branches reopened not long after the storm. Elton was rebuilt and reopened in the summer of 2006 (Davis 2010).

Jefferson Parish Public Library. All branches were damaged or destroyed by Katrina. East Bank Regional Branch reopened October 2005, with repairs continuing into 2006. West Bank Regional Branch also reopened October 2005, with repairs continuing into 2009. Belle Terre Branch reopened with new furnishings and a new collection in August 2008. Gretna Branch operated out of a temporary building for two years; a newly built branch opened in March 2010. Harahan Branch reopened in October 2005, with repairs continuing into 2009. Lafitte Branch was gutted and replaced by a new building in March 2010. Live Oak Branch reopened November 2006. North Kenner Branch reopened May 2006. Old Metairie, River Ridge, Rosedale, and Terrytown all reopened October 2005. Wagner Branch reopened October 2008, with repairs continuing into 2010. Westwego Branch reopened October 2005, with repairs complete in 2007. The destroyed Grand Isle Branch has been replaced by two donated bookmobiles. Lakeshore Branch is housed in a temporary building and there is no set date for construction of the new library. (Dickerson 2010).

Lafourche Parish Public Library. Golden Meadow Branch was heavily damaged by Katrina. The building that the branch was to move into was damaged by Rita. Golden Meadow reopened in its new location January 2006 (Plaisance 2010).

New Orleans Public Library. All branches were damaged or destroyed by Katrina, but all have reopened. Two branches, Algiers Regional and East New Orleans, were temporarily closed in June 2011 so that they could be moved to a new location. Five of the branches housed in temporary buildings are waiting for their new facilities to be ready (New Orleans Public Library 2010).

Plaquemines Parish Public Library. Katrina destroyed the main library and one branch and damaged the other branch. Rita added to the flood damage of the one building still standing. Belle Chase Library has reopened. Port Sulphur Branch is in a temporary building; whether to rebuild it has not been decided. Buras Branch reopened in February 2011. The bookmobile was not damaged and is running (Schouest 2010).

St. Bernard Parish Library. Katrina destroyed both branches. They all reopened in temporary buildings in the fall of 2007. The library moved from temporary quarters to long term termporary housing on July 5, 2011. (Llamas 2010).

St. Tammany Parish Public Library. Pontchartrain and Madison-ville branches were destroyed by Katrina. Pontchartrain has not been rebuilt. The parish is working on rebuilding Madisonville on a new lot and may break ground in October 2011. (Kaack 2010).

Terrebonne Parish Public Library. Two branches were flooded during Rita. Grand Caillou Branch was rebuilt and reopened in 2009. Chauvin Branch was moved into a new building after the storm and reopened (LeBoeuf 2010).

Vermillion Parish Public Library. Five branches were damaged by Rita. Pecan Island and Cow Island branches were completely destroyed and are now replaced by a bookmobile. Erath, Kaplan, and Gueydan branches have been repaired and reopened (Trosclair 2010).

Washington Parish Public Library. Headquarters and Main Branch, which shared a building, were destroyed by Katrina. That building was rebuilt and reopened on the two-year anniversary of the storm. Since then four branches that were not damaged have been closed because of budget cuts, and there are no plans to reopen them (Sbisa 2010).

—*Naomi Hurtienne Magola*

References

All the telephone interviews were conducted by Naomi Hurtienne. Information on damage was also given in State Library of Louisiana (see State Library of Louisiana 2010).

Davidson, Judy. 2010. Telephone interview, October 20.

Davis, Gary. 2010. Telephone interview, October 20.

Dickerson, Lon. 2010. Status report, October 1, 2010, Jefferson Parish Library. http://www.jefferson.lib.la.us/katrina/statusreport.

Kaack, Diane. 2010, 2011. Telephone interviews, October 20, 2010 and July 27, 2011.

LeBoeuf, Mary. 2010. Telephone interview, October 28.

Llamas, Ethel. 2010, 2011. Telephone interviews, October 28, 2010 and July 27, 2011.

Morgan, Barbara. 2010, 2011. Cameron Parish libraries damaged by Katrina and Rita. Message to Naomi Hurtienne, October 20, 2010; telephone interview, August 2, 2011.

New Orleans Public Library. 2010, 2011. Our recovery in progress (gives updates on constructions and reopenings). http://www.nutrias.org/~nopl/recovery/recovery.

Plaisance, Annette. 2010. Telephone interview, October 20.

Trosclair, Charlotte. 2010. Libraries damaged in hurricanes Katrina and Rita. Message to Naomi Hurtienne, October 20.

Sbisa, Joseph. 2010. Telephone interview, October 28.

Schouest, Todd. 2010, 2011. Libraries damaged in Katrina and Rita. Messages to Naomi Hurtienne, October 21, 2010 and July 27, 2011.

State Library of Louisiana. 2010. *Bullet Points 04-06*. http://tinyurl.com/38go5kf.

HUTSON, JEAN BLACKWELL, 1914–1998   Librarian. Born Sommerfield, FL, on September 7, 1914. She attended Barnard College; earning a BA in 1935, she was only the second black person to graduate there (the first was Zora Neale Hurston). After graduating from the library school at Columbia University, she joined the New York Public Library (NYPL) as librarian of the 135th Street Branch in Harlem. She was a strong promoter of research in the African American experience. In 1925 the branch had a Division of Negro Literature, History, and Prints, promoted by Arthur Schomburg. After a period of teaching and working as a school librarian in Baltimore, Hutson returned to NYPL in 1942. In 1940 the 135th Street Branch had been renamed the Schomburg Collection of Negro Literature, History, and Prints. She collaborated in creating a printed catalog of the collection and contributed to its extraordinary growth. In 1972 the Schomburg Collection was designated as a research facility of NYPL. Hutson was a library adviser in Ghana, 1964–1965. She became assistant director of collection management and development at NYPL in 1980. Death came in a Harlem hospital on February 4, 1998. *DALB*, 2nd supplement.

HUXLEY PUBLIC LIBRARY, IA   602 N. Main St., Huxley, IA 50124. Founded 1972. Population served: 2,959. Circulation: 39,387. Holdings: 25,373. LJ February 15, 2009, and November 15, 2009: 3-star library; October 1, 2010: 4-star library.

I

IDA LONG GOODMAN MEMORIAL LIBRARY, ST. JOHN, KS   306 N. Fifth St., St. John, KS 66536. Founded 1969. Population served 1,224. Circulation: 31,725. Holdings: 28,549. 3 branches. LJ February 15, 2009; November 15, 2009; and October 1, 2010: 5-star library.

INDEPENDENCE, MO. *See* MID-CONTINENT PUBLIC LIBRARY, INDEPENDENCE, MO.

INDIAN LAKE, NY. *See* TOWN OF INDIAN LAKE PUBLIC LIBRARY, NY.

INDIANAPOLIS-MARION COUNTY PUBLIC LIBRARY, IN   2450 N. Meridian St., Indianapolis, IN 46208. Founded 1872. Population served: 832,693. Circulation: 15,940,690. Holdings: 1,800,000. 22 branches. The central library was designed by Paul Cret (1917). A business branch opened in 1918. LJ February 15, 2009; November 15, 2009; and October 1, 2010: 4-star library. Directors: Charles Evans, 1872–1878; Albert B. Yohn, 1878–1879; Arthur W. Tyler, 1879–1883; William Hooper, 1883–1888; Eliza G. Browning, 1888–1889; Charles Evans, 1889–1892; Eliza G. Browning, 1892–1917; Charles E. Rush, 1917–1928; Luther L. Dickerson, 1928–1944; Marian McFadden, 1944–1956; Harold J. Sander, 1956–1971; Raymond E. Gnat, 1972–1994; Edward M. Szynaka, 1994–2003; Linda Mielke, 2004–2007; and Laura Bramble, 2008–.

INFORMATION LITERACY INSTRUCTION

Terminology

Neither *Merriam* nor *American Heritage* has an entry for "information literacy." Within the library field the term, like others that are centered on "information," has resisted precise description. *ODLIS* defines it as "skill in finding the information one needs, including an understanding of how libraries are organized, familiarity with the resources they provide (including information formats and automated search tools), and knowledge of commonly used research techniques." Esther Grassian, while noting that "there is no totally agreed upon and standard definition," gives one of her own: "a way of knowing how to deal with information, a way of finding out about information resources, and a way of interacting with information" (Grassian and Kaplowitz 2001, 7, 8).

The term arose in the 1980s, replacing "bibliographic instruction" (BI) and "library instruction" (LI) in library publications and in the names of library programs. BI and LI "may be used interchangeably to connote teaching the use of access tools such as catalogs of library holdings, abstracts, encyclopedias, and other reference sources that aid library users searching for information . . . both terms concern the transmission of the knowledge necessary for individuals to teach themselves after formal education has been completed" (Tucker 1994, 364). Thus, it seems that if online sources are included among "access tools," BI and LI are much the same as information literacy instruction (ILI).

A distinction that frames BI as "tool based" and ILI as "concept based" is valid only if supported by the instruction methodology; good teaching of BI, as well as ILI, is founded on concepts. And both BI and ILI must describe and utilize specific tools. The distinction is rejected by Grassian (2004), who considers ILI "not as a wholly new and different approach, but as an umbrella that encompasses and expands on the BI efforts we've all been engaged in for many years" (51).

Historical Summary

LI dates back to Melvil Dewey, who gave lectures on use of the library at Columbia College in 1884 (Wiegand 1996, 88). In doing so he fleshed out his idea that "the library is a school and the librarian is in the highest sense a teacher" (Dewey 1876, 5). That teaching function was most clear in the academic domain, where the library's clients were all students, ready if not eager to learn. Indeed, LI as a formal education educational activity developed in colleges and is now a standard component of freshman instruction. Most writing and discussion about BI is by academic librarians. In the late 1930s school librarians also took up LI. Public librarians, who have traditionally assisted readers in using resources on a one-to-one basis, began formal group instruction in the 1980s, usually under its new designation, ILI.

Two groups in the American Library Association are active in the field: the Library Instruction Round Table and the Bibliographic Instruction Section of the Association of College and Research Libraries; both were founded in 1975. They offer conference presentations, publications, and websites.

Current Practice and Issues

A survey published in 2009 showed that 29.8 percent of public libraries offered some form of ILI for patrons (McClure and Jaeger 2009, 31). The review of library websites conducted in the writing of this handbook indicates that nearly all larger libraries have formal ILI programming of some kind, the incidence declining with size of population served. A typical pattern in libraries with ILI programs is the scheduling of free one- or two-hour classes in computer basics and Microsoft Word. Details on such beginning offerings are in, for example, the websites of the Des Plaines (IL) Public Library, the Brooklyn (NY) Public Library, and the Lafourche Parish Public Library (Thibodaux, LA). More extended programs cover Internet searching (Enoch Pratt Free Library, Baltimore, MD, and Cuyahoga County Public Library, Parma, OH), Excel (Cuyahoga County, and Denver Public Library, CO), Microsoft Publisher (Denver), PowerPoint (Cuyahoga County), and digital photography (Enoch Pratt). Some libraries have developed elaborate teaching programs on a level with community college offerings. For example, Johnson County Library (Overland Park, KS) gives courses in basic PCs, Internet, Excel, and Word, with detailed, well-illustrated syllabi accessible online. Santa Clara County Library (Los Gatos, CA) has presented since 1985 a six-month course, two hours weekly, in adult basic reading, writing, math, and computer skills. The Literacy Center of Boston Public Library has a computer lab and language lab for patron use. Four-week courses (two hours weekly) are scheduled in adult basic literacy, email, and computer literacy. The Memphis (TN) Public library and Information Center received a national award in 2007 from the Institute of Museum and Library Services for innovative literacy programs, including the use of an "InfoBUS" to reach neighborhoods with high immigrant populations.

Adult patrons are the focus of most ILI, but children are not forgotten. For example, Fairfax County (VA) Public Library launched an Early Literacy Outreach Program in 2004 to teach reading skills to preschoolers. A staff specialist and volunteer helpers visit off-site schools, child care centers, community centers, parent groups, and teachers. She distributes picture books and other materials, reaching some 8,600 children in four years of the program (Clay and Bangs 2008). An innovative approach to ILI is at work in Portsmouth (VA) Public Library. To induce parents and children to participate in literacy programs, Family Reading Nights (for 25 invited families) begin with spaghetti dinner (Enrich and Burton 2004; the program is continuing).

All these offerings are free of charge and noncredit. There is no research at this time to demonstrate how effective they are, a matter of concern considering the imposing amount of staff time devoted to them. Even before BI became ILI, its value was questioned. Actual competencies (learning objectives) did not exist then: "goals for instruction remain in the stage of vague generalities." And lesson planning was ignored, without which "little of value will result from instruction . . . other than a potpourri of nonsequential programs which are little better than tours of the agency's facilities" (Penland 1975, 117, 136). Today's ILI manifestations are clearly more sophisticated than the rudimentary BI offerings that Penland criticized. But it does seem appropriate to question the overall aims and structures of many programs in public libraries. In the academic context, where BI originated and ILI now prospers, there are specific goals, tests, grades, prerequisites, student evaluations, and instructors with established credentials. In the public library the ILI offerings are loosely presented by staff who may need training in learning theory, modes of instruction, and learning outcomes (Grassian and Kaplowitz 2001, chaps. 3 and 7). Commendably, most libraries (86.4 percent of them, according to one study) are endeavoring to train staff in these matters and in the complex subjects involved (McClure 2009, 33). The future success of ILI may be a product of greater formalization of programs and mastery of teaching approaches by public library staff.

References

Clay, Edwin S., III, and Patricia Bangs. 2008. Fairfax County Public Library—Reaching out to readers. *Virginia Libraries* 54, no. 3 (July–December): 13–17.

Dewey, Melvil. 1876. The profession. *American Library Journal* 1, no. 1 (September 30): 5–6.

Enrich, Rachel, and Susan Burton. 2004. Dinner and a book: Portsmouth combats illiteracy with food for mind and body. *Virginia Libraries* 50, no. 4 (October–November–December): 15–17.

Grassian, Esther S. 2004. Building on bibliographic instruction. *American Libraries* 35, no. 9 (October): 51–53.

Grassian, Esther S., and Joan R. Kaplowitz. 2001. *Information Literacy Instruction: Theory and Practice*. New York: Neal Schuman.

Lindauer, Bonnie Gratch. 2004. The three arenas of information literacy assessment. *Reference & User Services Quarterly* 44, no. 2 (Winter): 122–29.

McClure, Charles R., and Paul T. Jaeger. 2009. *Public Libraries and Internet Service Roles: Measuring and Maximizing Internet Services*. Chicago: American Library Association.

Penland, Patrick R. 1975. Library use, instruction in. In *Encyclopedia of Library and Information Science* 16: 113–47. New York: Marcel Dekker.

Reichel, Mary, and Mary Ann Ramey, eds. 1987. *Conceptual Frameworks for Bibliographic Instruction: Theory into Practice*. Littleton, CO: Libraries Unlimited.

Tucker, John Mark. 1994. Library instruction. In *Encyclopedia of Library History*, 364–66. New York: Garland.

Wiegand, Wayne A. 1996. *Irrepressible Reformer: A Biography of Melvil Dewey*. Chicago: American Library Association.

INFORMATION RETRIEVAL. *See* INFORMATION TECHNOLOGY.

INFORMATION SCIENCE

Terminology

Participants at the 1969 conference of the International Federation of Library Associations (IFLA) heard this proclamation by Frank Francis, president of the association:

> In this complex and changing world the narrow concept of the library as we have known it is giving place to a much wider concept, that of library service—or perhaps I ought to amplify that to library and information service. ... It will indeed be possible in the not distant future to move information from place to place from library to library and from libraries to individuals even more easily than we have hitherto moved books and documents. ... We have extraordinary new prospects before us which we have to open our minds to, and prepare ourselves for. (Francis 1969, 18)

The author of this entry was among those in the Copenhagen audience for that presidential address and, like many others present, came away with a wish that the "extraordinary new prospects" had been elucidated in more detail by Sir Frank. He did say that the computer should be a part of the future project, along with coordination and unity in terminology. Although he did not use the phrase, his topic belonged to what came to be "information science" (IS). The computer is indeed a part of IS, and there is coordination at some levels, but unity in terminology is yet to be achieved.

Before examining various definitions of IS, two vocabulary elements need explanation: "documentation," and "information." *Merriam says* that "documentation" is equivalent to "information science," but that is too simple, as the following will show. *American Heritage* says that "documentation" is "the act or an instance of supplying documents, references, or records." A narrower usage for documentation appeared in 1931, when an organization dating from 1896 changed its name from Institut International de Bibliographie to Institut International de Documentation. The institute (which had further name changes in 1937 and 1988 before dissolving in 2002) maintained a vast card file of citations in scientific fields and responded to specific queries. Documentation was a library-like activity exercised independently of an actual library, but by the 1950s it seemed to have become a branch of librarianship. "Librarians typically organize, analyze and provide access for all kinds of users to contents of documents. Documentalists do the same thing, but tend to exploit a wider variety of media and formats, and traditionally limit their work to science-technology documents and users" (Ingwersen 1992, 102). In fact it was generally understood at that time that documentation was nothing more than science librarianship with an open mind about formats—microprint, having just come into wide use, was the wonder medium of the documentalist. A number of documentation centers were created by national governments to handle such files and queries. In the United States the American Documentation Institute was established in 1937; its journal was *American Documentation* (1950–1969).

But documentation as a term and field was abandoned when the computer came to the scene. Today it exists no more (e.g., see the third edition of the *World Encyclopedia of Library and Information Services* [1993], where it was mentioned only three times, in the special library context). It was succeeded by "information science" when its tools achieved computerized sophistication. A new organization in Britain marked the switch; it was named Institute of Information Scientists (1958). The American Documentation Institute altered its name to American Society for Information Science in 1968 and gave its journal a new name in 1970, *Journal of the American Society for Information Science*. Later the society added "& Technology" to its name. The Institut International de Documentation, which had become the Fédération Internationale de Documentation in 1937, resisted the changeover but ultimately compromised, becoming the Fédération Internationale d'Information et de Documentation in 1988. IFLA did not follow the wave; it added "and Institutions" to its name but not "information." (Indeed, IFLA has maintained a clear preference, in its organization and programs, for traditional library matters. Of its 48 sections, only one is in the information camp, dealing with "information technology.") In the American Library Association (ALA), an Information Science and Automation Division was created in 1966; it became the Library and Information Technology Association in 1978.

For the name IS to gain prominence, it was necessary to redefine "information." The traditional meaning, as inscribed in the third edition (1961) of *Merriam Webster's New International Dictionary*, was "knowledge obtained from investigation, study, or instruction . . . = intelligence, news, advices, data." A murky statement, perhaps, but one that conveys the notion of information as a body of facts and data. Such accumulations of facts and data were of course the materials of library reference service. But a new look at the term detached information from the reference desk: an ALA task force stated in 1973 that information "includes not only facts and data, but also ideas and the products of man's creative endeavors" (quoted in Williams 1988, 110). Even so, information seemed to remain within the scope of librarianship. The separation of the new information scientist from the venerable librarian needed a fresh element. The Institute of Information Scientists had found it in "scientific qualifications," without which the work of information science would be "merely some extension of librarianship" (Dyson 1961, 72). But that solution stemmed from a narrow view of information science as a sort of scientific bibliography—the space that had been occupied by documentation. What finally produced the separation was the computer.

Compared to today's computers, those of the 1960s were large, slow, mechanically unreliable, and laborious to use. They had no monitors or floppy discs. The operator gave them commands with a key punch device. Their applications were rudimentary ancillaries to bookkeeping. Their design and maintenance was the work of mathematically trained computer scientists. In time computers were designed that could capture files of data or titles of publications (information storage) and that could return those items when queried (information retrieval). Librarians who made special study of such applications were not computer scientists; they took on the new name "information scientists." From its early days information science was a hard field to define. There were redundancies like the description of Anthony Debons, which considered IS to encompass "all scientific study of communication of information in society" (Ingwersen 1992, 108), thus conflating IS with the old field of communications. There was the very big umbrella concept described by Harold Borko (1968):

> Information science is that discipline that investigates the properties and behavior of information, the forces governing the flow of information, and the means of processing information for optimum accessibility and usability. It is concerned with that body of knowledge relating to the origination, collection, organization storage, retrieval, interpretation, transmission, transformation, and utilization of information. This includes the investigation of information representations in both natural and artificial systems, the use of codes for efficient message transmission, and the study of information processing devices and techniques such as computers and their programming systems. It is an interdisciplinary science derived from and related to such fields as mathematics, logic, linguistics, psychology, computer technology, operations research, the graphic arts, communications, library science, management, and other similar fields. (3–5)

One difficulty posed by that array of disciplines imputed to IS is that the information scientist has little if any knowledge of any of them, except perhaps library science, which in fact stands out in the definition as a field that embraces nearly all the activities Borko ascribed to IS. The major difficulty with the definition is in fact that it overlaps with librarianship:

> Since librarians have always been concerned with documents that carry information, we may wonder in what distinctive way Borko's information science differs from librarianship. We would say that librarianship has only been concerned with certain elements or properties of Borko's definition—the processing and accessibility aspects—but it does have that field staked out. We cannot say that the discipline that investigates the means of processing information for optimum accessibility and usability is information science, since the subject of that definition can also take the predicate librarianship. (Marco 1996, 12)

The rest of Borko's definition, dealing with properties and behavior of information, is also the province of other disciplines: communication and computer science.

The definition issue has been persistent. As late as 2003 the president of the American Society for Information Science and Technology wondered in print, "Just what constitutes our field as separate from other fields such as computer science, librarianship, chemistry, engineering, medicine, management, law, or education?" (Hahn 2003, 1).

General dictionaries did not define IS until their latest editions came out. *Merriam* offers, "The collection, classification, storage, retrieval, and dissemination of recorded knowledge treated both as a pure and as an applied science." This statement could be applied as well to library science. *American Heritage* says that IS is "the science that is concerned with the gathering, manipulation, classification, storage, and retrieval of recorded knowledge." This is also a description of library science.

It is of interest to compare the definitions in *ODLIS* of library science and information science. Library science is "the professional knowledge and skill with which recorded information is selected, acquired, organized, stored, maintained, retrieved, and disseminated to meet the needs of a specific clientele, usually taught at a professional library school qualified to grant a post-baccalaureate degree of MLS or MLIS. The term is used synonymously in the U.S. with librarianship."

Information science: "systematic study and analysis of the sources, development, collection, organization, dissemination, evaluation, use, and management of information in all its forms, including channels (formal and informal) and technology used in its communication."

Another approach to the field of information science comes from occupational titles. The *Dictionary of Occupational Titles* (*DOT*; U.S. Department of Labor, Bureau of Labor Statistics. 2007) has an entry for information scientist, giving as alternate titles chief information officer, information broker, information manager, information resources director, and information resources manager. The work is described this way:

> Designs information system to provide management or clients with specific data from computer storage, utilizing knowledge of electronic data processing principles, mathematics, and computer capabilities. Develops and designs methods and procedures for collecting, organizing, interpreting, and classifying information for input into computer and retrieval of specific information from computer, utilizing knowledge of symbolic language and optical or pattern recognition principles. Develops alternate designs to resolve problems in input, storage, and retrieval of information. May specialize in specific field of information science, such as scientific or engineering research, or in specific discipline, such as business, medicine, education, aerospace, or library science. (*DOT* online, code 109.0678-010)

This picture is one that demands a higher knowledge and skill set than has been suggested in the definitions above. It appears that for *DOT* an information scientist is in fact a computer scientist. There is no *DOT* title for computer scientist, but there is a title for "computer engineer," defined as one who can "analyze data processing requirements to plan electronic data processing system to provide system capabilities required for projected workloads. Plans layout and installation of new system or modification of existing system. May set up and control analog or hybrid computer systems to solve scientific and engineering problems."

A final perspective comes from actual job vacancy advertising. A search of several online posting services, ALA *Career Leads*, and the *Chronicle of Higher Education* brought up no openings for "information scientist" but offered many vacancies for "computer scientist"—with work descriptions along the line of *DOT* for computer engineer.

With this excursion at an end, it is clear that the field of information science is one that is still undefined after half a century in business. There is a runover between its qualifications and tasks with computer science and computer engineering on one end and with library science on the other end. How this matters in the public library world is the topic of the next section.

Current Situation

The unsettled nature of IS has had no special effect on staffing in public libraries: they still seek and engage librarians who can handle the traditional activities. Use of the computer—which had made information scientists out of documentalists—is no longer a specialty but part of everyday library work. Tasks that do require very technical skills, like setting up a website or an in-house database, may be handled by the library's parent organization or by outside experts engaged for the occasion. Large libraries may have a unit that deals with complex computer matters.

If the impact of IS on library schools has been powerful enough to change fundamentally their goals and methods, it may be that the outcome has become more attentive to information technology, with separate tracks for qualified persons in the area of computer science. "Core competencies" relating to the actual work of librarians are under consideration (*see* EDUCATION OF PUBLIC LIBRARIANS).

A number of practicing librarians and writers in the library press have voiced displeasure with the whole "information" enterprise. A recent protest by the New Jersey Library Association over the removal of "library studies" from the name of the Rutgers library program is one example (*Library Journal*, May 1, 2009, 12; for a description of the incident, *see* EDUCATION OF PUBLIC LIBRARIANS). John Berry said in an editorial, "I don't think librarianship or any other profession is some kind of subdiscipline of that ill-defined, over broad field of 'information'" (*Library Journal*, June 15, 2009, 10).

Will the next years in public libraries focus less on technology (which may be taken for granted as a tool) and more on human interchange with patrons? There are signs that point to such a shift, such as a new focus on instruction of patrons and expanded services to immigrants, minorities, and disabled persons. Wayne Wiegand has pointed out that factual, work-related, nonfiction reading has held a higher value than leisure, fiction reading. That position was strengthened when information science arrived, with its emphasis on facts. Library schools have neglected fiction reading. The recent renewal of readers' advisory services may be a harbinger of change, with greater attention to what people really want to read (Wiegand 2001, 10).

The writer of this entry, two years after the Copenhagen IFLA conference cited at the beginning of this entry, suggested that there might be historic cycles in librarianship, alternating in generational preferences between people and machines (Marco 1971). Is it possible that the current cycle, keyed to the computer and its sciences, may be yielding to a new cycle that is closer to the library's pioneer devotion to personal service? *See also* Information Technology.

References

Bawden, D. 2006. The history of information and documentation." *Journal of Documentation* 62, no. 2: 169–70.

Borko, Harold. 1968. Information science: What is it? *American Documentation* 19, no. 1 (January): 3–5.

Dyson, G. Malcolm. 1962. The aims of the Institute of Information Scientists, Ltd. *Journal of Chemical Documentation* 2, no. 2 (April): 72–74.

Francis, Frank. 1969. Presidential address. *IFLA General Council Proceedings* [Copenhagen], 1969, 18–24. Copenhagen: Scandinavian Library Center.

Hahn, Trudi Bellardo. 2003. What has information science contributed to the world? *Bulletin of the American Society for Information Science and Technology* 30 (April–May): 1–7. Accessed online, May 2010.

Ingwersen, Peter. 1992. Information and information science in context." *Libri* 42, no. 2 (April/June): 99–135.

Lilley, D. B., and R. W. Trice. 1989. *A History of Information Science, 1945–1985*. San Diego: Academic Press.

Marco, Guy A. 1971. Tomorrow's public library: A conjecture about cycles. In *Proceedings of the Public Libraries Conference, Blackpool*, 60–64. London: Library Association.

Marco, Guy A. 1996. Two false dogmas of information science. *New Library World* 97, no. 1131: 11–14.

U.S. Department of Labor, Bureau of Labor Statistics. 2007. *Dictionary of Occupational Titles*. 4th ed. Washington, DC: U.S. Department of Labor, Bureau of Labor Statistics. Online version. http://www.occupationalinfo.org. Accessed May 2010.

Wiegand, Wayne. 2001. Missing the real story: Where library and information science fails the library profession. In *Readers' Advisors' Companion*, ed. Kenneth D. Shearer and Robert Burgin, 7–14. Westport, CT: Libraries Unlimited.

Williams, Patrick. 1988. *The American Public Library and the Problem of Purpose*. New York: Greenwood Press.

INFORMATION SYSTEMS. *See* INFORMATION TECHNOLOGY.

INFORMATION TECHNOLOGY

Terminology

Technology is "the application of science, esp. to industrial or commercial objectives" (*American Heritage*), or "the practical application of knowledge, esp. in a particular area" (*Merriam*). The common thread of those definitions is "application"—a technology applies what is known to actual tasks. Science is theory, technology is practice. It would follow that information technology (IT) is the application of what is known about information to actual tasks. However, the *American Heritage* definition of IT is more restrictive: "the development, installation, and implementation of computer systems and applications." Information technology is thus limited to applications of computer knowledge or science instead of information knowledge or science. To look at it another way, computer knowledge or science is equivalent to information knowledge or science, leading to computer science = information science. In fact, this equivalency appears to hold in the literature of information science, although definitions are unsatisfactory there (*see* INFORMATION SCIENCE). *Wikipedia* assigns the grandest concept to the term:

> IT spans a wide variety of areas that include but are not limited to things such as processes, computer software, computer hardware, programming languages, and data constructs. In short, anything that renders data, information or perceived knowledge in any visual format whatsoever, via any multimedia distribution mechanism, is considered part of the domain space known as Information Technology.

The library perspective on information technology is expressed in *ODLIS*: "a very broad term encompassing all aspects of the management and processing of information by computer, including the hardware and software required to access it." The underlying thought, of machine assistance in management and processing, preceded the advent of the computer under the name of "automation." Automation is an "automatically controlled operation of an apparatus, process, or system by mechanical or electronic devices to take the place of human labor" (*Merriam*) or "the automatic operation or control of equipment, a process, or a system" (*American Heritage*). One brings to mind a modern assembly line, with robotic devices putting caps on bottles or wheels on cars. Library automation was not so dramatic or so free of human labor; the term has been attached to almost any operation with a machine doing certain repetitive tasks but also to operations with labor-saving devices (like punch cards) that require constant human involvement. Automation was one term of choice for all such machine-assisted work in the 1960s. Several surveys were published that described automation by American libraries (e.g., American Library Association 1969; Parker 1965).

Simultaneously another term entered the picture: "data processing: the storing or processing of data by a computer" (*American Heritage*). The literature of the 1960s (e.g., Howe and Weidner1962; Jenkins 1966) displayed this term along with automation, the two having the same meaning. In library schools courses in data processing appeared in the early 1960s, in some cases with ambitious descriptions. For example, the Kent State University library school catalog for 1966 offered (for the first time) the following:

> Data Processing in the Library—Application of data processing techniques to library operations. Library systems analysis: theory, procedural description. Equipment: computer logic and programming, machine language, representation of data, recording media. Evaluation of operating systems.

This reads today like a course in information science. Another term entered the vocabulary in the 1960s. It was reflected in the new course given by Kent State University, described in the 1967 catalog this way:

> Fundamentals of Information Retrieval—Organization of information; classification, indexing and subject analysis. Syntax and semantics, coding, thesaurus. Storage, search, and retrieval. Computer systems.

Information retrieval—or information storage and retrieval—was soon a standard course in library schools. Again, it resembles information science as conceived today. Another look at the Kent State catalog, this time for 1974, suggests the expansion of both data processing (renamed with the old term automation) and information retrieval:

> Library Automation—Computer and other machine applications to library cataloging: acquisitions work; book selection; serials control; circulation routines; inventory control; reference work; and administrative uses, including personnel and budget work. Laboratory work on OCLC computer terminals.
>
> Information Retrieval in the Library—Basic functions of an IS&R (information storage and retrieval) system. Concepts and techniques. Networks. Data bases. Intensive studies of major existing information retrieval centers throughout the country using telelecture and remote on-line searching of computerized data bases. Laboratory work includes searching ERIC data base on-line.

Finally, there is the current (2010) Kent State manifestation of these topics:

> Library Automation—Analysis, design and selection of automated library systems. Considers system analysis and requirements, networking technologies, database management systems, multimedia and hypermedia, and client-serving computing. Also,

proposals to vendors, contract negotiation, implementation, staffing, training, system maintenance and evaluation.

Information Storage and Retrieval Systems—Fundamentals of information storage and retrieval systems: components, models, file structure, information representation, human-computer interaction, standards, protocols and evaluation of system performance. Design and evaluation of information storage and retrieval including contributions from artificial intelligence and cognitive research.

The Kent State catalog has numerous courses dealing with computers. It is of interest to read what comes forth under information technology and information science:

Information Technology for Library and Information Professionals—Provides basic information technology concepts and skills necessary for library and information professionals. Topics include computer hardware and software basics; operating systems; file management; software installation and configuration; basic PC applications; information systems concepts, development, and evaluation; search skills; Internet and web concepts, tools, and applications; emerging technologies and tools.

Information Science—Focal areas of information science; information retrieval systems, bibliometrics, citation analysis, systems analysis and evaluation, information technologies, information theory, information architecture, knowledge management and user experience.

Examination of other library school catalogs indicates that the Kent State descriptions are rather typical. Library education offers a thorough if overlapping set of learning experiences, clustered under a vague set of course titles (*see also* EDUCATION OF PUBLIC LIBRARIANS).

The definition scenario reflects the situation of the library and information field of today, which moves on steadily without a philosophical foundation that explains what the field is really about.

Historical Summary

Many developments in automation and IT have been related to cataloging and are covered in the chronology of cataloging (*see* CATALOGING). In the precomputer era mechanization centered on punch (or punched) cards, invented by Herman Hollerith of the Census Bureau and used by him in tabulating census figures for 1890. In 1896, Hollerith formed the Tabulating Machine Company, which later became IBM. Library application of punch cards waited until 1936, when Ralph Parker devised a circulation system that utilized them at the University of Texas. Various circulation systems followed, with elaborations of this simple technology, notably the charge machines set up by IBM at the Montclair (NJ) Public Library in 1942.

The Library of Congress produced *Serial Titles Received* with punch cards in 1950; King County (WA) Library created a book catalog with punch cards in 1951. Union catalogs and circulation systems proliferated in the 1950s. The County of Los Angeles Public Library published book catalogs with nearly full entries for all its branches in 1955. Decatur (IL) Public Library had by 1959 automated acquisitions and other routines.

Libraries began using computers in the 1960s, primarily for accounting functions then for acquisitions, circulation, and cataloging. A well-publicized example of computer application was the program at Florida Atlantic University, which included an integrated acquisitions, cataloging, and serials component and a printed book catalog (1964); the book catalog had numerous defects and was abandoned in 1967. A consultant survey at the Library of Congress was issued in 1963 as *Automation and the Library of Congress.*

In the late 1960s online circulation systems were widely used, pioneered by the Illinois State Library in 1966. With the creation of OCLC (1967, online 1971) and MARC II (1968; *see* CATALOGING), automated cataloging became normal practice. Online interactive systems followed in the 1970s, with early work at the University of Chicago, Northwestern University, and Stanford University. The 1970s also brought commercial online systems and computerized databases. Online public access catalogs (OPACs) arrived in the 1980s, facilitated by the marketing of minicomputers (PCs), and card catalogs were closed. In the 1990s, CD-ROMs became available for offline storage of databases. Vendor corporations began to take control of the distribution of online databases (e.g., of periodical files) in aggregated packages. Most libraries of any size had integrated library systems that allowed users to interact with information about their collections. It became increasingly difficult for patrons to utilize these systems, leading to enhanced library efforts at information literacy instruction. Most libraries created websites with information about their services, often including access to the OPAC from home computers (*see* INFORMATION LITERACY INSTRUCTION).

Current Situation

"Technology is a major component in the modern public library that has become almost indispensible in numerous aspects," according to the *Public Library Data Service 2010 Report* (American Library Association 2010). That report identifies the types of technological features offered in the 1,105 libraries sampled, with percents of libraries having them. Among the results, 96.99 percent of the libraries have a website, 91.82 percent have an OPAC, and 94.18 percent have wireless Internet access. Data from the 2009 report show that 68.9 percent have online reference services, 84.3 percent of the libraries purchase online data bases, and virtual reference services are available via email in 62.1 percent of the libraries, by chat in 31.4 percent, and by instant messaging in 19.5 percent.

Another study found that online homework resources are offered in 79.6 percent of the libraries sampled, audio content by 73 percent, e-books by 55 percent, and video content by 51 percent. Internet services are provided by 71 percent of the libraries (Davis et al. 2009, 50). In 2005 there were 185,179 Internet terminals for patron use in the nation's public libraries (U.S. National Center for Education Statistics 2007, table 6) (*see* INTERNET).

Recent Issues

The obvious blessings of IT in libraries have been accompanied by numerous concerns. The review of such concerns in Leckie and Buschman (2009) is the basis for what follows here:

- The substitution of computer displays for printed books brings a number of problems. The reader may be disadvantaged by incompatible texts and reading devices. A nonliterate culture is promoted in which data replace narrative memory (Postman 1993). Invariably some protocols need to be mastered by the user for access to the displays, and not everyone can do it. Research with children indicates they have major problems in this area (Large 2009).

- Control of what is available to library users no longer follows entirely from library decisions on selection but is to a growing extent in the hands of media corporations (*see* DIGITAL MEDIA).

- Users tend to accept what is given to them with all its flaws in the uncritical belief that technology must be good; librarians tend to acquire and use defective IT products for the same reason (Segal 2005).

- The "digital divide" separates more educated, sophisticated users from those with less preparation to handle computer devices. OPAC and Internet access is in effect limited to a more fortunate segment of the community (*see* INTERNET).

- The work of librarians changes subtly with each technological innovation. More time is spent on choosing and learning to use new products and less time on such traditional tasks as reference and collection development. Further, librarians have become unpaid test marketers for new technologies (Winter 2009). There is decreasing lack of recognition for librarians, as IT makes possible self-service approaches to facts and texts. Librarians are becoming viewed as handlers of technology, a role in which they compete with other occupational groups instead of (uniquely) masters of reference and literature.

- The opportunity offered by library websites has been squandered, as most websites are poorly designed, incomplete, and confusing (Leckie, Given, and Campbell 2009).

- OPACs usually give the user more trouble than card catalogs in locating given items. For example, a search in the Chicago Public Library OPAC for William Faulkner's novel *The Hamlet* pursued through the author's name gives 433 results, unsorted; or the title gives 629 results, mostly Shakespeare, unsorted. There is a way to search for Faulkner and *Hamlet*, by joining them (*without* a + symbol) as "key words," but there is no suggestion in the OPAC about this or indeed about the meaning of key word. An advanced search mode is accessible through a link and would yield the same results, but the typical user would probably keep away from that.

Two other areas of concern are broadband speed (*see* INTERNET) and staff training. The latter is approached in two useful volumes published by Neal-Schuman: Burke (2009), and Thompson (2009).

It was a long twisting road from the early punch card to the OPAC; along the way many technologies came to prominence and were superseded. Moore's law and similar laws and trends point to the rapid obsolescence of computer hardware. New optical or quantum technologies may totally replace the current integrated circuit technology. Costs are rising at impressive doubling rates as well. What appears to be a fairly stable technological picture in public libraries may well be totally redrawn in a decade. The library profession has always met the challenges of change and will continue to do so. IT is only a complex manifestation of data processing: a handy tool to be mastered and utilized efficiently, with knowledge and with caution.

References

American Library Association. 1969. *Library Automation: A State of the Art Review*. Chicago: American Library Association.

American Library Association. 2010. *Public Library Data Service 2010 Report* Chicago: American Library Association, Public Library Association. http://www.publiclibrariesonline.org. Accessed December 2010.

Becker, Joseph. 1964. Automating the serial record. *American Library Association Bulletin* 58, no. 6 (June): 557–60.

Becker, Joseph. 1964a. Circulation and the computer. *American Library Association Bulletin* 58, no. 12 (December): 1001–1010.

Burke, John J. 2009. *Neal-Schuman Library Technology Companion: A Basic Guide for Staff*. New York: Neal-Schuman.

Davis, Denise M., et al. 2009. How to work a crisis. *American Libraries* 40, no. 11 (November): 50–52.

Hamilton, Robert E. 1968. Illinois State Library computer system. *Wilson Library Bulletin* 43, no. 3 (March): 721–22.

Heiliger, Edward. 1966. Florida Atlantic University Library. In *Proceedings of the 1965 Clinic on Library Applications of Data Processing*, ed. Francis B. Jenkins, 92–111. Urbana: University of Illinois Press.

Howe, Mary T., and Mary K. Weidner. 1962. Data processing in the Decatur Public Library. *Illinois Libraries* 44 (November): 593–97.

Jenkins, Francis B., ed. 1966. *Proceedings of the 1965 Clinic on Library Applications of Data Processing.* Urbana: University of Illinois Press.

King, Gilbert W. et al. 1963. *Automation and the Library of Congress.* Washington: Library of Congress.

Large, Andrew. 2009. Children and information technology. In *Information Technology in Librarianship: New Critical Approaches*, ed. Gloria J. Leckie and John E. Buschman, 181–204. Westport, CT: Libraries Unlimited.

Leckie, Gloria J., and John E. Buschman, eds. 2009. *Information Technology in Librarianship: New Critical Approaches.* Westport, CT: Libraries Unlimited.

Leckie, Gloria J., Lisa Given, and Grant Campbell. 2009. Technologies of social regulation: An examination of library OPACs and web portals. In *Information Technology in Librarianship: New Critical Approaches*, ed. Gloria J. Leckie and John E. Buschman, 221–60. Westport, CT: Libraries Unlimited.

Parker, Ralph H. 1936. The punched card method in circulation work. *Library Journal* 61 (December): 903–5.

Parker, Ralph H. 1965. The machine and the library. *Library Resources & Technical Services* 9, no. 1 (Winter): 100–103.

Postman, Neil. 1993. *Technopoly: The Surrender of Culture to Technology.* New York: Vintage.

Public Library Data Service 2010 Report. 2010. Chicago: American Library Association, Public Library Association. www.publiclibrariesonline.org. Accessed December 2010.

Salmon, Stephen R. 1975. Library automation. In *Encyclopedia of Library and Information Science* 14: 338–445. This is the principal reference article for early automation projects.

Segal, H. P. 2005. *Technological Utopianism in American Culture.* Syracuse, NY: Syracuse University Press.

Thompson, Susan M., ed. 2009. *Core Technology Competencies for Librarians and Library Staff: A LITA Guide.* New York: Neal-Schuman.

U.S. National Center for Education Statistics. 2007. *Public Libraries in the United States: Fiscal Year 2005.*Washington, DC: U.S. Department of Education.

Winter, Michael F. 2009. Librarianship and the labor process: aspects of the rationalization, restructuring, and intensification of intellectual work. In *Information Technology in Librarianship: New Critical Approaches*, ed. Gloria J. Leckie and John E. Buschman, 143–64. Westport, CT: Libraries Unlimited.

INSTITUTE OF MUSEUM AND LIBRARY SERVICES   The Institute of Museum and Library Services (IMLS) was established by the Museum and Library Services Act (MLSA) of 1996 within the National Foundation on the Arts and Humanities. It is located at 1800 M Street NW, Washington, DC 20036–5802. The new agency combined the Institute of Museum Services, which had been in existence since 1976, and the Library Programs Office, which had been part of the Department of Education since 1956. The Library Services and Technology Act (LSTA; *see* GOVERNMENT ROLE) became a subtitle of MLSA. In 2003, MLSA was reauthorized. Effective in early 2008, the activities of the National Commission on Libraries and Information Science were consolidated under IMLS, along with some of the activities of the National Center for Education Statistics having to do with libraries. In December 2010, President Obama signed another reauthorization of MLSA, again including LSTA.

IMLS expresses its mission this way: "to create strong libraries and museums that connect people to information and ideas. The Institute works at the national level and in coordination with state and local organizations to sustain heritage, culture, and knowledge, enhance learning and innovation, and support professional development" (U.S. Institute of Museum and Library Services 2010). IMLS is the federal agency that collects and publishes statistical data about libraries (*see* STATISTICS) and distributes funds to libraries in accordance with LSTA. IMLS also makes grants of interest to libraries independent of LSTA; current programs include national leadership grants, library recruitment and education grants, and grants to support library services to Native Americans. The budget request for IMLS, fiscal year 2011, was $265,869,000.

Beginning in 2000, IMLS has presented national awards, later national medals, to distinguished libraries. These are the award winners by year:

2000	B. B. Comer Memorial Library, Sylacauga, AL
	Queens Borough Public Library, Jamaica, NY
2001	Alaska Resources Library and Information Service, Anchorage
	Hancock County Library System, Bay St. Louis, MS
	Providence Public Library, RI
2002	Boundary County District Library, Bonners Ferry, ID
	Hartford Public Library, CT
	Southwest Georgia Regional Public Library System, Bainbridge, GA
2003	Bozeman Public Library, MT
	Free Library of Philadelphia
	Pocahontas County Free Libraries, Marlinton, WV
2004	Flint Public Library, MI
2005	Johnson County Library, Overland Park, KS
	Matthews Memorial Library, Matthews, VA
	St. Paul Public Library, MN
2006	Frankfort Community Public Library, IN
	Charlotte-Mecklenburg Public Library, NC
	San Antonio Public Library, TX
2007	Georgetown County Library, SC
	Kim Yerton Branch, Humboldt County Library, Hoopa, CA
	Memphis Public Library, TN
	Ocean County Library, Toms River, NJ
2008	Kansas City Public Library, MO
	Miami-Dade Public Library System, FL
	Skidompha Library, Damariscotta, ME
	Skokie Public Library, IL

Reference

U.S. Institute of Museum and Library Services. 2010. About us: Legislation and budget. http://www.imls.gov/about/services1996/shtm.

INTELLECTUAL FREEDOM

Terminology

A number of expressions relating to this topic need to be carefully defined for it to make sense. The professional literature has given little useful guidance regarding these expressions, so it is necessary to put general dictionary statements into a reasonable context. "Intellectual freedom" itself is a rather hazy concept. It is not defined in *Merriam* or *American Heritage*. The American Library Association (ALA), its principal sponsor in the United States, has "never endorsed a uniform definition of intellectual freedom (Krug 2003, 1379). *Merriam* does have entries for the two individual words, "intellectual" and "freedom." "Intellectual" means "engaged in activity requiring the creative use of the intellect." "Freedom" "has a broad range of application from total absence of restraint to merely a sense of not being unduly hampered or frustrated." And "freedom" is also "the absence of necessity, coercion, or restraint in choice or action." Assembling these descriptions, it may be said that "intellectual freedom is a state of affairs in which activities requiring creative use of the intellect may occur without necessity, coercion, or restraint." Now "necessity" and "coercion" may be germane in totalitarian environments but not in mature democracies. "Restraint" is the only issue faced in the United States or other modern states. So a refined definition is "intellectual freedom is a state of affairs in which activities requiring creative use of the intellect may occur without restraint."

It is noteworthy that this definition is value free. The "restraint" involved is not imputed to be good or bad, right or wrong. However, there appears to be a fairly general view today that freedom is a good condition for humans to have, which would make restraints on freedom bad. This position is eloquently pronounced in the UN *Universal Declaration of Human Rights*: "Everyone has the right to freedom of opinion and expression; this right includes freedom to hold opinions without interference and to seek, receive and impart information and ideas through any media and regardless of frontiers" (United Nations 1948, Article 19). Americans also have the First Amendment to the Constitution, which reads, "Congress shall make no law respecting an establishment of religion, or prohibiting the free exercise thereof, or abridging the freedom of speech or of the press."

This seems clear enough, yet there is a controversial aspect to it. A long history of disputes in American society has been founded on the idea that the freedoms under consideration are not absolute. It is acceptable to yield a certain measure of freedom under specific conditions in the interest of a higher good. Sometimes restraints are required. For instance, "libel" is defined in *Merriam* as "a statement or representation published without just cause and tending to expose another to public contempt"; such a statement is subject to legal challenge. A person is not free to make such statements, and the legal system is empowered to restrain her from doing so.

Another example of a limitation on freedom, in this case to read as one chooses, lies with "classified" documents: those "withheld from general circulation for reasons of national security." (A history of such restrictions in the United States is given in Milevski 1990.) Other legal curbs on the freedom of speech have been associated with blasphemy, fraud, deceit, and misrepresentation (Wilson 1990, 95). An incident of a book deemed to be fraudulent by the court was reported in 2003, as Judge Lloyd D. George of the Federal District Court in Las Vegas enjoined Irwin Schiff from selling his book *The Federal Mafia*. Judge George wrote that the book offered "fraudulent tax advice" and represented "false commercial speech," which "is not protected by the First Amendment" (*American Libraries*, August 2003, 23). A further area of restraint, child pornography, will be taken up shortly.

In public librarianship a major realm of principal concern has been restraint of freedom for reasons of morality. (The other troubling area has to do with political ideas; this is not a definition problem. It is addressed in the section "Historical Summary" below.) Challenges and disputes have marked the morality issue since the pioneer days of the profession. It is easy to see why: since "morality" means "right human conduct," there will inevitably be difference of opinion about what that right conduct is. It is, after all, a question that has occupied philosophers for 2,500 years. In many societies the answer to the puzzle has been discovered in religious codes of conduct—giving solutions that are subjective and unsettled. In a given time and place there may be unanimity about the meaning of morality; in such a situation a like unanimity may follow regarding restraints on the products of creative intellect. This was the philosophical ambience of the mid-nineteenth-century United States as the public library idea took form. Librarians, like most Americans of the time, tended to accept the Christian tradition of morality and affirmed that tradition in library practice by approving restraints on publications that broke from it. In the formative decades of the profession, its leaders "endorsed the librarian as moral censor" (Geller 1984, xv).

The shame of Adam and Eve as they left Eden is an enduring image in Christian thought. That shame was about their nudity, which they sought to cover, and the concept of nudity as an indecent condition lingers in our own time. Nudity—and the sexual activities it implies—are subjects of restraint on publications and representations, drawn from the idea that morality must be protected, even at the expense of freedom of expression. Arguments against such restraints cannot succeed if they simply deny the validity of all restraints. Arguments have to be based on priority: the establishment of freedom as a higher good than traditional morality. Without that priority, intellectual freedom remains indeterminate, a concept that applies in certain situations and not in others.

"Censorship" is the term that is drawn from the idea of "restraint." *Merriam* says that censorship is the "practice of censoring," which means "to examine in order to suppress or delete anything considered objectionable." A bit fuzzy; it could be describing the normal practice of editing as well as censoring. And it leaves one to wonder, who does this deed? *American Heritage* is also vague: "Censorship—The act, process, or practice of censoring," which leads to "censor—One authorized to examine books, films, or other material and suppress what is considered objectionable." This does bring in the concept of authorization but leaves dangling the key term "objectionable." A more useful depiction of censorship appears in *ODLIS*: "Censorship—Prohibition of the production, distribution, circulation, or display of a work by a governing authority on grounds that it contains objectionable or dangerous material."

Among librarians censorship is usually construed as a wrongful act, but the definition is value free. Indeed, censorship, as a protective device for society, is possibly laudable. A useful view of censorship would be that it is neither right nor wrong in principle, but—like any other legislative action or regulation—it may be abused in practice. Librarians who are disturbed by censorship might well think of accepting it as a value-free practice but opposing its abuses. There is "prohibition" in the *ODLIS* definition, meaning that a censored item would be forbidden to everyone, with the possible exception of certain privileged groups, within the sphere of the censor's authority.

Who is to say whether a censor is effective or ineffective in determining what may bring harm to society? Clearly it must be the society for which the censor acts, in the spirit of the social contract. Members of the society authorize censors, just as they authorize their political leaders, teachers, and librarians, to do what operates for the communal good. Social forces impinge on the censor to act in accord with the general will. Open societies like the United States and the European democracies do not have officials with the title "censor," and indeed they do not routinely practice censorship. Strategic documents in wartime and certain governmental writings may have restricted access, and there are limits on who may share certain kinds of information about individuals (*see* PRIVACY AND CONFIDENTIALITY). Such actions do not censor but apply common sense to situations that have the potential of bringing harm to the society. Controversies develop not over the principle of censorship but about the question of application in given cases.

Although the United States has no official censor, it has a judicial system that has the power to restrain or prohibit promulgation of certain documents. American courts, with the Supreme Court as last resort, have interpreted the First Amendment in a manner that allows a number of abridgements specifically forbidden in the amendment. Major actions of the Court in this arena are examined in the section "Historical Summary" below.

Many thoughtful librarians have reflected on the possibility that the library profession itself may be a censoring body (Asheim 1953). The community that engages a public or school librarian gives that person a mission, part of which is to protect the community from harmful books and visual materials. As a consequence librarians, acting like "gatekeepers," keep certain materials away from their users. Although the librarian's sphere of control is local, applied only to one library or system, the result is a censoring of specific documents on the grounds that they are potentially harmful to society. This gatekeeper theory was described by Kenneth Shearer (1983):

> Library selectors not only stand at the gate to admit or deny entry on the basis of local system needs, but they also follow regulations in general to remove, for instance the obscene/"adult" materials, the inaccurate, and the inept, ungrammatical, or clumsily produced publication. ... Twenty years ago astrology, numerology, and witchcraft were, like modern erotic materials, generally barred from American libraries. (86)

Troubling gatekeeper decisions arise regarding extremist writings of all kinds. Holocaust deniers present a neat problem: do books exhibiting that persuasion have a place on public library shelves, as statements of opinion, or should they be denied space as potentially harmful? (Wolkoff 1996). Are librarians invariably neutral? Should they be? This issue is discussed in the section "Historical Summary" below. If librarians accept this gatekeeper role, they cannot rationally engage in the opposition to censorship. And the ALA's imprecation (*Library Bill of Rights* [ALA 1948]) that librarians "co-operate with all persons and groups concerned with resisting abridgment of free expression" rings hollow since librarians appear to be among those "persons and groups"!

Three other terms need to be addressed. Unfortunately the dictionaries are weak regarding two of them. "Pornography" is defined by *Merriam* as "the depiction of erotic behavior (as in pictures or writing) intended to cause sexual excitement." This is all right except for the last five words, which center on someone's intentions, unknowable factors. *American Heritage* gives us this: "Sexually explicit pictures, writing, or other material whose primary purpose is to cause sexual arousal." The intention factor intrudes here also. *Merriam*'s "erotic" is defined as "strongly marked or affected by sexual desire." It is no better explicated by *Heritage*: "of or concerning sexual love and desire; amatory." By taking out the subjective terms "love" and "desire" and putting in the objective "behavior," there is a usable definition of erotic: "sexual behavior." This works well in the context of "erotica," which is "literature or art concerning erotic behavior."

It is possible to assemble these expressions in a useful way. All depiction of erotic (sexual) behavior is pornography, while a segment of pornography that is occupied by literature or art is erotica. These are value-free definitions: neither pornography nor erotica is necessarily good or bad in principle. Much of the disputation over censorship has turned on vague definitions of these terms.

"Obscene" and "obscenity" fare poorly in *Merriam*. "Obscene" is "abhorrent to morality or virtue" *specif.* designed to incite to lust or depravity." The intentional problem arises again, and there is the difficulty of applying subjective ideas like "morality" and "virtue." *American Heritage* is a little better: "obscene" is "offensive to accepted standards of decency or modesty." What is better about it is the reference to "accepted standards," which is the basis for commonly accepted thinking about the term. "Decency" and "modesty" are loaded words, not really apt in this context. A simple definition of obscenity is "socially unacceptable pornography." Deciding what is socially acceptable has been a task on the one hand for the American legal system and on the other for librarians as they decide what is appropriate for their collections. The following section tells the story from both angles. Evelyn Geller (1984, xvi) has identified three periods of American library history with respect to restraints on certain materials: 1876–1900, with values of populism, neutrality, and censorship; 1900–1922, censorship eroding but still reflected in closed shelf policies; and 1923–1939, with the emerging value of freedom to read.

Historical Summary

With regard to pornography and obscenity, American courts have labored long to produce practical definitions. The most relevant efforts are summarized here. At the same time librarians were examining their beliefs about these matters. Both the legal and the philosophical meditations occurred amidst shifting social attitudes; those attitudes varying along a scale from permissive to restrictive. And "librarians have generally been in accord with the intellectual leaders of their times" (Daily 1970, 228). In the mid-19th century the social climate was clearly restrictive. The British courts, then very influential in American jurisprudence, had settled on a test for obscenity in *Regina v. Hicklin* (1868): a book is obscene if its tendency "is to deprave or corrupt those whose minds are open to such immoral influences, and who might come into contact with it" (Ernst and Schwartz 1964, 76). The corruption issue affected American judges and librarians as well. Neither group rose to oppose Anthony Comstock, a self-appointed crusader against the corrupting power of sex in writing or illustration. Comstock persuaded Congress in 1873 to prohibit "mailing obscene or crime-inciting matter." Books and magazines that could not be mailed could hardly be sold in quantity, so the impact of the law was to suppress publications that the Post Office determined to have "any indecent or immoral purpose" (Ernst and Schwartz 1964, 32). The new law was quickly effective: Comstock, appointed to the Post Office as a special agent, announced in 1874 that he had already seized 194,000 obscene pictures and photographs and 134,000 pounds of books. Thirty states had antiobscenity laws by 1900.

If the pioneer public librarians who were Comstock's contemporaries did not approach the obscenity question with his vigor and bias, they shared his worry about cheap and vulgar literature. They saw themselves as benevolent censors, in fact, gatekeepers.

> Although there was a genuine wish to improve the lot of the less fortunate and even to further the cause of democracy among many of the public-spirited elites that built the majority of the first public libraries, there was also a great deal of careful screening of the books that stocked those shelves. The elevation of taste

and development of skills took precedence over access to any potentially unsettling ideas and literature. (Swan 1994, 283)

William F. Poole, librarian of the Chicago Public Library and one of the founders of the ALA, expressed the common concern of professional leaders in support for the so-called ladder theory: "When the habit of reading is once acquired, the reader's taste, and hence the quality of his reading, progressively improves." However, "the librarian who should allow an immoral novel in his library for circulation would be as culpable as the manager of a picture gallery who should hang an indecent picture on his walls" (Poole 1876, 49, 51). In the 1870s this ambivalence was widespread. Librarians wished to meet reader demand, even for material of dubious quality, expecting them to climb the ladder to better things, but they did not wish to give readers anything unrespectable, even if they wanted it. A sly mechanism was available, and many librarians grasped it: restriction on use of dubious books (allowing them in the hands only of mature patrons and serious students). The locked case, or "inferno," was a stock feature of public libraries. As open shelves became the norm by the 1890s, such policies became obvious to readers, for closed shelves remained only for restricted volumes.

This dilemma over provision of wants, as opposed to supposed needs, has never been eliminated from professional concerns. A 1961 article spoke of it this way:

Serving the reader means "helping" him, learning his wishes and satisfying them. This comes dangerously close to the position taken by a minority of librarians, that their duty is to give the people what they want. In such a conception ... he yields a central meaning of service, the commitment to run personal risks in order to fulfill a high obligation to society. ... This strain between the wishes and the real needs of a clientele is perhaps to be found in all professions, but in established professions more often it is resolved by the professional's decision. (Goode 1961, 316–17)

The prevailing censorious attitude of the early librarians remained constant into the twentieth century. Arthur Bostwick, ALA president in 1908, gave an address to the association titled "The Librarian as a Censor"; it was a role that was comfortable for him (Bostwick 1908). Others who favored restrictions included Justin Winsor, Henry Edward Legler, William Howard Brett, and William Isaac Fletcher. Lutie Stearns in 1911 attacked the "sensualism" of current magazines but defended presentation of unpopular political expression. Voices for a more liberal position included John Cotton Dana and Frederick Morgan Crunden. Lindsay Swift, in an 1899 *Library Journal* article, cautioned against the "tendency to regulate and decide for others, which is antipathetic to the democratic principles of least possible government" (Stielow 1983, 331). Other librarians were uneasy about excluding books that were regarded as classics.

On the legal front, there was change in the air after the turn of the century. In 1913, Federal District Judge Learned Hand "suggested that legal obscenity be defined not in terms of moral corruption, but simply as 'the present critical point in the compromise between candor and shame at which the community may have arrived here and now'" (Boyer 2002, 47). Judge Hand's statement fits well with the definition offered above in *Terminology*: "obscenity is socially unacceptable pornography." How much candor will the community tolerate? This is a test that can be graded easily enough since the community will make its will known.

Censor advocates lost ground from this point. Some librarians, like Mary Wright Plummer, ALA president in 1916, called on her colleagues to resist censorship. In 1922 an important judicial milestone was reached, in the case involving the book *Mademoiselle de Maupin* (in English translation) by Théophile Gautier:

> It is significant that the Court [of Appeals, New York] took into consideration these points: (a) the reputation of the author; (b) the regard in which the novel had been held by eminent critics since its first publication in 1835; (c) a reading of the book in its entirety and not just selected passages; (d) the fact that even the language complained of was not "of the street"; (e) the effect of the translation from the French. (Ernst and Schwartz 1964, 57)

The book was not obscene, and the court's approach to it set the standard for future decisions.

World War I battered the neutrality claim of librarians. They easily acceded to the exclusion of propaganda and pacifist literature, putting their role as citizens ahead of their role as professionals (Geller 1984, 109). The books provided for the military through the ALA were carefully screened; indeed, there was a substantial list of titles not to be put into the hands of the boys "over there." Thus, the concept of social responsibility trumped neutrality, just as the value of free reading was replacing broad censorship. At the 1923 ALA conference there was an interesting exchange of opinion on the censorship question. A paper given by Mary Rothrock of Knoxville Public Library said that it is not a librarian's duty to exclude books "on the grounds of their possible moral effect on mature readers." But Mary Eileen Ahern, editor of the journal *Public Libraries*, responded that certain books should be avoided, specifically novels of "neurotic exploration" and fiction that made no contribution to the "happiness of mankind." Censoring such material, she claimed, should not trouble the librarian (Boyer 2002, 115). It was the Rothrock position that dominated the profession in the Roaring Twenties: a period of social liberality, the "jazz age" of flappers and speakeasies. A New York critic said that the 1926–1927 Broadway season had "the dirtiest lot of shows . . . ever put on view in the New York legitimate theaters" (Boyer 2002, 162). The rise of motion pictures in this era presented a new medium for sensual exploration. (Filmmakers ultimately decided to avoid censor trouble by self-imposed restraints.) Book censorship was relaxed, in part over growing apprehension about images. Radclyffe Hall's novel about lesbians, *The Well of Loneliness*, was cleared of obscenity charges by an appeal court in 1929; the judges observed the criteria set out in the *Mademoiselle de Maupin* case. Their decision also removed another lingering criterion of obscenity: the theme of a work. In 1926, ALA president Charles Belden (librarian of the Boston Public Library) could announce that "the true public library must stand for intellectual freedom of access to the printed word" (Belden 1926, 274). Nevertheless, the *ALA Catalog* of recommended books for libraries, 1926 edition (the previous edition was 1904), remained on the brink: the list (with its 1926–1931 supplement) covered most of the controversial books that had not made the 1904 list but still omitted the works of Marcel Proust, William Faulkner, and F. Scott Fitzgerald.

A legendary obscenity case of 1930 dealt with James Joyce's unique novel *Ulysses*. Judge John M. Woolsey of the New York District Court presided, and a more fortunate choice for the liberal cause could not have been made. Woolsey read and studied the work closely for weeks, concluding that it was "not pornographic"—note the ongoing conflation of pornography and obscenity—and did not tend "to stir the sex impulses or to lead to sexually impure and lustful thoughts" on the average reader. Such a tendency would have marked the book as "obscene" in Woolsey's view. Instead he found the novel to be innocent in that regard, being rather "a sincere and serious attempt to devise a new literary method for the observation and description of mankind" (quotes from Ernst and Schwartz 1964, 99–100). *Ulysses* did not bring censorship pressures to an end. There were instances in the 1930s of backlash against the new liberality. "The ambivalent attitude of the profession as a whole regarding censorship" was reflected in an "inconsistent position" by the ALA. "Review of library literature manifests relatively few articles on intellectual freedom prior to the late 1930s, and many of the articles appearing supported censorship and only quibbled over the degree and nature of it" (Krug and Harvey 1974, 171). It was not until 1939 that the ALA, responding to widespread challenges to John Steinbeck's *Grapes of Wrath*, adopted a policy statement on intellectual freedom: *Library's Bill of Rights* (later called the *Library Bill of Rights*). The statement was close to a verbatim rendering of a pronouncement issued in 1938 by the Des Moines Public Library. A year later the forerunner to the association's Intellectual Freedom Committee was established. After a decade of consideration, the *Library Bill of Rights* was published in 1948 in this form:

The ALA affirms that all libraries are forums for information and ideas, and that the following basic policies should guide their services.

> I. Books and other library resources should be provided for the interest, information, and enlightenment of all people of the community the library serves. Materials should not be excluded because of the origin, background, or views of those contributing to their creation.

II. Libraries should provide materials and information presenting all points of view on current and historical issues. Materials should not be proscribed or removed because of partisan or doctrinal disapproval.

III. Libraries should challenge censorship in the fulfillment of their responsibility to provide information and enlightenment.

IV. Libraries should cooperate with all persons and groups concerned with resisting abridgment of free expression and free access to ideas.

V. A person's right to use a library should not be denied or abridged because of origin, age, background, or view.

VI. Libraries which make exhibit spaces and meeting rooms available to the public they serve should make such facilities available on an equitable basis, regardless of the beliefs or affiliations of individuals or groups requesting their use.

Adopted 18 June 1948, amended 2 Feb 1961 and 23 Jan 1980, inclusion of "age" reaffirmed 23 Jan 1996 by the ALA Council.

The ALA position is based on a strict reading of the First Amendment and on the extension of First Amendment rights through the Fourteenth Amendment. A number of so-called interpretations have been issued by ALA Council, clarifying policy and procedure. The interpretations cover "Access for Children and Young Adults to Nonprint Materials," "Access to Digital Information, Services, and Networks," "Q&A: Access to Electronic Information, Services, and Networks," "Access to Library Resources and Service Regardless of Sex, Gender Identity, or Sexual Orientation," "Access to Resources and Services in the School Media Program," "Challenged Materials," "Diversity in Collection Development," "Economic Barriers to Information Access," "Evaluating Library Collections," "Exhibit Spaces and Bulletin Boards," "Expurgation of Library Materials," "Free Access to Libraries for Minors," "Importance of Education to Intellectual Freedom," "Intellectual Freedom Principles for Academic Libraries," "Labeling and Rating Systems," "Minors and Internet Interactivity," "Questions and Answers on Labels and Rating Systems," "Library-Initiated Programs as a Resource," "Meeting Rooms," "Privacy," "Questions and Answers on Privacy and Confidentiality," "Restricted Access to Library Materials," "Services to People with Disabilities," and "The Universal Right to Free Expression."

In general, the library community has accepted the *Library Bill of Rights*, except for concerns about the unlimited access to materials granted to minors (more of this in the next section of this entry). There have been critiques of the document that addressed its departure from accepted legal standards (Baldwin 1996; Wiegand 1996). Further, the beliefs of people who do not sympathize with the "absolutism" of the *Library Bill of Rights* "are as legitimately held as those of anyone else" so that "there seems to be a need for some deeper inquiry into intellectual freedom" (Budd 2007, 129). Deeper inquiry is also indicated to resolve the conflict between the neutrality of the *Library Bill of Rights* and the position taken by the mainstream profession that favors "advocacy of a host of democratic values: civil liberties, pacifism, antifacism, racial equality" (Geller 1984, 164). The University of Chicago Graduate Library School was a center for advocacy ideals in the 1930s and 1940s. Truth was proclaimed to be a goal that superseded neutrality and presentation of all sides on political issues. Leon Carnovsky (1939) visualized a librarian "whose predilections are for established truths and who then bases his book selection upon those truths ... the principle of wide representation ... should never be applied to justify the equal provision of established truths and their denials" (32). But since not everyone agrees on which truths are actually "established," this enterprise appears to collapse into one of personal preferences.

The courts have continued to refine the legal position of printed and graphic materials with respect to obscenity. A liberal trend continued through the 1950s, but concerns over such things as "prurient interests" lingered. The Supreme Court, in *U.S. v. Roth* (1957), defined a work as obscene if "to the average person, applying contemporary community standards, the dominant theme of the material taken as a whole appeals to the prurient interests." A work thus defined as legally obscene would have no protection under the First Amendment and would be subject to suppression. Clearly there are subjective aspects to this definition that led to confusion in the courts; what is an average person, what community is designated, and what are those prurient interests? None of these questions have yet found answers. On a practical level, it seems that "whatever is published and withstands a test in court establishes the community standards" (Daily 1970, 344).

The year 1966 brought a remarkable and curious pair of legal events. The Supreme Court in one decision upheld the conviction of publisher Ralph Ginzburg, who had been issuing a magazine named *Eros* since 1962. In the same year the Court reversed an earlier ban on the book *Memoirs of a Woman of Pleasure*, also known as *Fanny Hill* (1749), by John Cleland. That book was declared to be "prurient" but with "redeeming social importance" because of its literary value. Evidently the 1960s were a time of social uncertainties. Conservative opposition emerged to the various youth movements of the time and to rock music. But "girlie magazines" were published without much outcry, nudity in Broadway shows was accepted, and a "porn movie industry" flourished, moving to the mainstream in Hollywood.

President Lyndon Johnson appointed a Commission on Obscenity and Pornography to analyze the whole problem. They reported back in 1970 with a recommendation against federal or local legislation that interfered with the right of adults to read or view explicit sex materials. President Nixon rejected the report, and the U.S. Senate did likewise by a vote of 60 to 5. So it came to pass that while the library profession and to some extent the legal profession were in essential agreement in resisting censorship, the mood in the country at large was growing repressive. In 1973, Chief Justice Burger disposed of the *Fanny Hill* criterion about redeeming social value, substituting the statement that a work could not be protected if it lacked "serious literary, artistic, political, or scientific value." Of course all these "values" lay in the subjective realm, requiring dispute and interpretation. The Burger court also determined that "community standards" meant any local community, not a sort of national community; as a result challenges to materials were brought in highly conservative jurisdictions. The ALA reported that in 1981 alone, nearly 1,000 challenges to print or graphic materials were made (Boyer 2002, 325). When President Reagan set up an "Obscenity Unit" in the Department of Justice, it secured 135 convictions, mostly of films and videos, between 1987 and 1991. However, political writings, subject of so much agitation from the 1930s into the 1950s, faded as objects of restraint.

Recent Issues

The proliferation of videocassettes in the 1980s and 1990s and of the successor medium DVD brought numerous challenges to library policies. Local pressures led in some cases to limitations on the use of certain videos by younger users (e.g., the Omaha Public Library barred those under 18 years of age from charging out videos with "R" ratings; reported in *American Libraries*, May 2005, 15). But such ratings, devised by the motion picture industry and lacking legal power, have lost their value through dilution; "objectionable" scenes appear in films with more general ratings, with the "R" rating falling into disuse. Judging from reports in the library press of the past few years, the video/DVD arena seems not to be particularly active.

Libraries with meeting rooms that are available to the public may encounter difficulties. According to the *Library Bill of Rights*, such facilities should be offered "on an equitable basis, regardless of the beliefs or affiliations of individuals or groups requesting their use." But what about the events themselves? A relevant case was reported (*American Libraries*, October 2008, 33) regarding the Upper Arlington (Ohio) Public Library, whose meeting room policy barred "inherent elements of religious service." When a group named Citizens for Community Values scheduled a program in the meeting room about the role of Christians in politics that was to include "a time of prayer ... and singing praise and giving thanks to God ... " the library director objected, and the citizens' group filed suit against the library. On August 14, 2008, District Judge George C. Smith found for the citizens, stating that "the prayer and singing elements ... do not constitute mere religious worship, divorced from the otherwise permissible discussion elements of plaintiff's event," but he added that "the court expresses no opinion on the constitutionality of defendant library's policy of precluding religious services" per se. To what extent libraries are permitted to restrict what goes on in their meeting rooms is an issue grounded in the concept of "public forum." Such a forum is a locus within a facility operated by government with public funds where community residents may express their views without restriction except for breaking of laws. A park is such a forum, and so is an advertising space on a public bus. The rule of thumb is that accepting one person's speech or writing in such a forum carries the duty of accepting everyone's. This absolute permission becomes problematic in the library situation. There are rules for behavior in a public library to preserve an environment for reading and study. Some loud talking is tolerated but just up to a point. A librarian may disagree with a user whose actions or hygiene disturbs others that the matter is one of "rights." Libraries are, in fact, "limited public forums" in which reasonable regulations, applicable evenly to all, may be imposed on behavior so that the principal work of the institution may go on without hindrance. This distinction between public forum and limited public forum was the crux of a dispute in the Vidalia (GA) Public Library in 2002. When community objections were raised to the presence on a library giveaway table of a newspaper named *Gay Guardian*, the director and the regional library board decided to limit materials on the table to governmental and library-related materials. The owner of the newspaper brought a suit that was eventually decided by the U.S. Court of Appeals for the Eleventh Circuit. A library, said the decision, is a limited public forum, able to limit "expressive activity"; the court ruled in favor of the library on this basis (Helms 2004, 12–16).

Three acts of Congress energized the censorship debate in the 1990s. The Communications Decency Act (CDA) of 1996 was the first notable attempt by Congress to regulate objectionable material on the Internet. The CDA imposed criminal sanctions on anyone who knowingly sends via computer to a person under 18 years of age "any comment, request, suggestion, proposal, image, or other communication that, in context, depicts or describes, in terms patently offensive as measured by contemporary community standards, sexual or excretory activities or organs." It also criminalized the transmission of materials that were "obscene or indecent" to persons known to be under 18. The Supreme Court upheld a lower court in stating that the "indecency" provisions of the CDA were unconstitutional. An amended CDA was approved in Congress in 2003, but the Supreme Court rejected it as well. This issue was not a direct concern for libraries, but it did demonstrate that the mood of the country (reflected in Congress) was again on the repressive side, while again the legal position was on the permissive side.

The Child Online Protection Act (COPA) of 1998 rendered liable to prosecution a website owner who posts a commercial online communication "that includes any material that is harmful to minors" (meaning sexually explicit materials, with a minor here defined as someone 17 or younger) unless the website keeps minors out through a digital age-verification gateway. COPA brought on a decade of litigation and two decisions that were returned to lower courts by the Supreme Court for further review. On July 22, 2008, a determination by the Third Circuit Court of Appeals ruled the act unconstitutional, observing that blocking software (filters) would be a less restrictive means of shielding youngsters from sexually explicit material. The ALA had filed several amicus curiae briefs on behalf of the plaintiffs and might have felt those efforts to be fully successful except for the reference to filters.

Filters, computer software programs designed to prevent the display of "objectionable" depictions or a pornographic nature, were mandated in the Children's Internet Protection Act (CIPA) of 1998. In the national debate that followed, the ALA was a prominent member of the opposition to this act. As one librarian put it, filters are not capable of blocking so-called objectionable material. "They block things they should not, and do not block things that they aspire to block ... filters not only do not work but also *cannot* work. ... Filtering is just the latest tattered banner under which the bigots and the censors march" (Gorman 2005, 153). An ironic support for that position emerged when the Virginia General Assembly, considering a bill to require public libraries to install filters, was advised that such filters on the computers in one school had blocked the Code of Virginia because some of the laws in it had sexually explicit language (Reported in *American Libraries*, April 2005, 20). When CIPA came before the Supreme Court in 2003, the ALA argued that filtering was a content-based restriction on access to a public forum. By shielding children, the filter also prevented adults from access to legal materials. Public libraries, attorneys for the ALA stated, served "primarily as forums for private speech." However, Chief Justice Rehnquist disagreed, observing that the primary mission of the public library is to facilitate learning and a cultural environment. It does not need to create a forum for Web publishers to express themselves. So much for the philosophical argument. On the technical side, it was clear that a librarian could readily disable the filters to allow an adult unfettered access to the Internet and could still protect the children as appropriate. The ALA position came to be seen as insensitive to the special responsibilities of serving children and also vague on the mandate that society gives to public libraries. CIPA was upheld.

Two thoughtful articles about this conclusion are bright spots in the professional literature. Leonard Kniffel, editor of *American Libraries*, acknowledged the ALA's weak presentation to the court, notably in the insistence on giving children access to everything (as stated in the *Library Bill of Rights*): "We cannot be so fearful of being painted with the censor's brush that we become unable to acknowledge that there are materials that librarians should not offer in the children's room. As long as Internet pornography is readily available to minors in public libraries, can we expect a sympathetic public reaction?" (Kniffel 2003, 36). Ron McCabe suggested three lessons to be learned from the CIPA decision: the ALA should obtain balanced rather than ideologically driven legal advice; we should recognize that the primary purpose of public libraries is educational, not to act as forums for private speech; we should confess to our "arrogant disregard for the concerns of the vast majority of Americans regarding CIPA"' and we must "approach serious public issues with more openness to other points of view." He concludes that "we are not always wiser that the citizens we serve" (McCabe 2003, 16). Respect for those citizens who advocate restrictive policies has been lacking.

> While there are good reasons for resisting the intrusion of community members (other than legal entities) into selection decisions, such resistance often takes the form of derision or contempt for those who come forward to complain. Thus, the freedom of speech so vibrantly defended by the librarian acting as selector is denied by the librarian responding to complaints. It is strange to see community members characterized as "would-be censors" and "book banners" when they are in fact exercising the rights that librarians are pledged to support. (Marco 1995, 19)

Challenges do continue, some successful and others not. There were 513 of them reported to the ALA in 2008 (*American Libraries*, June/July 2009, 15). The ALA has its annual Banned Books Week and lists of most challenged books. Some of the materials that community members find reprehensible are puzzling to librarians, just as many library patrons are puzzled by some library choices and policies. Blending these interests, despite the complications they present, will guide librarians to true intellectual freedom. As Thomas Paine admonished, "Those who expect to reap the blessings of freedom must . . . undergo the fatigue of supporting it". *See also* AMERICAN LIBRARY ASSOCIATION, COLLECTION DEVELOPMENT, PHILOSOPHY OF PUBLIC LIBRARIANSHIP, PRIVACY AND CONFIDENTIALITY.

References

The closing quote from Paine is from *The Crisis* (1776). Much of the material on censorship in this entry is based on Marco (1995).

American Library Association. 1948. *Library Bill of Rights*. Chicago: American Library Association. Amended in 1961, 1980.
Asheim, Lester. 1953. Not censorship but selection. *Wilson Library Bulletin* 28, no. 1 (September): 63–67.
Baldwin, Gordon B. 1996. The *Library Bill of Rights*—A critique. *Library Trends* 45, no. 1 (Summer): 7–8.
Belden, Charles. 1926. Looking forward. *Bulletin of the American Library Association* 20, no. 10 (October): 274–78.
Bostwick, Arthur E. 1908. The librarian as censor. *Library Journal* 33, no. 7 (July): 247–64.
Boyer, Paul S. 2002. *Purity in Print: Book Censorship in America from the Gilded Age to the Computer Age*. 2nd ed. Madison: University of Wisconsin Press.
Budd, John M. 2007. *Self-Examination: The Present and Future of Librarianship*. Westport, CT: Libraries Unlimited.
Carnovsky, Leon. 1939. *The Practice of Book Selection*. Chicago: University of Chicago Press.

Daily, Jay. 1970. Censorship, contemporary and controversial aspects of. In *Encyclopedia of Library and Information Science* 4: 338–81. New York: Marcel Dekker.

Ernst, Morris L., and Alan U. Schwartz. 1964. *Censorship: The Search for the Obscene.* New York: Macmillan.

Geller, Evelyn. 1984. *Forbidden Books in American Libraries, 1876–1939.* Westport, CT: Greenwood Press.

Goode, William J. 1961. Librarianship: from occupation to profession? *Library Quarterly* 31, no. 4 (October): 300–318.

Gorman, Michael. 2005. *Our Own Selves: More Meditations for Librarians.* Chicago: American Library Association.

Helms, Cathy Harris. 2004. Lessons learned from the *Gay Guardian* newspaper vs. Ohoopee Regional Library System. *Georgia Library Quarterly* 41, no. 2 (Summer): 12–16.

Kniffel, Leonard. 2003. Editorial: Why we lost the CIPA case. *American Libraries* 34, no. 8 (September): 36–37.

Krug, Judith F. 2003. Intellectual freedom and ALA: A historical overview. In *Encyclopedia of Library and Information Science*, 2nd ed., 2: 1379–89. New York: Marcel Dekker.

Krug, Judith F., and James A. Harvey. 1974. Intellectual freedom and librarianship. In *Encyclopedia of Library and Information Science* 12: 169–85. New York: Marcel Dekker.

Marco, Guy A. 1995. Two false dogmas of censorship. *New Library World* 96: 15–19.

McCabe, Ron. 2003. The CIPA ruling as reality therapy. *American Libraries* 34, no. 7 (August): 16–17.

Milevski, Sandra N. 1990. Federal policy-making and national security controls on information. *Library Trends* 39, no. 1/2 (Summer/Fall): 132–44.

Poole, William F. 1876. Some popular objections to public libraries. *American Library Journal* 1, no. 1 (September): 45–57.

Shearer, Kenneth D. 1983. Applying new theories to library selection. *Drexel Library Quarterly* 19, no. 2 (Spring): 73–90.

Stielow, Frederic J. 1983. Censorship in the early professionalization of American libraries. *Journal of Library History* 18, no. 1 (Winter): 37–54.

Swan, John. 1994. Intellectual freedom. In *Encyclopedia of Library History*, 280–85. New York: Garland.

United Nations. 1948. *Universal Declaration of Human Rights.* New York: United Nations.

Wiegand, Shirley A. 1996. Reality bites: The collision of rhetoric, rights, and reality and the *Library Bill of Rights*. *Library Trends* 45, no. 1 (Summer): 75–76.

Wilson, Patrick. 1990. Copyright, derivative rights, and the First Amendment. *Library Trends* 39, no. 1/2 (Summer/Fall): 92–110.

Wolkoff, Kathleen Nietzke. 1996. The problem of Holocaust denial literature and libraries. *Library Trends* 45, no. 1 (Summer): 87–88.

INTERLIBRARY LOAN

Terminology

As defined by the *Interlibrary Loan Code for the United States*, "Interlibrary loan is the process by which a library requests material from, or supplies material to, another library" (American Library Association [ALA]2008, 1). The process is also known as "interloan," "interlending," "document delivery," and "document supply."

Historical Summary

The earliest known instance of a library lending to another dates from March 26, 1754, when Harvard College loaned a book to Yale College (Stone 1977, 189). However, that event, which was probably a personal favor, did not lead to systematic interlending. It was in the landmark year 1876 that such a system was first proposed. Samuel Swett Green wrote a letter to the editor of the *American Library Journal* that was published in the first issue. He suggested an agreement among libraries "to lend books to each other for short periods of time" (Green 1876, 1). The idea was well received, and interlibrary loans began. University libraries in California began interlending in 1894. By 1900 the practice was well established in public and academic libraries. The ALA attempted to rationalize the process with a number of "codes," beginning in 1919. The codes spelled out the responsibilities of the borrowing and lending libraries. The first code excluded current fiction from lending, but that restriction was ignored and dropped from later codes. A second code appeared in 1940, with later revisions. A new code came out in 1994, revised in 2001 and in 2008 (ALA 2008).

Current Situation

Federal government surveys show a remarkable rise in the number of public library interloans over the past 15 years. The number of items received on loan was 7,952,000 in fiscal year 1993, 38,043,000 in fiscal 2005, and 55,467,000 in fiscal 2008. One reason for the boom is that the Library Services and Technology Act (1996) provides for funding of cooperative ventures like library systems that handle interlibrary loan. Another reason is that the computer has streamlined the activity. The requesting library used to search printed sources like union catalogs to see which library has a desired item, then would fill out a standard request form and put it in the mail. At the responding library the staff had to determine whether they actually had the item (author or title information might have been misstated in the request) and then whether to lend it; finally they would put the item in the mail. Today there are two easier ways to accomplish the task. The borrowing library may consult a large online database like *WorldCat* to discover who has the desired item and request it online. There is no possibility of misinformation and no manual form to fill out. The supplying library can make an immediate reply online. The other procedure in use is even smoother: a group of libraries form a system, all of them consenting to lend to one another and all of them putting their catalogs into a single online database. A useful handbook published by the ALA describes the details in these approaches (Boucher 1997).

The latest revision of the ALA *Interlibrary Loan Code for the United States* (ALA 2008) lists these responsibilities of the requesting library: have a written interlibrary loan policy, ensure confidentiality of the user, describe requested material accurately, follow policies of lending libraries, observe copyright law, take responsibility for loss or damage, honor due dates and restrictions, and package material carefully. Supplying libraries should "consider filling all requests regardless of format," ensure confidentiality of the user, and process requests in a timely manner. The code is published with an "explanatory supplement."

Although the system in general is functioning admirably, some problems remain to be solved. One is the matter of formats, mentioned in the ALA code. Libraries have been reluctant to lend audio and visual materials as well as items like maps and photographs. The current mood, supported by the code, is more liberal regarding format (*see* AUDIOVISUAL COLLECTIONS). A related issue concerns noncirculating materials, a category that used to be limited to reference books and rare items but seems to be growing to cover whatever a library does not want to send out. Another problem is that rising costs for shipping may not be met by federal and other subsidies, as competition for funds is a developing factor. From the user point of view, an ongoing problem is the length of time—weeks or months—absorbed in the filling of requests. Inadequately trained staff seems to be the prime cause for canceled requests (those that could not be filled). One study showed that 12 percent of cancellations by a college library "were actually on campus but had not been found" (Gibson 2008, abstract).

References

American Library Association. Reference and User Services Association. 1994. *Guidelines and Procedures for Telefacsimile and Electronic Delivery of Interlibrary Loan Requests and Materials*. Chicago: American Library Association.

American Library Association. Reference and User Services Association. 1997. *Interlibrary Loan Packaging and Wrapping Guidelines*. Chicago: American Library Association.

American Library Association. 2008. *Interlibrary Loan Code for the United States*. Chicago: American Library Association. http://www.ala.org/ala/mgrps/divs/rusa/resources. Accessed December 2010.

Boucher, Virginia. 1997. *Interlibrary Loan Practices Handbook*. 2nd ed. Chicago: American Library Association.

Gibson, Tess. 2008. Cancelled requests: A study of interlibrary lending. *Journal of Access Services* 5, no. 3: 383–89.

Green, Samuel Swett. 1876. Letter to the editor of *American Library Journal* 1, no. 2 (October 1876): 1.

Johnson, Herbert F., and Geraldine King. 1974. Interlibrary loan (ILL). In *Encyclopedia of Library and Information Science* 12: 196–211. New York: Marcel Dekker.

Stone, Elizabeth. 1977. *American Library Development*. New York: H. W. Wilson.

INTERNET   This entry deals only with aspects of the Internet that are of direct concern to public librarians.

Terminology

Definitions and dates are from *Merriam* unless otherwise noted. "Internet," usually capitalized, often preceded by "the," came into the language in 1985 as "an electronic communications network that connects computer networks and organizational computer facilities around the world." "World Wide Web" is a term dating from 1990 meaning "a part of the Internet accessed through a graphical user interface and containing documents often connected by hyperlinks—called also Web." Web documents, or pages, are gathered into "Web sites." A Web site (1992) is "a group of World Wide Web pages usually containing hyperlinks to each other and made available online by an individual, company, educational institution, government, or organization." ("Web site" is more commonly written as "website" today.) "Online" (1950) is "connected to, served by, or available through a system and especially a computer or telecommunication system, as the Internet."

An Internet service provider (ISP), or server, gives individual users access to the Internet, usually via cable systems or telephone lines. A "browser" is "a program that accesses and displays files and other data available on the Internet and other networks," and a "search engine" is "a software program that searches indexed websites and reports locations containing specified information" (*American Heritage*). More specifically a search engine includes a program known as a "spider" (or "crawler" or "bot") that reads all searchable websites; it creates an index from those pages; it compares the index terms to terms in a search request and returns results (from the online technology dictionary *Whatis.com*). So the three base components that are engaged when a person searches the Internet are ISP (e.g., AT&T, RCN, Comcast, AOL), browser (e.g., Netscape, Internet Explorer), and search engine (e.g., Yahoo, Google).

"E-mail" or "e-mail" or "email" is "a system for sending and receiving messages electronically over a computer network" (*American Heritage*). It requires an ISP but is independent of the browser and search engine.

It is not possible to take up the numerous technical terms associated with Internet. But one should be mentioned since it is of considerable current interest. "Broadband = high speed data transmission, commonly used in reference to Internet access via cable modem, DSL, or wireless network, which provides higher bandwidth than slower dial-up (modem) connection" (*ODLIS*). The threshold varies from T1 (1.5 Mbps) to T3 (45 Mbps), where Mbps = Microbits per second. The Federal Communications Commission sets basic broadband speed at no less that 4 Mbps from computer to user and 1 Mbps from user to computer (see the section "Current Issues" below).

Historical Summary

The Internet was not invented by any one person or developed by any single institution. It was an outgrowth of theoretical explorations in technology and communications (e.g., Norbert Wiener's cybernetics) as well as socio-philosophical ideas (e.g., Marshall McLuhan's global village). Those foundations date from the post–World War II period. The basis for the Internet was a network that developed under direction of the U.S. Advanced Research Projects Agency (ARPA). Its purpose was to share resources among computers—which had been operating in isolation—primarily among scientific users in universities and government agencies. Development of that network came about through the work of many scientists, including Leonard Kleinrock, J. C. R. Licklider, Lawrence Roberts, Paul Baran, and Donald Davies. A special computer was designed to implement the network, which began operating in October 1969 under the name ARPANET. The first network connection between two computers (at the University of California, Los Angeles, and Stanford University) was made on September 2, 1969, and the first message was transmitted on October 29, 1969. "Packet switching" technology, first presented by Kleinrock in a 1962 paper, was the foundation of ARPANET and the later Internet. The World Wide Web was designed in 1989 by Timothy Berners-Lee at CERN in Geneva.

ARPANET became NSFNET, a function of the National Science Foundation, in 1990. A vast increase in use led to the transfer of the system from the U.S. government to independent organizations starting in 1995. The first widely popular browser was Netscape, designed by Mark Andreeson at the University of Illinois. In August 1995, Microsoft introduced Windows 95, which included the browser Internet Explorer. By the fall of 1996, Internet Explorer had a third of the market, and by 1999 it had passed Netscape to be the leading Web browser.

Yahoo!, started in 1994, was the principal search engine until the debut of Google in 1998. Google achieved prominence in the United States with 72 percent of all searches in 2009.

Library Applications

Libraries have made provision of Internet access to their communities a top priority. Virtually all public libraries are connected and offer free access.

Public librarians engage the Internet in four ways: (1) for email among staff and between a staff member and a patron, (2) by constructing and maintaining a library website, (3) in searching for information, and (4) in provision and maintenance of public access terminals.

An important use of email is for responding to reference or information queries from patrons. Many libraries have a quick answer service named "Ask a Librarian" or the like. This service is announced on the library's website. All U.S. public libraries except the smallest now have websites that guide the patron to the library's programs and services. Frequently a section of the website titled "About Us" or "About the Library" offers institutional history; information about the building and plans for new buildings, if any; library policies; and contact information with staff. There is no standard format for a library website or any established set of facts to be included in it.

Searching for information on the Internet is a normal part of reference work today, a practice that is edging out consultation of printed sources. Online databases that used to be accessed individually can now be searched via Internet (*see* REFERENCE AND INFORMATION SERVICES).

Availability of Internet terminals rose from 1.9 per 5,000 residents in 2000 to 3.6 per 5,000 residents in 2007, an increase of 90 percent (Henderson 2009, 4). Provision of these terminals, or workstations, is the booming service in modern public libraries. The vast majority of libraries report the need for more workstations, which is also a reflection of community wishes (Public Agenda 2006, 48). Public use of Internet workstations covers many interests. It was reported in 2009 that the most popular application was access to databases. Other uses, in declining order, were homework resources, audio content, digital/virtual reference, e-books, video content, online instruction, digitized special collections, and videoconferencing (American Library Association 2008, quoted in Davis, Rose, and Clark 2009, 52). Most library terminals run on T-1 bandwidth, leading to problems of congestion.

Current Issues

Unquestionably the primary Internet concern among librarians is quantitative. Everyone calls for more workstations and many require increased bandwidth. Sixty percent of libraries say their current Internet speed is insufficient. The Bill and Melinda Gates Foundation has been addressing the problem of bandwidth, most recently with grants to five states and technical assistance to 14 others. Nearly $3.4 million was committed in December 2009 (reported in *American Libraries*, January/February 2010, 31). Federal funds for broadband enhancement are provided through the National Telecommunications and Information Administration's Broadband Technology Opportunity Program. Slow Internet speeds often result in congestion that makes certain websites unavailable and may temporarily disable all access. One response to this problem, pending improved broadband, is to limit access to certain popular websites that consume bandwidth. Greensboro Public Library (NC) reported installation of a "bandwidth shaper" that "categorizes different websites and adjusts how much bandwidth each category receives" (*American Libraries*, January/February 2010, 31). The shaper makes it harder to access sites with "adult content"—thus doing the controversial task of "filtering." Filters that obstruct patron access to certain websites have been a point of dispute for many years (*see* INTELLECTUAL FREEDOM). It is useful for a library to prepare a policy statement on Internet use. A model statement appears on the website of the Akron-Summit County Public Library.

It has been suggested that the emphasis on more workstations lacks a research foundation. Librarians have not adequately examined community needs and resources to find out what the people actually want in their Internet access and what other agencies in the community are providing (McClure and Jaeger 2009, 57). In their wish to build up numbers, they may also have neglected the desirability to choose services that coordinate with traditional activities, that can be evaluated, and that can be effectively handled by the staff. There may be insufficient attention to the impact of equipment upgrades and the staff training entailed by them (McClure 2009, 67). More generally, there is no useful research so far to justify the costs of acquiring and managing the range of electronic resources in the library (Koehn and Hawamdeh 2010). Those costs are for the most part controlled by commercial vendors. There is concern that certain costs are "completely out of hand" (McCrory 2009, 1).

While Internet use is a rising metric across the library spectrum, a "digital divide" remains to be addressed. "Unequal access to information technology, based on income, race, ethnicity, gender, age, and geography" was the situation a decade ago, and no later research has contradicted it (Mossberger et al. 2003, 1, 47). Those most likely to need assistance in using the computer and Internet are the elderly, blacks, Hispanics, the poor, and those with no more than a high school education. The situation brings implications for instruction of library patrons in computer matters. One study reported that only 29.8 percent of public libraries are offering formal technology instruction (McClure and Jaeger 2009, 31); another report put the figure at 35 percent (American Library Association 2008, 3) (*see* INFORMATION LITERACY INSTRUCTION). Patrons with disabilities need to have full access to computer and Internet services (*see* SERVICES TO PEOPLE WITH DISABILITIES).

Staff training is also problematic. While 86.4 percent of public libraries in a study reported in 2007 gave Internet training to staff, only 27.9 percent trained them to use federal documents, and 26.3 percent trained them in local government information sources (McClure and Jaeger 2009, 33).

An overarching issue, albeit one that is not high on the discussion agenda, is what the Internet is doing to libraries. An obvious result of the growing emphasis on computer services is that less money and less staff time will be given to traditional acquisitions and activities. A more subtle transformation may also be taking shape: the public library may be viewed primarily through the technological prism. "Autonomy of the library may be eroding as the federal government more closely links public libraries not to established social roles but to providing Internet access." Other agencies could assume that role of accessing the Internet (schools, government offices, bookstores), and much of that access is already passing to home computers (McClure and Jaeger 2009, 54). However, at the present time, in three-fourths of U.S. communities, residents have only the public library for free access to the Internet. It is important to develop means of assessing users' perceptions of Internet access on their own lives as librarians make plans in this area (Bertot et al. 2008).

References

American Library Association. 2008. Libraries and technology. In State of America's libraries: a report from the American Library Association. www.ala.org/ala/mewspresscenter. Accessed May 2010.

American Library Association. 2008 *Libraries Connect Communities 3: Public Library Funding and Technology Access Study 2007–2008*, ed. Larra Clark. Chicago: American Library Association. http://www.ala.org/plinternetfunding. Accessed November 2010. Summary in Davis, Rose, and Clark (2009).

Bertot, John Carl, et al. 2008. The impact of free public Internet access on public library patrons and communities. *Library Quarterly* 78, no. 3 (July): 285–301.

Bertot, John Carl, et al. 2010. *Public Libraries and the Internet: Roles, Perspectives, and Implications*. Santa Barbara, CA: Libraries Unlimited.

Carson, Bryan M. 2007. *The Laws of Libraries and Archives*. Lanham, MD: Scarecrow Press.

Davis, Denise, Norman Rose, and Larra Clark. 2009. How to work a crisis. *American Libraries* 40, no. 11 (November): 50–52.

Griffiths, J. M., and D. W. King. 2008. *Interconnections: The IMLS National Study on the Use of Libraries, Museums, and the Internet*. Washington: Institute of Museum and Library Services, 2008.

Henderson, Everett. 2009. *Service Trends in U.S. Public Libraries, 1997–2007*. IMLS Research Brief 1, December. Washington, DC: Institute of Museum and Library Services.

Koehn, Shona L., and Suliman Hawamdeh. 2010. The acquisition and management of electronic resources: can use justify cost? *Library Quarterly* 80, no. 2 (April): 161–74.

McClure, Charles R., and Paul T. Jaeger. 2009. *Public Libraries and Internet Service Roles: Measuring and Maximizing Internet Services*. Chicago: American Library Association.

McCrory, Loren. 2009. Have we created a monster? *Library Journal* 134, no. 15 (September 15): 82.

Mossberger, Karen, et al. 2003. *Virtual Inequality: Beyond the Digital Divide*. Washington, DC: Georgetown University Press.

Public Agenda. 2006. *Long Overdue: A Fresh Look at Public and Leadership Attitudes about Libraries in the 21st Century*. New York: Public Agenda. http://www.publicagenda.org/research.

IRVINE, CA. *See* ORANGE COUNTY LIBRARY, SANTA ANA, CA.

ISLAND FREE LIBRARY, BLOCK ISLAND, RI   520 Dodge St., Block Island, RI 02807. Population served: 1,033; Circulation: 44,762; Holdings: 23,920. LJ February 15, 2009; November 15, 2009; and October 1, 2010: 5-star library.

ISOM, MARY FRANCES, 1865–1920   Librarian. Born Nashville, TN, February 27, 1865. She attended Wellesley College, 1883–1884, and left because of poor health. She graduated from Pratt Institute library school in 1901 and joined the Library Association of Portland (OR) as cataloger, then in January 1902 became librarian. Isom helped secure enactment in 1905 of a state law creating the Oregon Library Commission. She was vice president of the American Library Association, 1912–1913. At the opening of the new central library in Portland, September 6, 1913 she spoke of the public library mission, which included collecting on "all the trades carried on in the community." During World War I she spent six months organizing libraries for American hospitals in France. Isom and Cornelia Marvin Pierce (1873–1957), state librarian, are credited with particular influence "in the introduction, growth, and professionalization of library service in the state of Oregon ... they promoted tax-supported libraries ... and the advantages of staffing them with formally trained librarians" (Gunselman 2004). They were cofounders of the Pacific Northwest Library Association. Isom died on April 15, 1920. *DAB.*

Reference

Gunselman, Cheryl. 2004. Cornelia Marvin and Mary Frances Isom: Leaders of Oregon's library movement. *Library Trends* 52, no. 4 (Spring): 877–904.

J

J. C. CLEGG PUBLIC LIBRARY, CENTRAL CITY, IA   137 4th St. N, Central City, IA 52214. Founded 1895. Population served: 2,137. Circulation: 11,253. Holdings: 8,864. LJ November 15, 2009: 3-star library.

JACKSON, WY. *See* TETON COUNTY LIBRARY, JACKSON, WY.

JACKSON COUNTY LIBRARY SERVICES, MEDFORD, OR   205 S. Central Ave., Medford, OR 97501. Founded 1970 (individual cities had libraries earlier). Population served: 189,000. Circulation: 1,271,177. Holdings: 539,400. 15 branches. An economic downturn in 2005 resulted in library levies being rejected by the voters of the county, and all 15 branches closed in April 2007. The county contracted with Library Systems and Services (LSSI) to operate the libraries with reduced hours and staff, and all branches were again open at the end of October 2007 (information from the library).

JACKSON-MADISON COUNTY LIBRARY, JACKSON, TN   433 E. Lafayette St., Jackson, TN 38301. "In 1886 the Jackson Free Library Association established a circulating public library" (library website). The county library board announced on September 6, 2006, that it was outsourcing library management to Library Systems and Services. (LSSI).

JACKSONVILLE PUBLIC LIBRARY, FL   303 N. Laura St., Jacksonville, FL 32202. Founded 1903. Population served: 809,394. Circulation: 5,000,000. Holdings: 2,721,642. 20 branches. LJ November 15, 2009: 3-star library.

JAMAICA, NY. *See* QUEENS BOROUGH PUBLIC LIBRARY, JAMAICA, NY.

JAMES KENNEDY PUBLIC LIBRARY, DYERSVILLE, IA   320 First Ave. E, Dyersville, IA 52040. Founded 1956, opened September 11, 1959 (library website). Population served: 4,035. Circulation: 134,836. Holdings: 61,859. LJ February 15, 2009, and November 15, 2009: 3-star library; October 1, 2010: 4-star library. HAPLR 2009, 2010.

JEFFERSON, OH. *See* HENDERSON MEMORIAL PUBLIC LIBRARY ASSOCIATION, JEFFERSON, OH.

JEFFERSON DAVIS PARISH LIBRARY, JENNINGS, LA   118 W. Plaquemine St., Jennings, LA 70546. Population served: 32,000. Circulation: 85,596. Holdings: 77,135. 3 branches, 1 bookmobile. Hurricane Rita (2005) destroyed one outlet (Elton) and damaged three others. All reopened by summer 2006, Elton being rebuilt (*see* HURRICANES KATRINA AND RITA).

JEFFERSON PARISH LIBRARY, METAIRIE, LA   4747 W. Napoleon Ave., Metairie, LA 70009. Founded 1949. Population served: 452,824. Circulation: 1,548,565. Holdings: 732,219. 13 branches. Three branches, Gretna, Grand Isle, and Lakeshore, were totally destroyed by Hurricane Katrina, and the other branches were damaged. By July 2011 all branches were open and operational, although Grand Isle bookmobile and Lakeshore were still in temporary quarters. No date has been set for construction to begin on the new Lakeshore Branch. (*see* HURRICANES KATRINA AND RITA).

JEMEZ PUEBLO COMMUNITY LIBRARY, NM   20 Mission Rd., Jemez Pueblo, NM 87024. Population served: 3,377. Circulation: 5,702. Holdings: 13,870. LJ February 15, 2009: 3-star library.

JENNINGS, JUDSON TOLL, 1872–1948   Librarian. Born September 24, 1872, in Schenectady, NY. He attended Union College, 1894–1895, then the New York State Library School. He was appointed librarian of the Carnegie Free Library, Duquesne, PA, in 1903, remaining to 1906. As librarian of the Seattle Public Library, 1907–1942, he developed the branch system, libraries in schools, and professionalization of the staff. He successfully promoted state aid to libraries. Jenning administered library services to the U.S. Army of occupation after World War I, working out of the American Library Association (ALA) office in Paris. He was ALA president in 1923, speaking for the public library role in adult education. His idea of that role was that the library should be a facilitator and aid to education groups and to individual learners but should not itself engage in classroom teaching. He headed the ALA Adult Education Commission, 1924–1926. Jennings died in Seattle on February 8, 1948. *DALB*; LJ Hall of Fame.

JERICHO PUBLIC LIBRARY, NY   One Merry Lane, Jericho, NY 11753. Population served: 14,036. Circulation: 562,991. Holdings: 152,376. LJ February 15, 2009: 4-star library; November 15, 2009: 3-star library.

JERSEY CITY FREE PUBLIC LIBRARY, NJ   472 Jersey Ave., Jersey City, NJ 07032. Founded 1891. Population served: 240,055. Circulation: 206,900. Holdings: 438,384.

JEWETT, CHARLES COFFIN, 1816–1868   Librarian. Born Lebanon, ME, August 12, 1816. He graduated from Brown University, 1835, and Andover Theological Seminary, 1840. In 1841 he was appointed librarian of Brown University. He prepared a printed catalog of the library by author and subject and made important book-buying trips to Europe, 1843–1845. Jewett resigned 1847 to become librarian of the Smithsonian Institution. Among his innovative ideas there was the idea of centralized cataloging for libraries, to be carried out at the Smithsonian. Although that plan did not materialize, Jewett created—in preparation for it—a set of catalog rules and an inventory of public libraries in the United States (1851, the first of its kind). He presided at the 1853 conference of librarians, an event that led to the 1876 founding of the American Library Association. Conflicts with the secretary of the Smithsonian led to Jewett's dismissal in January 1855. He moved on to the Boston Public Library as cataloger, then acquisitions librarian, and from 1858 to his death as superintendent of the library. Jewett modernized procedures, improved public access to the materials, invented a new circulation system, and built the collection to 150,000 volumes. He died in Braintree, MA, on January 9, 1868. Through his many achievements across the spectrum of library practice, Jewett was a major force in the development of American librarianship. *DAB*; *DALB*; *LJ* Hall of Fame.

JOECKEL, CARLTON BRUNS, 1886–1960   Librarian. Born Lake Mills, WI, January 2, 1886. After a BA from the University of Wisconsin in 1908, he went to the New York State Library School, earning a BLS in 1910. From 1911–1914 he was a reference librarian and superintendent of circulation at the University of California, Berkeley. Joeckel was librarian of the public library in Berkeley from 1914 to 1927, with a two-year leave for military service in 1917–1919. His next position was associate professor in the library school at the University of Michigan (promoted to professor in 1930). He spent a year's leave at the Graduate Library School (GLS), University of Chicago, earning a PhD in 1934. From 1935 to 1945 he was on the GLS faculty, pursuing research and conducting surveys, the most important being an examination with Leon Carnovsky of the Chicago Public Library (1940).

Joeckel's dissertation on public library governance developed into a focus on administration and organization and a promotion of larger units of service. He was also an advocate of federal aid to libraries, playing a strong part in the creation of a library services division in the U.S. Office of Education (1937) and pressing for passage of the Library Services Act in 1956. He was the principal author of the American Library Association (ALA) *Post-War Standards for Public Libraries* (1943) and coauthor of the ALA *A National Plan for Public Library Service* (1948). Joeckel was dean of the GLS from 1942 to 1945, then resigned to return to Berkeley, where he was a professor in the University of California library school until his retirement in 1950. He died in Oakland on April 15, 1960. *DALB.*

References

Joeckel, Carlton B. 1935. *The Government of the American Public Library.* Chicago: University of Chicago Press. His dissertation.
Joeckel, Carlton B., and Leon Carnovsky. 1940. *A Metropolitan Library in Action: A Survey of the Chicago Public Library.* Chicago: University of Chicago Press.

JOHN A. STAHL LIBRARY, WEST POINT, NE   330 N. Colfax, West Point, NE 68788. Population served: 3,660. Circulation: 48,977. Holdings: 20,232. HAPLR 2010.

JOHN F. KENNEDY LIBRARY, HIALEAH, FL   190 W. 49th St., Hialeah, FL 33012. Population served: 233,566. Circulation: 204,327. Holdings: 109,706. 4 branches.

JOHNSON COUNTY LIBRARY, OVERLAND PARK, KS   9875 W. 87th St., Overland Park, KS 66212. Population served: 381,237. Circulation: 5,105,952. Holdings: 1,200,000. 13 branches. IMLS award 2005. LJ February 15, 2009: 4-star library; November 15, 2009, and October 1, 2010: 3-star library.

JORDAN BRAMLEY LIBRARY, JORDAN, NY   15 Mechanic St., Jordan, NY 13080. This is a suburban member of Onondaga County Public Library, the central library of Syracuse, NY. It is a free, association library (information from the library). LJ February 15, 2009: 4-star library; November 15, 2009, and October 1, 2010: 5-star library.

JULIA L. BUTTERFIELD MEMORIAL LIBRARY, COLD SPRING, NY   10 Morris Ave., Cold Spring, NY 10516. Founded 1913. Population served: 1,983. Circulation: 31,389. Holdings: 25,523. LJ February 15, 2009: 3-star library; November 15, 2009, and October 1, 2010: 4-star library.

K

KANSAS CITY PUBLIC LIBRARY, MO   14 W. 10th St., Kansas City, MO 64105. Founded 1898. Population served: 257,940. Circulation: 2,276,383. Holdings: 2,423,747. 9 branches. The Young People's Corner, serving ages 14 to 20, opened in September 1944. Notable extension activities of the library, dating from the 1970s, include services in nursing and retirement homes, hospitals, and correctional facilities. It was the first large public library in the United States to offer home delivery for handicapped users. IMLS award 2008. LJ February 15, 2009: 3-star library; November 15, 2009, and October 1, 2010: 4-star library. Directors: James Greenwood (superintendent of schools and library supervisor), 1874–1881; Carrie Whitney (first appointed librarian), 1881–1910; Purd B. Wright, 1911–1936; Irene Gentry (acting), 1936–1939; Louise M. Nourse, 1939–1942; Priscilla Burd (acting), 1942–1943; Harold Hamill, 1943–1947; Harry Brinton (acting), 1947–1950; Richard B. Sealock, 1950–1968; Stephen Kirk, 1968–1973; Idris Smith (acting), 1973–1974; Harold R. Jenkins, 1974–1983; Daniel J. Bradbury, 1983–2003; Joseph H. Green, 2003–2004; Roger Pearson (acting), 2004–2005; and R. Crosby Kemper III, 2005–.

KENNEDY LIBRARY OF KONAWA, OK   700 W. South, Konawa, OK 74849. Founded 1991. Operates as a public and high school library. Population served: 1,449. Circulation: 35,082. Holdings: 17,852. LJ November 15, 2009: 4-star library.

KENT DISTRICT LIBRARY, MI   814 W. River Center Dr., Comstock Park, MI 49321. Founded 1936. Population served: 362,312. Circulation: 4,060,039.

Holdings: 757,237. 18 branches. Issues a free online service and a print version of "What's next?" that lists books in series. LJ October 1, 2010: 3-star library.

KERN COUNTY LIBRARY, BAKERSFIELD, CA   701 Truxton Ave., Bakersfield, CA 93301. Founded 1911. Population served: 753,070. Circulation: 1,871,420. Holdings: 1,155,438. 26 branches.

KILBOURN PUBLIC LIBRARY, WISCONSIN DELLS, WI   620 Elm St., Wisconsin Dells, WI 53965. Population served: 3,032. Circulation: 75,461. Holdings: 37,031. LJ February 15, 2009: 5-star library; November 15, 2009, and October 1, 2010: 3-star library.

KILGORE PUBLIC LIBRARY, TX   301 Henderson Blvd., Kilgore, TX 75662. Founded 1933. Population served: 14,037. Circulation: 84,470. Holdings: 33,000. A French provincial building, still in use after a 1978 expansion, was built with Works Progress Administration funds in 1939. Architect George M. Marble designed "a magical building" that "looks like a stone witch's cottage" (Rabkin and Rabkin 1994, 250). The structure was designated a Texas historical site in 1993.

Reference

Rabkin, Marty, and Anna Rabkin. 1994. *Public Libraries: Travel Treasures of the West*. Golden, CO: North American Press.

KILLINGTON, VT. *See* SHERBURNE MEMORIAL LIBRARY, KILLINGTON, VT.

KING COUNTY LIBRARY SYSTEM, ISSAQUAH, WA   960 Newport Way, Issaquah, WA 98027. Population served: 1,183,851. Circulation: 19,000,000. Holdings: 3,345,860. 47 branches. HAPLR 2009, 2010.

KINSMAN FREE PUBLIC LIBRARY, OH   6420 Church St., Kinsman, OH 44428. Population served: 6,806. Circulation: 300,264. Holdings: 78,277. HAPLR 2009, 2010.

KNOX COUNTY PUBLIC LIBRARY SYSTEM, KNOXVILLE, TN   500 W. Church Ave., Knoxville, TN 37902. A subscription library from 1886, opened as a free public library, 1917; became county system, 1967; county took over the library, 2003. Population served: 392,995. Circulation: 2,374,152. Holdings: 975,355. 18 branches.

KNOXVILLE, TN. *See* KNOX COUNTY PUBLIC LIBRARY SYSTEM, KNOXVILLE, TN.

KONOWA, OK. *See* KENNEDY LIBRARY OF KONOWA, OK.

L

LA VETA PUBLIC LIBRARY DISTRICT, CO 310 S. Main St., La Veta, CO 80026. Founded 1974. Population served: 1,391. Circulation: 32,251. Holdings: 10,992. LJ February 15, 2009; November 15, 2009, and October 1, 2010: 5-star library.

LACYGNE, KS. *See* LINN COUNTY LIBRARY DISTRICT #2, LACYGNE, KS.

LAFOURCHE PARISH PUBLIC LIBRARY, THIBODAUX, LA 303 W. Fifth St., Thibodaux, LA 70301. Population served: 92,157. Circulation: 338,480. Holdings: 62,000. 9 branches. Golden Meadow Branch was severely damaged in Hurricane Katrina, and its intended replacement building was damaged by Hurricane Rita; it finally reopened in 2006 (*see* HURRICANES KATRINA AND RITA).

LAKE CHARLES, LA. *See* CALCASIEU PARISH LIBRARY SYSTEM, LAKE CHARLES, LA.

LAKE OSWEGO PUBLIC LIBRARY, OR 706 Fourth St., Lake Oswego, OR 97034. Population served: 42,953. Circulation: 1,306,937. Holdings: 153,395. HAPLR 2009.

LAKE WHITNEY PUBLIC LIBRARY, TX 106 N. Colorado St., Whitney, TX 76692. Founded (became a city department) 1995. Population served:

2,073. Circulation: 11,000. Holdings: 13,570. LJ October 1, 2010: 3-star library.

LAKE ZURICH, IL. *See* ELA AREA PUBLIC LIBRARY DISTRICT, LAKE ZURICH, IL.

LAKESIDE, AZ. *See* LARSON MEMORIAL PUBLIC LIBRARY, LAKESIDE, AZ.

LAKEWOOD PUBLIC LIBRARY, OH   15425 Detroit Ave., Lakewood, OH 44107. Population served: 54,842. Circulation: 1,753,165. Holdings: 341,494. 1 branch. LJ February 15, 2009: 3-star library; November 15, 2009, and October 1, 2010: 4-star library. HAPLR 2009, 2010.

LARAMIE COUNTY LIBRARY SYSTEM, CHEYENNE, WY   2200 Pioneer Ave., Cheyenne, WY 82009. Population served: 84,083. Circulation: 649,741. Holdings: 254,805. 2 branches, 1 bookmobile. "Oldest continuing operating county library system in the U.S." (library website). LJ Library of the Year 2008.

LAREDO PUBLIC LIBRARY, TX   1120 E. Calton Rd., Laredo, TX 78041. Population served: 203,212. Circulation: 50,557. Holdings: 55,000. 2 branches, 1 bookmobile.

LARNED, JOSEPHUS NELSON, 1836–1913   Librarian, journalist, historian. Born Chatham, Ontario (of American parents), May 11, 1936. Taken to Buffalo as a child, he attended high school there. He had no college study. He joined the editorial staff of the *Buffalo Express* in 1859, remaining to 1872. In 1877 he was superintendent of the Buffalo Young Men's Association, which he reorganized into the Buffalo Library. Larned cataloged the collection, making it the first library to be completely classified by the Dewey Decimal Classification. Buffalo had one of the early children's rooms. He was president of the American Library Association (ALA) in 1894. When the library was taken over by the city in 1897, he resigned over disagreements with the new trustees. He turned to scholarly writing, with *Literature of American History: A Bibliographic Guide* (1902) and *Larned's History of the World* (1915). In his presidential address to the ALA in 1894, he presented his thoughts on the public library mission: it is educational above all. "We fight against ignorant opinions," which have "a capacity for harm enormously increased over that of the elder times." Libraries fight not with "books" but with "good books" (Bostwick 1929, 411). "In our time we have brought the library to the help of the school, and the world is just opening its eyes to perceive the enormous value of the reinforcement that is gained from this new power. And the discovery has come none too soon; for a desperate need of more and stronger forces in the work of popular education is pressing on us" (quoted in Williams 1988, 25). Larned died on August 15, 1913, in Buffalo. *DAB*; LJ Hall of Fame.

References

Bostwick, Arthur E. 1929. *The American Public Library*. 4th ed. New York: Appleton.
Williams, Patrick. 1988. *The American Public Library and the Problem of Purpose*. New York: Greenwood Press.

LARSON MEMORIAL PUBLIC LIBRARY, LAKESIDE, AZ   1595 Johnson Dr., Lakeside, AZ 85929. Population served: 4,055. Circulation: 90,212. Holdings: 36,723. LJ February 15, 2009: 4-star library; November 15, 2009: 3-star library.

LAS VEGAS-CLARK COUNTY LIBRARY DISTRICT, NV   833 Las Vegas Blvd. N, Las Vegas, NV 89101. Population served: 1,400,000. Circulation: 13,200,000. Holdings: 2,900,000. 23 branches. LJ Library of the Year 2003. LJ February 15, 2009: 3-star library.

LAWRENCE PUBLIC LIBRARY, MA   51 Lawrence St., Lawrence, MA 01841. Established as Franklin Library Association, 1847; free public library, 1872. Population served: 71,858. Circulation: 141,933. Holdings: 179,453.

LAWRENCEVILLE, NJ. *See* MERCER COUNTY LIBRARY, LAWRENCEVILLE, NJ.

LEAKEY, TX. *See* REAL COUNTY LIBRARY, LEAKEY, TX.

LEDBETTER, ELEANOR EDWARDS, 1870–1954   Librarian. After graduating from the New York State library school, she spent 13 years in various libraries, in Massachusetts, New York, Indiana, Texas, and Ohio. In 1910 she was head of the Broadway branch, Chicago Public Library (CPL), serving a largely foreign-speaking neighborhood. Ledbetter made home visits to encourage reading by the residents (mostly German and eastern European). She put placards in shops and factories and inserted library information in foreign language newspapers. By 1916 the branch had 30,000 borrowers and 1,749,980 circulation. She promoted immigrant services in the American Library Association (ALA), participating in the Committee on Work with the Foreign Born (chair, 1920–1926). In 1923 and 1925 she made book-buying trips to southern and eastern Europe for CPL, also acquiring materials for the libraries of Indianapolis, Gary, Detroit, Pittsburgh, and Lakewood (OH). She had acquired proficiency in German, Polish, and Czech. In the 1920s Ledbetter lectured on immigrant services at the library schools of Western Reserve University and the Carnegie Library School

(Pittsburgh), gave presentations at the ALA and to various organizations, and wrote bibliographies and articles. She retired in 1938.

Reference

Jones, Plummer Alston, Jr. 1999. *Libraries, Immigrants, and the American Experience.* Westport, CT: Greenwood Press.

LEESBURG, VA. *See* LOUDON COUNTY PUBLIC LIBRARY, LEESBURG, VA.

LEGLER, HENRY EDWARD, 1861-1917   Librarian. Born in Palermo, Italy, on June 22, 1861. Following early years spent in Switzerland, he emigrated to the United States after the Civil War and settled in La Crosse, WI. The high school he attended there provided his only formal education. Legler became a reporter and editor for the *Milwaukee Journal* and in 1888 secretary of the Milwaukee School Board. In 1904 he was secretary of the state's library commission, situated in Madison. He promoted traveling libraries and pressed for a library school in Madison. He became librarian of the Chicago Public Library (CPL) in 1909, remaining eight years. During his tenure the library's stock increased from 800,000 to 6,000,000 volumes and the number of branches from one to 40. He wanted to arouse a reading habit in the community although advocating a restrictive policy on fiction selection. There were open shelves in the main library. Service to immigrants was a priority with Legler. CPL had 65 German magazines and 21 newspapers and 21 French magazines and two newspapers. Legler "made the library a factor in the lives of the people," and "died from overwork and too great devotion to the cause of learning" (*DAB*). Death came on September 13, 1917. *DAB.*

LEIGH, ROBERT DEVORE, 1890-1961   Political scientist, library educator. Born September 13, 1890, in Nelson, NE. He graduated 1914 from Bowdoin College and earned an MA at Columbia University in 1915. Leigh was on the faculty of Reed College, 1917-1919, then worked as assistant educational director of the U.S. Public Health Service, 1917-1919. After lecturing in political science at Columbia, 1919-1922, Leigh earned a PhD in political science there in 1927. From 1928 to 1941 he was president of Bennington College. He had wartime government positions, including director of the foreign broadcast intelligence service. Leigh made his first mark in the library field as editor of the *Public Library Inquiry*, a project undertaken by the Social Science Research Council in 1947-1950. That extensive critique of the public library situation was the work of social science investigators, none of them librarians (*see* HISTORY OF PUBLIC LIBRARIES; PHILOSOPHY OF PUBLIC LIBRARIANSHIP). He was then appointed visiting professor in the Columbia School of Library Service and became acting dean in 1954 and dean in 1956-1959. Leigh retired in 1959 and took up a survey of public and school libraries in Hawaii—one volume was published in 1960. He died after a heart attack suffered on a plane landing at O'Hare on January 31, 1961. *DALB*.

LENOX LIBRARY ASSOCIATION, MA   18 Main St., Lenox, MA 01240. Founded 1856. Although the first appropriation for the library from the town of Lenox did not occur until 1989, there had been previous support from a "dog tax," and "the library has always been free and open to the public" (communication from the library). The original building, designed by Isaac Damon, has been used by the library since 1856. It is on the National Register of Historic Places. Population served: 5,162. Circulation: 71,953. Holdings: 71,018. LJ February 15, 2009: 3-star library.

LETTIE W. JENSEN PUBLIC LIBRARY, AMHERST, WI   278 N. Main St., Amherst, WI 54406. Founded 1931. Population served: 1,037. Circulation: 24,022. Holdings: 15,802. LJ February 15, 2009; November 15, 2009, and October 1, 2010: 4-star library.

LEWISTON PUBLIC LIBRARY, UT   33 S. Main, Lewiston, UT 84320. Population served: 1,781. Circulation: 85,402. Holdings: 37,635. LJ February 15, 2009, and November 15, 2009: 5-star library; October 1, 2010: 4-star library.

LEXINGTON PUBLIC LIBRARY, KY   140 E. Main, Lexington, KY 40507. Founded 1899 as a free public library after more than a century as a subscription library. Population served: 266,358. Circulation: 2,331,545. Holdings: 602,891. 5 branches.

LIBRARIANS. *See* PUBLIC LIBRARIANS.

LIBRARIANSHIP

Terminology

Neither *Merriam* nor *American Heritage* has an entry for "librarianship"; in both dictionaries the word appears at the end of the "librarian" entry, indicating the work that a librarian does. "Library science" has its own entries, in *Merriam* as "the study or the principles and practices of library care and administration" and in *American Heritage* as "the principles, practice, or study of library administration."

ODLIS is more expansive. For librarianship it gives "the profession devoted to applying theory and technology to the creation, selection, organization, management, preservation, dissemination, and utilization of collections of information in all formats." Although *ODLIS* says that in the United States librarianship is used synonymously with library science, there is a rather different angle in the library science definition: "the professional knowledge and skill with which recorded information is selected, acquired, organized, stored, maintained, retrieved, and disseminated to meet the needs of a specific clientele, usually taught at a professional library school qualified to grant a post-baccalaureate degree of MLS or MLIS."

It is not too clear from these ventures whether librarianship is a set of principles, a state of knowledge, or the activity of running a library and how librarianship is distinguished, if at all, from library science. This brief definition is used in the present handbook: "librarianship (= library science): the activity of developing, staffing, managing, and operating libraries." When "information" moved into the field of librarianship it seemed to have confiscated its definition (*see* INFORMATION SCIENCE).

Although Melvil Dewey declared in 1876 that librarianship is a profession (Dewey 1876, 5), librarians have continued to discuss the matter. While the question may seem abstract, there is a pragmatic angle to it: professions are treated differently from other occupations in the academic hierarchy and in the job classification of their practitioners. Ralph Beals (1948, 296) suggested that a profession has certain attributes: moral purpose, a scholarly literature, techniques that apply principles in specific instances, and systematic theory. His approach was widely shared, as was the conclusion that librarianship fit the described mold. Beals was dean of the Graduate Library School, University of Chicago, which gained acceptance in the university's organization on a level with older professional schools. That achievement came slowly to other library science programs, but by the 1960s most university administrators had granted professional school status to their library education units. As the profession was recognized, so were its practitioners (*see* PUBLIC LIBRARIANS).

The issues today are about the purposes and theory of the profession. A special concern relates to the impact of information science on library science, viewed by some in a negative light (Gorman 2005; Budd 2007; Crowley 2008). Fundamentally, the library profession is still having difficulty articulating its principles (Marco 1997) and purposes (Williams 1988). Such uncertainties create an unstable position for the profession in confronting the implications of "information" and in the area of censorship. *See* INTELLECTUAL FREEDOM; PHILOSOPHY OF PUBLIC LIBRARIANSHIP.

References

Budd, John M. 2007. *Self-Examination: The Present and Future of Librarianship*. Westport, CT: Libraries Unlimited.

Crowley, Bill. 2008. *Renewing Professional Librarianship: A Fundamental Rethinking*. Westport, CT: Libraries Unlimited.

Dewey, Melvil. 1876. The profession. *American Library Journal* 1 (September 30): 5–6.

Gorman, Michael. 2005. *Our Own Selves: More Meditations for Librarians*. Chicago: American Library Association.

Marco, Guy A. 1997. Our troubled search for principles. In *Essays in Honor of Prof. P. B. Mangla*, ed. R. G. Prasher, 21–30. New Delhi: Concept Publishing.

Williams, Patrick. 1988. *The American Public Library and the Problem of Purpose.* New York: Greenwood Press.

LIBRARIES IN SOCIETY. *See* PHILOSOPHY OF LIBRARIANSHIP.

LIBRARY. *See* PUBLIC LIBRARY.

LIBRARY ASSOCIATION OF PORTLAND, OR   205 NE Russell St., Portland, OR 97212. Founded 1902 as a free, tax-supported library for the city, dating back to 1864 as a subscription library ("oldest public library in the West" according to the library website). Population served: 717,880. Circulation: 21,513,255. Holdings: 1,955,041. 17 branches.

LIBRARY AT CEDAR CREEK LAKE, SEVEN POINTS, TX   410 E. Cedar Creek Parkway, Seven Points, TX 75143. Population served: 15,725. Circulation: 48,783. Holdings: 32,001. LJ October 1, 2010: 3-star library.

LIBRARY EDUCATION. *See* EDUCATION OF PUBLIC LIBRARIANS.

LIBRARY EXTENSION. *See* BOOKMOBILES; OUTREACH.

LIBRARY INSTRUCTION. *See* INFORMATION LITERACY INSTRUCTION.

LIBRARY JOURNAL/GALE LIBRARY OF THE YEAR   A recognition accorded to outstanding libraries since 1992. "The $10,000 prize celebrates the library that most profoundly demonstrates service to the community; creativity and innovation in developing specific community programs or a dramatic increase in library usage; and leadership in creating programs that can be emulated by other libraries" (Gale press release, July 2010).

The libraries cited are the following:

1992—Redwood City Public Library, CA

1993—Austin Public Library, TX

1994—Brown County Public Library, Green Bay, WI

1995—Charlotte Mecklenburg Library, NC

1996—Broward County Library, Fort Lauderdale, FL

1997—Ann Arbor District Library, MI

1998—Medina County District Library, OH

1999—Oregon State University, The Valley Library

2000—Gwinnett County Public Library, Lawrenceville, GA

2001—Richland County Public Library, Columbia, SC

2002—Kalamazoo Public Library, MI

2003—Las Vegas-Clark County Library District, NV

2004—San Jose Public Library/San Jose State University, CA

2005—Fayetteville Public Library, AR

2006—Salt Lake City Public Library, UT

2007—Worthington Public Library, OH

2008—Laramie County Library System, WY

2009—Queens Library, NY

2010—Columbus Metropolitan Library, OH

LIBRARY OF THE YEAR. *See* LIBRARY JOURNAL/GALE LIBRARY OF THE YEAR.

LIBRARY SCIENCE. *See* LIBRARIANSHIP.

LIED PIERCE PUBLIC LIBRARY, PIERCE, NE   207 W. Court St., Pierce, NE 68767. Population served: 1,774. Circulation: 31,849. Holdings: 16,801. LJ February 15, 2009: 3-star library.

LIED PUBLIC LIBRARY, ESSEX, IA   508 Iowa St., Essex, IA 51638. Population served: 884. Circulation: 7,285. Holdings: 12,922. LJ February 15, 2009, and November 15, 2009: 3-star library.

LIGONIER PUBLIC LIBRARY, IN   300 S. Main St., Ligonier, IN 46767. Founded 1908. Population served: 4,357. Circulation: 25,889. Holdings: 31,467. LJ October 1, 2010: 4-star library.

LIMON MEMORIAL LIBRARY, CO   205 East Ave., Limon, CO 80828. Population served: 2,101. Circulation: 34,426. Holdings: 17,438. LN November 15, 2009: 3-star library.

LINCOLN CITY LIBRARIES, NE   136 S. 14th St., Lincoln, NE 68508. "A municipal, tax-funded public library in 1877" (communication from the library). Population served: 260,995. Circulation: 3,100,000. Holdings: 960,000. 7 branches, 1 bookmobile. HAPLR 2009, 2010.

LINCOLN LIBRARY, VT   222 W. River Rd., Lincoln, VT 05443. Population served: 1,254. Circulation: 18,167. Holdings: 15,150. LJ February 15, 2009, and November 15, 2009: 3-star library.

LINCOLN PUBLIC LIBRARY, NH   22 Church St., Lincoln, NH 03521. Founded 1905. Population served: 1,310. Circulation: 22,502. Holdings:

15,137. LJ February 15, 2009; November 15, 2009; and October 1, 2010: 5-star library.

LINCOLNSHIRE, IL. *See* VERNON AREA PUBLIC LIBRARY DISTRICT, LINCOLNSHIRE, IL.

LINDALE LIBRARY, TX   200 E. Hubbard St., Lindale, TX 75771. Founded 1993. "Funded mostly through donations and fundraising events; some funds from city" (library website). Population served: 5,000. Circulation: 69,632. Holdings: 40,000. LJ November 15, 2009: 3-star library.

LINN COUNTY LIBRARY DISTRICT #2, LACYGNE, KS   209 N. Broadway, Lacygne, KS 66040. Population served: 1,722. Circulation: 35,000. Holdings: 24,696. LJ October 1, 2010: 4-star library.

LINN COUNTY LIBRARY DISTRICT #4, MOUND CITY, KS   509 Main St., Mound City, KS 66056. Population served: 1,437. Circulation: 20,029. Holdings: 14,285. LJ February 15, 2009: 3-star library.

LITHOPOLIS, OH. *See* WAGNALLS MEMORIAL LIBRARY, LITHOPOLIS, OH.

LITTLE VALLEY, NY. *See* MEMORIAL LIBRARY OF LITTLE VALLEY, NY.

LONG BEACH PUBLIC LIBRARY AND INFORMATION CENTER, CA   101 Pacific Ave., Long Beach, CA 90822. Founded 1896. Population served: 491,564. Circulation: 1,467,069. Holdings: 1,120,645.

LOPEZ ISLAND LIBRARY DISTRICT, WA   2265 Fisherman Bay Rd., Lopez Island, WA 98261. Population served: 98,261. Circulation: 55,745. Holdings: 20,700. LJ November 15, 2009, and October 1, 2010: 3-star library.

LORD, MILTON EDWARD, 1898–1985   Born June 12, 1898, Lynn, MD. He attended Harvard, 1915; left for army service, 1917–1919; then returned to finish his degree. He pursued graduate study and worked in the library. In 1925–1926 he was at the University of Paris. Lord had four years in Rome as librarian of the American Academy. He returned to the United States in 1930 as director of the University of Iowa library and library school but moved on to the Boston Public Library as assistant librarian in 1931. A year later he was promoted to librarian; he stayed with the library until his retirement in 1965. Lord initiated a training class for staff, negotiated for increases in endowments, and pressed for international activities. In 1952 the trustees backed his refusal to remove so-called communist materials from the library. Lord's "greatest contribution to the profession was as an international ambassador for American librarianship" (*DALB*). He died in Salem, MA, on February 12, 1985. *DALB* 1st supplement.

LOS ANGELES COUNTY LIBRARY. *See* COUNTY OF LOS ANGELES PUBLIC LIBRARY, DOWNEY, CA.

LOS ANGELES PUBLIC LIBRARY, CA   630 W. Fifth St., Los Angeles, CA 90071. Founded 1872. Population served: 4,000,000. The library (LAPL) serves residents of Los Angeles, CA; the County of Los Angeles Public Library serves residents of suburban communities. Circulation: 17,182,815. Holdings: 6,433,495. 71 branches. A private subscription library of 1872 was organized as LAPL in 1878. Tessa Kelso, city librarian, 1889–1895, opened shelves to the public and started a training program for librarians that became a library school (later taken over by the University of Southern California). Librarian Mary L Jones (1900–1905) initiated the branch system. The central library moved five times in rented spaces before Everett Robbins Perry (city librarian, 1911–1933) led successful campaigns to fund a new building. When that structure, designed by Benjamin Goodhue, opened on July 6, 1926, it held 250,000 volumes. There were subject departments, a children's room, a municipal reference library, and many specialized collections. The library was heavily used from its opening and soon achieved the highest per capita circulation of any large U.S. public library.

A 1986 fire in the central library destroyed 375,000 books; more of the collection was damaged by water used to put out the flames. Earthquakes of 1987 and 1994 destroyed several branches. These misfortunes inspired the citizens to raise funds to rebuild; 16 new branches were constructed, and the central building—which had been closed for seven years after the fire—reopened on October 3, 1993, with a 340,000-square-foot addition. LAPL would become a key in the revitalization of downtown Los Angeles. Another significant building program was completed in 2005, including a further renovation and expansion of the central library and new construction in 64 branches. The Hollywood Branch, specializing in film and performing arts, was designed by Frank Gehry.

City librarians have been the following: John Littlefield, 1872–1879; Patrick Connolly, 1879–1880; Mary E. Foy, 1880–1884; Jessie A. Gavitt, 1884–1889; Lydia Prescott, 1889; Tessa Kelso, 1889–1895; Clara B. Fowler, 1895–1897; Harriet Child Wadleigh, 1897–1900; Mary L. Jones, 1900–1905; Charles Fletcher Lummis, 1905–1910; Purd B. Wright, 1910–1911; Everett Robbins Perry, 1911–1933; Althea Warren, 1933–1947; Harold L. Hamill, 1947–1970; Wyman Jones, 1970–1990; Elizabeth Martinez, 1990–1994; Susan Kent, 1995–2004; Fontayne Holmes, 2004–2009; and Martin Gomez, 2009–.

References

Holmes, Fontayne. 2001. Los Angeles Public Library. *International Dictionary of Library Histories*, 419–21. Chicago: Fitzroy Dearborn.
Siegel, Ernest, and John D. Bruckman. 1975. Los Angeles Public Library. In *Encyclopedia of Library and Information Science* 15: 337–43. New York: Marcel Dekker.

LOS GATOS, CA. *See* SANTA CLARA COUNTY LIBRARY, LOS GATOS, CA.

LOUDON COUNTY PUBLIC LIBRARY, LEESBURG, VA   908 Trailview Blvd. SE, Leesburg, VA 20175. Population served: 225,830. Circulation: 2,800,000. Holdings: 520,000. LJ February 15, 2009: 3-star library HAPLR 2009, 2010.

LOUDONVILLE PUBLIC LIBRARY, OH   122 E. Main St., Loudonville, OH 44842. Population served: 8,341. Circulation: 164,989. Holdings: 55,534. LN February 15, 2009; November 15, 2009; and October 1, 2010: 4-star library.

LOUISVILLE FREE PUBLIC LIBRARY, KY   301 York St., Louisville, KY 40203. A private library from 1816, became public 1908. Population served: 700,000. Circulation: 4,000,000. Holdings: 1,500,000. 18 branches, 3 bookmobiles. The library began giving service to African Americans through a colored branch in 1905; it was headed by Thomas Fountain Blue (see entry for him). Jennie Flexner was head of circulation in 1912 and wrote the first textbook on the subject (see entry for her).

LOWER MERION LIBRARY SYSTEM, ARDMORE, PA. *See* ARDMORE FREE LIBRARY, PA.

LUBBOCK PUBLIC LIBRARY, TX   1306 Ninth St., Lubbock, TX 79401. Population served: 240,310. Circulation: 972,748. Holdings: 385,199. 3 branches.

LYDENBERG, HARRY MILLER, 1874–1960   Librarian. Born November 18, 1874, Dayton, OH. He worked as a page in Dayton Public Library in his teens. At Harvard he worked in the college library, graduating in 1896 magna cum laude. Lydenberg was employed at the New York Public Library (NYPL) as a cataloger, then assistant to the director, John Shaw Billings, and head of reference. In 1928 Lydenberg was assistant director, rationalizing collection development and policies. He became NYPL director in 1934, remaining in the post until he retired in 1941. In his tenure the reference collections were strengthened, notably in unique materials and books in more than 1,000 foreign languages and dialects. He was an early advocate of preservation, setting up a preservation laboratory in NYPL A strong internationalist, he directed the Biblioteca Benjamin Franklin in Mexico City for two years after leaving NYPL and headed the American Library Association (ALA) Board of International Relations, 1943–1946. Lydenberg was an active adviser in Europe and Latin America. In 1931–1932 he was president of ALA. Among his important publications is the *History of the New York Public Library* (1923). He died on April 16, 1960, in Westerville, Ohio. *ANB.*

M

MACSHERRY LIBRARY, ALEXANDRIA BAY, NY   112 Walton St., Alexandria Bay, NY 13607. Population served: 1,068. Circulation: 24,113. Holdings: 15,111. LJ February 15, 2009; November 15, 2009; and October 1, 2010: 4-star library.

MADISON PUBLIC LIBRARY, OH   6111 Middle Ridge Rd., Madison, OH 44057. Population served: 18,864. Circulation: 562,010. Holdings: 105,764. HAPLR 2009, 2010.

MADISON PUBLIC LIBRARY, WI   201 W. Mifflin St., Madison, WI 53703. Founded 1875. Population served: 210,000. Circulation: 3,900,000. Holdings: 954,370. 8 branches. LJ February 15, 2009; November 15, 2009; and October 1, 2010: 3-star library. HAPLR 2009, 2010.

MADISON VALLEY PUBLIC LIBRARY, ENNIS, MT   210 Main St., Ennis, MT 59729. Population served: 1,129. Circulation: 25,127. Holdings: 25,127. LJ February 15, 2009, and November 15, 2009: 5-star library; October 1, 2010: 4-star library. HAPLR 2009, 2010.

MAGAZINES. *See* SERIALS.

MALVERN PUBLIC LIBRARY, IA   502 Main St., Malvern, IA 51551. Founded 1916. Population served: 1,256. Circulation: 12,814. Holdings: 13,623. LJ November 15, 2009: 5-star library.

MANAGEMENT AND ORGANIZATION

Terminology

Librarianship shares with other fields the key terms in this area and has no peculiar usages for them. *Merriam* says that management is "the conducting or supervising of something (as a business)." This statement equates management with supervision. For "manage" *Merriam* offers "to exercise executive, administrative and supervisory direction of . . . ," which equates the management act with that of administration and supervision. For "administration" there is "performance of executive duties." And for "executive" there appears "having administrative or managerial responsibility." Sorting that out, it seems that for *Merriam*, management and administration carry similar if not identical meanings.

American Heritage says that management is "the act, manner, or practice of managing, handling, supervision, or control." To "manage" is "to direct or control the use of . . . ; to exert control over." There is a suggestion that management and administration are somewhat different in the definition of "administration": "the management of a government or large institution." Putting these rather imprecise labels together, it may be said that administration is management but perhaps on a large scale.

ODLIS has no entry for "management." For "administration" it says "the range of activities normally associated with the management of a government agency, organization, or institution, such as a library or library system."

"Scientific management," a term not in the general dictionaries, is defined in a management textbook as "that kind of management which conducts a business or affairs by standards established by facts or truths gained through systematic observation, experiment, or reasoning" (Kreitner 1986, 51). In library contexts, this approach leans on data gathering and analysis (inputs and outputs), surveys and user studies, "operational" studies of employees at work, and experiments with organization and policy.

There are other terms to consider. "Middle management" refers to a tier of the authority line that lies between the highest tier and the supervisor tier. "Supervisor" is the lowest tier of the authority line, resting at the day-to-day operations of the organization. If the top tier is named "administration," this schema results:

- Administration
- Middle management
- Supervisors
- Employees

At each level there are units that may have various names. The top tier is often named "office" or "department," the middle tier "division," and the lower tiers (if any) "sections" or "services." Or the elements may be named simply by their functions, such as "human resources" or "public relations."

The person in charge of a public library may be a "director," "executive director," "librarian," "chief librarian," "commissioner," "city librarian," or "president," with "director" being the preferred designation today. Titles in lower tiers include "assistant director" and assistant to the other top titles, "head," "manager," "supervisor," "coordinator," and "librarian" (as in "youth services librarian").

Historical Summary

The father of scientific management was Frederick Winslow Taylor (1856–1915), who analyzed the operations of steel production and devised means of making the tasks more efficient. His 1911 book *The Principles of Scientific Management* laid the groundwork for time studies; such studies were enhanced by Frank Gilbreth (1868–1924) and Lillian Gilbreth (1878–1972). They considered the physical movements made during a work operation. After World War II these techniques, known as time and motion studies, were refined into operations management.

Another pioneer was Henri Fayol, whose 1916 publication in French (translated into English in 1949) codified his own experience into practical guidelines for the direction of all types of organizations (this summary of scientific management is drawn from Sager 1982; Kreitner 1986). His 14 principles are still in effect, although they have been criticized as too rigid. The principles state that management must establish division of work, authority accompanied by responsibility, discipline, unity of command, unity of direction, subordination of the individual to the organization, fair remuneration, centralization, formal chain of command, everyone and everything in their proper place, equity of treatment for all, stability and tenure of personnel, initiative, and esprit de corps.

Translating human behavior into numbers was certain to raise objections. Time and motion was "rightly criticized for alienating workers ... [by] treating them as mindless, emotionless, and easily replicable factors of production" (*Business Dictionary* 2010). The approach has not been popular in library contexts, but a recent book has revived the concept as "workload measurement," with time study becoming "numeric analysis" and motion study becoming "process analysis":

> Numeric measures can range from the very general (average number of books circulated per staff hour) to very specific (number of steps and minutes needed to process each new videotape). ... Process analysis is a key tool in solving operational problems. (Mayo and Goodrich 2002, 9, 11)

The counterbalance to operations management and the authoritarian aspects of Fayol was the human relations movement, which called on managers to be sensitive to the needs of employees. "Supportive supervision" involves sincere concern for subordinates and implementation of policies that vivify that concern. Douglas McGregor's "theory Y" (expounded in his *The Human Side of Enterprise*, 1960) was an enlightened assumption about human nature: he viewed employees as energetic and creative, wanting only opportunity to present excellent results.

In the 1990s libraries were attracted to the idea of "total quality management" (TQM), drawn from the work of W. Edwards Deming. The novel principles advocated by Deming were in part based on the success of Japanese industry and were applicable primarily to business enterprises. But some of Deming's so-called 14 points made their way into library administrative philosophy. Those points were the following:

- Drive out fear, so that everyone may work effectively for the company.
- Break down barriers between departments. People . . . should work as a team.
- Eliminate management by objective . . . substitute leadership.
- Remove barriers that rob people . . . of their right to pride of workmanship.
- Institute a vigorous program of education and self-improvement.
- Put everybody in the company to work to accomplish the transformation (Stevens 1994, 28).

Deming also wanted to eliminate performance evaluations of staff, because you cannot measure performance. Appraisal of people is ruinous (Stevens 1994, 24). Good performance should not be rewarded because the real reward is "joy on the job."

Administrative and Managerial Work in a Library

There are two sets of activities that may be named "administration" and "management." This is what they involve:

Administration:

- Interacting with the mission giver
- Organizing the units of the library
- Long-range planning
- Organizational budgeting
- Overall deployment of resources
- Staffing management positions
- Directing and controlling major units
- Creating organizational policies
- Coordinating unit policies
- Dealing with building and facilities needs
- Collecting and analyzing data

- Interacting with community groups and with media
- Interacting with state, national, and international agencies and organizations
- Implementing applicable laws and regulations
- Developing and maintaining cooperation with other libraries
- Reporting to the mission giver

Management:

- Interacting with administration
- Short-term planning
- Unit budgeting
- Deployment of unit resources
- Making unit policies
- Staffing within units
- Directing and controlling unit work
- Reporting to administration

Administration takes the long, wide-angle view of the organization, while management takes the close, narrow view. In a small organization, such as a library with only one qualified librarian, the administrative and managerial roles are merged. But as the staff size grows, even to two persons, the division of roles begins to occur. In a library staff of two, one will be the superior of the other and will have the responsibility of dealing with entities outside the library (mission givers) along with the responsibility of supervising the other person and replacing that person if necessary. The same patterns hold in libraries of any size.

The concepts of "mission" and "mission giver" are poorly treated in library literature and in statements issued by libraries. Indeed, one of the general dictionaries points in two directions. *Merriam* has for "mission" "a specific task with which a person or group is charged" and also "a preestablished and often self-imposed objective or purpose [statement of a company's ...]." In *American Heritage* "mission" is "a special assignment given to a person or group." The essence of all the approaches to "mission" is that it identifies a task given by someone to someone else. That first someone is the mission giver.

A public library is tasked by its community, those persons who pay for its operations, to do something that the community finds beneficial. This task, the library's mission, is unfortunately left unstated, or it is stated in such vague language as to be of little use to the library that must accomplish it. The community's expression of mission is usually put in the hands of a select number: the trustees, library board, or city officials. Those selected individuals may have a try at stating the mission or may also leave it unexpressed. So this is the primary challenge to the library administration: interpreting the mission it has received.

Given the uncertainties that are usually presented by the community, administration has two options. It may seek to gain a more distinct mission from the people, or it may invent its own mission. The second choice is indicated as a possibility in the second *American Heritage* definition above. Both options are difficult to handle, but the second—self-made mission—is after all easier since it requires only a high-level meeting or two. Yet it is the first option that is more desirable since the community will respond to the library's programs and activities in terms of its task (even if unstated) and how well the library has met it. The community will not be interested in the library's invented mission for itself unless that invention is congruent with community wishes. This is a good example of such a statement, one that appears to express what the community wants from the library:

The mission of the San Diego Public Library is to:

- Respond to the information needs of San Diego's diverse communities
- Ensure equal access to local, national, and global resources
- Anticipate and address the educational, cultural, business, and recreational interests of the public
- Develop and provide welcoming environments. (Greiner 2004, 114)

For more on mission statements, *see* PLANNING.

The administration's first job, then, is to interact with the mission giver and clarify the library's tasks. Only then can a rational set of activities, as listed above, begin (*see* ACQUISITIONS; BOOKMOBILES; BRANCH LIBRARIES; BUILDINGS AND FACILITIES; COLLECTION DEVELOPMENT; COOPERATION; EVALUATION; FIXTURES, FURNISHINGS, AND EQUIPMENT; FUNDING OF PUBLIC LIBRARIES; INFORMATION TECHNOLOGY; PLANNING; POLICY STATEMENTS; PUBLIC RELATIONS; PUBLIC SERVICES; SPECIAL SERVICES; STAFFING; STATISTICS; TECHNICAL SERVICES; TRUSTEES).

Only a word is offered here about planning, which is the making of a plan, and a plan is a statement that describes the important steps to be taken for the accomplishment of a mission or the solution of a problem. Planning occurs at both the administrative and the managerial level of the library (*see* PLANNING).

To carry out the plan it is necessary to organize the resources available. A library's organization is a formal hierarchical design of unit relationships and lines of authority. It is documented visually in an organization chart. The chart exhibits units or offices in the library, with or without job titles associated with them but not individual persons. Many types of organization design are found in libraries: functional, topical, geographical, and so on. The approach may be centralized or decentralized. In all cases there are basic principles to observe: there must be unity of command, delegation, a reasonable span of control, and clarity between line and staff functions. Unity of command means that each unit is responsible to one higher level unit only. (In practice that means that nobody has more than one boss.) Span of control is the range of subordinate units assigned to one larger unit; it must be a number that the officer of the larger unit can readily supervise (not more than 10 in most cases). A line function is one that carries authority from a higher point of the organization to a lower point, "down the line"; a staff function is one without authority at all, employed as an adjunct to another unit. In a properly devised organization chart, it will be clear to any observer which units deal with which tasks and which units are in control of other units. The names given to the units do not matter.

This would be a typical set of elements for the organization chart in a medium-size public library:

Director- - - -Office Manager		
Assistant Director	Assistant Director	Assistant Director
Public Services	Technical Services	Administrative Services
Head, Reference	Head, Acquisitions	Financial Officer
Head, Circulation	Head, Collection Development	Head, Human Resources
Head, Outreach	Head, Cataloging	Head, Maintenance
	Head, Information Technology	Head, Mail and Shipping
		Head, Security

Such a plan follows venerable principles, drawn from public administration, and articulated at a 1938 conference at the University of Chicago Graduate Library School. Since around 1970 there have been creative efforts to modify this standard form of organization and to reflect new patterns in the charts. The hierarchical design, thought to give an impression of declining importance and empowerment of units and their occupiers at lower points of the chart, has been criticized. Various visual presentations of the authority situation have been devised. The matrix design visualizes library operations as a set of over-lapping circles or similar forms. One ingenious design placed the administration at the bottom of the chart. But in fact none of them altered the basic power structure—nor could they if the library were to function. All the innovative charts can be redrawn along traditional lines.

The library's work can be characterized as a multiplicity of decisions about what to do next. A hierarchical organization chart displays the impact area of specific decisions. Decisions made by any unit affect all units on the same chart line and all units below. At the bottom line, the nonsupervisory employee makes decisions about how to carry out his or her own work assignment. At the top of the hierarchy the trustees (of a public library), representing the community served, make the overarching decisions that affect the very life of the institution.

Staff participation in decision making, apart from what is suggested in the unit array of an organization chart, is a hallmark of modern scientific management. In general such participation means that the hierarchical lines of the chart are modified to allow a vertical flow of inputs that will be used in decision making. There are numerous intensities of participation. A low-intensity participation is found in the suggestion box. Evidently suggestions will be offered from units on a certain line of the chart to higher units; a downward-flowing suggestion would in fact be a direction. Suggestion boxes are effective if the receiving unit is responsive (Sager 1982, 21; this source underlies much of the following).

A sizable library will have committees of staff members. These groups may be permanent (standing committees) or temporary (committees with a specific function only, meant to end at a certain time). There are also task forces, which are groups that take on certain issues or problems, usually of immediate concern; they may include persons with special competence from outside the library. Committees and task forces are not found on the organization chart. Their role is advisory; they make recommendations to the unit that established them. They do not make decisions, although they may be very influential in guiding decisions.

Representation of a unit in the deliberations of a higher-level unit is a form of participation that is gaining favor in public libraries. The library director may sit with the trustees, usually in a nonvoting capacity. Recently some trustees have invited representation from young people in the community (*see* TRUSTEES).

Librarians who took up TQM believed that it required a new organization plan (breaking down barriers) and intensive staff participation (putting everybody in the company to work to accomplish the transformation). Their reports in the literature spoke of success in meeting elusive goals, albeit with considerable expenditure of staff time and a bit of illusion about having made all the units equal once the old organization chart was upgraded (an example of such an account is given in Fitch et al. 1993). TQM is no longer a topic of great interest among librarians, to judge from the lack of literature about it.

Common sense needs to be activated in consideration of staff participation of any kind. "No employee can effectively participate in decision making if he or she is denied power over the ultimate methods they will have to employ to carry out the task required. Conversely, no manager can function effectively if all the decisions rest in the hands of the employees" (Sager 1982, 21). Staff participation seems best when it is limited to process changes in task execution and if management refrains from vetoing employee decisions. Staff should not be expected to select their supervisors or to overrule them. Problems about staff participation remain to be dealt with. One is that there is little research to support its value. And staff may be unwilling to do it—much time and effort need to be invested in the activity. Managers who insist on doing it may be viewed as authoritarian. Civil service rules may be another deterrent. In large libraries, dissemination of the information required (e.g., financial data) to all employees given decision responsibility would be costly. In the end, staff and management will probably perceive that just about any form of participation is really advisory. If decision proposals are not satisfactory to the unit that receives them, they will not be implemented. "Between 75 and 80 percent [of decision making] is participative," said one library director. "I am a team manager. But the remaining 20 to 25 percent is the responsibility of the administrator. Someone has to be responsible—this is where the buck stops" (Pamela Pridgen, director at Hattiesburg, MS, quoted in Greiner 2004, 129).

Policymaking at the administrative or managerial level refers to codification in writing of the library's position in given situations. Policy statements found in public libraries include circulation policy, reference service policy, interlibrary loan policy, Internet policy, personnel policy, security policy, preservation policy, and disaster policy. All but the last named are dealt with in their own entries in this handbook. A disaster policy is important because there is no time in a sudden crisis to formulate one. Several topics should be covered in the policy (or plan, as it is also called). One author (Kahn 2003) takes up response, recovery, prevention, and planning; she gives useful details on dealing with damage and moving toward restoration of normal service. Library response to Hurricanes Katrina and Rita of 2005 is a valuable example of what can be done in such a desperate situation through professional cooperation (for details on recovery by Louisiana libraries, see HURRICANES KATRINA AND RITA).

With an organization chart in place and policy statements issued, administrators and managers are situated to take appropriate actions in the interest of fulfilling library mission. A primary step is to acquire funds (see FUNDING OF PUBLIC LIBRARIES) and use them to fill staff positions (see STAFFING) and purchase materials (see COLLECTION DEVELOPMENT). These administrative chores are accomplished by directing the unit personnel to do specific things and controlling (checking up on) the results. How they direct and control is an expression of "management style" or "leadership style." This style is not easy to characterize, but it might be described as a point between two extremes: authoritarian and yielding. One who practices the extreme authoritarian manner will issue orders and demand timely results, accepting no excuses for failure. It is a military style and one that obviously breeds successful outcomes in appropriate situations. One who engages in the extreme yielding style gives suggestions instead of orders and is flexible about the timing and value of results. This style may lead to a pleasant work atmosphere but without much accomplishment. Between the extremes is where most administrators see themselves. Machiavelli's guideline, it is better to be feared than loved, was operative in library administration until modern times; today managers seem to need at least some love, but fear is always lurking. Basically, good directing calls for leadership skills. Those skills are nebulous; there is no suitable list of traits that identify a good leader and no single profile of such a person (Hernon et al. 2003, 14). There are, according to Daniel Goleman, four preferred leadership styles:

- Authoritative = come with me
- Democratic = what do you think?

- Coaching = try this
- Affiliative = people come first

And there is one poor style:

- Coercive = do what I say

Of course these leadership qualities overlap managerial qualities. A good library leader, manager, or administrator should have communication skills, integrity, vision, knowledge of trends, knowledge of current library practices, skill in planning, skill in finance, and commitment to intellectual freedom (Hernon et al. 2003, 94; for a review of recent theories of leadership, see Stueart and Moran 2007, 321–45). Colin Powell (1995) observed that "leadership is the art of accomplishing more than the science of management says is possible" (255).

Acquiring the money to run the library is a central administrative challenge. While some money comes from donations and fines, most of the operating expenses come from the library's governing authority (which raises it through taxes, levies, fees, and bond issues or receives it in funding from higher levels). There is a standard process in which funds move from the governing authority to the library. Once a year there is a "budget call" that advises the library director when to submit a funding request and under what conditions. Those conditions may impose limits on the request; for example, a stipulation might be that the new request should not exceed what was granted in the prior year. The authority identifies the type of request to be made: it may be a "line-item budget" (which assumes continuation of existing services and is based on previous allocations for each of them), a "formula budget" (which requests funds according to predetermined standards), or a "performance budget" (which requests funds on the basis of what each unit in the library does and what it costs to do it). An elaboration of the performance budget is the "planning, programming, and budgeting system," (PPBS), which examines the goals and objectives of the library, considers what activities are needed to accomplish those ends, and determines what funds are required for those activities (these systems are described in Stueart and Moran 2007, 444–52).

The term "budget" is loosely applied in this process and may be confusing to the outside observer. When the librarian makes a presentation to the governing authority asking for a certain sum, that is the "budget request"— often described as the "budget." When the authority determines how much to give the library, that is the "allocation," sometimes named the "budget." As the library spends its allocation, it is adding up "operating expenditures" or "operating expenses."

With the year's allocation settled, the director moves the process down the organization, asking each major unit for its budget request. Or, more likely in practice, the director establishes an allocation for each unit.

The final step in the budget process is an annual report from the director to the governing authority, relating the library's activities and accomplishments to the way allocations were expended. This report is often published in the library website. Thus, the mission giver (governing board, city officials, and the community) may judge how well resources have been used.

Recent Issues

Probably the premier puzzle of administrators in the current dismal economic climate of libraries has to do with outsourcing. This term is defined by *Merriam*: "to procure (as some goods or services needed by a business or organization) under contract with an outside supplier." The dictionary gives 1979 as the earliest usage date for outsourcing. Should any of the library's functions be handed over to an outside entity? Clearly the reason for doing so would be to save money, primarily in staff time. One type of outsourcing, the granting of certain acquisition privileges to commercial agents, is now quite ordinary. Some cataloging and classification functions have been outsourced to vendors or the Library of Congress or OCLC for 100 years. Aspects of reference service have been turned over to Internet database operators. What remains to outsource? It is the administration itself. This drastic action is not one that an administrator would choose; in fact, it comes from the library's controlling board or municipal authority, with the voice of the citizens playing a variable role. A few examples will be useful.

The first public library to outsource its management functions was Riverside (CA) County Library. It engaged Library Systems and Services (LSSI) to handle all administrative/management activities in 1997. The city of Moorpark, CA, contracted with LSSI in 2007 to operate the new city library, which opened January 13, 2007. Moorpark was experienced in contracting out services, having outsourced the sheriff's office, bus service, and waste collection. It was expected the LSSI could save on personnel costs since it did not have to pay civil service benefits. A well-publicized outsourcing event came from Jackson County (TN) Public Library. Citizen opposition has been involved in some outsourcing decisions. Bedford, TX, voted not to outsource its public library in 2007. "Little research surrounds the phenomenon of public library management outsourcing," according to a recent report (Hill 2009). It remains an open project, awaiting definitive accounts of results achieved and the cost of them.

References

Barnard, Susan B. 1998. Total quality management. *Encyclopedia of Library and Information Science* 61: 311–325. New York: Marcel Dekker.

Bernfeld, Betsy A. 2004. Developing a team management structure in the public library. *Library Trends* 53, no. 1 (Summer): 112–29.

Business Dictionary. 2010. http://www.Businessdictionary.com. Accessed January 15, 2010.

Dawson, Alma, and Kathleen de la Peña McCook. 2006. Rebuilding community in Louisiana after the hurricanes of 2005. *Reference & Users Services Quarterly* 45, no. 4 (Summer): 292–96.

Evans, G. Edward, and Patricia Layzell Ward. 2007. *Management Basics for Information Professionals.* 2nd ed. New York: Neal Schuman.

Fitch, Donna K., et al. 1993. Turning the library upside down: Reorganization using total quality management principles. *Journal of Academic Librarianship* 19, no. 5 (November): 294–99.

Greiner, Joy M. 2004. *Exemplary Public Libraries: Lessons in Leadership, Management, and Service.* Westport, CT: Libraries Unlimited.

Gulick, Luther, and L. Urwick, eds. 1937/1969. *Papers on the Science of Administration.* New York: Institute of Public Administration. Reprint, New York: Augustus M. Kelley.

Hernon, Peter, et al. 2003. *The Next Library Leadership: Attributes of Academic and Public Library Directors.* Westport, CT: Libraries Unlimited.

Hill, Heather. 2009. Examining the power relationships in public library management outsourcing. Paper given at the American Library Association Conference, Chicago, July 12.

Joeckel, Carleton B., ed. 1939. *Current Issues in Library Administration.* Chicago: University of Chicago Press.

Kahn, Miriam B. 2003. *Disaster Response and Planning for Libraries.* Chicago: American Library Association.

Kreitner, Robert. 1986. *Management.* 3rd ed. Boston: Houghton Mifflin.

Matthews, Joseph R. 2004. *Measuring for Results: The Dimensions of Public Library Effectiveness.* Westport, CT: Libraries Unlimited.

Mayo, Diane, and Jeanne Goodrich. 2002. *Staffing for Results: A Guide to Working Smarter.* Chicago: American Library Association.

McGregor, Douglas M. 1960. *The Human Side of Enterprise.* New York: McGraw-Hill.

Miller, Paula J. 2001. Implementing Total Quality Management. In *Library Evaluation: A Casebook and Can-Do Guide,* ed. Danny P. Wallace and Connie Van Fleet, 25–40. Englewood, CO: Libraries Unlimited,

Nelson, Sandra et al. 2000. *Managing for Results: Effective Resource Allocation for Public Libraries.* Chicago: American Library Association.

Olbrich, William L, Jr. 1994. Organization of libraries. *Encyclopedia of Library History:* 477–81. New York: Garland.

O'Neil, Rosanna M. 1994. *Total Quality Management in Libraries: A Sourcebook.* Englewood, CO: Libraries Unlimited.

Powell, Colin. 1995. *My American Journey.* New York: Ballantine Books.

Rosenberg, Jane A. 1994. Library management. *Encyclopedia of Library History:* 373–77. New York: Garland.

Rubin, Rhea Joyce. 2006. *Demonstrating Results: Using Outcome Measures in Your Library.* Chicago: American Library Association.

Sager, Donald J. 1982. *Participatory Management in Libraries.* Metuchen, NJ: Scarecrow Press.

Stevens, Tim. 1994. Dr. Deming: Management today does not know what its job is. *Industry Week,* January 17, 21–28.

Stueart, Robert D., and Barbara Moran. 2007. *Library and Information Center Management.* 7th ed. Westport, CT: Libraries Unlimited.

Woodward, Jeanette. 2005. *Creating the Customer-Driven Library: Building on the Bookstore Model.* Chicago: American Library Association.

MANCHESTER CITY LIBRARY, NH   405 Pine St., Manchester, NH 03104. Founded 1854 as a free public library (library website). Population served: 109,966. Circulation: 1,200,000. Holdings: 555,000. 1 branch.

MANSFIELD-RICHLAND COUNTY PUBLIC LIBRARY, OH   43 W. Third St., Mansfield, OH 44902. Founded 1908 as a free public library; had been a private library since 1887. Population served: 129,000. Circulation: 2,000,000. Holdings: 542,000. 8 branches. LJ February 15, 2009, and November 15, 2009: 3-star library.

MARICOPA COUNTY LIBRARY DISTRICT, PHOENIX, AZ   2700 N. Central Ave., Phoenix, AZ 85004. Population served: 591,012. Circulation: 3,716,445. Holdings: 617,000. 15 branches. The whole system is converting from Dewey Classification to BISAC (*see* CLASSIFICATION).

MARIETTA, OH. *See* WASHINGTON COUNTY PUBLIC LIBRARY, MARIETTA, OH.

MARIN COUNTY FREE LIBRARY, SAN RAFAEL, CA   3501 Civic Center Dr., San Rafael, CA 94903. Founded 1927. Population served: 150,000. Circulation: 1,420,286. Holdings: 438,631. 10 branches, 1 bookmobile. The main library is part of the civic center designed by Frank Lloyd Wright. LJ February 15, 2009: 3-star library.

MARINETTE COUNTY CONSOLIDATED PUBLIC LIBRARY SERVICE, MARINETTE, WI   1700 Hall Ave., Marinette, WI 54143. Founded 1878. Population served: 44,471. Circulation: 227,324. Holdings: 96,462. 6 branches. Lutie E. Stearns (see entry for her) rode a horse-drawn book wagon from the library in 1905, initiating a service that ended in 1983.

MARION CITY LIBRARY, KS   101 Library St., Marion, KS 66861. Population served: 2,009. Circulation: 40,000. Holdings: 24,000. The library is located in the newly restored Santa Fe depot. LJ February 15, 2009: 3-star library.

MARION COMMUNITY LIBRARY, TX   500 Bulldog Blvd., Marion, TX 78124. Population served: 12,686. Circulation: 113,643. Holdings: 44,636. LJ February 15, 2009: 4-star library; October 1, 2010: 5-star library.

MARKETING. *See* PUBLIC RELATIONS.

MARLINGTON, WV. *See* POCAHONTAS COUNTY FREE LIBRARIES, MARLINTON, WV.

MARY RILEY STYLES PUBLIC LIBRARY, FALLS CHURCH, VA   120 N. Virginia Ave., Falls Church, VA 22046. Founded 1928 as Falls Church Public Library. Population served: 10,000. Circulation: 350,000. Holdings: 157,338. LJ February 15, 2009, and November 15, 2009: 3-star library; October 1, 2010: 4-star library.

MARY WILLIS FREE LIBRARY, WASHINGTON, GA. *See* BARTRAM TRAIL REGIONAL LIBRARY, WASHINGTON, GA.

MASSILLON PUBLIC LIBRARY, OH   208 Lincoln Way E, Massillon, OH 44646. Founded 1899 (year of opening: chartered 1897) as McClymonds Public Library. Changed to present name in 1922. Population served: 30,447. Circulation: 864,435. Holdings: 170,173. HAPLR 2010.

MASTICS-MORICHES-SHIRLEY COMMUNITY LIBRARY, SHIRLEY, NY   407 William Floyd Parkway, Shirley, NY 11967. Population served: 45,704. Circulation: 650,000. Holdings: 150,000. LJ February 15, 2009; November 15, 2009; and October 1, 2010: 4-star library.

MATHEWS MEMORIAL LIBRARY, MATHEWS, VA   251 Main St., Mathews, VA 23109. Population served: 9,500. Circulation: 30,064. Holdings: 31,947. IMLS award 2005.

MATTITUCK-LAUREL LIBRARY, NY   13900 Main Rd., Mattituck, NY 11952. Population served: 5,770. Circulation: 125,604. Holdings: 62,000. LJ November 15, 2009: 3-star library.

McCAMEY, TX. *See* UPTON COUNTY PUBLIC LIBRARY, MCCAMEY, TX.

McMURRAY, PA. *See* PETERS TOWNSHIP PUBLIC LIBRARY, MCMURRAY, PA.

Mc PHEETERS, ANNIE LOU WATTERS, 1908–1994   Librarian. Born in Floyd County, GA, February 22, 1908. She graduated from Clark University in 1929 and earned a library degree from the Hampton Institute in 1933. In 1957 she completed a master's degree in library science from Columbia University. In 1934 she became assistant librarian in the Auburn Branch of the Carnegie Library of Atlanta, a segregated black branch. McPheeters was the first black librarian with a library degree in the Atlanta system. From 1936 to 1949 she was head of the branch, creating an active program of story hours, radio broadcasts, reading clubs, and discussion groups; she wrote newspaper columns. She began assembling a collection of books by black writers and took it with her when she moved to the new West Hunter Branch, one of three designated for blacks. As head of the new Negro department, she emphasized provision of political information in the three branches, including instruction in voting. She was a leading voice in efforts to desegregate the library system. When McPheeters retired from the public library in 1966, she worked as a reference librarian at Georgia State University until 1975. She received many awards and a special recognition from the Atlanta-Fulton County Library System in 1993 as the West Hunter Branch was renamed in her honor. The collection she began in Auburn moved to West Hunter and then to the main library; it finally settled in the new Auburn library in 1994 as the Auburn Avenue Research Library on African-American Culture and History. McPheeters is most remembered for that collection and for her lifelong efforts to end segregation in public libraries of the South. She died in Atlanta on December 23, 1994. *DALB*, 2nd supplement.

MEADE PUBLIC LIBRARY, KS   101 E. West Plains, Meade, KS 67864. Founded 1936 as a tax-supported library; earlier library from 1895. Population served: 1,625. Circulation: 39,000. Holdings: 24,000. LJ February 15, 2009: 5-star library.

MEADOW GROVE PUBLIC LIBRARY, NE   215 Main St., Meadow Grove, NE 68752. Population served: 311. Circulation: 11, 614. Holdings: 6,952. HAPLR 2009, 2010.

MEDFORD, OR. *See* JACKSON COUNTY LIBRARY SERVICES, MEDFORD, OR.

MEDIA. *See* AUDIOVISUAL COLLECTIONS; DIGITAL MEDIA; MICROFORM.

MEDINA COUNTY DISTRICT LIBRARY, OH   215 S. Broadway, Medina, OH 44256. Population served: 140,904. Circulation: 2,171,536. Holdings: 588,149. 5 branches, 1 bookmobile. LJ Library of the Year 1998. LJ October 1, 2010: 3-star library. HAPLR 2009, 2010.

MEEKINS LIBRARY, WILLIAMSBURG, MA   2 Williams St., Williamsburg, MA 01096. Population served: 2,443. Circulation: 69,750. Holdings: 35,096. LJ November 15, 2009, and October 1, 2010: 3-star library. HAPLR 2009, 2010.

MEMORIAL LIBRARY OF LITTLE VALLEY, NY   110 Rock City St., Little Valley, NY 14755. Population served: 1,130. Circulation: 15,880. Holdings: 19,814. LJ February 15, 2009: 4-star library.

MEMPHIS PUBLIC LIBRARY AND INFORMATION CENTER, TN   3030 Poplar Ave., Memphis, TN 38111. Population served: 808,113. Circulation: 2,480,472. Holdings: 1,637,596. 25 branches. IMLS medal 2007.

MENTONA, IN. *See* BELL MEMORIAL LIBRARY, MENTONA, IN.

MERCER COUNTY LIBRARY, LAWRENCEVILLE, NJ   275 Brunswick Pike, Lawrenceville, NJ 08648. Population served: 143,288. Circulation: 1,200,000. Holdings: 684,600. LJ February 15, 2009; November 15, 2009; and October 1, 2010: 5-star library.

MESA, AZ. *See* CITY OF MESA LIBRARY, AZ.

METAIRIE, LA. *See* JEFFERSON PARISH LIBRARY, METAIRIE, LA.

METROPOLITAN LIBRARY SYSTEM IN OKLAHOMA COUNTY, OKLAHOMA CITY, OK   300 Park Ave., Oklahoma City, OK 73102. Founded 1901 as a tax-supported Carnegie library; an earlier private library dates from 1898. In 1964 the city-county system was established. The present name was taken in 1977. Population served: 672,487. Circulation: 6,125,875. Holdings: 1,114,788. 17 locations.

MEXICO PUBLIC LIBRARY, NY   3269 Main St., Mexico, NY 13114. Founded 1964. Population served: 1,577. Circulation: 14,068. Holdings: 10,329. LJ November 15, 2009: 3-star library.

MIAMI-DADE PUBLIC LIBRARY SYSTEM, MIAMI, FL   101 W. Flagler St., Miami, FL 33130. Founded 1936 as Miami Public Library; became Miami-Dade Public Library system, 1971. Population served: 2,123,688. Circulation: 7,834,828. Holdings: 4,199,940. 43 branches, 2 bookmobiles. IMLS award 2008. Directors: Frances E. Gates (later Mrs. Frances Gates Parsons), 1936–1952; Frank B. Sessa, 1952–1968; Edward Sintz, 1968–1989; Ronald Kozlowski, 1989–1994; Mary Somerville, 1994–1999; and Raymond Santiago, 1999–.

MICROFORM

Terminology

Microform is "a process for reproducing printed matter in a much reduced size; matter reproduced by microform" (*Merriam*). The images are commonly reduced about 25 times. There are three principal microform formats: microfilm, microfiche, and microcard. Microfilm, those most common medium, is a 35-mm film roll stored on open reels. One roll, with the standard length of 100 feet, may carry 800 images of newspaper pages or 3,200 pages of periodical pages. Microfiche is a flat film, 105 × 148 mm in size, displaying about 100 pages of book-size material. Microcard, a format no longer made, is similar to microfiche but is printed on hard paper rather than film and is smaller—about the size of a catalog card.

Historical Summary

Microphotographs were produced by several experimenters in the mid-nineteenth century but treated as novelties. In the early twentieth century, Paul Otlet and Robert Goldschmidt suggested the use of microfiche as a substitute for printed documents. In the 1920s microfilm had commercial use in the banking industry for copying checks. Several library applications followed, including the publication of the *New York Times* on microfilm in 1935 by Kodak. Harvard University began filming foreign newspapers in 1938.

Microfilm gained acceptance in libraries with the establishment of University Microfilms International (UMI) by Eugene Powers in Ann Arbor, Michigan. UMI soon dominated the field, offering dissertations and back files of periodicals. By the 1950s it was standard practice for librarians to dispose of hard-copy magazines in favor of the little UMI cartons. UMI was absorbed by ProQuest in 2001.

Although microfiche had some advantages over microfilm (easy to store in binders and easy to put into reading machines), it did not gain mass production and never found a secure place in public libraries. Microcards had benefits too, being readable with portable viewers and readily filed in catalog drawers, but they were not mass-produced and were mostly ignored by public librarians.

Current Situation

Librarians have weighed the pros and cons of microform for more than half a century and have decided it is good. Its great benefit is space saving. Compared to print formats, microform reduces storage requirements by as much as 95 percent. Microform also provides security against vandalism and does not deteriorate like paper. In its typical library format, microfilm, it is easy to view (once it is properly placed in the reading machine), requiring no software or elaborate instructions. On the negative side, it is costly: replacing a paper file with film means buying the file twice. It is difficult to use the reading machines, which require careful threading of the film and invariably a tutorial for each patron ("It slides between the two glass plates ... "). The images are black and white, so certain kinds of research are not feasible. Above all there is poor patron response. "Microforms have several drawbacks, chief among them the fact that library users hate them" (Gorman 2000, 63).

Microfilm readers today usually have a copy function to produce paper copies of given pages. And new machines have a conversion feature that enables the user to scan an image and save it as a digital document. Automatic scanners are used for large-scale projects, allowing microfilm rolls to be digitized at the cost of pennies a page. The resulting digital files are convenient to use but do require technological support that encounters the familiar problems of hardware/software obsolescence. And the life span of digital media has not been determined, while microfilm has a shelf life estimated at 500 years.

Reference

Gorman, Michael. 2000. *Our Enduring Values: Librarianship in the 21st Century.* Chicago: American Library Association.

Microform. 2010. *Wikipedia.* http://en.wikipedia.org/wiki/microform. Accessed December 2010.

Otten, Klaus W. 1976. Microform. In *Encyclopedia of Library and Information Science* 18: 76–99. New York: Marcel Dekker.

MID-CONTINENT PUBLIC LIBRARY, INDEPENDENCE, MO   15616 E. Highway 24, Independence, MO 64050. Founded 1965. Population served: 668,425. Circulation: 8,003,080. Holdings: 3,076,599. 30 branches. LJ February 15, 2009, and November 15, 2009: 4-star library.

MIDDLE COUNTRY PUBLIC LIBRARY, CENTEREACH, NY   101 Eastwood Blvd., Centereach, NY 11720. Founded 1960. Population served: 60,689. Circulation: 1,834,544. Holdings: 353,260. 1 branch. LJ February 15, 2009; November 15, 2009, and October 1, 2010: 5-star library.

MIDDLETON PUBLIC LIBRARY, WI   7425 Hubbard Ave., Middleton, WI 53562. Founded 1964. Population served: 27,207. Circulation: 755,727. Holdings: 125,869. LJ October 1, 2010: 3-star library. HAPLR 2009, 2010.

MILFORD PUBLIC LIBRARY, UT   400 S. 100W, Milford, UT 84751. Population served: 1,414. Circulation: 27,138. Holdings: 17,895. LJ February 15, 2009: 4-star library; November 15, 2009: 5-star library; October 1, 2010: 4-star library.

MILTON, NY. *See* SARAH HULL HALLOCK FREE LIBRARY, MILTON, NY.

MILWAUKEE PUBLIC LIBRARY, WI   814 W. Wisconsin Ave., Milwaukee, WI 53233. Founded 1878. Population served: 593,367; Circulation: 2,944,880. Holdings: 2,494,834. 12 branches. Lutie E. Stearns, head of circulation, 1890–1897, was responsible for establishing traveling libraries in the state and advancing library work with children (see entry for her). The central library building, designed by Ferry & Clas (Frank Lloyd Wright competed unsuccessfully for the contract), opened 1898.

MINERVA PUBLIC LIBRARY, OH   677 Lynnwood Dr., Minerva, OH 44657. Founded 1917. Population served: 12,526. Circulation: 312,767. Holdings: 63,320. LJ February 15, 2009: 4-star library.

MINNEAPOLIS, MN. *See* HENNEPIN COUNTY LIBRARY, MINNETONKA, MN.

MISSION. *See* PLANNING.

MONROE, LA. *See* OUACHITA PARISH LIBRARY, MONROE, LA.

MONROE COUNTY PUBLIC LIBRARY, BLOOMINGTON, IN   303 E. Kirkwood, Bloomington, IN 47408. Founded 1915 as city library; merged with county library system, 1965. Population served: 120,053. Circulation: 2,211,189. Holdings: 385,587. 1 branch, 1 bookmobile. LJ February 15, 2009, and November 15, 2009: 3-star library. HAPLR 2009, 2010.

MONTCLAIR FREE PUBLIC LIBRARY, NJ   50 S. Fullerton Ave., Montclair, NJ 07042. Founded 1893. Population served: 38,977. Circulation: 3,384,480. Holdings: 210,507. 1 branch. During the administration of Margery Quigley (1927–1956; see entry for her), Montclair came to typify excellence in suburban library service, transforming the suburban role "from a quiet source of light reading to a dynamic information center" (Curley 1976, 269). The library initiated home delivery service and a staff exchange with foreign libraries. The library produced a film about itself in 1940, depicting its varied programs; it was shown worldwide under the auspices of the U.S. Department of State. The idea of automating circulation and registration was Quigley's, leading to a model system designed by IBM that included a pilot book charging machine (1942). The main library that opened in 1955 was innovative as well, designed by Ralph Walker of Voorhees, Walker, Foley & Smith with "broad expanses of glass, structural concavity to create a psychological effect of external space flowing inward, internal ebb and flow of space, complete absence of interior load-bearing walls, and inclusion of furnishings in a planned harmony of proportions" (Curley 1976, 270). Directors: Mary F. Weeks, 1893–1897; S. Augusta Smith, 1897–1909; Katherine Scholl, 1909–1912; Helen M. Hereling, 1912–1915; Alta M. Barker, 1915–1927; Margery C. Quigley, 1927–1956; Ruth P. Tubby, 1956–1968; Arthur Curley, 1968–1975; Betty J. Turock, 1975–1977; Phillip M. Clark and Ellen Foth, 1977–1979; Michael L. Connell, 1979–1999; Carol W. Robinson (acting), 1999–2000; Howard W. Curtis, 2000–2001; Cheryl M. McCoy (interim) 2001–2001; Cheryl M. McCoy 2002–2006; Mary Lou Skillin (acting), 2006; and David Hinkley, 2006–.

MONTGOMERY COUNTY PUBLIC LIBRARIES, ROCKVILLE, MD   21 Maryland Ave., Rockville, MD 20850. Population served: 948,000. Circulation: 10,000,000. Holdings: 2,338,184. 23 branches, 1 bookmobile. LJ February 15, 2009: 4-star library; November 15, 2009, and October 1, 2010: 3-star library.

MONTICELLO TOWNSHIP LIBRARY, IL   201 N. State St., Monticello, IL
61856. Population served: 5,604. Circulation: 75,176. Holdings: 34,194.
LJ October 1, 2010: 5-star library.

MOORE, ANNE CARROLL, 1871–1961   Librarian. Born Limerick, ME,
July 12, 1871. She graduated from Bradford Academy for Women 1891,
then studied law, but finding no employment for women in the field, turned
to librarianship. In 1895 she took the library course at Pratt Institute in
Brooklyn, then designed the new children's library there. Moore was
engaged by New York Public Library in 1906 to establish library service
for children in the main library (opened 1911) and branches. Moore promoted love of reading unrelated to school work and free of moral preaching.
She bought books for use by immigrant children in their family languages
and promoted storytelling. Her column on children's books, "The Three
Owls," ran in the *New York Herald Tribune* from 1924 to 1930. From
1936 until her death she wrote a column for the *Horn Book*. Moore retired
in 1941. She died on January 20, 1961. *DAB*; *DALB*.

References

Sayers, Frances Clarke. 1972. *Anne Carroll Moore: A Biography*. New York: Ath-
     eneum.
Spain, Frances Lander. 1956. Reading without Boundaries: Essays Presented to Anne
     Carroll Moore. New York: New York Public Library.

MORRILL PUBLIC LIBRARY, HIAWATHA, KS   431 Oregon, Hiawatha, KS
66434. Population served: 3,285. Circulation: 87,373. Holdings: 40,390.
LJ October 1, 2010: 3-star library.

MORTON COUNTY LIBRARY, ELKHART, KS   410 Kansas, Elkhart, KS
67950. Founded 1922. Population served: 3,269. Circulation: 116,024.
Holdings: 41,782. LJ February 15, 2009; November 15, 2009, and October 1, 2010: 5-star library.

MORTON GROVE PUBLIC LIBRARY, IL   6140 Lincoln Ave., Morton Grove,
IL 60053. Founded 1938. Population served: 22,451. Circulation: 262,760.
Holdings: 117,194. The library developed "Fiction-L," an electronic mail
list for readers' advisory librarians, in 1995. It is still running (2010).

MOTION PICTURES. *See* AUDIOVISUAL COLLECTIONS.

MOUND CITY, KS. *See* LINN COUNTY LIBRARY DISTRICT #4, MOUND
CITY, KS.

MOUNT PLEASANT PUBLIC LIBRARY, UT   24 E. Main, Mount Pleasant, UT 84647. Population served: 2,588. Circulation: 103,597. Holdings: 23,459. LJ February 15, 2009; November 15, 2009; and October 1, 2010: 3-star library. HAPLR 2009, 2010.

MULTNOMAH COUNTY LIBRARY, PORTLAND, OR   205 NE Russell St., Portland, OR 97212. Founded 1902 as a tax-supported library; earlier library dates to 1864. The oldest public library west of the Mississippi (library website). Population served: 717,880. Circulation: 21,513,255. Holdings: 1,955,041. 17 branches. The 1912 building is on the National Register of Historic Places. LJ February 15, 2009, and November 15, 2009: 5-star library; October 1, 2010: 3-star library. HAPLR 2009, 2010. Directors: Mary Frances Isom, 1902–1920; Anne M. Mulheron, 1920–1937; Nell Avery Unger, 1937–1953; Bernard Van Horne, 1953–1959; Mary E. Phillips (acting), 1959–1960; William B. Wood, 1961–1963; Mary E. Phillips, 1963–1972; James E. Burghardt, 1972–1984; Cecile L. Carpenter (acting), 1984–1985; Sarah Ann Long, 1985–1989; Charles Davis, 1989–1990; Ginnie Cooper, 1990–2002; Ruth Metz (interim), 2003; Molly Raphael, 2003–2009; and Vailey Oehlke, 2009–.

MUNDELEIN, IL. *See* FREMONT PUBLIC LIBRARY DISTRICT, MUNDELEIN, IL.

MUNN, RALPH, 1894–1975   Born Aurora, IL, September 19, 1894. Munn grew up in Colorado, attending the University of Denver (AB, 1916; LLB 1917). He served in the army in France, 1917–1919. He earned a BLS from New York State Library School, 1921. Munn was a reference librarian in the Seattle Public Library, 1921–1925, then assistant librarian, 1925–1926. He directed the public library in Flint, MI, 1926–1928, then went to the Carnegie Library of Pittsburgh in 1928, remaining to 1964. He was also director, then dean of the Carnegie Library School, 1928–1962. He made library surveys in Australia and New Zealand in 1934 and three years later made a tour of Central and South American libraries, representing the American Library Association (ALA) and the U.S. Department of State. He advocated the merger of the Carnegie Free Library of Allegheny with Carnegie Library of Pittsburgh in 1956 and extended service to all residents of Allegheny County. His efforts at library development in the state brought a distinguished service award from the Pennsylvania Library Association in 1959. Munn introduced modern management practices, public relations, and library cooperation. He insisted on quality over demand in book selection policy. He saw the public library role as service to "opinion leaders" (Williams 1988, 73). He was president of the Pennsylvania Library Association, 1930–1931, and of the ALA, 1939–1940. Death came on January 2, 1975, in Pittsburgh. *DALB*.

Reference

Williams, Patrick. 1988. *The American Public Library and the Problem of Purpose.* New York: Greenwood Press.

MUSIC COLLECTIONS

Terminology

For library purposes, "music" is taken to mean materials (print, nonprint, or digital) in musical notation, and recordings of performances in video or audio formats. "Notation" means any system of symbols used to write down music. Library collections of music also include writings about music, generally labeled "music literature." Music periodicals are a segment of music literature.

The term "score" is used to describe "the copy of a musical composition in written or printed notation" (*Merriam*). When the composition consists of more than one part sounding simultaneously, the score is written down so that "the simultaneous moments of all voices or parts are aligned vertically" (*New Harvard Dictionary of Music* 1986). A music collection consists primarily of scores, recordings, and music literature. The collection may also include films, photographs, and other illustrative materials; musical instruments; objects associated with musicians; realia of all kinds; and literature on topics related to music.

Scores have their own terminology. A "full score" is one that presents notation for all the parts of a composition, each on its own staff. "Full" here means "complete." However, the same phrase is applied to a score that is "full size," meaning one of physical dimensions suitable for reading by a conductor in performance; it is sometimes referred to as a "conductors' score." Such a score measures about 32 cm high by 22 cm wide. A full (complete) score may also appear in smaller dimensions under the name "miniature score." A miniature score, usually measuring about 18 cm by 13 cm, is full (in the sense of complete) but is suitable for study rather than performance. It is necessary to confront these distinctions when a library makes collection development decisions.

Works for voices and instruments, such as operas and oratorios, are usually published in full score (large and miniature) and in "vocal score" (also called "piano-vocal score"). A vocal score has notation for all the vocal parts of the work, just as they appear in the full score. But instead of notation for all the instrumental parts, there is a condensation of those parts into a single part for piano. A vocal score is well suited for study, for "following along" a performance, and for rehearsal of the voice parts. In most public libraries it is the accepted format of opera and oratorio publications.

In ensemble playing, each instrumentalist and singer is provided with a partial score, one that displays only the individual part to be performed. This format is known simply as a "part." A library that serves a performing ensemble, like a band or orchestra, will need to have a full (complete, conductors' score) of each work to be played, along with individual parts for each performer: a set known as "score and parts." In practice, such sets are often rented from the publisher as required.

"Sheet music" refers to a score made up of one or more unbound sheets of music; the genre encompasses popular songs as well as shorter classical works.

"Arrangements," in which an original composition is rendered for other voices or instruments, may be written out in full score format or presented in a kind of shorthand that notates only melody lines and chords.

The recording collection presents another vocabulary. The preeminent format today is the disc, "a flat circular object employed to receive and retain sound signals" (Marco 1993, 189). From 1887 to 1924 discs were recorded by the "acoustic" method, in which all the energy comes from the sound waves themselves. Such discs are often referred to as "acoustics." Electrical energy has been used in recording since 1924. A "78" is a disc made to revolve at about 78 rpm, the industry norm from around 1920 to 1948. An "LP" is a "long-playing" disc made to revolve at 33[[comp: Please use a piece fraction for 1/3.]]1/3 rpm; it was the final form of the "analog" recording process. In the analog process the form of the input signal resembles that of the stored signal. Analog was succeeded by "digital" recording, in which the input signal is converted to a series of digits in computer-readable form. The computer examines the signal thousands of times per second ("sampling") and generates chains of pulses. A laser beam cuts corresponding pits into the storage surface. In playback mode, the pulses are reconverted to the original signal values to re-create the initial audio input. Digital technology is the basis for the "compact disc," or "CD," introduced in 1983 by Philips and SONY. Public library collections are now focused on the CD, although some libraries retain LPs. Except in research libraries, the 78 has been eclipsed.

Research collections will give their users detailed information about recordings, at least those of special interest. Facts presented may include the issue date or release date (usually not on the record itself), the "matrix number" (on 78s and LPs), the "take" (the performance, of several recorded, that was actually published), and the recording session date.

Another recording format uses rolls of moving tape (originally steel wire). Varying magnetic patterns that correspond to sound waves can be imposed on a moving magnetizable surface, and such patterns can be played back on appropriate equipment. The first working magnetic recorder, devised by Valdemar Poulsen, dates from 1898; it used a steel wire. In 1928 the first patents for paper or plastic recording tape were issued. In the 1930s machines suitable for broadcasting were available. With the introduction of Mylar plastic tape and high-quality "reel-to-reel" equipment, in the late 1940s, the format achieved high quality and wide popularity. Philips introduced the audiocassette (or "cassette") in 1963, creating a convenient device that competed with LP discs. Public libraries were interested in the cassette, but it presented the problem of easy damage by users. With the rise of the CD, prerecorded audiocassettes of music lost their place in the market, but cassettes of spoken material retained a niche. Today the principal function of cassettes is for copying material from radio, live performance, or other formats.

Two older formats should be mentioned since they appear in collections of public libraries that support research. One is the original medium used to record and replay sounds, the "cylinder" invention of Thomas Edison in 1877. Edison's company continued to market cylinders until 1929; they carry a rich repertoire not available on discs. The cylinder player was called a "phonograph," as opposed to the "gramophone," which was the disc player; however, this distinction faded with the demise of the cylinder.

Piano rolls and player pianos were popular in the United States from the early 1900s. The basic type of roll was a paper roll with holes punched into it at the factory. Those holes activated a mechanism that depressed corresponding piano keys. A more interesting variant was the "reproducing piano roll," which was created by a pianist in actual performance. A substantial repertoire of those rolls emerged from 1904 to the end of the 1920s. Special "reproducing pianos" were needed to make this happen. Recently, digital technology has been used to transfer the music of the rolls to modern formats (Permut 1993). Piano rolls were available at the Evanston (IL) Public Library in 1907 and in several other libraries within a few years.

Historical Summary

Systematic collection of music materials in American public libraries began near the end of the nineteenth century. (In Britain music scores were acquired and circulated by public libraries from the outset.) A few American libraries did begin earlier to develop collections of music. Boston Public Library was buying music as early as 1855 and made a major purchase, of the DeKoudelka collection, in 1858 (Marco 1976a; Bradley 1981; Bowles 1993; these sources provided most of the facts in this section). In 1894, Boston acquired the important collection of Allen Brown. In New York, the Drexel and Lenox libraries, which would be part of the New York Public Library in 1895, had music materials for reference use.

The first known circulating library of music was that of Brooklyn Public Library, which commenced "an experiment" in lending scores in 1882 (Bardwell 1887). Music was available in the St. Louis Public Library sometime before 1889, the Providence Public Library in 1892, the Newton (MA) Free Library and Syracuse (NY) Public Library in 1893, and the Brookline (MA) and Hartford (CT) libraries in 1895. When New York Public Library was established in 1895, it offered musical materials. In 1896, Forbes Library in Northampton, MA, circulated music. Other pre-1900 libraries to do so were Buffalo, Milwaukee, and Lowell, MA.

Evanston (IL) Public Library seems to have been (as mentioned above) the first to circulate sound recordings; they were in the piano roll format. Cylinder records were in the Forbes Library in 1912. A 1913 report by the Music Teachers National Association found piano rolls in seven New York libraries and gramophone (disc) records in seven New York and four California libraries (Bowles 1993, 674). St. Paul reported a circulation of 3,505 in 1914, from a stock of 600 records. A survey of 1917–1918 disclosed that 1,016 libraries had music sections or music collections of some kind. Despite objections from some librarians "that recordings were fragile and easily damaged, that their sound quality was poor and deteriorated with use, and that they were very expensive for only three minutes of sound" (Bowles 1993, 674), public demand resulted in wide acceptance of records in public libraries. By 1949, such collections were of sufficient consequence to merit a separate volume in the important survey issued by Columbia University, the *Public Library Inquiry* (Luening 1949). Today it would be a curiosity to find a central public library without any sound recordings, although that situation does appear in branches. Scores are another matter: they are still collected by larger libraries but are rare in smaller ones.

Two organizations have influenced the growth and quality of music collections in public and academic libraries. The Music Library Association (MLA) was established in 1931 and soon became the focus of research in all aspects of music librarianship. Its quarterly journal, *Notes*, began publication in 1934. A series of "technical reports" commenced in 1973 (31 issued through April 2010). The Association for Recorded Sound Collections was organized in 1966. Its *ARSC Journal* first appeared in 1968, offering research articles and reviews.

Several publications signaled the maturity of music librarianship. An overview of the music library field, emphasizing British public library tradition, appeared in 1959 (Bryant 1959); its second edition introduced elements of American practice (Bryant 1985). Printed catalogs of the music collections in the New York Public Library (New York Public Library 1964) and the Boston Public Library (Boston Public Library 1972) revealed the remarkable development of music as a public library domain of interest. The New York division moved from the library's central building on Fifth Avenue to Lincoln Center in 1965, named the Rodgers and Hammerstein Archives of Recorded Sound. The collections in the archives, numbering more than half a million items, are second in size and importance only to those of the Library of Congress. The *Encyclopedia of Library and Information Science* devoted 165 pages to a state-of-the-art group of articles on "Music Libraries and Collections" in 1976 (Marco 1976b). A detailed inventory of music collections in American libraries appeared in 1981 (Bradley 1981).

Current Practice and Issues

In large urban libraries the typical organizational plans have either a separate music department (variously titled) or a unit that combines music with fine arts. Scores, recordings, and literature on music are brought into proximity. Medium-size libraries are less likely to have separate departments. If there is a separate department, its head usually reports to the director of public services. A survey of organizational matters with a useful bibliography appeared in *Encyclopedia of Library and Information Science* (Marco 1976c).

Collection development is the first task. A detailed policy, based on the library's general policy, is important (*see* COLLECTION DEVELOPMENT). It specifies the types of scores, recordings, and literature that the department intends to have, with some kind of "intensity" values (Coover 1973; Luttman 2004). Building collections in special areas is often simplified by checking lists of selected titles (e.g., concerned with lists of popular music; Halliday 2001). Acquisition is the next task, and it offers a range of problems. Lack of bibliographic control, in the sense of inventories of what has been published, has been a pervasive challenge to librarians who work with scores and recordings. While national and trade bibliographies are fairly adequate in covering the output of printed books and periodicals, they are deficient with respect to music materials. There are no comprehensive, or continuing, lists of scores, nor is there a musical equivalent to *Books in Print*. Sound recordings have never been under bibliographic control (Marco 1989). However, individual libraries are making their catalogs available online, and *WorldCat* offers a union catalog of holdings reported by member libraries. Amazon presents purchase options for scores and CDs in popular and classical genres. In practice, library acquisition—and to some extent selection—is now centered on Web resources. A number of vendors offer packages to libraries that facilitate the entire acquisition process (*see* ACQUISITIONS). Reviews of new music and recordings are featured in *Notes* and *ARSC Journal*. One of the MLA's Basic Manuals gives guidance on the whole acquisitions procedure, with extensive references to other writings (Fling 2004).

Cataloging and classification of scores and recordings has long been a special preoccupation of music librarians (Bradley 2003). A particular challenge has been the variability of titles that a single composition may have. A score or recording may identify a work in its original language or in translation by its key, number in its series, opus number, or popular title. Of course these representations need to be brought together in the library catalog, along with arrangements of all kinds:

> The confusion arising from the common problem of the same piece of music being stocked in different editions with varying title pages, because of publication in one or other of a number of countries, has been solved with a high degree of success by the use of what was called (in the 1941 MLA code) the conventional title, but is now called (in AACR) the uniform title ... it is now standard practice in the well catalogued music collection. (Bryant 1985, 161–62)

Recent thinking on the matter of uniform title may not be supportive of the concept. In the "Dublin Core" approach, for instance, the cataloger takes the title and other information directly from the source before her (Coleman 2005). The idea is that a key word search of a computer catalog will bring up a needed work regardless of the title chosen. Bringing together all the permutations of a title serves a purpose in a card catalog but seems less relevant in a computer catalog where there is no actual "together." Nevertheless, the MLA has provided a technical report on uniform titles (Koth 2008) that follows tradition.

Several cataloging codes have been promulgated, most of them in two or more editions. Responsible parties have been the MLA, the American Library Association, the Library of Congress, the International Association of Music Libraries, the British Library, and the (British) Library Association. The history of cataloging codes for music has been narrated in detail by Bryant (1985). For recent developments in cataloging codes, which include practice for music materials, *see* CATALOGING.

Classification schemes for music also have a long history. The early designs (Brown, Cutter, Bliss) have disappeared by conversion to other systems. Today's music librarian chooses to follow one of the two major classifications: Dewey Decimal Classification (DDC) or Library of Congress Classification (LCC). These quite different structures have been modified through many editions. The DDC, "the best known and most widely used system in the world today," is nevertheless much criticized for its music schedules, which "can only be regarded as unsatisfactory, both in outline and in difficulties of consistent application" (Bryant 1985, 214; this work offers a critical comparison of several DDC editions). The first edition of the music classification in LCC was published in 1904. It has been through many revisions, and despite its oddities—such as the creation of a hazy section of works labeled MT, for "music theory"—seems to be the current system of choice. The MLA has issued a technical report to assist catalogers in its use (Smiraglia 2008). Another MLA document reviewed various classification systems (McKnight 2002), and Carol Bradley (2003) has examined classification practice in American libraries. Some issues in cataloging popular music are taken up in an article by Terry Simkins (2001).

Describing sound recordings, whether to catalog them in a library or to list them in a discography, is an activity that is becoming more formalized (Smolian 1976; Marco 1994; Brooks 2000) after years without clear rules and regulations. A great deal of information is required for a description that meets scholarly standards, and much of that information is usually not on the disc—whatever the format—or in the accompanying notes. Thus, the discographer (or the library cataloger of discs) is pressed to do research in a variety of sources, many of them ephemeral. Discography is a topic that goes beyond description of recordings into the history of sound recording, industry matters, technical developments, and so on; thorough cataloging will often draw on knowledge of these areas (Stevenson 1972; Bowles 1993; Marco 1993).

Sound recordings have been troublesome for classifiers. Since classification leads to shelving arrangement, the issue is one of importance for library users who go directly to the collection without looking up items in the catalog. Instead of classification with its call numbers, many librarians have suggested shelf arrangement of recordings by manufacturer number, accession number, composer and medium, arrangement by medium, and arrangement by genre. Clearly some of these plans prove awkward for browsing (for a discussion of all these possibilities and a detailed bibliography, see Buth 1975). In the end, what seems practical and simple is to classify recordings (LPs and

CDs) by DDC or LCC. The inherent problem remains: both LP and CD formats, as opposed to the 78 format, promote multiple titles on one disc, so the classifier must decide which title will be the basis for classification, and the user must have recourse to the catalog after all to identify those other titles that eluded classification.

A recent concern relative to sound recordings is whether they will prevail in current disc formats or be replaced by downloading from web sources (Hoek 2009). This question was discussed at the MLA 2009 conference. As of 2010, the transformation has not yet occurred.

Reference service in music departments, like reference service elsewhere, has been radically simplified in the online environment. It is now quick and easy to find facts through Google, bibliographic data through *WorldCat* or library online catalogs, and music and words to individual pieces through such services as ebrary. Citations can be gathered through ProQuest, often with downloadable full texts. Libraries may have to pay considerable sums for access to such websites—ebrary, for example, costs $3,000 per year. One disadvantage in the online universe is multiplicity; another is lack of standards. These are matters of general interest to librarians (*see* REFERENCE AND INFORMATION SERVICES). So-called virtual reference is an aspect of modern music reference service (Szymanski and Fields 2005).

Preservation of music materials has become a significant concern in the digital age. While 78s and LPs could last "forever" if handled carefully, the newer media may be less durable (Swartzburg 1993). All media demand appropriate storage. Richard Warren (1993) presented a detailed picture of good storage practice, covering building specifications, temperature, humidity, shelving, cleaning, containers, and sleeves. His measures and suggestions serve as a basis for practice in music departments. The National Institute of Standards and Technology (2003) presented a guide for handling CDs and DVDs, with the reassuring prediction that those media have a respectable life span; library CDs may well last 100 to 200 years. Conditions that affect life span include humidity, light, solvents, magnetism, X-rays, microwaves, radiation, smudges, dirt, dust, and even wear from repeated playing. An important symposium about preservation of audio collections was held in Austin in 2003. The papers have been published (Matz 2004).

Apart from digital formats, preservation is a concern for libraries with cylinder collections. Hardly any of the extant records have been copied into durable media. A project at University of California, Santa Barbara, is one effort to digitize a large (6,000 titles) collection. (Farrington 2007).

Printed music deteriorates like any other paper medium. Conservation methods include copying and enclosure in plastic. Bindings and enclosures need attention to prevent damage. MLA has issued guidelines for handling printed music (Carli 2003).

For copyright matters, *see* COPYRIGHT; specific concerns of music librarians with digital media are addressed in a regular column, "Copyright and Fair Use," in *ARSC Journal*.

Finally, in this account of recent issues, there is a long-standing concern about qualifications and training of music librarians. Writings on the topic may be traced to a 1937 article by Otto Kinkeldey, musicologist and chief of the New York Public Library Music Division. His view, still widely held, was that a music librarian is first of all a librarian and, second, one with a certain knowledge of music:

> A reasonable acquaintance with musical theory in the widest acceptance of the word; knowledge of all its principles and technical terms is a fair requirement. A music librarian who did not recognize a fugue when he heard it, or saw it on paper, or who did not know the meaning of the term double counterpoint, would be as useful as a literary librarian who did not know the difference between a sonnet and an epic, or a science librarian who could not recognize an equation of the second degree when he saw it, or who could not distinguish between a genus and species name. (Kinkeldey 1937, 300)

A continuing discussion in the profession has left unanswered the fundamental questions on training: Is the Kinkeldey formula, library training plus musical knowledge, the right one? Or is the reverse combination preferable? Should advanced degrees in both librarianship and music be necessary qualifications? What should library schools teach? (Solow et al. 1974; Marco and Freitag 1975; Morrow 2000; Oates 2004). The present situation in the accredited library schools points to a number of paths. Most schools have no courses or programs in music librarianship. Some, like the University of Illinois and Kent State University, offer a course in music bibliography or music librarianship. A master's program in music librarianship is offered at Buffalo. The most intense program is available at Dominican University in cooperation with Northwestern University School of Music: it leads to dual master's degrees in librarianship and music. Among all these possibilities, the person who wishes to be a music specialist, particularly in a public library, must have—to quote Kinkeldey (1937) again—"a deep interest in, and even a love for, the art of music. I cannot conceive of anyone who would want to become a music librarian without this" (300).

References

Bardwell, W. A. 1887. A library of music. *Library Journal* 12, no. 4 (April): 159.

Boston Public Library. 1972. *Dictionary Catalogue of the Music Collection*. 20 vols. Boston: G. K. Hall.

Bowles, Garrett H. 1993. Sound recordings and the library. In *Encyclopedia of Recorded Sound in the United States*, ed. Guy A. Marco, 673–77. New York: Garland.

Bradley, Carol June. 1973. *Reader in Music Librarianship*. Washington: Microcard Editions.

Bradley, Carol June. 1976. Music libraries in North America. In *Encyclopedia of Library and Information Science* 18: 358–425. New York: Marcel Dekker.

Bradley, Carol June. 1981. *Music Collections in American Libraries*. Detroit Studies in Music Bibliography, 46. Detroit: Information Coordinators.

Bradley, Carol June. 2003. Classifying and cataloging music in American libraries: a historical review. *Cataloging & Classification Quarterly* 35, no. 3/4 (March): 467–81.

Bradley, Carol June. 2005. *American Music Librarianship: A Research and Information Guide*. New York: Routledge.

Brooks, Tim. 2000. Discographical guidelines for the *ARSC Journal*: Identifying sources in discographies. *ARSC Journal* 31, no. 2 (Fall): 276–81.

Bryant, E. T. 1959. *Music Librarianship: A Practical Guide*. London: Clarke; New York: Hafner.

Bryant, E. T. 1985. *Music Librarianship: A Practical Guide*. 2nd ed., with the assistance of Guy A. Marco. Metuchen, NJ: Scarecrow Press.

Buth, Olga. 1975. Scores and recordings. *Library Trends* 22, no. 3 (January): 427–50.

Carli, Alice. 2003. *Binding and Care of Printed Music*. Music Library Association Basic Manuals. Lanham, MD: Scarecrow Press.

Coleman, Anita S. 2005. From cataloging to metadata: Dublin Core records for the library catalog. In *Metadata: A Cataloger's Primer*, ed. Richard P. Smiraglia, 153–81. Binghamton, NY: Haworth.

Coover, James B. 1973. Selection policies for a university music library. In *Reader in Music Librarianship*, ed. Carol June Bradley, 236–46. Washington, DC: Microcard Editions.

Farrington, Jim. 2007. Cylinder preservation and digitization project. *Notes* 64, no. 1 (September): 121–24.

Fling, R. Michael. 2004. *Library Acquisition of Music*. Music Library Association Basic Manuals, 4. Lanham, MD: Scarecrow Press.

Halliday, Blane. 2001. Identifying library policy issues in list checking. In *Library Evaluation: A Casebook and Can-do Guide*, ed. Danny P. Wallace and Connie Van Fleet, 140–52. Englewood, CO: Libraries Unlimited.

Hoek, D. J. 2009. The download dilemma. *American Libraries* 40, no. 8/9 (August/September): 54–57.

Kinkeldey, Otto. 1937. Training for music librarianship: aims and opportunities. *American Library Association Bulletin* 31, no. 8 (August): 459–63. Reprinted in *Reader in Music Librarianship*, ed. Carol June Bradley, 299–302. Washington, DC: Microcard Editions.

Koth, Michelle S. 2008. *Uniform Titles for Music*. Music Library Association Technical Reports, 31. Lanham, MD: Scarecrow Press.

Luening, Otto. 1949. *Music Materials and the Public Library*. New York: Columbia University Press.

Luttman, Stephen. 2004. Selection of music materials. *Acquisitions Librarian* 16, no. 31/32 (February): 11–25.

McKnight, Mark. 2002. *Music Classification Systems*. Music Library Association Basic Manuals, 1. Lanham, MD: Scarecrow Press.

Marco, Guy A., ed. 1976a. Historical survey. In *Encyclopedia of Library and Information Science* 18: 340–58. New York: Marcel Dekker.

Marco, Guy A., ed. 1976b. Music libraries and collections. [A collection of 11 articles by various authors.] In *Encyclopedia of Library and Information Science* 18: 318–493. New York: Marcel Dekker.

Marco, Guy A., ed. 1976c. Nature and organization of music libraries. In *Encyclopedia of Library and Information Science* 18: 328–40. New York: Marcel Dekker.

Marco, Guy A., ed. 1989. Bibliographic control of sound recording: An international view. *Audiovisual Librarian* (England) 15, no. 1 (February): 19–24.

Marco, Guy A., ed. 1993. *Encyclopedia of Recorded Sound in the United States.* New York: Garland.

Marco, Guy A., ed. 1994. Bibliographic and bibliothecal considerations for discographers. *ARSC Journal* 25: 1–8.

Marco, Guy A., and Wolfgang Freitag. 1975. Training the librarian for rapport with the collection. *Library Trends* 23, no. 3 (January): 541–45.

Matz, Judith. 2004. *Sound Savings: Preserving Audio Collections.* Washington, DC: Association of Research Libraries.

Morrow, Jean. 2000. Education for music librarianship. *Notes* 56, no. 3 (March): 655.

National Institute of Standards and Technology. 2003. *Care and Handling of CDs and DVDs: A Guide for Librarians and Archivists.* NIST Special Publication 500-252, by Fred. R. Byers. Washington, DC: U.S. Department of Commerce.

New Harvard Dictionary of Music. 1986. Cambridge, MA: Harvard University Press.

New York Public Library. 1964. *Dictionary Catalog of the Music Collection.* Boston: G. K. Hall, 1964/1965. 33 vols. and 2 supplements. 2nd ed., 1982, 45 vols.

New York Public Library. 1981. *Dictionary Catalog of the Rodgers & Hammerstein Archives of Recorded Sound.* Boston: G.K. Hall. 15 vols.

Oates, Jennifer. 2004. Music librarianship education: Problems and solutions. *Music Reference Services Quarterly* 8, no. 3 (March): 1–24.

Permut, Steven. 1993. Reproducing piano rolls. In *Encyclopedia of Recorded Sound in the United States*, ed. Guy A. Marco, 582–85. New York: Garland.

Simkins, Terry. 2001. Cataloging popular music recordings. *Cataloging & Classification Quarterly* 31, no. 2: 1–35.

Smiraglia, Richard. 2008. *Shelflisting Music: Guidelines for Use with the Library of Congress Classification M.* Music Library Association Technical Reports, 30. Lanham, MD: Scarecrow Press.

Smolian, Steven. 1976. Standards for the review of discographic works. *ARSC Journal* 7, no. 3: 47–55.

Solow, Linda, et al. 1974. Qualifications of a music librarian. Issued by the Music Library Association Committee on Professional Education. *Journal of Education for Librarianship* 15, no. 1 (Summer): 53–59.

Stevenson, Gordon. 1972. Discography: Scientific, analytical, historical, and systematic. *Library Trends* 21, no. 1 (July): 101–35.

Swartzburg, Susan. 1993. Preservation of sound recordings. In *Encyclopedia of Recorded Sound in the United States*, ed. Guy A. Marco, 542–46. New York: Garland.

Szymanski, Gerald, and Mary Alice Fields. 2005. Virtual reference in the music library. *Notes* 61, no. 3 (March): 634–59.

Warren, Richard, Jr. 1993. Storage of sound recordings. *ARSC Journal* 24, no. 2 (Fall): 130–75.

N

NAMPA PUBLIC LIBRARY, ID   101 E. 11th Ave., Nampa, ID 83651. Founded 1904. Population served: 81,840. Circulation: 741,087. Holdings: 140,607. It was reported in April 2008 that in response to a challenge by a resident, the library board had relocated *The New Joy of Sex* and *The Joy of Gay Sex* to the director's office, accessible to patrons only by specific request. Pressure from the American Civil Liberties Union of Idaho led to reconsideration by the board, which voted on September 5, 2008, to return both books to open circulation.

NAPERVILLE PUBLIC LIBRARY, IL   200 W. Jefferson Ave., Naperville, IL 60540. Founded 1898. Population served: 138,400. Circulation: 4,665,000. Holdings: 800,000. 2 branches. LJ February 15, 2009; November 15, 2009; and October 1, 2010: 5-star library. HAPLR 2009, 2010.

NASHVILLE PUBLIC LIBRARY, TN   615 Church St., Nashville, TN 37219. Founded 1901 (library website). The Howard Library, 1901, was the city's first free circulating library. Population served: 570,785. Circulation: 4,203,335. Holdings: 2,011,149. 23 branches. The 1904 building was designed by Ackerman and Ross. Blacks were not allowed in the library until community agitation led to a Carnegie grant for a separate Negro branch. Marian Hadley, a black librarian, went to Louisville (which had a colored branch since 1910) for training, then took up duties as head of the new branch; it opened February 10, 1916. There was a standard branch collection, augmented by materials by black authors, books on the Old South, and books on the Negro experience in America. Directors: Mary Hannah

Johnson, 1904–1912; Margaret Kercheval, 1912–1920; G. H. Baskette, 1920–1927; Harold F. Brigham, 1927–1931; Francis K. Drury, 1931–1946; Robert S. Alvarez, 1946–1959; David Marshall Stewart, 1960–1985; Caroline Phillippe Stark, 1985–1994; Donna D'Arminio Nicely, 1995–.

Reference

Malone, Cheryl Knott. 2003. The adult collection at Nashville's Negro Public Library, 1915–1916. In *Libraries to the People: Histories of Outreach*, ed. Robert S. Freeman and David M. Hovde, 148–156. Jefferson, NC: McFarland.

NATIONAL CITY PUBLIC LIBRARY, CA   1401 National City Blvd., National City, CA 91950. Population served: 63,773. Circulation: 305,000. Holdings: 110,000. LJ November 15, 2009: 4-star library; October 1, 2010: 3-star library.

NEDERLAND COMMUNITY LIBRARY, CO   20 Lakeview Dr., Nederland, CO 80466. Founded 2002. Population served: 1,621. Circulation: 15,879. Holdings: 8,552. LJ November 15, 2009: 3-star library.

NELIGH PUBLIC LIBRARY, NE   710 Main St., Neligh, NE 68756. Founded 1905. Population served: 1,651. Circulation: 42,553. Holdings: 16, 508. LJ February 15, 2009: 5-star library; November 15, 2009, and October 1, 2010: 4-star library. HAPLR 2009, 2010.

NELSONVILLE PUBLIC LIBRARY (ATHENS COUNTY PUBLIC LIBRARIES), OH   95 W. Washington, Nelsonville, OH 45764. Founded 1935 as a school district library under the name Public Library of the City of Nelsonville and Athens County. Although the legal name is Nelsonville Public Library, it is commonly known as the Athens County Public Libraries. Population served: 62,062. Circulation: 597,121. Holdings: 254,987. 7 locations. In 1802 or 1804 the "Coonskin Library" opened in Ames Township, Athens County. Pioneer settlers collected coonskins and sold them for cash to buy books. The library operated until 1861. A Coonskin Library Museum opened in May 1994.

NEODESHA, KS. *See* W. A. RANKIN MEMORIAL LIBRARY, NEODESHA, KS.

NETWORKS OF LIBRARIES. *See* COOPERATION.

NEW BERLIN LIBRARY, NY   15 S. Main St., New Berlin, NY 13411. Population served: 1,129. Circulation: 16, 974. Holdings: 21,493. LJ February 15, 2009; November 15, 2009, and October 1, 2010: 5-star library.

NEW CARLISLE AND OLIVE TOWNSHIP PUBLIC LIBRARY, IN   408 S. Bray St., New Carlisle, IN 46552. Founded 1918. Population served: 3,914.

Circulation: 103,545. Holdings: 41,116. LJ November 15, 2009: 5-star library; October 1, 2010: 4-star library.

NEW CARLISLE PUBLIC LIBRARY, OH   111 E. Lake Ave., New Carlisle, OH 45344. Founded 1936. Population served: 5,652. Circulation: 194,108. Holdings: 63,522. LJ February 15, 2009; November 15, 2009, and October 1, 2010: 5-star library. HAPLR 2009, 2010.

NEW CUMBERLAND PUBLIC LIBRARY, PA   One Benjamin Plaza, New Cumberland, PA 17070. Population served: 7,349. Circulation: 267,021. Holdings: 75,244. LJ February 15, 2009: 3-star library; November 15, 2009: 4-star library; October 1, 2010: 3-star library. HAPLR 2009, 2010.

NEW ORLEANS PUBLIC LIBRARY, LA   219 Loyola Ave., New Orleans, LA 70112. Founded 1896. Population served: 484,674. Circulation: 1,272,033. Holdings: 705,339. 11 branches. All the branches were damaged or destroyed by Hurricane Katrina. While all have since reopened, they are in temporary locations. Two branches, Algiers Regional and East New Orleans, were closed temporarily in June 2011 so that they could be moved to new locations. *See also* HURRICANES KATRINA AND RITA.

NEW SHOREHAM, RI. *See* ISLAND FREE LIBRARY, NEW SHOREHAM, RI.

NEW WINDSOR, MD. *See* CARROLL COUNTY PUBLIC LIBRARY, NEW WINDSOR, MD.

NEW WOODSTOCK FREE LIBRARY, NY   2106 Main St., New Woodstock, NY 13122. Founded 1939. Population served: 900. Circulation: 55,439. Holdings: 25,900. HAPLR 2009, 2010.

NEW YORK PUBLIC LIBRARY

Terminology and Present Situation

The official name of the library is New York Public Library, Astor, Lenox, and Tilden Foundations (referred to here as NYPL). Founded in 1895, it serves the New York City boroughs of Manhattan, Bronx, and Staten Island; the other two boroughs, Queens and Brooklyn, have separate public libraries. NYPL consists of a central building at 476 Fifth Avenue (10018) and a number of branches. Some of the 113 units designated as branches (*ALD* 2009–2010) are departments housed in the central building, while others are circulating libraries located throughout the three boroughs. The count by borough is Manhattan, 35; Bronx, 34; and Staten Island, 12. Administratively NYPL is cast in two principal segments: the research libraries (named the reference department until 1966) and the branch libraries (named the circulation department until 1966). Materials in the research libraries—which is to say the holdings in the central building—are noncirculating, while materials in the branch libraries are, with exceptions for reference books and the like, available for borrowing. With holdings in excess of 20 million volumes (including 5,169,953 volumes in the circulating branches), NYPL is one of the largest libraries in the United States. Circulation was 16,556,899 in 2008. If the primary population served is taken to be that of Manhattan, Bronx, and Staten Island (i.e., 3,669,005), the circulation count per capita is 4.5. However, NYPL offers library cards and borrowing privileges beyond that geographical border: to all residents, students, or taxpayers of New York State. The state resident population (2008) is 19,490,297. Evidently the usual per capita calculations are awkward to apply in this case.

As a resource for scholarship, NYPL ranks with the major libraries of the world. In all fields of knowledge, imposing collections, including great rarities, are to be found. These collections originated in the library's ancestors: the Astor and Lenox libraries. A volume describing many of the remarkable materials has been published (Davidson and McTigue 1988).

The central building, opened in 1911, is highly regarded for its architectural qualities and its functional design. It is a New York City landmark building and (since 1965) a National Historic Landmark. Some facts about the structure are given in the section "Historical Summary" below.

In terms of organization and administration, NYPL is unique among U.S. public libraries. The officer in charge is titled president; the office has been filled only by nonlibrarians. There is a director who is responsible to the president; that office has been held by librarians. In 2010 the president was Paul LeClerc. Effective July 1, 2011, the president will be Anthony W. Marx. David Ferriero, appointed director in 2004, resigned in 2009 to accept President Obama's nomination as archivist of the United States; he assumed that office (the first librarian to hold it) on November 13, 2009. The total staff of NYPL in 2009 was 3,147 persons.

Historical Summary

NYPL came into being on May 23, 1895, when an agreement of consolidation, reached after extensive negotiation, was signed by the trustees of three earlier organizations: the Astor Library, the Lenox Library, and the Tilden Trust. This amalgamation was enhanced in the years following by the acquisition of 10 other libraries, listed here with their founding years and the years when they joined NYPL: Harlem Library (1825–1903), Washington Heights Library (1868–1901), New York Free Circulating Library (1878–1900), Aguilar Free Library (1866–1903), Cathedral Library (1887–1904), University Settlement Library (1887–1903), Webster Free Library (1892–1903), St. Agnes Free Library (1893–1901), and Tottenville Library

(1899–1903). These founding dates (from Lydenberg 1923, vii) are not necessarily firm since such dates are variously reckoned (by trustee agreement, by incorporation, by actual opening, and so on). A brief account of the major libraries involved is in order.

The library of John Jacob Astor, incorporated in 1849, was the "first large public library designed and developed primarily for scholars and research workers" (Dain 1972, 5). It opened in 1854 in a landmark building (still standing) on Lafayette Place with some 80,000 volumes. Joseph Green Cogswell was superintendent; he remained until 1861. Astor and Cogswell shared a vision for the library: a general, nonspecialized collection open to researchers across the disciplines, with all material noncirculating and the shelves closed to readers. There was criticism of the closed-shelf policy, but Cogswell was fixed in his view; he wrote in a letter to George Ticknor on January 18, 1854, "It would have crazed me to have seen a crowd ranging lawlessly among the books, and throwing everything into confusion" (Lydenberg 1923, 22). Without access to the shelves, readers—who had to be at least 16 years of age—had a challenge in finding anything since there was initially no public catalog of any kind. Staff used a "slip catalog" of author entries, but not even they had a subject catalog. Cogswell labored nobly to remove this deficiency, doing all the work himself on the catalogs that became available in the next few years. These were printed catalogs by department (1855) and a full printed catalog by author in four volumes (1857–1861). Plans for a subject catalog did not materialize. The Astor Library grew to 189,114 volumes by the end of 1879. Another printed catalog, not by Cogswell, who had resigned on November 30, 1864, appeared in 1886–1888 in four volumes. It was supplemented by a public card catalog for post-1880 acquisitions. These catalogs were criticized for errors and inconsistent categorizations, the latter problem resulting from the lack of a solid classification system. Bequests from the Astor family began to dry up, and readership declined because of the access situation mentioned and "uncivil staff" (Dain 1972, 7). By 1894, with 260,611 volumes, many of bibliographic importance, the Astor Library was a grand monument ready for fresh leadership.

James Lenox founded a library, incorporated January 20, 1870, to display his splendid collection of rare and beautiful items (including 4,000 Bibles). The building, designed by Richard Morris Hunt, was situated on Fifth Avenue between 70th and 71st streets; it opened to the public on January 15, 1877. Lenox treated the collection in an eighteenth-century manner, offering it primarily for exhibits with limited access (after 1882) to a few scholars. Samuel Austin Allibone was librarian from March 6, 1879, remaining to 1888. Wilberforce Eames was assistant librarian from May 1, 1892, then librarian from June 2, 1893. A dictionary catalog (authors and subjects interfiled) was available on 100,000 cards in November 1894. According to a *New York Times* report of April 16, 1911, the collection included 150,000 volumes. Only a plaque remains of the Lenox Library building, which was acquired by Henry Clay Frick, razed in 1912, and replaced by a mansion and art gallery (the Frick Collection) designed by the architects of the NYPL central building, Carrère and Hastings.

Samuel J. Tilden, former governor of New York, endowed a free circulating library in his will (1886), but his testament was contested by his heirs. In the end, only a portion of his intended $2.4 million bequest was available for the library.

The New York Free Circulating Library (NYFCL), founded in 1878 and incorporated in 1880, was a flourishing institution. Beginning in two small rooms at 36 Bond Street, it circulated 69,000 items in its first year. Moving to larger quarters at 49 Bond Street in 1883, the library posted a circulation of 81,233 items in the year ending October 1883, with a collection of only 8,000 volumes. Card and book catalogs were available to the public. Distinctively among libraries of the time, NYFCL had a female librarian and a staff who were nearly all women as well, and 19 of the 40 persons who served as trustees from 1880 to 1901 were women. Ellen M. Coe, chief librarian, 1881–1895, led a remarkable growth of the library; by 1886 the collection had grown to 20,000 volumes, and circulation had reached 200,000. A study of NYFCL appeared in the *Evening Post* of March 10, 1886. It cited the titles most frequently charged out: a remarkably wholesome list but probably all that was available. Shakespeare was the most popular poet and Thackeray the favored novelist. NYFCL did not join the NYPL until 1901 after a term as chief librarian by the noted library administrator Arthur E. Bostwick (1895–1899). The library had 11 branches, 172,029 registered readers, and a circulation of 1.5 million per year.

The New York Free Circulating Library for the Blind (NYFCLB), incorporated June 3, 1895, was located at the Church of the Messiah, Brooklyn, and then settled at 121 West 91st Street in the parish house of St. Agnes Church. On opening day, November 9, 1896, it had just 60 volumes, but in seven years it grew to 1,548 volumes and 412 music scores. These materials were in embossed print. As NYFCLB joined the NYPL consolidation on February 21, 1903, it had 248 readers and a circulation of 8,020 items annually.

The Aguilar Free Library, founded in 1878, was intended for the use of the Jewish population, principally immigrants. In 1903 it joined NYPL and remains today as one of the branches.

Although permissive legislation had been enacted by the New York State legislature in 1892, allowing communities to tax themselves to finance public libraries, New York City was slow to move. Dain (1972, 32) observes that public anxiety over a corrupt municipal government running it was a factor that held back development of a proper city library. That a public library finally came to light must be credited to the influence and civic motivation of a consolidated board of trustees that, on May 23, 1895, brought together the Astor, Lenox, and Tilden corporations—after long and difficult negotiations with all parties—into a formal institution named the New York Public Library, Astor, Lenox, and Tilden Foundations. All male, all wealthy, and all distinguished, the 21 members of the board were able to get things done. They made a felicitous appointment of library director, John Shaw Billings, in January 1896 and did not try to micromanage him.

NYPL lived at first in the Astor and Lenox buildings. It shared the weaknesses of its ancestors: inadequate catalogs, closed shelves, and a staff with minimal training (only one of the 42 personnel had been to a library school). Billings made quick improvements. He prepared a classification scheme of his own (finding neither the Cutter nor the Dewey system satisfactory), organized the library into four major departments (catalog, shelf, readers, and periodicals), began an exchange program with other libraries (1896), and opened a public documents department (1897; the first in a large public library), a Slavonic department (1899), and a print room (1899). In 1897 the library began issuing the *Bulletin of the New York Public Library*; it was published to 1977, then again from 1992 to 2001. The reference department was organized in 1901. by which time the NYPL collections amounted to 538,000 books and 182,370 pamphlets.

Legislation for a new building was enacted on May 19, 1897. Competition for architect led to the choice of John Merven Carrère and Thomas Hastings, chosen to the surprise of many over the bid of McKim, Mead, and White (designers of the Boston Public Library) and the firm of Howard and Cauldwell. Construction began on May 23, 1900, on the site of an abandoned reservoir. Even before completion of the main building, construction of branches began with a gift by Andrew Carnegie: he financed 65 buildings at $80,000 each. Most of the branches served immigrant populations and stocked books in the languages of their communities. These were circulating collections, and in 1901 a circulation department was initiated to handle them under the leadership of Arthur E. Bostwick, late of the NYFCL.

The cornerstone for the new building was laid on November 10, 1902, and the formal opening of the structure took place on May 23, 1911, in a grand ceremony that included remarks by President William Howard Taft. John Shaw Billings was not on the program that day and was not mentioned by any of the speakers. The building, graced by its two famous lions by Edward C. Potter, had an area of 115,000 square feet "including boiler and engine rooms, but excluding the south court" (Lydenberg 1923, 514). The exterior was of Vermont marble and the interior mostly of white oak from Indiana. It is considered one of the country's finest examples of beaux arts architecture. It was the first large public library designed for function as well as appearance, the interior plan having been developed by Billings himself. The imposing main reading room is 297 feet long and 78 feet wide.

Public response to NYPL in its new quarters was rewarding. In 1911, 7,914.882 volumes were circulated for home use; in 1915, the count was 9,516,482; and in 1920, it was 9,658,977. The books were chosen in a manner that became standard for public libraries: there were weekly selection meetings in which branch librarians inspected approval books and discussed new items, while subject specialists from outside the library (one was John Dewey) were consulted. One individual was assigned the task of weeding the collections. Branches were stocked with materials in the prominent languages of their communities; by 1913 there were 99,609 foreign language items in 25 languages. It will be recalled that New York City in the early years of the twentieth century was very much a haven for immigrants; the population was 41 percent foreign born in 1910. The librarians "worked with foreign born out of compassion for their struggle to make a new life for themselves" (Dain 1972, 291). Branches held lectures and programs, made meeting rooms available to nonpolitical groups, and presented exhibits. A traveling library was initiated to supplement the branch program, serving 802 stations in 1910, and a "Library for the Blind" sent reading materials throughout the United States.

The first specific program for cooperation between a public library and the public schools dates from 1906, when Edwin White Gaillard was given direction of the effort. Anne C. Moore was appointed on January 1, 1906, to be "supervisor of children's rooms" in the branches. In her 35 years at NYPL she raised children's work to respected status. Moore offered story hours in profusion: there were 1,929 noted by 1913. Mabel Williams, named supervisor of work with schools in 1919, began the first public library program for young adults.

A Carnegie donation enabled the library to start a training school in 1912, directed by Mary Wright Plummer. The program transferred to Columbia University in 1926.

With the retirement of Billings on March 3, 1913 (he died a week later and was buried with military honors at Arlington Cemetery), Edwin Hatfield Anderson was appointed director; he served to 1934. Anderson was succeeded by Harry Miller Lydenberg, who had been chief of the reference department since 1928. Lydenberg's tenure, to 1941, was marked by significant growth in the reference collections across the disciplines, including materials in 1,000 languages and dialects.

Ernestine Rose, librarian of the 135th Street Branch from 1920 to 1942, developed a splendid collection of materials on African American life and culture, documenting the Harlem Renaissance as well as the past century. A gift by Arthur Schomburg in 1926 created what is now the Schomburg Center for Research in Black Culture, the principal library of its kind. The center now has its own building (1980, enlarged 1991) at 515 Malcolm X Boulevard; its holdings exceed 150,000 volumes (see SERVICES TO AFRICAN AMERICANS).

The Music Division, dating back to 1915, is second only to the Library of Congress in extent of holdings. A circulating collection of music scores was established in 1920 at the 58th Street Branch near Carnegie Hall. Music staff and materials transferred to the new Lincoln Center complex in 1966. The New York Public Library for the Performing Arts includes, in addition to music (644,400 volumes), the Jerome Robbins Dance Division (38,500 volumes), the Rodgers & Hammerstein Archives of Recorded Sound (9,500 volumes), and the Billy Rose Theatre Collections.

Franklin F. Hopper was director from 1941 to 1946. He had been head of the branches. His tenure was marked by serious annual deficits, as funds from both the city and outside sources were greatly diminished. Ralph A. Beals, director from 1946 to 1954, improved the financial picture by determined lobbying of the city and foundations for increased support. Edward

G. Freehafer became director in 1954. The major event of Freehafer's tenure was the opening of the Donnell Library Center in 1955. This facility at 20 West 53rd Street provided a large circulating collection in midtown. See the section "Recent Events" below for more about Donnell. Telephone reference service has been available since 1968. It is now running seven days a week, 24 hours a day, as Ask NYPL.

The card catalog closed (no new entries) on December 31, 1971; it was replaced by book catalogs. In 1979–1983 there appeared the 800-volume *Dictionary Catalog of the Research Libraries of the New York Public Library, 1911–1971*. This imposing publication, like all book catalogs, presented users with two burdens: only one person could consult one volume at one time, and updating required still another catalog in some form. These annoyances were abated with the computer catalog described below. In 1974, NYPL joined with the libraries of Columbia University, Harvard University, and Yale University to create the Research Libraries Group. (RLG). This consortium, with numerous national and international affiliates, developed a database of their holdings, the Research Libraries Information Network, which was the base for cooperative acquisitions and lending. NYPL is a participant in Google Books Library Project.

NYPL has an important history in the presentation of programs. One may be cited: the discussion and reading group known as "Exploring the American Idea" (EAI). This series of events was an outgrowth of the Great Books series initiated by Ralph Beals in 1947. In 1950, NYPL began to hold public meetings for discussion of democracy and other "American ideas." EAI was the basis for a national program offered by the American Library Association as its "American Heritage Project." As a book discussion vehicle, EAI was not a huge success (average attendance was only 10 persons), but when films were added to the books being explored, there was a surge in participation, with attendance in one year of 39,994 persons.

Recent Events

In 1995 the Science, Industry & Business Library opened at 188 Madison Avenue. It is a major research collection that includes extensive patent files from the United States and Europe.

On January 21, 2006, the Bronx Library Center opened to the public. It is a three times the size of the Fordham Library Center, which had served the borough for 82 years. The five-story building offers 127 desktop computers with 200,000 books and other materials.

The Donnell Library Center was sold in 2007 to the Orient-Express Hotel, which was to build a larger structure on the site. Within that structure a smaller Donnell Library will operate. The decision to dispose of the original Donnell was made when necessary renovations were estimated as $48 million.

Extensive renovation of the main building, made possible by the philanthropy of Stephen A. Schwarzman, was announced in 2007. Schwarzman's name is to be inscribed on the facade and included in the official name of the library.

In July 2009 a new catalog was put into operation, one that integrated for the first time the research and circulating collections. As described in *American Libraries* (August/September 2009), the new catalog offers researchers advanced research tools that draw materials from "all the library's collections, throughout various divisions and formats," and makes Boolean searches possible. (*see* ANDERSON, EDWIN HATFIELD; BILLINGS, JOHN SHAW; BOSTWICK, ARTHUR E.; COGSWELL, JOSEPH GREEN; LYDENBERG, HARRY MILLER; MOORE, ANNE C.; ROSE, ERNESTINE).

References

Much of the historical material in this entry was drawn from Dain (1972, 2001) and Lydenberg (1923).

Dain, Phyllis. 1972. *The New York Public Library: A History of Its Founding and Early* Years. New York: New York Public Library.

Dain, Phyllis. 2001. New York Public Library. In *International Dictionary of Library Histories* 2: 614–20. Chicago: Fitzroy Dearborn.

Davidson, Marshall B., and Bernard McTigue. 1988. *Treasures of the New York Public Library*. New York: Abrams.

Lydenberg, Harry Miller. 1923. *History of the New York Public Library, Astor, Lenox and Tilden Foundations*. New York: New York Public Library. Reprint, Boston: Gregg Press, 1972.

Preer, Jean L. 2001. Exploring the American idea at the New York Public Library. In *Libraries as Agencies of Culture*, ed. Thomas Augst and Wayne Wiegand; an issue of *American Studies* 42, no. 3 (Fall 2001), 135–54.

NEWARK PUBLIC LIBRARY, NJ   5 Washington St., Newark, NJ 07101. Founded 1888. Population served: 273,546. Circulation: 247,905. Holdings: 1,610,344. 10 branches. The Newark circulation system was used from 1896 (*see* CIRCULATION SERVICES). John Cotton Dana was director, 1902–1929; in 1904 he established a branch to serve local business and industry, known from 1907 as the Business Branch.

NEWARK VALLEY, NY. *See* TAPPAN-SPAULDING MEMORIAL LIBRARY, NEWARK VALLEY, NY.

NEWPORT BEACH PUBLIC LIBRARY, CA   130 Avocado Ave., Newport Beach, CA 92660. Founded "in the 1920s" (library website). Population served: 83,361. Circulation: 1,443,178. Holdings: 305,289. LJ February 15, 2009, and November 15, 2009: 3-star library; October 1, 2010: 4-star library.

NEWSPAPERS. *See* SERIALS.

NEWTON FREE LIBRARY, NEWTON CENTRE, MA   330 Homer St., Newton Centre, MA 02459. Founded 1876. Population served: 83,802. Circulation:

1,898,781. Holdings: 521,093. 4 branches. LJ February 15, 2009, and November 15, 2009: 3-star library. HAPLR 2009, 2010.

NICHOLSON MEMORIAL LIBRARY SYSTEM, GARLAND, TX   625 Austin St., Garland, TX 75040. Founded as a private library 1933; "shortly after World War II became a member of the Dallas County Library System … a department of the city of Garland in 1957" (library website). Population served: 235,000. Circulation: 1,000,000. Holdings: 500,000. 4 branches.

NONPRINT MATERIALS. *See* AUDIOVISUAL COLLECTIONS; DIGITAL MEDIA; MICROFORM; MUSIC COLLECTIONS.

NORA E. LARABEE MEMORIAL LIBRARY, STAFFORD, KS   108 N. Union St., Stafford, KS 67578. Population served: 1,077. Circulation: 45,775. Holdings: 22,940. LJ November 15, 2009: 5-star library; October 1, 2010: 3-star library.

NORFOLK LIBRARY, CT   9 Greenwoods Rd. E, Norfolk, CT 06058. Founded 1889. Population served: 1,687. Circulation: 33,491. Holdings: 28,000. LJ February 15, 2009: 4-star library; November 15, 2009: 5-star library; October 1, 2010: 4-star library.

NORFOLK PUBLIC LIBRARY, VA   301 E. City Hall Ave., Norfolk, VA 23510. Founded 1904. Population served: 234,100. Circulation: 1,059,103. Holdings: 771,918. 9 branches, 1 bookmobile.

NORMAL MEMORIAL LIBRARY, FAYETTE, OH   301 N. Eagle St., Fayette, OH 43521. Population served: 2,726. Circulation: 56,653. Holdings: 28,186. LJ February 15, 2009: 3-star library.

NORMAN, OK. *See* PIONEER LIBRARY SYSTEM, NORMAN, OK.

NORTH CANTON PUBLIC LIBRARY, OH   185 N. Main St., North Canton, OH 44720. Founded 1929. Population served: 28,076. Circulation: 1,079,429. Holdings: 95,157. LJ February 15, 2009: 4-star library. HAPLR 2009, 2010.

NORTH LOGAN CITY LIBRARY, UT   475 E. 2500 N., North Logan City, UT 84341. Population served: 9,647. Circulation: 215,866. Holdings: 44,434. LJ February 15, 2009: 4-star library.

NORTH MANCHESTER PUBLIC LIBRARY, IN   405 N. Market St., North Manchester, IN 46962. Founded 1908. Population served: 6,260. Circulation: 120,611. Holdings: 53,133. LJ October 1, 2010: 3-star library.

NORTHAMPTON, MA. *See* FORBES LIBRARY, NORTHAMPTON, MA.

NORTHPORT-EAST NORTHPORT PUBLIC LIBRARY, NORTHPORT, NY   151 Laurel Ave., Northport, NY 11768. Founded 1914. Population served: 36,602. Circulation: 465,711. Holdings: 256,920. 1 branch. LJ February 15, 2009; November 15, 2009, and October 1, 2010: 4-star library.

O

OAK BLUFFS PUBLIC LIBRARY, MA   56R School St., Oak Bluffs, MA 02557. Population served: 3,900. Circulation: 84,000. Holdings: 25,000. LJ November 15, 2009, and October 1, 2010: 3-star library.

OAK PARK PUBLIC LIBRARY, IL   834 Lake St., Oak Park, IL 60301. Founded 1902. Population served: 52,524. Circulation: 913,247. Holdings: 256,170. 2 branches.

OAKLAND PUBLIC LIBRARY, CA   125 14th St., Oakland, CA 94612. Founded 1878. Population served: 446,320. Circulation: 2,426,465. Holdings: 1,428,897. 17 branches.

OAKWOOD, OH. *See* WRIGHT MEMORIAL PUBLIC LIBRARY, OAKWOOD, OH.

OBERLIN PUBLIC LIBRARY, OH   65 S. Main St., Oberlin, OH 44074. Founded in 1947 through a contract between the city and Oberlin College. The public library was located on the campus until 1990, when it occupied its own building at the present location. Population served: 8,245. Circulation: 295,748. Holdings: 110,000. LJ October 1, 2010: 3-star library.

OCEAN COUNTY LIBRARY, TOMS RIVER, NJ   101 W. Washington, Toms River, NJ 08753. Population served: 509,638. Circulation: 4,500,000.

Holdings: 1,200,000. 21 locations. IMLS award 2007. LJ October 1, 2010: 4-star library.

OKLAHOMA CITY, OK. *See* METROPOLITAN LIBRARY SYSTEM IN OKLAHOMA COUNTY, OKLAHOMA CITY, OK.

OLD SAYBROOK, CT. *See* ACTON PUBLIC LIBRARY, OLD SAYBROOK, CT.

OLEAN PUBLIC LIBRARY, NY   134 N. Second St., Olean, NY 14700. Founded 1906. Population served: 16,818. Circulation: 203,585. Holdings: 113,007. LJ November 15, 2009: 3-star library.

OMAHA PUBLIC LIBRARY, NE   215 S. 15th St., Omaha, NE 68102. Founded 1877. Population served: 448,205. Circulation: 2,100,000. Holdings: 787,000. 10 branches.

ONIDA, SD. *See* SULLY COUNTY LIBRARY, ONIDA, SD.

ORANGE BEACH PUBLIC LIBRARY, AL   26267 Canal Rd., Orange Beach, AL 36561. Founded 1992. Population served: 3,784. Circulation: 47,644. Holdings: 37,359. LJ February 15, 2009: 3-star library; November 15, 2009: 5-star library. HAPLR 2010.

ORANGE COUNTY LIBRARY SYSTEM, ORLANDO, FL   101 E. Central, Orlando, FL 32801. Founded 1920. Population served: 970,601. Circulation: 6,642,591. Holdings: 1,542,118. 15 branches.

ORANGE COUNTY PUBLIC LIBRARIES, SANTA ANA, CA   1501 E. St. Andrew Place Santa Ana, CA 92705. Founded 1919. Population served: 1,503,964. Circulation: 6,500,000. Holdings: 2,000,000. 33 branches. The library produced an early book catalog in 1971. Michael Graves designed the San Juan Capistrano Branch, 1983.

ORLANDO, FL. *See* ORANGE COUNTY LIBRARY SYSTEM, ORLANDO, FL.

ORLEANS, MA. *See* SNOW LIBRARY, ORLEANS, MA.

ORLEANS TOWN AND TOWNSHIP PUBLIC LIBRARY, ORLEANS, IN   174 N. Maple St., Orleans, IN 47452. Population served: 2,273. Circulation: 15,583. Holdings: 19,287. LJ February 15, 2009: 4-star library.

ORONO PUBLIC LIBRARY, ME   16 Goodridge Dr., Orono, ME 04473. Founded 1930. Population served: 9,006. Circulation: 48,022. Holdings:

37,660. The public library shares space with Orono High School and includes two students on its board of trustees.

ORRVILLE PUBLIC LIBRARY, OH   230 N. Main St., Orrville, OH 44667. Founded 1925. Population served: 13,000. Circulation: 426,358. Holdings: 80,000. LJ February 15, 2009: 4-star library; November 15, 2009: 5-star library; October 1, 2010: 4-star library. HAPLR 2009, 2010.

OSTERVILLE FREE LIBRARY, MA   43 Wianno Ave., Osterville, MA. Population served: 3,262. Circulation: 91,667. Holdings: 34,497. LJ February 15, 2009: 5-star library; November 15, 2009: 4-star library; October 1, 2010: 5-star library.

OUACHITA PARISH PUBLIC LIBRARY, MONROE, LA   1800 Stubbs Ave., Monroe, LA 71201. Population served: 149,259. Circulation: 845,000. Holdings: 480,644. LJ October 1, 2010: 3-star library.

OUTREACH

Terminology

Outreach has had several meanings in public librarianship, and terms related to it have signified various concepts. *Merriam* defines outreach as "the extending of services or assistance beyond current or usual limits." In the library context this kind of activity has been known as "library extension," "library development," "service to the disadvantaged," and "serving the unserved." Outreach is also a word for services to people with disabilities and persons with other problems in using library materials. The terminology is so entangled with evolution of library services that this entry treats it from an historical perspective.

Library extension is the oldest member of the vocabulary. A current definition is "programs and activities that enable a library or library system to deliver traditional services outside the physical walls of its facilities, including bookmobiles, books-by-mail, and direct delivery of library materials to patrons" (*ODLIS*). In a sense, extension began with building of branch libraries in 1870; they were outside the walls of the central libraries and offered traditional services (*see* BRANCHES). Traveling libraries left the library walls to bring materials to remote patrons, beginning in New York State in 1893. Book wagons hit the country roads of Wisconsin and Maryland in 1905 (*see* BOOKMOBILES). As state library commissions and formed, starting in Rhode Island in 1875, the term "library development" arose and in time took over the conceptual territory from library extension.

Extension and development, the early manifestations of outreach, were directed at rural areas, which a century ago were clearly perceptible as farms and ranches. *American Heritage* says that rural means "of, relating to, or characteristic of the country." For country it has "an area or expanse outside cities and towns." Farms and ranches were outside the towns. *ODLIS* preserves this idea in defining "rural library" as "a library or library system that serves a population living primarily on farms and ranches, and in remote communities, rather than in a town or city." Attaching a population figure to "rural" is troublesome. A specialist in rural librarianship has suggested that rural is a place with 2,500 or fewer population but notes that other definitions give 15,000 or even 25,000 population as rural (Vavrek 1988, 193). Any of those numbers would exceed the population of any farm or ranch and might include towns of substantial size. Another writer has described a "rural library" in Brown County (OH), a county with a population of 40,000 (Spencer 2000). Rurality was muddled after World War II with the emergence of suburbia and exurbia. How to classify those places, with small populations but next to large cities? The U.S. Census Bureau retains 2,500 as the population break point between urban and rural but has other characteristics as well. The definition issue has occupied specialists in many fields; for example an educator has wondered whether rural is "a concept beyond definition? (Rios 1988). Without knowing what rural is, one may question "whether or not there is something called rural librarianship" (Vavrek 1988, 201). Knowing what farmers are, one may wonder if they have special library or information needs. One writer has listed several areas they should keep up with: farming methods, legislation, market trends, farming organizations, publications for farmers, and resources from the U.S. Department of Agriculture (Nason 2007).

Back in the 1930s, when rural still referred to farms, ranches, and small remote communities, librarians could point them out as "unserved," meaning that no public library offered them any of the extension services. Louis Round Wilson, in a landmark study, showed where those unserved populations were, asked why such a situation existed, and proposed improvements. In 1926, 43 percent of the population were without public library service; in 1935, it was 37 percent (Wilson 1938). The American Library Association (1947) estimated that 32 million rural residents were still without public library services in 1945. State libraries, notably in California, were the focal points of extension in the 1930s and 1940s and remain so today, pressing what is known as library development, along with state library commissions (*see* STATE LIBRARY AGENCIES). When the Library Services Act (LSA) was authorized in 1956, its purpose was to "promote extension by the several states of public library service to rural areas without such service or with inadequate services." The estimates by the U.S. Office of Education were that 26 million rural citizens still had no library service and that 50 million others had inadequate service. Progress was satisfying, thanks to the effective work of state library agencies; by 1961, 34 million rural persons had improved library service, 1.5 million receiving service for the first time. "Rural" was removed from the LSA goal when the act was amended in 1964. Emphasis shifted to the "disadvantaged"—the urban poor. The successor to LSA, the Library Services and Construction Act (1964) and its amendments, cited programs to meet the needs of disadvantaged persons in both urban and rural areas. Clarion University created a Center for the Study of Rural Librarianship in 1978 and published a journal called *Rural Libraries*; both the center and the journal closed down in 2008.

Outreach acquired a distinctive meaning in the 1960s as public libraries endeavored to make library patrons of disadvantaged residents in poverty areas. Admirable efforts were made to attract those citizens with popular programming, movies, music, and a spirit of fun. Brooklyn Public Library gave away paperbacks in poor districts. In a bold experiment the University of Maryland library school established a library in an impoverished Baltimore neighborhood, staffed by students, watched by researchers, named "High John." A promising beginning brought nationwide attention to High John, but three years later it closed down. (An encyclopedia article about the Maryland library school, published in 1976, does not mention it.) High John's failure to take root in a poverty area was symbolic of the outreach movement of the time. Other outreach programs folded as well, and "by 1971 librarians ... realized that the traditional public library cannot help the disadvantaged very much, that the library is a middle-class institution, alien and irrelevant in the ghetto" (Williams 1988, 105).

So outreach took on the meaning that it still holds. The term refers now to "library programs and services designed to meet the information needs of users who are unserved or underserved, for example those who are visually impaired, homebound, institutionalized, not fluent in the national language, illiterate, or marginalized in some other way" (*ODLIS*). Attention to the marginalized patron used to fall under "special services". *See also* INFORMATION LITERACY INSTRUCTION; READERS' ADVISORY SERVICES; REFERENCE AND INFORMATION SERVICES; SERVICES TO AFRICAN AMERICANS; SERVICES TO HISPANICS; SERVICES TO IMMIGRANTS; SERVICES TO NATIVE AMERICANS; SERVICES TO PEOPLE WITH DISABILITIES; SERVICES TO SENIORS; SPECIAL SERVICES.

References

American Library Association. 1947. *The Equal Chance: Books Help to Make It.* Chicago: American Library Association. Originally published 1936; 2nd ed. 1943 with supplement 1947.

Nason, Lisa. 2007. The farmer and the library. *Rural Libraries* 27, no. 2: 19–45.

Rios, Betty Rose. 1988. *"Rural"—Concept beyond Definition?* ERIC Document ED 296820. http://www.ericdigests.org/pre-929/concept. Accessed December 2010.

Rosser-Hogben, Debra M. 2004. Meeting the challenge: an overview of the information needs of rural America. *Rural Libraries* 24, no. 1: 25–49.

Spencer, Roxanne Myers. 2000. The rural library in an urban environment: A study of the Brown County Public Library. *Rural Libraries* 20, no. 1: 7–32.

Vavrek, Bernard. 1988. Rural librarianship. In *Encyclopedia of Library and Information Science* 43 (Supplement 8): 191–202.

Williams, Patrick. 1988. *The American Public Library and the Problem of Purpose.* New York: Greenwood Press.

Wilson, Louis Round. 1938. *The Geography of Reading: A Study of the Distribution and Status of Libraries in the United States.* Chicago: American Library Association.

OVERLAND PARK, KS. *See* JOHNSON COUNTY LIBRARY, OVERLAND PARK, KS.

P

PAGE PUBLIC LIBRARY, AZ   479 S. Lake Powell Blvd., Page, AZ. Population served: 12,306. Circulation: 116,157. Holdings: 70,653. LJ February 15, 2009: 3-star library; November 15, 2009: 4-star library; October 1, 2010: 5-star library.

PALO ALTO CITY LIBRARY, CA   1213 Newell Rd., Palo Alto, CA 94303. Founded 1902. Population served: 62,148. Circulation: 1,280,547. Holdings: 260,468. 4 branches. The 1958 building, designed by Edward Durrell Stone, was remodeled in 1984. The Palo Alto Children's Library (1940) was the only library in the United States expressly for children. LJ February 15, 2009; November 15, 2009, and October 1, 2010: 4-star library.

PARKER PUBLIC LIBRARY, AZ   1001 S. Navajo Ave., Parker, AZ 85344. Population served: 9,125. Circulation: 61,102. Holdings: 16,983. LJ November 15, 2009, and October 1, 2010: 5-star library.

PARMA, OH. *See* CUYAHOGA COUNTY LIBRARY, PARMA, OH.

PASADENA PUBLIC LIBRARY, CA   285 E. Walnut St., Pasadena, CA 91101. Population served: 135,000. Circulation: 1,647,393. Holdings: 1,111,188. 9 branches. Main library designed by Myron Hunt, 1927, is on the National Register of Historic Places. LJ February 15, 2009: 5-star library; November 15, 2009, and October 1, 2010: 4-star library.

PAWTUCKET PUBLIC LIBRARY, RI   13 Summer St., Pawtucket, RI 02860. Founded 1852. Population served: 74,033. Circulation: 246,617. Holdings: 167,624. 1 bookmobile. The library innovations included open shelves (1879) and a separate children's area with appropriate furnishings and open shelves (1887).

PELHAM FREE PUBLIC LIBRARY, MA   2 S. Valley Rd., Pelham, MA 01002. Founded 1891. It is a combination of public library and elementary school library (library website). Population served: 1,422. Circulation: 28,837. Holdings: 25,926. LJ November 15, 2009: 4-star library; October 1, 2010: 5-star library.

PELICAN PUBLIC LIBRARY, AK   32 Harbor Way, Pelican, AK 99832. Population served: 115. Circulation: 5,434. Holdings: 8.916. HAPLR 2009, 2010.

PELICAN RAPIDS PUBLIC LIBRARY, MN   25 W. Mill Ave., Pelican Rapids, MN 56572. Founded 1988. Population served: 4,861. Circulation: 168,455. Holdings: 39,266. LJ February 15, 2009: 4-star library; November 15, 2009: 3-star library.

PENINSULA LIBRARY AND HISTORICAL SOCIETY, OH   6105 Riverview Rd., Peninsula, OH 44264. Founded 1946. Population served: 2,800. Circulation: 82,655. Holdings: 37,153. 1 branch. LJ November 15, 2009, and October 1, 2010: 3-star library.

PERIODICALS. *See* SERIALS).

PERKINS, FREDERIC BEECHER, 1828–1899   Librarian. Born Hartford, CT, September 27, 1828. He earned an MA from Yale University, 1860. He taught school in New York City and New Jersey, then was librarian of the Connecticut Historical Society, 1874–1879. In 1880 he was bibliographer and cataloger, Boston Public Library, then chief librarian, San Francisco Public Library, to 1887. Perkins was a contributor to the U.S. Bureau of Education *Public Libraries in the United States* (1876). He was associate editor of *Library Journal*, 1877–1880. A paper, read at the American Library Association conference of 1885, was an early presentation of comparative performance data on public libraries in large cities. He died on January 27, 1899. *DAB.*

Reference

Perkins, Frederic Beecher. 1885. Public libraries and the public. Paper read at the American Association conference, Lake George, New York, September 1885. Printed in Arthur E. Bostwick, *The American Public Library*, 4th ed., 231–41. New York: Appleton, 1929.

PERRY PUBLIC LIBRARY, OH   3753 Main St., Perry, OH 44081. Population served: 3,650. Circulation: 247,135. Holdings: 52,158. LJ February 15, 2009: 5-star library.

PERRYSBURG, OH. *See* WAY PUBLIC LIBRARY, PERRYSBURG, OH.

PERSONNEL. *See* STAFFING.

PETERBOROUGH TOWN LIBRARY, NH   2 Concord St., Peterborough, NH 03458. Founded 1833. Population served: 6,134. Circulation: 77,939. Holdings: 46,456. This was the first publicly supported library open to all. It began with 100 books, housed in Smith and Thompson's General Store, in the post office building. Annual appropriations averaged $100 to 1849, the money coming from a "literary fund." In 1893 the library gained its own building, which continues to serve it after two expansions.

PETERS TOWNSHIP PUBLIC LIBRARY, MCMURRAY, PA   616 E. McMurray Rd., McMurray, PA 15317. Founded 1957. Population served: 17,566. Circulation: 397,672. Holdings: 102,384. HAPLR 2009, 2010.

PETERSBURG PUBLIC LIBRARY, AK   12 Nordic Dr., Petersburg, AK 99833. Population served: 3,155. Circulation: 57,678. Holdings: 29,455. LJ February 15, 2009: 3-star library; November 15, 2009: 4-star library.

PHILADELPHIA, PA. *See* FREE LIBRARY OF PHILADELPHIA, PA.

PHILLIPS, EDNA, 1890–1968   Librarian. Born in Newark, NJ; she studied art but did not earn a degree. In 1913–1914 she was a library assistant in the Madison (NJ) Public Library, then librarian in Edgewater, NJ, 1914–1918. During World War I, Phillips volunteered as a canteen operator in France and Germany. From 1921 to 1923 she was librarian in East Orange, NJ. She was appointed to the Massachusetts Division of Public Libraries in 1923 as secretary for library work with foreigners; service to immigrants became her career focus. She supported "Americanization" with retention of the cultural heritage of those who came to the United States In 1925, Phillips surveyed the national situation of public library service to immigrants for the U.S. Bureau of Education. She chaired the American Library Association (ALA) Committee on Work with the Foreign Born, 1927–1928, and was in demand as a speaker, consultant, and author; she wrote bibliographies on practical subjects that could be used by immigrant patrons. Her *Easy Books for New Americans* was published by the ALA in 1926, revised edition 1927. She received a Carnegie Fellowship for the study of adult education at Columbia University, then went to Gloucester, MA, as librarian, 1934–1939, and Norwood, MA, as librarian, 1939–1962.

Reference

Jones, Plummer Alston, Jr. 1999. *Libraries, Immigrants, and the American Experience*. Westport, CT: Greenwood Press.

PHILMONT PUBLIC LIBRARY, NY   101 Main St., Philmont, NY 12565. Founded 1898 (permanent charter; a provisional charter had been granted in 1893). Population served: 1,480. Circulation: 23,644. Holdings: 14,322. LJ February 15, 2009, and November 15, 2009: 4-star library; October 1, 2010: 5-star library.

PHILOSOPHY OF PUBLIC LIBRARIANSHIP

Terminology

In *Merriam* "philosophy" is "a theory underlying or regarding a sphere of activity or thought." This is the *Merriam* definition that applies best to "philosophy of . . . ." For "theory" the same source gives "a plausible or scientifically acceptable general principle or body of principles offered to explain phenomena." For "theory," *American Heritage* offers "the branch of a science or art consisting of its explanatory statements, accepted principles, and methods of analysis, as opposed to practice." Philosophy is thus concerned with the theory of the "science or art" of public librarianship and with its principles and explanations.

The definition in this handbook of a public library is "a library that is open without charge for reference and circulation to all members of the community that is taxed to support it." Now to "librarianship." Neither *Merriam* nor *American Heritage* gives a definition. This one will serve: "the activity of developing, staffing, managing, and operating libraries." Public librarianship will add a word: "the activity of developing, staffing, managing, and operating public libraries." The principles and explanations of that activity are the philosophy of public librarianship.

A principle is "a comprehensive and fundamental law, doctrine, or assumption" (*Merriam*); "a basic truth, law, or assumption" (*American Heritage*). The body of principles that applies to an activity is comprehensive and universal (covering all examples of the activity), and it is distinct to that activity, not applicable to any other. For public libraries a set of principles like these would meet the criteria:

- The documents of the public library are acquired because they exhibit one or both of these characteristics: (1) they have intrinsic merit as reflections of the accumulated knowledge and experience of the world, and (2) they are of interest to the community served.
- The documents are systematically described and organized.
- The documents are made accessible to the community served.

Other statements that might appear to be principles seem to fail on analysis. For instance, "the documents are preserved from deterioration and hazards" is promising but not universal since not all public libraries engage in preservation. Some statements might be classed as principles but would be rejected because of triviality. Thus, the statement that "tables and chairs are provided in the public library for the use of persons as they read or consult materials" is universal—unless there is a library with no tables or chairs—but it is not "fundamental" to the nature of public libraries. Other statements would be rejected as not being distinct to public libraries, such as "a file is maintained with the names and addresses of users," which would apply to many organizations as well as libraries.

So one group of statements may be valid as principles because they are universal, fundamental, and distinct to the public library. But other types of principles are recognized in the definitions: those that make assumptions. It is just in this area that that library thinking has displayed the most variety. Some of the notable variants are taken up in the section "Historical Summary" below. For the most part, assumptions relate to the proper role of the public library: to its basic purpose in society. An assumption, which is "a fact or statement taken for granted" (*Merriam*) or "something taken for granted or accepted as true without proof; a supposition" (*American Heritage*), covers the idea of purpose, which is usually presented with arguments but without proof.

"Purpose," in *Merriam*, is "an object or end to be attained"; in *American Heritage*, "an aim or goal." The purpose of public librarianship is the aim or goal that underlies the universal principles; it is what they are for. With a clear purpose, librarians can give emphasis to one principle or another. They can concentrate on what is important to the purpose. Their work, including all that is involved in management of a library, comes into focus. Individual libraries may choose to promote services and act on positions that are not universally observed, based on assumptions of certain purposes that will suit their own communities. For example, "documents are utilized for the enlightenment of the community," while not universal, could be a guiding assumption in a particular library (as it is indeed in many) and thus a principle for that library. Some ideas of public library purpose are in the next section.

Another term to be addressed is "values." For "value," Merriam gives something (as a principle or quality) intrinsically valuable or desirable"; *American Heritage* gives "a principle, standard, or quality considered worthwhile or desirable." The connection to "principle" is again through the concept of "assumption." But a value implies more than a belief that something is desirable; it moves to the area of action. A philosophical dictionary gives a more thorough treatment:

> A theory of value is a theory about what things in the world are good, desirable and important. The theory implies action, since to conclude that a state of affairs is good is to have a reason for acting so as to bring it about, or if it exists already, to maintain it. (Flew 1979, 338)

From that point of view, to say that "a value is something that is of deep interest (often and quite reasonably self interest) to an individual or a group" (Gorman 2000, 5) is incomplete, merely as an assumption that something is desirable. On the other hand, to add an action component to a value statement seems to conflate the term with purpose, or goal (*see* PLANNING).

To sum up, public librarianship is the activity of developing, staffing, managing, and operating public libraries. A philosophy of public librarianship consists of its underlying theory, theory consists of a body of principles, and principles include universal laws and assumptions. Assumptions about the purpose of the public library may be argued but not proved; assumptions that refer to action are values, which may be expressed as purposes or perhaps goals.

Historical Summary

It will be convenient to examine the emergence of public library philosophy under three headings; they correspond to aspects of theory mentioned in the section "Terminology" above. The earliest category of theory to be discussed and written about consisted of assumptions. Much later there were endeavors to discover universal principles, and recently there has been interest in values. This historical overview deals with assumptions and universal principles. Values are examined in the section "Recent Issues" below.

The history of assumptions about public libraries began with the trustees of the Boston Public Library as they worked to establish that institution in the 1850s. Their assumptions were about the role of the public library in society. While assumptions usually follow on study of examples of a phenomenon, that is, empirically, in the case of public libraries the trustees had no examples to examine. They knew a good deal about the character of American society, but their ideas about library roles had to be intuitive. They settled rather quickly on a position and presented it in their July 1852 report: "We consider that a large public library is of the utmost importance as the means of completing our system of public education ... by opening to all the means of self culture through books" (quoted in Williams 1988, 4; this source underlies much of the following exposition). The view of public libraries as educational institutions has survived the debate of 150 years and remains a significant assumption in library theory. The trustees also reasoned about the social benefit of the educational venture, which would give the general population the opportunity of understanding issues of the day and to make sound decisions regarding them. Divisions of opinion followed among library leaders about what kind of books would best serve the educational cause and what kind of books might debilitate it; this was the issue of fiction reading along with the concerns about harmful consequences of immoral reading. These problems, which lingered for a century on the professional agenda, are taken up in other entries within this book (*see* COLLECTION DEVELOPMENT; HISTORY OF PUBLIC LIBRARIES; INTELLECTUAL FREEDOM; READERS' ADVISORY SERVICES). In 1906, John Cotton

Dana put forth, almost as an afterthought in an article about stimulating reading, another role assumption for the public library: that it provide "a quiet corner for rumination . . . a place apart" (Dana 1906, 16). This idea of the public library as a special place has had a modern revival. Perhaps it stands more among universal principles—since all public libraries must be tokens of it—than among unprovable assumptions.

An added role for the public library, beyond the generally accepted educational function, was the provision of recreational reading. Samuel Swett Green, speaking in 1876 at the founding meeting of the American Library Association (ALA), said that "popular libraries are not established merely for instruction. It is meant that they should give entertainment also . . . by giving people a harmless source of recreation" (Williams 1988, 16). Librarians were uneasy. But justification for recreational reading (although immoral books were still excluded) was found in the "ladder theory," which proposed that lower tastes would be gradually uplifted by continued reading. In time the recreational role of public libraries became a settled assumption, although no evidence to support the ladder theory was ever produced.

By 1876, then, the three fundamental roles currently ascribed to public libraries—education, information, and recreation—were already mainstream assumptions within the new profession. In the sense that modern American public libraries exhibit all three roles, they are elements of a universal principle, perhaps like this: "The documents of the public library include materials of educational, informational, and recreational character; and library staff utilize them to satisfy the needs and interests of the community served." This principle could be appended to the first one suggested above under "Terminology."

Ernest Cushing Richardson, writing primarily about the qualities of the ideal librarian (one who knows books), attributed a grand task to libraries: they were not only the memory of the race but also "a common basis of unity . . . which gives reality and stability to human society or civilization." Librarianship serves this goal by offering "cooperation with persons who wish to know books" (Richardson 1927, 57, 59).

The ALA raised its collective voice in philosophical matters for the first time in 1933, with its *Standards for Public Libraries*, wherein a statement of purpose appeared: "The public library is maintained by a democratic society in order that every man, woman, and child may have the means of self-education and recreational reading." This was the mainstream position of library leaders at the time. It was elaborated later in the ALA *National Plan for Libraries*; a section on library objectives stated,

> The objectives of a library are to assemble and preserve books and related materials in organized collections and, through stimulation and guidance, to promote their use to the end that children, young people, men and women may have opportunity and encouragement. (both quotes from Williams 1988, 46, 47)

There the discussion seemed to rest; it took the form of a universal principle plus some assumptions about purposes. But there were soon fresh ideas in the mix.

In his *Introduction to Library Science*, Pierce Butler (1933) proposed that librarianship had a clear-cut social function. He, like many others connected with the Graduate Library School of the University of Chicago, visualized libraries in social science terms. This orientation was expressed in a rather remarkable assertion:

> The knowledge that comes from reading has no social signifi-cance unless it is acquired by such persons as can inject it into the vital stream of communal life. For an American banker to know Sanskrit may be a source of great satisfaction to himself and to his friends, but it will probably add nothing to his voca-tional skill or to his more general qualifications as a citizen.

Butler seemed to leap quickly back from that announcement:

> On the other hand the welfare of the whole community may be indirectly affected if this same banker possesses a general knowl-edge of Hindu religion; this might, under conceivable circum-stances, tend to liberalize his mind and determine where the weight of his influence will be placed when the people are in dan-ger of making a short-sighted decision of permanent consequen-ces. (Butler 1933, 48)

What emerges from this rather cloudy conception is a priority of social good over private interest. The librarian has the responsibility to exploit the cul-tural archives "for communal advantage to the utmost extent of his ability. Therefore, a major phase of the library's service to any individual reader will be to assist him to an effective method for achieving his own private purpose, so long as this is not anti-social" (Butler 1933, 106). A codification of this social role for public libraries was soon to come, in the *Public Library Inquiry*, to be examined shortly.

J. Periam Danton voiced impatience, in 1934, over the lack of a comprehen-sive philosophy of librarianship, the lack of "a systematic body of general concepts" (Danton 1934, 64). He took note of the "five laws" of S. R. Ranganathan (1931) but found them deficient as "an open-minded enquiry" (Danton 1934, 67). Those laws below are examined below. Danton's own sug-gestions as the basis for thinking about a philosophy included "achievement of a definite and recognized place for the library in the social order" and "a sound, scientific framework for practical procedures" (Danton 1934, 74). But to find that place for the library in the social order, "there must be an understanding and recognition of the ideals and purposes of the society into which that philoso-phy must fit... before a library philosophy can be formulated there must be a philosophy of life for the world today" (Danton 1934, 81). This is a dispiriting conclusion, for the ideals and purposes of society are not easily enshrined in a paradigm; they constitute one of the perennial problems of philosophers.

Alvin Johnson (1938) proclaimed the public library to be "a people's university." In Johnson's view, the library did not serve that role well by providing ephemeral books or even genealogical works. However, some fiction could be more educational than some nonfiction. True adult education would leave the user free to choose one side or another in controversial matters, and libraries should offer him materials to make such choices (Johnson 1938, 1, 28). This rather severe outlook was echoed by the University of Chicago's Douglas Waples (1938), who recommended that public libraries leave popular literature to the rental libraries and stores (Waples 1938).

Concentration of library efforts on opinion leaders was advised by Lester Asheim, who observed that the majority is never reached by the library anyway and that it is always the higher level of society that uses libraries. By serving this level, the library will serve the majority in the best way possible (Asheim 1947). This was the attitude projected in a set of volumes issued under the name of *The Public Library Inquiry* (*PLI*) in the early 1950s. In the keynote volume, titled *The Public Library in the United States*, author Robert Leigh surveyed the numerous statements and ideas about library purposes. He then disclosed that the "natural public library audience" was "the group of adults whose interest, will, and ability lead them to seek personal enrichment and enlightenment" (Leigh 1950, 48, 50). This minority sector included persons of importance in the community; serving them was socially valuable. Bernard Berelson's contribution to *PLI* was a study of "the library's public." He found that a small minority of the community actually used the library; about 18 percent of adults used the library once a year. He concluded that "the proper role of the public library is deliberately and consciously to serve the 'serious' and 'culturally alert' members of the community rather than attempt now to reach all the people." The library "might leave the field of popular entertainment to the commercial media" (Berelson 1949, 130, 131). So much then, for meeting popular demand, the ladder theory, and meeting the interests of the community served. These *PLI* findings were not well appreciated by the library community, which continued to insist on meeting demands of the public. Although some library leaders spoke up for the *PLI*, the profession in general ignored it; it offered too strong a contradiction to traditional purposes. "By ignoring *PLI* the library community gave up serious discussion of the purpose of public libraries" (Williams 1988, 81) may be too strong a statement; there were some philosophic efforts later. But for the most part, library thought in the 1950s seems to have settled on a broad consensus:

> The library plays a distinctive role in American civilization, encouraging reading both for good citizenship and for the pure pleasure of knowing. Its purpose is to conserve and make available the record of Man's mind for any who seek it. The librarian is obligated to try to stimulate a desire for the meaning contained in this record, but must also tolerate all points of view and all kinds and forms of expression, while at the same time favoring the highest, truest, best, and most useful. (McCrimmon 1975, xxiii)

An extension of the range of philosophic meditation was provided by the ALA. Responding at last to decades of censorship controversy, the association issued in 1939 the first version of its *Library Bill of Rights*. Assumptions of the document included the need for libraries to "challenge censorship" and "cooperate with all persons and groups concerned with resisting abridgment of free expression and free access to ideas" (for this statement and the background that led to it, *see* INTELLECTUAL FREEDOM). In its new standards for public libraries of 1943, the ALA inserted the idea that the library "plays a significant role in making democracy work by helping citizens to be enlightened participants in public affairs." The other library purposes given were the classical roles of education, recreation, and information provision. The commitment to democracy may not seem especially novel, but it did present libraries as proponents of one style of government. From this humble beginning, the advocacy of particular styles within democracy were to follow. Later goal statements by the ALA fostered enlightened citizenship along with an enriched personal life for library users (1946) and provision of "information and educational materials" (1948) (Williams 1988, 55, 58).

A British librarian writing in 1949 introduced a fresh concept into library philosophy, at least one that had not been stated as clearly. A. Broadfield took issue with the idea that public libraries have the prime role of serving societal needs. For him, public libraries exist "for the sake of freedom of thought." They must "help a man to form his judgment by giving him access, through catalogues, bibliographies and shelves, to unsuspected interrelations of knowledge ... he could not judge wisely without the library, which places before him unexpected truths" (Broadfield 1949, 25). The contrast between Broadfield's views and those of Pierce Butler (mentioned above) sum up the debate in librarianship about social and individual emphases of service. Butler wants a good citizen, but Broadfield says that to produce one, "an exemplary citizen," makes men copyists (for elaboration on the Butler–Broadfield differences, see Marco 1966).

The "five laws" of S. R. Ranganathan are frequently cited as useful library principles. He stated them in various books beginning in 1931; they are taken here from his 1952 work *Library Book Selection*. Here are his laws (which are expressed as universal principles) with some comments (this review is based on Marco 1997):

1. "Books are for use." The author treats this statement as a prescription to librarians to find ways to have their books used. They can do this if their books match the interests and abilities of the community. Comment: This is a kind of general guideline, not a law or principle in the sense taken in this entry.

2. "Every reader his book." The author explains that reader's wants (not defined) must be observed. He recommends direct contact with the community, talking to individuals to ascertain their preferences. It does not seem that there is much

added here to the first law. And it is misleading to suggest that every reader should have whatever book he wants.

3. "Every book its reader." This is redundant to the first law and indeed the second law as well. It tells librarians to get the right books, which are those the community will read.

4. "Save the time of the reader." This seems to tell librarians: do a good job, and you will save the user's time. Do accurate cataloging and reference since time is lost when users act on the errors of librarians. Have good signage and regulations. The first two laws could be subsumed here since the user's time is saved by proper acquisitions.

5. "The library is a growing organism." The metaphor is faulty: most libraries do not die, and none of them reproduce. Up to a point, growth is a process that organisms share with libraries, but some libraries do not grow, others grow for a time and then stabilize, and some get smaller over time. But assuming that growth is typical in most libraries, what then? Librarians who study this law will find nothing to work with.

The five laws hardly merit the ongoing reverence they have acquired (e.g., Gorman 1998, 2). Two further endeavors to identify laws of a universal nature may be noted. James Thompson (1977) made a list that came in part from Ranganathan: "Libraries are for all," "Libraries must grow," and "Every book is of use," with some additions: "A librarian must be a person of education" and "A librarian needs training and/or apprenticeship." These educational points would apply to other professions and occupations as well. Another statement that fits all occupations is "A librarian's role can only be an important one if it is fully integrated into the prevailing social political system." Thompson's ideas do not seem to form a coherent theory.

Michael Gorman (1997) has presented a "reinterpretation" of Ranganathan's laws as follows:

1. Libraries serve humanity.

2. Respect all forms by which knowledge is communicated.

3. Use technology intelligently to enhance service.

4. Protect free access to knowledge.

5. Honor the past and create the future.

These prescriptions are interesting as starting points for discussion, if they do not stand well as formal laws (principles). Numbers 1 and 3 would apply generally to professions. Numbers 2 and 5 are vague. Number 4 is a worthy statement of purpose in the American context.

In 1956, the ALA restated earlier goals—education, recreation, and information, along with "appreciation"—in the document *Public Library Service*; they repeated those goals in the 1966 *Minimum Standards*. Service to all remains a key purpose of public libraries in the presentations of the ALA (compare *A Strategy for Public Library Change* [1972] and *Planning and Role Setting for Public Libraries* [1987]).

Recent Issues

Several new concepts have enlivened philosophical thought. One is the cluster of topics centered on the expansive definition of "information": information science, information studies, and information technology. Arriving on the scene in the 1960s, information science was at first an equal partner with traditional librarianship (note the 1968 *Encyclopedia of Library and Information Science* and the newly renamed Schools of Library and Information Science). Then in some respects information became the senior partner (a chronology of events that brought this about is given in Crowley 2008, 52–55). This complex subject has its own entry (*see* INFORMATION SCIENCE); what needs to be said here is that the purpose of libraries has been altered, in many minds, from the traditional standpoints to one that focuses on provision of factual statements. In its most extensive form this focus seems to deconstruct public libraries, even to the point of renaming them "information centers."

"Values" have been given much attention for about 20 years. It is not entirely clear just what a value is in the minds of those librarians who identify them. The definition given in the first section above, from a philosophical dictionary, is more precise than the current library usage. A suggested list of library "core values" by Michael Gorman (2000, 26) is typical:

- Stewardship
- Service
- Intellectual freedom
- Rationalism (order)
- Literacy and learning
- Equity of access
- Privacy
- Democracy

It appears that the named topics represent desirable states of affairs. In 1999, the ALA set up a task force to identify professional values (Sager 2001). Their report presented "connection of people to ideas; assurance of free and open access to recorded knowledge, information, and creative works; commitment to literacy and learning; respect for the individuality and diversity of all people; freedom for all people to form, to hold, and express their own beliefs; preservation of the human record; excellence in professional service to our communities; formation of partnerships to advance these ideas" (Budd 2007, 44; Sager 2001). The ALA council did not accept this report. A second task force reported in 2004 with these values: "access; confidentiality/privacy; democracy; education and lifelong learning; intellectual freedom; preservation; the public good; professionalism; service; social responsibility." This set was approved by the council.

Librarians have not greeted such value lists with uniform enthusiasm. One writer noted that "the profession is still unable to fashion a succinct statement of values ... each new statement focused more on orientations, civic obligations, and ethics, than on values unique to our profession" (Haycock 2005, 64). While values, adequate or inadequate, serve to illuminate areas of concern in librarianship, they seem to provide little else, and the assumptions underlying them are for the most part murky. The point raised by Haycock regarding what might be called today "mission creep" has been a discussion topic since the 1970s. It refers to the entrance into specific library concerns of issues that are not directly connected to libraries. "Advocacy" and "social responsibilities" are the applicable terms (*see* AMERICAN LIBRARY ASSOCIATION).

A commendable perspective of self-criticism has evolved since the 1970s, touching on the most fundamental library activities. Assumptions about library roles had been traditionally garbed in tacit favorability; in saying that libraries assembled "books and related materials in organized collections and through stimulation and guidance" would "promote their use" (ALA 1935, 92–93), the unvoiced expectation was that those tasks would be executed competently. But research and reflection began to throw shadows over the competence of librarians to assemble the right materials (half the books in large libraries were unused), to organize them most effectively (faults with Library of Congress subject headings, prominent classification systems, and cataloging practice), to guide readers in their use (flawed attempts at readers' advisory), and to use materials skillfully in answering reference questions (as many as half the questions asked received incorrect answers) (for a discussion of these concerns, *see* COLLECTION DEVELOPMENT; CATALOGING; CLASSIFICATION; READERS' ADVISORY SERVICES; REFERENCE AND INFORMATION SERVICES).

Fresh models of library service continue to appear. The library as a business model is centered on lowering operational costs (Crowley 2008, 37). An aspect of this viewpoint is the library as a bookstore model (Woodward 2005). The library as "a place" is an idea that is receiving exploration (Buschman and Leckie 2006). The "library in the life of the user" is a different way of looking at the old relationship (Wiegand 2005).

Research studies of public library use have refreshed thinking about its mission. It is the traditional library services that members of the community want (Public Agenda 2006; *Perceptions* 2005). The main purposes of the library, as expressed by its public, are to provide information, books, research assistance, and entertainment, in a comfortable environment. (*Perceptions of Libraries and Information Resources* 2005, 339). With such facts in hand, library philosophers may proceed beyond intuition in formulating their assumptions; and in time those stronger assumptions may take on universal character, leading to a set of universal principles: the long-anticipated theory of librarianship. *See also* AMERICAN LIBRARY ASSOCIATION;

CATALOGING; CLASSIFICATION; COLLECTION DEVELOPMENT; ETHICS FOR LIBRARIANS; INTELLECTUAL FREEDOM; PLANNING; READERS' ADVISORY SERVICES; REFERENCE AND INFORMATION SERVICES.

References

American Library Association. 1935. A national plan for libraries. *ALA Bulletin* 29, no. 2 (February): 91–98.

Asheim, Lester. 1947. What kinds of books? What kinds of readers? *College and Research Libraries* 10, no. 2 (March): 247–48.

Berelson, Bernard. 1949. *The Library's Public: A Report of the Public Library Inquiry*. New York: Columbia University Press.

Broadfield, A. 1949. *A Philosophy of Librarianship*. London: Grafton.

Budd, John M. 2007. *Self-Examination: The Present and Future of Librarianship*. Westport, CT: Libraries Unlimited.

Buschman, John E., and Gloria J. Leckie, eds. 2006. *The Library as Place: History, Community, and Culture*. Westport, CT: Libraries Unlimited.

Butler, Pierce. 1933. *An Introduction to Library Science*. Chicago: University of Chicago Press.

Crowley, Bill. 2008. *Renewing Professional Librarianship: A Fundamental Rethinking*. Westport, CT: Libraries Unlimited.

Dana, John Cotton. 1906. Many-sided interest: how the library promotes it. *School Journal*, December 22. Reprinted in *American Library Philosophy*, ed. Barbara McCrimmon, 10–19. Hamden, CT: Shoe String Press, 1975. Pagination cited is from the reprint.

Danton, J. Periam. 1934. Plea for a philosophy of librarianship. *Library Quarterly* 4, no. 4 (October): 527–51. Reprinted in *American Library Philosophy*, ed. Barbara McCrimmon, 62–87. Hamden, CT: Shoe String Press, 1975.

Flew, Antony [sic]. 1979. *A Dictionary of Philosophy*. New York: St. Martin's.

Gorman, Michael. 1995. Five new laws of librarianship. *American Libraries* 26, no. 4 (September): 784–88.

Gorman, Michael. 1998. *Technical Services Today and Tomorrow*. 2nd ed. Westport, CT: Libraries Unlimited.

Gorman, Michael. 2000. *Our Enduring Values: Librarianship in the 21st Century*. Chicago: American Library Association.

Haycock, Ken. 2005. Librarianship: Intersecting perspectives from the academy and from the field. In *Perspectives, Insights and Priorities: Seventeen Leaders Speak Freely of Librarianship*, ed. Norman Horrocks, 63–72. Lanham, MD: Scarecrow Press.

Johnson, Alvin. 1938. *The Public Library: A People's University*. New York: American Association for Adult Education.

Leigh, Robert D. 1950. *The Public Library in the United States*. New York: Columbia University Press.

Marco, Guy A. 1966. Old wine in new bottles. *Ohio Library Association Bulletin* 36, no. 4 (October): 8–14. Reprinted in *American Library Philosophy*, ed. Barbara McCrimmon, 191–201. Hamden, CT: Shoe String Press, 1975.

Marco, Guy A. 1997 Our troubled search for principles. In *Essays in Honor of Prof. P. B. Mangla*, 21–30. New Delhi: Concept Publishing.

McCrimmon, Barbara, ed. 1975. *American Library Philosophy*. Hamden, CT: Shoe String Press. A reprinting of 19 articles by various writers on library philosophy.

Perceptions of Libraries and Information Resources: A Report to the OCLC Membership. 2005. Dublin, OH: OCLC.

Public Agenda. 2006. *Long Overdue: A Fresh Look at Public and Leadership Attitudes about Libraries in the 21st Century*. New York: Public Agenda.

Ranganathan, S. R. 1931. *Library Book Selection*. Delhi: Indian Library Association.

Richardson, Ernest Cushing. 1927. The book and the person who knows the book. *ALA Bulletin* 21, no. 10 (October): 289–95. Reprinted in *American Library Philosophy*, ed. Barbara McCrimmon, 51–62. Hamden, CT: Shoe String Press, 1975.

Sager, Donald J. 2001. The search for librarianship's core values. *Public Libraries* 40, no. 3 (May/June): 149–53.

Thompson, James. 1977. *A History of the Principles of Librarianship*. London: Bingley.

Waples, Douglas. 1938. People and libraries. In *Current Issues in Library Administration*, ed. Carlton Joeckel, 355–70. Chicago: University of Chicago Press.

Wiegand, Wayne A. 2005. To reposition a research agenda: What American studies can teach the LIS community about the library in the life of the user. *Library Quarterly* 73, no. 4 (October): 369–82.

Williams, Patrick. 1988. *The American Public Library and the Problem of Purpose*. New York: Greenwood Press, 1988.

Woodward, Jeanette. 2005. *Creating the Customer-Driven Library: Building on the Bookstore Model*. Chicago: American Library Association.

PHOENIX PUBLIC LIBRARY, AZ   1221 N. Central Ave., Phoenix, AZ 85004. Founded 1902. Population served: 1,416,055. Circulation: 12,264,467. Holdings: 1,717,169. 14 branches. A national study, *Public Agenda* (2006) recognized the library as an "exemplar for a successful library system" despite being below the national average in funding. The Desert Broom Branch received an American Library Association/American Institute of Architects Library Building Award in 2007, and the Palo Verde Branch received an award in 2009. A financial crisis in 2009 threatened the continuation of six branches, but it was announced in March 2010 that they would stay open. Directors: Mrs. Claude Berryman, 1900–1903; Mrs. N. A. Morford, 1903–1912; Addie P. Ingalls, 1912–1918; Delia E. Button (acting), 1917; Maude L. Hiatt, 1918–1923; Mary L. Christy (Lambert), 1923–1927; Effie Carmichael, acting 1927, librarian 1929–1932; Jane Hudgins, 1932–1959; Winston R. Henderson, 1959–1981; Rosemary Nelson (acting), 1981; Ralph Edwards, 1981–1995; Rosemary Nelson (acting), 1996; Toni Garvey, 1996–.

Reference

Public Agenda. 2006. *Long Overdue: A Fresh Look at Public Attitudes about Libraries in the 21st Century*. New York: Public Agenda. http://www.publicagenda .org/research.

PIEDMONT PUBLIC LIBRARY, WV   1 Child Ave., Piedmont, WV 26750. Population served: 1,417. Circulation: 9,750. Holdings: 19,529. LJ February 15, 2009, and November 15, 2009: 4-star library; October 1, 2010: 5-star library.

PIERCE, NE. *See* LIED PIERCE PUBLIC LIBRARY, PIERCE, NE.

PIKE'S PEAK LIBRARY DISTRICT, COLORADO SPRINGS, CO   20 N. Cascade Ave., Colorado Springs, CO 80903. Founded 1962. Earlier library service in Colorado Springs dates back to 1885. A special taxing district was created in 1962. Population served: 535,537. Circulation: 7,733,371. Holdings: 1,132,440. 11 branches. HAPLR 2008.

PIMA COUNTY PUBLIC LIBRARY, TUCSON, AZ   101 N. Stone Ave., Tucson, AZ 85701. Tucson had a Carnegie Free Library in 1901, which became the Tucson Public Library in 1957. Tucson Pima Public Library was created in 1990, changing to Pima County Public Library in 2006. Population served: 931,210. Circulation: 6,249,123. Holdings: 1,427,983. 22 branches. LJ February 15, 2009: 4-star library; November 15, 2009, and October 1, 2010: 5-star library.

PIONEER LIBRARY SYSTEM, NORMAN, OK   225 N. Webster Ave., Norman, OK 73069. Population served: 318,255. Circulation: 1,390,000. Holdings: 316,124. 9 branches.

PITKIN COUNTY LIBRARY, ASPEN, CO   120 N. Mill St., Aspen, CO 81611. Founded as a free county library in 1940. Population served: 11,860. Circulation: 175,877. Holdings: 95,331. The library maintains the archive of the Aspen Music Festival. LJ February 15, 2009; November 15, 2009, and October 1, 2010: 3-star library.

PITTSBURGH, PA. *See* CARNEGIE LIBRARY OF PITTSBURGH, PA.

PLAINS COMMUNITY LIBRARY, KS   500 Grand Ave., Plains, KS 67869. Founded 1987. Population served: 1,153. Circulation: 16,938. Holdings: 18,218. LJ February 15, 2009: 3-star library; November 15, 2009: 4-star library; October 1, 2010: 3-star library.

PLAINVIEW-OLD BETHPAGE PUBLIC LIBRARY, PLAINVIEW, NY   999 Old Country Rd., Plainview, NY 11803. Founded 1955. Population served: 28,138. Circulation: 437,358. Holdings: 194,296. LJ October 1, 2010: 5-star library.

PLANNING

Terminology

Library planning has often been hampered by the lack of an accepted vocabulary for the process. Published plans by individual libraries, as well as the literature on planning, indicate the need for a standardized terminology. Since most of the terms used in library planning appear in other fields as well (notably business management), a sensible starting point for definitions is the general dictionaries.

"Plan" in *Merriam* is "a detailed formulation of a program for action." In *American Heritage* it is "a scheme, program, or method worked out beforehand to accomplish an objective." The term "objective" will be discussed in detail shortly. It is well to consider the purpose of planning (making of a plan), or—in accord with the *American Heritage* definition—the basis for the objective of the plan. In the library context, planning stems from the purpose or role of the library, which is expressed in its "mission." *Merriam* says that "mission" is "a specific task with which a person or group is charged"; *American Heritage* says that "mission" is "a special assignment given to a person or group." Both definitions make clear that the mission comes to the person or group (or library) from an outside source; in other words, it is imposed on the library. That outside source may be conveniently named "mission giver."

A mission giver is likely to speak in very general terms, so the nature of the "task" or "assignment" imposed on the library requires interpretation. *ODLIS* states, for "mission," that it is "the basic purpose or role of an organization, expressed succinctly in abstract terms." Therefore, antecedent to the creation of a plan is the preparation of a "mission statement" that clarifies the assignment. A mission statement expresses the library's role as given to it by the mission giver. The actual writing down of the statement falls to the planner, but the sense of it must derive from the mission giver.

In a public library situation, the ultimate mission giver is the community being served. Typically, the community speaks through a board of trustees or through a designated public official. "Evidently, the planner's first challenge is to interpret correctly the institutional mission, for a misunderstanding at this initial stage will result in disconnections later. Although the mission giver may be vague in its mission statement, it will still assess the library according to mission accomplishment" (Marco 1996a, 18). Much of the present discussion is drawn from this article and Marco (1996b).

Several types of plans may emerge in response to the mission. The basic "overall" plan may be conceived as a "short-term" program—encompassing a time period of a few months—or a "long-term" program—covering a period of years. Other words in use are "tactical plan" for the short term and "long-range plan" or "strategic plan" for the long term. Strategic planning, "in contrast to tactical planning (which focuses at achieving narrowly defined interim objectives . . .) looks at the wider picture" (*Business Dictionary* 2010). The last definition takes in the concept of scope as well as time frame. Many subsidiary plans may be formulated in support of the overall plan. *ODLIS* cites approval, contingency, disaster, and emergency plans; others are collection development plans and building plans.

"Goal" and "objective" are two terms that have uncertain places in the vocabulary of planning. In many sources they appear to be synonyms; for example, *American Heritage*: "goal—a purpose toward which effort is directed; an objective." General management literature tends to equate the two terms. Even when they are distinguished, they may well receive descriptions that vary from place to place. It is useful to give each word its own conceptual space since planning involves two separate steps for them (see below in the section "The Planning Process"). *ODLIS* is useful: "goal—a general direction or aim that an organization commits itself to in order to further its mission . . . usually expressed in abstract terms with no time limit for realization" and "objective—a specific achievable outcome of actions taken to achieve a stated goal, usually expressed in measurable terms and subject to time limit." Thus, there are two things implied: one is a general intention to be fulfilled at some undetermined time, and the other is a measurable outcome to be fulfilled by a deadline. It does not matter what tag is attached to each statement. Goal may be expressed as a "vision" and objective as a "target." What is important is a distinction between the two ideas. The goal idea carries a number of hazards in operation which are discussed in "The Planning Process" below.

"Strategy" as a component in planning has given rise to some definitional complications. *Merriam* takes it to mean "a careful plan or method," and *American Heritage* falls back on itself: "a plan of action resulting from strategy or intended to accomplish a specific goal." *ODLIS* does not define "strategy." This language has been suggested: "strategies" are" proposed activities that will lead to the condition described in one or more objectives" (Marco 1996b, 20). As proposed activities translate into perceptible movement within the library, each strategy is matched to an "action" (sometimes called a "tactic").

"Outcome" or "result" is the name given to what has been accomplished by the plan: how goals have been met. Outcome is sometimes a factual position, expressed in numbers or other tangible forms. But outcome may also be filtered through subjective opinion. "Interpretation" is a term that accounts for the way an outcome is understood and promulgated. An interesting aspect of interpretation is that it is not fully under the planner's control since the mission giver will also appraise the outcome.

"Feedback" is the last step in the process. *Merriam* says that it is "the transmission of evaluative or corrective information about an action, event, or process to the original or controlling source; also the information so transmitted." And *American Heritage* says that it is "feedback—a return of information about the result of a process or activity; an evaluative response." While the planner may observe and act on feedback—and ought to do so— as soon as the action stage of the process in under way, the critical feedback comes from the mission giver, who is usually concerned only with the result.

In brief, the terminology of planning consists of mission (the purpose of the plan, originating with the mission giver), goals (general, long-term intentions, drawn from the mission), objectives (specific, time-bound, measurable intentions drawn from the goals), strategies (proposed activities that will fulfill objectives), actions (implementations of strategies), outcomes or results (accomplishments), interpretations of outcomes (by the planner and mission giver), and feedback (corrective or evaluative information).

Historical Summary

Formal library planning has had a short history. The pioneer public librarians seem to have shaped visions of what their libraries ought to be and to work out means of actualizing those visions from day to day. Their plans remained unstated and unwritten, in their heads. In the mid-twentieth century "management in the classic sense—planning and organizing to achieve specific objectives—was not commonly practiced in libraries" (Rosenberg 1994, 375). For many years the American Library Association (ALA) offered uncertain guidance to librarians through its own standards and plans. The *National Plan* of 1934 had no measurable objectives (Williams 1988, 47). "Areas of concentration" took the place of goals and objectives in the 1943 *Post-War Standards*, and goals and objectives were conflated in the 1946 *National Standards*. The *Planning Process for Public Libraries* of 1980 was "obscure and confused" (Williams 1988, 120). Finally, in 1987 the ALA issued a useful guide in *Planning and Role Setting for Public Libraries*—it used consistent terminology and said that objectives should be measurable.

Meanwhile another impetus to systematic planning emerged from federal agencies that responded to grant applications from libraries after the 1956 Library Services Act. Applicants were required to express their intentions and strategies in unequivocal terms. Innovative planning designs in the business world, like management by objectives (MBO) were ubiquitous in the 1960s and influenced library administrators. Planning was seen as a division of scientific management (*see* MANAGEMENT AND ORGANIZATION), discussed in library science textbooks. Interest in public library planning waned, however, and has become tangential (see the section "Current Trends and Issues" below).

The Planning Process

As suggested in the section "Terminology" above, planning involves a number of coordinated steps.

1. Mission statement. Drawing on indications from the mission giver, the library staff articulates its mission in a written document, "a short, succinct statement focusing on the purpose of the organization, its reason for existence, and what it hopes to accomplish ... defining its mission is the most important strategic step an organization can take" (Stueart and Moran 2007, 109). The Kansas City (MO) Public Library offers a brief mission statement, identifying the library as "a doorway to knowledge for all people in our community." Since the planning goals are drawn from the mission statement, a more comprehensive view seems desirable; for example, the Indianapolis-Marion County Public Library states that the library "is the community's place to access essential information resources, technology, programs, and services, foster reading and learning and promote the social, economic, recreational and lifelong learning interests of its diverse population."

2. Goals. These long-term intentions provide the starting point for accomplishing the mission. They have been described as "broad aspirations defined

in operation terms, leading to measurable objectives with strategies and activities emanating from them" (Stueart and Moran 2007, 110). There are several pitfalls to avoid in writing goals. One is the "improvement goal," which proposes only to do better at some present activity. Often such a goal can be met easily and quickly if one allows that even a small change is an improvement. Suppose the case of a goal to improve reference service. "Service is improved by the addition of a staff member, or a service point, or better lighting, or a new sign pointing to the information desk. Surely we would not consider our improvement goal to be completed by putting up a sign" (Marco 1996a, 21). The words "improve" and "strengthen" are best omitted in goal statements. Another pitfall is the "continuation goal," in which the library states an intention to "keep" or "maintain" a certain level of service. If there is no reason why it should *not* be kept, there is no reason for the goal. Goals may also be evaluated as to their relevance: some are ideal (essential to mission accomplishment), some are useful (supportive of mission accomplishment but not essential), some are useless (irrelevant to mission accomplishment), and some may even be counterproductive (obstructing mission accomplishment by draining resources away from mission-essential work).

3. Objectives. These specific, measurable, time-bound projections give energy to the plan. Without them the plan remains at the level of vision (goals), and there is no systematic means of moving to the next step: strategies. Difficulties in writing measurable objectives are imposing, and libraries have not been very successful at the task. "Most objectives are tangible and measurable, but others are not" (Stueart and Moran 2007, 113), meaning that some objectives are really goals and that is the situation that is typically found in published public library plans. This is a matter deserving of serious consideration by planners. There is adequate guidance in the literature, notably in the ALA *Planning and Role Setting* document, which presents useful criteria for objectives, such as "Is the objective measurable or verifiable, that is, how will librarians know if the objective has been achieved?" and "Is the objective related to at least one goal?"(McClure et al. 1987, 52). Objectives may be classed, as goals were above, according to their relevance; in the case of objectives, the relevance is to one or more goals. The categories are ideal, useful, useless, and counterproductive.

4. Strategies. These are the proposed actions to be taken in order to meet each objective. Without properly designed objectives, no useful strategies will emerge. With good objectives in place, strategies can be developed; they will reflect ambient factors like the state of resources, cost–benefit calculations, and community impact. If success eludes the planner, the reason may often lie with ill-chosen strategies. A single objective may generate one strategy or any number of strategies, and a single strategy may account for a single objective or for several objectives. What is needed is a clear connection between the conceptual steps. It may be that, on study of the situation, no strategy can result in the meeting of a certain objective. Then the objective—and the goal from which it stems—will need to be modified.

5. Actions. With this step the plan exhibits its first perceptible movement. The four earlier steps have been thought pieces, desk work; to an outside observer, the library at the end of step 4 will be as it was at step 1. But step 5 starts the engine. Actions (or tasks, tactics, or initiatives) are implementations of the strategies, which are directly related to the objectives. Not every strategy is implemented, and not every action results from a strategy since there are intervening events that may affect the relationship. But in proper execution, an action will always be something done to implement a strategy, or it will be of no use.

Most planning documents are weak at steps 4 and 5. Many say nothing about strategies but leave off with the statement of objectives or stop at goals. A further complication, not unusual in plans, is the blending of objectives with strategies so that "doing something"—an action—is read as an objective. Having a conference or issuing a publication may be taken as an objective, but such matters are means to a further end: strategies toward another objective, perhaps not stated.

6. Outcome. Whether anything has been accomplished as a result of the planning process is the final test of its worth. Since there are so many possible deflections from clarity in the previous steps, the outcome may be read variously. It is natural for the planners and their constituencies to want success: no one announces failure. A good statement of outcome would connect all the specific objectives to the definite results that they engendered. The outcome is a factual report.

7. Interpretation. It is the planner who offers the final appraisal of the outcome, and it may be shaped to reflect satisfaction with the completed process. Even if no tangible outcomes can be discovered at the end of the day, the planner may put matters under a favorable light. One director, asked about the success of a five-year plan just completed, answered, in part,

> Successive plans reflect the dynamics of growth, change, and new trends. They build on the foundations of the previous report. It is not so much that our six goals have been achieved, but that they have changed to reflect accomplishments, new ideas, and social and economic shifts in state and local populations. (quoted in Marco 1996b, 22)

8. Feedback. With the issuance of step 7, the planner's interpretation of the outcome, response from the mission giver may be expected. This feedback phase closes the loop that began with the mission in step 1 (feedback may have occurred at step 5 as well). Feedback works more easily in some types of plan than in others. A building plan will lead to a tangible structure for all to see and criticize. But there is less opportunity for scrutiny of other types of plans, such as those that lead to administrative reorganizations, or collaborations, or revised policies. It would be valuable for the planner to determine in some way the extent of satisfaction that the plan outcome has in the community. But what is likely to occur is a vague response, as nebulous as the mission itself. Or the mission giver may be overwhelmed by the scope of the plan, the time

it consumed, or the polished publication of outcome and interpretation, and the response may be praise without understanding.

So this is the ultimate challenge to the planner: to give the mission giver a clear and dispassionate outcome statement that will not only show what has been accomplished but also demonstrate the worth of the effort and the library that exercised it. Libraries that achieve this purpose are those that have reason to survive and prosper in any economic and political climate.

Current Trends and Issues

The present condition of public library planning is problematic. On the theoretical side, there have been useful books, articles, and ALA publications, most of which define the planning process along the lines given above. On the practical side, few public libraries have strategic plans (to judge from an extensive examination of library websites). Those that have plans have adopted a rather free approach, not consistent with the guidance of the professional literature. This approach is strong on vision statements and weak on measurable objectives. Indeed, goals and objectives are invariably conflated. Accomplishments, if any are pronounced, may seem disconnected from intentions.

The ALA, which has offered good theoretical instruction for planners, has concurrently given them a poor example to follow in its *ALA Ahead to 2010* strategic plan. This plan presents six "goal areas," each with a "goal statement" and "strategic objectives." Goal area 1, "Advocacy/Value of the Profession," carries the goal statement "ALA and its members are the leading advocates for libraries and the library profession." This sentence announces the present state of affairs rather than a long-term intended outcome and is neither a goal nor an objective. The six strategic objectives follow:

1. Increase support for research and evaluation to provide evidence regarding the value and impact of libraries.
2. Increase public awareness of the value and impact of libraries of all types.
3. Increase public awareness of the value and impact of librarians and library staff.
4. Mobilize, support, and sustain grassroots advocacy for libraries and library funding at local, state, and federal levels.
5. Increase collaboration on securing legislation favorable to libraries.
6. Increase public awareness of the importance of intellectual freedom and privacy and the role of libraries in a democracy.

All these are goal statements rather than objectives; none can be measured as to outcome (it is interesting that none of them pertain to quality of library service). All except number 4 are "improvement goals" (see above), which can be achieved with minimal effort. Number 4 is a proper long-range goal.

So the whole "goal area" is without objectives, strategies, or actions; it is merely a checklist of good things to work on. When the time comes to say what the outcome of such a "goal area" has been, odd things appear. For example, "objective" 2 is credited with this "accomplishment" on the ALA website:

> According to the new Harris Poll (Harris interactive), 68% of Americans have a library card, up 5% since 2006. This is the greatest number since ALA began to measure library card usage in 1990. In person visits are also up 10% compared with a 2006 ALA household survey.

These are favorable findings, and librarians may take satisfaction with them. But it is curious for the ALA to claim credit for bringing them about through the activation of "objective" 2. In fact the website shows no activity was initiated with regard to that item. In a 2009 report on the plan's progress, the ALA's executive director cited numerous changes and events related to the goal areas; however, it seems to be largely an account of commendable daily activities at the ALA (and elsewhere in the profession) rather than a list of results from distinct "actions" generated by *ALA Ahead* (Fiels 2009, 10–11).

Time will tell whether planning, as "a scheme, program, or method worked out beforehand to accomplish an objective," can be restored to the panoply of fundamental activities in public libraries.

References

Business Dictionary. 2010. http://www.businessdictionary.com. Accessed May 2010.
Fiels, Keith Michael. 2009. Strategic planning. *American Libraries* 40, no. 11 (November): 10–11.
McClure, Charles R., et al. 1987. *Planning and Role Setting for Public Libraries.* Chicago: American Library Association.
Marco, Guy A. 1996a. The terminology of planning. Part 1. *Library Management* 17, no. 2: 17–23.
Marco, Guy A. 1996b. The terminology of planning. Part 2. *Library Management* 17, no. 7: 17–24.
Nelson, Sandra. 2008. *Strategic Planning for Results.* Chicago: American Library Association.
Rosenberg, Jane A. 1994. Library management. In *Encyclopedia of Library History*, 373–77. New York: Garland.
Stueart, Robert D., and Barbara Moran. 2007. *Library and Information Center Management.* 7th ed. Westport, CT: Libraries Unlimited.
Williams, Patrick. 1988. *The American Public Library and the Problem of Purpose.* New York: Greenwood Press.

PLANO PUBLIC LIBRARY SYSTEM, PLANO, TX   2501 Coit Rd., Plano, TX 75075. Founded 1965. Population served: 273,923. Circulation: 1,510,560. Holdings: 322,694. 6 branches.

PLAQUEMINES PARISH LIBRARY, BELLE CHASE, LA   8442 Highway 23, Belle Chase, LA 70037. Founded 1959. Population served: 26,049. Circulation: 18,546. Holdings: 26,624. 2 branches, 1 bookmobile. Hurricane Katrina destroyed the main library and one branch, damaging the other (for present status, *see* HURRICANES KATRINA AND RITA).

PLUMMER, MARY WRIGHT, 1856–1916   Librarian. Born in Richmond, IN, March 8, 1856. In 1881–1882 she studied at Wellesley College but was mostly self-educated. She was a member of the first class (1887) in Melvil Dewey's library school at Columbia College, and reported on it at the American Library Association (ALA) conference. Plummer worked as a cataloger in the St. Louis Public Library, then went to the Pratt Institute Free Library in Brooklyn as librarian and instructor in the training program. In 1895 she was head of the library and the school and in 1904 of the school only. From 1911 to 1916 she headed the new library school of the New York Public Library. Plummer was the second woman elected to the presidency of the ALA (1915–1916). She advocated an end to censorship and promoted librarianship as a profession, one that should be grounded in ethics. LJ Hall of Fame; *DALB*.

PLYMOUTH DISTRICT LIBRARY, MI   223 S. Main St., Plymouth, MI 48170. Founded 1923. Population served: 46,719. Circulation: 891,519. Holdings: 220,949. HAPLR 2009.

POCAHONTAS COUNTY FREE LIBRARIES, MARLINTON, WV   500 Eighth St., Marlinton, WV 24954. Population served: 9,131. Circulation: 47,361. Holdings: 54,114. IMLS award 2003.

POLAND PUBLIC LIBRARY, NY   8849 Main St., Poland, NY 13431. Founded 1919. The library is autonomous, with its own board. It chose to affiliate with the Mid-York Library System in 1960. Population served: 451. Circulation: 30,797. Holdings: 16,410. HAPLR 2009.

POLICY STATEMENTS

Terminology

The relevant terms are "policy," "procedure(s)," "regulation(s)," and "practice." *Merriam* says of policy, "A definite course or method of action selected from among alternatives and in light of given conditions to guide and determine present and future decisions." *American Heritage* says that policy is "a plan or course of action, as of a government, political party, or business, intended to influence and determine decisions, actions, and other matters." A recent book on library policy defines the word as "a set of guidelines that define managerial actions and decisions" or "procedures, regulations, and other documents that relate to the policy" (Larson and Totten

2008, 3). *ODLIS* has no entries for these terms, but a sense of "policy" may be drawn from the entry on "information policy," which reads in part "a governing principle, plan, or course of action."

"Procedure" in *Merriam* is "a series of steps followed in a regular definite order." *American Heritage* gives "a series of steps taken to accomplish an end." In Larson and Totten (2008, 4), "procedures are step-by-step action guides that standardize the methods by which repetitive tasks are performed, usually by listing the steps in order of performance."

"Regulation" in *Merriam* is "an authoritative rule dealing with details or procedure." In *American Heritage* it is "a principle, rule, or law designed to control or govern conduct." Larson and Totten (2008, 4) has "rules and regulations indicate actions that should and should not occur in response to policy."

"Practice" is "a repeated or customary action" (*Merriam*), "a habitual or customary action or way of doing something" (*American Heritage*), or "the way things are actually done" (Larson and Totten 2008, 4).

Sorting this out and applying it all to the library context leads to these definitions:

> Policy: a general expression of the library's position on matters that will require decisions.
>
> Procedures: steps taken to implement library policy, including decisions, regulations, and routines.
>
> Regulations (rules): directions given to staff and patrons in order to implement library policy.
>
> Practice: customary actions of staff and patrons, whether or not based on library policy.

All these entities exist in every library, but they may be unverbalized, simply "understood." It is desirable for policy, procedures, and regulations to be written and available to staff and patrons. A written policy statement is a managerial tool, a segment of the library's documentation, a public relations tool, a training tool, and a basis for handling legal issues that may arise (Larson and Totten 2008, 5).

Types of policy statements include those concerning staff (*see* STAFFING), access to the collections and services (*see* CIRCULATION SERVICES; INTERNET; REFERENCE AND INFORMATION SERVICES; SERVICES TO PEOPLE WITH DISABILITIES), interlibrary loan (*see* INTERLIBRARY LOAN), patron conduct, patron right to privacy and confidentiality (*see* PRIVACY AND CONFIDENTIALITY), materials selection (*see* COLLECTION DEVELOPMENT), and use of facilities. There are useful descriptions with sample texts for these statements in Larson and Totten (2008). The American Library Association (ALA 1993) has issued a guide for public library policy writers.

An examination of public library websites reveals a variety of approaches to policies and the presentation of them to the community. Most of the libraries with individual entries in this handbook offer no information about their policies, except perhaps for procedures on how to get a library card and regulations on fines. Libraries that do mention their policies give texts for just a few of them, suggesting either that there are no others or that the public would not be interested in others. For example, the Chicago Public Library provides Web access to these "library policies": confidentiality of patron and circulation records, customer bill of rights, guidelines for computer and Internet use, guidelines governing use of the library, library borrowing policies, meeting room policies, photo reproduction policy, policy of unattended children and disruptive behavior, and reciprocal borrowing policy (many of these statements are in fact regulations and procedures rather than policies). Conspicuous by their absence are policies for collection development, reference services, and staffing. Only a few of the statements given in the website are posted in the main library.

While the Chicago Public Library offers a typical approach to the policy issue, some libraries are more thorough in their presentations. For example, the Topeka and Shawnee County (KS) Public Library provides website texts of its "policies" (again, many are regulations and procedures) dealing with circulation, computer use, patron conduct, exhibits and displays, materials selection, privacy, confidentiality, programs, and unattended children. The Denver Public library offers website texts of policies (or regulations) on getting library cards, library use, child safety, collection development, computer/Internet use, and privacy. Although one might hold that certain policies, such as those about staffing or collection development, need not be readily available to the public, it is a fact that in public libraries they are public documents.

Most of the topics covered by policy, regulations, and procedures are treated in other entries in this volume, as indicated above. Policies on patron conduct do not appear in other entries, so this issue has a place here. It seems to be a subject of much concern, often leading into curious pathways. The Chandler (AZ) Public Library, for example, lists 20 prohibited behaviors. Some are sensible enough, such as carrying firearms, exhibitionism, bathing, soliciting, and fighting. Others are cloudy, such as "roaming aimlessly" or "loitering." One is in violation of *The Library Bill of Rights* and common sense: "Adults not accompanied by a child or researching children's materials in the Youth Area."

The policy domain is one that can be viewed as satisfactory in terms of theory (textbooks and official guidelines) but less so in terms of practice. Public libraries need to develop policies (distinguishing them from procedures and regulations) if they do not have them, publish them on websites if they do have them, and post them in main libraries and branches. Policies should be created in concert between trustees and library administration and authorized by appropriate authority. They should be amplified and revised periodically.

References

American Library Association. 1993. *Handbook for Writers of Public Library Policies*. Chicago: American Library Association.

Larson, Jeanette C., and Herman L. Totten. 2008. *The Public Library Policy Writer: A Guidebook with Model Policies on CD-ROM.* New York: Neal-Schuman.

POMEROY PUBLIC LIBRARY, IA   114 S. Ontario St., Pomeroy, IA 50575. Population served: 1,120. Circulation: 10,371. Holdings: 9,523. LJ October 1, 2010: 3-star library.

POOLE, WILLIAM FREDERICK, 1821–1894   Librarian. Born in Salem, MA, December 24, 1821. He graduated from Yale in 1849. While a student he compiled an index to the magazine collection of a student literary organization. In 1851 he began working as assistant librarian in the Boston Athenaeum, then moved to the Mercantile Library Association of Boston as librarian. He published a printed catalog (1854) of the holdings, with author, title, and subject entries in one sequence, the form that came to be known as a dictionary catalog. Poole's first index was revised and published in 1853; it was shown at the first meeting of American librarians in New York, 1853. He became librarian of the Athenaeum, remaining to 1869. From 1871 to 1874 he directed the Cincinnati Public Library, bringing it quickly to second place after Boston among American libraries. In 1874 he became the first librarian of the Chicago Public Library, where he set about devising a classification system and building up circulation. Recognized as one of the leading librarians of his day, he was elected vice president of the new American Library Association, established in 1876, and later for two terms as president. His interest in indexing continued, and he issued *Poole's Index to Periodical Literature* in 1882. He moved a few blocks away in 1887 to become the founding director of the Newberry Library. His idea of a building divided into subject departments was opposed by the architect Henry Cobb, but Poole seems to have prevailed; however, the present structure has no such divisions. Poole was an adherent of the "ladder theory" of selection, defending a library's acquisition of fiction as a means of inculcating good reading habits. He wanted only respectable fiction, however: "The librarian who should allow an immoral novel in his library for circulation would be as culpable as the manager of a picture gallery who should hang an indecent picture on his walls" (Poole 1876, 50). Poole died in Evanston, IL, on March 1, 1894. LJ Hall of Fame; *DALB.*

Reference

Poole, William Frederick. 1876. Some popular objections to public libraries. *American Library Journal* 1, no. 1 (September): 45–51.

PORT JEFFERSON FREE LIBRARY, NY   100 Thompson St., Port Jefferson, NY 11777. Founded 1909 with a provisional state charter; received absolute charter 1912. Population served: 7,502. Circulation: 321,978. Holdings: 141,161. LJ February 15, 2009; November 15, 2009, and October 1, 2010: 5-star library.

PORT WASHINGTON PUBLIC LIBRARY, NY   1 Library Dr., Port Washington, NY 11050. Population served: 29,687. Circulation: 438,474. Holdings: 244,158. LJ February 15, 2009: 4-star library; November 15, 2009, and October 1, 2010: 5-star library.

PORTLAND, OR. *See* LIBRARY ASSOCIATION OF PORTLAND, OR; MULTNOMAH COUNTY LIBRARY, PORTLAND, OR.

PORTSMOUTH PUBLIC LIBRARY, VA   601 Court St., Portsmouth, VA 23704. Population served: 99,000. Circulation: 368,824. Holdings: 318,089. 3 branches. The library's innovative "dinner and a book" program to combat illiteracy (Enrich and Burton 2004) was ongoing in 2010.

Reference

Enrich, Rachel, and Susan Burton. 2004. Dinner and a book: Portsmouth combats illiteracy with food for mind and body. *Virginia Libraries* 50, no. 4 (October–November–December): 15–17.

POWER, EFFIE LOUISE, 1873–1969   Librarian. Born near Conneautville, PA, February 12, 1873. With no academic degree, she was brought to the Cleveland Public Library (CPL) by its director (and a family neighbor) William Howard Brett. She started as an apprentice in 1895 and took charge of the Junior Alcove, which became a children's room in 1898. Power was the first children's librarian in the CPL. After studying children's work in the training program of the Carnegie Library of Pittsburgh Power earned a diploma in 1904. She later earned a teacher's certificate from Columbia University. She went on to Pittsburgh as first assistant in the children's department in 1909 and taught in the school. In 1911 she became supervisor of children's work in the St. Louis Public Library but returned to Pittsburgh in 1914 to supervise the Carnegie Library schools division and head the children's department. A final library assignment came in 1920, when she returned to CPL as director of children's work. Power taught in several library schools and finished her career with two years as instructor in the Columbia University library school. Her wide experience was reflected in the first text on children's work, *Library Service for Children* (American Library Association 1930). She also compiled stories for children in various volumes. A driving force in the development of children's work in three major public libraries and a significant instructor/author, Power was a leader in the movement to give attention to children the highest professional attention. She died in Pompano Beach, FL, on October 8, 1969. *DALB*.

Reference

Kimball, Melanie A., et al. 2004. Effie Louise Power: librarian, educator, author. *Library Trends* 52, no. 4 (Spring): 924–72.

PRESERVATION

Terminology

Preservation is the act of preserving; to preserve is to "keep safe from injury, harm, or destruction; to keep alive, intact, or free from decay; to keep or save from decomposition" (*Merriam*). In the library (and archive) context, the meaning has the extra element of repair; if harm to a library product has occurred, there are remedies available. This definition conjoins the two aspects: "Preservation is the maintenance of objects in their original condition through retention, proper care, and, if the object has been damaged, restoration" (Jordan 2003, 210). Conservation—"careful preservation and protection of something" (*Merriam*)—and restoration—"a bringing back to a former position or condition" (*Merriam*)—are terms usually applied to art works but are germane with respect to printed materials as well.

Historical Summary

Art scholars and curators were the early practitioners of preservation. Decades or centuries of neglect confronted them when they began to restore paintings. In 1565 a project began to restore parts of the Sistine Chapel frescoes (the first of many restorations, the latest taking from 1989 to 1994). There was an attempt in 1726 to restore Leonardo's *Last Supper*. After a fire in 1734 there was an extensive repair of paintings in the royal Spanish collections. In the late eighteenth century the basic concepts of conservation were developed. Technical analysis of original pigments advanced in France and Britain in the early nineteenth century, and cleaning of old paintings was common if often questionable. Michael Faraday carried out analytical and deterioration studies for the National Gallery, London, in 1850–1853, reporting on varnishes, cleaning methods, and the impact of fog, coal smoke, and gas lighting, but his findings were not influential. Later technical studies began to have more impact, and systematic restorations took their place in the curatorial work. Laboratories and conservation departments were established in major museums, and training programs were offered. International conferences and publications followed. An Italian scholar published a handbook of restoration in 1936 (Mancia 1936). An early scientific work in English was *The Conservation of Antiquities and Works of Art: Treatment, Repair, and Restoration* by Harold Plenderleith and Alfred E. Werner (1956) (for details on recent work, see *Arthur M. Sackler Colloquium* 2005).

The energy expended in the conservation of paintings has not been matched in the preservation of books and other library formats. The early history of library preservation was sporadic (Higginbotham 1990). In the mid-twentieth century the expressed concerns were about repair ("mending") and binding. Serious attention to paper chemistry and deterioration emerged a generation ago. The Yale University Library and the New York Public Library had formal preservation programs in 1972, and the Newberry Library had a conservation and preservation department in 1974. The New England Document Conservation Center was established by the New

England Library Association in 1973. A degree in conservation was offered by Columbia University in 1981, and other library schools had preservation courses. A *Library Trends* issue in 1981 dealt with preservation and conservation, covering paper problems, sound recording preservation, photograph preservation, and microform as a replacement medium.

Current Practice

A significant difference between painting preservation and book preservation is that paintings can be kept in protected condition, never to be handled by the public, while books, even rare books, are available for direct use by library patrons. This factor has led to a deemphasis on prevention of harm to the materials, such as in the sense of temperature and humidity controls, since environmental conditions need to be set at levels of human comfort. Preservation in public libraries is generally limited to materials in "special collections," which may have some measure of environmental control and restrictions on photocopying, use of pens in reading rooms, and the like. Books in the general open-shelf collection receive no preservative protection. Large research libraries have programs to preserve certain collections, such as old newspapers and periodicals (see below). Libraries of all sizes are preparing policies and procedures for dealing with disasters (Fortson 1992).

Research has provided guidance for librarians who are in a position to implement it. It is possible to stabilize the condition of books with deteriorating paper although not possible to reverse the decay, to clean books systematically with proper solvents that will not cause harm, to repair books in a way that brings back much of their original situation, and to retain the intellectual content of materials that are too far gone for physical restoration. And while the ideal temperature (65 to 68 degrees Fahrenheit) and humidity (48 to 52 percent relative humidity) for a book may be impossible to maintain in a public library, lighting can be designed for the benefit of the materials without affecting the users. What should be avoided is daylight—high in damaging ultraviolet and infrared wavelengths—and fluorescent illumination—high in ultraviolet. Air quality can be controlled to some extent with filters to exclude various pollutants and pests.

"By far the largest preservation problem quantitatively are 'brittle books' printed after 1860" (Banks 1978, 181). Because of the acidic content of paper used in books and newspapers after about 1860, the paper gradually becomes brittle and ultimately crumbles when handled. A library that wants to have a usable file of local newspapers needs to take certain steps. A page-by-page examination of the file will determine which pages are brittle (or otherwise damaged with mold or insects). If a brittle page is not yet crumbling, it can be sheathed in Mylar. Deacidification is an option but a slow and expensive one (see description in Banks 1978, 201). If the paper is too much damaged, it can be replaced with a photocopy made on the spot (see American Library Association 1990). If an entire run is seriously brittle, it may be best to replace it with a microfilm or a digital copy. Microfilming and digitizing preserve the intellectual content but destroy the artifactual element that may be significant in research. If a file is to be bound or rebound, special considerations apply, such as regarding adhesives, trimming, and sewing. "Preservation binding" is done with acid-free and lignin-free materials. The American National Standards Institute, the National Information Standards Organization, and the Library Binding Institute have prepared standards for preservation binding (Merrill-Oldham and Parisi 2008).

Large public libraries may have dedicated departments that deal with preservation (e.g., Cleveland Public Library), but for the most part the function is subsumed in special collections or collection management. The American Library Association has a Preservation and Reformatting Section in its Association for Library Collections & Technical Services; it issues useful publications and holds a "preservation week" each year to draw attention to the issues involved. *See also* DIGITAL MEDIA; MUSIC COLLECTIONS.

References

American Library Association. Association for Library Collections & Technical Services. 1990. *Preservation Photocopying of Replacement Pages*. Chicago: American Library Association.

Arthur M. Sackler Colloquium on Scientific Examination of Art: Modern Techniques in Conservation and Analysis. 2005. Washington, DC: National Academies Press.

Ballofet, Nelly, and Jenny Hille. 2004. *Preservation and Conservation for Libraries and Archives*. Chicago: American Library Association.

Banks, Paul N. 1978. Preservation of library materials. In *Encyclopedia of Library and Information Science* 23: 180–222. New York: Marcel Dekker.

Cloonan, Michele V., and Ross Harvey, eds. 2007. Preserving Cultural Heritage. An issue of *Library Trends 56*, no. 1 (Summer).

Cunha, George M., and D.G. Cunha. 1971. *Conservation of Library Materials*. 2nd ed. Metuchen, NJ: Scarecrow Press.

Fortson, Judith. 1992. *Disaster Planning and Recovery: A How-to-Do-It Manual for Librarians and Archivists*. New York: Neal-Schuman.

Higginbotham, Barbara. 1990. *Our Past Preserved: A History of American Library Preservation, 1876–1910*. Boston: G. K. Hall.

Jordan, Sophia K. 2003. Preservation of library materials. In *Encyclopedia of Library and Information Science*, 2nd ed., 3: 2352–62.

Mancia, Renato. 1936. *L'esame scientifico delle opera d'arte ed il lore restauro*. Privately published. 2nd ed. Milan: Hoepli, 1944.

Merrill-Oldham, Jan, and Paul Parisi. 2008. *Guide to the ANSI/NISO/LBI Library Binding Standard*. Chicago: American Library Association.

Plenderleith, Harold, and Alfred E. Werner. 1956. *The Conservation of Antiquities and Works of Art: Treatment, Repair, and Restoration*. London: Oxford University Press.

Schecter, Abraham. 1999. *Basic Book Repair Methods*. Englewood, CO: Libraries Unlimited.

Swartzburg, Susan.1980. *Preserving Library Materials.* Metuchen, NJ: Scarecrow Press.

Teper, T. H. 2005. Current and future challenges for library and archive preservation. *Library Resources & Technical Services* 49, no. 1 (January): 32–39.

PRINCETON PUBLIC LIBRARY, NJ   65 Witherspoon St., Princeton, NJ 08542. Founded 1909, opened 1910. Population served: 33,450. Circulation: 573,200. Holdings: 177,500. LJ February 15, 2009; November 15, 2009, and October 1, 2010: 4-star library.

PRINCIPLES. *See* PHILOSOPHY OF PUBLIC LIBRARIANSHIP.

PRIVACY AND CONFIDENTIALITY

Terminology

Merriam defines "privacy" as "the quality or state of being apart from company or association; freedom from unauthorized intrusion." *American Heritage* says that privacy is "the quality or condition of being secluded from the presence or view of others. The state of being free from unsanctioned intrusion." Privacy in the first sense given here seems not to be a library concern; users do not expect a situation where they are secluded from others. In the second sense, having to do with intrusion, the case moves to library territory. But in what way could library practice be an "intrusion"? Back to the dictionaries: *Merriam* offers "intrusion" as "the act of intruding," which is "to thrust or force in or upon someone or something, esp. without permission, welcome or fitness." *American Heritage* states that "intruding" is "to put or force in inappropriately, esp. without invitation, fitness, or permission." It is difficult to say how libraries do that. But it is clear that the dictionaries are restricting their purview to physical privacy. They do not approach what has come to called data privacy or informational privacy. In this area libraries may have a role to perform.

Adult individuals are likely to regard personal information about themselves as private. For one reason or another, a person may not want others to know of her religion, political affiliations, relationships, medical problems, sexual orientation, financial condition, Internet use, or recreational preferences. American society has developed some traditions and legal safeguards regarding certain personal information; this is most evident in doctor–patient and lawyer–client relationships. Since this is the type of privacy that will apply to libraries, it is worth thinking about how it actually works. Medical information about an individual is private, intended for the use of a particular person: the doctor. But the doctor shares the information, at least some of it, rather widely: among his own staff, with specialist colleagues, with pharmacists, with various technicians, and with insurance companies. Lawyers share information with their staff and with appropriate officers of the court. In both doctor and lawyer situations, waiting rooms are public spaces in which anyone may observe who is there and draw inferences about their situations.

Another relevant term is "confidentiality." It is not a headword in either of the reference dictionaries, but since it is drawn from "confidential," one may construct a definition. *Merriam* has "confidential": "entrusted with confidence"; *American Heritage* has "confidential": "entrusted with the confidence of another." "Confidence" is "reliance on another's discretion" (*Merriam*) or "a feeling of assurance that a confidant will keep a secret." So confidentiality emerges as a state of affairs in which an agent discloses private matters to another agent (a confidant), assuming that agent to be discrete. The doctor or lawyer holds the role of confidant for the patient or client. The difference between data privacy and confidentiality seems to be that the former is fundamental and ongoing, while the latter depends on deliberate sharing of information.

It is time to find a place for public libraries. As already noted, libraries seem to have no part to play in the field of physical privacy. Libraries are like doctors' waiting rooms, open places where anyone is observed and observing. But there is no intrusion on anyone's physical self as there is in security areas like airports. This kind of privacy is simply not a library issue. As for data privacy, public libraries do require a limited amount of information about those who want to register for library cards. Typically, such information is no more than what is available in open sources: street address, phone number, and the like.

What may apply to library–patron situations is confidentiality. In this state of affairs the patron shares with the library staff various personal facts (not available in open sources): what books and other materials he charges out and what Internet sites he looks at. If he assumes that the staff will be discrete in handling this information about his practices, the confidentiality situation applies. But if he does not make that assumption, out of indifference or skepticism, then there is no confidentiality situation. Still there is much that is implicit here. Librarians may impute to the patrons a desire for discretion since it is reasonable that a rational person would prefer to have his information handled discretely rather than made available to anyone. And even though many, even most, patrons do not care about the matter at all, some will, and policy must be made for all not for individuals. The section "Library Policy and Practice" below considers how public libraries and the American Library Association (ALA) have approached this complex issue.

Historical Summary

The U.S. Constitution does not mention privacy or confidentiality, and it was a hundred years before the issue was mentioned in legal literature. An article published in 1890 by Samuel Warren and Louis Brandeis dealt with the impact of new technologies, such as photography, on the exposure of private information; they asserted that privacy is the "right to be let alone." The earliest legal case to enshrine that right was *Griswold v. Connecticut* 381

U.S. 479 (1965), in which the Supreme Court identified it as a "penumbra"—a right not explicitly stated in the Constitution but existing as a concomitant to expressed rights. Primary among those expressed rights that bear the privacy penumbra is the Fourth Amendment, protecting individuals "in their persons, homes, papers, and effects from unreasonable searches and seizures" by the government. In *Katz v. United States* 389 U.S. 347 (1967), the Supreme Court held that what a person "seeks to preserve as private even in areas accessible to the public may be constitutionally protected." In his concurring opinion, Justice Harlan said that a right to privacy exists if a person "has exhibited and actual (subjective) expectation of privacy" and that the expectation is "one that society is prepared to recognize as reasonable" (according to the definitions in the first section of this entry, *Katz v. United States* was about confidentiality). The Privacy Act of 1974 and Amendments (5 USC Sec. 552a) deals with the responsibilities of government agencies in protecting privacy. There are further subtleties that cannot be pursued in this summary, but it should be mentioned that laws of individual states must be considered since they may restrict the zone of privacy. Except Hawaii and Kentucky, all the states in 2009 had passed legislation to provide some level of protection for the confidentiality of library circulation records.

The U.S. Senate ratified on June 8, 1992, the UN *Covenant on Civil and Political Rights*, which follows the 1948 *Universal Declaration of Human Rights* in stating that "No one shall be subjected to arbitrary interference with his privacy, family, home or correspondence" (United Nations 1948, article 12).

The legal scene was abruptly turned from this established support of confidentiality on October 26, 2001, as the USA Patriot Act was signed into law by President Bush (Public Law 107-56). The measure had wide bipartisan support in Congress; the only senator to vote against it was Russell Feingold. In 2006 and 2010 the act was reauthorized. The purpose of the Patriot Act was to increase the ability of law enforcement agencies to search telephone, email, financial, medical, and other records of individuals in the effort to discover terrorist activities. Section 215 is of greatest concern to public librarians since it allows the FBI to apply for an order to a library to produce books, records, papers, and other documents, including information on materials charged out by individuals. Despite protests and legal challenges from organizations concerned with civil liberties, the act remains in force.

Library Policy and Practice

There was no particular alarm about patron privacy or confidentiality among public librarians before the Patriot Act arrived. But there were troubling incidents. In 1970, U.S. Treasury agents requested permission of the Milwaukee Public Library to examine the circulation records of books and other materials on explosives. The ALA responded with a statement that read in part,

> The Executive Board of the ALA believes that the efforts of the
> federal government to convert library circulation records into

"suspect lists" constitute and unconscionable and unconstitutional invasion of the right of privacy of library patrons and, if permitted to continue, will do irreparable damage to the educational and social value of the libraries of this country. (McQuarie 1984, 44)

An ALA "Policy on Confidentiality of Library Records" was formally adopted by the ALA Council on January 20, 1971. It declared "circulation records and other records identifying the names of library users to be confidential in nature" and that such records should not be made available to any agency without court order or subpoena.

Actually there had been an earlier assertion by the ALA in a code of ethics that dealt with confidentiality, but the focus was on personal information provided by patrons rather than circulation records: "It is the librarian's obligation to treat as confidential any private information obtained through contact with library patrons" (ALA 1939). The provision was amplified in the 1995 code to read, "We protect each library user's right to privacy and confidentiality with respect to information sought or received and resources consulted, borrowed, acquired, or transmitted" (ALA 1995). Confidentiality is treated as an ethical issue; the ALA also places it within the bounds of intellectual freedom (see INTELLECTUAL FREEDOM).

These positions of the professional association have been echoed in policy statements of public libraries. An example, cited in the ALA website, is the "Confidentiality Policy" of the Seattle Public Library, which reads in part, "Staff members and volunteers may not convey information about borrower records, including loan transactions, requests for information, or materials and online sites accessed, to individuals or to any private or public agency without an order from a court of competent jurisdiction, or as otherwise required by law." Also, "The Seattle Public Library keeps the minimum number of records necessary for maintaining operations. When a customer logs off a library computer, information about that user session is automatically deleted. Also, when a customer returns materials to the library, information about what was checked out is automatically deleted at day-end, unless the customer has fines or has been referred to a materials recovery agency" (Seattle Public Library 2010).

Some useful advice to librarians has been published by ALA (Chmara 2009, from which the following is drawn). First, what should be done if a law enforcement agent requests library records? Distinguish between a search warrant, which is a binding court order, and a subpoena, which is not a court order. Search warrants have to be obeyed, although the librarian may request time for discussing the matter with legal counsel. A subpoena may be refused, but legal counsel should be involved. Internet records are protected as well as book circulation records. Protect confidentiality by avoiding public "hold shelves" that have patron names attached to requested books. Arrange computer screens to minimize observation by staff or other patrons. See that there is a gap in the queue at the charge-out desk so that one patron does not have another patron watching what is being taken out. "Intellectual freedom is threatened if readers are inhibited by possible observation of others" (Gorman 2005, 85). The "waiting room" situation described in the first section of this entry is still operative in the library, but there are ways to make it less onerous. Finally, write a confidentiality policy, post it, and see that all staff are trained accordingly.

References

American Library Association. 1939. *Code of Ethics for Librarians.* Chicago: American Library Association.
American Library Association. 1995. *Code of Ethics for Librarians.* Chicago: American Library Association.
Chmara, Theresa. 2009. *Privacy and Confidentiality Issues: A Guide for Librarians and Their Lawyers.* Chicago: American Library Association.
Gorman, Michael. 2005. *Our Own Selves: More Meditations for Librarians.* Chicago: American Library Association.
McQuarie, Heather McNeil. 1984. Confidentiality of library records. In *Encyclopedia of Library and Information Science* 41 (Supplement 6): 44–46. New York: Marcel Dekker.
Seattle Public Library. 2010. Confidentiality policy. Seattle: Seattle Public Library. http://www.spl.org. Accessed January, 2010.
United Nations. 1948. *Universal Declaration of Human Rights.* New York: United Nations.

PROSPECT COMMUNITY LIBRARY, PA   357 Main St., Prospect, PA 16052. Population served: 3,526. Circulation: 31,097. Holdings: 14,374. LJ November 15, 2009: 3-star library.

PROVIDENCE PUBLIC LIBRARY, RI   150 Empire St., Providence, RI 02903. Opened February 4, 1878, a private library open free to all. Registration in the first month of operation was 5,763. Today the system is run by a nonprofit organization, not by the city. Population served: 175,901. Circulation: 792,000. Holdings: 2,581,704. 9 branches. It was reported in May 2009 that the trustees had turned the branches over to the city for operation by "Providence Community Library." It was not determined what to do about the central library. The library has had the highest percent of funding from private sources (40 percent) of any U.S. public library. IMLS award 2001. Directors: William E. Foster, 1877–1930; Clarence E. Sherman, 1930–1957; Stuart C. Sherman, 1957–1968; F. Charles Taylor, 1968–1977; Annalee Bundy, 1977–1987; and Dale Thompson, 1988–.

PROVINCETOWN PUBLIC LIBRARY, MA   356 Commercial St., Provincetown, MA 02657. Population served: 3,450. Circulation: 42,833. Holdings: 24,811. LJ February 15, 2009: 4-star library; November 15, 2009, and October 1, 2010: 5-star library.

PUBLIC LIBRARIANS

Terminology

The *Dictionary of Occupational Titles* (U.S. Department of Labor 2007) describes a librarian as "a person who administers library services, provides patrons access to and assistance with library resources; and selects, acquires, processes, and organizes library materials for patron use." A public librarian, then, is one who carries on those activities in a public library (*see* PUBLIC LIBRARY). The distinction between a librarian and a member of the library support staff is cloudy, but it must revolve around the scope of duties and responsibilities for each category (*see* STAFFING). Persons with the job title "librarian" are likely to have a library school degree, but many do not (see the section "Current Situation" below).

Historical Summary

American public librarians created their occupation. There was no formal training or credential for the work in the mid-nineteenth century when the early libraries appeared in New England. Nor was there a structured apprenticeship for those who aspired to positions in those libraries. They learned by doing, through conversations with colleagues, by sharing experiences in journals, and by discussing issues at conferences. Pioneers like John Shaw Billings, Arthur Bostwick, John Cotton Dana, Melvil Dewey, Joseph Cogswell, Gratia Alta Countryman, Samuel Swett Green, and William F. Poole attended no library training courses, and some expressed their doubts about the wisdom of such programs. Dewey's library training school at Columbia College (1887) altered the landscape, and before long it was desirable for librarians to take formal study and display certificates attesting to it (*see* EDUCATION OF PUBLIC LIBRARIANS). Dewey's New York State library school had such notable alumni as Edwin H. Anderson, Sarah Askew, George Bowerman, Charles Compton, and Mary Frances Isom.

Whether formally trained or not, the librarians who directed or served in public libraries during the first decades of the twentieth century were book people: they were conversant with literature and history, and they knew languages and arts. The model librarian was exhibited in *Living with Books* by Helen Haines in 1935—it was a person who knew the significant writings in every field of knowledge. Librarians were eager to raise the reading taste and cultural level of the public and put their energies into appropriate collection development and readers' advisory (*see* COLLECTION DEVELOPMENT; PHILOSOPHY OF PUBLIC LIBRARIANSHIP; READERS' ADVISORY SERVICES). At the same time there arose a recognition that bookish learning did not fill out the skill set needed to manage a library budget, to recruit and organize a staff, or to oversee the design of a branch system. So the idea of the librarian as a manager competed with the "person who knows books" (Richardson 1927, 293). A managerial emphasis grew with the rise of scientific management in the business world. Nevertheless, the notion of the scholar, without professional training, as prepared to operate a library has persisted. Librarians of Congress have almost always been professors in some nonlibrary subject; and directors of the New York Public Library and the Newberry Library have been nonlibrarians.

With the rationalization of library schools that began after a scathing report about them in 1923 (Williamson 1923), professional degrees took on more luster. And with the research achievements of faculty at the Graduate Library School at the University of Chicago in the 1930s and 1940s, the idea that scholarship could operate within the library field itself was established. At mid-century the public ideal librarian was visualized as a person with a good academic background—usually in the humanities but increasingly in the social sciences (Bryan 1952)——competence in management, comfortable with research, and trained in the technical tasks of a library. A neophyte laid claim to that array of skills on the basis of a graduate degree from a library school accredited by the American Library Association (ALA). The arrival of the computer in the 1960s put some major cracks in that tidy picture.

Public librarians and other librarians became, in their laudable attempt to master the computer with its myriad applications, technically oriented. In library school they learned rudiments of scientific topics like communication and computer design. They had less time to study the standard library science subjects like cataloging and academic topics in the humanities. They learned about "information" and took on titles connected to it, like "information scientist" (*see* INFORMATION SCIENCE). Complexities of management became daunting (*see* PLANNING). By the beginning of the twenty-first century, there were grave uncertainties in the field about what librarians knew and should know, giving rise to the analysis of "competencies" required for the work (ALA Reference and User Services Association 2003; Helmick and Swigger 2006. Library schools (or information schools, in the new style) were criticized for failing to prepare graduates with those competencies.

Current Situation

Basic data about public librarians show an increase in numbers and compensation in recent years. There were 111,944 full-time equivalent (FTE) staff in public libraries in fiscal year (FY) 1993. Of those, 37,353 were "librarians," and of the librarians, 24,825 held MLS degrees. For FY 2008 the FTE staff was 145,243; there were 47,925 librarians, of whom 32,561 held MLS degrees (U.S. National Center for Education Statistics 1995; U.S. Institute of Library and Museum Services 2010). There have been about four public librarians per 25,000 population since 1999.

Librarians have been doing well with regard to salaries. The mean salary reported in a new survey was $60,734 in 2010. Steady increases are shown from 2005 ($53,779) in every year but one. In public libraries the mean salaries are strong for top administrators and less inspiring for new staff. In 2010 the mean salary for public library directors was $100,106; for deputy directors, $77,633; for department and branch heads, $65,875; for nonsupervisory librarians, $52,851; and for entry-level staff, $48,749. All the categories show increases of 3 to 6 percent over 2009, except director, which grew by 20 percent (ALA 2010). The job market is flat: the 5,192 graduates of library schools in 2009 found positions with difficulty.

Questions remain about which path to follow in educating new librarians. Recent "competencies" approved by the ALA council emphasize traditional areas (ALA 2009; *see* EDUCATION OF PUBLIC LIBRARIANS). Yet the computer applications are there and need to be understood. Public library management is a skill that seems to need amplification. In the preparation of this handbook, hundreds of library plans, organization charts, websites, and policy statements were examined. It must be said that most of them suggest the heavy hand of the amateur.

Attitude is the last frontier for public librarians. Research points to the negative feelings that patrons often have about their librarians (*Perceptions of Library and Information Resources* 2005). The present writer used to advise his students that as a patron approached, they should radiate joy and anticipation! Such a display in the real world of today would indeed be cause for celebration.

References

American Library Association. 2009. *Core Competencies of Librarianship*. Chicago: American Library Association. http://www.ala.org/ala/aboutala/governance/council/councildocuments/2009mw. Accessed February 2010.

American Library Association. 2010. *Salary Survey: 2010 Librarian Pay Up 3 Percent despite Economic Woes*. Chicago: American Library Association. http://www.ala.org/newsletter/2010/11/01/salary-survey. Accessed December 2010.

American Library Association. Reference and User Services Association. 2003. Professional competencies for reference and user services librarians. By the Task Force on Professional Competencies. *Reference & User Services Quarterly* 42, no. 4 (Summer): 290.

Bryan, Alice I. 1952. *The Public Librarian: A Report of the Public Library Inquiry*. New York: Columbia University Press.

Helmick, Catherine, and Keith Swigger. 2006. Core competencies of library practitioners. *Public Libraries* 45, no. 2 (March/April): 54–69.

Perceptions of Library and Information Resources: A Report to the OCLC Membership. 2005. Dublin, OH: Online Computer Library Center. http://www.oclc.org/reports/2005.

Richardson, Ernest Cushing. 1927. The book and the person who knows the book. *Bulletin of the American Library Association* 21, no. 10 (October): 289–95.

U.S. Department of Labor. 2007. *Dictionary of Occupational Titles*. 4th ed. Washington, DC: U.S. Department of Labor, Bureau of Labor Statistics. http://www.occupationalinfo.org. Accessed February 2010.

U.S. Institute of Museum and Library Services. 2010. *Public Libraries in the United States, FY 2008*. Washington, DC: U.S. Department of Education.

U.S. National Center for Education Statistics. 1995. *E. D. TABS: Public Libraries in the United States: 1993*. Washington, DC: U.S. Department of Education.

Williamson, Charles C. 1923. *Training for Library Service: A Report Prepared for the Carnegie Corporation of New York.* New York: Carnegie Corporation of New York.

PUBLIC LIBRARY   This entry deals with the definition of the public library and the various names that are used to identify it. It is necessary first to define library. In *Merriam*, "library" is "a place in which literary, musical, artistic, or reference materials (as books, manuscripts, recordings, or films) are kept for use but not for sale." *American Heritage* is similar: "library": "a place in which literary and artistic materials, such as books, newspapers, and tapes, are kept for reading, reference, or lending." Both definitions describe a place, and in fact libraries have always been physically located in actual places. The concept of "virtual library" dispenses with place. *ODLIS* says this about it: "virtual library—a library without walls in which the collections do not exist on paper, microform, or other tangible form at a physical location but are electronically accessible in digital format via computer networks ... the term digital library is more appropriate." Since no American public library is a virtual library, this entry (and this handbook) will not deal with virtual libraries (*see also* DIGITAL MEDIA).

Merriam has no entry for public library. *American Heritage* offers "a noncommercial library often supported with public funds, intended for use by the general public." Several problems are noticeable with this definition. "Often" is misleading since a library not supported by public funds—that is, one that is privately financed—is probably not going to be available to the general public. And "use" is left in a cloudy area: it could simply mean that the public may walk through and admire the art works as in a museum. Finally, "general public" is contrary to real-world custom, which limits use of a given public library to a particular population.

ODLIS has this entry for public library: "a library or library system that provides unrestricted access to library resources and services free of charge to all the residents of a given community, district, or geographic region, supported wholly or in part by public funds." This is satisfactory, except for "unrestricted," which runs contrary to normal usage regarding various special collections.

The National Center for Education Statistics has a long definition of public library: "an entity that is established under state enabling laws or regulations to serve a community, district, or region, and that provides at least the following: (1) an organized collection of printed or other library materials, or a combination thereof; (2) paid staff; (3) an established schedule in which services of the staff are available to the public; (4) the facilities necessary to support such a collection, staff, and schedule; and (5) that is supported in whole or in part with public funds" (U.S. National Center for Education Statistics 2007, B-9). What is missing is the kind of service provided and the fact that service is free.

The working definition of public library employed in this volume is "a library that is open without charge for reference and circulation to all members of the community that is taxed to support it." "Community" is taken in the widest sense to cover any geographic division. By including "circulation," the definition omits governmental libraries at all levels. By saying "taxed to support it," the definition leaves open the possibility of some private financing in addition to public funding.

Historically, "public library" did not always mean what these definitions suggest. "The Bureau of Education's celebrated report of 1876 used 'Public Libraries' to cover every institution it could learn about which was not maintained strictly for its owner's use" (Jackson 1973, 104). The term "free library" was frequently conflated, in the nineteenth century, with "public library." There were also "circulating libraries," which were public—open to all—but were fee-based lending libraries.

Taxing authority may be assigned by state legislation to municipalities (towns, cities, and villages), counties, or special "districts" (see COUNTY AND REGIONAL LIBRARIES; STATE LIBRARY AGENCIES).

It might be expected that over time, one designation would become the general name for a public library. However, there remains a plethora of choices in current American practice. Most municipal public libraries have a direct name, like Dallas Public Library. But some have retained the "free" in their names, omitting "public": Free Library of Philadelphia, Elbridge (NY) Free Library. Others use the word "library" with the town/city name, without "public" or "free": Dover Town (MA), perhaps adding "city" as in North Logan (UT) City Library or "community" as in Fairfax (VT) Community Library. Libraries that began with private donations may record the benefactor's name, often adding "memorial" to it: Eleanor Daggett Memorial Public Library (Chama, NM), Carnegie Library of Pittsburgh, or Enoch Pratt Free Library (Baltimore). Or the "memorial" may stand without a donor name at all: Limon (CO) Memorial Library. Some libraries have personal names attached, without notice of memorial or beneficence as in Lincoln Library (Springfield, IL), and some memorialize a group as in Bismarck Veterans Memorial Library.

Names representing the earlier status of a public library are found: Stockbridge (MA) Library Association or Rye (NY) Free Reading Room. It is becoming common for a library name to identify its type: Carroll County Public Library, Westminster MD; Medina County District Library (OH); Barrington Public Library District (IL); or Montgomery (AL) City-County Public Library System. An added complication is change of name; thus, the Public Library of Columbus and Franklin County (OH) is now the Columbus Metropolitan Library. Mergers are unusual, but Minneapolis Public Library has been absorbed into Hennepin County Library.

What makes this bewildering nomenclature tolerable is the basic nature of all these institutions whatever they are called. The American public library today is invariably open "free" to all of its community, available for information, recreation, and education. People always refer to it as "the library."

References

Jackson, Sidney L. 1973. Free libraries. In *Encyclopedia of Library and Information Science* 9: 103–4. New York: Marcel Dekker.

U.S. National Center for Education Statistics. 2007. *Public Libraries in the United States: Fiscal Year 2005.* Washington, DC: Department of Education.

PUBLIC LIBRARY OF BROOKLINE, MA   361 Washington St., Brookline, MA 02445. Founded 1857. Population served: 55,000. Circulation: 1,055,000. Holdings: 350,000. 2 branches. In 1878 it was one of four libraries directed by a woman (Mary A. Bean). In 1890 or 1891 the library had the first U.S. public library children's room, although it was only a small area in the basement, with a few picture books and nothing circulating.

PUBLIC LIBRARY OF CHARLOTTE AND MECKLENBURG COUNTY. *See* CHARLOTTE MECKLENBURG LIBRARY, CHARLOTTE, NC.

PUBLIC LIBRARY OF CINCINNATI AND HAMILTON COUNTY, OH   800 Vine St., Cincinnati, OH 45202. Founded 1853; opened March 14. Originally a school district library, located in the Central School House. A new building opened December 9, 1870. Population served: 806,652. Circulation: 14,344,449. Holdings: 9,608,333. 50 branches. The library issued a printed catalog in 1871, supplemented by a card catalog. Other innovations included an art department (probably the first subject department in an American public library) and a collection of juvenile books. Cincinnati, under director William Frederick Poole (1869–1873), "was considered second only to Boston among the public libraries of the day" (Stone 1977, 164). LJ October 1, 2010: 4-star library. HAPLR 2009, 2010. Grave financial difficulties have obstructed services for several years. While the library's primary source of funding (the state's public library fund) dropped by nearly 30 percent since 2000, demand for services grew by more than 20 percent. There has been a 20 percent reduction in staff and a 10 percent reduction in hours of operation. Fortunately the county voters approved a levy in 2009 that will provide a dependable source of revenue, projected as $20 million annually. Directors: John D. Caldwell, 1855–1857; N. Peabody Poor, 1857–1866; Lewis Freeman, 1866–1869; William Frederick Poole, 1869–1873; Thomas Vickers, 1874–1879; Chester W. Merrill, 1880–1886; Albert W. Whelpley, 1886–1900; Nathaniel D. C. Hodges, 1900–1924; Chalmers Hadley, 1924–1945; Carl Vitz, 1946–1955; Ernest I. Miller, 1955–1971; James R. Hunt, 1971–1991; Robert D. Stonestreet, 1991–1998; Kimber L. Fender, 1999–.

References

Fleischman, John. 2003. *Free and Public: One Hundred Fifty Years at the Public Library of Cincinnati and Hamilton County, 1853–2003.* Cincinnati: Orange Frazer Press.

Stone, Elizabeth. 1977. *American Library Development.* New York: H. W. Wilson.

PUBLIC LIBRARY OF NASHVILLE AND DAVIDSON COUNTY, TN. *See* NASHVILLE PUBLIC LIBRARY, TN.

PUBLIC RELATIONS

Terminology

Several related terms need to be sorted out. The following definitions are from *Merriam*:

> Public relations: "the business of inducing the public to have understanding for and goodwill toward a person, firm, or institution."
>
> Publicity: "the dissemination of information or promotional material."
>
> Advertising: "the action of calling something to the attention of the public, esp. by paid announcements."
>
> Marketing: "the process or technique of promoting, selling, and distributing a product or service."
>
> Promotion: "the act of furthering the growth or development of something, esp. the furtherance of the acceptance and sale of merchandise through advertising, publicity, or discounting."
>
> Advocacy: "the act or process of advocating or supporting a cause or proposal."

According to the dates when the terms were first used, "public relations" is the newest one; it embraces the ideas expressed in the five earlier ones. A feeling of goodwill toward an institution (such as public libraries) is a necessary (if not sufficient) condition for gaining support. Promotion or advocacy of specific causes (such as better financing of public libraries) is therefore an aspect of library public relations. This connection is recognized in *ODLIS*: "Public relations: publicity designed to create favorable public opinion and boost awareness of the benefits of library services, resources, and programs, and promote the interests of libraries in society."

In recent years "advocacy" has taken center stage, giving a name to various public relations strategies. *ODLIS* has a detailed account: "Advocacy: concerted action taken in support of libraries, particularly political action aimed at securing adequate funding for library operations and capital improvements, which may include lobbying legislators and government officials, organizing voter rallies, securing media coverage, etc."

Historical Summary

The first glimmers of library public relations were the ideas of William E. Foster (*see* FOSTER, WILLIAM E.). In 1880 he wrote an article outlining "of what service may the library be?" He noted that a public library supports industries, societies, public lectures, college classes, school teachers, and reading for children (Foster 1880). Later he offered an inventory of library services that brought actual financial return to the community; for example, a city saving thousands of dollars in a contract negotiation by consulting data held in the library (Foster 1891). From such beginnings has emerged the modern "library value calculator" (see the section "Current Situation" below). Foster's ideas were fleshed out by John Cotton Dana (*see* DANA, JOHN COTTON). In his 1896 presidential address to the American Library Association (ALA), Dana urged making libraries as appealing as retail stores, with all their best features: "Deny your people nothing which the book-shop grants them" (Dana 1896, 5). In a later article he urged that the library "must make known its powers ... [for] if it make itself widely known for what it is, present interests will be fed, new interests will be aroused. I am aware that these remarks smell more of commerce than of the lamp" (Dana 1906, 13, 15). That commercial "odor" was a disturbing one to public librarians, who tended to prefer a more passive philosophy. Most of them believed that a public library, like a hospital, needed only to "be there" for the community to engage with it (indeed, growing use and support for libraries seemed to make that case through the first half of the twentieth century). However, the ALA did establish a committee on publicity in 1906, "when librarians had come generally to recognize the importance of the subject" (Bostwick 1929, 380).

There were some efforts at promotion of library services, such as to users distant from central libraries (*see* BOOKMOBILES; OUTREACH), to immigrants (*see* SERVICES TO IMMIGRANTS), and to those in the military (*see* AMERICAN LIBRARY ASSOCIATION). During the 1970s there was a concerted initiative to bring library materials to the disadvantaged (*see* OUTREACH). Such programs seem to fall under the rubric "publicity." Publicity for targeted services expanded to public relations—getting the community to feel favorably toward the library as an institution—in the 1940s. *Library Literature* introduced the subject heading "Public Relations of Libraries" in 1943. The ALA and the H. W. Wilson Company established the John Cotton Dana Library Public Relations Award in 1946. The topic was formalized in several books of the 1970s (e.g., Sherman 1971; Rice 1972; Angoff 1973). Still the whole enterprise remained problematic, as illustrated by a 1974 protest in *Library Journal*: "No other essential public service finds it necessary to peddle its wares as if they were new appliances for a consumer public" (Berry 1974, 85).

"Marketing" was the name of choice in the 1970s and 1980s. It appeared in the titles of numerous books and articles (e.g., Wasserman and Ford 1980; Weingand 1987; Wood 1988). Basically it was a movement to increase library use (circulation) through an emphasis on recreational reading. Another *Library Journal* editorial stood in the road, decrying marketing as a "fad" (Berry 1979, 1605). But the ALA was an active marketer, through sponsorship of National Library Week from 1975, and provision of posters, publications, and publicity. At the White House Conference on Library and Information Services of 1979, one of the resolutions called for "an aggressive, comprehensive national public awareness campaign coordinated at the federal level." A recommendation of the second White House

Conference of 1991 proposed "that model programs be created to market libraries to their publics" (Barber 1993, 691). One such model program, in the form of a guidance manual, appeared in 1993 (Baker 1993). No actual library can be cited as a marketing model, although strong initiatives appeared in many of them. The resurgence of readers' advisory in the 1980s provided a valuable fulcrum for promotional activities. But the essential ingredient for a professionally unified public relations campaign for libraries came from declining library support, a challenge that emerged in the 1990s (Free 1993).

Current Situation

Perhaps a final name change for the public relations enterprise came in the new century as the commercial taint of "marketing" was dissolved and the very old term "advocacy" was poured into its new bottle. Under this fresh banner, the profession has marched in step for 10 years. The ALA is at the head of the parade. Its Office for Library Advocacy has this stated mission:

> OLA supports the efforts of advocates seeking to improve libraries of all types by developing resources, a peer-to-peer advocacy network, and training for advocates at the local, state and national level ... on behalf of particular types of libraries or particular issues, in order to help better integrate these efforts into the overall advocacy planning and strategies of the association. (ALA 2010, 1)

The ALA website lists 13 publications in the series "Advocacy Fact Sheets." They cover such topics as cultivating relationships, involving community partners, developing a plan and message, and working with legislators and decision makers. Four sessions at the ALA annual conference in 2010 made up an "advocacy institute workshop"; the primary subject was fundraising. The ALA's commitment to advocacy has been emphasized by recent presidents of the association. Roberta Stevens listed three ways in which she intended to advance the cause during her term of office: "frontline fundraising," "'Why I Need My Library' contest," and "our authors, our advocates." She pledged to "dedicate myself wholeheartedly and unreservedly to representing and advocating for our association, our libraries, and library staff everywhere" (Stevens 2010, 5).

A recent statement of the "advocacy message" is the following:

> Libraries should be thought of as: an essential part of an organization's learning community; critical to any information, research, or education mission; an organization's or community's connection to the print and online world of knowledge and information; a balancing act of an investment in the future and preservation of the past. Goals include: getting others' attention and then getting them to listen; getting others to think about things you want them to think about and consider in a positive way;

getting others to support part or all of your needs and requests;
and getting others to carry your message and your specific needs.
(Todaro 2007, 29)

An issue yet to be fully addressed is the lack of a research base to justify the
time and effort expended on public relations. One study discovered that
there was no relationship between public opinion about libraries and funding levels over time (Allen 2003). But the clear success of individual libraries
in promotion does offer a pragmatic rationale for advocacy programs. A
notable example was the campaign of the Salinas (CA) Public Library
to overturn a planned closure of the system in 2004 due to a budget crisis.
"A delegation of national and state library leaders, as well as celebrities,
traveled to Salinas in February 2005 to rally on its behalf. In November 2005
nearly 9,000 voters passed the Measure V referendum, which raised a half-
cent tax to fund libraries and other essential services . . . the libraries remain
open seven days a week" (*American Libraries*, November 2009, 22).

One public relations technique that a number of libraries are using is the
"library value calculator"—a specification of library services and what they
would cost the community if the library did not provide them. This idea goes
back to the pioneer thoughts of William E. Foster, as mentioned in the section "Historical Summary" above (Foster 1891). A useful model appears in
the website of the Mid-Continent Public Library in Independence, MO.
Headed "How much can the library save you?" the calculator lists various
library services (books borrowed, movies borrowed, interlibrary loan, hours
of computer use, adult programs and classes, and so on) and invites patrons
to put a dollar value on them (the worksheet was adapted from an original
by the Massachusetts Library Association).

Online public relations begins with the character of the library website,
just as in-house public relations begins with the staff members first encountered by the patrons. Both areas would benefit from careful review by library
directors. One study of public library websites concluded that they were less
than effective and that "libraries need to apply logic and schemes of knowledge organization to produce user-friendly and consistent representation
structure for web access" (Tang and Thelwall 2008, 435). Above all, websites need to be easily open to patron input. Many websites fail to give email
contacts to staff, or let users ask questions without cumbersome routines.
Staff that meet the public are usually not the advocacy-dedicated administrators but rather low-classification library technicians in the circulation area
who may not share the public relations philosophy of their superiors (*see*
STAFFING) or reference librarians who may lack appropriate skills and attitudes for inspiring good feelings in the public. Only 11 percent of patrons in
a study reported in 2005 had positive associations with library staff (*Perceptions of Libraries and Information Resources* 2005, item 3.21).

Public relations, advocacy in particular, needs a solid basis of institutional
quality. "The foundation of any organization's public relations must be the
actual product or service which the organization supplies" (Norton 1975, 368).

References

Allen, Bryce. 2003. Public opinion and the funding of public libraries. *Library Trends* 51, no. 3 (Winter): 414–23.

Alman, Susan Webreck. 2007. *Crash Course in Marketing for Libraries*. Westport, CT: Libraries Unlimited.

American Library Association. 2010. Office for Library Advocacy [untitled statement]. Chicago: American Library Association. http://www.ala.org/ala/aboutala/offices/index/cfm.

Angoff, Allan, ed. 1973. *Public Relations for Libraries: Essays in Communication*. Westport, CT: Greenwood Press.

Baker, Sharon L. 1993. *The Responsive Public Library Collection: How to Develop and Market It*. Englewood, CO: Libraries Unlimited.

Barber, Peggy. 1993. Public relations. In *World Encyclopedia of Library and Information Services*, 3rd ed.: 688–92. Chicago: American Library Association.

Berry, John N., III. 1974. The selling of the library (editorial). *Library Journal* 99, no. 2 (January 15): 85.

Berry, John N., III. 1979. The test of the marketplace (editorial). *Library Journal* 104, no. 15 (September 1): 1605.

Dana, John Cotton. 1896. Hear the other side. *Library Journal* 21, no. 12 (December): 1–5.

Dana, John Cotton. 1906. Many-sided interest: How the library promotes it. *School Library Journal*, December 22. Reprinted in *American Library Philosophy: An Anthology*, ed. Barbara McCrimmon, 10–19. Hamden, CT: Shoe String Press, 1975. Pagination cited is from the reprint.

Foster, William E. 1880. Methods of securing the interest of a community. *Library Journal* 5, no. 8/9 (September/October). Reprinted in *The American Public Library*, 4th ed., by Arthur E. Bostwick, 193–97. New York: Appleton, 1929. Pagination cited is from the reprint.

Foster, William E. 1891. Arguments for public support of public libraries. Paper given at the American Library Association conference, San Francisco, CA, 1891. Reprinted in *The American Public Library*, 4th ed., by Arthur E. Bostwick. New York: Appleton, 1929. Pagination cited is from the reprint.

Free. 1993. Free libraries: Are they becoming extinct? *Omni* 15, no. 10 (August): 4.

Gould, Mark R., ed. 2009. *The Library PR Handbook: High-Impact Communications*. Chicago: American Library Association.

Norton, Alice. 1975. Library public relations. In *Encyclopedia of Library and Information Science* 15: 386–89. New York: Marcel Dekker.

Perceptions of Libraries and Information Resources: A Report to the OCLC Members. 2005. *Perceptions of Libraries and Information Resources: A Report to the OCLC Members*. Dublin, OH: OCLC. http://www.oclc.org/reports/2005.

Reed, Sally Gardner. 2009. Amalgamating for advocacy. *American Libraries* 40, no. 3 (March): 34–36.

Rice, Betty. 1972. *Public Relations for Public Libraries*. New York: H. W. Wilson.

Sherman, Steve. 1971. *ABCs of Library Promotion*. Metuchen, NJ: Scarecrow Press.

Stevens, Roberta. 2010. Advancing advocacy. *American Libraries* 41, no. 8 (August): 5.

Tang, Rong, and Mike Thelwall. 2008. Hyperlink analysis of web sites. *Library Quarterly* 78, no. 4 (October): 419–35.

Todaro, Julie Beth. 2007. Advocacy today—a broadened approach. In *Bowker Annual*, 52nd ed., 23–31. New Providence, NJ: Bowker.

Wasserman, Paul, and Gary T. Ford. 1980. Marketing and library research: What the library manager should learn. *Journal of Library Administration* 1, no. 1 (Spring): 19–29.

Weingand, Darlene E. 1987. *Marketing/Planning Library and Information Services*. Littleton, CO: Libraries Unlimited.

Wolfe, Lisa A. 2005. *Library Public Relations, Promotions, and Communications: A How-to-do-it Manual*. 2nd ed. New York: Neal-Schuman.

Wood, Elizabeth J. 1988. *Strategic Marketing for Libraries: A Handbook*. Westport, CT: Greenwood.

PUBLIC SERVICES   *ODLIS* describes public services as those "activities and operations of a library that bring the staff into regular direct contact with users, including circulation, reference, online services, bibliographic instruction, serials assistance, government documents, and interlibrary loan document delivery, as distinct from technical services, which are performed behind the scenes, out of contact with library users." Library programs and exhibits fall under public services (PS) as well, and so does readers' advisory work. Children's and young adult services are in part PS. Branch libraries and bookmobiles belong in PS too, with outreach/extension activities.

PS and technical services (TS) are the two principal tracks in the library structure. Administrative services (AS) round out the organization chart. All the functions go by various names, and headings like PS and TS may not even appear on a chart. For example, the Denver Public Library organization chart has upper-level boxes for PS and AS, but instead of TS there is a box for Collections and Technology; the Ferguson Library (Stamford, CT) has director-level boxes for PS and AS but none for TS.

In this handbook the activities of PS are distributed among several entries (*see* BOOKMOBILES; BRANCH LIBRARIES; CIRCULATION SERVICES; INFORMATION LITERACY INSTRUCTION; INTERLIBRARY LOAN; INTERNET; MUSIC COLLECTIONS; OUTREACH; READERS' ADVISORY SERVICES; REFERENCE AND INFORMATION SERVICES; SERVICES TO AFRICAN AMERICANS; SERVICES TO BUSINESS AND INDUSTRY; SERVICES TO CHILDREN AND YOUNG ADULTS; SERVICES TO GAY, LESBIAN, BISEXUAL, AND TRANSGENDERED PERSONS; SERVICES TO HISPANICS; SERVICES TO IMMIGRANTS; SERVICES TO NATIVE AMERICANS; SERVICES TO PEOPLE WITH DISABILITIES; SERVICES TO SENIORS; SPECIAL SERVICES).

Reference

Evans, G. Edward, and Thomas L. Carter. 2008. *Introduction to Library Public Services*. 7th ed. Westport, CT: Libraries Unlimited.

PUBLICITY. *See* PUBLIC RELATIONS.

PULASKI PUBLIC LIBRARY, NY   4917 N. Jefferson St., Pulaski, NY 13142. Population served: 2,398. Circulation: 25,816. Holdings: 25,028. LJ October 1, 2010: 5-star library.

PUTNAM, HERBERT, 1861–1955   Librarian. Born in New York City on September 20, 1861. He graduated from Harvard in 1883, then studied law. He directed the library of the Minneapolis Athenaeum in 1884, then went to the Minneapolis Public Library—which had absorbed the Athenaeum—in 1887 as its first director. He left in 1891, practiced law for a time, then took the appointment of superintendent of the Boston Public Library in 1895. He reorganized the administration, established a new children's room, and initiated interlibrary loan. Putnam considered public libraries to be educational institutions entirely and opposed their acceptance of cheap fiction. He participated in congressional hearings about the role of the Library of Congress in 1896. Supported by the American Library Association (ALA), Putnam was appointed Librarian of Congress in 1899. His achievements there included the new classification, distribution of printed catalog cards, and a national union catalog. In general he expanded the role of the library for the benefit of all libraries in the country. When he retired in 1939, the ALA cited him as "dean of our profession." He was ALA president in 1898 and in 1903–1904. Putnam died in Woods Hole, MA, on August 14, 1955. *DALB*.

Q

QUARTZSITE PUBLIC LIBRARY, AZ 465 N. Plymouth Ave., Quartzsite, AZ 85346. Population served: 3,550. Circulation: 52,730. Holdings: 28,272. LJ February 14, 2009: 3-star library; November 15, 2009: 4-star library; October 1, 2010: 3-star library.

QUEENS BOROUGH PUBLIC LIBRARY, JAMAICA, NY 89–11 Herrick Blvd., Jamaica, NY 11432. Founded 1896. Population served: 2,225,486. Circulation: 23,041,425. Holdings: 6,632,209. 70 branches. A recent innovation of the Queens Library (as it is known) was creation of the Queens Library for Teens (O'Connor and Kenney 2008). LJ February 15, 2009, and November 15, 2009: 3-star library. IMLS award 2000. LJ Library of the Year 2009.

Reference

O'Connor, Maureen, and Brian Kenney. 2008. Make it new: The Queens Library for Teens and Dallas's Bookmarks. *School Library Journal* 54, no. 7 (July): 38–42.

QUIGLEY, MARGERY CLOSEY, 1886–1968 Librarian. Born in Los Angeles, CA, September 16, 1886. She graduated from Vassar College in 1908 and went to St. Louis Public Library as an assistant in circulation in 1909, becoming a branch librarian in 1911. From 1918 to 1925 Quigley was librarian in Endicott, NY. She went to the New York State Library School, earning a certificate in 1923. She was elected president of the New York Library Association in 1924. After serving as a branch head in the District of Columbia

Public Library (1925–1927), she moved to Montclair, NJ, as director. Montclair soon gained national recognition as a model suburban library. It offered home delivery, had staff exchanges with European libraries, dispensed with fines for children, and gained wide community support. Her book *Portrait of a Library* (1936) attracted the attention of filmmaker Hans Burger, who turned it into a film of the same name; it was distributed by the Museum of Modern Art and shown worldwide by the Department of State. Quigley persuaded IBM to set up a demonstration system of data processing for the library's circulation and inventory, the first of its kind. In 1955 she saw the opening of a new building; she had influenced the innovative, open design of architect Ralph Walker. In the American Library Association she was on the executive board, 1935–1939. She taught public relations at Columbia and other library schools. On her retirement she headed the most famous American suburban library in the world. Quigley died in Montclair on April 17, 1968. *DALB.*

Reference

Curley, Arthur. 1976. Montclair Free Public Library. In *Encyclopedia of Library and Information Science* 18: 268–71. New York: Marcel Dekker.

QUOGUE LIBRARY, NY   40 Quogue St., Quogue, NY 11959. Population served: 1,206. Circulation: 17,053. Holdings: 28,850. LJ November 15, 2009: 3-star library; October 1, 2010: 4-star library.

R

RALEIGH, NC. *See* WAKE COUNTY PUBLIC LIBRARY SYSTEM, RALEIGH, NC.

RANGEVIEW LIBRARY DISTRICT, THORNTON, CO   8992 Washington St., Thornton, CO 80229. Founded as a library district 2004; formerly Adams County Public Library. Population served: 250,000. Circulation: 825,000. Holdings: 300,000. 6 locations. The library attracted national interest when it dropped the Dewey Classification in favor of BISAC, a book industry system (*see* CLASSIFICATION).

RANSOMVILLE FREE LIBRARY, NY   3733 Ransomville Rd., Ransomville, NY 14131. Population served: 1,488. Circulation: 38,828. Holdings: 30,786. HAPLR 2009, 2010.

RAQUETTE LAKE FREE LIBRARY, NY   1 Dillion Rd., Raquette Lake, NY 13436. Population served: 200. Circulation: 9,068. Holdings: 16,379. HAPLR 2009, 2010.

RAVENNA PUBLIC LIBRARY, NE   121 W. Seneca, Ravenna, NE 68869. Population served: 1,341. Circulation: 19,859. Holdings: 11,493. LJ February 15, 2009: 5-star library.

RAYMOND A. WHITWER TILDEN PUBLIC LIBRARY, TILDEN, NE   202 S. Center, Tilden, NE 68781. Founded 1925. Population served: 1,078. Circulation: 20,210. Holdings: 3,791. LJ October 1, 2010: 3-star library.

READERS' ADVISORY SERVICES

Terminology

ODLIS does not define readers' advisory (RA) services but offers this description of the work: "a readers' advisor recommends specific titles and/ or authors, based on knowledge of the patron's past reading preferences, and may also compile lists of recommended titles." It is further understood that RA work deals with leisure, recreational reading, as opposed to fact searching, and that while books are the prime media of concern, any formats may be covered. Thus, RA is the activity of recommending materials to meet the recreational needs of patrons. It is distinct from any educational programs that a library may offer (as noted below, recreation and education were blended in the early philosophy of RA).

Current library practice has settled on the plural form of "readers" so that the apostrophe follows the word, but the alternative singular form remains in use, particularly in publications (*The Reader's Encyclopedia*). "Adviser" and "advisor" are accepted in the dictionaries and both are found in library situations.

Historical Summary

In the pioneer epoch of public librarianship, roughly the last quarter of the nineteenth century, library leaders were fervent promoters of the educational role of libraries. "We consider that a large public library is of the utmost importance as the means of completing our system of public education ... by opening to all the means of self culture through books," stated the trustees of the Boston Public Library in 1852 (Williams 1988, 4). There was a structural belief in the power of reading to improve individual lives and society—to achieve "self-culture." Disagreements arose over what kind of reading would best serve that goal, with debates over the suitability of popular fiction occupying many minds and publications (*see* COLLECTION DEVELOPMENT; PHILOSOPHY OF PUBLIC LIBRARIANSHIP). What emerged was the so-called ladder theory, which held that reading taste improved itself over time—that taste climbed a ladder from some lower rung toward the topmost steps. On those upper rungs resided the classics of literature, history, biography, and the like.

Such an upward movement in reading taste might well occur independently of assistance by a librarian (or anyone else), or possibly it would benefit from some guidance. There was no research to support either of those viewpoints, both of which remained viable in the nineteenth century (indeed there has never been any scientific validation or disposal of the ladder theory). The earliest advocate of some guidance was Samuel Swett Green, librarian of the Worcester (MA) Free Library. An article he wrote in 1876 advocated staff assistance to patrons in locating factual information and in identifying suitable recreational reading—giving "every person ... the best book he is willing to read" (Green 1876). Others, like Melvil Dewey, preferred to let readers do their own selection. Dewey was one of many librarians of his time and later who disliked the air of paternalism that clouded guidance of readers. "It is in no sense your business to dictate to others as to what they may or may not, should or should not, read" (Dewey 1897, 266). Nevertheless, Dewey was an advocate of library collection guides that identified preferred titles.

As open stacks became common in the later nineteenth century, self-selection through browsing was practical. Another point in favor of reader laissez-faire was the lack of knowledge among librarians (or the clerical circulation staff who tended to be the readers' first encounter) of the whole range of traditional and popular literature; it was not a situation that promised important results in guidance up the ladder.

So two attitudes reigned simultaneously for a long period: (1) reading tastes improved over time, and (2) patrons could choose for themselves what to read—patrons' choices being limited, of course, to materials librarians considered suitable for their collections.

Then, in the 1920s, librarians were energized by the new adult education movement. As formal programs swept the country, involving courses, discussion groups, and self-study programs, there was a clear spot for the public library. It was to assist patrons in their self-study through individualized consultation and planning of systematic reading. Mabel Booton of the Cleveland Public Library was an early practitioner. Cleveland had a separate room in the early 1920s labeled "Readers' Consultation Service." There Booton would conduct an interview, a sort of two-way book chat, resulting in the formation of a reading plan on topics of interest. In addition to those studious projects, suggestions could be offered for recreational reading (Booton 1939). Such activities soon materialized in other large libraries: Chicago, Boston, Milwaukee, Indianapolis, Detroit, New York, and Cincinnati making noteworthy progress. Milwaukee created 1,207 individualized reading plans in 1927 (Dilevko and Magowan 2007, 93). At the New York Public Library, Jennie Flexner set up an RA department in 1929. During 1933–1939 she and her staff held 5,336 personal interviews. By 1941 the library had RA service in 30 branches. Flexner retained a faith in the ladder theory; she promoted "serious reading" and useful knowledge, with each topic explored systematically, proceeding from easy to difficult in treatment (Flexner and Edge 1934).

By this time RA was definitely a professional task, no longer an adjunct to circulation desk duties. It required a wide knowledge of literature, old and new, posing a challenge to librarians in their own self-cultural efforts. The model reader adviser was vividly delineated in a 1935 treatise, *Living with Books: The Art of Book Selection*, by Helen Haines (1935). Not many librarians could match the erudition displayed by the polymathic Haines, but they set their goals and tried. Those who succeeded could work with

"Haines's compromise," uniting the best books with books in demand: with sufficient knowledge of what has been written, it would usually be possible to find a title that exemplified literary quality and also suited the interest of a patron.

In the 1930s, with the flowering of the Graduate Library School at the University of Chicago and a stream of studies by its faculty and students, "research" was the fresh occupation of serious librarians. Through the work of Chicago scholars, librarianship was given a scientific basis, or so it was claimed. Douglas Waples led the way into reading studies, writing (with Ralph Tyler) the most acclaimed tract in the field, *What People Want to Read About* (1931). Waples and Tyler explored reading habits in topical areas, passing over recreational reading. There were community studies as well, analyzing the patrons and their reading habits of towns and neighborhoods. It is not clear that any practical results came from all these examinations in the sense of building library collections or guiding individual users; for example, the search for a connection between reading preferences and occupation, age, or education did not bear fruit (later investigations support the position that voluntary [recreational] reading does lead to improvements in reading; Krashen 2004). What did emerge was a sense that the community and its individuals have particular wants and needs and that public libraries ought to support them. Thus, the "demand theory" of books selection appeared (Drury 1930; Wellard 1937), never to be uprooted.

The American Library Association (ALA) had various involvements with RA. From 1925 to 1933 it published *Reading with a Purpose*, 66 volumes of formal reading lists on diverse subjects: study outlines with recommended books, all written by experts. By the end of 1931, 850,000 copies had been sold. The "national plan for libraries" (ALA 1935) promoted RA. Patrons were entitled to "skilled personal advice and counseling necessary to effective self study." This was a period of emphasis on serious reading. That perspective was emphasized by the findings of the *Public Library Inquiry*, which concluded that public library service would best concentrate on the small number of "opinion leaders" in the community and drop out of the entertainment-reading business for the mass of the population (Leigh 1950). As things turned out, that suggestion was ignored; public libraries were too heavily committed by then to meeting the demands of their patrons. Circulation of fiction had been established as the principal factor in overall library use, running around 60 to 65 percent of total transactions—a proportion more or less retained ever since.

As library patronage increased, it became less feasible to conduct thousands of private interviews. And the adult education movement faded in the postwar years for various reasons, one being the emergence of relatively free local educational opportunity in junior colleges. The RA concept got lost in the 1950s. "Fewer than ten large libraries" had RA services in 1959, compared to forty-four in 1935 (Dilevko and Magowan 2007, 131).

A revival of RA took place in the 1980s. It was marked, perhaps initiated, by a book that once again emphasized recreational reading, Betty Rosenberg's

Genreflecting (1982). Rosenberg's book, now in its sixth edition (Herald and Wiegand 2006), took reader interest in fiction—fiction in all its modern varieties—at face value. The new RA is directed toward the quality of the reading experience rather than the quality of the reading matter—which is not to say that the matter must be poor in quality. Fiction classification by genre had begun in the late 1970s when Sharon L. Baker separated romance and mystery from other fiction in three branches of the Davidson County (NC) Public Library and reported a circulation increase. The plan, known as "genrefication," was adopted by other libraries. In a 1984 report, 46 of 49 public libraries surveyed used some kind of fiction categories for shelving. What Rosenberg did in her 1982 book was tie this categorization to reader guidance. Fiction lists, in ever more subdivisions, marked subsequent editions of *Genreflecting*. In the fifth edition there were 32 subgenres for westerns. Before long book-length treatments of numerous genres appeared (a number are listed in the "References" section below). The point was to find exactly what kind of book a patron liked, in such terms as pacing, characterization, story line, and background frame, and then to locate a match in one of the genre lists.

Technology soon became the partner of the revived RA. EBSCO offers a Web-based service named NoveList that presented in 2010 a list of 150,000 fiction titles for all ages, with some 4,000 articles, and another list of 50,000 nonfiction titles. Some 36,000 subject terms can be combined in Boolean fashion to identify novels in very particular ways (a detailed account of NoveList with user comments can be found in Dilevko and Magowan 2007, 173–85). An even greater database, BIR (Book Index with Reviews), by EBSCO and Baker & Taylor, was available in 2004: it offered about 3.8 million titles and 800,000 full-text reviews, all the entries being nonfiction. Other tools, such as Bowker's Fiction/Nonfiction Connection and Booklist Online, appeared, claiming their usefulness as RA tools. In 2006, Libraries Unlimited launched The Reader's Advisor Online, which provides all the content of their popular *Genreflecting* series and advice from well-known experts in the field. New attention to nonfiction is evident in RA (Saricks 2005). The type known as narrative nonfiction has drawn special notice (Alpert 2006).

Another trend that gained momentum in the 1990s was the application of "appeal features" to reading material, as described in Saricks and Brown's *Readers' Advisory Service in the Public Library*, first published in 1989 and now in its third edition. The approach here was for the adviser to identify underlying characteristics of books—pacing, characterization, frame, and story line—to match readers with books they would enjoy.

A turn toward quality reading was marked by Nancy Pearl's *Book Lust* and its sequel *More Book Lust* (2003, 2005); they listed studious works along with popular titles in topical groupings (details on these books are in Dilevko and Magowan 2007, 185–94). Very favorable reception for Pearl's approach suggests that librarians are ready once again to seek out the best reading for every person "that he is willing to read."

Current Issues

A fundamental transformation in the reading habits of Americans was reported by the National Endowment for the Arts in 2004. The study *Reading at Risk* analyzed a sample of 17,000 adults and found that the practice of reading literature (fiction, poetry, and drama) showed a steady decline. In 1982, 56.9 percent of adults had read something in the literature category; in 1992, the percent was 54, and in 2002, it was 46.7. The percent of adults who had "read any book" fell from 60.9 in 1982 to 56.6 in 2002. Literary reading (fiction, poetry, and drama) declined among whites, African Americans, and Hispanics—in all educational levels and in all age-groupsbut most sharply among persons 18 to 24 years of age. In contrast to earlier studies that showed book readers as heavy users of other communication media, this one reported that the "decline in reading correlates with *increased* participation in a variety of electronic media, including the Internet, video games, and portable digital devices." "*Reading at Risk* reveals ... a culture at risk" (National Endowment for the Arts 2004). In other words, the likely audience for public library fictional recreational reading is growing smaller, as individuals in that group turn to electronic media. Public library circulation figures support this finding: while national circulation remains around seven items per capita, the items of increasing interest are audio and video materials rather than books. In this context the library service goals are understandably shifting toward supplying users with books they want most.

As libraries move toward the "bookstore model," they appear to support giving readers "what they want" regardless of quality issues. Many libraries have announced their intention follow an entertainment orientation. Philosophically, this attitude may be traced to the revisionist histories of public librarianship presented by Michael H. Harris (1973) and Dee Garrison (1979). They denounced libraries as elitist and paternal, supporters of a conservative value system. To escape this trap, it was said, control needs to be given to the patron. Writers like Bill Crowley (2008) and Joyce Saricks (2005, 2009) "put the reader in the driver's seat" (Dilevko and Magiwan 2007, 45), thus the direction described above, toward finding close matches between reader interest and actual publication. What makes this an issue is that patrons appear to become consumers, and the products they consume are the commercialized products of megacorporations, packaged as genre titles, best-sellers, celebrity books, and prize winners. So goes the critique of Dilevko and Magowan (2007). Nancy Pearl's program notwithstanding, it seems to such authors that the RA project has dissolved into a mechanical process that gives patrons immediate satisfactions but no long-term benefit. Indeed the current RA literature gives credence to the decline of the ladder theory among librarians. As for long-term benefit, it may be asked how RA practice, concentrated on popular fiction, assists or impedes the advance of information literacy. Literacy levels, one author reports, are rising, but "literacy demands of a complex, modern society are going up even faster" (Ross 2006, 3). Libraries are working on the problem (*see* INFORMATION LITERACY INSTRUCTION) but may be overlooking the RA implications of it.

The idea of uplift in reading tastes may be obsolete. The distinction between popular culture and high culture, on which the ladder theory stands, could well be put aside as a historical curiosity (Ross 2006, 186). Yet the personal reading experiences of readers, librarians among them, may yet speak to a measure of truth in the uplift project. Who can say—since, as noted above, no research has demonstrated the value of the theory. Is it an idea to be discarded or one to be revisited?

Another concern is about the quality of RA. The RA role is "one that only the most dedicated, adept, and passionate readers' advisers employ. It is a role that few have been educated to assume." The result is often "unprofessional and unsatisfactory" (Smith 2001, 62, 65). Unobtrusive observation of RA librarians at work produced a troubling report. When 54 libraries in Nassau County, NY, were visited by researchers posing as patrons, staff responses ranged "from delight to trepidation to bafflement to downright dismissal of the request for a good book." Many librarians were unreceptive and irritated and often gave poor guidance (May 2001, 134). Like so many professional problems, this one may be attributed to the library schools. Most ALA-accredited programs did not pay any attention whatever to readers' advisory in the core curriculum in the 1998–1999 academic year. RA was covered to some extent in elective courses of 26 schools (Shearer and Burgin 2001, 21). Recently textbooks used in reference courses have included attention to RA.

It is not clear what the library schools should be doing other than identifying the many RA genre aids. There is no time in the graduate year to activate the Helen Haines model of scholarship with students whose breadth of knowledge is likely to be modest. And unfortunately, many students "are resistant to genre reading . . . and, until actually assigned, have never read a romance or a western . . . [and] may not be able to deal with certain themes (sexual abuse, violence) or types of literature (horror)" (Van Fleet 2008, 3). At least the professors are addressing the issue (Watson 2000).

In connection with the writing of this entry, a pair of questions was sent by email to 30 large and medium-size libraries. The questions were the following: (1) Does your library have a librarian specifically assigned to RA work? (2) If so, is it a full-time assignment? Twenty-three libraries responded. Twenty answered "no" to question 1. The three that answered "yes" to question 1 also answered "yes" to question 2. A number of responses clarified the present situation: RA is a responsibility of many, perhaps all, public service librarians. The concept of a true specialist seems to be fading. For example, consider this response from New York Public Library:

> No, NYPL does not have one librarian specifically assigned to Readers' Advisory duties—RA is performed by librarians across our 90 locations who assist patrons at our public service desks, as well as through this virtual service. Depending on the subject, we might refer a patron to a particular bibliographer for RA in

one of the research centers. Additionally, NYPL provides indirect Readers' Advisory through the regular production of recommended booklists, generally compiled by committees made up of staff members who have many other duties, and the creation of book displays in the neighborhood libraries.

Remnants of the earlier epoch are found in the libraries that reported full-time assigned readers' advisers. They are the Charleston County (SC) Public Library System, which has a Readers' Advisory Department, staffed by a full-time librarian, and the Laramie County (WY) Library System in Cheyenne, which has an RA desk, also staffed by a full-time librarian. The Seattle Public Library presents the most elaborate structure, with two full-time and three part-time readers' advisers. The Seattle website has a "Reader's Corner" with an inviting array of reading lists, blogs, and book groups; patrons are invited to sign up for NextReads (an EBSCO service), "which automatically notifies you about new books in your favorite subject areas. We will e-mail you a short annotated list of titles every few weeks, with links to our catalog so you can place items on hold." Other libraries, even without assigned readers' advisers, have inviting websites that include lists of books by genre, age, awards, and the like—commercial products and local blogs. The Madison (WI) Public Library is a good example, with many lists displayed and the names of about 25 email book letters available to patrons.

The present scene is a blend of happy and sad elements. It is a good thing to recognize the importance of recreational reading and to put the reader "in the driver's seat" without a paternalistic critique of his or her preferences. It is less good to put the enterprise into the hands of librarians who may lack the education and enthusiasm to carry it out and to have more or less deleted the idea of an RA specialist. It is both good and bad, perhaps, to have the corporate contributions of digital title lists since they present voluminous choices and information but may slant libraries in the direction of becoming consumer outlets.

RA service has been philosophically enriched by recent attention to reading as a social act rather than a solitary pursuit. For thousands of years reading was a public deed: authors read their books aloud, and individual readers spoke aloud the words before them. Our familiar mode of solitary, silent reading is relatively new to the scene. Augustine was surprised to find Ambrose, in the late fourth century AD,

> reading like this in silence, for he never read aloud.... The implication is that this method of reading, this silent perusing of the page, was in his time something out of the ordinary, and that normal reading was performed out loud. Even though instances of silent reading can be traced to earlier dates, not until the tenth century does this manner of reading become usual in the West. (Manguel 1996, 41)

Today, authors on book marketing tours read parts of their new works to the audience, but otherwise that oral activity is little evident. However, the importance of reading as associational behavior—in the sense of persons coming together to discuss a book, or the unifying impact that a given book has on all of those who partake of it—is gaining recognition. Shared texts provide common sets of experiences, making a foundation for community feeling and even nationalism (Anderson 2006). On a personal level, shared reading stimulates the construction of common narratives that served to bind individuals together (Long 2003). The demand for popular novels, for so long an object of concern among librarians, may be interpreted as serving this need for communal unity. Librarians foster the social nature of reading through provision of desired materials, storytelling, book discussion groups, author events, writing workshops, and other programs. In doing so, they forge for libraries a place in the lives of their readers, becoming a part of the communities they serve. A lucid account of this philosophy by one of its spokespersons makes a good introduction to the topic (Wiegand 2006).

References

Anderson, Benedict R. 2006. *Imagined Communities: Reflections on the Origin and Spread of Nationalism.* Rev. ed. London: Verso.

Alpert, Abby. 2006. Incorporating nonfiction in the readers' advisory services. *Reference & User Services Quarterly* 46, no. 1 (Fall): 25–33.

American Library Association. 1935. A national plan for libraries. *American Library Association Bulletin* 29, no. 2 (February): 91–98.

Baker, Sharon L. 2002. *The Responsive Public library: How to Develop and Market a Winning Collection.* 2nd ed. Englewood, CO: Libraries Unlimited.

Booton, Mabel. 1939. A close view of advisory service in a large library. In *Helping Adults to Learn: The Library in Action,* ed. John Chancellor, 9–26. Chicago: American Library Association.

Bosman, Ellen, et al. 2008. *Gay, Lesbian, Bisexual, and Transgendered Literature: A Genre Guide.* Westport, CT: Libraries Unlimited.

Burgin, Robert. 2001. Readers' advisory and nonfiction. In *Readers' Advisors' Companion,* ed. Kenneth D. Shearer and Robert Burgin, 213–27. Westport, CT: Libraries Unlimited.

Chelton, Mary K. 2002. Readers' advisory work. In *Reference and Information Services in the 21st Century,* 2nd ed., by Kay Ann Cassell and Uma Hiremath, 293–305. New York: Neal-Schuman.

Crowley, Bill. 2008. *Renewing Professional Librarianship: A Fundamental Rethinking.* Westport, Ct: Libraries Unlimited.

Dawson, Alma, and Connie Van Fleet. 2001. The future of readers' advisory in a multicultural society. In *Readers' Advisors' Companion,* ed. Kenneth D. Shearer and Robert Burgin, 249–68. Westport, CT: Libraries Unlimited.

Dewey, Melvil. 1897. Advice to a librarian. *Public Libraries* 2, no. 6 (June): 266–67.

Dilevko, Juris, and Candice F. C. Magowan. 2007. *Readers' Advisory Service in North American Public Libraries, 1870–2005: A History and Critical Analysis.* Jefferson, NC: McFarland.

Drury, Francis. 1930. *Book Selection.* Chicago: American Library Association.

Flexner, Jennie M., and Sigrid A. Edge. 1934. *A Readers' Advisory Service.* New York: American Association for Adult Education.

Fonseca, Anthony J., and June Michele Pulliam. 2009. *Hooked on Horror II*. Westport, CT: Libraries Unlimited.

Garrison, Dee. 1979. *Apostles of Culture: The Public Librarian and American Society, 1876–1920*. New York: Macmillan.

Green, Samuel Swett. 1876. Personal relations between librarians and readers. *American Library Journal* 1, no. 2 (October): 74–81.

Haines, Helen. 1935. *Living with Books; The Art of Book Selection*. New York: Columbia University Press.

Harris, Michael H. 1973. The purpose of the American public library: a revisionist interpretation of history. *Library Journal* 98, no. 16 (September 15): 2509–14.

Herald, Diana Tixier. 2006. *Genreflecting: A Guide to Popular Reading Interests*. 6th ed. Edited by Wayne A. Wiegand. Westport, CT: Libraries Unlimited. 1st ed., see Rosenberg (1982). See also Wiegand (2006).

Johnson, Sarah L. 2009. *Historical Fiction II*. Westport, CT: Libraries Unlimited.

Kimball, Melanie A. 2006. A brief history of readers' advisory. In *Genreflecting: A Guide to Popular Reading Interests*, by Diana Tixier Herald, 6th ed., 15–24.

Krashen, Stephen. 2004. The *Power of Reading: Insights from Research*. 2nd ed. Westport, CT: Libraries Unlimited.

Leigh, Robert D. 1950. *The Public Library in the United States: The General Report of the Public Library Inquiry*. New York: Columbia University Press.

Long, Elizabeth. 2003. *Book Clubs: Women and the Uses of Reading in Everyday Life*. Chicago: University of Chicago Press.

Manguel, Alberto. 1996. *A History of Reading*. New York: Penguin Books USA.

Martinez, Sara L. 2009. *Latino Literature: A Guide to Reading Interests*. Westport, CT: Libraries Unlimited.

May, Anne K. 2001. Readers' advisory service: explorations of the transaction. In *Readers' Advisors' Companion*, ed. Kenneth D. Shearer and Robert Burgin, 123–48. Westport, CT: Libraries Unlimited.

Meloni, Christine. 2009. *Teen Chick Lit: A Guide to Reading Interests*. Westport, CT: Libraries Unlimited.

Mort, John. 2006. *Read the High Country: A Guide to Western Books and Films*. Westport, CT: Libraries Unlimited.

Moyer, Jessica E. 2008. *Research-Based Readers' Advisory*. Chicago: American Library Association.

National Endowment for the Arts. 2004. *Reading at Risk: A Survey of Literary Reading in America*. Washington, D.C.: National Endowment for the Arts, Research Division, Report #46. www.nea.gov/pub/readingatrisk. Accessed August 2010.

Niebuhr, Gary Warren. 2009. *Caught Up in Crime: A Reader's Guide to Crime Fiction and Nonfiction*. Westport, CT: Libraries Unlimited.

Pawuk, Michael. 2006. *Graphic Novels: A Genre Guide to Comic Books, Manga, and More*. Westport, CT: Libraries Unlimited.

Pearl, Nancy. 1999. *Now Read This: A Guide to Mainstream Fiction, 1978–1998*. Englewood, CO: Libraries Unlimited.

Pearl, Nancy. 2002. *Now Read This II: A Guide to Mainstream Fiction, 1990–2001*. Englewood, CO: Libraries Unlimited.

Pearl, Nancy. 2003. *Book Lust: Recommended Reading for Every Mood, Moment, and Reason*. Seattle: Sasquatch Books.

Pearl, Nancy. 2005. *More Book Lust: Recommended Reading for Every Mood, Moment, and Reason*. Seattle: Sasquatch Books.

Pitman, Randy. 2001. Viewers' advisory: handling audiovisual advisory questions. In *Readers' Advisors' Companion*, ed. Kenneth D. Shearer and Robert Burgin, 229–36. Westport, CT: Libraries Unlimited.

Radway, Janice A. 1991. *Reading the Romance: Women, Patriarchy, and Popular Literature*. With a new introduction by the author. Chapel Hill: University of North Carolina Press.

Readers' Advisor Online. 2010. Includes all the titles in the Genreflecting series. Santa Barbara, CA: Libraries Unlimited. http://www.abc-clio.com.

Redefining RA. *Library Journal* July 15, 2007; November 1, 2008; October 15, 2009.

Rosenberg, Betty. 1982. *Genreflecting*. Littleton, CO: Libraries Unlimited.

Ross, Catherine Sheldrick. 1991. Readers' advisory service: new directions. *RQ* 30, no. 4 (Summer): 503–18.

Ross, Catherine Sheldrick. 2006. *Reading Matters: What the Research Reveals about Reading, Libraries, and Community*. Westport, CT: Libraries Unlimited.

Saricks, Joyce G. 2005. *Readers' Advisory Service in the Public Library*. 3rd ed. Chicago: American Library Association.

Saricks, Joyce G. 2009. *Readers' Advisory Guide to Genre Fiction*. 2nd ed. Chicago: American Library Association.

Saricks, Joyce G., and Nancy Brown. 1989. *Readers' Advisory Service in the Public Library*. 2nd ed. Chicago: American Library Association.

Shearer, Kenneth D., and Robert Burgin, eds. 2001. *Readers' Advisors' Companion*. Westport, CT: Libraries Unlimited.

Shearer, Kenneth D., and Robert Burgin, eds. 2001a. Partly out of sight: not much in mind: master's level education for adult readers' advisory services. In *Readers' Advisors' Companion*, ed. Kenneth D. Shearer and Robert Burgin, 15–25. Westport, CT: Libraries Unlimited.

Smith, Duncan. 2001. Reinventing readers' advisory. In *Readers' Advisors' Companion*, ed. Kenneth D. Shearer and Robert Burgin, 59–76. Westport, CT: Libraries Unlimited.

Van Fleet, Connie. 2008. Education for readers' advisory service in library and information science programs: Challenges and opportunities. *Reference & User Services Quarterly* 47, no. 3 (Spring): 224–30.

Waples, Douglas, and Ralph W. Tyler. 1931. *What People Want to Read About*. Chicago: American Library Association.

Watson, Dana. 2000. Time to turn the page: Library education for readers' advisory services. *Reference & User Services Quarterly* 40, no. 2 (Winter): 143–46.

Webber, Carlisle K. 2010. *Gay, Lesbian, Bisexual, Transgender, and Questioning Teen Literature: A Genre Guide*. Santa Barbara, CA: Libraries Unlimited.

Wellard, James Howard. 1937. *Book Selection: Its Principles and Practice*. London: Grafton.

Wiegand, Wayne A. 2006. The social nature of reading. In *Genreflecting: A Guide to Popular Reading Interests*, by Diana Tixier Herald, 6th ed., 3–14. Westport, CT: Libraries Unlimited.

Williams, Patrick. 1988. *The American Public Library and the Problem of Purpose*. New York: Greenwood Press.

Wyatt, Neal, et al. 2007. Core collections in genre studies: romance fiction 101. *Reference & User Services Quarterly* 47, no. 2 (Winter): 120–27.

REAL COUNTY PUBLIC LIBRARY, LEAKEY, TX   225 Main St., Leakey, TX 78873. Population served: 1,398. Circulation: 24,011. Holdings: 13,375. LJ February 15, 2009: 3-star library; November 15, 2009, and October 1, 2010: 4-star library.
   Recordings (*see* MUSIC COLLECTIONS).

RED HOOK PUBLIC LIBRARY, NY   7444 S. Broadway, Red Hook, NY 12571. Founded 1898. Population served: 1,805. Circulation: 38,497. Holdings: 14,884. The 1935 building, by Orson Squire Fowler, is "one of the finest examples of octagonal architecture in the Hudson Valley" (communication from the library). LJ October 1, 2010: 3-star library.

REDLANDS, CA. *See* A. K. SMILEY PUBLIC LIBRARY, REDLANDS, CA.

REDWOOD CITY PUBLIC LIBRARY, CA   1044 Middlefield Rd., Redwood City, CA 94063. Founded 1865. Population served: 75,986. Circulation: 982,962. Holdings: 228,530. 2 branches. LJ February 15, 2009: 5-star library; November 15, 2009, and October 1, 2010: 4-star library. LJ Library of the Year 1992.

REFERENCE AND INFORMATION SERVICES

Terminology

   Defining the activity of "reference service(s)"—or recently "reference and information service(s)"—has proved troublesome. One writer has observed that "many definitions of reference service have been offered over the years, all of them illustrative, none definitive; part art, part science, it is better described than defined" (Rettig 1993, 703). Textbook authors have tended to sidestep the definition issue, either by citing uncritically several definitions by others (e.g., Bopp and Smith 2001) or by saying nothing about it (e.g., Katz 1997). Cassell and Hiremath (2009, 5) presents a definition of "reference transactions" as "information consultations in which library staff recommend, interpret, evaluate, and/or use information resources to help others to meet particular information needs"—this being a statement of the Reference and User Services Association (RUSA) of the American Library Association (ALA). "Information service" for Cassell "is the process of assisting library users to identify sources of information in response to a particular question, interest, assignment, or problem. Sometimes referred to as reference service."
   ODLIS offers a lengthy account:

> Reference services: All the functions performed by a trained librarian employed in the reference section of a library to meet the information needs of patrons (in person, by telephone, or electronically), including but not limited to answering substantive questions, instructing users in the selection and use of

appropriate tools and techniques for finding information, conducting searches on behalf of the patron, directing users to the location of library resources, assisting in the evaluation of information, referring patrons to resources outside the library when appropriate, keeping reference statistics, and participating in the development of the reference collection.

Another RUSA statement reads, "Reference work includes reference transactions and other activities that involve the creation, management, and assessment of information or research resources, tools, and services" (ALA, RUSA 2008). This last description engages the term "reference work," which was in common use before "reference service." Neither statement offers "information service" as a partner to "reference service." That partnership, reference and information, actually makes an uneasy union since it is hardly clear what the difference may be between the players. Nevertheless, there it is in the title of this entry, as a concession to current usage.

An implication in the *ODLIS* definition is that to "meet the information needs of patrons" the reference service will provide useful and correct answers or guidance. As Patrick Wilson (1977) has expressed it, this means that answers will be drawn from "verified public knowledge" (109). This point is taken up under the section "Current Practice of Reference Service" below.

By assembling these ideas, one may offer a definition of reference service: "a structured activity that is designed to respond to direct questions with answers, and to unexpressed information needs with guidance; in both cases providing useful statements which are correctly drawn from appropriate segments of verified public knowledge." How this activity is designed is discussed below under the section "Current Practice of Reference Service."

Until the rise of the Internet, reference service was centered on a class of printed materials known as reference books. A reference book was traditionally defined as "a book designed by the arrangement and treatment of its subject matter to be consulted for definite items of information rather than to be read consecutively" (ALA 1983, 188). A later definition encompasses nonbook media and considers materials with any approach: "reference source: any material, published work, database, website, etc., which is used to obtain authoritative information" (*Harrod's Librarians' Glossary and Reference Book* 2000, 618). While the first definition seems too restrictive (even if expanded to include media and websites), the second seems too broad since it has everything in it. But the second is closer to contemporary reality; a Google search will explore a database comprising multiple formats—just about everything. Reference "source" is the preferred expression today since it covers books, other printed materials, nonprint media, and websites.

A recent addition to the terminology of the field is "virtual reference," defined by RUSA as "reference service initiated electronically where patrons employ computers or other technology to communicate with public services staff without being physically present." The communication channels include chat, email, and instant messaging. While the transaction is computer based, the sources used by staff in responding to the patron (typically by giving the answer to a question) may be electronic or traditional. RUSA has issued guidelines covering this aspect of reference work (ALA, RUSA 2010).

Finally there is the creation of novel terms to describe reference work. It may now be called "information delivery service," and its staff may be named "information management specialists." "Cybrarians" and "knowledge engineers" are also found. The reference desk is often an "information center." It is an open question whether such linguistic turns enhance public appreciation of the service or diminish it (Gorman 2005, 57–58).

Historical Summary

At the first conference of librarians in 1853, there was no allusion to reference work. By the 1876 founding of the ALA, the notion was in the air, albeit hard to distinguish from what was later called readers' advisory service. An article by Samuel Swett Green in the first issue of the *American Library Journal* introduced the idea of personal assistance to readers in contrast to the prevailing practice of letting them find their way independently. Green, like other library leaders of his day, was ever seeking to elevate reading tastes, and he found in personal assistance a means of promoting that cause. But his article also noted that readers often had trouble finding information and that librarians should be "cordially" ready to help (Green 1876). His own Worcester, MA, library had a separate section of "reference books."

Of course the array of reference books, especially in English, was modest in the nineteenth century. Taking the field of religion as an example, these standard works were not written until the end of the century or early in the twentieth century: *Encyclopedia of Religion and Ethics* (ed. James Hastings; 1911–1927), *Schaff-Herzog Encyclopedia of Religious Knowledge* (1st English ed., 1908–1912), *Dictionary of the Bible* (ed. James Hastings, 1898–1902), James Strong's *Exhaustive Concordance of the Bible* (1894), and the *Westminster Commentaries* (1907–1927). The pioneer index to American and English periodicals was compiled by William F. Poole in 1891; it covered about 590,000 articles in 470 periodicals issued from 1802 to 1881, with subject entries only. The *Reader's Guide to Periodical Literature* began in 1905. The only substantial English-language encyclopedia in the nineteenth century was the *Britannica*, first issued in 1768–1771. *Who's Who in America* began in 1899 and the *Dictionary of American Biography* in 1928. It would seem that a reference section in a public library in Samuel Green's time would require only a few shelving units and that librarians would need relatively little application to master its contents. But publication of reference sources accelerated, inspiring ALA to issue in

1902 a *Guide to the Study and Use of Reference Books* by Alice Bertha Kroeger. This modest work was expanded in 1908, and there have been subsequent editions with varying titles under the editorship of Isidore Gilbert Mudge, Constance Winchell, Eugene Sheehy, and Robert Balay. After the eleventh edition of *Guide to Reference Books*, the ALA abandoned the print format and put forth an online version of the work titled *Guide to Reference* (2009).

Returning to the later nineteenth century, we find the profession running ahead of the reference book publishers. Personal assistance in guiding patrons "to the best books and sources of information" became a major readers' service by 1883 (Rothstein 1953, 4). In 1885, Melvil Dewey, then director of the Columbia College Library, assigned two librarians to aid inquirers. By 1893 there were librarians with specific reference duties in the public libraries of Boston, Providence, Milwaukee, Detroit, Newark, Chicago, St. Louis, and Brooklyn. The first journal article to name the new service in its title appeared in *Library Journal* (October, 1891): "Reference work in libraries." From 1896, presentations about reference work appeared regularly on ALA conference programs. "By the end of the century its place in the library order was securely established in a form essentially the same as today's" (Rothstein 1953, 13). Mary Eileen Ahern, editor of the journal *Public Libraries*, wrote that "the reference work of the library gives the institution its greatest value and may be called the heart of the work. The very best talent obtainable should be placed in the reference room. . . . Here is where the real educative work is done" (Ahern 1904, 55).

With the service established, it was possible to organize its concepts and procedures in articles and then a textbook (Wyer 1930). Writers began to separate reference inquiries into various types, such as "scholarly-popular" (McCombs 1943), "elementary-intermediate-advanced" (Butler 1943), and those that fell into the librarian's field (or a related field) or an unknown field (Alexander 1936). In its *Post-War Standards for Public Libraries*, the ALA set a standard: a public library's minimum number of reading and reference questions per year should be from one-half to one for each person in the population served over five years of age (ALA 1943, 27). It is interesting to see the 2005 figure of reference transactions per capita in public libraries: 1.1 (U.S. National Center for Education Statistics 2007, table 4). The ALA's 1943 goal is being met today.

The next innovation in reference service came in the early 1970s under the rubric "information and referral" (I & R). It was intended to connect patrons (especially the disadvantaged) with agencies providing social services. The effort was a part of the social responsibility activities that affected public libraries at the time (*see* AMERICAN LIBRARY ASSOCIATION; OUTREACH). Despite considerable publicity about it, such as an entire issue of *Drexel Library Quarterly* in 1976 (Braverman 1976), I & R did not have a secure footing. It was "mostly I and relatively little R," according to Thomas Childers, who surveyed and visited libraries in 1978–1980 (Williams 1988, 106). It seems that after the 1970s, I & R was more or less absorbed into traditional reference services. Bill Katz (1997) noted that reference librarians commonly called on outside experts for assistance in meeting patron needs for social resources, offered meeting space for community groups, and provided "files, pamphlets, booklists, and so on, which give users information on topics ranging from occupations to local housing regulations" (22).

The 1970s brought a more lasting alteration to traditional reference services: computerized resources (a history of online information services is provided by Bourne and Hahn 2003). Lockheed offered its DIALOG database in 1972. Through the application of skilled searching, a DIALOG user could acquire a printed list of book and article titles on chosen subjects. DIALOG and similar databases that followed (ORBIT, BRS, and LEXIS-NEXIS) were too complicated for direct access by library patrons, so reference staff conducted the searches. Special study, in workshops for active librarians and in full courses for library school students, was necessary. Databases appeared in CD-ROM format in the 1980s, reducing the need for online time, but the whole search process remained forbidding. With the arrival of the Internet in the early 1990s, access to the older databases and to new sources was gradually simplified. OCLC First Search, available from 1991, was usable by patrons. Massive information structures emerged: Yahoo! (1994), now indexing 4 billion pages, and Google (1998), now indexing 8 billion pages. These marvels and others like them soon dominated reference activity, bringing up two complications taken up below under the section "Recent Issues": the need for instruction (patron and staff) in use of the new sources and the problem of reliability in the sources.

In the twenty-first century, library users with modest searching skills can do much of their own "reference work" on their home computers. It may be that, as one writer sees it, "the reference book is fading into the sunset" (Gorman 2005, 110), and reference service is fading as well. Or perhaps the role of the reference librarian is simply changing from that of providing and pointing to resources to educating patrons to evaluate resources and manage the deluge of data that the Internet presents to them (*see* INFORMATION LITERACY INSTRUCTION).

Current Practice of Reference Service

A public library reference department, under whatever name it may be known, engages in a wide span of activities. An account of those activities in the sixth edition of *Guide to Reference Books* remains essentially valid:

> The work of a reference department covers everything necessary to help the reader in his inquiries, including the selection of an adequate and suitable collection of reference books, the arrangement and maintenance of the collection in such a way that it can be used easily and conveniently, the making of such files, indexes and clipping collections as are needed to supplement the library catalog and the book collection, the training of a capable staff

of reference assistants and their supervision is such a way as to insure skilful and pleasant service and good teamwork, the provision of posted signs, printed directions, lists and bulletins to help the reader who can profit by such guides, expert aid in the use of the catalog and other records, suggestions as to books to be used for special purposes, instruction of individuals, groups, or classes in the use of reference books and reference methods, and constant work in answering individual questions. (Mudge 1936, 1)

What one would change in describing today's reference department in action are emphases on one task or another. For example, the clipping collection (or "vertical file") is far less important now than it was before Internet access to the contents of newspapers and magazines, although the great convenience of finding a folder of clips and pictures on a subject has been lost. Aid in use of the catalog, however, seems to take more time than it once did now that the catalog is computerized and often tricky to navigate (for a discussion of such assistance and related guidance to use of library and online materials, *see* INFORMATION LITERACY INSTRUCTION).

Selection of materials to be used in reference work involves choosing of print materials, nonprint media, and online sources. Choosing dependable reference books has been facilitated over the years by a growing body of critical assessments covering general works and specialized titles. The ALA's *Guide to Reference Books* has been mentioned. *American Reference Books Annual (ARBA)* has reviewed new publications in many fields since 1970. Reviews are also found in *Library Journal, Booklist,* and *Reference & User Services Quarterly* and in specialized journals of diverse fields. It is more challenging to select appropriate online sources since the materials are in flux and less subject to bibliographic control. Useful guides include *Best of the Web,* produced by the New York Public Library (Best Free Reference Websites 2010), the University of Washington *Information Gateway* (2010), *Web Research* (Radford et al. 2006), and an annual list in *Reference & User Services Quarterly.*

While many online sources are free to the user, such as *Wikipedia,* others require subscription. The issue of permanence is important in consideration of Internet reference tools since a website could be taken down at any time—nearly all are commercial ventures, after all—leaving the library with no equivalent of "back files." There are numerous advantages that online sources have over book materials: currency (not in all cases), ease of access (not in all cases), and capability of serving multiple users at once. Disadvantages include too many results to a query, incomplete free access to full texts and materials dated before about 1980, and above all the "lack of regulated quality control" (Cassell and Hiremath 2009, 276; chapter 13 of Cassell's book is a valuable discussion of Internet materials). Lack of standard protocols for searching the various websites is perennially troublesome.

The quality of the source affects the nature of the librarian's response to a query. In the older world of reference books, the sources became familiar, with their strong features and weaknesses, and such factors could be weighed by a reference librarian in deciding where to look for an answer and how to present the answer to a patron. Nevertheless, many studies indicated that finding correct answers was sporadic. A considerable literature developed in the area of evaluating reference service, particularly the question–answer transaction. Obtrusive (disclosed to the librarian) and unobtrusive (not disclosed) methods have been used (Bundy 1982; Weech and Goldhor 1982; Gatten and Radcliff 2001) along with patron surveys. The pioneer work was done by Terence Crowley and Thomas Childers (Crowley and Childers 1971; Childers 1980). Librarians cannot be satisfied with the results. "A consistent pattern of responses has emerged. In responding to questions about facts, library reference departments give correct answers about 55% of the time" (Bopp and Smith 2001, 254). A guide to evaluative procedures has been published by the ALA (Whitlach 2000). RUSA has issued "Guidelines for Behavioral Performance of Reference and Information Service Professionals" (ALA, RUSA 2004), an approach to improving results in reference transactions. It seems there is a long road ahead before the profession can reach the hard goal set for it by Patrick Wilson (see the section "Terminology" above). Wilson proposed "a true information service" that would vouch for the accuracy of the information given as being part of public knowledge. The status of public knowledge in a field is discovered in the consensus of experts on given points; agreement creates verified public knowledge, while conflict of experts on certain points reflects an indeterminate status of knowledge for those areas. In general, everyone seeks the best available story about the world; it is the librarian's task to find that story in an array of subjects, most of them outside his or her personal scope of expertise (Wilson 1977, 6, 109).

At present, reference librarians are not able to "vouch for the accuracy" of responses they present. It is curious that despite the research attention to gross weaknesses in reference service, the situation has not engendered panic and alarms. Indeed the textbook treatment of the issue is usually brief and nearly unconcerned:

> It is difficult to escape the consistent finding from more than twenty studies that has come to be called the "55% rule." Many comments about the "crisis" in reference service are based on the widely held opinion that reference services should be doing better than this. The results of unobtrusive testing have pointed out areas in which substantial improvement can be made. . . . Libraries are now turning their attention to staff training, collection improvement, and other techniques to improve the accuracy of responses to factual questions. (Bopp and Smith 2001, 254)

Success or failure in the reference transaction often depends on the quality of the so-called reference interview, which is the initial exchange between patron and librarian. This episode has been a favorite topic in the reference literature (summaries in Bopp and Smith 2001, chap. 3; Katz 2002, vol. 2, chap. 7; Cassell and Hiremath 2009, 15–17; longer studies in Lynch 1978; Jennerich and Jennerich 1997; Radford et al. 2010). The steps to be taken in this interview are establishing rapport, negotiating the question (finding out exactly what is wanted), designing a search strategy and sharing it with the patron, finding the answer (and citing the source for the patron), following up with the patron (does this fully answer your question?), and closing the interview (be sure to come back if anything is unclear or you need something else). One domain of trouble found in the research is that the librarian unconsciously adapts the patron's query to fit it into his own comfort zone of expertise or to sources he knows; this leads to an answer that is responsive to a question not asked, but the patron may be inclined to accept it anyway.

Another departure from the ideal has been uncovered by a study of telephone reference service in large public libraries: in 68.8 percent of the encounters, the librarians gave no sources for their answers. That report also noted that librarians rarely asked the follow-up question, did not always identify themselves professionally, did not seem to take the question seriously, and "exhibited an alarming lack of confidence in their own answers" (Agosto and Anderton 2007). The worst-case scenario is no reference interview at all, which is the situation encountered by the home Internet user.

Public libraries today often have written reference policies. These statements express what a library will do (and sometimes will not do) with regard to inquiries from patrons. An example follows:

> Reference service, reader's advisory, and related materials are available to all persons who reside in the Warren-Newport Public Library District regardless of the patron's age, race, sex, or economic status. Reference service, reader's advisory, and related materials are available during all hours the library is open and are provided in response to inquiries of all forms, including but not limited to inquiries from patrons in the library, by telephone, by facsimile, by e-mail, by virtual reference, and by TTY. The reference and reader's advisory questions of patrons are given the highest priority. All requests for information receive an answer or status report within one working day. Questions that cannot be answered with on-site resources are referred to another agency. Such referrals are verified and/or mediated by library staff. In the instance of legal, medical, investment, consumer information, computer assistance, or tax reference questions, the staff will only guide the patron to the material available on the topic of interest. (Warren-Newport Public Library District 2005)

A useful collection of model library policies includes a chapter on reference policies (Larson and Totten 2008).

Recent Issues

The ongoing concerns about quality of online resources have been mentioned. Most issues today have to do with those resources and how best to integrate them into the service. RUSA has guidelines for this area (ALA, RUSA, 2006). Virtual reference was described under the section "Terminology."

Competencies for reference librarians and other staff have drawn attention, and a RUSA guideline (ALA, RUSA 2004) (*see* EDUCATION OF PUBLIC LIBRARIANS). The use of support staff for reference work is controversial but widespread (*see* STAFFING).

Cooperative reference services, in which libraries agree to assist each other in handling queries, are developing. RUSA has issued a guideline for such collaboration (ALA, RUSA 2006a) (For instructions to patrons in the use of reference resources, from the library catalog to research websites, *see* INFORMATION LITERACY INSTRUCTION).

It may be that the overarching challenge to reference librarians in the new century is to assign a proper weight to the offerings of technology. As one writer says,

> It is quite possible that sections of the community are punch drunk with the availability of "shiny new toys." It is quite possible that large chunks of this new technology will glitter for a period and fall away into oblivion. It is even possible for reference departments to continue with business as usual, much as there are libraries that continue to use card catalogs. What is not possible is to pretend that it is not happening. (Cassell and Hiremath 2009, 413)

See also INTERNET; READERS' ADVISORY SERVICES; SERVICES TO BUSINESS AND INDUSTRY.

References

Among the several valuable textbooks treating the reference field, these may be mentioned: Bopp and Smith (2001), Katz (2002), and Cassell and Hiremath (2009). Important journals include *Reference & User Services Quarterly* and *Reference Services Review*.

Agosto, Denise E., and Holly Anderton. 2007. Whatever happened to "Always cite the source"? *Reference & User Services Quarterly* 47, no. 1 (Fall): 44–55.

Ahern, Mary Eileen. 1904. Reference work with the general public. *Public Libraries* 9, no. 2 (February): 55.

Alexander, Carter. 1936. The technique of library searching. *Special Libraries* 17, no. 7 (September): 230–38.

American Library Association. 1943. *Post-War Standards for Public Libraries*. Chicago: American Library Association.

American Library Association. 1983. *ALA Glossary of Library and Information Science*. Chicago: American Library Association.

American Library Association, Reference and User Services Association. 2004. Guidelines for behavioral performance of reference and information service providers. *Reference & User Services Quarterly* 44, no. 1 (Fall): 9–14.

American Library Association, Reference and User Services Association. 2006. Guidelines for cooperative reference service. http://www.ala.org/rusa. Accessed April 2010.

American Library Association, Reference and User Services Association. 2006a. Guidelines for the introduction of electronic information resources for users. www.ala.org/rusa, accessed April 2010.

American Library Association, Reference and User Services Association. 2008. Definition of reference work. http://www.ala.org/rusa. Accessed April 2010.

American Library Association, Reference and User Services Association. 2010. Guidelines for implementing and maintaining virtual reference services. http:// www.ala.org/rusa. Accessed April 2010.

Bell, Suzanne S. 2009. *Librarian's Guide to Online Searching*. 2nd ed. Englewood, CO: Libraries Unlimited.

Best Free Reference Websites. 2009. 11th annual list. *Reference & User Services Quarterly* 49, no. 1 (Fall): 43–49.

Bopp, Richard E., and Linda C. Smith. 2001. *Reference and Information Services: An Introduction*. 3rd ed. Englewood, CO: Libraries Unlimited.

Bourne, Charles P., and Trudi Bellardo Hahn. 2003. *A History of Online Information Services*. Cambridge, MA: MIT Press.

Braverman, Miriam, ed. 1976. Information and referral services in the public library. *Drexel Library Quarterly* 12 (January/April). Entire issue (12 articles).

Breeding, Marshall. 2008. An analytical approach to assessing the effectiveness of web-based resources. *Computers in Libraries* 28, no. 1 (January): 20–22.

Bundy, Mary Lee. 1982. Public library reference service: myth and reality. *Public Library Quarterly* 3, no. 3 (Fall): 11–22. Reprinted in *Library Lit 14: The Best of 1983*, ed. Bill Katz, 113–23. Metuchen, NJ: Scarecrow Press.

Butler, Pierce, ed. 1943. *The Reference Function of the Library: Papers Presented before the Library Institute at the University of Chicago, June 29 to July 10, 1942*. Chicago: University of Chicago Press.

1943. Survey of the reference field. In *The Reference Function of the Library: Papers Presented before the Library Institute at the University of Chicago, June 29 to July 10, 1942*, ed. Pierce Butler, 1–15. Chicago: University of Chicago Press.

Cassell, Kay Ann, and Uma Hiremath. 2009. *Reference and Information Services in the 21st Century*. 2nd ed. New York: Neal-Schuman.

Childers, Thomas. 1980. The test of reference. *Library Journal* 105, no. 8 (April 15): 924–28.

Crowley, Terence, and Thomas Childers. 1971. *Information Service in Public Libraries: Two Studies*. Metuchen, NJ: Scarecrow Press.

Gatten, Jeffrey, and Carolyn J. Radcliff. 2001. Assessing reference behaviors with unobtrusive testing. In *Library Evaluation: A Casebook and Can-Do Guide*, ed. Danny P. Wallace and Connie Van Fleet, 105–15. Englewood, CO; Libraries Unlimited.

Gorman, Michael. 2005. *Our Own Selves: More Meditations for Librarians*. Chicago: American Library Association.

Green, Samuel Swett. 1876. Personal relations between librarians and readers. *American Library Journal* 1, no. 2 (October): 74–81.

Harrod's Librarians' Glossary and Reference Book. 2000. 9th ed., ed. Ray Prytherich. Aldershot Gower.

Hernon, Peter, and Charles R. McClure. 1986. Unobtrusive reference testing: the 55 percent rule. *Library Journal* 111, no. 7 (April 15): 37–41.

Information Gateway. 2010. Seattle: University of Washington. http://www.lib.washington.edu/subject.

Jennerich, Elaine Z., and Edward J. Jennerich. 1997. *The Reference Interview as a Creative Art*. 2nd ed. Englewood, CO: Libraries Unlimited.

Katz, William. 1997. *Introduction to Reference Work*. 7th ed. 2 vols. New York: McGraw-Hill.

Katz, William. 2002. *Introduction to Reference Work*. 8th ed. 2 vols. New York: McGraw-Hill.

Larson, Jeanette C., and Herman L. Totten. 2008. *The Public Library Policy Writer: A Guidebook with Model Policies on CD-ROM*. New York: Neal-Schuman.

Lynch, Mary Jo. 1978. Reference interviews in public libraries. *Library Quarterly* 48, no. 2 (April): 119–42.

McCombs, Charles. 1943. The reference function in the large public library. In *The Reference Function of the Library: Papers Presented before the Library Institute at the University of Chicago, June 29 to July 10, 1942*, ed. Pierce Butler, 16–35. Chicago: University of Chicago Press.

Mudge, Isidore Gilbert. 1936. *Guide to Reference Books*. 6th ed. Chicago: American Library Association.

Murfin, Marjorie E., and Lubomyr R. Wynar. 1977. *Reference Service: An Annotated Bibliographic Guide*. Littleton, CO: Libraries Unlimited.

Murfin, Marjorie E., and Lubomyr R. Wynar. 1984. *Reference Service: An Annotated Bibliographic Guide. Supplement, 1976–1982*. Littleton, CO: Libraries Unlimited

Radford, Marie L., et al. 2006. *Web Research: Selecting, Evaluating, and Citing*. Boston: Pearson/Allyn Bacon.

Radford, Marie L., ed. 2010. *Reference Renaissance: Current and Future Trends*. New York: Neal-Schuman.

Reference Work in Libraries. 1891. Comments by W. A. Bardwell, W. B. Child, and Mary C. Mosman. *Library Journal* 16, no. 1 (October): 297–302.

Rettig, James. 1993. Reference and information services. *World Encyclopedia of Library and Information Services*, 3rd ed., 703–8. Chicago: American Library Association.

Roncevic, Mirela, ed. 2009. *Library Journal Guide to E-Reference Resources*. New York: Neal-Schuman.

Rothstein, Samuel. 1953. The development of the concept of reference service in American libraries. *Library Quarterly* 23, no. 1 (January): 1–15.

U.S. National Center for Education Statistics. 2007. *Public Libraries in the United States: Fiscal Year 2005*. Washington, DC: U.S. Department of Education.

Wallace, Danny P., and Connie Van Fleet. 2003. Strange bedfellows: evidence of accuracy in professional performance. *Reference & User Services Quarterly* 43, no. 2 (Winter): 109–10.

Warren-Newport Public Library District. 2005. Reference and readers' advisory service. In Board of Trustees *Policy Manual*, #3035. Gurnee, IL: Warren-Newport Library District.

Weech, Terry L., and Herbert Goldhor. 1982. Obtrusive versus unobtrusive evaluation of reference service in five Illinois public libraries: A pilot study. *Library Quarterly* 51, no. 4 (October): 305–24.

Whitlach, Jo Bell. 2000. *Evaluating Reference Services: A Practical Guide*. Chicago: American Library Association.

Williams, Patrick. 1988. The American Public Library and the Problem of Purpose. New York: Greenwood Press.

Wilson, Patrick. 1977. *Public Knowledge and Private Ignorance: Toward a Library and Information Policy.* Westport, CT: Greenwood Press.

Wyer, James I. 1930. *Reference Work: A Textbook for Students of Library Work and Librarians.* Chicago: American Library Association.

RENO, NV. *See* WASHOE COUNTY LIBRARY SYSTEM, RENO, NV.

RESEARCH

Terminology

"Research" is a term, a concept, and an approach to understanding that is frequently misunderstood. The term is ubiquitous in a variety of contexts but is at the same time fundamentally ambiguous. Corporations engage in market research to cement their competitive positions. Consumers engage in comparative research to make informed product choices. Students complete research papers as a standard component of the process of learning composition.

Dictionary definitions of "research" tend to be generic and ultimately rather unsatisfying. The *Oxford English Dictionary* provides an extensive definition, including these essential elements: "1) The act of searching carefully for or pursuing a specified thing or person; an instance of this; 2) Systematic investigation or inquiry aimed at contributing to knowledge of a theory, topic, etc., by careful consideration, observation, or study of a subject. In later use also: original critical or scientific investigation carried out under the auspices of an academic or other institution." Each of these definitions is pertinent in the context of the many possible understandings of research, with the second one the most pertinent to the view of research explored in this essay.

Herbert Goldhor (1969), in his classic *An Introduction to Scientific Research in Librarianship*, defined research as "any conscious premeditated inquiry—any investigation which seeks to increase one's knowledge of a given situation" (7). This simple, straightforward definition incorporates the elements necessary to distinguish research from other approaches to understanding. The requirement that research be *conscious* establishes research as being a structured, designed enterprise rather than a natural, organic process. Research does not just happen; it must be made to happen for a recognized purpose. The element of *premeditation* reinforces the structured, designed nature of research and adds the need for careful planning and an explicitly systematic approach to gathering data. Research happens only in the context of careful preparation and a project orientation. The inclusion of the term "inquiry" underlines the fundamental nature of research as a process of seeking an answer to a question. Research does not set out to prove a preestablished contention or to reveal an undeniable truth about the state of the world. A research project poses a question for which there is no established answer and sets out to determine the answer.

Goldhor, whose distinguished career included serving as director of the Library Research Center at the University of Illinois Graduate School of Library and Information Science, was known to lament that librarians frequently—nearly constantly—engage in activities that are almost research, some of which qualify as evaluation and some of which are misguided and unnecessary attempts at improvement. It is common practice for a librarian who observes that a particular service or program seems to be underutilized or ineffective to take action to change some aspect of the service or program in the interest of improvement. Sometimes the desired improvement actually accompanies the change, but sometimes it does not. The problem with any such ad hoc modification based on anecdotal evidence is that, even if the desired improvement follows the change, the lack of systematic assessment makes it impossible to know what would have happened if the "improvement" had not been implemented.

Research requires that data be gathered systematically, not accidentally or anecdotally, in a manner that can be documented to be an accurate representation of the phenomenon of interest. Research is generally perceived to be best when the results of a research project can be readily reproduced in a comparable environment. These are the essential research concepts of *validity* and *reliability*.

Validity has to do with the extent to which those entities to be studied are described accurately and any relationships among such entities are correctly identified. Establishing validity for a research project requires relating conceptual definitions that are frequently too broad or vague to be directly studied to operational definitions that establish a researchable base for the concepts of interest. Ability to provide a correct answer to a reference question is a readily understood concept but one that requires substantial operationalization to be made amenable to research. Hernon and McClure (1986), building on the work of Bunge (1968), Crowley and Childers (1971), and others, both established precedent and sparked controversy in their study of reference effectiveness based on unobtrusive observation carried out by student surrogate library patrons asking preformulated questions. Although the study clearly provided an easily researched approach to assessing correctness of answers, many commentators questioned the extent to which it was an accurate or appropriate representation of reference success, with some expressing outrage at Hernon and McClure's conclusion that 55 percent of questions were answered correctly.

Reliability has to do with the extent to which the results of a research process can be replicated. Subsequent to Hernon and McClure's exposition on the "55 percent rule," additional studies, including those by Wallace (1983, 1984) and Richardson (2002), found that the variation in success rates for unobtrusive studies of reference, even when the same procedure was carried out across multiple years, was substantial (*see* REFERENCE AND INFORMATION SERVICES).

Research and Evaluation

Research and evaluation tend to be very closely linked in any service-oriented profession such as librarianship (*see* EVALUATION). Although there are distinct and numerous similarities in the methods and tools of research and evaluation, the purposes of the two endeavors are different. Evaluation focuses on improving the quality of a specific service, product, activity, or institution. Evaluation and its outcomes are fundamentally local in nature. The quality of an evaluation process is determined by its contribution to effective decision making. Research is at its core dedicated to the advancement of knowledge and, in the context of a service-oriented profession, focuses on improving the overall quality of the benefit the profession returns to the public. The quality of a research project is reflected in its contribution to the professional or societal knowledge base. Although public library research can and does contribute to improvement of local library operations, much library research serves primarily as a basis for understanding the roles, purposes, and contributions of libraries in their societal contexts.

Historical Summary

Research focusing on libraries and librarianship followed very closely on the rise of libraries and the professionalization of librarianship in the United States in the late nineteenth century. The efforts of Dewey (1876), Cutter (1876), and others to formalize processes for organizing library collections can be understood to be research-based development efforts. In 1876, the year that the American Library Association (ALA) was founded and *Library Journal* began publication, the U.S. Bureau of Education, now the Department of Education, published *Public Libraries in the United States: Their History, Condition, and Management*, an attempt at a comprehensive examination of the state of American public libraries. On a more limited but quite meaningful scale, some of the earliest efforts that can be understood as systematic research were the studies of reading among young people in public libraries initiated by Caroline Hewins in 1882 (McDowell 2009).

Later attempts at comprehensive examinations of public librarianship in the United States included Learned's (1924) *The American Public Library and the Diffusion of Knowledge*; the ALA's *Survey of Libraries in the United States*, issued in four volumes in 1926 and 1927; Wilson's (1938) *The Geography of Reading: A Study of the Distribution and Status of Libraries in the United States*; and the massive *Public Library Inquiry*, a series of 19 research projects published in 10 reports from 1949 to 1952.

Such early research efforts were primarily the activities of individuals, sometimes supported by governmental or professional agencies, interested in understanding the nature and status of librarianship. Although formal education for librarians began as early as 1887 with the founding of the School of Library Economy at Columbia University, research was neither a focus nor an interest of formal library education programs for several decades. The Williamson Reports, a pair of studies conducted in 1920 and 1921 and sponsored by the Carnegie Corporation, severely criticized library education programs as failing to distinguish between professional education and technical training, unable to provide leadership for the profession, and intellectually empty. The Williamson reports prompted a shift to a more academic focus for library education, perhaps best exemplified by the founding of the Graduate Library School (GLS) at the University of Chicago in 1929. GLS assembled a faculty from a variety of social sciences disciplines with a focus on scholarship as well as professionalism and launched the research journal *Library Quarterly* in 1931. Richardson (1982) provides an excellent overview of the formative years of GLS.

Beals (1942) criticized the existing body of library literature as consisting of "Glad Tidings, Testimony, and Research," with the last constituting a very small component of the literature. Williamson (1931), in the inaugural issue of *Library Quarterly*, explained the paucity of research in the library literature as having its origin in "a deep-rooted prejudice among library workers against subjecting their activities to scientific scrutiny" (10). Thompson (1931) questioned the need for, desire for, and wisdom of viewing librarianship as a science, preferring a fundamentally humanistic view.

Lynch (1984) explored the "uneasy connection" between research and librarianship, attributing it in part to other activities in which librarians frequently engage as part of their professional responsibilities. These include the numeric fact gathering that librarians routinely carry out by counting such activities as circulation of materials, attendance at programs, and reference questions asked; consultant reports that provide an external view of library performance; and demonstration and development of new approaches to library service. Lynch was concerned that these pseudoresearch activities might substitute in the minds of librarians for true research and thereby impede the production of more formal research activities.

Despite concerns about the development and status of research in librarianship, research continues to be a component of professionalism in the field. As Schwartz and Hernon (1999) have pointed out, most library associations have some sort of research division or committee, support one or more periodicals that publish research, provide opportunities for research presentations at conferences and workshops, and sponsor research through grants and awards.

The ALA's Library Research Round Table, established in 1968, has as its mission "to contribute toward the extension and improvement of library research; to provide public program opportunities for describing and evaluating library research projects and for disseminating their findings; to inform and educate ALA members concerning research techniques and their usefulness in obtaining information with which to reach administrative decisions and solve problems; and expand the theoretical base of the field" (ALA, Library Research Round Table 2010). The ALA also supports an Office for Research and Statistics, the mission of which is "to provide leadership and expert advice to ALA staff, members, and public on all matters related to research and statistics about libraries, librarians, and other library staff; represent the Association to Federal agencies on these issues; and initiate projects needed to expand the knowledge base of the field through research and the collection of useful statistics" (ALA, Office for Research and Statistics 2010). *Public Libraries*, the official journal of the Public Library Association, provides an outlet for research articles related to public librarianship (*see* AMERICAN LIBRARY ASSOCIATION).

Families of Research Methodologies

Research methodologies can be understood in the context of three essential focuses or families of methodologies characterized by differing core purposes: (1) historical, (2) descriptive, and (3) experimental. Historical research is based on observation of the past and addresses questions that can be summarized as "what happened?" Descriptive research focuses on observation of the present and asks "what is happening?" Experimental research manipulates the present to ask "what might happen?" Each of these families of research methodologies is characterized by many different specific methodological approaches and tools. All three families have pertinence to public library research.

Historical Research and Public Libraries

The essential component of historical research is a focus on understanding what happened in the past. The ALA established its Library History Round Table (LHRT) in 1950, lending an element of official support to the role of history in librarianship. Dain (2000), in an issue of *Libraries and Culture* dedicated to the fiftieth anniversary of LHRT, emphasized the role of history in support of librarianship as "a humanistic endeavor, concerned with preserving and organizing [the records of human activity and thought] and with serving the human need for cultural continuity and intellectual nourishment as well as practical information" (241).

Although understanding the past may have implications for action in the present or the future, such implications are in no way essential in determining the quality of historical research. The quality of historical research is determined by the appropriateness, completeness, authority, and accuracy of the historical sources examined and the quality of the interpretation provided by the historical researcher. Even though the essential nature of historical research is exploration of the past, simply associating dates with events—building a chronology—is not history. Historical research requires careful interpretation of the past as represented in the artifacts of the past.

Harris's and Dain's studies of the origins and history of public libraries in the United States, examining the same time period and using essentially the same historical sources, provide a solid example of the role of interpretation in historical research. Harris (1973) challenged the popular view of the origin of the American public library as "dedicated to the continuing education of the 'common man' and that its collections and services be as broadly popular as possible" (2509). In his exploration of the historical influences of such library pioneers as George Ticknor, Justin Winsor, Edward Everett, William I. Fletcher, William F. Poole, Melvil Dewey, and Andrew Carnegie, Harris found evidence of "the mindlessness of public librarianship" in the first several decades of public library history in the United States. Ticknor, who was involved in the founding and development of the Boston Public Library, is described as a "frank elitist living in an era of rampant equalitarianism" (2511). Everett viewed the Boston Public Library as "principally a library intended for scholarly research" (2511). Winsor is described as a "technician" who supported the view that the public library could be viewed "as a derrick, lifting the inert masses and swinging them round to be sure foundations upon which the national character shall rise" (2512). Fletcher viewed the librarian as a cook (2512). Poole is quoted as having instructed the public library's staff that "ample arrangements having been made for washing, the attendants are instructed to deliver no periodical or book into unclean hands" (2512–13). Dewey is characterized as being among a category of librarians who "nearly succeeded in their goal of making the library a new bureaucracy adhering to more and more inflexible rules of operation" (2513). Carnegie's philanthropy toward libraries is presented in terms of a goal of the "elevation of the Masses" (2513). Throughout Harris's analysis, library leaders are presented as "patrician" and "elitist" and generally out of touch with the publics their libraries claimed to serve.

Dain (1975) presented a critique of Harris's interpretation of public library history, noting that an exploration of the origins of the Boston Public Library cannot be assumed to serve as a "prototype for public libraries elsewhere" (262). She describes the influences of other leaders not mentioned by Harris, such as Horace Mann. Dain also suggested that public library history cannot be properly understood without placing it in the contemporary context of the development of other types of libraries, noting that there were numerous other types of libraries that played parallel roles in society, including "mercantile, mechanics, and apprentices libraries," "the libraries of charitable organizations (and later of settlement houses), endowed free reference libraries, and libraries of ethnic and religious minority groups" (262). Dain rejected Harris's criticism that librarians in the nineteenth century were primarily middle class, commenting that "librarianship was a bookish profession, and ... bookish people, like intellectuals generally, seldom came from the unpropertied and poorly educated masses" (262). Ultimately, Dain concluded that "the public library, like all socially sanctioned agencies, is and has been an instrument to serve the needs of an existing society to which it is tied by economic, social, and ideological bonds" (264).

This interchange between Harris and Dain is representative of the interactive exchange that characterizes an active research climate. There is no obvious "winner" in this debate in the literature other than the profession, which benefits from multiple views of the phenomenon of interest. As the historical picture is made more complete through identification of new sources and novel explications for existing sources, the profession's ability to assess where it has been and how it arrived at its current state is enhanced, and its general knowledge base grows (*see* HISTORY OF PUBLIC LIBRARIES).

Descriptive Research and Public Libraries

Descriptive research has long been the dominant family of research methodologies focusing on public libraries. Direct observation of activity within a library, distribution of questionnaires to individuals or groups, and interviews are examples of common approaches to descriptive research. Descriptive research can be thought of as aligned with one or both of two dominant research paradigms or models of thought: (1) the quantitative paradigm and (2) the qualitative paradigm.

Quantitative descriptive research seeks to measure and summarize phenomena of interest by representing them numerically. The quantitative paradigm is characteristic of most research in the physical and biological sciences and of much research and the social and behavioral sciences and was the model for nearly all early public library research. The essential characteristic of quantitative research is the identification of approaches to describing phenomena with numbers—counts, sums, percentages, averages, and other numeric functions. If a study presents information numerically, the study is at least in part quantitative. The use of sophisticated or advanced statistical analysis, although it may accompany and enhance quantitative research and is frequently an appropriate approach to understanding numbers, is not an essential component of quantitative research.

Gross and Saxton's (2001) study of the imposed query phenomenon is an example of quantitative descriptive research carried out in a public library setting. Based on earlier work by Gross (1995), Gross and Saxton explored the distinction between self-generated questions that arise from the direct needs of the questioner and imposed questions that are asked by the questioner on behalf of or at the behest of another individual. Adults asking questions in 13 public libraries were asked to fill out a questionnaire related to the reference transaction just completed and to report on their personal characteristics. About 25 percent of the more than 1,000 respondents indicated that they had asked a question as a representative of someone else, including a child, a spouse, another family member, an instructor, or an employee, among others. This study provided the first clear, quantified indicator that public library patrons may frequently be acting as agents of other people rather than seeking information for themselves.

Qualitative descriptive research focuses on detailed exploration of the fundamental characteristics of phenomena of interest, emphasizing richness and expressiveness rather than quantity. Qualitative methods may incorporate elements of ethnographic research, in-depth reflective interviews, focus group experiences, or other nonquantifiable approaches to understanding. Qualitative research is not intended to determine the quality or value of any given phenomenon and has no direct relationship to evaluation, although qualitative methods and tools can be used in evaluation as well as in research. The term "qualitative" in this context refers to determining or summarizing the qualities or characteristics of some phenomenon.

Antell (2004) explored college student use of public libraries by conducting open-ended interviews with student patrons of public libraries in three cities. In keeping with the focus of qualitative research on depth rather than numbers, a total of 17 students were interviewed. Each interview took place at a time and place convenient to the student and lasted between 15 and 20 minutes. The researcher recorded each interview for later analysis. The interviews were essentially loosely structured conversations, with the researcher asking only three predetermined questions. Results revealed five broad "themes" that characterized the students' choices to use public libraries rather than the libraries of the academic institutions at which they were enrolled. These themes included (1) convenience, such as the geographic location of the public library; (2) ease of use and prior familiarity with the public library; (3) choice of materials; (4) staff characteristics, such as perceived friendliness and helpfulness; and (5) subjective appeal based on factors such as the attractiveness of the public library environment. Antell found that there was no central "typical" reason for student choices to use public libraries, noting that "college students using public libraries are a diverse group" motivated by a variety of reasons and perceptions (234). Although Antell did use some quantification in her article, the emphasis was on the richness and expressiveness of the specific comments made by the respondents, which were extensively quoted in the article.

These two descriptive research projects, although quite different in approach, execution, and reporting, share the essential common characteristic of lending understanding to a real-life concern in public librarianship. Both strive to increase understanding of the motives that lie behind familiar, observable patron behaviors. Although neither of these studies resulted in any specific targets for public library action, research that explores public library patrons can be especially valuable in increasing the profession's knowledge base regarding how specific services can be envisioned and implemented to best serve the library's public.

Experimental Research and Public Libraries

Experimental research involves an element of manipulating the environment to explore a phenomenon that may not exist in nature or that cannot be understood through observation of the natural environment. Experimental research is the most controlled family of research methodologies and is very closely allied with quantification. Experimentation involves the introduction of some planned change into a predictable, observable situation to explore the impact of that change. In the physical and biological sciences, experimental research typically takes place in highly controlled laboratory settings. Experimental research in libraries usually has to be adapted to fit an otherwise naturally occurring environment.

Baker (1986) studied the "display phenomenon" in public libraries. The display phenomenon describes the commonly observed tendency for books or other materials that are prominently displayed in a public library to garner more patron use than materials that are not displayed. Baker, building on earlier works, such as Goldhor's (1972) documentation and quantification of the display phenomenon and Morse's (1970) exploration of browsing, addressed the question of *why* displaying library materials is associated with increased use. Baker posed two explicit hypotheses:

1. "That fiction books placed in a prime display location will circulate significantly more than their counterparts on the regular shelves or in a nonprime display location simply because they are more physically accessible and visible to browsers."

2. "That fiction books marked as 'recommended' will circulate more than their counterparts in the prime display area, in the nonprime display area, or on the regular shelves because such a recommendation serves to narrow the browser's choice of materials, thus providing a type of selection guidance that overcomes the effects of information overload" (239).

Baker (1986) addressed these two hypotheses through two experiments in two small public libraries. In the first experiment, circulation of a defined set of fiction books from each library was recorded for a three-month period with the books in their normal shelf locations. During a subsequent three-month period, the books were randomly assigned to one of three groups: a group in which books were placed on display racks in a highly visible "prime location" near the circulation desk, a group in which books were deliberately placed in a nonvisible location far from the library entrance, and a group in which books remained on their usual shelves. The prime and nonprime titles were reversed for a subsequent three-month period. In the second experiment, a random selection of books was marked with red dots to indicate that those books were "recommended," and signs were posted to notify patrons of the meaning of the dots. A subsequent round of the second experiment involved removing the recommendation dots and placing them on books that had previously not been marked. Baker found that displayed books did indeed circulate more than nondisplayed books but that the "recommendation" feature was not associated with increased circulation. Her conclusion was that prime display location alone is the critical factor accounting for increased circulation of displayed books.

The very tightly structured and controlled nature of Baker's experiments is characteristic of experimental research. There is to some extent less room for flexibility in an experiment than in historical research, which is frequently deliberately kept open ended in the interest of making sure that the best sources are consulted, or descriptive research, which frequently allows the researcher to modify some aspects of the project as it progresses. The need for extremely careful design, attention to detail, and understanding of complex methodological and analytical processes may explain why experimental research in librarianship is the least populated of the three methodological families. The specific appeal of experimental research is explanatory capacity; a carefully constructed experiment is the only approach to research that has any real potential for exploring cause-and-effect relationships.

Secondary Analysis and Public Libraries

Although most research projects involve directly gathering and analyzing new data, there is a wealth of preexisting data about public libraries that can be mined to produce research results. The U.S. Institute of Museum and Library Services (IMLS), through its annual public library survey, provides a wealth of publicly available data about public libraries, including numbers of libraries, numbers of branches, numbers of bookmobiles, facility sizes, sizes of service populations, types of services provided, circulation counts for library materials, numbers of publicly available computers, collection volume figures, staff breakdowns, and financial information (*see* STATISTICS). Data are also gathered and made available by state library agencies and professional associations (*see* STATE LIBRARY AGENCIES). Davis (2010) brought together data from the ALA Office for Research and Statistics, IMLS, the Kaiser Family Foundation and Health Research and Educational Trust, and other sources to present a comprehensive picture of trends in U.S. public library finances, staffing, and services.

Generalization, Cumulation, and Public Library Research

None of the research studies summarized here is in and of itself definitive or exhaustive, nor is that the role or goal of any single study. Research contributes to the knowledge base of the profession incrementally by presenting results of projects carried out in a manner that ensures some level of generalizability—the ability to, with reasonable confidence, extend from the results of the study to inferences about other situations. Baker's (1986) study of the display phenomenon, for instance, built on the work of others and has itself been used as a foundation for subsequent work. The care built into a study such as Baker's allows for at least the implication that the display phenomenon and its relationship to use of library materials can be expected to provide a general model for understanding one aspect of library service and use behavior. Furthermore, the results of the study have implications for other environments, such as bookstores. The cumulative body of literature related to the display phenomenon lends further credibility to the results of the individual studies of which it is comprised. It is in this way, through the generation of multiple iterations and generations of generalizable results, that research in general contributes to the profession and to society and that public library research contributes to public librarians and the publics they serve. *See also* EVALUATION.

—*Connie Van Fleet and Danny P. Wallace*

References

American Library Association, Library Research Round Table. 2010. Mission. http://www.ala.org/ala/mgrps/rts/lrrt/index.cfm. Accessed December 2010.

Antell, Karen. 2004. Why do college students use public libraries? A phenomenological study. *Reference & User Services Quarterly* 43, no. 3 (Spring): 227–36.

Baker, S. L. 1986. The display phenomenon: An exploration into the factors causing the increased circulation of displayed books. *Library Quarterly* 56, no. 3 (July): 237–57.

Beals, Ralph A. 1942. Implications of communications research for the public library. In *Print, Radio, and Film in a Democracy*, ed. Douglas Waples, 165–67. Chicago: University of Chicago Press.

Bunge, Charles A. 1968. Professional Education and Reference Efficiency. PhD diss., University of Illinois at Urbana-Champaign.

Crowley, Terence, and Thomas Childers. 1971. *Information Service in Public Libraries: Two Studies*. Metuchen, NJ: Scarecrow Press.

Cutter, Charles Ammi. 1876. *Rules for a Printed Dictionary Catalogue*. In U.S. Bureau of Education, *Public Libraries in the United States Their History Condition, and* Management. Washington, DC: Government Printing Office.

Dain, Phyllis. 1975. Ambivalence and paradox: The social bonds of the public library. *Library Journal* 100, no. 3 (February 1): 261–66.

Dain, Phyllis. 2000. The historical sensibility. *Libraries and Culture* 35, no. 1 (Winter): 240–43.

Davis, Denise M. 2010. Public libraries: An economic and service outlook. *Public Libraries* 49, no. 2 (March/April): 14–21.

Dewey, Melvil. 1876. *A Classification and Subject Index for Arranging the Books and Pamphlets of a Library*. Amherst, MA: Amherst College.

Goldhor, Herbert. 1969. *An Introduction to Scientific Research in Librarianship*. Washington, DC: U.S. Department of Education.

Goldhor, Herbert. 1972. The effect of prime display location on public library circulation of selected titles. *Library Quarterly* 42, no. 4 (October): 371–89.

Gross, Melissa. 1995. The imposed query. *RQ* 35, no. 2 (Winter): 236–43.

Gross, Melissa, and Matthew L. Saxton. 2001. Who wants to know? Imposed queries in the public library. *Public Libraries* 40, no. 3 (May/June): 170–76.

Harris, Michael H. 1973. The purpose of the American public library: A revisionist interpretation of history. *Library Journal* 98, no. 16 (September 15): 2509–14.

Henderson, Everett, et al. 2010. *Public Libraries Survey: Fiscal Year 2008*. Washington, D.C.: Institute of Museum and Library Services.

Herald, Diana Tixier. 2006. *Genreflecting: A Guide to Popular Reading Interests*. 6th ed. Edited by Wayne A. Wiegand. Westport, CT: Libraries Unlimited. 1st edition 1982 by Betty Rosenberg.

Hernon, Peter, and Charles R. McClure. 1986. Unobtrusive reference testing: The 55 percent rule. *Library Journal* 111, no. 7 (April 15): 37–41.

Kimball, Melanie. 2006. A brief history of readers' advisory. In *Genreflecting: A Guide to Popular Reading Interests*, 6th ed., by Diana Tixier Herald, 15–24. Westport, CT: Libraries Unlimited.

Learned, William S. 1924. *The American Public Library and the Diffusion of Knowledge*. New York: Harcourt Brace.

Leigh, Robert. 1950. *The Public Library in the United States: The General Report of the Public Library Inquiry*. New York: Columbia University Press.

Lynch, Mary Jo. 1984. Research and librarianship: an uneasy connection. *Library Trends* 32, no. 4 (Spring): 367–83.

McDowell, Kate. 2009. Surveying the field: The research model of women in librarianship, 1882–1898. *Library Quarterly* 79, no. 3 (June): 279–300.

Morse, Philip M. 1970. Search theory and browsing. *Library Quarterly* 40, no. 4 (October): 391–408.

Office for Research and Statistics. 2010. Mission. http://www.ala.org/ala/aboutala/offices/ors/index.cfm. Accessed December 2010.

Richardson, John V. 1982. *The Spirit of Inquiry: The Graduate Library School at Chicago, 1921–1951.* Chicago: American Library Association.

Richardson, John V. 2002. Reference is better than we thought: Refuting the 55% rule. *Library Journal* 127, no. 7 (April 15): 41–42.

Rosenberg, Betty. 1982. *Genreflecting.* Littleton, CO: Libraries Unlimited. 6th edition by Diana Tixier Herald, 2006.

Schwartz, Carolyn S., and Peter Hernon. 1999. Professional associations and LIS research. *Library and Information Science Research* 21, no. 2: 145–51.

Thompson, C. S. 1931. Do we want a library science? *Library Journal* 56, no. 13 (July): 581–87.

U.S. Bureau of Education. 1876. *Public Libraries in the United States of America: Their History, Condition, and Management.* Washington, DC: Government Printing Office.

Wallace, Danny P. 1983. An index of quality of Illinois public library service. In *Illinois Library Statistical Report 10*, 1–46. Springfield: Illinois State Library.

Wallace, Danny P. 1984. An index of quality of Illinois public library service, 1983. In *Illinois Library Statistical Report 14*, 61–84. Springfield: Illinois State Library.

Wiegand, Wayne A. 2006. On the social nature of reading. In *Genreflecting: A Guide to Popular Reading Interests*, 6th ed., by Diana Tixier Herald, 3–14. Westport, CT: Libraries Unlimited.

Williamson, Charles C. 1931. The place of research in library service. *Library Quarterly* 1, no. 1 (January): 1–17.

Williamson, Charles C. 1971. *The Williamson Reports of 1921 and 1923, Including Training for Library Work (1921) and Training for Library Service (1923).* Metuchen, NJ: Scarecrow Press.

Wilson, Louis Round. 1938. *The Geography of Reading: A Study of the Distribution and Status of Libraries in the United States.* Chicago: American Library Association.

RICEVILLE PUBLIC LIBRARY, IA   307 Woodland Ave., Riceville, IA 50466. Population served: 1,188. Circulation: 19,048. Holdings: 11,947. LJ February 15, 2009: 3-star library.

RICHBURG, NY. *See* COLONIAL LIBRARY, RICHBURG, NY.

RICHLAND COUNTY PUBLIC LIBRARY, COLUMBIA, SC   1431 Assembly St., Columbia, SC 29201. Founded 1924. Population served: 334,609. Circulation: 2,000,000. Holdings: 615,682. LJ February 15, 2009, and November 15, 2009: 3-star library. LJ Library of the Year 2001.

RIDGWAY PUBLIC LIBRARY, CO   300 Charles St., Ridgway, CO 81432. Population served: 2,182. Circulation: 28,127. Holdings: 14,867. LJ October 1, 2010: 3-star library.

ROCHESTER PUBLIC LIBRARY, NY   115 South Ave., Rochester, NY 14604. Founded 1911. Population served: 219,773. Circulation: 1,430,162. Holdings: 1,157,888. 10 branches, 1 bookmobile. A business branch opened in 1917, but in 1938 business services moved into the new main library building.

ROCK CREEK PUBLIC LIBRARY, OH   2988 High St., Rock Creek, OH 44084. Founded 1937. Population served: 11,617. Circulation: 93,072. Holdings: 24,562. LJ November 15, 2009, and October 1, 2010: 5-star library. HAPLR 2010.

ROCKLAND PUBLIC LIBRARY, ME   80 Union St., Rockland, ME 04841. Founded 1904. Population served: 12,000. Circulation: 213,322. Holdings: 54,000. LJ February 15, 2009: 3-star library; November 15, 2009: 4-star library; October 1, 2010: 3-star library.

ROCKPORT, IN. *See* SPENCER COUNTY PUBLIC LIBRARY, ROCK-PORT, IN.

ROCKSPRINGS, TX. *See* CLAUD H. GILMER MEMORIAL LIBRARY, ROCKSPRINGS, TX.

ROCKVILLE, MD. *See* MONTGOMERY COUNTY PUBLIC LIBRARIES, ROCKVILLE, MD.

RODEN, CARL BISMARCK, 1871–1956   Librarian. Born in Kansas City, MO, June 7, 1871. At age 15 he became a page in the Chicago Public Library (then located in City Hall) and worked in the library 64 years to his retirement in 1950. He rose through the ranks from assistant cataloger to chief cataloger, acting librarian, and in 1918 librarian. Roden was committed to developing branches, which grew to 61 in his tenure. He developed regional branches in three parts of the city. He also created the most extensive readers' advisory program of any public library at the time. Disappointed with the status of American libraries, he said in a 1923 speech that "we stand today in the placid esteem of our communities somewhere between the tulip beds and monkey cages of the parks and the compulsory processes of the public schools" (Williams 1988, 42). He called for intensive emphasis on personal service. Roden died in Palatine, IL, on October 25, 1956. *DALB.*

Reference

Williams, Patrick. 1988. *The American Public Library and the Problem of Purpose.* New York: Greenwood Press.

ROGERSVILLE PUBLIC LIBRARY, AL   74 Bank St., Rogersville, AL 35652. Population served: 1,199. Circulation: 31,281. Holdings: 26,895. LJ November 15, 2009: 3-star library; October 1, 2010: 4-star library.

ROLLINS, CHARLEMAE HILL, 1897–1979   Librarian. Born Yazoo City, MS, June 20, 1897, a descendant of slaves. She attended black high schools in Mississippi, Missouri, and Kansas and studied one year at Howard University. Although she took courses at the University of Chicago and Columbia, she had no college degree. In 1926 she was a children's librarian in the Chicago Public Library (CPL), working in the multiethnic Hardin Square Branch. From 1926 to 1963, Rollins was children's librarian in the George Cleveland Hall branch, serving a black community. She assisted Vivian Harsh in efforts to enhance the image of blacks in children's books, writing to publishers, and greatly improved children's reading lists. Her bibliography of suitable books for black children, *We Build Together*, was published by the National Council for Teacher Education in 1941, bringing her national attention. Subsequently much of her time went into lecturing and teaching. She taught children's literature at Roosevelt University from 1946. Active in the American Library Association (ALA), she was a member of council in 1951–1954 and president of the Children's Library Association, which later became the Children's Service Division of the ALA. She retired on August 29, 1963. Among her numerous awards and honors was a special recognition of her accomplishments at the CPL. The library dedicated a room to her, with a portrait, in the Woodson Regional Branch on November 19, 1977. Her collection of materials on the black experience was made a part of the Vivian G. Harsh Collection at Woodson. She wrote several other books, of which the most popular was *Christmas Gif'* (Follett, 1963), a collection of stories, poems, and recollections about black Christmas traditions in the United States. Rollins died in Chicago on February 3, 1979. *DALB*, 1st supplement.

ROOS, JEAN CAROLYN, 1891–1982   Librarian. Born Buffalo, NY, March 9, 1891. She attended the University of Buffalo, the Cleveland School of Education, and Cleveland College. In 1927 she earned a library certificate from Western Reserve University. From 1916 to 1918, Roos was a children's librarian in the Cleveland Public Library (CPL). She worked as a school librarian, 1919–1922, then returned to the CPL as director of the new Robert Louis Stevenson Room for young adults, remaining to 1940. Roos headed the new Office for Service to Youth (later the Youth Department), 1940–1959. She provided mainly recreational reading for the teen clientele, along with poetry groups, book discussions, and programs with other youth agencies. She emphasized personal service to the readers, believing that tastes and interests could be guided to higher levels. Roos was active in the American Library Association, which published her book *Patterns in Reading* in 1954. She died March 21, 1982. *DALB*.

ROSE, ERNESTINE, 1880–1961   Librarian. Born in Bridgehampton, NY. She graduated from Wesleyan in 1902 and went to the New York State Library School, earning a BLS in 1904. She started working in the New York Public Library in 1905, remaining to 1942, except for time at the Carnegie Library School and library war service in 1918–1920. At the 135th Street Branch in New York, Rose (who was white) developed the collections and programs relating to African American culture. There were concerts, literary and art workshops, and theater. A believer in the "people's university," Rose promoted adult education activities and self-education and advocated serving immigrants with foreign languages speakers on the staff and books in European languages. Her most renowned contribution was the development of the Schomburg Collection (*see* NEW YORK PUBLIC LIBRARY; SERVICES TO AFRICAN AMERICANS). She taught at Columbia library school and published a book, *Public Library in American Life* (1954). Rose died on March 28, 1961. *DALB.*

ROSLYN, NY. *See* BRYANT LIBRARY, ROSLYN, NY.

ROTHROCK, MARY UTOPIA, 1890–1976   Librarian. Born Trenton, NJ, September 19, 1890. She earned an MA at Vanderbilt University in 1912 and a BS at the New York State Library School in 1922. After serving as head of circulation in the Cossitt Library, Memphis, she went to Knoxville as its first librarian in 1917 as the public library replaced the earlier subscription library. She developed branches in Knoxville and the first statewide regional system. The East Tennessee Historical Society, which she founded, was based in the library. Rothrock supervised library services for the Tennessee Valley Authority in 1934–1948. From 1949 to 1955 she was librarian of Knox County. As a leader in library development in the Southeast, she was invited to be an adviser for the U.S. Office of Education. She was active in the American Library Association (ALA; president, 1946–1947), the Southeastern Library Association (president, 1922–1924), and the Tennessee Library Association (president 1932 and 1937). Rothrock opposed censorship, observing in a paper given at the ALA conference in 1923 that it is not a librarian's duty to exclude books for mature readers in fear of moral consequences. She died in Knoxville on January 30, 1976. *DALB.*

ROUND MOUNTAIN, NV. *See* SMOKY VALLEY LIBRARY DISTRICT, ROUND MOUNTAIN, NV.

RUNALS MEMORIAL LIBRARY, EDGERTON, MN   750 First Ave. N, Edgerton, MN 56128. Founded 1922. Population served: 1,033. Circulation: 47,664. Holdings: 16,328. LJ February 15, 2009, and November 15, 2009: 5-star library.

RYE FREE READING ROOM, NY   1060 Boston Post Rd., Rye, NY 10580. Population served: 14,955. Circulation: 237,134. Holdings: 82,943. LJ February 15, 2009: 4-star library.

S

SACRAMENTO PUBLIC LIBRARY, CA   828 I St., Sacramento, CA 95814. Founded 1879. Population served: 1,270,000. Circulation: 5,581,130. Holdings: 2,021,227. 27 branches. The 1918 Carnegie building is preserved in today's central library.

ST. BERNARD PARISH LIBRARY, CHALMETTE, LA   1125 E. St. Bernard Hwy, Chalmette, LA 70043. Population served: 63,364. Circulation: 50,829. Both branches were destroyed by Hurricane Katrina and are still in temporary quarters (*see* HURRICANES KATRINA AND RITA).

ST. CHARLES CITY-COUNTY LIBRARY DISTRICT, ST. PETERS, MO   77 Boone Hills Dr., St. Peters, MO 63376. Founded 1973. Population served: 350,000. Circulation: 4,890,790. Holdings: 803,375. 12 branches. LJ February 15, 2009: 3-star library. HAPLR 2009, 2010.

ST. CHARLES PUBLIC LIBRARY DISTRICT, IL   1 S. Sixth Ave., St. Charles, IL 60174. Founded 1906. Population served: 47,855. Circulation: 1,170,949. Holdings: 251,370. LJ October 1, 2010: 3-star library. HAPLR 2009, 2010.

ST. HELENA PUBLIC LIBRARY, CA   1492 Library Lane, St. Helena, CA 94574. Founded 1892. Population served: 6,006. Circulation: 254,247. Holdings: 92,549. LJ February 15, 2009: 5-star library; November 15, 2009: 4-star library; October 1, 2010: 5-star library.

ST. JOHN, KS. *See* IDA LONG GOODMAN MEMORIAL LIBRARY, ST. JOHN, KS.

ST. JOSEPH COUNTY PUBLIC LIBRARY, SOUTH BEND, IN   304 S. Main St., South Bend, IN 46601. Founded in 1888 as South Bend Public Library; name changed, 1930. Population served: 172,627. Circulation: 2,400,000. Holdings: 475,000. 8 branches, 1 bookmobile. LJ February 15, 2009: 4-star library; November 15, 2009: 3-star library.

ST. LOUIS PUBLIC LIBRARY, MO   1301 Olive St., St. Louis, MO 63103. Opened 1865 as St. Louis Public School Library, assessing fees for taking out books; became free to all city residents, April 4, 1893. Population served: 348,189. Circulation: 2,266,618. Holdings: 2,851,601. 15 branches, 3 bookmobiles. New central library 1912, designed by Cass Gilbert. During the directorship of Frederick M. Crunden (1877–1909), the library gained recognition for promoting service to children (a children's room opened in 1897) and foreign-born citizens. He pressed the concept of the library as a "people's university" with adult classes and expanded the branch system. The next librarian, Arthur E. Bostwick (1909–1938), established a municipal reference branch in city hall and initiated telephone reference service. Music, art, and applied science departments were organized. In 1925 there was a readers' advisory service. A training program dating from 1905 became a library school in 1917, recognized by the American Library Association in 1921 (the school closed in 1932). LJ February 15, 2009: 3-star library. Directors: Ira C. Divoll, superintendent of schools, headed the subscription library in 1865; John J. Bailey, 1865–1877; Frederick M. Crunden, 1877–1909; Arthur E. Bostwick, 1909–1938; Charles H. Compton, 1938–1950; Louis M. Nourse, 1950–1966; F. Charles Taylor, 1966–1968; Paxton P. Price, 1969–1978; Mary Joan Collett, 1978–1986; Glen E. Holt, 1987–2004; and Waller McGuire, 2004–.

ST. PAUL PUBLIC LIBRARY, MN   90 W. Fourth St., St. Paul, MN 55102. Founded 1883. The public library succeeded a mercantile library association dating back to 1857. Population served: 287,151. Circulation: 3,339,830. Holdings: 1.021,923. 12 branches. The central library, 1917, was designed by Electus Litchfield. A branch program financed by Andrew Carnegie produced three branches; two more branches were added in 1930. The library was collecting phonograph records by 1914, offered hospital services from 1921, and opened a young adults room in 1939. Community relations has been a prominent activity since the 1960s. LJ February 15, 2009: 4-star library; November 15, 2009: 3-star library; October 1, 2010: 4-star library. IMLS award 2005. Directors: Helen J. McCaine, 1877–1913; W. Dawson Johnson, 1914–1921; Webster Wheelock, 1922–1931; Jennie T. Jennings, 1931–1936; Perrie Jones, 1937–1956; J. Archer Eggen, 1956–1978; Gerald Steenberg, 1978–1997; Carole Williams, 1997–2002; Gina La Force,

2002–2005; Kathleen Flynn (interim), 2005–2006; Melanie Huggins, 2006–2009; and Kit Hadley, 2009–.

ST. PETERS, MO. *See* ST. CHARLES CITY-COUNTY LIBRARY DISTRICT, ST. PETERS, MO.

ST. TAMMANY PARISH LIBRARY, COVINGTON, LA   310 W. 21st Ave., Covington, LA 70433. Founded 1951. Population served: 80,000. Circulation: 885,990. Holdings: 450,000. 10 branches. Two branches were destroyed by Hurricane Katrina; one has been rebuilt (*see* HURRICANES KATRINA AND RITA).

SALISBURY, CT. *See* SCOVILLE MEMORIAL LIBRARY, SALISBURY, CT.

SALT LAKE CITY PUBLIC LIBRARY, UT   209 E. 500 St. S, Salt Lake City, UT 84111. Founded 1897, opened February 14, 1898. Population served: 178,605. Circulation: 3,489,616. Holdings: 600,000. 5 branches. The new building (2003) was designed by Moshe Safdie. LJ February 15, 2009, and November 15, 2009: 5-star library. HAPLR 2009, 2010. LJ Library of the Year 2006. Directors: Annie E. Chapman, 1897–1903; Joanna H. Sprague, 1903–1940; Julie T. Lynch, 1940–1943; Ethel E. Holmes, 1943–1952; Margaret E. Block, 1952–1959; Robert E. Thomas, 1960–1969; Richard J. Rademacher, 1969–1976; J. Dennis Day, 1976–1995; Nancy Tessman, 1996–2007; and Beth Elder, 2008–.

SALT LAKE COUNTY LIBRARY SERVICES, SALT LAKE CITY, UT   2197 E. Fort Union Blvd., Salt Lake City, UT 84121. Founded 1939. Population served: 753,597. Circulation: 4,500,000. Holdings: 1,285,453. 19 branches. LJ October 1, 2010: 3-star library. HAPLR, 2009, 2010.

SAN ANTONIO PUBLIC LIBRARY, TX   600 Soledad St., San Antonio, TX 78205. Founded 1900, opened 1903. Population served: 1,500,000. Circulation fiscal year 2009: 6,616,776 (communication from the library). Holdings: 1,671,158 (communication from the library). 30 branches, 2 bookmobiles. IMLS award, 2006.

SAN DIEGO COUNTY LIBRARY, CA   5555 Overland Ave., San Diego, CA 92123. Population served: 655,025. Circulation: 8,500,000 (library website). Holdings: 1,600,167. 33 branches, 2 bookmobiles. LJ November 15, 2009: 5-star library.

SAN DIEGO PUBLIC LIBRARY, CA   820 E St., San Diego, CA 92101. Founded 1882. Population served: 1,316,837. Circulation: 7,167,104. Holdings: 3,080,633. 35 branches. In 1922 the circulation was highest per capita in the United States (Thorne 1979, 297). Directors: Augustus Wooster, 1884–1887; Lulu Younkin, 1887–1895; Mary Walker, 1895–1903; Hanna P. Davison, 1903–1916; Althea Warren, 1916–1926; Cornelia D. Plaister, 1926–1945; Clara E. Breed, 1945–1970; Marco G. Thorne, 1970–1978; L. Kenneth Wilson, 1978–1979; William W. Sannwald, 1979–1997; Anna Tatár, 1997–2008; and Deborah L. Barrow, 2008–.

References

Breed, Clara E. 1983. *Turning the Pages: San Diego Public Library History, 1882–1982.* San Diego: Friends of the San Diego Public Library.
Thorne, Marco. 1979. San Diego Public Library. In *Encyclopedia of Library and Information Science* 26: 296–98. New York: Marcel Dekker.

SAN FRANCISCO PUBLIC LIBRARY, CA   100 Larkin St., San Francisco, CA 94102. Founded 1879. Population served: 764,976. Circulation: 9,638,160. Holdings: 5,860,577. 27 branches. San Francisco Public Library (SFPL) opened its doors, on the second floor of Pacific Hall, on June 7, 1879, offering 17,000 volumes. Albert Hart was librarian for a few months only; he resigned in November. The next librarian also served briefly: C. H. Robinson, who resigned on June 1, 1880. The library occupied various locations for the ensuing years. A Carnegie Foundation grant of $750,000 in 1901, plus a successful bond issue, gave promise of a permanent building, and Chicago architect Daniel Burnham prepared a plan for one, in a new civic center. Those plans were put aside after the 1906 earthquake, which destroyed the main library and two of the six branches, leaving only some 30,000 books in usable condition. Another temporary location, at Hayes and Franklin streets, was utilized until a new central library could be financed. Meanwhile a branch, North Beach, acquired a collection of books in Italian, becoming the "first library to cater to the needs of a minority group" (Ramirez and Gumina 1979, 301). Another notable branch, Chinatown, opened in a Carnegie building in 1915. A new main library opened in the Civic Center on February 15, 1917. George W. Kelham was the architect, drawing inspiration from the Boston Public Library building. Robert Rea, a political appointee without library qualifications, was city librarian from 1913 to 1945.

In 1929 a business library opened in the financial district (it closed in 1987 because of budget cuts). During the 1950s there were extensive service cuts and strong criticism of the library in the local press. A progressive period followed with the appointment of William R. Holman as librarian in 1960. A curious circumstance attached to the engagement of Kevin Starr as acting librarian, then as city librarian in July 1974. Starr, a historian, had no library qualifications; when there were protests over his appointment, he took up the study of library science at the University of California, Berkeley.

Plans for a new main library began after an earthquake in 1989 damaged the main building, requiring the stacks to be closed to the public. On April 18, 1996, the new structure opened in the Civic Center (the old library was converted to an Asian Art Museum). Architects were Pei Cobb Freed and Partners (of New York City) and Simon Martin-Vegue Winkelstein Moris (of San Francisco); the total cost was given at $104.5 million. With 376,600 square feet of space, the building is expected to serve the community's needs for many years.

These persons have served as city librarians: Albert Hart, June 1878–November 1879; C. H. Robinson, November 1879–May1880; Fred B. Perkins, June 1880–June? 1888; John Vance Cheney, June? 1888–November 24, 1894; George T. Clark, June? 1895–March 1907; William R. Watson, October 1907–March 1912; Robert Rea, March 1913–November 1945; Laurence J. Clarke, January 1946–April 1960; Frank Clarvoe (acting), April 1960–November 1960; William R. Holman, November 1960–July 1967; Harold D. Martelle Jr. (acting), July 1967–July 1968; John F. Anderson, July 1968–September 1973; Kevin Starr, September 1973–July 1976; Vivian Goodwin (acting), July 1976; William Ramirez (acting; August 1976), Edwin Castagna (acting, August 1976–January 1977), John C. Frantz (February 1977–March 12, 1987), Karen Scannell (acting), March 12, 1987–; Kenneth Dowlin, October 1987–January 21 1997; Regina Minudri (acting), August 4, 1997–May 1999; Susan Hildreth (acting, May 1999; permanent, April 9, 2001–June 30, 2004); Paul Underwood (acting, July 1, 2004–); and Luis Herrera, February 15, 2005–.

References

Ramirez, William, and Deanna Gumina. 1979. San Francisco Public Library. In *Encyclopedia of Library and Information Science* 26: 299–307. New York: Marcel Dekker.
Wiley, Peter Booth. 1996. *A Free Public library in This City: The Illustrated History of the San Francisco Public Library.* San Francisco: Weldon Owen.

SAN JOSE PUBLIC LIBRARY, CA   150 E. San Fernando St., San Jose, CA 95112. Founded 1880. Population served: 1,066,892. Circulation: 19,000,000. Holdings: 1,900,000. 16 branches. The library has offered joint service for the public and for San Jose State University since 2003. It was reported in May 2009 that the city council had voted not to use filters in the public library computers. Since 2004 patrons have been able to access and download e-books from any location. LJ February 15, 2009, and November 15, 2009: 4-star library; October 1, 2010: 3-star library. LJ Library of the Year 2004. Directors: William Redding, 1880–1887; Agnes Berry, 1887–1889; Nellie Egan, 1889–1900; Mary Barnby, 1900–1911; Nell McGinley, 1911–1917; Charles Wood, 1917–1923; Edith Daley, 1923–1943; Geraldine Nurney, 1943–1970; Homer Fletcher, 1970–1990; Jim Fish, 1990–1997; and Jane Light, 1997–.

SAN MATEO COUNTY LIBRARY, CA   125 Lessingia Court, San Mateo, CA 94402. Population served: 274,807. Circulation: 2,902,035. Holdings:

479,579. 12 branches. LJ February 15, 2009; November 15, 2009; and October 1, 2010: 4-star library.

SAN MIGUEL LIBRARY DISTRICT #1, TELLURIDE, CO   100 W. Pacific Ave., Telluride, CO 81435. Population served: 5,524. Circulation: 252,121. Holdings: 44, 867. LJ February 15, 2009; November 15, 2009, and October 1, 2010: 5-star library.

SAN RAFAEL, CA. *See* MARIN COUNTY FREE LIBRARY, SAN RAFAEL, CA.

SANDERS, MIVERVA AMANDA LEWIS, 1837–1912   Librarian. Born Marblehead, MA, February 11, 1837. Little is known of her early life. She was appointed town librarian of Pawtucket, RI, in 1876 and spent her career there, retiring in 1910. Sanders was an advocate of open shelves, and Pawtucket was one of the first libraries to implement that policy (1879). Her other initiative was in children's services. She created a children's section in the library in 1877, perhaps the first of its kind, with small furniture to accommodate 70 children. She was "the first librarian to do something for children who were roaming the streets" and was "most interested in children at a time when they were considered noisy nuisances" (Cramer 1972, 62). Sanders arranged cooperative ventures with schools, bringing classes to the library for orientation. She also pioneered public relations, sending a placard to every house in town reading "Consult the public library for anything you want to know." Pawtucket was a leader in offering Sunday hours to the public (1890). Sanders was active in the American Library Association, elected to the council in 1904. She died March 20, 1912. *DALB*.

Reference

Cramer, Clarence H. *Open Shelves and Open Minds: A History of the Cleveland Public Library*. Cleveland: Case Western Reserve University Press, 1972.

SANIBEL PUBLIC LIBRARY, FL   770 Dunlop Rd., Sanibel, FL 33957. Population served: 6,272. Circulation: 145,094. Holdings: 54,362. LJ October 1, 2010: 3-star library.

SANTA ANA, CA. *See* ORANGE COUNTY PUBLIC LIBRARY, SANTA ANA, CA.

SANTA CLARA CITY LIBRARY, CA   2635 Homestead Rd., Santa Clara, CA 95051. Population served: 109,106. Circulation: 2,630,001. Holdings: 339,124. 1 branch. LJ February 15, 2009: 4-star library; November 15, 2009: 3-star library; October 1, 2010: 4-star library. HAPLR 2009, 2010.

SANTA CLARA COUNTY LIBRARY, LOS GATOS, CA 14600 Winchester Blvd., Los Gatos, CA 95032. Population served: 409,853. Circulation: 10,000,000. Holdings: 1,600,000. 8 branches. LJ February 15, 2009: 4-star library; November 15, 2009: 3-star library; October 1, 2010: 4-star library. HAPLR 2009, 2010.

SANTA CLARA PUEBLO COMMUNITY LIBRARY, ESPAÑOLA, NM 1 Kee St., Española, NM 87532. Population served: 2,278. Circulation: 9,173. Holdings: 10,147. LJ February 15, 2009: 5-star library. "Funded in part by a grant from IMLS Native American Library Programs Enhancement Grant" (library website).

SANTA CRUZ PUBLIC LIBRARIES, CA 224 Church St., Santa Cruz, CA 95060. Founded 1882. Population served: 205,000. Circulation: 1,899,739. Holdings: 572,739. 10 branches. "Santa Cruz Public Libraries is a city-county library system" (library website). LJ February 15, 2009: 3-star library.

SANTA MONICA PUBLIC LIBRARY, CA 601 Santa Monica Blvd., Santa Monica, CA 90401. Founded 1890. Population served: 90,000. Circulation: 1,600,000. Holdings: 340,869. 3 branches. LJ November 15, 2009: 4-star library; October 1, 2010: 5-star library.

SARAH HULL HALLOCK FREE LIBRARY, MILTON, NY 56 Main St., Milton, NY 12547. Founded 1887 "as a New York State library association" (communication from the library). Population served: 1,251. Circulation: 11,729. Holdings: 16,279. LJ February 15, 2009: 3-star library.

SCARSDALE PUBLIC LIBRARY, NY 54 Olmsted Rd., Scarsdale, NY 10583. Founded 1928. Population served: 17,823. Circulation: 441,060. Holdings: 141,562. LJ February 15, 2009; November 15, 2009, and October 1, 2010: 4-star library.

SCHAUMBURG TOWNSHIP DISTRICT LIBRARY, IL. 130 S. ROSELLE RD., SCHAUMBURG, IL 60193 Founded 1963. Population served: 129,839. Circulation: 2,000,000. Holdings: 506,732. 2 branches. LJ February 15, 2009; November 15, 2009, and October 1, 2010: 5-star library. HAPLR 2009.

SCHUYLERVILLE PUBLIC LIBRARY, NY 52 Ferry St., Schuylerville, NY 12871. Population served: 1,197. Circulation: 14,438. Holdings: 16,791. LJ February 15, 2009: 3-star library.

SCOGGIN, MARGARET C., 1905–1968 Librarian. Born in Caruthersville, MO, April 14, 1905. She graduated from Radcliffe; worked a summer at

New York Public Library (NYPL), developing an interest in youth services; and took a degree at the School of Librarianship, University of London. Returning to NYPL, Scoggin pursued a client-centered approach to serving young people, listening to their ideas and opinions. She set up book discussions and individual conversations. In 1935 she was supervising the NYPL work with vocational and industrial schools; she arranged class visits and made presentations. She helped design the Nathan Straus Branch for children and young people (opened 1941) and made it a model of its kind. Straus was absorbed into the Donnell Library Center in 1955. In 1945, Scoggin initiated an award-winning radio program in which teenagers talked about books. While supervising children's work at NYPL, she also taught at the Simmons College library school and wrote many books and articles. *Gateways to Readable Books* (1952) became a landmark in guidance for young patrons. After the war, Scoggin spent six months in Germany helping to establish an International Youth Library; it opened in 1949. Scoggin died in New York on July 11, 1968.

SCOTTSDALE PUBLIC LIBRARY, AZ   3839 N. Drinkwater Rd., Scottsdale, AZ 85251. Founded 1960. Population served: 221,000. Circulation: 2,050,807. Holdings: 800,000. 3 branches. Arabian Branch won AIA/ALA design award 2009; architects Richard + bauer.

SCOVILLE MEMORIAL LIBRARY, SALISBURY, CT   38 Main St., Salisbury, CT 06068. Founded 1803 (the library website erroneously gives 1805). Caleb Bingham donated some books to the town, stipulating that the collection be maintained by the authorities. The library was named the Bingham Library for Youth. This is the oldest American public library. The town had a subscription library even earlier, when Richard Smith donated 200 books in 1771.

SEATTLE PUBLIC LIBRARY, WA   1000 Fourth Ave., Seattle, WA 98104. Founded 1890 (municipally supported from 1890 but not by tax until 1899). Population served 571,900. Circulation: 11,196,338. Holdings: 2,000,000. 29 branches, 4 bookmobiles. The library has been noted for excellent designs since 1960, when it opened one of the early modular buildings. It won several AIA/ALA design awards: temporary central library facility by LMN Architects, 2003; central library by Office for Metropolitan Architecture and LMN Architects, 2005; and Ballard Branch by Bohlin Cywinski Jackson, 2007. LJ October 1, 2010: 5-star library.

Reference

Marshall, John Douglas. 2004. *Place of Learning, Place of Dreams.* Seattle: University of Washington Press.

SELECTION OF LIBRARY MATERIALS. *See* COLLECTION DEVELOPMENT.

SENECA FREE LIBRARY, KS   606 Main St., Seneca, KS 66538. Founded 1931. Population served: 2,070. Circulation: 58,567. Holdings: 25,157. LJ February 15, 2009: 4-star library; November 15, 2009: 3-star library; October 1, 2010: 5-star library. HAPLR 2009, 2010.

SERIALS

Terminology

This is a general concept, covered in the general dictionaries. *Merriam* says that a serial is "a publication (as a newspaper or journal) issued as one of a consecutively numbered and indefinitely continues series." *American Heritage* simply states that a serial is a publication "produced in installments." The treatment of related terms is less clear. For "periodical" *Merriam* offers, "a publication with a fixed interval between the issues of numbers," which seems to impinge on the definition of serial, and in fact that fixed interval is not essential in practice. "Periodical" in *American Heritage* has a special requirement to distinguish it from newspaper: "a publication issued ... at regular intervals of more than one day." A "magazine" is "a periodical containing miscellaneous pieces, as articles, stories, poems" (*Merriam*).

Library terminology is more detailed. These definitions are from *ODLIS*:

> Serial—"a publication in any medium issued under the same title in a succession of discrete parts, usually numbered (or dated) and appearing at regular or irregular intervals with no predetermined conclusion."

> Periodical—"a serial publication with its own distinctive title, containing a mix of articles, editorials, reviews, columns, short stories, poems, or other short works, written by more than one contributor, issued in softcover more than once, generally at regular stated intervals of less than a year, without prior decision as to when the final issue will appear."

> Magazine—"a popular interest periodical usually containing articles on a variety of topics, written by various authors in a nonscholarly style."

Further refinements from *ODLIS* are the following:

> Journal—"a periodical devoted to dissemination of original research and commentary on current developments in a specific discipline."

> Little magazine, or literary magazine—a magazine "devoted to poetry, fiction, essays, and art."

> Zine—"a small, low circulation magazine or newspaper, self published."

> Fanzine—"a serial in electronic or print for enthusiasts of a pastime or person."

> Annual—"a serial issued once a year."

The glossary in *Anglo-American Cataloguing Rules*, 2nd ed. (AACR2; 1978) gives a definition similar to the one in *ODLIS*: "serial—a publication in any medium issued in successive parts bearing numerical or chronological designations and intended to be continued indefinitely. Serials include periodicals; newspapers; annuals (reports, yearbooks, etc.); the journals, memoirs, proceedings, transactions, etc., of societies; and numbered monographic series."

Newspapers are serials and, according to *Merriam* and *ODLIS* but not *American Heritage*, also periodicals. *Merriam*: "newspaper: a paper that is printed and distributed usu. daily or weekly and that contains news, articles of opinion, features, and advertising."

The vocabulary is further extended by consideration of electronic materials, usually identified as "e-journals" or "e-newspapers."

One might gather from this complex of nuances that a library's work with serials would be a confusing enterprise, but librarians have made a straightforward business of it. In practice all the types and definitions cited above are clustered under one designation: usually serials but sometimes periodicals. The library usually has one serials or periodicals department or unit within another department that handles the selection, acquisition, cataloging, and delivery to the users of all publications "produced in installments." This approach is congruent with that of publishers of indexes or lists of serials (consider *Readers' Guide to Periodical Literature*, *Union List of Serials*, and *Magazines for Libraries*—all of which include magazines, journals, and periodicals).

Historical Summary

This is a chronology of important events relating to library serials work.

Seventeenth century—The earliest newspapers and scholarly journals.

Eighteenth century—the earliest general magazines.

1848—William Frederick Poole's *An Alphabetical Index to Subjects Treated in the Reviews and Other Periodicals to Which No Indexes Have Been Published*. A subject guide to articles in the library of a student society at Yale College, it was the first published (G. P. Putnam) consolidated periodical index. Poole issued an expanded periodical index in 1853, published by C. B. Norton. See also 1882.

1858—A serials division created in the Boston Public Library. By 1911 the library was acquiring 1,809 titles.

1876—Charles Ammi Cutter, librarian of the Boston Athenaeum, issued *Rules for a Printed Dictionary Catalogue*, printed in the U.S. Bureau of Education's *Public Libraries in the United States*. Serials were to be entered in the catalog by title or issuing body. Subsequent catalog rules followed this prescription.

1876—Ainsworth Rand Spofford, Librarian of Congress, appealed for systematic collecting and cataloging of serials and their preservation in a chapter of the U.S. Bureau of Education's *Public Libraries in the United States.*

1876—*New York Daily Tribune Index* appeared; published annually 1876–1907.

1880—*Ayer Directory of Publications* issued; continued under various titles. A directory of newspapers and magazines.

1882—*Poole's Index to Periodical Literature, 1802–81* (Boston: Houghton, 1882; rev. ed. 1891). Supplements covered through 1906. A subject index to about 580,000 articles in 479 American and English periodicals. See Poole's original index at 1848.

1886—F. W. Faxon was the first agent to handle serials for libraries.

1892—*Cooperative List of Periodical Literature* published by the University of California, Berkeley. It was the first regional union catalog showing actual holdings of the member libraries.

1897—Serials division created in the Library of Congress.

1901—*Readers' Guide to Periodical Literature* published by H. W. Wilson, covering 15 popular periodicals. Greatly expanded coverage in later issues and numerous offshoot indexes.

1906—A report noted the existence of 35 union lists of periodicals in U.S. and Canadian libraries.

1911—Serials division created in the New York Public Library.

1913—Kardex marketed by Rand Co. A flipover arrangement of cards for periodical titles, showing issues received.

1913—*New York Times Index* issued; publication continues. "Prior series" and "in-house indexes" covering back to 1851 were made available later.

1927—*Union List of Serials in Libraries of the United States and Canada* published by H. W. Wilson. Contained entries for around 75,000 titles held in 225 libraries. Later editions covered to 1949, then the work was replaced by *New Serial Titles* (1953–).

1927—Swets & Zeitlinger began subscription service for libraries in Amsterdam.

1932—*Periodicals Directory* published by R. R. Bowker; later title (1943–1963) *Ulrich's Periodical Directory*; current title (1965–) *Ulrich's International Periodicals Directory.*

1937—Harris Gable, *Manual of Serials Work* published; first text for the topic.

1944—EBSCO Industries began offering subscription service for libraries.

1955—Andrew D. Osborn, *Serial Publications: Their Place and Treatment in Libraries* published by the American Library Association.

1969—*Magazines for Libraries* published by R. R. Bowker, ed. William Katz.

1970—MARC format for serials issued.

1975—ISSN (International Standard Serial Number) established, based on ISO (International Organization for Standardization) 3297; ANSI/NISO Z39.9. On application to the Library of Congress, U.S. publishers of serials may acquire a unique identifier number called ISSN. Serials with ISSN are entered into *WorldCat*.

1976—CONSER (Cooperative Online Serials Project). A national database of serial records, now maintained by OCLC. It provides MARC cataloging for serials.

1977—ISBD-S (International Standard Book Number—Serials) created by International Federation of Library Associations and Institutions.

1982—SISAC (Serials Industry Advisory Committee) established; consists of publishers, librarians, and agents.

1985—NASIG (North American Serials Interest Group) created; consisting of publishers, librarians, and agents.

1989—*Newsletter on Serials Pricing Issues* published.

Organization and Routines

A serials department or unit is found in larger libraries, often within the larger unit for technical services. In a small library, one librarian looks after serials. Much of the serials routine is the same as that for monographic materials. It includes request, verification, searching, placing the order, noting receipt, and paying the invoice Vendors are available to simplify much of this work (*see* ACQUISITIONS). "For most libraries, it is not cost-effective to place serial subscriptions directly with the publisher ... if a library uses a serials vendor for most orders, there will be more time for other problem-solving activities related to serials" (Evans et al. 2002, 219). Principal subscription vendors include EBSCO (Birmingham, AL), Swets & Zeitlinger (Amsterdam), and Gale Cengage Learning (Farmington Hill, MI). Vendors assess a service charge, variable according to the library situation. Serials acquisition requires a means of indicating which issues of a given periodical have been received. The manual approach to this task has traditionally involved a Kardex file, a flipover arrangement of cards with grids that provide for checking individual issues as they come in. Regular examination of the Kardex by serials staff discloses missing issues and leads to "a claim" to the publisher or vendor. In many libraries the Kardex has been retired; they use their integrated systems for check in, claiming, and binding.

A serials subscription produces a file of individual issues ("back files"). It is possible—and inexpensive—to keep the individual issues together in dated cartons or in metal containers ("Princeton files"). Back files can thus be kept on public shelves or in a storage area. A common approach is to display recent issues and keep earlier years in storage. Smaller libraries may choose to discard certain back files after a given period of time. Another approach to back files is binding the issues of a year (or other period) together with a date inscription on each binder spine showing the coverage. Bound volumes are easy to arrange on public or storage shelves, and they offer defense against disorder among the issues. Large libraries may do their own binding, but most libraries engage commercial binderies. Binding involves a number of decisions by the library, such as how many issues to bind together and when to bind them. A publisher's annual index to a periodical may not appear for some time after the final issue indexed, which is one reason to delay binding. Another reason for delay is that binding removes a group of issues from availability: the recent issues, most in demand, should not be in the bindery when the public asks for them.

Microprint presents another means of handling back files. The paper issues are discarded and replaced by microprint (reels of microfilm or microfiche) that can be read on special machines. The basic problem with microprint is user resistance: it is a cumbersome and inconvenient medium in action (*see* MICROFORM). There is also a cost consideration to the library since the system involves buying the same issues twice. And of course the reading machines have to be bought. Many regard microfilm as an archaic format and will select digitized files instead, but if a microfilm file is already in place, it is prudent to maintain it.

For serials available in electronic format, the problem of back issues takes care of itself. But if the content is the property of a vendor, a library's subscription to it is subject to variable pricing. For example, a vendor may assess fees for the number of times a file is searched beyond a certain agreed-on number. And a given title may not be available alone. Some titles come only in a publisher's package containing a subset of its publications, and some are available only in a third-party aggregator's database (see below). A library may not save money in acquiring journals online, but it does gain convenience and—for the user—enhanced searching capabilities. However, there are problems with search protocols. There is no standardization of terms and procedures among journals, and when periodicals are bundled in databases like *ProQuest*, the reader may need to master a hard learning situation before looking at an actual page of text.

Current Issues

As suggested above, cost of serials is an overriding concern. Pricing of print and electronic subscriptions, binding, and microprint reading machines is ever escalating, beyond the other costs of doing business in a library. Migration to electronic formats may not be a cost cutter. Subscriptions to journals may require subscription to an aggregated database of many titles, some or which the library would not have selected. In 2010 a dispute between EBSCO and Gale Cengage highlighted "exclusivity"—a contract between a journal publisher and a vendor to give that vendor exclusive rights to market its online content. This privilege, it was alleged, could lead to exorbitant pricing. Nonetheless, libraries realize savings in labor (no check-in, claiming, or binding) and shelf space.

Apart from acquisition routines, public librarians face the growing challenge of selecting titles to be acquired, whether in print or electronic format. *Ulrich's International Periodicals Directory* lists over 200,000 U.S. and foreign serials. A useful, annotated guide to general periodicals, covering more than 6,850 magazines and databases, has been published by Bowker since 1969: *Magazines for Libraries*, now in its eighteenth edition. The concept of a core list of journals has been discussed; one author considered 10 proposed characteristics of a core journal: "subjective judgment, use, indexing coverage, overlapping library holdings, citation data, citation network/co-citation analysis, production of articles, Bradford's Law, faculty publication data, and multiple criteria methods" (Nisonger 2007, abstract). His focus was on academic libraries, but most of the ideas are relevant to public libraries as well (*see* PUBLIC SERVICES; SPECIAL SERVICES; TECHNICAL SERVICES).

References

Black, Steve. 2006. *Serials in Libraries: Issues and Practices*. Westport, CT: Libraries Unlimited.

Evans, G. Edward, et al. 2002. *Introduction to Technical Services*. Greenwood Village, CO: Libraries Unlimited.

Gale Directory of Databases. 1993. Farmington Hills, MI: Gale. Annual. Online at www.gale.cengage.com.

Gale Directory of Publications and Broadcast Media. 1990. Farmington Hills, MI: Gale. Annual. Online at www.gale.cengage.com.

Magazines for Libraries. 1969–. New York: Bowker. Irregular. http://www .ulrichsweb.com.

McReynolds, Rosalee. 1994. Serials librarianship. In *Encyclopedia of Library History*: 574–77. New York: Garland.

Mouw, James R. 1999. Acquiring serials. In *Understanding the Business of Library Acquisitions*, 2nd ed., ed. Karen Schmidt, 157–78. Chicago: American Library Association.

New Serial Titles. 1953–1999. Washington, DC: Library of Congress.

Nisonger, Thomas E. 2007. Journals in the core collection: Definition, identification, and applications. *Serials Librarian* 51, no. 3/4: 51–73.

Osborn, Andrew D. 1955. *Serial Publications: Their Place and Treatment in Libraries*. Chicago: American Library Association.
Serials Librarian. 1976–. New York: Haworth. Quarterly.
Standard Periodical Directory. 1989–. New York: Oxbridge. Annual. Online at www.mediafinder.com.
Ulrich's International Periodicals Directory. 1932–. New York: Bowker. Annual. http://www.ulrichsweb.com.
Union List of Serials in the U.S. and Canada before 1950. 1965. New York: H. W. Wilson.

SERVICES. *See* PUBLIC SERVICES; SPECIAL SERVICES; TECHNICAL SERVICES.

SERVICES TO AFRICAN AMERICANS

Terminology

American Heritage gives some assistance in this murky area. It identifies a "black" (or "Black") as "a member of a racial group having brown to black skin, esp. one of African origin"; or "an American descended from peoples of African origin having brown or black skin." But the "racial" connection is dubious, according to another *American Heritage* statement: "Many cultural anthropologists now consider race to be more a social or mental construct than an objective biological fact." That observation would seem to dispose of "Negro," which is described as "(often offensive): a Black person; a member of the Negroid race. Not in scientific use." Finally there is the term that has gained favor in recent years: "African American: a Black American of African ancestry." None of these definitions is precise enough to include everyone intended or to exclude unintended individuals.

There is one more term in the mix: "As a racial label, *colored* can simply mean *non-white*, but in the United States its usage has generally been restricted to persons of African descent. Though long a preferred term among Black Americans, it lost favor as the 20th century progressed, and its use today is often taken to be offensive." Nevertheless the venerable National Association for the Advancement of Colored People has retained its name.

In library usage "Negro" and "colored" have been abandoned. Institutions and writings refer with apparent impartiality to "blacks" (sometimes capitalized) or "African Americans."

Historical Summary and Current Situation

"Are you serious?" E. J. Josey shouted at the 1964 American Library Association (ALA) conference when the ALA had honored the National Library Week activities of the Mississippi Library Association. Josey, librarian at Savannah State College, pushed a resolution prohibiting ALA officers and staff from participating at conferences of any state library associations that refused membership to African Americans (Josey 1970, 315). While the ALA had been open to blacks, it had been meeting in segregated cities where black members were subjected to racist humiliation. The journey to Josey's resolution had been long and difficult. Most blacks came to America as slaves. In the North they were often permitted to read, but in the South they were usually forbidden to read and write. Many practiced reading in secret. Such efforts at self-education constituted the first steps of the journey to equal access (Wheeler and Johnson-Houston 2004, 42).

Initially public libraries in the South were not segregated: African Americans simply could not use them. A 1935 survey reported that only 83 of 565 southern libraries reporting provided any services to African Americans (Wheeler and Johnson-Houston 2004, 43). Although the Supreme Court in *Plessy v. Ferguson* (163 U.S. 537, 1896) legitimated the concept of "separate but equal" and allowed states to segregate public spaces, facilities and services were far from equal. Public school systems in the South underfunded black schools. "Black development had to proceed, if at all, at a respectful distance behind white progress" (Lamon 1977, 62). *Plessy* was not overturned by the Supreme Court until *Brown v. Board of Education* (347 U.S. 483, 1954).

In 1905, Thomas Fountain Blue became the first African American to head a public library facility when he was appointed to manage the Western Colored Branch of the Louisville (KY) Free Public Library. This was the first American branch to serve blacks with an entirely black staff. Blue's accomplishments included establishment of a second colored branch in 1915 and a notable training program for black librarians (see entry for Blue).

With a grant from Andrew Carnegie, the Atlanta Public Library opened its Auburn Branch for blacks in 1921 (many southern libraries declined Carnegie grants in order to avoid serving blacks). Under dynamic leadership by Annie L. McPheeters and other African American female managers, the branch became an important center for the study of black culture. The Negro History Collection was formally organized in 1934, when McPheeters was assistant librarian. She later headed a second colored branch, West Hunter, in 1949. Auburn closed in 1959 as the library system was desegregated and the collection moved to the central library. It was named the Samuel W. Williams Collection on Black America in 1971. A final move took place in 1994 as the collection was relocated to the newly constructed Auburn Branch, which is officially named the Auburn Avenue Research Library on African American Culture and History.

Other important public library research centers on the black experience are those in Broward County (FL) Library (African American Research Library and Cultural Center, 2002), Denver Public Library (Blair-Caldwell African American Research Library, 2003), and New York Public Library (Schomburg Center for Research in Black Culture, 1905) (*see* NEW YORK PUBLIC LIBRARY).

The need for African American librarians was addressed by another Carnegie Grant in 1925; it funded the establishment of a library school at the traditionally black Hampton Normal Agricultural Institute (later the Hampton Institute and finally, in 1984, Hampton University) in Hampton,

VA. When the school closed in 1939 (Smith 1940, 54), Carnegie assisted in the founding of a library education program at Atlanta University in 1941. That school provided black staff for public libraries across the country until it closed in 2005. Efforts to recruit African Americans to librarianship have had mixed results. They make up 12.3 percent of the U.S. population (according to the 2000 census) but only 5 percent of the library profession. Perhaps this low proportion is explained by the fact that African Americans are "less likely to earn advanced degrees," such as the ALA-accredited master's degree (Lance 2005, 42). Recruitment of black students has been a priority in library schools for decades; the project has been aided by scholarships and grants from the ALA and the federal government.

Energized by Effie Lee Morris and E. J. Josey, the ALA formed a Black Caucus in 1970. Its purpose was to "monitor any aspect of librarianship as it related to African Americans as librarians and library users" (Ham 2001, 101). In addition, the caucus reviews records and analyzes the platform statement of candidates for ALA office and checks on activities of public library boards with regard to service policy toward blacks (*see* AMERICAN LIBRARY ASSOCIATION).

It has taken one hundred years for African Americans to become "visible" (Marshall 1976, 77). Public libraries are endeavoring to serve them as well as other minority groups. In the second century of American librarianship, libraries "should make color invisible by absorbing the Afro-American into the mainstream of U.S. life and allowing release of pent-up abilities and emotions, exploding the dream, no longer deferred" (Marshall 1976, 77). Public libraries can be a strong influence in the lives of African Americans, as illustrated by Supreme Court Justice Clarence Thomas, author Toni Morrison, and President Barack Obama.

—*Aisha M. Johnson*

References

American Library Association. 2006. Diversity counts (press release). ala.org/ala/newspresscenter/pressreleases2006. Accessed August 2010.

Battles, David M. 2009. *The History of Public Access for African Americans in the South, or, Leaving Behind the Plow*. Lanham, MD: Scarecrow Press.

Ham, Debra N. 2001. Black Caucus of the American Library Association. In *Organizing Black America: An Encyclopedia of African American Associations*, 100–101. New York: Garland.

Josey, Elonie J. 1970. *The Black Librarian in America*. Metuchen, NJ: Scarecrow Press.

Lamon, L. 1977. *Black Tennessee: 1900–1930*. Knoxville: University of Tennessee Press.

Lance, Keith C. 2005. Racial and ethnic diversity of U.S. library workers. *American Libraries* 36, no. 5 (May): 41–43.

Marshall, A. P. 1976. Service to Afro-Americans. In *A Century of Service: Librarianship in the United States and Canada*, ed. Sidney L. Jackson et al., 62–78. Chicago: American Library Association.

McPheeters, Annie L. 1988. *Library Service in Black and White: Some Personal Rec-ollections, 1921-1980*. Metuchen, NJ: Scarecrow Press.

Musmann, Klaus. 1998. The ugly side of librarianship: segregation in library services from 1900 to 1950. In *Untold Stories: Civil Rights, Libraries, and Black Librarianship*, ed. John Mark Tucker, 78–92. Champaign: University of Illinois, Graduate School of Library and Information Science.

Smith, S. L. 1940. The passing of the Hampton Library School. *Journal of Negro Education* 9, no. 1 (January): 51–58.

Wheeler, Maurice, and Debbie Johnson-Houston. 2004. A brief history of library service to African Americans. *American Libraries* 35, no. 2 (February): 42–45.

SERVICES TO BLIND USERS. *See* SERVICES TO PEOPLE WITH DISABILITIES.

SERVICES TO BUSINESS AND INDUSTRY   Business activities lacked a research base until the late nineteenth century. The University of Pennsylvania established the Wharton School of Finance and Commerce in 1881, placing business in the academic context, and other universities followed suit: the University of Chicago, Harvard University, Northwestern University, and the University of Pittsburgh had business schools by 1908. All large universities have created schools or departments of business, with the necessary library collections. Those collections contain census data, city directories, industry directories, market information, descriptions of individual businesses, and other reference materials of interest to business persons of all kinds. Similar collections began to appear in libraries operated by individual firms; there were 39 of them by 1900.

Public libraries entered the business field in the early twentieth century. Earlier writings laid the groundwork (Green 1889; Foster 1898). The pioneer leader was John Cotton Dana, who established a business branch in the Newark (NJ) Public Library in 1904. It was a specialized branch located in the city's financial district (see Dana 1910). Newark was the model for other large city libraries; business branches were opened in Minneapolis (1916), Rochester (1917), Indianapolis (1918), Detroit (1920), and Boston (1930). In cases where the main library was conveniently located with respect to the business district, business departments were set up in the central building.

After World War II public library business services faced growing competition from their own customers, as business and industrial firms tended to develop their own corporate libraries. Those that did so incurred costs for materials and staff that had been available free in the public library. Access to digital information sources influenced the move to independence. Gradually this move toward on-site libraries in business firms reduced usage in public library business units. All the business branches mentioned above have closed, most recently that of the Boston Public Library in 2009. The Cleveland Public Library had an annex to the main library that functioned as a business and science library from 1959 to 1994. It was demolished then and replaced by a new wing of the main library that includes business services, among various other functions. The San Francisco Public Library closed its business branch. Separate branches remain in the Brooklyn Public Library, the New York Public Library, and the Carnegie Library of Pittsburgh.

Factors militating against the maintenance of separate business branches include the large size of many new central libraries, such as the one in Chicago, which makes it reasonable for them to accommodate all the business materials.

The American Library Association, Reference and User Services Association, has a Business Reference and Services Section that offers guidance to business resource and serves to bring business librarians together at annual conferences. Its programs and publications are noted at http://www.ala.org/ala/mgrps/divs/rusa/sections/brass.

References

Dana, John Cotton. 1910. *The Business Branch*. Woodstock, VT: Elm Tree Press.
Foster, William E. 1898. Use of a library by artisans. *Library Journal* 23, no. 5 (May): 188–91.
Green, Samuel Swett. 1889. The library and its relation to persons engaged in industrial pursuits. *Library Journal* 14, no. 5/6 (May/June): 215–25.
Vormelker, Rose L. 1970. Business and the public library. *Encyclopedia of Library and Information Science* 3: 573–92. New York: Marcel Dekker.

SERVICES TO CHILDREN AND YOUNG ADULTS

Terminology

The ambiguous vocabulary of this field has been discussed in the "Prologue on Terminology" earlier in this book. Because of the vague borders between children and young adults it seems as well to discuss their library services together in one entry.

Historical Summary

This is a chronology of significant events in the development of children's and young adult services in American public libraries.

1803—Caleb Bingham donated books to the town of Salisbury, CT, requesting that the town maintain it as the Bingham Library for Youth.

1833—The new public library in Peterborough, NH, included children's books.

1869—Children were generally barred from public libraries, but they were welcomed in Cleveland at the opening of the new public library building.

1876—The U.S. Bureau of Education report on *Public Libraries in the United States* had no index citations for "child" or "children." However, a chapter in the report by William I. Fletcher of the

Hartford Public Library was titled "Public Libraries and the Young." Fletcher asked, "What shall the public library do for the young, and how?" (Jackson 1976, 21). He answered his own question in part: "the library ought to bring its influence to bear on the young as early as possible." To prevent development of taste for dime novels and cheap stories, libraries should provide children with good books that are "instructive and stimulating to the better nature" (Walter 2001, 1).

1879—Cooperation between public and school libraries initiated by the Worcester (MA) Public Library. Similar efforts followed by the public libraries of Providence, Boston, Quincy, and Rochester.

1882—The first story hours for children were offered by Caroline M. Hewins in the Hartford Public Library. She was the author of *Books for the Young: A Guide for Parents and Children*, published in 1882.

1884—William Howard Brett named director of the new Cleveland Public Library; among his interests was service to children. By 1891 the library had 61 deposit collections in Cleveland schools.

1885—A children's room in New York City was established under the direction of Emily S. Hanaway at 243 Ninth Avenue; it became a branch of the New York Free Circulating Library in 1888 (Bostwick 1929, 11–12).

1885—Children's Library Association created by Melvil Dewey.

1886—The Aguilar Free Library (serving the Jewish population) in New York City opened a children's library at 624 Fifth Street.

1887—A children's area, with appropriate furniture and open shelves, was set up in the Pawtucket (RI) Public Library.

1888—A new branch of the New York Free Circulating Library had a children's room.

1890 or 1891—A small basement room, with a few picture books, noncirculating, was opened for children in the Brookline (MA) Public Library (Stone 1977, 179).

1890—An American Library Association (ALA) recommended list of *Reading for the Young* was published in Boston by the Library Bureau.

1893—The Minneapolis Public Library put all children's books in a basement corridor as an open shelf circulating collection, with a special attendant.

1894—Seventy percent of public libraries still did not serve children (Williams 1998, 30). The Denver Public Library was one of the exceptions, opening a separate children's room with open shelves. The Cambridge (MA) Public Library also set up a children's room in this year.

1895—The new Boston Public Library building opened with no separate children's room, but in response to popular demand it created one two months later. In the Cleveland Public Library, the first librarian to be appointed specifically to work with children was Effie Louise Power.

1896—Children's rooms in Cambridge and Brookline, MA. "Corners, alcoves, or tables" in Buffalo, Lowell, Medford, and Pawtucket, RI (Bostwick 1929, 12). Anne Carroll Moore began story hours at the Pratt Institute (Brooklyn).

1896–1897—Children's rooms in the libraries of Omaha, Seattle, New Haven, San Francisco, Detroit, Pittsburgh, and Brooklyn's Pratt Institute.

1897—First discussion of children's work at an ALA conference (Philadelphia). Schools department established in the New York Free Circulating Library. First librarian designated as director of children's work, Frances Jenkins Olcott, at the Carnegie Library of Pittsburgh.

1898—Schools department established in Buffalo Public Library. The first courses in children's work were offered at the New York State Library School and at the Pratt Institute.

At the turn of the century, children's rooms had become a common feature in larger urban libraries. They usually had appropriate furniture, cheerful décor, and a female librarian in charge. The pattern of service to the young was laid down and remains the norm: special collections of age-specific materials, a separate room or area, staff with special training, programs to enhance use, and working relations with schools. Promotion of lifelong reading was an accepted goal since only 10 percent of children remained in school to age 14.

1900—Carnegie Library of Pittsburgh began offering a two-year training course in children's work; it began with five students and had 65 in 1907. In the ALA, a Children's Library Club was established, becoming the Children's Service Section in 1901.

1905—The ALA began publishing *Booklist*, which included reviews of children's books. The Louisville Public Library offered story hours in its colored branch by Rachel D. Harris and sent out 35 classroom collections to black neighborhood schools.

1905—Various recommended lists of children's books were published around this time, such as *Books for Children* by Gertrude Weld Arnold.

1906—The New York Public Library initiated a training course for children's librarians and opened a children's room in the central library. Anne Carroll Moore was the head from 1906 to 1941.

1909—First edition of the *Children's Catalog*, a basic collection for public libraries, issued by H. W. Wilson. The Western Reserve University library school offered a course for children's librarians.

1919—Mabel Williams appointed supervisor of work with schools, New York Public Library, remaining to 1959.

1922—First Newbery Medal awarded for outstanding children's book of the year.

1924—First issue of the journal for children's librarians, *Horn Book*.

1925—The Robert L. Stevenson Room for service to young adults opened in Cleveland Public Library; Jean Roos was head of special services to young people, 1925–1940, then supervisor of the youth department, 1940–1959.

"By the end of the 1920s, even the smallest public libraries stocked books for children and provided some of the services that were becoming standard, such as summer reading and storytelling programs. Andrew Carnegie did his part by including designated space for children in his massive public library building program" (Walter 2010, 2).

1933—Margaret A. Edwards instituted "Y work" at the Enoch Pratt Free Library, continuing to 1962.

1938—First award of the Caldecott Medal for outstanding illustrated children's book of the year.

By the end of the 1930s, service for youth was found nationwide in separate alcoves, rooms, and buildings.

1947—*Children and Books* by May Hill Arbuthnot.

1948—The ALA published *A Public Library Plans for the Teen Age*, suggesting standards and programs, describing the work of several libraries.

1950—*The Public Library Inquiry*, a multivolume study published by Columbia University, did not consider children's services.

The several youth movements that began in the 1960s brought uncertainties to public libraries. Young people were harder to reach or to satisfy with traditional materials and programs. The outreach efforts of libraries, aiming to increase usage by the young (and by disadvantaged adults), did not demonstrate lasting impact. By the early 1970s many libraries had cast aside their efforts to hold young patrons. Decline of services followed, with elimination or downgrading of children's and young adults positions and closing of children's rooms in central libraries (Jackson 1976, 38).

1977—The ALA *Directions for Library Service to Young Adults* stressed traditional approaches, but patronage continued to decline into the 1980s.

1988—A report from the National Center for Educational Statistics (NCES) announced that while one of four public library patrons was 12 to 15 years of age, libraries were giving up their specialists in children's and young adult services and that almost all young adult areas or rooms had been closed (Steinfirst 1994).

1992—The ALA published *Output Measures for Public Library Service to Children* by Virginia A. Walter, part of a general public library effort to demonstrate accountability.

1993—The NCES reported on circulation of children's materials and attendance at children's programs. This was the first NCES public library report to give data on children (defined as 14 years of age or younger). Nationwide circulation of children's materials was nearly 462.9 million, or over 29 percent of total circulation. Attendance at children's programs was nearly 35.6 million.

2005—The NCES reported that circulation of children's materials was 716.4 million, or 35 percent of total circulation. Attendance at children's programs was 54.6 million.

Current Situation

The downward trend of public library services to children and young adults that ran into the 1980s was stemmed in the 1990s and early years of the twenty-first century. Public library usage by all age-groups increased, in part because of the economic recession but also because of the greater attention libraries gave to the Internet:

> National per person visitations and circulation have both increased solidly over the past decade . . . the increased demand for library services may not have occurred if these institutions had not recognized and adapted to new patron demands by drastically increasing the availability of Internet workstations, and allocating greater proportions of collection expenditures to electronic materials and providing a wider range of targeted programs. (Henderson 2009, 6)

Internet access proved especially attractive to younger patrons who may not always be in the library to access information or forbidden websites; "mostly, librarians tell me and my own observations confirm, they want to play games" (Walter 2009, 53). Whatever their motives, teenagers have become library users again. A 2007 Harris Poll found that "78 percent of teen respondents have library cards, and participation in library programs by youth under age 18 has been rising steadily; further, three-quarters of Americans believe it is a high priority for public libraries to offer a safe place where teenagers can study and congregate" (*State of America's Libraries* 2010, 2). According to the 2007 Public Library Data Service (PLDS) report, "nearly ninety percent of the public libraries surveyed offer young adult programs, with more than half (51.9 percent) employing at least one full-time equivalent dedicated to fostering young adult programs and services, up dramatically from eleven percent in 1995" (*Statistical Report* 2007, 45). Examples of these programs are noted below. Most adults surveyed felt that these were important library activities for children: summer reading programs, homework help, after-school activities, story hour, computer classes, and teen programs (*State of America's Libraries* 2010, 3).

The demise of library positions designated as children's or young adult librarians that had been ongoing 20 years ago seems to have subsided, at least for the children's category. Around two-thirds of public libraries in a small sample examined in the writing of this entry have a person in charge of children's work. The sample consisted of public libraries in Texas that reported their administrative titles to the *American Library Directory 2009–2010*. There were 22 libraries that did so, ranging in total staff size from six (Tyler and Plano) to 209 (Fort Worth). While 16 libraries had someone identified with children's services, only two had someone identified with young adult services. Fort Worth mentioned neither a children's nor a young adult services specialist. The only two young adult persons were in Bastrop (total staff of eight) and Fort Bend County (total staff of 83). There is further information on Austin Public Library below. A check of various important libraries nationwide displayed results that matched that of the Texas libraries. Many large libraries had no specified administrator for children or young adult services (Boston, Brooklyn, Queens, New York Public Library, Newark, Detroit, Louisville, Indianapolis, and Denver), suggesting that work with younger patrons was directed at a subsidiary administrative level. In other libraries there is someone identified with children's services but not with young adult services, suggesting that the latter is included with the former (Enoch Pratt, Evanston, and San Diego). The Chicago Public Library has a person titled director of children's and young adult services. There is someone in charge of youth services in Columbus, Cleveland, Los Angeles, and St. Louis—which evidently includes children. Philadelphia is one library with both children's and "teen services" administrators. Putting this information next to the finding of the PLDS noted above, that 51.9 percent of libraries have a full-time-equivalent staff person dedicated to young adult programs (which means nearly half of them do not), the current situation that emerges is of children's specialists most often taking responsibility for young adult work.

The need for a new career ladder and position descriptions for children's librarians has been noted (Walter 2001, 115). While some concerns have been expressed about the weakness of library school curricula in these areas, a review of current programs in a number of the schools finds that they do offer courses in both children's and young adult services as well as instruction in administration of school media centers. The ALA's Association for Library Service to Children (ALSC) has prepared "core competencies" for children's librarians (1989, revised 1999 and 2009). The list refers to persons working with children up to age 14. It may be expected that library educators will make appropriate adjustments in their offerings to reflect these skill sets.

With the resurgence of public library attention to young patrons, there has been a fresh interest in reader's advisory work. A number of books with guidance and title lists have proved valuable to librarians; a selection of them is included in the "References" section below.

Groundwork for a philosophy of children's work has been laid by Virginia Walter. She offered three concepts of the child in the library: child as reader, child of the information age, and child in the community (Walter 2001, 91). Two new concepts were suggested later: the global child and the empowered child (Walter 2009, 52). The same author has outlined a research agenda to buttress library service to the young. She presents four "significant unanswered questions": (1) How have these services developed over time? (2) How and why do young people use public libraries? (3) How can they be evaluated? and (4) How to justify funding for these services? (Walter 2003).

The ALA, through the ALSC and the Young Adult Library Services Association (YALSA), provides support for professional activities with a vigorous publication program, including two journals: *Children and Libraries* and *Young Adult Library Services*. The ALSC and YALSA offer programs at ALA conferences and continuing education for members. The American Association of School Librarians, another ALA organization, issues *Knowledge Quest*. The International Federation of Library Associations and Institutions (IFLA) has prepared guidelines for service to children and to young adults. Principal ALA and IFLA publications are included in the "References" section below.

Book selection is a growing challenge for librarians working with the young since the number of new juvenile titles now exceeds 5,000 per year in the United States. Useful core lists have been issued by the H. W. Wilson Company since 1909. See the "References" section for details on *Children's Catalog, Junior High School Library Catalog,* and *Senior High School Library Catalog*. Journals with valuable book reviews include *Booklist, Horn Book,* and the ALA publications noted above; see the "References" section for publication details.

As a concluding note, some imaginative programs may be cited. The Queens (NY) Library has created a distinct "Library for Teens," and the Dallas Public Library has a library (named "Bookmarks") for youngsters located where youngsters go, in a shopping center (O'Connor and Kenney 2008). The Austin Public Library has story times and live stage events for children and a range of teen activities: anime club, comic books club, gaming tournament, manga book club, mother–daughter book club, plus access to 11 gaming websites (adventure and educational). Austin has an outreach program called "Second Chance Books," a collaboration with the local juvenile detention center. Around the country there are new young adult rooms (e.g., Port Jefferson, NY, and Worthington, OH). The Charlotte-Mecklenburg (NC) Public Library has collaborated with the Children's Theater of Charlotte to create ImaginOn, a building opened in 2005 that brings stories to life in dynamic modules (Kenney 2005). And libraries are concentrating on service to preschool children and improving early childhood literacy. Parents are included in the planning of facilities: specially designed spaces are set aside for them to read, play, and learn with their youngsters and to consult parenting materials.

References

American Library Association. 1948. *The Public Library Plans for the Teen Age.* Prepared by the Committee on Post-war Planning of the American Library Association, Division of Libraries for Children and Young People, and its section, the Young People's Reading Round Table. Chicago: American Library Association.

Arbuthnot, May Hill. 1947. *Children and Books.* Chicago: Scott, Foresman.

Arbuthnot, May Hill. 1948. *Children's Books Too Good to Miss.* Cleveland: Press of Western Reserve University.

Arnold, Gertrude Weld. 1905. *Books for Children.* Jamaica, NY: Marion Press.

Baker, Susan F., and Erin Holden. 2007. Preschool outreach plus: Rapides Parish Library award-winning preschool outreach service. *Bookmobile and Outreach Services* 10, no. 2: 9–6.

Barr, Catherine, and John T. Gillespie. 2010. *Best Books for Children: Preschool through Grade 6.* 9th ed. Santa Barbara: Libraries Unlimited.

Bartel, Julie, and Pamela Spencer Holley. 2009. *Annotated Book Lists for Every Teen Reader.* Titles chosen by members of the American Library Association, Young Adult Library Services Association. New York: Neal-Schuman.

Bobinski, George S. 2007. *Libraries and Librarianship: Sixty Years of Challenge and Change, 1945–2005.* Lanham, MD: Scarecrow Press.

Booklist. 1905–. Chicago: American Library Association. Monthly. Title varies. *ALA Booklist,* 1905–1917; *Booklist,* 1917–1956; *Booklist and Subscription Books Bulletin,* 1956–1968; *Booklist,* 1969–.

Bostwick, Arthur E. 1929. *The American Public Library.* 4th ed. New York: Appleton. 1st ed. 1910.

Brehm-Heeger, P. 2008. *Serving Urban Teens.* Westport, CT: Libraries Unlimited.

Burek, Pierce J. 2008. *Sex, Brains and Video Games: A Librarian's Guide to Teens in the Twenty-first Century.* Chicago: American Library Association.

Butler, Florence W. 1970. Children's libraries and librarianship. *Encyclopedia of Library and Information Science* 4: 559–66. New York: Marcel Dekker.

Cerny, R., et al. 2006. *Outstanding Library Service to Children: Putting the Core Competencies to Work.* Chicago: American Library Association.

Chelton, Mary K. 2000. *Excellence in Library Services to Young Adults.* 3rd ed. Chicago: American Library Association, Young Adult Library Services Association.

Children and Libraries: The Journal of the ALSC. 2003–. Continues in part *Journal of Youth Services in Libraries,* 1987–2002. Chicago: American Library Association. 3 times per year.

Children's Catalog. 1909–. New York: H. W. Wilson. Quinquennial; supplements.

Competencies for Librarians Serving Children in Public Libraries. 1999. Chicago: American Library Association, Association for Library Service to Children.

Dresang, E.T., et al. 2006. *Dynamic Youth Services through Outcome-Based Planning and Evaluation*. Chicago: American Library Association.

Fasick, Adele M., and Leslie.E. Holt. 2008. *Managing Children's Services in the Public Library*. 3rd ed. Westport, CT: Libraries Unlimited.

Feinberg, Sandra, et al. 1998. *Learning Environments for Children: Rethinking Library Spaces and Services*. Chicago: American Library Association.

Fellows, May J., ed. 1998. *Smart Training, Smart Librarians: Competency-Based Training for Youth Services*. Chicago: American Library Association.

Flowers, Sarah. 2008. Guidelines for library services to teens. *Young Adult Library Services* 6, no. 3 (Spring): 4–6.

Freeman, Judy. 2007. *Once upon a Time*. Westport, CT: Libraries Unlimited.

Gerhardt, Lillian N. 1997. *School Library Journal's Best: a Reader for Children's, Young Adult, and School Librarians*. New York: Neal-Schuman.

Gillespie, John T. 2005. *The Children's and Young Adult Literature Handbook: A Research and Reference Guide*. Westport, CT.: Libraries Unlimited.

Greene, Ellen, and Janice M. Del Negro. 2010. *Storytelling: Art and Technique*. 4th ed. Santa Barbara: Libraries Unlimited.

Guidelines for Children's Libraries Services. 2003. The Hague: International Federation of Library Associations and Institutions, Libraries for Children and Young Adults Section.

Guidelines for Library Service for Young Adults. 2001. The Hague: International Federation of Library Associations and Institutions, Libraries for Children and Young Adults Section. A revision of the 1996 publication.

Henderson, Everett. 2009. *Service Trends in U.S. Public Libraries, 1997–2007*. IMLS Research Brief, 1. Washington, D.C.: Institute of Museum and Library Services.

Honnold, Rosemary. 2006. *The Teen Reader's Advisor*. New York: Neal-Schuman.

Horn Book Magazine. 1945–. Boston: Horn Book. Continues *Horn Book*, 1924–1944. 6 times per year; publisher varies.

Jackson, Clara O. 1976. Service to urban children. In *A Century of Service: Librarianship in the United States and Canada*, ed. Sidney L. Jackson et al., 20–41. Chicago: American Library Association.

Jenkins, Christine A. 1994. Children's services, public. In *Encyclopedia of Library History*: 127–31. New York: Garland.

Junior High School Library Catalog. 1965–. New York: H. W. Wilson. Quinquennial.

Kenney, Brian. 2005. Imagine this. *School Library Journal* 57, no. 12 (December): 52–55.

Knowledge Quest. 1997–. Chicago: American Library Association. 5 times per year. A publication of the American Association of School Libraries. Continues *School Libraries*, 1952–1972, which continued as *School Media Quarterly*, 1972–1981, and *School Library Media Quarterly*, 1981–1997.

LaMaster, Jennifer. 2005. Collaboration of Indiana public and school media center youth services: a survey analysis of current practices. *Indiana Libraries* 24, no. 1: 38–41.

Lewis, Dan. 1993. *Directions for Library Service to Young Adults*. 2nd ed. Chicago: American Library Association, Young Adult Library Services Association. 1st ed. 1977.

Lima, Carolyn W., and Rebecca L. Thomas. 2010. *A to Zoo: Subject Access to Children's Picture Books*. 8th ed. Santa Barbara: Libraries Unlimited.

Long, Harriet G. 1969. *Public Library Service to Children: Foundation and Development*. Metuchen, NJ: Scarecrow Press.

Mahood, Kristine. 2006. *A Passion for Print: Promoting Reading and Books to Teens*. Westport, CT: Libraries Unlimited.

Martin, Hillias J. 2006. A library outing: serving queer and questioning teens. *Young Adult Library Services* 4, no. 4 (Summer): 138–39.

Mediavilla, Cindy. 2001. *Creating the Full-Service Homework Center in Your Library*. Chicago: American Library Association.

Miller, Donna P. 2008. *Crash Course in Teen Services*. Westport, CT: Libraries Unlimited.

Miller, Marilyn L. 2003. *Pioneers and Leaders in Library Services to Youth: a Biographical Dictionary*. Westport, CT: Libraries Unlimited.

Miller, Steve. 2005. *Developing and Promoting Graphic Novel Collections*. New York: Neal-Schuman.

O'Connor, Maureen, and Brian Kenney. 2008. Make it new: The Queens Library for Teens and Dallas's Bookmarks. *School Library Journal* 54, no. 7 (July): 38–42.

Perez, Marlene. 2006. Going all the way in teen literature. *Young Adult Library Services* 4, no. 2 (Winter): 20–21.

Power, Effie Louise. 1943. *Work with Children in Public Libraries*. Chicago: American Library Association.

School Library Journal. 1961–. New York: Bowker. Monthly. Continues *Junior Libraries*, 1954–1960.

Senior High School Library Catalog. 1926–1928–. New York: H. W. Wilson. Quinquennial; supplements. Title varies. *Standard Catalog for High School Libraries*, 1928–1962.

State of America's Libraries. 2010. Chicago: American Library Association. http://www.ala.org/ala/newspresscenter/mediapresscenter/americaslibraries. Accessed October 2010.

Statistical Report. Public Library Data Service. 2007. Chicago: Public Library Association. Summarized in *Young Adult Library Services* 6, no. 1 (Fall): 45.

Steinfirst, Susan. 1994. Young adult services. In *Encyclopedia of Library History*, 663–65. New York: Garland.

Stone, Elizabeth. 1977. *American Library Development*. New York: H. W. Wilson.

Van Orden, Phyllis, and Patricia Pawelak-Kort. 2005. *Library Service to Children*. 2nd ed. Lanham, MD: Scarecrow Press. Includes a bibliography of bibliographies, 428 items from 1876 to 2003.

Vardell, Sylvia M. 2008. *Children's Literature in Action: A Librarian's Guide*. Westport, CT: Libraries Unlimited.

Walter, Virginia A. 1992. *Output Measures for Public Library Service to Children: A Manual of Standardized Procedures*. Chicago: American Library Association, Association for Library Service to Children and Public Library Association.

Walter, Virginia A. 1995. *Output Measures and More: Planning and Evaluating Young Adult Services in Public Libraries*. Chicago: American Library Association.

Walter, Virginia A 2001. *Children and Libraries: Getting It Right*. Chicago: American Library Association.

Walter, Virginia A. 2003. Public library service to children and teens: A research agenda. *Library Trends* 51, no. 4 (Spring): 571–75.

Walter, Virginia A. 2009. The children we serve. *American Libraries* (October): 52–55.

Walter, Virginia A. 2010. Children's services in libraries. In *Encyclopedia of Library and Information Sciences*. 3rd ed. Read in proof.

Williams, Patrick. 1998. *The American Public Library and the Problem of Purpose*. New York: Greenwood Press.

Young Adult Library Services. 2002–. Chicago: American Library Association. A publication of the Young Adult Library Services Association. Quarterly. Continues *Top of the News*, 1942–1987; continues in part *Journal of Youth Services in Libraries*, 1987–2002.

SERVICES TO DISABLED USERS. *See* SERVICES TO PEOPLE WITH DISABILITIES.

SERVICES TO FOREIGN POPULATIONS. *See* SERVICES TO IMMIGRANTS.

SERVICES TO GAY, LESBIAN, BISEXUAL, AND TRANSGENDERED PERSONS

Terminology

These definitions are from *American Heritage*: "gay" = "a person whose sexual orientation is to persons of the same sex"; "lesbian" = a woman whose sexual orientation is to women"; "bisexual" = "a person whose sexual orientation is to persons of either sex"; "transgendered" = one "appearing as, wishing to be considered as, or having undergone surgery to become a member of the opposite sex." The older term "homosexual" (a person with a sexual orientation to persons of the same sex) is out of favor. The *American Heritage* usage note states, "Many people now avoid using *homosexual* because of the emphasis the term places on sexuality ... *gay* and *lesbian* are frequently better choices."

The initialism GLBT, in common use since the 1990s, signifies gay, lesbian, bisexual, and transgendered persons. An alternative, LGBT, reverses the first two letters to emphasize lesbians. Sometimes a Q is added to the LGBT to account for "questioning" persons, who have uncertainties about their place.

"Queer," meaning a homosexual person, "was once used solely as a slur but has been semantically overturned by members of the maligned group, who use it as a term of defiant pride" (*American Heritage*). It applies to all GLBT persons. Nevertheless, "its use by heterosexuals is often considered offensive."

The Library Situation

What public librarians are doing with respect to GLBT patrons is first of all to see that they are treated equally with other users, then to provide specific materials of interest to the group. The American Library Association's (ALA's) Gay, Lesbian, Bisexual and Transgendered Round Table promotes the provision of such materials, unrestricted access to them, elimination of job discrimination, and removal of derogatory terminology from classifications and subject heading lists. The Library of Congress has replaced its subject heading "homosexuality" with headings for "Lesbians," "Gay Men," "Bisexuals," and "Transgendered People."

The ALA's *Library Bill of Rights* has an interpretation titled "Access to library resources and services regardless of sex, gender identity, gender expression, or sexual orientation." It expects librarians to "resist efforts that systematically exclude materials dealing with any subject matter, including sex, gender identity, or sexual orientation" (for the *Library Bill of Rights*, *see* INTELLECTUAL FREEDOM). The GLBT Round Table material is at htttp://www.ala.org/ala/mgrps/glbt.

How large is the GLBT patron group?

> Traditionally, the gay and lesbian community has been estimated to be about ten percent of the population based on the ground-breaking Kinsey report published over a half century ago. Other surveys have ranged anywhere from one percent to nine percent ... however, these figures may not include bisexuals and most likely do not include transgender or questioning individuals. (Greenblatt 2003, 21)

Of course not all GLBT persons are library users, and those who are do not identify themselves as GLBT, so the size of the library patron group remains uncertain. Libraries have generally not tried to bring GLBT patrons together or to segregate resources of interest to them. Efforts to serve them have focused on materials selection, an area well served by recent bibliographies (see the "References" section). Special concern for teens is reflected in a growing literature for and about them. The publishing industry is offering a small but steady flow of fiction. "Since the turn of the millennium, roughly a dozen YA novels featuring queer characters have been released each year" (Martin 2006, 1). Patrons who seek such stories or who ask related reference questions must not be made uncomfortable by librarians, but such things do happen (Curry 2005).

References

American Library Association. Gay, Lesbian, Bisexual, Transgendered Round Table. *GLBTRT Newsletter*. Online at www.ala.org/mgrps/glbt.

Bosman, Ellen, et al. 2008. *Gay, Lesbian, and Transgendered Literature: A Genre Guide*. Westport, CT: Libraries Unlimited.

Curry, Ann. 2005. If I ask, will they answer? Evaluating public library reference service to gay and lesbian youth. *Reference & User Services Quarterly* 45, no. 1 (Fall): 65–75.

Greenblatt, Ellen. 2003. Lesbian, gay, bisexual, transgender library users: overcoming the myths. *Colorado Libraries* 29, no. 4 (Winter): 21–25.

Martin, Hillias J. 2006. A library outing: Serving queer and questioning teens. *Young Adult Library Services* 4, no. 4 (Summer): 38–39.

Meezan, William, and James I. Martin. 2009. *Handbook of Research with Lesbian, Gay, Bisexual, and Transgender Populations*. New York: Routledge.

Webber, Carlisle K. 2010. *Gay, Lesbian, Bisexual, Transgender, and Questioning Teen Literature: A Genre Guide*. Santa Barbara, CA: Libraries Unlimited.

SERVICES TO HANDICAPPED USERS. *See* SERVICES TO PEOPLE WITH DISABILITIES.

SERVICES TO HISPANICS

Terminology

Making a distinction between "Hispanic" and "Latino" presents some difficulties. One writer characterized "Hispanic" as "one of the most amorphous and elusive" human categories, but he found that in the United States today, "all persons of Spanish-language heritage, whether they speak Spanish, Spanish and English, or only English" are in the Hispanic category (Gorman 2005, 221). *American Heritage* has a helpful usage note under "Hispanic," which it defines as follows: "A Spanish-speaking person; a US citizen or resident of Latin-American or Spanish descent":

> Though often used interchangeably in American English, *Hispanic* and *Latino* are not identical terms. *Hispanic* has the broader reference, potentially encompassing all Spanish-speaking peoples of both hemispheres. *Latino* refers more exclusively to persons or communities of Latin-American origin. For a certain segment of the Spanish-speaking population, *Latino* is a term of ethnic pride and *Hispanic* a label that borders on the offensive. . . . These views are strongly held by some but are by no means universal. . . . *Latino* [is] widely preferred in California and *Hispanic* . . . in Florida and Texas. Even in those regions, however, usage is often mixed, and it is not uncommon to find both terms used by the same writer or speaker.

The U.S. Census Bureau has settled on "Hispanic," reporting that in 2008 the Hispanic population was 46,891,456—in a total U.S. population of 304,060,000. Seven states had Hispanic populations exceeding 20 percent of total population: New Mexico, 44.9 percent; California, 36.6 percent; Texas, 36.5 percent; Arizona, 30.1 percent; Nevada, 25.7 percent; Florida, 21 percent; and Colorado, 20.2 percent (all census figures reported in *World Almanac 2010*). Seventy percent of Hispanics are from Mexico.

The Library of Congress subject heading is "Hispanic Americans and Libraries." It seems, for the purposes of library practice, that the designation "Hispanic" is generally satisfactory. A recent book on serving that population treats "Hispanic" and "Latino" as synonyms (Avila 2008, x); however, the title of that book brings in yet another designation: *Crash Course in Serving Spanish-Speakers*. And that descriptor was the preference of the American Library Association, Reference and User Services Association (ALA, RUSA 2007), in naming its "Guidelines for Library Services to Spanish-Speaking

Library Users." It remains to be seen whether the "Spanish speaker" will replace "Hispanic."

One last term needs to be noticed: Chicano. This designation for a Mexican American was common into the 1970s but has fallen out of favor, having developed "strong political associations" (*American Heritage*).

Historical Summary

For the tale of American library service to immigrant groups, *see* LIBRARY SERVICES TO IMMIGRANTS. Hispanics do not figure significantly in that story until the 1970s, when librarians became aware of the growing populations from Spanish-speaking countries. The early wave of immigration was from Puerto Rico (900,000 came to New York City in the 1950s), while more recent arrivals have been from Mexico. Federal funds from the Library Services and Construction Act and other programs were the catalysts for library activities aimed at Hispanics. Public libraries with early efforts were the New York Public Library, South Bronx Branch (for Puerto Ricans), and the Albuquerque, Tucson, and Los Angeles public libraries (all for Mexicans). As immigration grew in the next decades, library attention to it increased. The Census Bureau's number of Hispanics in the United States in selected years follows:

1970	9.6 million
1980	14.6 million
1990	22.4 million
2000	35.3 million
2008	46.9 million
2010	49.7 million (projected)
2020	66.4 million (projected)

Current Situation

Virtually all medium-size and large public libraries have program features that are targeted to the Hispanic community (Buck 2004; Guerra 2006; Marquis 2003). Library websites have presentations in Spanish. Branch libraries with Spanish-speaking staff and Spanish collection priorities are opening (the latest is the Hispanic Branch of Miami-Dade Public Library, open on July 13, 2010). Educational programs for children and adults are common. Details on the extensive programs at the East Las Vegas Library Service Plan appear in Avila (2008). Research studies are appearing that deal with the needs of Spanish-speaking persons and their attitudes toward public libraries. The ALA/RUSA has issued guidelines for serving those persons (see below). The aggregate scene is one of dedication and considerable accomplishment.

Training of librarians for work with Hispanics is gaining attention. A recent program that serves as a model is "Hola! Hispanic Outreach Library Action Project" of the Wisconsin Department of Public Instruction. Between

November 2007 and May 2008, one-day workshops were offered in the state for public librarians, helping them to understand the Hispanic culture, how to build links to their community, and what services the patrons especially want.

Recent research offers a mixed picture of the library venture. WebJunction and 40 state libraries sponsored a study of Latino library usage. Their 2008 report showed that 54 percent of Hispanics visited a library in the previous year, with 17.8 percent making monthly visits. They go to the library primarily to borrow movies or music, to learn English, to use computers, and to take children. Library use increases with age, education, income, and each new generation. There were concerns expressed about possible misuse of personal information, insufficient supply of Spanish materials, staff unable to speak Spanish, staff being generally unhelpful, and just feeling unwelcome in the library (*Latinos and Public Library Perceptions* 2008 and summary in *Library Journal*, September 17, 2008).

Such research—and the benefit of experience—has led to specific efforts at maximizing service. Those efforts are well encapsulated in the ALA/RUSA's *Guidelines* (2007) mentioned above. In brief, the recommendations cover materials selection (Spanish and bilingual needed); bibliographic access (Spanish subject headings in the online public access catalog, bibliographies, and instructional items in Spanish), use of Spanish vendors and local bookstores, programming (bilingual and Spanish, reflecting community culture), community profiles outreach to nonusers, cultural events and holiday observations, library and computer instruction in Spanish, bilingual policy statements, recruitment and training of staff with language skills, training of staff in Spanish, and signage and brochures in Spanish.

Although the United States is not officially a bilingual nation, like Belgium or Finland, census data indicate that it has become one in many ways. Public librarians have demonstrated a desire to serve well this new profile of the citizenry.

References

Alire, Camila, and Jacqueline Ayala. 2007. *Serving Latino Communities: A How-to-do-it Manual for Librarians*. 2nd ed. New York: Neal-Schuman.

American Library Association, Reference and User Services Association. 2007. *Guidelines for Library Services to Spanish-speaking Library Users*. Chicago: American Library Association. http://www.ala.org/template.cfm. Accessed August 2010.

Avila, Salvador. 2008. *Crash Course in Serving Spanish-Speakers*. Westport, CT: Libraries Unlimited.

Buck, Katie. 2004. Library services for Hispanic patrons. *Indiana Libraries* 23, no. 1: 23–29. http://www.scholarworks.iupui.edu. Accessed August 2010.

Gorman, Michael. 2005. *Our Own Selves: More Meditations for Librarians*. Chicago: American Library Association.

Guerra, Anna Marie. 2006. Innovative library programs for the Hispanic population. In *Advances in Library Administration and Organization* 24: 249–317.

Haro, Robert P. 1971. Bicultural and bilingual Americans: a need for understanding. *Library Trends* 20, no. 2 (Fall): 271–79.

Herrera, Luis. 1990. Managing administrative change for ethnic collection development. In *Developing Library Collections for California's Emerging Majority*. ed. Katherine T.A. Scarborough. Berkeley: Bay Area Library and Information System.

Josey, E.J. 1976. Minority groups, library service for. In *Encyclopedia of Library and Information Science* 18: 188–98. New York: Marcel Dekker.

Latinos and Public Library Perceptions. 2008. http://www.webjunction.org. Accessed August 2010.

Marquis, Solina Kasten. 2003. Collections and services for the Spanish-speaking: Issues and resources. *Public Libraries* 42, no. 2 (March/April): 106–12.

Miller, Elissa, and Salvador Güerña. 1990. Resources for Chicano/Latino collection development. In *Developing Library Collections for California's Emerging Majority*. ed. Katherine T.A. Scarborough, 215–65. Berkeley: Bay Area Library and Information System.

SERVICES TO IMMIGRANTS

Terminology

An immigrant is "a person who comes to a country to take up permanent residence" (*Merriam*). Immigrants are sometimes called "foreign born" or "ethnic minorities."

Historical Summary and Current Situation

From 1876 to 1924 there were about 26 million immigrants to the United States; by 1973 the number had reached about 37 million. The influx lessened during World War I, then resumed. So-called nativists in this country tried to restrict immigration and were supported by the "Red Scare" of 1918–1920. The National Origins Act of 1924 encouraged immigration from northern and western Europe while limiting immigration from eastern and southern Europe and anywhere outside Europe. There were fewer persons coming to the United States after 1924, but around 1935 a new group began to arrive from Spanish-speaking countries and the Far East. It is the Oriental and Hispanic immigrants that are most numerous today.

Although there was no national movement among librarians to serve immigrants in the nineteenth century, several large libraries developed foreign language collections (Chicago had 65 German magazines and 21 newspapers in 1893). Librarians generally favored open immigration, and from 1904 to 1918 they worked enthusiastically to build foreign language collections. There were specific appropriations for the purpose in Brooklyn and Queens in 1910. Cleveland acquired foreign books from its opening in 1869 and sent staff to Europe to acquire materials (Jones 1999; that article and McMullen 1976 are principal sources for this section).

In some cases there was mutual benefit as community members assisted library staff in cataloging materials. Branch libraries in immigrant neighborhoods appeared in Buffalo (1906), Philadelphia (1907), New Orleans

(1908), St. Louis (1910), New York (1913), and Denver (1913). Central libraries had foreign language departments as well: Providence (1907), Cleveland (1909), Los Angeles (1920), and Detroit (1924). Reading lists in various languages were written in Cleveland (1876), Detroit (1889), and San Francisco (1898). The whole idea of accommodating newcomers in their native languages was controversial at first but was soon embraced, strongly advocated by leaders like Gratia Countryman in Minneapolis and Henry Legler in Chicago.

Leadership came also from the American Library Association (ALA). Its Committee on Work with the Foreign Born was active from 1918 to 1948, guided by chairman John Foster Carr. A philosophy of support for Americanization of immigrants (citizenship; blending into the society) and respect for the native cultures, promoted by Carr, became the general library point of view. A survey published by the ALA in 1926–1927 reported considerable foreign language holdings in 28 public libraries. The most popular languages were French, German, Italian, Yiddish, Spanish, Polish, Czech, and Russian, in that order. In 1923, Edna Phillips became secretary for library work with foreigners in the Massachusetts Division of Public Libraries. She supported Carr's idea of Americanization plus preservation of native cultures. She surveyed the national situation of library service to immigrants for the U.S. Bureau of Education in 1925, served as chair of the ALA committee after Carr, and wrote extensively on immigrant issues (see entry for her). Another great advocate of services to foreigners was Eleanor Ledbetter, who directed the Broadway branch in Cleveland, a neighborhood of Germans and eastern Europeans. She learned their languages, bought books for them in Europe, and lectured in library schools. Ledbetter chaired the ALA committee in 1920–1926 (see entry for her).

During the Depression the Works Progress Administration assisted public libraries with programs for immigrants and with processing of foreign publications. Fewer immigrants were coming in the early 1930s, but refugees in the later 1930s and 1940s gave libraries a new clientele. Mainly there was a decline in attention to the foreign born, as second-generation immigrant children turned away from the traditions and languages of their parents. Libraries diminished their attention to immigrants in the late 1940s. The series of studies titled *Public Library Inquiry* of the early 1950s did not mention them.

Hispanics and Asians are the principal immigrant groups today. They enjoy a range of library services, including collections and programs in their languages and classes in English. Such activities are virtually universal in public libraries (*see* SERVICES TO HISPANICS). Research has disclosed useful information about how immigrants use libraries and how they feel about the experience. Barriers to use are identified, and several means of reaching immigrants are suggested by these studies. For example, "the literature identified several means of reaching immigrants, such as focus groups at community centers, door to door interviewing, and street-corner canvassing" (Burke 2008, 9).

Jones (1999) offered this assessment of the public library's accomplishments with regard to immigrants:

> The American public library, through its educational mission with the immigrant community, shaped, perpetuated, and transferred culture from one generation to another. American librarians, in their collective role as sovereign alchemists, raised our national consciousness to the point where ethnic differences were not just tolerated, but more fully understood and respected. (204)

References

Burke, Susan K. 2008. Use of public libraries by immigrants. *Reference & User Services Quarterly* 48, no. 2 (Winter): 164–75.

Dawson, Alma, and Connie Van Fleet. 2001. The future of readers' advisory in a multicultural society. In *Readers' Advisors' Companion*, ed. Kenneth D. Shearer and Robert Burgin, 249–68. Westport, CT: Libraries Unlimited.

Jones, Plummer Alston, Jr. 1999. *Libraries, Immigrants, and the American Experience*. Westport, CT: Libraries Unlimited.

Luevano-Molina, Susan, ed. 2001. *Immigrant Politics and the American Public Library*. Westport, CT: Libraries Unlimited.

McMullen, Haynes. 1976. Service to ethnic minorities other than Afro-Americans and American Indians. In *A Century of Service: Librarianship in the United States and Canada*, ed. Sidney L. Jackson et al., 42–61. Chicago: American Library Association.

SERVICES TO NATIVE AMERICANS

Terminology

According to *Merriam*, a Native American is "a member of any of the aboriginal peoples of the western hemisphere, esp . . . of North America and esp. the U.S." The definition of "American Indian" is identical, except for the addition of "except Eskimos." In *American Heritage*, Native American is "a member of any of the aboriginal peoples of the Western Hemisphere," and an American Indian is "a member of any of the peoples indigenous to the Americas except the Eskimos, Aleuts, and Inuits." From this it seems correct to say that not all Native Americans are American Indians, but all American Indians are Native Americans. The usage note in *American Heritage* helps clarify this matter:

> Many Americans have come to prefer *Native American* over *Indian*. . . . For some, *Indian* is seen as wrong and offensive, while for others it smacks of bureaucracy and the manipulation of language for political purposes. The controversy appears to have subsided somewhat, and the two terms are now commonly used interchangeably in the same piece of writing. . . . Most Indian writers have continued to use *Indian* at least as often.

Federal terminology in the United States remains with the earlier designation: there is the Bureau of Indian Affairs and the National Museum of the American Indian (opened 2004 in Washington). The Census Bureau tabulates American Indians.

To avoid ambiguity, it is customary to capitalize Native American; without the capital letters, the expression refers to any person born in the United States (a further distinction is made to identify persons from India who have become American citizens: Indian Americans).

Library practice accepts both terms. One recent book is titled *Tribal Libraries in the United States: A Directory of American Indian and Alaska Native Facilities* (2007). There is an American Indian Library Association (founded 1979; see below). The Library of Congress subject heading is "Indians of North America."

Among Native Americans, the term "Native American" suggests a polite address; the people themselves do not use it much. Elders still say American Indian.

A final term of interest is "indigenous," defined by *American Heritage* as "originating and living or occurring naturally in an area or environment." It is used to indicate cross-border concepts and peoples (Roy 2009). See also the section "Library Associations" below.

Public Library Services

The Native American population in 2008 was estimated at 2,443,442 by the Census Bureau. About one-third of those persons live in three states: California, Arizona, and Oklahoma. All Native Americans are citizens of the United States, as per the Indian Citizenship Act of 1924. The federal government recognizes 562 tribal governments, which have most of the functions of states. About half the Native Americans in the United States live on reservations. There are some 285 federal and state Indian reservations that are variously named: in California about half the reservations are "Rancherias," in New Mexico most are "Pueblos," and in some western states they are "Indian Colonies." As citizens, Native Americans are entitled to use public libraries that serve their geographic areas.

Many public libraries, especially in the states with large Native American populations, have special collections about Indians in general or about local tribes (e.g., the Fresno County [CA] Public Library and the Bartlesville [OK] Public Library).

The County of Los Angeles Public Library established an American Indian Resource Center in 1979; it has become the largest collection of its kind. Coverage spans the American Indian experience from pre-Columbian times to the present, with arts, biographies, education, fiction, history, languages, literature, government relations, federal and tribal law, and studies of individual tribes and geographic areas. There are more than 5,000 volumes on the Indian experience, with Indian periodicals, recordings in several formats, films and videocassettes. Government publications from the mid-nineteenth century to the present are collected. Staff makes visits to Indian gatherings (Poon 1990; County of Los Angeles Public Library 2010). Some public libraries are located on reservations, such as the Kim Yerton Memorial Library, a branch in Hoopa of the Humboldt County Library, Eureka, CA.

To supplement standard public library service, many Native American communities have established their own libraries. A 2007 directory describes 237 of them. These libraries "have collections similar to regular public libraries with a special focus on American Indian history and culture" (Peterson 2007, 1; much of the following is derived from this source). Tribal libraries may have unique materials, such as native language recordings, children's books in native languages, oral histories, arts and crafts, and tribal archives. They have meeting rooms, story hours, and programs. Support for the libraries comes mostly from tribal business councils and federal grants, but in some states the institutions have "public library status, allowing them the same funding and support as other public libraries." The Institute of Museum and Library Services (IMLS) began in 1979 to provide some funds for tribal library operations in the form of small basic grants and larger, competitive enhancement grants. Total grants came to $1.3 million in 2006. A grant of $1,495,000 was made in 2010 to 218 Indian tribes and Alaska native villages and corporations, enabling librarians to strengthen their core services for the benefit of tribal communities and villages they serve (*Library Journal*, September 1, 2010).

A report issued by the National Commission on Libraries and Information Science (NCLIS), the predecessor agency to IMLS, concluded that the "development of tribal libraries has remained static for the past decade" (NCLIS 1992). A review of the situation published in 2003 said that "outreach to tribes has been notably non-existent" but pointed to progress in New Mexico, where state funds were being provided, and the New Mexico Library Association had a Native American Libraries Special Interest Group. New York State was showing "exemplary progress," as Indian libraries became part of the public library system and were getting good support. Activity was also noted in Arizona, Montana, and Alaska (Patterson 2003, 157, 161).

Perusal of the Peterson directory indicates that some of the libraries have staff and service comparable to those of public libraries in communities of the same size; indeed the situation may be better in some cases. One instance of advanced service is the Bay Mills Library and Heritage Center, Brimley, MI, which serves the Bay Mills Indian Community. Tribal enrollment is 1,462; the collection holds more than 5,000 books plus oral histories and tribal archives; it is open to the public six days a week and has a paid staff of four. A more typical situation is found in the Ponca Tribe Library, Ponca City, OK, which has a tribal enrollment of 2,618 but a staff composed of only three volunteers.

Library Associations

A task force on American Indians was formed within the ALA Social Responsibilities Round Table in 1971; at the same time, a Committee on

Library Service for American Indian People was formed within the ALA Advisory Committee to the Office for Library Service to the Disadvantaged. Following a preconference (Denver, 1978) to the White House Conference on Library and Information Services in 1979, the American Indian Library Association (AILA) was established; it became an ALA affiliate in 1985. Committed to disseminating information about Indian cultures, languages, and values, the AILA has been "the focal point for bringing awareness to a broad audience regarding the need for tribal libraries on reservations" but has not been able to offer assistance to tribal librarians (Biggs 2004, 42; information given here about associations comes from this source). As mentioned above, there is a Native American Librarians Special Interest Group in the New Mexico Library Association (formed 1979). A Native Libraries Round Table was established in the California Library Association in 2003. There is also a new group in the Oklahoma Library Association and an active group in the Alaska Library Association. A Five State Project led to the National Tribal Archives, Libraries, and Museums Conferences, the last of which was held in Portland, OR, in October 2009.

The International Indigenous Librarians Forum first met in 1999 in New Zealand. There have been biennial meetings in different countries. Its purpose is "to provide a focused exploration of the significant issues facing libraries and institutions that care for indigenous and cultural information" (Sixth International Indigenous Librarians' Forum 2009). At the third forum, in Santa Fe, NM, in 2003, a manifesto was offered for discussion by Lotsee Patterson. It stated that "traditional knowledge is the intellectual property of indigenous peoples and that protection of their cultural heritage is their right" and called for the adoption of "culturally responsive guidelines for use by all information providers." The International Federation of Library Associations and Institutions has a special interest group for indigenous matters. The indigenous perspective was described in a recent article (Roy 2009).

References

Biggs, Bonnie. 2004. Strength in numbers. *American Libraries* 35, no. 3 (March): 41–43.

County of Los Angeles Public Library. 2010. http://www. colapublib.org/services/ethnic/Indian. Accessed February 2010.

Indigenous Matters. 2010. Copenhagen: International Federation of Library Associations and Institutions. Special Interest Group on Indigenous Matters. www.ifla.org/en/indigenous-matters. Accessed October 2010.

National Commission on Libraries and Information Science. 1992. *Pathways to Excellence: A Report on Improving Library and Information Services for Native American People.* Washington, DC: National Commission on Libraries and Information Science.

Patterson, Lotsee. 2003. On tribal libraries. In *Libraries to the People: Histories of Outreach,* ed. Robert S. Freeman and David M. Hovde, 157–62. Jefferson, NC: McFarland.

Patterson, Lotsee. 2005. Reflections on a Passion. In Perspectives, Insights and Priorities: Seventeen Leaders Speaking Freely of Librarianship, ed. Norman Horrocks, 107–13. Lanham, MD.: Scarecrow Press.

Peterson, Elizabeth. 2007. *Tribal Libraries in the United States: A Directory of American Indian and Alaska Native Facilities.* Jefferson, NC: McFarland.

Poon, Wei Chi. 1990. Collection development principles, guidelines, and policies. In *Developing Library Collections for California's Emerging Majority: A Manual of Resources for Ethnic Collection Development,* ed. Katherine T. A. Scarborough, 22–35. San Francisco: Bay Area Library and Information System.

Roy, Loriene. 2009. Indigenous matters in library and information science: An evolving ecology. *Focus on International Library and Information Work* 40, no. 2 (July): 8–12.

Sixth International Indigenous Librarians' Forum. 2009. Aotearoa, New Zealand. www.trw.org.nz/iilf2009. Accessed January 2010.

SERVICES TO PEOPLE WITH DISABILITIES

Terminology

Usage in this field is in flux. The current situation is described in *American Heritage*:

> Although *handicapped* is widely used in both law and everyday speech to refer to people having physical or mental disabilities, those described by the word tend to prefer the expressions *disabled* or *people with disabilities*. The term *handicapped* may imply an inequality in functioning, while *disability* implies functioning equally but in different ways. The word *handicapped*, therefore, is best reserved to describe a disabled person who is unable to function owing to some property of the environment. Thus people with a physical disability requiring a wheelchair may or may not be *handicapped*, depending on whether wheelchair ramps are made available to them.

Libraries are making the accommodation suggested by that entry, although the name of the National Library Service for the Blind and Physically Handicapped remains unchanged, and public libraries have parking spaces reserved for the handicapped. The meaning of the term "disability" is stated in the Americans with Disabilities Act:

> A person with a disability is anyone who has a physical or mental impairment that substantially limits one or more of the person's major life activities; has a record of such impairment; or is regarded as having such an impairment. (Rubin 2001, 45)

Exactly what those disabilities are remains uncertain; terminology is not standardized, even among federal agencies (Rubin 2001, 69). In the library context, it may be sufficient to describe people with disabilities as those who have impairments of vision, hearing, mobility, or physical activity.

Other kinds of impairment, such as mental illness or learning disabilities, are beyond the scope of library services.

Historical Summary

Few public libraries in the nineteenth century provided special services for blind patrons. The Boston Public Library made a Braille collection available in 1868, and the Free Library of Philadelphia set up a department for the blind in 1899. In 1897 a reading room for the blind opened at the Library of Congress (LC). In 1931, Congress authorized LC to organize a network of regional libraries for the distribution of materials to the blind. The name of the earlier LC division was changed in 1966 to the National Library for the Blind and Physically Handicapped. Materials provided by LC and other libraries serving the visually impaired include Braille (raised-type) books, talking books (using various recorded media), large-print (16- to 24-point type) books and magazines, and newer digital media. The American Library Association issued *Books for Tired Eyes: A List of Books in Large Print* in 1923 (there were three later editions, the last one published in 1951), and various libraries published their own lists.

Home delivery of library materials to disabled users began with a service in the Webster City (IA) Public Library in 1935. The Kansas City (MO) Public Library had home service in 1936. A structured home service offered by the Cleveland Public Library in 1941, under Clara Lucioli, became a model for other public libraries.

The idea of facilitating access to libraries by disabled persons emerged with the so-called modular revolution in building design that began in the late 1940s. New plans that replaced monumental library architecture with inviting, open designs often included consideration of patrons with special needs (Rogers 1976, 233).

A strong national effort to assist patrons with disabilities flowered with Public Law 101-336 (1990), the Americans with Disabilities Act (ADA). That law required that measures be taken to provide disabled persons with full access to goods and services. Libraries and other public buildings constructed "handicapped entrances" and facilitated mobility inside. ADA accessibility guidelines have been accepted and staff trained to implement them.

Current Situation

"Twenty-one percent of the U.S. population—more than one in every five people—has a disability as defined by the Americans with Disabilities Act" (Rubin 2001, x). This considerable number of persons includes those with visual or hearing impairment and those with mobility impairment. Also included are persons with learning disabilities and mental illnesses. The disability rate is rising, in part because of growing minority populations and in part because of longer life spans.

Libraries are addressing mobility issues by providing close-in parking spaces, ramps and curb cuts for wheelchair users, public elevators to all floors, access to all reading and seating areas, lowering heights of service counters and other furniture, and modifying bathrooms.

Services to the visually impaired have benefited from technological advance. In June 2010, LC initiated its digital talking-book system, using digital audio books and magazines and the Braille and Audio Reading Download(BARD) service, through which eligible patrons download materials from the Internet.

Hearing-impaired persons are assisted in many libraries by staff who know sign language. Among the libraries noted in *American Library Directory* for having such staff are Alameda County Library (Fremont, CA), Columbus (OH) Metropolitan Library, County of Los Angeles Public Library, Detroit Public Library, Enoch Pratt Free Library (Baltimore, MD), Los Angeles Public Library, Pike's Peak Library District (Colorado Springs, CO), and St. Louis Public Library. Patrons may use high-intensity headphones and on-screen texts to accompany visual images.

There is a national commitment among public librarians to enhance services to people with disabilities (Walling and Irwin 1995). Obstacles to their efforts are formidable: the large number of persons in the disabled category is one problem. Another is the likelihood that in addition to their disabilities, affected persons tend to have low economic and educational profiles (Rubin 2001, xi); thus, they may require "outreach" programs to bring them into the library where helpful services are offered. In recent years librarians have also focused on ways to improve Web accessibility for people with disabilities (Brophy and Craven 2007). Assistive technologies in workstations include screen enlargers, text magnification, voice output, large-print printers, and touch screens. Concerted efforts at staff training include attention to such technology as well as interpersonal issues (Deines-Jones and Van Fleet 1995) and legal considerations generated by the ADA (Torrans 2004, chap. 14).

References

Brophy, Peter, and Jenny Craven. 2007. Web accessibility. *Library Trends* 55, no. 4 (Spring): 950–73.

Cylke, Kurt. 1989. Blind and physically handicapped. In *Encyclopedia of Library and Information Science* 44 (Supplement 9): 27–64. New York: Marcel Dekker.

Deines-Jones, Courtney, and Connie Van Fleet. 1995. *Preparing Staff to Serve Patrons with Disabilities.* New York: Neal-Schuman.

Rogers, A. Robert. 1976. Library buildings. In *A Century of Service*, ed. Sidney L. Jackson et al., 221–42. Chicago: American Library Association.

Rubin, Rhea Joyce. 2001. *Planning for Library Services to People with Disabilities.* ASCLA Changing Horizons, 5. Chicago: American Library Association.

Torrans, Lee Ann. 2004. *Law and Libraries.* Westport, CT: Libraries Unlimited.

Walling, Linda Lucas, and Marilyn M. Irwin, eds. 1995. *Information Services for People with Disabilities: The Library Manager's Handbook.* Westport, CT: Libraries Unlimited.

SERVICES TO SENIORS

Terminology

A "senior," or "senior citizen" is "an elderly person: esp. one who has retired," according to *Merriam*, which defines "elderly" as "rather old; esp. being past middle age" and "middle age" as "the period of life from about 45 to about 64." The U.S. Bureau of the Census has an untitled category of population for persons 65 and over.

The research literature on the elderly has generally used the term "aging" to describe the group. There is also the term "older" as in the Older Americans Act of 1973. Most of the Library of Congress subject headings for seniors call them "older people." However, libraries have settled on the word "seniors."

Current Situation

While all public libraries serve seniors, not many identify them as a special group with special needs and interests. The American Library Association (ALA), Adult Services Division (ASD; now the Reference and Adult Services Division [RUSA]) appointed a committee on library service to an aging population in 1957. A policy statement emerged from the ASD that listed library responsibilities. These included provision of information on aging to the people themselves and those who work with them, facilitating physical access to the library and within the library, taking materials to the homebound and institutionalized, and use of the elderly as volunteers and in program planning (Casey 1975). Lately the ALA has been rather quiet about service to seniors. There are no designated committees or round tables. RUSA has a list of websites that should interest seniors and "21 ideas" for serving them. They include offering classes on Internet, genealogy, and finance; presenting programs on health issues and Social Security; and providing space for displays of crafts and hobbies (ALA, RUSA 2010).

A review of the websites of 20 five-star libraries in the *Library Journal* list of October 1, 2010, produced limited results. A few libraries present lists of useful websites and community agencies. Akron-Summit County and Stark County (OH) offer programs and classes slanted toward seniors. A model senior program is operating in the Schaumburg (IL) Public Library. Its "Senior Center" offers classes, homebound delivery, scooters for use in the library, freedom from overdue fines, field trips, and book discussions. Similar programs appear in the Westerville (OH) Public Library and the "Senior Spot" of the Cleveland Heights-University Heights (OH) Public Library.

As a percent of the U.S. population, persons aged 65 and over are a rapidly growing segment. In 1900 the Census Bureau reported only 4.1 percent of the population at 65 and over. In 1940 it was 6.8 percent; 1980, 11.3 percent; 2010, 13 percent, and projected 2020, 16.1 percent (*World Almanac* 2010). Public libraries are confronting a burgeoning cluster of patrons and seem, at this point in time, uncertain about how best to serve them.

References

American Library Association, Reference and User Services Association. 2010. *Library Services to an Aging Population: 21 Ideas for the 21st Century.* Chicago: American Library Association. http://www.ala.org/ala/mgrps/divs/rusa/sections/rss/rsssection. Accessed January 2011.

Casey, Genevieve M. 1975. Libraries and the aging. In *Encyclopedia of Library and Information Science* 14: 201–304. New York: Marcel Dekker.

Honnold, Rosemary, and Saralyn A. Mesaros. 2004. *Serving Seniors: A How-to-do-it Manual for Librarians.* New York: Neal-Schuman.

SERVICES TO YOUNG ADULTS. *See* SERVICES TO CHILDREN AND YOUNG ADULTS.

SEVEN POINTS, TX. *See* LIBRARY AT CEDAR CREEK LAKE, SEVEN POINTS, TX.

SEWARD COMMUNITY LIBRARY, AK   238 Fifth Ave., Seward, AK 99664. Founded 1930 (date of incorporation), became city department 1988 (information from the library). Population served: 5,000. Circulation: 74,000. Holdings: 30,000. LJ February 15, 2009: 4-star library; November 15, 2009: 3-star library; October 1, 2010: 4-star library.

SEWICKLEY PUBLIC LIBRARY, PA   500 Thorn St., Sewickley, PA 15143. Population served: 13,366. Circulation: 325,015. Holdings: 78,366. The library board has a teen member. LJ February 15, 2009: 3-star library; November 15, 2009, and October 1, 2010: 4-star library.

SHAKER HEIGHTS PUBLIC LIBRARY, OH   16500 Van Aken Blvd., Shaker Heights, OH 44120. Founded 1937. Population served: 32,989. Circulation: 1,138,903. Holdings: 217,324. 1 branch. LJ February 15, 2009; November 15, 2009, and October 1, 2010: 5-star library. HAPLR 2009, 2010.

SHELDON PUBLIC LIBRARY, IA   925 Fourth Ave., Sheldon, IA 51201. Population served: 4,914. Circulation: 66,861. Holdings: 33,782. LJ October 1, 2010: 3-star library.

SHELTER ISLAND PUBLIC LIBRARY SOCIETY, NY   37 N. Ferry Rd., Shelter Island, NY 11964. Founded 1896. Population served: 2,228. Circulation: 36,697. Holdings: 30,652. LJ February 15, 2009: 4-star library.

SHERBURNE MEMORIAL LIBRARY, KILLINGTON, VT   29989 River Rd., Killington, VT 05757. Population served: 1,122. Circulation: 30,110. Holdings: 18,830. LJ February 15, 2009; November 15, 2009, and October 1, 2010: 5-star library.

SHIRLEY, NY. *See* MASTICS-MORICHES-SHIRLEY COMMUNITY LIBRARY, SHIRLEY, NY.

SHUTER LIBRARY OF ANGEL FIRE, ANGEL FIRE, NM   11 S. Angel Fire Rd., Angel Fire, NM 87110. Founded 1978. Population served: 1,118. Circulation: 9,408. Holdings: 10,379. LJ February 15, 2009, and November 15, 2009: 5-star library; October 1, 2010: 3-star library.

SILVERTON PUBLIC LIBRARY, CO   1111 Reese, Silverton, CO 81432. Founded 1906. Population served: 548. Circulation: 36,000. Holdings: 18,000. HALPR 2009, 2010.

SIOUX RAPIDS MEMORIAL LIBRARY, IA   215 Second St., Sioux Rapids, IA 50585. Founded 1928. Population served, 1,199. Circulation 24,800. Holdings: 21,482. LJ October 1, 2010: 3-star library.

SKIDOMPHA PUBLIC LIBRARY, DAMARISCOTTA, ME   184 Main St., Damariscotta, ME 04543. Population served: 5,853. Circulation: 54,389. Holdings: 24,367. IMLS award 2008. LJ October 1, 2010: 4-star library.

SKOKIE PUBLIC LIBRARY, IL   5215 Oakton, Skokie, IL 60077. Founded 1941. Population served: 63,348. Circulation: 1,654,467. Holdings: 421,686. 1 bookmobile. IMLS award 2008. LJ February 15, 2009; November 15, 2009, and October 1, 2010: 4-star library.

SLATER PUBLIC LIBRARY, IA   105 N. Tama St., Slater, IA 50244. Founded 1970. Population served: 1,306. Circulation: 19,460. Holdings: 16,947. LJ February 15, 2009: 4-star library.

SMOKY VALLEY LIBRARY DISTRICT, ROUND MOUNTAIN, NV   73 Hadley Circle, Round Mountain, NV 89045. Population served: 1,868. Circulation: 39,759. Holdings: 35,000. LJ November 15, 2009, and October 1, 2010: 4-star library.

SNOW LIBRARY, ORLEANS, MA   67 Main St., Orleans, MA 02653. Founded 1876. Population served: 6,474. Circulation: 162,725. Holdings: 56,852. LJ November 15, 2009, and October 1, 2010: 3-star library.

SODUS COMMUNITY LIBRARY, NY   17 Maple Ave., Sodus, NY 14551. Founded 1907 as Sodus Circulating Library, with provisional state charter. Absolute charter, 1912; became Sodus Free Library, 1927; became Sodus Community Library, 2009, to serve residents of the school district (information from the library). Population served: 1,735. Circulation: 62,820.

Holdings: 29,425. LJ February 15, 2009; November 15, 2009, and October 1, 2010: 4-star library. HAPLR 2009, 2010.

SOLDOTNA PUBLIC LIBRARY, AK   235 N. Binkley St., Soldotna, AK 99669. Population served: 3,869. Circulation: 101,973. Holdings: 40,372. LJ February 15, 2009; November 15, 2009, and October 1, 2010: 3-star library.

SOMERSET COUNTY LIBRARY SYSTEM, BRIDGEWATER, NJ   One Vogt Dr., Bridgewater, NJ 08807. Founded 1930. Population served: 176,402. Circulation: 1,225,000. Holdings: 615,523. LJ February 15, 2009; November 15, 2009, and October 1, 2010: 3-star library.

SOUND RECORDINGS. *See* MUSIC COLLECTIONS.

SOUTH BEND, IN. *See* ST. JOSEPH COUNTY PUBLIC LIBRARY, SOUTH BEND, IN.

SOUTH HERO COMMUNITY LIBRARY, VT   75 South St., South Hero, VT 05486. Population served: 1,870. Circulation: 16,056. Holdings: 18,693. LJ November 15, 2009: 3-star library.

SOUTHWEST GEORGIA REGIONAL LIBRARY, BAINBRIDGE, GA   301 S. Monroe St., Bainbridge, GA 39819. Population served: 42,769. Circulation: 204,964. Holdings: 150,534. 3 branches, 1 bookmobile. IMLS award 2002.

SPECIAL COLLECTIONS

> The concept of "special collections" can be traced from initial steps at the end of the nineteenth century to identify and segregate rare books (while special collections were in fact subject collections) through the opening of treasure rooms and the organization of rare book departments in the first third of the 20th century to the interest in collecting unpublished source materials since the 1950s. With the increased collecting of a wide diversity of source materials in a multiplicity of formats, the concept of "special collections" has steadily broadened—very much like the scholarship it supports. (Joyce 1994, 597)

In the public library context, a special collection is more likely to be a subject concentration of source materials in a multiplicity of formats than a treasury of rare books, but the large research libraries have the rare books as well. Many of these subject concentrations stem from local industries, like the automotive history collection in the Detroit Public Library, the film and theater collection in the Los Angeles Public Library, and the chocolate collection in the Hershey (PA) Public Library. Others have grown around local persons of importance, like the H. L. Mencken Archives in the Enoch Pratt

Free Library in Baltimore and the John Steinbeck collection in the Salinas (CA) Public Library. Local attractions lead to collections of materials: the Orlando Public Library has a Disney World collection, and Buffalo and the Erie County Public Library has Niagara Falls photographs and prints.

Donors create special collections when they pass along their lifelong acquisitions in favorite topics. John G. White gave his materials on chess and checkers and also on folklore to the Cleveland Public Library. Among the donors of significant music collections were Allen A. Brown (Boston Public Library), Edwin A. Fleisher (Free Library of Philadelphia), and Sadie Coe (Evanston Public Library). Personal hobbies resulted in collections on unusual topics, such as the baseball player photos in the Boston Public Library, shopping bags in the Newark Public Library, and materials on magic in the Providence Public Library. One of the world's largest cookbook collections is in the New York State Library. Consultation of Ash and Miller (1993) will disclose hundreds of public library special collections.

Apart from such important concentrations, there are in nearly all public libraries collections of local history materials, such as newspapers, directories, academic yearbooks, and photographs. A natural interest in the past of one's community blends with a wish to learn about one's family history. Local history is often paired with genealogy to make a separate section or room. Genealogy, the "study and investigation of ancestry and family histories" (*American Heritage*), is a new national pastime. One survey reported that more than 120 million Americans had expressed interest in their family roots (Davidsson 2004, 142). Public libraries can help people get started in family research and in some cases can offer enough source material for extended investigations. A library wanting to provide a strong service in genealogy is well served by the Reference and User Services Association guidelines (American Library Association 1999) and documents issued by the National Genealogical Society (http://www.ngs genealogy.org) and the Association of Professional Genealogists (http://www.apgen.org).

Staff need training and patrons need guidance if a genealogical collection is to fulfill its promise. Complex tools are available, such as vital statistics issued by states and municipalities, U.S. military records, immigration and naturalization documents, and cemetery directories. Libraries may provide online access to databases that assemble blocks of these data. For example, the Chicago Public Library offers *Heritage Quest Online*, which includes indexing to 2.3 million articles; *Chicago Tribune* obituaries from 1849 to 1987; and *Ancestry Library Edition*, which contains Social Security death notices, immigration records, and draft registrations. While most public libraries have to be content with knowing about such sources and directing patrons to them, some attempt to collect research materials in quantity, print and online, and provide guidance to patrons using them. The Allen County Public Library, Fort Wayne, IN, is a strong example. Major collections of genealogy, while not parts of public libraries, are open for public use. The Family History Library of the Church of Jesus Christ of Latter-Day Saints in Salt Lake City is the largest of its kind. Chicago's Newberry Library has a notable research collection.

The rare books aspect mentioned at the start of this entry is limited to larger public libraries. Manuscripts, first editions, diaries, incunabula, and other items of scarcity and value may be segregated into a department with controlled atmospheric conditions (see PRESERVATION) and trained staff.

Some public library topical special collections are large enough to have their own buildings (see MUSIC COLLECTIONS; SERVICES TO BUSINESS AND INDUSTRY).

References

American Library Association. Reference and User Services Association. 1999. Guidelines for developing beginning genealogical collections and services. *Reference & User Services Quarterly* 39, no. 1 (Fall): 23–24.

Ash, Lee, and William G. Miller. 1993. *Subject Collections: A Guide to Special Book Collections and Subject Emphases as Reported by University, College, Public, and Special Libraries and Museums in the United States and Canada.* 7th ed. New Providence, NJ: R. R. Bowker.

Davidsson, Robert I. 2004. Providing genealogy research services in public libraries: Guidelines and ethics. *Public Libraries* 43, no. 3 (May/June): 142–44.

Joyce, William L. 1994. Special collections. In *Encyclopedia of Library History*, 595–97. New York: Garland.

Morgan, George G. 2009. *Genealogy.* 2nd ed. New York: McGraw-Hill.

SPECIAL SERVICES

Terminology

The services of a public library are organized under various headings. Technical services refers to acquisitions, cataloging, serials, and related areas. Public services refers to activities that involve direct contact with patrons, such as reference and readers' advisory; it divides into adult services and youth services. Administrative services refers to management support areas like human resources and buildings. The category of special services identifies groups of patrons with particular needs and interests. Today this category is often named "outreach services." Library organization charts indicate uncertainty over the prominence of these services; in most of the charts examined, neither special services nor outreach services appears. In some charts outreach has a low-level box; in one it exists only under youth services. When outreach does appear, it may suggest a sphere of activities limited to some kind of "disadvantaged" users. The *ODLIS* definition of outreach is "library programs and services designed to meet the information needs of users who are unserved or underserved, for example those who are visually impaired, homebound, institutionalized, not fluent in the national language, illiterate, or marginalized in some other way" (see OUTREACH).

There still needs to be a term to encompass groups of patrons who are not necessarily disadvantaged but who have particular needs and interests, such as businesspeople, Hispanics, and seniors. Special services seems acceptable, although it is no longer in common use. *See also* SERVICES TO AFRICAN AMERICANS; SERVICES TO BUSINESS AND INDUSTRY; SERVICES TO CHILDREN AND YOUNG ADULTS; SERVICES TO GAY, LESBIAN, BISEXUAL, AND TRANSGENDERED PERSONS; SERVICES TO HIS-PANICS; SERVICES TO IMMIGRANTS; SERVICES TO NATIVE AMER-ICANS; SERVICES TO PEOPLE WITH DISABILITIES; SERVICES TO SENIORS.

SPENCER COUNTY PUBLIC LIBRARY, ROCKPORT, IN   210 Walnut St., Rockport, IN 47635. Population served: 9,393. Circulation: 177,736. Hold-ings: 87,102. LJ February 15, 2009; November 15, 2009, and October 1, 2010: 5-star library.

SPRINGFIELD, IL. *See* LINCOLN LIBRARY, SPRINGFIELD, IL.

SPRINGMEIER COMMUNITY LIBRARY, TIFFIN, IA   311 W. Marengo Rd., Tiffin, IA 52340. Population served: 1,032. Circulation: 5,632. Holdings: 7,627. LJ November 15, 2009: 5-star library.

STAFFING

Terminology

The basic vocabulary of this area is shared by many fields. "To staff" is "to supply with a staff or with workers." The "staff" consists of "personnel who assist a director in carrying out an assigned task" and "personnel" means "a body of persons employed (as in a factory, office, or organization" (all from *Merriam*). Thus, staffing is the activity of providing personnel to do the work of an organization. Recently the term "personnel" has been super-seded in organizational contexts by "human resources." *Merriam* traces "human resources" to 1961 and defines it as equivalent to "personnel." A clear preference for the new term was exhibited in 1989 when the American Society for Personnel Administration changed its name to the American Society for Human Resources Management (Stueart and Moran 2007, 205). The switch has not been universal, and there remains in the federal government the Office for Personnel Management and such other units as the Civilian Personnel Office in the Department of the Army. In any case, the old word "personnel" is still applied to the staff itself.

In libraries, the staff consists of professional librarians and support per-sonnel. A professional librarian is, in current thinking, a person who holds a master's degree in library science or one of the "information" fields (Stueart and Moran 2007, 211). Support personnel may include persons with varied backgrounds: some with minimal education, others with advanced degrees. What the librarians do, according to the U.S. Bureau of Labor Statistics, is "administer library services; provide library patrons access to or instruction in accessing library resources; and select, acquire, process, and organize library materials and collections for patron use" (U.S. Department of Labor 2007, code 31502A). The tasks of a librarian are often carried out by individuals who do not have the library degree, bringing up the question of their status as "professional librarians" and rendering problematic the division of staff into "professional" and "support." It may be as well to set aside the educational qualification matter and concentrate on tasks performed by types of personnel in the library.

Support staff include persons with such designations as "paraprofessional," "clerical," "technical assistant," "library assistant," and "specialist." U.S. Department of Labor (2007, code 31505) states that "technical assistants, library": "assist librarians by furnishing information on library sciences, facilities, and rules; by assisting readers in the use of card catalogs and indexes to locate books and other materials; and by answering questions that require only brief consultation of standard reference. May catalog books or train and supervise clerical staff." Technical assistants may also be identified as "library technicians." While "paraprofessional" is a term that covers technicians, it is not used to label specific work. Thus, while there are "paramedics" and "paralegals" whose work can be described, there are no "paralibrarians," except in the sense that the expression would include all support staff.

A "library assistant" is described in the U.S. Department of Labor (2007, code 249.367–046) as equivalent to "library clerk" or "library attendant." Most of the work done by persons in this category is basic routine: shelving, writing overdues, issuing library cards, answering directional inquiries, repairing books, and typing.

In view of the general acceptance of "information science" as a partner occupational category for library science (*see* INFORMATION SCIENCE), it is of interest to see how the U.S. Department of Labor (2007, code 109.067-010) describes the work of an "information scientist":

> Designs information system to provide management or clients with specific data from computer storage, utilizing knowledge of electronic data processing principles, mathematics, and computer capabilities. Develops and designs methods and procedures for collecting, organizing, interpreting, and classifying information for input into computer and retrieval of specific information from computer, utilizing knowledge of symbolic language and optical or pattern recognition principles. Develops alternate designs to resolve problems in input, storage, and retrieval of information.

It is from this array of occupations that a library staff will be assembled. "Occupation" refers to a general category of work. Two other terms emerge from it: "job" (a group of positions with similar duties) and "position" (the work assignment of one person).

The Staffing Process

The first thing to do in staffing a library is to decide what jobs to include. If the whole staff will consist of one person, which is the situation of many very small public libraries, a single job will have to suffice, under the name of "librarian." That person, regardless of qualifications, will have to carry out the duties of support staff as well as management activities. If the situation allows for more than one person, the next question is "how many?" This decision is easier to deal with in a small library with very limited resources than in a larger library with more staffing options. There are no standards or guidelines to help here and no research on the topic (Lynch 2003). Two useful principles would be "form follows function" and "examine practice elsewhere." A library's function, which is what it does or will be doing, is obviously the baseline for staffing decisions. The function is derived from the mission and translates into goals, objectives, and actions (*see* PLAN-NING). What other libraries are doing would seem easier to observe since there are statistics on staff compiled by various agencies. For example, 75 percent of libraries serving 1 million or more persons have less that 0.51 staff per 1,000 persons served, whereas 25 percent of those libraries have between 0.51 and 1.00 staff per 1,000 persons served (Lynch 2003, 2). So a library in a community of 1 million would probably have no more than 1,000 staff and in most cases would have less than 500 staff. Actual figures from *American Library Directory (ALD)* for a few such public libraries offer a widely variable perspective. Looking at seven that serve populations in the range 800,000 to 1.5 million, we find the staff number as follows: San Diego, 330; San Antonio, 130; Dallas, 125; Philadelphia, 841; Atlanta, 454; Las Vegas 102; and Cincinnati, 836. The library with the largest population served and that reported staff size to *ALD* is Los Angeles; just 443 persons look after the community of 4.3 million. Evidently the answer to "how many staff?" will not be extracted easily from what is happening elsewhere.

So the managerial task of organizing (*see* MANAGEMENT AND ORGANIZATION) needs to precede the task of staffing. In a sense the library administration creates an organization chart that shows what "jobs" will be necessary for the library to operate. Then those jobs will be named according to their functions, not according to the title or ranking of the presumed hold-ers of the jobs. The function "circulation department" might be staffed by one circulation librarian, by a librarian plus technical assistants, or entirely by technical assistants. The determination of who fills the box "circulation department" is made on the basis of volume of work and available funds. To rationalize the array of job titles and functions in the library, the American Library Association (ALA) adopted a statement in 1969 entitled "Library Education and Personnel Utilization." The statement included a "lattice" with

> five levels of personnel, two professional and three support staff
> ...: senior librarian/senior specialist; librarian/specialist; library
> associate/associate specialist; library technical assistant/technical

assistant; and clerk. Library-related and nonlibrary qualifications were defined at each level, confirming the trend toward the employment of specialists without library credentials. The designations "librarian" and "specialist" were reserved for those personnel who engage in tasks requiring independent judgment, analytical skills, and the creative application of general principles. (Young 1994, 391)

In 2002, the ALA renamed the document as *Library and Information Studies and Human Resource Utilization: A Statement of Policy* (ALA 2002).

Funding for staff, in the context of total library funding, is another topic without clear rules. The figures compiled by the U.S. National Center for Education Statistics (NCES 2008, table 10) for fiscal year 2005 reveal a pattern that reflects a long tradition in public libraries: as percents of total expenditures, libraries used 65.9 percent for staff, 13.2 percent for collections, and 20.9 percent for other categories. But there appears to be a trend toward reducing the percent allocated to staff. A recent recommendation is for 33 percent to staff, 50 percent to materials (collections), and 17 percent for other categories (Stueart and Moran 2007, 211). And current practice as displayed in *ALD* figures show this reduction from the established (approximately) 65 percent. A selection of five libraries gives the staff percent of total expenditures as follows: Montclair, NJ, 54 percent; Oakland, CA, 46 percent; Nashville, 43 percent; Cincinnati, 47 percent; and Olean, NY, 41 percent.

Considering the librarian and support staff proportion, the NCES (2008, table 8) reported that of a total U.S. public library staff of 137,855 in fiscal year 2005, there were 45,354 (36 percent) classed as librarians, and 68 percent of those librarians had master's degrees (the NCES survey for fiscal year 1993 gave nearly identical percentages). We cannot readily scan the immediate situation in particular libraries since the *ALD* responses to separation of staff into professional and support are not reliable. But a recent survey indicates that core functions are being transferred from master's-degree librarians to persons without degrees. In 88 percent of responding libraries, nondegree persons do some of the reference work, and in 65 percent, they do some of the materials selection. Only 61 percent said that the master's degree is a necessary requirement for a branch head (at the New York Public Library the new title for branch head is "site manager": a job open to nondegree holders). Although the preferred master's degree is still the master of library science (or one with "information" in it), three-fourths of the respondents in the survey said they also hire persons with master's degrees in other fields (*Library Journal*, June 1, 2009, 44–46).

From all these numbers there emerges a somewhat typical image of public library staffing. The staff will require around 50 to 60 percent of the library's total expenditures. About one-third of the staff will be librarians, with the rest in the support category. There is a trend toward engaging non–master's degree holders as librarians and a trend toward giving more "professional" duties to nondegreed staff.

With the library organization chart in place and all these fiscal considerations in mind, the administration is ready to identify the "jobs" that will activate each function in the chart; the results are job titles. Here there is a burgeoning practice that departs from tradition. The standard job titles of the past have been of this nature: reference librarian, catalog librarian, children's librarian, interlibrary loan librarian, and so on. Lately those designations have often been renamed, not to everyone's satisfaction. Michael Gorman (2005) has decried "a virtually meaningless term such as 'information management specialist' for 'librarian" and titles that refer to "access services" or "information delivery services." Why change, he asks, terms that are familiar to everyone, like "reference," "circulation," and "cataloging"? (57–58). In any case, the heart of the job is in the description that fills out the title. The description lists the activities of the job, notes its place in the hierarchy of the organization, and expresses some of the qualifications of persons doing the job. All the library's job descriptions will encompass the entire work to be done in fulfilling its mission. The ALA has published a volume on personnel procedures that includes suggested work forms; it gives attention to job descriptions (Goodrich and Singer 2007).

A job description may apply to one or more positions, which are the work assignments of individuals. As individuals are recruited to fill positions, the job description is the basis for a vacancy notice. This notice may be published or simply posted in the library; in the former case it is assumed that the position may be filled from outside the library; in the latter it is expected that only current staff will be aware of the notice. It is sometimes necessary to change an internal posting to a public advertisement if there is insufficient interest from qualified persons on the current staff. In writing the vacancy notice, it is necessary to observe federal and local regulations; the notice may not suggest any preferences or limitations on hiring that involve race, color, religion, gender, age, disability, or national origin. Librarians have been concerned recently to enhance racial and ethnic diversity on their staffs, but this aspiration cannot be implemented through preferential hiring. In fact, a study made in 2005 reveals that libraries are already diverse in the sense that staff characteristics reflect the national picture among individuals with appropriate qualifications for librarian positions or support positions (Lance 2005).

As applications come in, a number of steps usually follow. Those who will make the selection (usually the direct supervisor with a staff committee) review the applicant pool and identify the most promising persons. A screening of the promising group, usually by telephone, may take place. Checking of credentials is done. A small number of the most qualified persons (perhaps four or five) are invited for interviews. There are various interview styles, but all of them are focused on the tasks to be performed, not on the personal life of the applicant. Selection is made after the final interview.

Orientation and training of new staff are standard personnel procedures (a useful checklist for these activities is in Stueart and Moran 2007, 238). Old and new staff need the means to expand their professional knowledge, especially in relation to their work assignments. Courses, workshops, and presentations are available to public library staff from various sources. The ALA began to offer guidance in this area in 1975, with the establishment of CLENE (Continuing Library Education Network and Exchange). In 2009 that unit changed its name to LearnRT (for a discussion of directing and controlling staff, with a discussion of staff participation, *see* MANAGEMENT AND ORGANIZATION).

The next large field of attention is performance appraisal (PA), also known as performance evaluation. PA serves three purposes: it determines what personnel action to take regarding an employee, it provides the employee with motivation for improved performance, and it produces information that will help in review and revision of the personnel system. Two types of PA are found in libraries: formal and informal. A formal PA is held on a regular schedule, usually once a year, the schedule being known to the employees. An informal PA is without a regular schedule, when the supervisor thinks it is needed. As to content, a formal PA has written guidelines for the employee's work, a confidential, documented meeting between supervisor and employee, and appropriate follow-up actions. The informal PA amounts to an unstructured critique of the employee's work. Whether to follow a formal or an informal approach to PA is a management decision, but in libraries with more than a few workers the formal path is usually followed, and it is that type that is discussed here.

A job description is essentially a goal statement: it points out what is intended to happen in general terms. It cannot be used to evaluate results, which are specific events. But the job description may be the basis for "performance standards." For example, a job description for acquisitions librarian might read, "Under the general supervision of the head of Technical Services, trains and supervises acquisitions staff, orders library materials, pays invoices, prepares reports of expenditure, and does related work as required." For clarity and for ease of appraisal, those duties may be clustered under a few task headings, also known as elements, each of which identifies a group of related activities. This job could have the task headings (elements): training, supervising, ordering, paying, and reporting. Each task leads to specific performance standards. The supervisor rates job performance according to the standards.

It is an unsettled issue whether those performance standards should be relatively structured or unstructured. The more structured they are, the more objective and the less likely they are to depend on personal opinions in the rating process. However, it is difficult to develop highly structured standards that will be acceptable to the employees and indeed to write them at all. Modern texts and guidelines usually settle for less structured standards (e.g., Goodson 1997, in which all the proposed standards are unstructured). An example of an unstructured standard for the acquisitions librarian, task heading "training," would be as follows: "Gives proper orientation and job instruction to new employees in the department in timely fashion." A fully structured version would be as follows: "Gives proper orientation and job instruction to new employees in the department, individually or in groups, doing so for each person during the first week of employment, and receiving no more than three supervisor criticisms for failing to do so during the rating period."

Each of the task headings, or elements, has its standards. Certain headings may identify realms of the work that are essential to it; they are named "critical." On the basis of the number and kind of standards that are met (or not met) or exceeded, the supervisor rates the employee according to a scheme such as "outstanding," "excellent," "very good," "satisfactory," "marginal," or "unsatisfactory," If the employee is rated unsatisfactory in a critical element, the work is not being done, and the employee needs to be retrained, transferred, or even terminated. None of these disciplinary actions may be taken without serious counseling, opportunity to improve performance, and a careful management record of those procedures. In a library with a human resources office, that unit should be involved in difficult cases.

PA is difficult, time consuming, and often distressing to employees; it is not surprising that librarians—following total quality management principles—might wish to avoid it entirely. Still, decisions have to be made about which employees to reward, promote, retrain, and so on. And there is the point of employee motivation, which results in part from favorable appraisals. Furthermore, the outcomes of performance appraisal may lead to reconsideration by management of the personnel system itself.

It was noted that one reason for PA is to provide employees with motivation for improved performance. Motivation is a characteristic of the worker, not an activity of the manager. One definition of motivation is "a willingness to expend energy to achieve a goal or a reward" (Stueart and Moran 2007, 304). Although managers cannot produce such willingness in the workforce, they can optimize the conditions that will inspire people to "expend energy." Some working conditions are potentially negative with regard to motivation but have little positive meaning. Frederick Herzberg and colleagues (1959) called them "hygiene factors"; today they might be "environmental factors." They include cleanliness, safety, noise, lighting, temperature, air quality, equipment, privacy, parking, status symbols, and the general atmosphere of the library. If any of these factors are weak, employees will suffer diminished motivation. But even if they are all favorable, they will not in themselves increase motivation; favorable environmental factors are usually taken for granted. The true motivating factors have to do with the content of the work. Herzberg and colleagues listed these: opportunity for achievement, responsibility, recognition, advancement, and personal growth. Other writers have considered salary to be an important motivator, but there is uncertainty about this since it seems that employees accept salary increases somewhat like favorable environmental factors: they take the new salary for granted.

Relations with fellow workers are important as well but are generally beyond the control of management, except that discriminatory or harassing actions must be stopped. Motivation can improve with flexible work schedules, with job enlargement (not just piling on extra duties), with efforts to reduce stress, with opportunity to make more decisions about the work, with explanation of the meaning of the work to others, and with continued feedback. If one concept is dominant in motivation theory, it is that all people want to have their self-esteem protected and enhanced (all aspects of job satisfaction are covered by Sager 1982).

Recent Trends

The above account has identified some of the current issues before the profession. Essentially the concerns of the past decade or so have centered on the transfer of tasks from librarians to support staff and the proportional reduction in library expenditure for staff of all types. With the growing focus on support staff, there has been a concomitant interest in training of that group. Particular attention has turned on persons serving at the lowest compensation levels: clerical employees and library assistants. A 2008 article dealt concisely with questions of motivation and worker satisfaction at those levels (Morrison 2008). Circulation staff may need special consideration since they present an image of the library to the patron. They have been regarded as requiring the least qualifications and people skills—in contrast, as one writer notes, to the sales desk employees in a bookstore (Woodward 2005, 32). Indeed, all library workers might benefit from attention to improved interactions with patrons since users have recorded considerable dissatisfaction with their librarian encounters (only 36 percent were satisfied with their most recent library experience, and only 11 percent had positive associations with library staff; *Perceptions of Libraries and Information Resources* 2005, items 2.26 and 3.21).

Flexibility and willingness to multitask are the optimal qualities of librarians and support staff as the profession adjusts to economic conditions and technological change.

References

Four useful sources not cited above are Creth (1986), Avery et al. (2001), Mayo and Goodrich (2002), and Evans and Ward (2007).

American Library Association. 2002. *Library and Information Studies and Human Resource Utilization: A Statement of Policy.* Chicago: American Library Association. http://www.ala.org/ala/hrdr/educprofdev/lepu. Accessed February 2010.

Avery, Elizabeth Fuseler, et al. 2001. *Staff Development: A Practical Guide.* 3rd ed. Prepared by the Staff Development Committee, Human Resources Section, Library Administration and Management Association, American Library Association. Chicago: American Library Association. Includes an annotated bibliography, pp. 174–82.

Brumley, Rebecca R. 2005. *The Neal-Schuman Directory of Public Library Job \Descriptions.* New York: Neal-Schuman.

Creth, Sheila D. 1986. *Effective On-the-Job Training: Developing Library Human Resources.* Chicago: American Library Association.

Evans, G. Edward. 2004. *Performance Management and Appraisal*. New York: Neal-Schuman.

Evans, G. Edward, and Patricia Layzell Ward. 2007. *Management Basics for Information Professionals*. 2nd ed. New York: Neal-Schuman.

Goodrich, Jeanne, and Paula M. Singer. 2007. *Human Resources for Results: The Right Person for the Right Job*. Chicago: American Library Association.

Goodson, Carol. 1997. *The Complete Guide to Performance Standards for Library Personnel*. New York: Neal-Schuman.

Gorman, Michael. 2005. *Our Own Selves: More Meditations for Librarians*. Chicago: American Library Association.

Herzberg, Frederick et al. 1959. *The Motivation to Work*. 2nd ed. New York: Wiley.

Lance, Keith Curry. 2005. Racial and ethnic diversity of U.S. library workers. *American Libraries* 36, no. 5 (May): 41–43.

Lynch, Mary Jo. 2003. Public library staff: How many is enough? *American Libraries* 34, no. 5 (May): 58–59.

Mayo, Diane, and Jeanne Goodrich. 2002. *Staffing for Results: A Guide to Working Smarter*. Chicago: American Library Association.

Morrison, Douglas. 2008. In the name of service. *American Libraries* 39, no. 6 (June/July): 51.

Perceptions of Libraries and Information Resources: A Report to the OCLC Membership. 2005. Dublin, OH: OCLC. http://www.oclc.org/reports/2005. Accessed December 2009.

Sager, Donald J. 1982. *Participatory Management in Libraries*. Metuchen, NJ: Scarecrow Press.

Stueart, Robert D., and Barbara Moran. 2007. *Library and Information Center Management*. 7th ed. Westport, CT: Libraries Unlimited.

U.S. Department of Labor. 2007. *Dictionary of Occupational Titles*. 4th ed. Washington, DC: U.S. Department of Labor, Bureau of Labor Statistics. http://www.occupationalinfo.org. Accessed February 2010.

U.S. National Center for Education Statistics. 2008. *Public Libraries in the United States: Fiscal Year 2005*. Washington, DC: U.S. Department of Education.

Woodward, Jeanette. 2005. *Creating the Customer-driven Library: Building on the Bookstore Model*. Chicago: American Library Association.

Young, Arthur P. 1994. Library staffing patterns. In *Encyclopedia of Library History*, 387–94. New York: Garland.

STAFFORD, KS. *See* NORA E. LARABEE MEMORIAL LIBRARY, STAFFORD, KS.

STAMFORD, CT. *See* FERGUSON LIBRARY, STAMFORD, CT.

STANDARDS. *See* EVALUATION.

STARK COUNTY DISTRICT LIBRARY, CANTON, OH   715 Market Ave. N, Canton, OH 44702. Population served: 258,311. Circulation: 4,600,000. Holdings: 1,250,000. 10 branches, 4 bookmobiles. IMLS award 2009. LJ February 15, 2009: 4-star library; November 15, 2009, and October 1, 2010: 5-star library. HAPLR 2009, 2010.

STATE LIBRARY AGENCIES

Terminology

Each of the 50 states has one or more units of government with the responsibilities of meeting the information needs of legislators and officials, administering library services to the blind and physically handicapped, providing library services to state institutions, and advancing public library development through finance and guidance. The nomenclature for those units is somewhat dense. One common name is "state library," defined in *ODLIS* as "a library supported by state funds for the use of state employees and citizens, usually located in the state capital, containing a comprehensive collection of the state's official documents." This description suggests a large structure in the civic center of the capital, convenient to the state legislature and government offices, and that is the case in many of the states (e.g., New York, Illinois, California, and Ohio). But a state library may be a small organization with few staff and a modest collection (e.g., Georgia and Massachusetts) offering only basic service to government employees. Some state libraries do not have "state" in their names: Library of Michigan and Library of Virginia. All state libraries have legal collections; indeed state library agencies began as law libraries (see the section "Historical Summary" below).

What every state has is an office that advances public library development in the state. This office provides consultant services, keeps statistics, distributes financial aid from state and federal sources, and runs various programs for the benefit of libraries around the state. The name of this office is variable; it usually carries the term "division," "department," or "commission." Examples are the Delaware Division of Libraries, Oklahoma Department of Libraries, and Nebraska Library Commission. In some states, such as Ohio, this development office is a unit in the state library; in others, such as Massachusetts, it is a separate entity. State development offices gained prominence with the passage of the Library Services Act in 1956 since they were the designated channels for applications and appropriations.

The principal officer of the state library or commission may be called state librarian, director, commissioner, or executive secretary. In Illinois the secretary of state is also the state librarian.

Historical Summary

In the early years of the republic, state legislators realized that they needed collections of legal materials to support their work. Pennsylvania established the first state library in 1816, followed by Ohio in 1817 and New York, New Hampshire, and Illinois in 1818. By 1829 all 24 states had such libraries, which were essentially law libraries. Most of them expanded their collections beyond legal works to state and local records, federal documents, and general reference materials. An active reference service emerged in many libraries. Melvil Dewey, New York state librarian (1888–1905), created the position of legislative reference librarian. Dewey also established a children's library (1898) on the fifth floor of the Capitol building, under direction of the library school (which he directed), staffed by students. The New York State Library had a half million volumes in the mid-1890s, ranking fifth in size among U.S. libraries of all types.

The concept of library development as a state responsibility arose later in the century. State library agencies or commissions were established in Rhode Island, 1875; Massachusetts, 1890; New Hampshire, 1891; Vermont, 1895; Wisconsin, 1895; Ohio, 1896; Georgia, 1897; Indiana, 1899; Maine, 1899; Colorado, 1899; Pennsylvania, 1899; Kansas, 1899; and Michigan, 1899. Formation of such commissions continued to 1949, when Arizona created the last of them. One early initiative of the development agencies was the traveling library: a carton of books sent to remote parts of the state that were otherwise unserved. Again it was Melvil Dewey leading the way (1893), followed by Michigan (1895). Those programs evolved into book wagons and bookmobile services (see BOOKMOBILES).

James Louis Gillis, state librarian of California (1899–1917), was a vibrant leader of the state library movement. He worked to rationalize state laws that affected libraries, set up traveling libraries, circulated Braille books, wrote a newsletter, and promoted county libraries (see entry for him). Another pioneer was Essae M. Culver, first state librarian of Louisiana (1925); she organized demonstration projects that led to tax levies and permanent library service (see entry for her.)

The American Library Association (ALA) had a state library section in 1889. It evolved into the American Association of State Librarians, then into a division called the Association of Specialized and Cooperative Library Agencies, State Library Agency Section (ASCLA). The ALA published an important review of *The Library Functions of the States* (Monypenny and Garrison 1966) and proposed standards for state library agencies (ALA, AASL 1970; ALA, ASCLA 1985).

Current Situation

State library agencies have been damaged by budgetary reductions but remain strong, in large part because they handle federal funds that come through the Library Services and Technology Act (LSTA) of 1966. In fiscal year 2010 the appropriation under the act was $213,523,000 (*see* GOVERNMENT ROLE). The kinds of activities financed by LSTA, and with state funds, are exemplified by programs in three state libraries reported in a *Public Libraries* article (Hilyard 2006). The California State Library produces research and data reports for state officials. It dispenses financial aid to libraries, offers consultant assistance, serves blind and disabled persons, operates a research bureau, gives students online tutoring, and boosts diversity and informational literacy. The Illinois State Library has a special interest in training librarians; nearly 2,000 persons have joined online training sessions on topics like automation, collection development, preservation, grant preparation, interlibrary loan, and new technologies. Weeklong institutes are held for library directors and conferences for government document librarians. Fifteen scholarships are awarded annually for library school students. There are grants and programs to enhance literacy and workplace skills.

North Dakota State Library provides cataloging services to libraries across the state, helping them to add their catalogs to the Online Dakota Information Network. Several online databases have been created. A radio information service broadcasts daily with local news, senior center activities, and content aimed at persons with disabilities.

Many state libraries have substantial subject collections that represent the culture and history of their state and region. The Indiana State Library, for example, has extensive coverage of Indiana authors, books about Indiana, city directories and telephone books, county histories, biographies, maps and atlases, state documents since the mid-1800s, photographs, sheet music, private papers, Civil War diaries and letters, and papers of political figures. The newspaper collection holds nearly 100,000 reels of microfilm. Genealogy is one of the principal strengths (Brooker 2008).

The ALA remains active in the state library arena. It published a compilation of American library laws (Ladenson 1983) and, through ASCLA, revised standards for state agencies (Himmel and Wilson 2000). An independent group named the Chief Officers of State Library Agencies promotes cooperation among state libraries and addresses issues of common concern; it holds annual meetings.

References

American Library Association, American Association of State Librarians. 1970. *Standards for Library Functions at the State Level*. Chicago: American Library Association.

Association of Specialized and Cooperative Library Agencies. 1985. *Standards for Library Functions at the State Level*. 3rd ed. Chicago: American Library Association.

Brooker, Roberta L. 2008. The Indiana State Library: Open for exploration. *Indiana Libraries* 27, no. 1: 92–93.

Hilyard, Nann Blaine. 2006. State libraries. *Public Libraries* 45, no. 5 (September/October): 18–24.

Himmel, Ethel E. 1994. State library agencies in the United States. In *Encyclopedia of Library History*: 602–04. New York: Garland.

Himmel, Ethel E., and William J. Wilson. 2000. *The Functions and Roles of State Library Agencies*. Chicago: American Library Association.

Ladenson, Alex. 1983. *American Library Laws*. 5th ed. Chicago: American Library Association.

Monypenny, Phillip. 1975. Library functions of the states. In *Encyclopedia of Library and Information Science* 15: 264–81. New York: Marcel Dekker.

Monypenny, Phillip, and Guy Garrison. 1966. *The Library Functions of the States*. Chicago: American Library Association.

STATISTICS

Terminology

Statistics are "numerical data" (*American Heritage*) or "a collection of quantitative data" (*Merriam*). Two types of statistics are collected about public libraries: individual library data and collective data. Individual library data are the foundation of scientific management. They are used in planning, budgeting, reporting, and public relations. A library's governing authority may require certain categories of data, and governmental or grant agencies and library associations may do so as well. As a minimum, a public library director maintains data series showing the number of card holders, circulation, inquiries, computer use, holdings, budget, and events. These areas have subcategories. Recently public libraries have issued data to demonstrate the cash value of their services (*see* PUBLIC RELATIONS).

Individual library statistics may be compiled to exhibit the quantitative situation at various geographic levels (state, regional, and national). For the most part such compilations have been created by state and federal agencies. Statistical reports may be accompanied by interpretations, comparative evaluations, and other commentary.

Historical Summary

Charles Coffin Jewett made the earliest survey of American public libraries, collecting basic data for a report he issued in 1831. Subsequently the education department of the federal government (under its varying names; *See* GOVERNMENT ROLE) gathered and published library statistics. This is a chronology of early federal reports.

> 1850—*List of Public Libraries in the United States, with the Number of Volumes of Printed Books in Each, Reported to the Smithsonian Institution, January 1950.* Washington, DC: Buell & Blanchard.

> 1870—*Report of the Commissioner of Education for the Year 1870.* Washington, DC: Government Printing Office. Gave founding dates, volumes, and acquisitions for the year; covered 161 libraries.

> 1876—*Public Libraries in the United States of America: Their History, Condition, and Management.* Special report, parts 1 and 2, of the Bureau of Education. Washington, DC: Government Printing Office. Included a 131-page list of 3,647 libraries holding at least 300 volumes; aggregate holdings of 12,276,964 volumes (on the criteria for inclusion, see McMullen 2000).

> 1886—*Statistics of Public Libraries in the United States.* In the report of the Commissioner of Education for the year 1884–1885. Washington, DC: Government Printing Office.

1888—Data on 670 public libraries were included in the Bureau of Education report.

1893—*Statistics of Public Libraries in the United States and Canada.* Washington, DC: Government Printing Office.

1897—*Public, Society, and School Libraries, in the United States, with Library Statistics and Legislation of the Various States.* Washington, DC: Government Printing Office.

1897—*Statistics of Libraries and Library Legislation in the United States.* From the report of the Commissioner of Education for 1895–1896. Washington, DC: Government Printing Office.

1901—*Public, Society, and School Libraries.* Washington, DC: Government Printing Office.

1904—*Public, Society, and School Libraries.* Washington, DC: Government Printing Office.

1909—*Statistics of Public, Society, and School Libraries having 5,000 Volumes and Over in 1908.* Office of Education Bulletin 1909, no. 5. Washington, DC: Government Printing Office.

1916–1958—*Biennial Survey of Education in the United States.* Issued as part of Office of Education Bulletin series, 1916/1918–1936/1938, then as an independent series, 1938/1940–1956/1958. Discontinued. Washington, DC: Government Printing Office.

1926—*A Survey of Libraries in the United States* published in four volumes by the American Library Association (ALA).

1931—*Statistics of Public, Society, and School Libraries, 1929.* Office of Education Bulletin, 2930, no. 37. Washington, DC: Government Printing Office.

1936—*The Equal Chance: Books Help to Make It* published by the ALA, revised in 1943 and supplemented in 1947. Gave public library circulation data, holdings, and expenditures by state.

When a library unit began operating within the Office of Education in 1939, data gathering became more systematic. Comprehensive statistical surveys were issued for 1938/1939, 1944/1945, 1950, 1955/1956, and 1962. Basic data surveys covering various types of public libraries and systems appeared regularly as well. The National Center for Education Statistics (NCES) issued surveys of public libraries in 1974 and 1978.

Current Reports

The computer age brought new capabilities. In 1985 a pilot project to standardize the collection of public library data by state library agencies was developed by the NCES and the ALA. A legislative mandate to collect public library statistics was in the 1988 amendments to the Elementary and Secondary School Act and later in the National Education Statistics Act of 1994 and the Education Sciences Reform Act of 2002. In 1989, the NCES developed a software program for states to use in collecting individual library data and generating statistical tables. Later programs have given the public online access to data about individual libraries as well as aggregate data.

In 1991, the NCES issued *Public Libraries in 50 States and the District of Columbia: 1989*. This was the first of a series of annual reports that continued to fiscal year (FY) 2005. On October 1, 2007, the survey was transferred from the NCES to the Institute of Museum and Library Services (IMLS). IMLS has issued reports for FY 2006 (published 2008), 2007 (published 2009, revised 2010), and 2008 (published 2010).

The Public Library Association, a division of the ALA, issues annual surveys of public libraries (*Public Library Data Service, 1988–*). These are sample surveys that bring responses from about a thousand libraries, including most of those serving populations of 100,000 or more and all those serving 1 million or more. Data given for each library relate to income sources, operating expenditures, and measures of operating expenditures. The ALA has also issued trend statistics in *The Condition of U.S. Libraries: Trends, 1999–2009* (Davis 2009a) and *The Condition of U.S. Libraries: Public Library Trends, 2002–2009* (Davis 2009b). The ALA Office for Research and Statistics, which issued these studies, also offers an annual report: *Libraries Connect Communities: Public Library Funding and Technology Access Study* (ALA, *Libraries Connect Communities*, 2008–).

Statistical Picture of Public Libraries

Because the historical sources cited above worked from variable definitions (*see* PUBLIC LIBRARY) and with different collection methods, comparisons from one year or period to another are suspect. It is more secure to examine trends in the recent era, specifically since the NCES initiated the *Public Libraries Survey* in 1991 (the first covering FY 1989). A selection of data from NCES and IMLS reports for FY 1993, 2005, and 2008 displays the recent lines of development.

	FY 1993	FY 2005	FY 2008
Number of public libraries (administrative entities)	8,929	9,198	9,221
Number of branches	7,017	7,503	7,629
Percent municipal	56 percent	53 percent	52.9 percent
Percent county	12 percent	10 percent	9.8 percent
Percent library districts	4 percent	14 percent	14.6 percent
Total income	$5 billion	$9.7 billion	$11.4 billion
Operating expenditures	4.7 billion	$9.1 billion	$10.72 billion
Per capita operating expenditures	$19.16	$31.65	$36.36
Full-time-equivalent staff	111,945	137,855	145,243
Holdings, print materials	656 million	815.6 million	816 million
Holdings, audiovisual materials	30 million	81.2 million	98.7 million

Circulation	1.6 billion	2.1 billion	2.28 billion
Circulation per capita	6.5	7.2	7.7
Circulation, children's materials	462.9 million	716.4 million	786.3 million

Absolute figures for the different years in these reports can be compared only in the light of U.S. population data and inflation. But the per capita numbers carry the message of increasing usage in terms of expenditures and circulation.

The NCES and IMLS reports are used in the individual library data profiles given in lib-web-cats (see this book's introduction). *See also* EVALUATION; FUNDING OF PUBLIC LIBRARIES; GOVERNMENT ROLE; INTERNET; PUBLIC RELATIONS.

References

NCES documents are at http://www.nces.ed.gov. IMLS documents are at http://www.imls.gov. ALA materials are at http://www.ala.org.

American Library Association. 1936. *The Equal Chance: Books Help to Make It.* Chicago: American Library Association. Revised in 1943; supplemented in 1947.
American Library Association. 2008–. *Libraries Connect Communities: Public Library Funding & Technology Access Study, 2007–2008*, ed. Larra Clark. Chicago: American Library Association. Annual. Issues for 2008–2009 and 2009–2010 have appeared. The study is funded by the Bill and Melinda Gates Foundation and the ALA. Continues the reporting of Bertot and McClure (next entry). http://www.ala.org/ala/research/initiatives/plftas.
Bertot, John C., Charles R. McClure, and Douglas L. Zweizig. 1994. *Public Libraries and the Internet: Study Results, Policy Issues, and Recommendations.* Prepared for the National Commission on Libraries and Information Science. Tallahassee: Florida State University, Information Institute. This was followed by reports for 1997, 1998, 2000, 2002, 2004, 2006, 2007, and 2008 by Bertot and McClure with various coauthors. The reports issued in 2008 and 2009 were drawn from the ALA's *Libraries Connect Communities: Public Library Funding & Technology Access Study* for those years.
Davis, Denise M. 2008. A comparison of public library data: PLDS in context. *Public Libraries* 47, no. 5 (September/October): 20–25. Compares the statistics issued by NCES and IMLS with those of the *Public Library Data Service.*
Davis, Denise M. 2009a. *The Condition of U.S. Libraries: Trends, 1999–2009.* Chicago: American Library Association. Covers public, school, and academic libraries. See the next entry.
Davis, Denise M. 2009b. *The Condition of U.S. Libraries: Public Library Trends, 2002–2009.* Chicago: American Library Association. Excerpted from previous entry.
Henderson, Everett. 2009. *Service Trends in U.S. Public Libraries, 1997–2007.* Research brief, 1. Washington: Institute of Museum and Library Services. www.imls.gov.
McMullen, Haynes. 2000. *American Libraries before 1876.* Westport, CT: Greenwood Press.

Public Library Data Service: Statistical Report. 1988–1991. Prepared by the Public Library Association, a division of the ALA. Chicago: American Library Association. Annual. http://www.publiclibrariesonline.org. Continued by *Statistical Report/Public Library Data Service.*

Schick, Frank L. 1970. A century of U.S. library statistics of national scope. In *Bowker Annual of Library and Book Trade Information, 1970,* 5–10. New York: R.R. Bowker.

Smith, Mark. 1996. *Collecting and Using Public Library Statistics: A How-to-do-it Manual for Librarians.* New York: Neal-Schuman.

Statistical Report/Public Library Data Service. 1992–. Prepared by the Public Library Association, a division of the ALA. Chicago: American Library Association. Annual. Continues *Public Library Data Service: Statistical Report.*

A Survey of Libraries in the United States. 1926. Chicago: American Library Association. 4 vols.

U.S. Bureau of Education. 1876. *Public Libraries in the United States of America: Their History, Condition, and Management.* Special report, parts 1 and 2. Washington, DC: Government Printing Office.

U.S. Bureau of Education. 1886. *Statistics of Public Libraries in the United States.* In the *Report of the Commissioner of Education for the Year 1884–1885.* Washington, DC: Government Printing Office.

U.S. Bureau of Education. 1888. *Report of the Commissioner of Education.* Washington, DC: Government Printing Office.

U.S. Bureau of Education. 1893. *Statistics of Public Libraries in the United States and Canada.* Washington, DC: Government Printing Office.

U.S. Bureau of Education. 1897a. *Public, Society, and School Libraries in the United States, with Library Statistics and Legislation of the Various States.* Washington, DC: Government Printing Office.

U.S. Bureau of Education. 1897b. *Statistics of Libraries and Library Legislation in the United States.* In the *Report of the Commissioner of Education for 1895–1896.* Washington, DC: Government Printing Office.

U.S. Bureau of Education. 1901. *Public, Society, and School Libraries.* Washington, DC: Government Printing Office.

U.S. Bureau of Education. 1904. *Public, Society, and School Libraries.* Washington, DC: Government Printing Office.

U.S. Institute of Museum and Library Services. 2008–. *Public Libraries in the United States, FY 2006–.* Washington, DC: Government Printing Office. Annual. Published: data for FY 2006, 2007, and 2008. Continues data gathering function of the NCES.

U.S. National Center for Education Statistics. 1978. *Survey of Public Libraries.* Washington, DC: Government Printing Office.

U.S. National Center for Education Statistics. 1982. *Statistics of Public Libraries, 1977–1978.* Washington, DC: Government Printing Office.

U.S. National Center for Education Statistics. 1991–2007. *E. D. TABS: Public Libraries in Fifty States and the District of Columbia: 1989–2005.* Annual. Title varies. Data gathering function transferred to the Institute of Museum and Library Services.

U.S. National Center for Education Statistics. 1996. *Public Library Structure and Organization in the United States.* NCES 96–229. Washington, DC: U.S. Office of Education.

U.S. National Center for Education Statistics. 2001. *Public Library Trends Analysis, Fiscal Years 1992–1996*. NCES 2001–324. Washington, DC: U.S. Department of Education.

U.S. Office of Education. 1870. *Report of the Commissioner of Education for the Year 1870*. Washington, DC: Government Printing Office.

U.S. Office of Education. 1909. *Statistics of Public, Society, and School Libraries Having 5,000 Volumes and over in 1908*. Office of Education Bulletin 1909, no. 5. Washington, DC: Government Printing Office.

U.S. Office of Education. 1916–1958. *Biennial Survey of Education in the United States*. Issued as part of the Office of Education Bulletin series, 1916/1918–1936/1938, then as an independent series, 1938/1940–1956/1958. Discontinued. Washington, DC: Government Printing Office.

U.S. Office of Education. 1931. *Statistics of Public, Society, and School Libraries, 1929*. Office of Education Bulletin 1930, no. 37. Washington, DC: Government Printing Office.

U.S. Smithsonian Institution. 1850. *List of Public Libraries in the United States, with the Number of Volumes of Printed Books in Each, Reported to the Smithsonian Institution, January 1850*. Washington, DC: Buell & Blanchard.

STEARNS, LUTIE EUGENIA, 1866–1943   Librarian. Born Stoughton, MA, September 13, 1866. The family moved to Wauwatosa, WI, in 1871. Stearns took teacher training at the Milwaukee State Normal School and taught two years in the Milwaukee schools. In 1888 she became head of circulation at the Milwaukee Public Library, holding the post to 1897. Active in the Wisconsin Library Association, she advocated creation of a state library agency; when legislation established the Wisconsin Free Library Commission in 1895, she became the commission secretary. She devoted herself to library extension, traveling personally among small towns with her book wagon, and sending out deposit collections to remote communities. In 1903 she was named head of the Department of Traveling Libraries. Having resigned because of illness and personal circumstances in 1914, she became a noted lecturer, visiting 38 states to speak on social issues. Later she wrote a regular column in the *Milwaukee Journal*. Stearns was a vigorous critic of the library profession, which she found engrossed in administrative and technical matters, lacking energetic outreach and social programs. In a 1911 article she attacked "sensualism" in *Cosmopolitan* and other mass-market magazines but defended publications that offered dissent on political issues. LJ Hall of Fame; *ANB*.

STEVENS COUNTY LIBRARY, HUGOTON, KS   500 Monroe, Hugoton, KS 67951. Founded 1924. Population served: 5,520. Circulation: 98,000. Holdings: 45,000. LJ October 1, 2010: 3-star library.

STOCKBRIDGE LIBRARY ASSOCIATION, MA   Population served: 2,250. Circulation: 44,735. Holdings: 28,578. LJ February 15, 2009, and November 15, 2009: 3-star library.

STOCKTON PUBLIC LIBRARY, KS   124 N. Cedar, Stockton, KS 67669. Founded 1911. Population served: 1,465. Circulation: 18,629. Holdings: 16,242. LJ November 15, 2009: 3-star library.

STOCKTON-SAN JOAQUIN COUNTY PUBLIC LIBRARY, CA   605 E. El Dorado St., Stockton, CA 95202. Founded 1881. Population served: 590,866. Circulation: 2,114,061. Holdings: 1,076,816. 12 branches.

STOW-MUNROE FALLS PUBLIC LIBRARY, OH   2512 Darrow Rd., Stow, OH 44224. Founded 1924. Population served: 37,890. Circulation: 746,169. Holdings: 117,368.

STOWE FREE LIBRARY, VT   90 Pond St., Stowe, VT 05672. Founded 1866. Population served: 4,300. Circulation: 110,000. Holdings: 29,000. LJ February 15, 2009: 3-star library.

STRATFORD, OK. See CHANDLER WATTS MEMORIAL LIBRARY, STRATFORD, OK.

STRATFORD PUBLIC LIBRARY, IA   816 Shakespeare St., Stratford, IA 50249. Population served: 1,374. Circulation: 18,296. Holdings: 6,791. LJ October 1, 2010: 3-star library.

SULLY COUNTY LIBRARY, ONIDA, SD   500 Eighth St., Onida, SD 57564. Population served: 1,607. Circulation: 11,545. Holdings: 23,728. LJ October 1, 2010: 4-star library.

SUPPLIES. See FIXTURES, FURNISHINGS, AND EQUIPMENT.

SUPPORT STAFF. See STAFFING.

SURVEYS AND USE STUDIES. See RESEARCH.

SWINK PUBLIC LIBRARY, CO   610 Columbia Ave., Swink, CO. Population served: 1,299. Circulation: 11,998. Holdings: 12,427. LJ October 1, 2010: 5-star library.

SYLACAUGA, AL. See B. B. COMER MEMORIAL LIBRARY, SYLACAUGA, AL.

SYRACUSE PUBLIC LIBRARY, NE   496 Sixth St., Syracuse, NE 68446. Founded 1901. Population served: 1,762. Circulation: 17,887. Holdings: 8,184. LJ February 15, 2009: 5-star library.

.

T

TAMPA-HILLSBOROUGH COUNTY PUBLIC LIBRARY, TAMPA, FL   900 N.
Ashley Dr., Tampa, FL 33602. Founded 1917. Population served:
1,131,546. Circulation: 3,000,000. Holdings: 1,100,000. 25 branches.

TAOS PUBLIC LIBRARY, NM   402 Camino de La Placita, Taos, NM 87571.
Founded 1923. Population served: 27,000 (communication from
the library). Circulation: 150,090. Holdings: 71,144. LJ February 15,
2009: 3-star library; October 1, 2010: 4-star library.

TAPPAN-SPAULDING MEMORIAL LIBRARY, NEWARK VALLEY, NY   6 Rock
St., Newark Valley, NY 13811. Population served: 1,071. Circulation:
14,795. Holdings: 12,866. LJ February 15, 2009: 3-star library; October 1,
2010: 5-star library.

TECHNICAL SERVICES   According to *ODLIS*, technical services are
"library operations concerned with the acquisition, organization (bibliographic control), physical processing, and maintenance of library collections
as opposed to the delivery of public services" usually performed "behind the
scenes" (*see* ACQUISITIONS; CATALOGING; CLASSIFICATION; COL-
LECTION DEVELOPMENT; PRESERVATION).
   "Behind the scenes" in contrast to "public" describes the difference
between any library's two principal spheres of action. The work of technical
services (TS) takes place in locations that are used by staff only. Acquisitions
librarians, catalogers, and other TS personnel interact among themselves

without direct patron contacts. Public service librarians are in regular contact with patrons. A library organization chart reflects these two fundamental operations. Some efforts have been made to bring TS staff out of the backroom and onto the public stage, working in reference a few hours a week (Evans et al. 2002, 6).

Book repair is an activity that used to engage hours of staff time, involving sewing and library paste. Today such mundane tasks are usually passed along to the library bindery. Binding of materials that are not in need of mending is largely confined to journal files (*see* SERIALS).

The American Library Association has had a division since 1957 devoted to TS: Association for Library Collections and Technical Services. Its principal publication is *Library Resources & Technical Services* (quarterly).

Reference

Evans, G. Edward, et al. 2002. *Introduction to Technical Services*. 7th ed. Greenwood Village, CO: Libraries Unlimited.
Schecter, Abraham. 1999. *Basic Book Repair Methods*. Englewood, CO: Libraries Unlimited.

TECHNOLOGY. *See* INFORMATION TECHNOLOGY.

TELLURIDE, CO. *See* SAN MIGUEL LIBRARY DISTRICT #1, TELLURIDE, CO.

TETON COUNTY LIBRARY, JACKSON, WY   125 Virginian Lane, Jackson, WY 83001. Founded 1938. Population served: 14,000. Circulation: 389,643. Holdings: 93,621. 1 branch. LJ February 15, 2009; November 15, 2009, and October 1, 2010: 3-star library.

THIBODAUX, LA. *See* LAFOURCHE PARISH PUBLIC LIBRARY, THIBODAUX, LA.

THOMAS B. NORTON PUBLIC LIBRARY, GULF SHORES, AL   221 W. 19th Ave., Gulf Shores, AL 36542. Founded 1963. Population served: 5,044. Circulation: 77,428. Holdings: 38,585. LJ November 15, 2009: 4-star library.

THORNTON, CO. *See* RANGEVIEW LIBRARY DISTRICT, THORNTON, CO.

TICKNOR, GEORGE, 1791–1871   Educator, literary scholar. Born in Boston, August 1, 1791. He was a precocious scholar, admitted to Dartmouth College at age 10; he graduated in 1807, a specialist in languages. Ticknor's exceptional talents were recognized by Thomas Jefferson, who commissioned him to buy books in Europe for the Jefferson library. He studied in

Germany, France, and Spain for several years, mastering numerous languages. An invitation from Harvard brought him back to the United States in 1819; he taught languages and literature with such students as James Russell Lowell, Charles Eliot Norton, and Henry David Thoreau. He resigned in 1835 (succeeded in his professorship by Henry Wadsworth Longfellow) and returned to Europe for three years. His great scholarly work *History of Spanish Literature* (1849 and later editions) was universally acclaimed. In 1852, Ticknor accepted an appointment to a committee to establish the Boston Public Library. He wrote most of the committee's famous planning report, which has been called "the charter of the American public library movement" (Lord 1970, 101) (*see* BOSTON PUBLIC LIBRARY), and when the library became a reality, he went again to Europe to acquire materials. Despite his own lofty culture, he wanted a public library to be a place for popular reading—holding that a taste for the best books would develop step-by-step with a beginning in ordinary fiction (*see* COLLECTION DEVELOPMENT; PHILOSOPHY OF PUBLIC LIBRARIANSHIP). When he was elected president of the trustees of the Boston library, he took charge of planning a new building and the move into it. He died two months before it opened on January 26, 1871. *ALB*; *DAB*.

Reference

Lord, Milton E. 1970. Boston Public Library. In *Encyclopedia of Library and Information Science* 3: 100–104. New York: Marcel Dekker.

TIFFIN, IA. *See* SPRINGMEIER COMMUNITY LIBRARY, Tiffin, IA.

TILDEN, NE. *See* RAYMOND A. WHITWER TILDEN PUBLIC LIBRARY, TILDEN, NE.

TITCOMB, MARY LEMIST, 1857–1932   Librarian. Born in Farmingham, NH, she attended the Robinson Female Seminary in Exeter, NH, and went to work as cataloger in the library of Rutland, VT, rising to head librarian. Appointed to the Vermont Library Commission, she organized new libraries and assisted old ones for 12 years. In 1900 she went to Hagerstown Public Library in Maryland (which became the Washington County Free Library, one of the earliest county libraries in the United States). There she set up book deposits in 66 locations, designed the first book wagon, and took it on the road in 1905 (*see* BOOKMOBILES). Active in the American Library Association, Titcomb was a member of council and second vice president in 1915. She organized training classes for librarians that functioned from 1924 to 1931.She died in Hagerstown on June 5, 1932. *DALB*.

TIVOLI FREE LIBRARY, NY   1 Tivoli Commons, Tivoli, NY 12587. Founded 1919. Population served: 1,163. Circulation: 21,349. Holdings: 11,520. LJ February 15, 2009: 4-star library; November 15, 2009: 3-star library; October 1, 2010: 4-star library.

TOLEDO-LUCAS COUNTY PUBLIC LIBRARY, OH   325 N. Michigan St., Toledo, OH 43604. Population served: 500,000. Circulation: 6,400,000. Holdings: 2,513,188. 18 branches, 1 bookmobile. LJ November 15, 2009, and October 1, 2010: 4-star library.

TOMS RIVER, NJ. *See* OCEAN COUNTY LIBRARY, TOMS RIVER, NJ.

TOPEKA AND SHAWNEE COUNTY PUBLIC LIBRARY, KS   1515 SW Tenth Ave., Topeka, KS 66604. Founded 1878. Population served: 167,747. Circulation: 2,061,000. Holdings: 546,000. 1 branch, 3 bookmobiles. LJ November 15, 2009: 4-star library.

TOWN OF INDIAN LAKE PUBLIC LIBRARY, NY   Pelon Rd., Indian Lake, NY 12842. Founded 1968. Population served: 1,471. Circulation: 18,748. Holdings: 25,500. LJ November 15, 2009, and October 1, 2010: 3-star library.

TOWN OF VAIL PUBLIC LIBRARY, CO   292 W. Meadow Dr., Vail, CO 81657. Founded 1983. Population served: 4,150. Circulation: 75,360. Holdings: 52,878. LJ February 15, 2009: 3-star library.

TRI-VALLEY COMMUNITY LIBRARY, HEALY, AK   Suntrana Rd., Healy, AK 99743. Population served: 1,012. Circulation: 14,009. Holdings: 21,836. LJ November 15, 2009: 3-star library; October 1, 2010: 4-star library.

TRUSTEES

Terminology

A trustee is "a member of a board elected or appointed to direct the funds and policy of an institution" (*American Heritage*). The library perspective is in *ODLIS*: "Library trustee—a member of an appointed or elected board responsible for overseeing the growth and development of a library or library system, including long-range planning and policy making, public relations, and fund-raising."

Structure and Duties of Library Boards

Although there is great variety in the way library boards are constituted and in the duties they pursue, this typical pattern emerges. A board's domain is coterminous with the library governing unit; members are appointed by the head of that unit (e.g., a mayor) or its governing body (e.g., county commissioners) or elected by citizens of that unit (e.g., in a library district). Members usually serve fixed terms of four to six years, subject to renewal. A board usually has five to nine members; they serve without salary but may be compensated for necessary expenses. The library board establishes policies and requests appropriations from the funding authority. It selects and supervises an administrator (director or librarian) who carries out policies and expends funds accordingly. Less tangibly,

> the board serves as a vital link between the library and the community, bringing the public's point of view and the needs of the community to the development of responsive library service. . . . The role of board members is seldom easy because of the varied composition of communities—the different interests, concerns, and social and economic levels that must be considered. Reconciling this diversity by representing the total community is the greatest accomplishment to which a board can aspire. (Commonwealth of Virginia 2005)

In representing the community, a board takes the role of mission giver: it determines what the community wants the library to do and shares that vision with the library director. Clarification of mission is essential for creation of goals and making of plans (see PLANNING).

Trustees do not take part in the daily management or operations of the library, but they may express their concerns to the director. They do not handle employee complaints or work issues except to see that applicable laws are enforced. If the board is dissatisfied with the library's performance, it has the final resource of replacing the director.

A library board usually produces written policies and assembles them in a handbook that is available to the public in printed form or on the library website. These statements are written in cooperation with the library director (see POLICY STATEMENTS).

Role of the American Library Association and State Library Associations

In 1890 the American Library Trustee Association was founded in the American Library Association (ALA). It was renamed Association for Library Trustees and Advocates (ALTA) in 1999. On February 1, 2009, ALTA joined with Friends of Libraries U.S.A. to become an expanded division of ALA known as the Association of Library Trustees, Advocates, Friends and Foundations (ALTAFF). The goals of ALTAFF are "helping trustees and friends work together at the local, state, and national levels to effectively promote and advocate for libraries, encouraging the development of library foundations, and engaging corporate supporters to unite and strengthen voices in support of libraries" (ALA 2010).

The ALA has vigorously promoted the idea of a partnership between trustees and librarians, minimizing their supervisor–subordinate relationship. Trustees have guidance from ALA regarding the public library situation and their role. Several useful publications are available, notably *The Complete Library Trustee Handbook* (Reed 2010).

Many state library associations have similar programs aimed at educating trustees and have prepared handbooks. Websites of the individual associations give details.

A number of library boards have appointed teen members who speak for the interests of young library users. These have been reported in the literature: Virginia Beach Public Library (city council ordinance of August 1992 stated that one member of the public library board shall be a high school senior; Caywood 2003), Harford County (MD) Public Library (first teen appointed 1994; Caplan 2003), Orono (ME) Public Library (2001; Rose 2003), and Sewickley (PA) Public Library (2001; Rose 2003). The teens are nonvoting members, excluded from discussions of personnel.

The trustee system has been successful. "The profession has generally increased its reliance on trustees for effective work for libraries" (Ihrig 1975, 108). It is surely preferably to the alternative: direct supervision of the library by a city official. That structure leads to political appointments and a muted voice of the community served.

References

American Library Association. 2010. *A New Voice for America's Libraries*. Chicago: American Library Association. http://www.ala.org/mgrps/divs/altaff. Accessed December 2010.

Caplan, Audra. 2003. Making a difference: Harford County Public Library's teen board member. *Young Adult Library Services* 1, no. 2 (Spring): 9–11.

Caywood, Carolyn. 2003. Giving back to the community: Virginia Beach Public Library's teen board member. *Young Adult Library Services* 1, no. 2 (Spring): 16–18.

Commonwealth of Virginia. 2005. *Becoming a Trustee*. Richmond: Library of Virginia. http://www.lva.virginia.gw/lib-edu/ldnd/trustee. Accessed December 2010.

Hage, Christine Lind, et al. 2010. *A Library Board's Practical Guide to Hiring Outside Experts*. Chicago: American Library Association, Association of Library Trustees, Advocates, Friends and Foundations. Available online only: www.ala.org/ala/mgrps/divs/altaff. Accessed December 2010.

Ihrig, Alice B. 1975. Library trustees. In *Encyclopedia of Library and Information Science* 16: 102–9. New York: Marcel Dekker.

Reed, Sally Gardner. 2010. *The Complete Library Trustee Handbook*. Published for the Association of Library Trustees, Advocates, Friends and Foundations. New York: Neal-Schuman.

Rose, Laurie, et al. 2003. Teen library board members: Three perspectives. *Young Adult Library Services* 1, no. 2 (Spring): 14–16.

Spillios, Nicholas, et al. 2010. *A Library Board's Practical Guide to Self-Evaluation*. Chicago: American Library Association, Association of Library Trustees, Advocates, Friends and Foundations. Available online only: www.ala.org/ala/mgrps/divs/altaff. Accessed December 2010.

TUCKER, HAROLD WALTON, 1915–1973   Librarian. Born in Waco, TX, March 24, 1915. His degrees were BA, Rice University, 1936; BLS, University of Illinois, 1938; and MA, Graduate Library School, University of Chicago, 1941. He was a reference assistant at Enoch Pratt Free Library, 1938–1940, then went to Dayton Public Library as head of technology. Tucker was in the

Medical Corps, 1942–1946. He was assistant librarian in Gary, 1946–1949; assistant director in St. Louis County, 1947–1950; and librarian in Gary, 1950–1954. He became director of Queens Public Library in 1954 and set about to enhance outreach programs, create 12 new buildings, and establish a major reference center in Jamaica, the headquarters city. There was a new central library in 1966. Tucker chaired the American Library Association project "Library USA" at the New York World's Fair of 1964–1965. He was a promoter of total access, especially to the disadvantaged (book trucks to inner city) and to very young patrons (operation "Head Start" for three- to five-year-olds). He was one of the advocates of the Library Services and Construction Act of 1964, which revised the former Library Services Act (1956) to include urban libraries. Tucker was president of the New York Library Association in 1964. He died on April 4, 1973.

TUCSON, AZ. *See* PIMA COUNTY PUBLIC LIBRARY, TUCSON, AZ.

TULSA CITY-COUNTY LIBRARY SYSTEM, OK   400 Civic Center, Tulsa, OK 74103. City library founded in 1916; became city-county library in 1962. Population served: 569,148. Circulation: 4,860,570. Holdings: 1,748,751. 26 branches, 1 bookmobile. LJ February 15, 2009: 5-star library; November 15, 2009: 4-star library; October 1, 2010: 3-star library.

TWINSBURG PUBLIC LIBRARY, OH   10050 Ravenna Rd., Twinsburg, OH 44087. Population served: 21,441. Circulation: 1,149,160. Holdings: 140,820. LJ February 15, 2009; November 15, 2009, and October 1, 2010: 4-star library. HAPLR 2009, 2010.

TYLER, ALICE SARAH, 1859–1944   Librarian. Born in Decatur, IL, April 27, 1859. She worked in the Decatur Public Library as an assistant in 1887 and completed a library training course at the Armour Institute in Chicago. In 1895 she was a cataloger in the Cleveland Public Library. Tyler moved to Iowa in 1900 as secretary of the new state library commission, remaining 13 years. She developed a traveling library system for small towns and pressed to increase the number of libraries in state hospitals, reform schools, prisons, and orphanages. When she left Iowa the number of public libraries had grown from 41 to 114 and the traveling libraries from 90 to 700. Tyler succeeded William Howard Brett as director of the library school at Western Reserve University (Cleveland) in 1913 and introduced new courses in special, school, and hospital libraries as well as children's librarianship. From 1925 to her retirement in 1929, she held the title of dean. She was elected to three presidencies: Ohio Library Association, 1916; Association of American Library Schools, 1918; and American Library Association, 1920. She died in Cleveland on April 18, 1944. *ALB.*

U

ULVELING, RALPH VINCENT ADRIAN, 1902–1980   Librarian. Born Adrian, MN, May 9, 1902. His family moved to Chicago, and he attended DePaul University, earning a BA in 1922. From 1924 to 1926 he was a reference assistant at the Newberry Library. After a brief term as librarian of the public library in Amarillo, TX, Ulveling went to the library school at Columbia University. On graduation he was appointed associate director of the Detroit Public Library, where he remained until retirement in 1967. He was director of the library from 1941. An advocate of the public library as the "people's university," he strongly supported meeting every individual's educational needs. To simplify access to the library collections, he devised in 1949 a "reader interest classification" and shelving arrangement for books in the branch libraries and the main library browsing collection. This alternative to the Dewey Decimal Classification evidently had mixed results, for it was abandoned when Ulveling retired. However, the concept behind it has been revived lately by libraries using the BISAC system (*see* CLASSIFICATION). Ulveling was a strong defender of the right to read. In 1944 he refused a police request to withdraw Lillian Smith's controversial novel *Strange Fruit*. Threats of retaliation and even dismissal did not weaken his resolve, and eventually he was successful in retaining the book. He also insisted on keeping communist literature available to the public during the Red Scare of the 1950s. His many pursuits included the advance of state library legislation, creation of Friends of the Library, and establishing the important research collection on automotive history. Ulveling was elected president of the American Library Association in 1945. He died in Boynton Beach, FL, on March 21, 1980. *DALB*, 1st supplement.

UNALASKA PUBLIC LIBRARY, AK   64 Eleanor Dr., Unalaska, AK 99685. Founded 1995. Population served: 4,297. Circulation: 96,632. Holdings: 21,216. LJ February 15, 2009: 4-star library; November 15, 2009, and October 1, 2010: 5-star library.

UNION, SC. *See* UNION COUNTY CARNEGIE LIBRARY, UNION, SC.

UNION COUNTY CARNEGIE LIBRARY, UNION, SC   300 E. South St., Union, SC 29379. Founded 1905. Population served: 28,862. Circulation: 52,752. Holdings: 48,113. LJ February 15, 2009: "best small library in the United States."

UNIVERSITY HEIGHTS, OH. *See* CLEVELAND HEIGHTS-UNIVERSITY HEIGHTS PUBLIC LIBRARY, OH.

UPPER ARLINGTON PUBLIC LIBRARY, OH   2800 Tremont Rd., Upper Arlington, OH 43221. Founded 1967. Population served: 31,860. Circulation: 1,500,000. Holdings: 500,000. 2 branches. LJ February 15, 2009; November 15, 2009, and October 1, 2010: 5-star library. HAPLR 2009, 2010.

UPTON COUNTY PUBLIC LIBRARY, McCAMEY, TX   212 W. Seventh St., McCamey, TX 79752. Population served: 1,270. Circulation: 38,575. Holdings: 20,138. LJ February 15, 2009: 5-star library; November 15, 2009, and October 1, 2010: 4-star library.

V

VAIL, CO. *See* TOWN OF VAIL PUBLIC LIBRARY, CO.

VALLEY MILLS PUBLIC LIBRARY, TX   405 Fifth St., Valley Mills, TX 76689. Founded 1990. Population served: 1,181. Circulation: 2,730. Holdings: 10,734. LJ October 1, 2010: 4-star library.

VAN WERT, OH. *See* BRUMBACK LIBRARY, OH.

VERNON AREA PUBLIC LIBRARY DISTRICT, LINCOLNSHIRE, IL   300 Olde Half Day Rd., Lincolnshire, IL 60069. Founded 1974. Population served: 41,107. Circulation: 966,432. Holdings: 261,023. LJ October 1, 2010: 3-star library.

VIDEOCASSETTES. *See* AUDIOVISUAL COLLECTIONS.

VINCENNES, IN. *See* KNOX COUNTY PUBLIC LIBRARY, VINCENNES, IN.

VINEYARD HAVEN PUBLIC LIBRARY, MA   200 Main St., Vineyard Haven, MA 02568. Founded 1895. Population served: 3,851. Circulation: 127,308. Holdings: 33,801. LJ February 15, 2009, and November 15, 2009: 3-star library.

VIRGINIA BEACH PUBLIC LIBRARIES, VA   4100 Virginia Beach Blvd., Virginia Beach, VA 23542. Founded 1959. Population served: 428,200. Circulation: 2,825,924. Holdings: 857,694. The library board has two teen members.

VITZ, CARL PETER PAUL, 1883–1981.   Librarian. Born in St. Paul, MN, on June 3, 1883. He graduated from Adelbert College in 1904 and earned a BLS at the New York State Library School in 1907. He had started working at the Cleveland Public Library (CPL) in his teens and stayed there to 1906. In 1907 he went to the District of Columbia Public Library as assistant director, and then he was assistant director of the New York State Library in 1909–1911. Returning to CPL in 1912, Vitz was second vice librarian under William Howard Brett, then vice librarian under Linda Eastman. He left in 1922 to head the Toledo Public Library, establishing six new branches, school services, and a technical department. Involvement in planning for a new building was the start of a career as library building consultant; he worked on more than 60 projects around the country. His book *Loan Work* was published by the American Library Association (ALA) in 1919, later revised as *Circulation Work*. From 1937 to 1946, Vitz was librarian in Minneapolis, initiating bookmobile service and a vocational information service for returning veterans. He was active in pressing for federal aid to public libraries. In Cincinnati from 1946, he supervised the planning for the 1955 building (designed by Frederick W. Garber) in a modular style. Vitz was president of the Ohio Library Association, 1920–1921 and 1933–1934, and the ALA, 1944–1945. He lectured in several library schools. Vitz died in Cincinnati on January 8, 1981. *DALB*.

W

W. A. RANKIN MEMORIAL LIBRARY, NEODESHA, KS   502 Indiana St., Neodesha, KS 66757. Founded 1914. Population served: 2,691. Circulation: 33,044. Holdings: 19,046. LJ February 15, 2009; November 15, 2009, and October 1, 2010: 4-star library.

WADSWORTH LIBRARY, GENESEO, NY   24 Center St., Geneseo, NY 14454. Founded 1869. Population served: 9,654. Circulation: 53,530. Holdings: 24,950. In 1878 it was one of four American libraries directed by women; the librarian was C. B. Olmsted.

WADSWORTH PUBLIC LIBRARY, OH   132 Broad St., Wadsworth, OH 44281. Founded 1922. Population served: 25,563. Circulation: 856,755. Holdings: 158,460. 2 bookmobiles. HAPLR 2009, 2010.

WAGNALLS MEMORIAL LIBRARY, LITHOPOLIS, OH   150 E. Columbus St., Lithopolis, OH 43136. Founded 1925. Population served: 615. Circulation: 107,755. Holdings: 67,612. HAPLR 2009, 2010.

WAKE COUNTY PUBLIC LIBRARIES, RALEIGH, NC   4020 Carya Dr., Raleigh, NC 27610. Founded 1901; became county library, 1985. Population served: 700,000. Circulation: 6,628,630. Holdings: 1,485,000. 19 branches.

WALTON AND TIPTON TOWNSHIP PUBLIC LIBRARY, NY   110 N. Main St., Walton, NY 46994. Founded 1914. Population served: 2,500. Circulation: 35,000. Holdings: 20,000. LJ February 15, 2009: 3-star library; November 15, 2009: 4-star library.

WARREN-NEWPORT PUBLIC LIBRARY DISTRICT, GURNEE, IL   224 N. O'Plaine Rd., Gurnee, IL 60031. Founded 1973. Population served: 58,237. Circulation: 1,333,321 (library website). Holdings: 276,332 (library website). 1 bookmobile.

WASHINGTON, DC. See DISTRICT OF COLUMBIA PUBLIC LIBRARY, WASHINGTON, DC.

WASHINGTON, GA. See BARTRAM TRAIL REGIONAL LIBRARY, WASHINGTON, GA.

WASHINGTON COUNTY FREE LIBRARY, HAGERSTOWN, MD   100 S. Potomac St., Hagerstown, MD 21740. Founded 1898, opened 1901. Population served: 141,050. Circulation: 859,003. Holdings: 345,215. 7 branches, 1 bookmobile. One of the nation's earliest bookmobile services was running in April 1905. Mary Titcomb's (see entry for her) "bookwagon," drawn by two horses, was the first vehicle. In 1912 it was superseded by a motorized wagon.

WASHINGTON COUNTY PUBLIC LIBRARY, MARIETTA, OH   615 Fifth St., Marietta, OH 45750. Founded as an association library in 1796 (the first of its type in the Northwest), it became a free public library in 1918 and was incorporated as the Marietta Library in 1830. Population served: 62,210. Circulation: 821,197. Holdings: 202,618. 5 branches, 1 bookmobile.

WASHINGTON-CENTERVILLE PUBLIC LIBRARY, CENTERVILLE, OH   111 Spring Valley Rd., Centerville, OH 45458. Founded 1930. Population served: 52,188. Circulation: 2,256,660. Holdings: 382,767. 1 branch. LJ February 15, 2009: 4-star library; November 15, 2009, and October 1, 2010: 5-star library. HAPLR 2009, 2010.

WASHOE COUNTY LIBRARY SYSTEM, RENO, NV   301 S. Center St., Reno, NV 89501. Founded 1904 (Reno city library), 1930 (county library). Population served: 400,000. Circulation: 2,000,000. Holdings: 905,000. 15 branches.

WATERLOO-GRANT TOWNSHIP PUBLIC LIBRARY, IN   300 S. Wayne St., Waterloo, IN 46793. Founded 1913. Population served: 3,114. Circulation: 50,847. Holdings: 26,007. LJ February 15, 2009: 5-star library; November 15, 2009, and October 1, 2010: 4-star library.

WAY PUBLIC LIBRARY, PERRYSBURG, OH   101 E. Indiana Ave., Perrysburg, OH 43551. Founded 1933. Population served: 16,947. Circulation: 516,256. Holdings: 96,577. LJ February 15, 2009: 5-star library; November 15, 2009: 4-star library. HAPLR 2009, 2010.

WAYLAND FREE PUBLIC LIBRARY, MA   5 Concord Rd., Wayland, MA 01778. Founded by a donation from Francis Wayland in 1847; opened 1851. Present building opened 1900. Population served: 13,063. Circulation: 236,892. Holdings: 79,355. It was the first free public library in Massachusetts and second in the United States.

WEBSITES. See INTERNET.

WEEDING. See COLLECTION DEVELOPMENT.

WELLFLEET PUBLIC LIBRARY, MA   55 W. Main St., Wellfleet, MA 02667. Population served: 2,841. Circulation: 82,483. Holdings: 43,933. LJ February 15, 2009; November 15, 2009, and October 1, 2010: 5-star library.

WEST BLOOMFIELD TOWNSHIP PUBLIC LIBRARY, MI   4600 Walnut Lake Rd., West Bloomfield, MI 48323. Population served: 96,597. Circulation: 1,600,000. Holdings: 230,000. 1 branch. HAPLR 2010.

WEST POINT, NE. See JOHN A. STAHL LIBRARY, WEST POINT, NE.

WEST TISBURY FREE PUBLIC LIBRARY, MA   1042A State Rd., West Tisbury, MA 02575. Founded 1969. Population served: 2,670. Circulation: 109,398. Holdings: 41,449. LJ February 15, 2009: 4-star library; November 15, 2009, and October 1, 2010: 5-star library. HAPLR 2009.

WESTERVILLE PUBLIC LIBRARY, OH   126 S. State St., Westerville, OH 43081. Founded 1930. Population served: 85,000. Circulation: 1,971,711. Holdings: 329,982. LJ October 1, 2010: 5-star library.

WESTHAMPTON FREE LIBRARY, WESTHAMPTON BEACH, NY   7 Library Ave., Westhampton Beach, NY 11978. Population served: 5,759. Circulation: 149,320. Holdings: 47,166. LJ February 15, 2009: 4-star library; November 15, 2009: 5-star library; October 1, 2010: 4-star library.

WESTLAKE PORTER PUBLIC LIBRARY, OH   27333 Center Ridge Rd., Westlake, OH 44145. Population served: 30,744. Circulation: 897,110. Holdings: 168,784. HAPLR 2009, 2010.

WESTPORT PUBLIC LIBRARY, CT   Arnold Bernhard Plaza, Westport, CT 06880. Founded 1908. Population served: 26,564. Circulation: 834,692.

Holdings: 193,331. LJ February 15, 2009, and November 15, 2009: 3-star library.

WHEELER, JOSEPH L., 1884–1970   Librarian. Born in Dorchester, MA, March 16, 1884. He earned a master's degree in social and political science from Brown University and a certificate from the New York State library school. Wheeler worked in the public libraries of Washington, D.C.; Jacksonville, FL; Los Angeles; and Youngstown, OH. In 1926 he became director of the Enoch Pratt Free Library in Baltimore, remaining to 1944. His tenure revitalized the library, gaining community and official support. He started a training class in 1928 and initiated a widely regarded series of book lists that sold hundreds of thousands of copies nationally. Youth work began under Margaret Edwards in 1932. His most conspicuous achievement was the new central building, designed by Edward Tilton, opened 1933. It was the first large American public library with an open design, unique for its time in having 12 large street-level windows for book displays. When Wheeler left Enoch Pratt, it had 26 branches and 792 classroom collections and was circulating more than 2.5 million volumes per year. He was a prolific library consultant, completing some 225 studies and surveys. He died in Benson, VT, on December 3, 1970. *DALB*.

WHITE PLAINS PUBLIC LIBRARY, NY   100 Marine Ave., White Plains, NY 10601. Founded 1899. Population served: 53,077. Circulation: 531,292. Holdings: 270,000. LJ November 15, 2009, and October 1, 2010: 3-star library.

WHITNEY, TX. *See* LAKE WHITNEY PUBLIC LIBRARY, WHITNEY, TX.

WICHITA PUBLIC LIBRARY, KS   223 S. Main St., Wichita, KS 67202. Founded as a subscription library; became free to the public in 1900. Population served: 353,875. Circulation: 1,700,000. Holdings: 610,000. 10 branches.

WICKLIFFE PUBLIC LIBRARY, OH   1713 Lincoln Rd., Wickliffe, OH 44092. Founded 1933. Population served: 13,754. Circulation: 459,974. Holdings: 100,535. LJ February 15, 2009; November 15, 2009, and October 1, 2010: 5-star library. HAPLR 2009, 2010.

WILLIAMSBURG, MA. *See* MEEKINS LIBRARY, WILLIAMSBURG, MA.

WILLIAMSBURG REGIONAL LIBRARY, VA   7770 Croaker Rd., Williamsburg, VA 23188. Founded 1909. Population served: 80,000. Circulation: 1,302,000. Holdings: 339,000. 1 branch, 2 bookmobiles. LJ February 15, 2009; November 15, 2009, and October 1, 2010: 5-star library.

WILLOUGHBY-EASTLAKE PUBLIC LIBRARY, WILLOWICK, OH   263 E. 305th St., Willowick, OH 44095. Founded 1956. Population served: 68,140. Circulation: 1,252,600. Holdings: 216,289. 4 branches. HAPLR 2009, 2010.

WILLOWICK, OH. *See* WILLOUGHBY-EASTLAKE PUBLIC LIBRARY, WILLOWICK, OH.

WINCHESTER PUBLIC LIBRARY, KS   203 Fourth St., Winchester, KS 66097. Population served: 1,299. Circulation: 8,545. Holdings: 16,731. LJ October 1, 2010: 3-star library.

WINDHAM PUBLIC LIBRARY, NY   Church and Mains Sts., Windham, NY 12496. Founded 1971. Population served: 1,660. Circulation: 21,909. Holdings: 12,264. LJ November 15, 2009, and October 1, 2010: 3-star library.

WINSOR, JUSTIN, 1831–1897   Librarian, historian. Born in Boston, January 2, 1831. He studied at Harvard College but left in 1852 without graduating. He spent two years in Paris and Heidelberg, learned French and German, and wrote poetry and criticism. Back in Boston he became a well-known literary figure. In 1866 he was named to the board of trustees of the Boston Public Library. Tasked with writing a review of the library's operations, he produced a balanced report that noted crowded conditions, low circulation, and insufficient fiction in the collection. On the death of Charles Coffin Jewett in 1868, Winsor became superintendent of the library. In his nine-year tenure Winsor improved services in several ways. He introduced interlibrary loan, opened the building on Sundays, reduced the age limit for borrowers, renovated the building, and established six branches (*see* BOSTON PUBLIC LIBRARY). After difficulties with the trustees, Winsor resigned in 1877 to take the post of librarian at Harvard. He was an active historian throughout his life, writing a history of Boston, other local histories, an eight-volume history of the United States, and many other standard works. He participated in the founding of the American Library Association (1876) and served as its first president. At first he was skeptical about the "ladder theory" but later seemed more optimistic, coming to believe that reading tastes could rise from low to high on the literary scale. He died in Boston on October 22, 1897. LJ Hall of Fame; *DALB*.

WINSTON-SALEM, NC. *See* FORSYTH COUNTY PUBLIC LIBRARY, WINSTON-SALEM, NC.

WINTHROP PUBLIC LIBRARY, IA   354 W. Madison St., Winthrop, IA 50682. Founded 1926. Population served: 1,751. Circulation: 13,421. Holdings: 8,965. LJ October 1, 2010: 3-star library.

WISCONSIN DELLS, WI. *See* KILBOURN PUBLIC LIBRARY, WISCONSIN DELLS, WI.

WITHERLE MEMORIAL LIBRARY, CASTINE, ME   41 School St., Castine, ME 04421. "In 1855 Castine was the first community in Maine to establish a public library supported by public funds" (library website). The library was originally a subscription library dating from 1801. Population served: 1,358. Circulation: 21,324. Holdings: 14,861. The 1913 building is on the National Register of Historic Places.

WOBURN PUBLIC LIBRARY, MA   45 Pleasant St., Woburn, MA 00801. Founded 1856. Population served: 37,448. Circulation: 152,598. Holdings: 76,897. The building, by H. H. Richardson (1876–1879), has a Gothic cathedral floor plan and Romanesque exterior. It is a National Historic Landmark.

WOMELSDORF COMMUNITY LIBRARY, PA   203 W. High St., Womelsdorf, PA 19567. Founded 2000. Population served: 2,599. Circulation: 50,022. Holdings: 10,077. LJ February 15, 2009: 3-star library.

WORCESTER PUBLIC LIBRARY, MA   Salem Square, Worcester, MA 01608. Founded in 1859 and open free to the public, April 30, 1860, with 11,500 volumes donated by John Green, tax support via city council. Population served: 200,000. Circulation: 700,000. Holdings: 900,000. 3 branches. The second librarian, Samuel Swett Green, administered the library from 1871 to 1909. He promoted personal service to readers (writing the first article on reference service in 1876 and establishing a reference section in the library), cooperation with schools, (from 1879), and Sunday openings (from 1872). See entry for him.

WORNSTAFF MEMORIAL PUBLIC LIBRARY, ASHLEY, OH   302 E. High St., Ashley, OH 47003. Population served: 1,265. Circulation: 50,772. Holdings: 31,044. LJ February 15, 2009, and November 15, 2009: 5-star library; October 1, 1010: 4-star library.

WORTHINGTON PUBLIC LIBRARY, OH   820 High St., Worthington, OH 43085. Founded 1925. Population served: 73,586. Circulation: 2,632,136. Holdings: 506,978 (data from *ALD*; no figures in *lib-web-cats*). 2 branches. LJ Library of the Year 2007. LJ February 15, 2009; November 15, 2009, and October 1, 2010: 5-star library. HAPLR 2009, 2010.

WRIGHT MEMORIAL PUBLIC LIBRARY, OAKWOOD, OH   1776 Far Hills Ave., Oakwood, OH 45419. Founded 1933. Population served: 9,215.

Circulation: 500,000. Holdings: 170,000. LJ February 15, 2009; November 15, 2009, and October 1, 2010: 3-star library. HAPLR 2009, 2010.

WYER, MALCOLM GLENN, 1877–1965   Librarian. Born August 21, 1877, in Concordia, KS. He graduated from the University of Minnesota in 1899, earned a master's degree in literature in 1901, and then went to the New York State Library School for a BLS in 1903. He was librarian of what is now the University of Iowa, then went to the University of Nebraska in 1913–1917. During World War I, Wyer served at Camp Hogan, TX, and was assistant librarian of the American Library Association (ALA) war service program. His main career was at the Denver Public Library (1924–1951), where he established a fine arts department, the Colorado collection, and the Bibliographic Center for Research. He organized the Western history department, the first project to preserve the records of the Western frontier. A promoter of a library school in Denver, he was its dean and also directed the University of Denver libraries. Wyer was ALA president in 1936–1937. After retiring in 1951, he wrote a book, *Books and People*, in which he observed that "libraries should accept and utilize all inventions and mechanics that increase efficiency of library operations. But they should remember that these are not the library but the framework of the real library, which is today, as always, the collection of books with staff members who know books, who like people, and who are given definite time for the function of bringing books and people together" (Eastlick 1971, 590). Wyer died in Denver on December 31, 1965.

Reference

Eastlick, John T. 1971. Denver Public Library. In *Encyclopedia of Library and Information Science* 6: 588–92. New York: Marcel Dekker.

WYMORE PUBLIC LIBRARY, NE   116 W. F St., Wymore, NE 68466. Population served: 1,656. Circulation: 15,643. Holdings: 18,161. LJ February 15, 2009; November 15, 2009, and October 1, 2010: 4-star library.

X

XENIA, OH. *See* GREENE COUNTY LIBRARY, XENIA, OH.

Y

YOAKUM COUNTY LIBRARY, DENVER CITY, TX   205 W. Fourth St., Denver City, TX 79323. Founded 1957. Population served: 3,857. Circulation: 138,000. Holdings: 34,433. LJ February 15, 2009, and November 15, 2009: 5-star library. HAPLR 2009, 2010.

YOUNG ADULTS' LIBRARY SERVICES. *See* SERVICES TO CHILDREN AND YOUNG ADULTS.

Z

ZEARING PUBLIC LIBRARY, IA   101 E. Main, Zearing, IA 50278. Founded 1976. Population served: 617. Circulation: 42,539. Holdings: 14,761. LJ October 1, 2010: 3-star library.

Index

The index cites all personal names mentioned in the text, including those in the lists of directors that appear in many entries, and those in the lists of award-winning architects. There are no citations for names, places, ideas, and titles that are mentioned only peripherally; and no citations to names and titles in the lists of references. In the case of multiple entries for one name the page numbers that give the primary information are in bold. The entries are in word-by-word sequence.

Advisory Board

About the Contributors

Stephen Bero (Advisory Board): Buildings and Facilities; Fixtures, Furnishings, and Equipment

Eric J. Hunter (Emeritus Professor of Information Management, Liverpool John Moores University): portions of Cataloging; Classification

Aisha M. Johnson (doctoral student, College of Information, Florida State University): Services to African Americans

Naomi Hurtienne Magola (Reference Librarian, Thibodaux Branch, Lafourche Parish Library, Thibodaux, Louisiana): Hurricanes Katrina and Rita

Connie Van Fleet (Advisory Board) and Danny P. Wallace (Professor, School of Library and Information Studies, University of Oklahoma): Evaluation; Research

About the Author

GUY A. MARCO (MALS, PhD, University of Chicago) has done virtually all the work of a public library and has taught virtually all the subjects. He has directed a public library service and been on a board of trustees. He was a division chief in the Library of Congress, dean/director of two library schools and visiting/adjunct professor in eight others. His publications include six books and about 150 articles and reviews. As a consultant, he advised national governments on library planning in Europe, Africa, and the Middle East. He was the first American since Melvil Dewey to be invited to address a conference of the (British) Library Association. At present, he is an instructor in the seminars program of the Newberry Library.